Introduction to Business and Marketing

PEARSON

At Pearson, we have a simple mission: to help people make more of their lives through learning.

We combine innovative learning technology with trusted content and educational expertise to provide engaging and effective learning experience that serve people wherever and whenever they are learning.

We enable our customers to access a wide and expanding range of market-leading content from world-renowned authors and develop their own tailor-made book. From classroom to boardroom, our curriculum materials, digital learning tools and testing programmes help to educate millions of people worldwide — more than any other private enterprise.

Every day our work helps learning flourish, and wherever learning flourishes, so do people.

To learn more, please visit us at: www.pearsoned.co.uk/personalised

Introduction to Business and Marketing

Compiled from:

Management: An Introduction
Sixth Edition
David Boddy

Essentials of Marketing
Fifth Edition
Jim Blythe

The Business Environment
Seventh Edition
Ian Worthington and Chris Britton

PEARSON

Harlow, England • London • New York • Boston • San Francisco • Toronto • Sydney • Auckland • Singapore • Hong Kong
Tokyo • Seoul • Taipei • New Delhi • Cape Town • Sao Paulo • Mexico City • Madrid • Amsterdam • Munich • Paris • Milan

Pearson Education Limited
Edinburgh Gate
Harlow
Essex CM20 2JE

And associated companies throughout the world

Visit us on the World Wide Web at:
www.pearson.com/uk

© Pearson Education Limited 2015

Compiled from:

Management: An Introduction
Sixth Edition
David Boddy
ISBN 978-1-292-00424-2
© Prentice Hall Europe 1998 (print)
© Pearson Education Limited 2002, 2005, 2008, 2011 (print)
© Pearson Education Limited 2014 (print and electronic)

Essentials of Marketing
Fifth Edition
Jim Blythe
ISBN 978-0-273-75768-9
© Financial Times Professional Limited 1998
© Pearson Education Limited 2001, 2012

The Business Environment
Seventh Edition
Ian Worthington and Chris Britton
ISBN 978-0-273-75672-9
© Ian Worthington and Chris Britton 1994, 1997, 2000, 2003 (print)
© Ian Worthington and Chris Britton 2006, 2009 (print and electronic)
© Pearson Education Limited 2015 (print and electronic)

All rights reserved. No part of this publication may be reproduced, stored in a retrieval system, or transmitted in any form or by any means, electronic, mechanical, photocopying, recording or otherwise, without either the prior written permission of the publisher or a licence permitting restricted copying in the United Kingdom issued by the Licensing Agency Ltd, Saffron House, 6–10 Kirby Street, London EC1N 8TS.

ISBN 978-1-78447-935-0

Contents

Foreword — viii

Managing in Organisations — 2
Chapter 1 in *Management: An Introduction*, Sixth Edition
David Boddy

What do Marketers do? — 32
Chapter 1 in *Essentials of Marketing*, Fifth Edition
Jim Blythe

The Marketing Environment — 52
Chapter 2 in *Essentials of Marketing*, Fifth Edition
Jim Blythe

Marketing Planning, Implementation and Control — 78
Chapter 10 in *Essentials of Marketing*, Fifth Edition
Jim Blythe

Consumer and Buyer Behaviour — 104
Chapter 3 in *Essentials of Marketing*, Fifth Edition
Jim Blythe

Segmentation, Targeting and Positioning — 130
Chapter 4 in *Essentials of Marketing*, Fifth Edition
Jim Blythe

Products, Branding and Packaging — 152
Chapter 6 in *Essentials of Marketing*, Fifth Edition
Jim Blythe

Pricing Strategies — 186
Chapter 7 in *Essentials of Marketing*, Fifth Edition
Jim Blythe

Distribution — 204
Chapter 8 in *Essentials of Marketing*, Fifth Edition
Jim Blythe

Marketing Communications and Promotional Tools — 224
Chapter 9 in *Essentials of Marketing*, Fifth Edition
Jim Blythe

Services Marketing — 266
Chapter 11 in *Essentials of Marketing*, Fifth Edition
Jim Blythe

Sustainable Marketing — 290
Chapter 12 in *Essentials of Marketing*, Fifth Edition
Jim Blythe

Models of Management — 322
Chapter 2 in *Management: An Introduction*, Sixth Edition
David Boddy

The Political Environment — 365
Chapter 4 in *The Business Environment*, Seventh Edition
Ian Worthington and Chris Britton

The Macroeconomic Environment — 403
Chapter 5 in *The Business Environment*, Seventh Edition
Ian Worthington and Chris Britton

The Demographic, Social and Cultural Context of Business — 439
Chapter 6 in *The Business Environment*, Seventh Edition
Ian Worthington and Chris Britton

The Resource Context: People, Technology and Natural Resources — 461
Chapter 7 in *The Business Environment*, Seventh Edition
Ian Worthington and Chris Britton

The Legal Environment — 487
Chapter 8 in *The Business Environment*, Seventh Edition
Ian Worthington and Chris Britton

The Ethical and Ecological Environment — 511
Chapter 9 in *The Business Environment*, Seventh Edition
Ian Worthington and Chris Britton

Managing Internationally — 530
Chapter 4 in *Management: An Introduction*, Sixth Edition
David Boddy

Organisation Cultures and Contexts — 560
Chapter 3 in *Management: An Introduction*, Sixth Edition
David Boddy

Planning — 588
Chapter 6 in *Management: An Introduction*, Sixth Edition
David Boddy

Managing Strategy 614
Chapter 8 in *Management: An Introduction*, Sixth Edition
David Boddy

Organisation Structure 646
Chapter 10 in *Management: An Introduction*, Sixth Edition
David Boddy

Decision Making 680
Chapter 7 in *Management: An Introduction*, Sixth Edition
David Boddy

Creativity, Innovation And Change 712
Chapter 13 in *Management: An Introduction*, Sixth Edition
David Boddy

FOREWORD

I have put together this textbook both to support and enhance your learning needs.

Each chapter is specifically chosen to give further depth and understanding to the content of my lectures. I hope you find the text both interesting and enjoyable and trust that it could be a useful tool both now and in the future.

Thanks

Richard Gough

Introduction to Business and Marketing

CHAPTER 1
MANAGING IN ORGANISATIONS

Aim

To introduce the tasks, processes and context of managerial work in organisations.

Objectives

By the end of your work on this chapter you should be able to outline the concepts below in your own terms and:

1. Explain that the role of management is to add value to resources
2. Give examples of management as a universal human activity and as a distinct role
3. Compare the roles of general, functional, line, staff and project managers, and of entrepreneurs
4. Compare how managers influence others to add value to resources through:
    a. the process of managing;
    b. the tasks (or content) of managing; and
    c. the contexts within which they and others work
5. Explain the elements of critical thinking and use some techniques to develop this skill
6. Suggest the implications the integrating themes of the book have for managing

Key terms

This chapter introduces the following ideas:

organisation
tangible resources
intangible resources
competences
value
management as a universal human activity
manager
management
management as a distinct role
role
general manager

functional manager
line manager
staff manager
project manager
entrepreneur
stakeholders
networking
management task
critical thinking
sustainability
corporate governance

Each is a term defined within the text, as well as in the glossary at the end of the book.

Case study: Ryanair www.ryanair.com

In 2012 Ryanair, based in Dublin, reported that it had carried almost 76 million passengers in the 12 months to the end of March, 5 per cent more than in the previous year. Revenue had grown by almost 20 per cent and profit by 25 per cent. It planned to continue to expand its route network, and therefore its staff and aircraft fleet to meet customer demand: in March 2013 it ordered 175 jets from Boeing.

Tony Ryan (1936–2007) founded the company in 1985 with a single aircraft flying passengers from Ireland to the UK. Ryan, the son of a train driver, left school at 14 to work in a sugar factory, before moving in 1954 to work as a baggage handler at Aer Lingus, the state-owned Irish airline. By 1970 he was in charge of the aircraft leasing division, lending Aer Lingus aircraft and crews to other airlines. This gave him the idea, which he quickly put into practice, to create his own aircraft leasing company. As Guinness Peat Aviation this became a world player in the aviation leasing industry, and is now part of GE Capital.

In 1985 he founded Ryanair, to compete with his former employer. Southwest Airlines in the US inspired this move by showing that a new business could enter the industry to compete with established, often state-owned, airlines. Tony Ryan turned Ryanair into a public company in 1997 by selling shares to investors.

In the early years the airline changed its business several times – initially competing with Aer Lingus in a conventional way, then a charter company, at times a freight carrier. The Gulf War in 1990 discouraged air travel and caused the company financial problems. Rather than close the airline, he and his senior managers (including Michael O'Leary, who is now Chief Executive) decided it would be a 'no-frills' operator, discarding conventional features of air travel like free food, drink, newspapers and allocated seats. It would serve customers who wanted a functional and efficient service, not luxury.

In 1997 changes in European Union regulations enabled new airlines to enter markets previously dominated by national carriers such as Air France and British Airways. Ryanair quickly took advantage of this, opening new routes between Dublin and continental Europe. Although based in Ireland, 80 per cent of its routes are between airports in other countries – in contrast to established carriers which depend on passengers travelling to and from the airline's home country (Barrett, 2009, p. 80). The company has continued to grow rapidly, regularly opening new routes to destinations it thinks will be popular. It now refers to itself as 'the world's largest international scheduled airline', and continues to seek new bases and routes.

In May 2012 the chairman of the board presented the company's results for the latest financial year.

© Thierry Tronnel/Corbis

Measures of financial performance in financial years ending 31 March 2011 and 2012

	2012	2011
Passengers (millions)	75.8	72.1
Revenue (millions of Euros)	4,325	3,630
Profit after tax (millions of Euros)	503	401
Earnings per share (Euro cents)	34.10	26.97

Sources: *Financial Times* 24 October 2011, 21 June 2012, 20 March 2013; Kumar (2006); O'Connell and Williams (2005); Doganis (2006); and company website.

Case questions 1.1

- Identify examples of the resources that Ryanair uses, and of how managers have added value to them (refer to Section 1.2).
- Give examples of three points at which managers changed what the organisation does and how it works.

1.1 Introduction

Ryanair illustrates several aspects of management. An entrepreneur, Tony Ryan, who had already created one new business, saw a further opportunity in the market, and created an organisation to take advantage of it. He persuaded others to provide the resources he needed – especially money for the aircraft and the costs of operating it – and organised these into a service which he sold to customers. The business changed frequently in the early years, and under the current chief executive, Michael O'Leary, it has continued to be innovative in how it operates, quick to identify new routes, and imaginative in identifying new sources of revenue.

Entrepreneurs thrive on innovation as they try to make the most of new opportunities. Managers in established businesses often face the different challenge of how to meet more demand with fewer resources. Those managing the United Nations World Food Programme struggle to raise funds from donor countries: aid is falling while hunger is increasing. In almost every public healthcare organisation managers face a growing demand for treatment, but fewer resources with which to provide it.

Organisations of all kinds – from rapidly growing operations like Facebook to established businesses like Royal Dutch Shell or Marks & Spencer – depend on people at all levels who can run the current business efficiently, and also innovate. This book is about the knowledge and skills that enable people to meet these expectations, and so build a satisfying and rewarding career.

Figure 1.1 illustrates the themes of this chapter. It represents the fact that people draw resources from the external environment and manage their transformation into outputs that they hope are of greater value. They pass these back to the environment, and the value they obtain in return (money, reputation, goodwill, etc.) enables them to attract new resources to continue in business (shown by the feedback arrow from output to input). If the outputs do not attract sufficient resources, the enterprise will fail.

The chapter begins by examining the significance of managed organisations in our world. It then outlines what management means and introduces theories about the nature of managerial work. It introduces the idea of critical thinking, and ends with a section on four integrating themes which conclude each chapter – entrepreneurship, sustainability, internationalisation and governance.

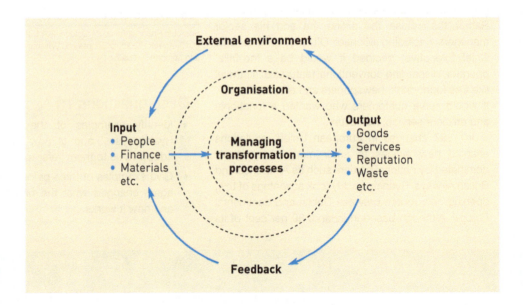

Figure 1.1 Managing organisation and environment

Activity 1.1 What is 'management'?

Write a few notes summarising what you think 'management' means.

- You may find it helpful to think of instances in which you have encountered 'management' – such as when you have been managed in your school or university.
- Alternatively, reflect on an occasion when you have managed something, such as a study project. Keep the notes so you can refer to them.

1.2 Managing to add value to resources

We live in a world of managed **organisations**. We experience many every day – domestic arrangements (family or flatmates), large public organisations (the postal service), small businesses (the newsagent), large businesses (the jar of coffee), or a voluntary group (the club we attended). They affect us and we judge their performance. Did the transaction work smoothly or was it chaotic? Was the service good, reasonable or poor? Will you go there again?

> An **organisation** is a social arrangement for achieving controlled performance towards goals that create value.

Key ideas Joan Magretta on the innovation of management

What were the most important innovations of the past century? Antibiotics and vaccines that doubled, or even tripled, human life spans? Automobiles and aeroplanes that redefined our idea of distance? New agents of communication, like the telephone, or the chips, computers and networks that are propelling us into a new economy?

All of these innovations transformed our lives, yet none of them could have taken hold so rapidly or spread so widely without another. That innovation is the discipline of management, the accumulating body of thought and practice that makes organisations work. When we take stock of the productivity gains that drive our prosperity, technology gets all of the credit. In fact, management is doing a lot of the heavy lifting.

Source: Magretta (2002), p. 1.

As human societies become more specialised, we depend more on others to satisfy our needs. We meet some of these by acting individually or within family and social groups: organisations provide the rest. Good managers make things work – so that aid is delivered, roads are safe, shops have stock, hospitals function and all the rest. They don't do the work themselves, but build an organisation with the resources *and* competences to deliver what people need. **Tangible resources** are physical assets such as plant, people and finance – things you can see and touch. **Intangible resources** are non-physical assets such as information, reputation and knowledge.

To transform these resources into valuable goods and services people need to work together. They need to know what to do, understand their customers, deal with enquiries properly, and generally make the transaction work well. Beyond that they look for opportunities to improve, innovate and learn from experience. Good managers bring out the best in other people so that they willingly 'go the extra mile': together they develop effective ways of working that become second nature. These 'ways of working' are **competences** – skills, procedures or systems which enable people to use resources productively. Managers' role is to obtain the resources, and develop the competences to use them, so that the organisation adds **value** – by producing things that are more valuable to customers than the resources it has used.

> **Tangible resources** are the physical assets of an organisation such as plant, people and finance.
>
> **Intangible resources** are non-physical assets such as information, reputation and knowledge.
>
> **Competences** are the skills and abilities which an organisation uses to deploy resources effectively – systems, procedures and ways of working.
>
> **Value** is added to resources when they are transformed into goods or services that are worth more than their original cost plus the cost of transformation.

Well-managed organisations create value by delivering goods and services which make the customer feel better off in some way – a cheap and punctual flight, a bright and well-equipped gym, a trendy phone, clothes that enhance their image. Others value good service, or a clear set of instructions. Good managers understand what customers value, and allocate resources (build an organisation) to satisfy them. They provide value through the performance of the product AND through the quality of the relationship the customer has with the company (O'Cass and Ngo, 2011).

Management in practice   **Creating value at DavyMarkham** www.davymarkham.com

Kevin Parkin was Managing Director (and part-owner) of DavyMarkham, a heavy engineering company. Although the company has a long history, by the mid-1990s it was making regular losses, and its survival was in doubt. Since Mr Parkin joined the company he had returned it to profit by concentrating on what the company is good at, and then using tough management and financial discipline to make sure staff follow the recipe for success. Mr Parkin removed poor managers, walked the shop floor twice a day to check on progress, and engaged closely with the workforce:

> It's been essential to tell people the truth about the business, whether it's good or bad, and giving them the enthusiasm they require to make them want to succeed . . . I also ask my 'mentors' – [people I have known in previous jobs] about key strategic decisions, people issues, market penetration, capital spending and general business solutions.

The business is now part of the IVRCL Group, and continues to win large orders for mining equipment, especially in South America.

Source: From an article by Peter Marsh and Andrew Bounds, *Financial Times*, 27 May 2009.

Commercial organisations of all kinds (business start-ups, small and medium-sized enterprises, large private sector businesses, often operating internationally) create wealth for their owners by adding value to resources, which they can only do if they offer goods and services that consumers want. Co-operatives (in 2012 there were 5900 co-operative enterprises in the UK, compared to 4800 in 2009, according to their trade body, Co-operatives UK: **www.uk.coop**) do the same, though with a different ownership structure. Some (like the many retail co-operatives, of which the largest is the Co-operative Group) are owned by customers, who receive a share of the profits as a dividend. Others are owned by their employees – the John Lewis Partnership (**www.johnlewispartnership.co.uk**) is the most prominent example. Similar examples include Circle (**www.circlepartnership.co.uk**), a healthcare company founded and owned by clinicians; and Suma (**www.suma.coop**) a worker-owned co-operative running a wholefoods distribution business.

Voluntary and charitable organisations aim to add value by educating people, counselling the troubled or caring for the sick (Handy, 1988). The British Heart Foundation (**www.bhf.org**) raised over £128 million from legacies, fundraising activities and the retail business in 2011–12, which enabled it to deliver its mission of caring for people with heart disease, and preventing others developing it in the first place. Raising the income, and ensuring that the research and other projects it supports give value for money, is a formidable management task – with over 700 shops, it is the largest charity retailer in the UK. Managing a large charity is at least as demanding a job as managing a commercial business, facing similar challenges of adding value to limited resources.

Theatres, orchestras, museums and art galleries create value by offering inspiration, new perspectives or unexpected insights. Other organisations add value by serving particular interests – such as Unison, a trade union that represents workers in the UK public sector, or the Law Society, which defends the interests of lawyers. Firms in most industries create trade organisations to protect their interests by lobbying or public relations work.

Table 1.1 Where people manage

Setting – industry or type	Examples in this book	'Unique' challenges
Business start-ups	innocent drinks in the early days (Chapter 2 case study)	Securing funding to launch, and enough sales to sustain cash-flow. Building credibility
Small and medium-sized enterprises (SMEs)	DavyMarkham (Management in practice, see above)	Generating enough funds to survive, innovate and enter new markets
Professional service firms	Hiscox (insurance) (Management in practice, Chapter 11)	Managing highly qualified staff delivering customised, innovative services.
Large private businesses, often working internationally	Virgin Group (Part 4 Case)	Controlling diverse activities, meeting shareholder expectations
Voluntary, not-for-profit organisations and charities	Eden Project (Chapter 15 case study)	Providing visitors with an experience which encourages them to return, raising funds for educational work, fulfilling mission.
Co-operatives – customer or employee-owned	The Co-operative Group (Chapter 5 case study)	Balancing democratic and commercial interests; raising capital.
Public sector organisations	Crossrail (Chapter 6 case study)	Managing high profile political and commercial interests.

While organisations aim to add value, many do not do so. If people work inefficiently they use more resources to make a product than customers will pay for, and so destroy value – as does pollution and waste. Motorways create value for drivers, residents of by-passed villages, and shareholders – but destroy value for some people if the route damages an ancient woodland rich in history and wildlife. Deciding if managers have created value can be subjective and controversial.

Some issues that managers face arise in most organisations (business planning or ensuring quality). Others are unique to the setting in which they operate (charities need to maintain the support of donors). Table 1.1 illustrates some of these diverse settings, and their (relatively) unique management challenges – which are in addition to challenges that are common to all.

Whatever its nature, the value an organisation creates depends on how well those who work there understand their situation, and use that knowledge to develop the right resources and competences. Even within the broad categories shown there is great variation in circumstances. As an example, 'professional services' includes legal, auditing, and engineering consultancy businesses, but they differ in terms of the nature of their knowledge base, their degree of jurisdictional control, and the nature of their client relationships.

Activity 1.2 Focus on diverse management settings

Choose ONE of the settings in Table 1.1 which interests you. Gather information about an organisation of that type (using, for example, case studies in this book or someone you know who works in that setting) so you can:

- name one organisation in that setting;
- identify how it adds value to resources, and the main management challenges it faces;
- compare your evidence with someone who has gathered data about a different setting, and summarise similarities or differences in the management challenges.

1.3 Meanings of management

Management as a universal human activity

As individuals we run our lives and careers: in this respect we are managing. Family members manage children, elderly dependants and households. Management is both a **universal human activity** and a distinct role. In the first sense, people manage an infinite range of activities:

> When human beings 'manage' their work, they take responsibility for its purpose, progress and outcome by exercising the quintessentially human capacity to stand back from experience and to regard it prospectively, in terms of what will happen; reflectively, in terms of what is happening; and retrospectively, in terms of what has happened. Thus management is an expression of human agency, the capacity actively to shape and direct the world, rather than simply react to it. (Hales, 2001, p. 2)

Rosemary Stewart (1967) expressed this idea when she described a **manager** as someone who gets things done with the aid of people and other resources, which defines **management** as the activity of getting things done with the aid of people and other resources. So described, management is a universal human activity – domestic, social and political – as well as in formally established organisations.

In pre-industrial societies people typically work alone or in family units, controlling their time and resources. They decide what to make, how to make it and where to sell it, combining work and management to create value. Self-employed craftworkers, professionals in small practices, and those in a one-person business do this every day. We all do it in household tasks or voluntary activities in which we do the work (planting trees or selling raffle tickets) and the management activities (planning the winter programme).

Management as a universal human activity occurs whenever people take responsibility for an activity and consciously try to shape its progress and outcome.

A **manager** is someone who gets things done with the aid of people and other resources.

Management is the activity of getting things done with the aid of people and other resources.

Activity 1.3 Think about the definition

Choose a domestic, community or business activity you have undertaken.

- What, specifically, did you do to 'get things done with the aid of people and other resources'?
- Decide if the definition accurately describes 'management'.
- If not, how would you change it?

Management as a distinct role

Human action can also separate the 'management' element of a task from the 'work' element, thus creating 'managers' who are in some degree apart from those doing the work. **Management as a distinct role** emerges when external parties, such as a private owner of capital, or the state, gain control of a work process that a person used to complete themselves. These parties may then dictate what to make, how to make it and where to sell it. Workers become employees selling their labour, not the results of their labour. From about 1750 factory production began to displace domestic and craft production in many economic sectors such as textiles and iron production. Factory owners took control of the physical and financial means of production and tried to control the time, behaviour and skills of those who were now employees rather than autonomous workers.

Management as a distinct role develops when activities previously embedded in the work itself become the responsibility not of the employee, but of owners or their agents.

The same evolution occurs when someone starts an enterprise, initially performing the *technical* aspects of the work itself – writing software, designing clothes – and also more *conceptual* tasks such as planning which markets to serve, or deciding how to raise money. If the business grows and the entrepreneur engages staff, he or she will need to spend time on *interpersonal* tasks such as training and supervising their work. The founder progressively takes on more management roles – a **role** being the expectations that others have of someone occupying a position. It expresses the specific responsibilities and requirements of the job, and what someone holding it should do (or not do). If the business grows the founder needs others to share the management role – and begins to build a management team. Levy (2011) traces how this proved controversial as Google grew. Founders Larry Page and Sergey Brin were not convinced that the hundreds of engineers whom they were recruiting needed managers – they could all just report to the head of engineering. The engineers disagreed:

> Page wanted to know why. They told him they wanted someone to learn from. When they disagreed with colleagues and discussions reached an impasse, they needed someone who could break the ties. (p.159)

A **role** is the sum of the expectations that other people have of a person occupying a position.

This separation of management and non-management work is not inevitable or permanent. People deliberately separate the roles, and can also bring them together. As Henri Fayol (1949) (of whom you will read more in Chapter 2) observed:

> Management ... is neither an exclusive privilege nor a particular responsibility of the head or senior members of a business; it is an activity spread, like all other activities, between head and members of the body corporate. (p. 6)

Key ideas — Tony Watson on separating roles

All humans are managers in some way. But some of them also take on the formal occupational work of being managers. They take on a role of shaping ... work organisations. Managers' work involves a double ... task: managing others and managing themselves. But the very notion of 'managers' being separate people from the 'managed', at the heart of traditional management thinking, undermines a capacity to handle this. Managers are pressured to be technical experts, devising rational and emotionally neutral systems and corporate structures to 'solve problems', 'make decisions', 'run the business'. These 'scientific' and rational–analytic practices give reassurance but can leave managers so distanced from the 'managed' that their capacity to control events is undermined. This can mean that their own emotional and security needs are not handled, with the effect that they retreat into all kinds of defensive, backbiting and ritualistic behaviour which further undermines their effectiveness.

Source: Watson (1994), pp. 12–13.

Someone in charge of, say, a production department will usually be treated as a manager, and referred to as one. Those operating the machines will be called something else. In a growing business like Ryanair the boundary between 'managers' and 'non-managers' will be fluid, with all being expected to perform a range of tasks, irrespective of their title. Hales (2006) shows how some first-line managers hold responsibilities usually associated with middle managers. They still supervise subordinates, but may also deal with issues of costs and customer satisfaction.

1.4 Specialisation between areas of management

As an organisation grows, senior managers usually create functions and a hierarchy, so 'management' becomes divided (there are exceptions, but these are a small minority).

Functional specialisation

General managers are responsible for the performance of a distinct unit of the organisation.

Functional managers are responsible for the performance of an area of technical or professional work.

Line managers are responsible for the performance of activities that directly meet customers' needs.

General managers typically head a complete unit, such as a division or subsidiary, within which there will be several functions. The general manager is responsible for the unit's performance, and relies on the managers in charge of each function. A small organisation will have just one or two general managers, who will also manage the functions. At Shell UK the most senior general manager in 2012 was Graham van't Hoff, the Chairman.

Functional managers are responsible for an area of work – either as line managers or staff managers. **Line managers** are in charge of a function that creates value directly by supplying products or services to customers: they could be in charge of a retail store, a group of nurses, a social work department or a manufacturing area. Their performance significantly affects business performance and image, as they and their staff are in direct contact with customers. At Shell, Melanie Lane was (in 2012) General Manager, UK Retail.

Management in practice   The store manager – fundamental to success

A manager with extensive experience of retailing commented:

> The store manager's job is far more complex that it may at first appear. Staff management is an important element and financial skills are required to manage a budget and the costs involved in running a store. Managers must understand what is going on behind the scenes – in terms of logistics and the supply chain – as well as what is happening on the shop floor. They must also be good with customers and increasingly they need outward-looking skills as they are encouraged to take high-profile roles in the community.

Source: Private communication from the manager.

Staff managers are responsible for the performance of activities that support line managers.

Project managers are responsible for managing a project, usually intended to change some element of an organisation or its context.

Entrepreneurs are people who see opportunities in a market, and quickly mobilise the resources to deliver the product or service profitably.

Staff managers are in charge of activities like finance, personnel, purchasing or legal affairs which support the line managers, who are their customers. Staff in support departments are not usually in direct contact with external customers, and so do not earn income directly for the organisation. Managers of staff departments act as line managers within their unit. At Shell, Bob Henderson was (in 2012) Head of Legal, and Paul Milliken was Vice-President of Human Resources.

Project managers are responsible for a temporary team created to plan and implement a change, such as a new product or system. Mike Buckingham, an engineer, managed a project to instal new machinery in a van factory. He still had line responsibilities for manufacturing, but worked for most of the time on the project, helped by a team of technical specialists. When the change was complete he returned to his line job.

Entrepreneurs are people who are able to see opportunities in a market which others have overlooked. They secure the resources and competences they need and use them to build a profitable business. John Scott (founder, at the age of 18, of the Scott Group, now Europe's largest supplier of pallets and other industrial services – www.scottgroupltd.com) recalls the early days – 'I went from not really knowing what I wanted to do … to getting thrown into having to make a plant work, employ men, lead by example. We didn't have an office – it was in my mum's house, and she did the invoicing. The house was at the top of the yard, and the saw mill was at the bottom' (*Financial Times*, 11 July 2007, p. 18).

Management hierarchies

Figure 1.2 shows the type of positions within a management hierarchy. The amount of 'management' and 'non-management' work within these positions varies, and the boundaries between them are fluid.

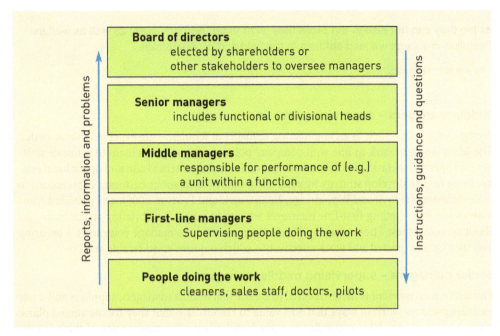

Figure 1.2
Illustration of generic levels within management hierarchies

People doing the work

People who do the manual and mental work needed to make and deliver products or services. These range from low paid cleaners or shop workers to highly paid pilots at Ryanair or software designers at Apple. The activity is likely to contain some aspects of management work, though in lower-level jobs this will be limited. People running a small business combine management work with direct work to meet customer requirements.

First-line managers – supervising those doing the work

Sometimes called supervisors, first-line managers typically direct and support the daily work of a group of staff, framed by the requirement to monitor, report and improve work performance (Hales 2005, p. 484). They allocate and co-ordinate work, monitor the pace and help with problems, and may work with middle managers to make operational decisions on staff or work methods. Examples include the supervisor of a production team, the head chef in a hotel, a nurse in charge of a hospital ward or the manager of a bank branch. They may continue to perform some direct operations, but will spend less time on them than subordinates. This role is especially challenging when 'subordinates' are skilled professionals with strong views on how to do the work.

Management in practice   Leading an army platoon

In the British Army an officer in charge of a platoon is responsible for 30 soldiers. Captain Matt Woodward, a platoon commander, describes the job:

> As a platoon commander at a regiment you're looking after up to 30 soldiers, all of whom will have a variety of problems you'll have to deal with – helping them [sort out financial difficulties], one of them might need to go to court for something, and you might go and represent them in court, try and give them a character reference, help them as best you can. Or a soldier who has got a girl pregnant, or a soldier who has got just got family problems and needs some help. Somebody else may want to take a posting back to England if they're based in Germany, or indeed if they're in England they might want to go to Germany. That's your job to try and help them out as best you can, to help manage their career to

> find them the best job they can but also in the place they want to be. And obviously as well as welfare and family and discipline problems we lead soldiers in the field and on operations.
>
> Source: Based on an interview with Matt Woodward.

Middle managers – supervising first-line managers

People in this role – such as an engineering manager at Ryanair – are expected to ensure that first-line managers work in line with company policies. This requires them to translate strategy into operational tasks, mediating between senior management vision and operational reality. Some help to develop strategy by presenting information about customer expectations to senior managers (Floyd and Wooldridge, 2000; Currie and Proctor, 2005), and provide a communication link – telling first-line managers what they expect, and briefing senior managers about current issues. Those working for charities are likely to manage volunteers – ensuring they turn up as expected and work effectively – which requires considerable skill.

Senior managers – supervising middle managers

The senior management team is expected to ensure that middle managers, suppliers and other business partners work in ways that add value to resources – that they follow agreed plans, suggest innovations, deliver supplies as agreed, and so on. The most senior of these is usually called the managing director (MD) or chief executive officer (CEO), and will be assisted by functional heads (such as the heads of engineering or marketing) or heads of the main product divisions. This senior team reports to the board of directors, the board of trustees in a charity like the British Heart Foundation, or the equivalent in public sector organisations.

Board of directors – managing the business

Managing the business is the work of a small group, usually called the board of directors, the most senior of whom is usually called the chairman. They establish policy and have a particular responsibility for managing relations with people and institutions in the world outside, such as shareholders, media or elected representatives. At Marks & Spencer the board focusses on corporate culture, strategy and succession planning. A board needs to be aware of the work of senior managers, but spends most of their time looking to the future or dealing with external affairs. The CEO is usually a member of the board, and some of the senior team may also be. The board usually includes non-executive directors – senior managers from other companies who should bring a wider, independent view to discussions. Such non-executive directors can enhance the effectiveness of the board, and give investors confidence it is acting in their interests. They can both support the executives in their leadership of the business and monitor and control executive conduct (Roberts *et al.*, 2005, p. S6) by challenging, questioning, discussing and debating issues with the executive members.

1.5 Influencing through the process of managing

Stakeholders are individuals, groups or organisations with an interest in, or who are affected by, what the organisation does.

Whatever their role, people add value to resources by influencing others, including internal and external **stakeholders** – those parties who affect, or who are affected by, an organisation's actions and policies. The challenge is that stakeholders will have different priorities, so managers need to influence them to act in ways they believe will add value.

They do this directly and indirectly. Direct methods are the interpersonal skills (Chapter 14) which managers use – persuading a boss to support a proposal, a subordinate to do more work, or a customer to change a delivery date. Managers also influence indirectly through:

- the process of managing (this section);
- the tasks of managing (Section 1.6); and
- shaping the context (Section 1.7).

Key ideas: Rosemary Stewart – how managers spend their time

What are managers' jobs like? One of the best-known studies was conducted by Rosemary Stewart (1967) of Oxford University, who asked 160 senior and middle managers to keep a diary for four weeks. This showed that they typically worked in a fragmented, interrupted fashion. Over the four weeks they had, on average, only nine periods of 30 minutes or more alone, with 12 brief contacts each day. They spent 36 per cent of their time on paperwork (writing, dictating, reading, calculating) and 43 per cent in informal discussion. They spent the remainder on formal meetings, telephoning and social activities.

The research team found great variety between managers, identifying five profiles based not on level or function but on how they spent their time:

- Emissaries spent most time out of the organisation, meeting customers, suppliers or contractors.
- Writers spent most time alone reading and writing, and had the fewest contacts.
- Discussers spent most time with other people and with their colleagues.
- Troubleshooters had the most fragmented work pattern, with many brief contacts, especially with subordinates.
- Committee members had most internal contacts, and spent much time in formal meetings.

Source: Stewart (1967).

Henry Mintzberg – ten management roles

Mintzberg (1973) observed how (five) chief executives spent their time, and used this data to create a frequently-quoted model of management roles. Like Stewart he noted that managers' work was varied and fragmented (see Key ideas), and contained ten roles in three categories – informational, interpersonal and decisional. Managers can use these to influence others to get things done. Table 1.2 describes them, and illustrates each with a contemporary example provided by the manager of a school nutrition project.

Informational roles

Managing depends on obtaining information about external and internal events, and passing it to others. The *monitor* seeks, receives and screens information to understand the organisation and its context, using websites, reports and chance conversations – such as with customers or new contacts at an exhibition. Much of this information is oral (gossip as well as formal meetings), building on personal contacts. In the *disseminator role* the manager shares information by forwarding reports, passing on rumours or briefing staff. As a *spokesperson* the manager transmits information to people outside the organisation – speaking at a conference, briefing the media or presenting views at a company meeting. Michael O'Leary at Ryanair is renowned for flamboyant statements to the media about competitors or officials in the European Commission with whose policies he disagrees.

Interpersonal roles

Interpersonal roles arise directly from a manager's formal authority and status, and shape relationships with people within and beyond the organisation. As a *figurehead* the manager is a symbol, representing the unit in legal and ceremonial duties such as greeting a visitor, signing legal documents, presenting retirement gifts or receiving a quality award. The *leader role* defines the manager's relationship with other people (not just subordinates), including motivating, communicating and developing their skills and confidence – as one commented:

> I am conscious that I am unable to spend as much time interacting with staff members as I would like. I try to overcome this by leaving my door open whenever I am alone as an invitation to staff to come in and interrupt me, and encourage them to discuss any problems.

Table 1.2 Mintzberg's ten management roles

Category	Role	Activity	Examples from a school nutrition project
Informational	Monitor	Seek and receive information, scan reports, maintain interpersonal contacts	Collect and review funding applications; set up database to monitor application process
	Disseminator	Forward information to others, send memos, make phone calls	Share content of applications with team members by email
	Spokesperson	Represent the unit to outsiders in speeches and reports	Present application process at internal and external events
Interpersonal	Figurehead	Perform ceremonial and symbolic duties, receive visitors	Sign letters of award to successful applicants
	Leader	Direct and motivate subordinates, train, advise and influence	Design and co-ordinate process with team and other managers
	Liaison	Maintain information links in and beyond the organisation	Become link person for government bodies to contact for progress reports
Decisional	Entrepreneur	Initiate new projects, spot opportunities, identify areas of business development	Use initiative to revise application process and to introduce electronic communication
	Disturbance handler	Take corrective action during crises, resolve conflicts amongst staff, adapt to changes	Holding face-to-face meetings with applicants when the outcome was negative; handling staff grievances
	Resource allocator	Decide who gets resources, schedule, budget, set priorities	Ensure fair distribution of grants nationally
	Negotiator	Represent unit during negotiations with unions, suppliers, and generally defend interests	Working with sponsors and government to ensure consensus during decision making

Source: Based on Mintzberg (1973), and private communication from the project manager.

Liaison refers to maintaining contact with people outside the immediate unit. Managers maintain networks in which they trade information and favours for mutual benefit with clients, officials, customers and suppliers. For some managers, particularly chief executives and sales managers, the liaison role takes a high proportion of their time and energy.

Management in practice — Strengthening interpersonal roles

A company restructured its regional operations, closed a sales office in Bordeaux and transferred the work to Paris. The sales manager responsible for south-west France was now geographically distant from her boss and the rest of the team. This caused communication problems and loss of teamwork. She concluded that the interpersonal aspects of the role were vital to the informational and decisional roles. The decision to close the office had broken these links.

> She and her boss agreed to try the following solutions:
>
> - A 'one-to-one' session of quality time to discuss key issues during monthly visits to head office.
> - Daily telephone contact to ensure speed of response and that respective communication needs were met.
> - Use of fax and email at home to speed up communications.
>
> These overcame the break in interpersonal roles caused by the location change.
>
> Source: Private communication.

Decisional roles

In the *entrepreneurial* role managers see opportunities and create projects to deal with them. Beamish Museum (www.beamish.org.uk) is England's biggest open-air museum, telling the story of working life in the north-east region in the 18th and 19th centuries. In 2008 the charity was in financial trouble as the number of visitors had stabilised, and government subsidy was declining. The director saw opportunities to attract visitors, create new attractions and devise new sources of revenue. In three years visitors increased by 70 per cent and revenue more than doubled – almost removing the need for subsidy. A manager becomes the *disturbance handler* when they deal with unexpected events, which draw their attention away from planned work. Surprise is a common feature of organisational life, caused by external events (a supplier's failure, say), an internal process fault, or a lack of information. Good managers put in place systems and procedures to deal with sudden shocks and limit their disruption – Bechky and Okhuysen (2011) show how some organisations have been especially successful at preparing for the unexpected.

> **Management in practice** Handling disturbance at Nokia www.nokia.com
>
> In early 2013 the management and staff at Nokia were handling disturbance on a scale that threatened the future of the business. As recently as 2008 it had been the world's leading supplier of mobile handsets, with a 40 per cent share of the market. The unexpected arrival of, and success of, the Apple iPhone began the challenge, which was soon followed by improved smartphones from Samsung. Cheap suppliers in emerging markets also brought stiffer competition at the lower end of the market. The company was urgently trying to recover, having dismissed their CEO and several senior managers, cut thousands of jobs, and formed an alliance with Microsoft to develop software for a new generation of devices.
>
> Source: Chapter 3 case.

The *resource allocator* chooses among competing demands for money, equipment, personnel and other resources. How much of her budget should the housing manager (quoted on page 22) spend on different types of project? What proportion of the budget should a company spend on advertising a product? The manager of an ambulance service regularly decides between paying overtime to staff to replace an absent team member, or letting service quality decline until a new shift starts. This is close to the *negotiator role*, in which managers seek agreement with other parties on whom they depend. Managers at Ryanair regularly negotiate with airport owners to agree on services and fees for a subsequent period.

Activity 1.4 Gather evidence about Mintzberg's model

Recall a time when you were responsible for managing an activity. Alternatively draw on your experience of being managed, and recall your manager at the time as the focus for the activity.

- Do the ten roles cover all of your work, or did you do things not on Mintzberg's list? What were they?
- Give examples of what you did under (say) five of the roles.
- On reflection, were there any of these roles to which you should have given more time? Or less?
- If possible compare your results with other members of your course
- Decide if the evidence you have collected supports or contradicts Mintzberg's theory.

Mintzberg observed that every manager's job combines these roles, with their relative importance depending on the manager's personal preferences, position in the hierarchy and the type of business. Managers usually recognise that they use many of the roles as they influence others.

Case study Ryanair – the case continues www.ryanair.com

Michael O'Leary joined the company in 1988 (he was previously financial adviser to founder Tony Ryan) and became chief executive in 1994. He depends on securing agreements with airport operators, and also on aviation authorities granting approval for Ryanair to open a route. This often leads him into public disputes with airport operators and/or with the European Commission over subsidies. O'Leary takes a deliberately aggressive stance to these controversies, believing that

as long as it's not safety-related, there's no such thing as bad publicity.

He is outspokenly dismissive of traditional high-cost airlines, the European Commission, airport operators, travel agents, and governments that subsidise failing airlines. Airline seats are perishable goods – they have no value if they are not used on the flight, so companies aim to maximise the proportion of seats sold on each one. Ryanair use a technique known as dynamic pricing, which means that prices change with circumstances. Typically fares rise the nearer the date is to departure, though if a flight has empty seats the company encourages sales by lowering fares.

It earns revenue by charging for services such as checking baggage into the hold or booking by credit card, selling insurance, priority boarding and refreshments. Each time a passenger rents a car or books a hotel room on the Ryanair website, it earns a commission. The company expects revenue from ancillary activities will continue to grow more rapidly than passenger revenue: in the last financial year they earned 21 per cent of revenue.

Sources: O'Connell and Williams (2005); Company website.

Case question 1.2
- Make notes showing which of Mintzberg's management roles you can identify in the case. Support your answer with specific examples.

Managers have noted two roles missing from Mintzberg's list – manager as subordinate and manager as worker. Most managers have subordinates but, except for those at the very top, they are subordinates themselves. Part of their role is to advise, assist and influence their boss – over whom they have no formal authority. Managers often need to persuade people higher up the organisation of a proposal's value or urgency. A project manager recalled:

> This is the second time we have been back to the management team, to propose how we wish to move forward, and to try and get the resources that are required. It is worth taking the time up front to get all members fully supportive of what we are trying to do. Although it takes a bit longer we should, by pressure and by other individuals demonstrating the benefits of what we are proposing, eventually move the [top team] forward.

Many managers spend time doing the work of the organisation. A director of a small property company helps with sales visits, or an engineering director helps with difficult technical problems. A lawyer running a small practice performs both professional and managerial roles.

Key ideas — **Managerial work in small businesses**

O'Gorman *et al.* (2005) studied the work of ten owner-managers of small growth-orientated businesses to establish empirically if the nature of their work differs from those in the large businesses studied by Mintzberg. They concluded that managerial work in these businesses is in some ways similar to that in large organisations, finding brevity, fragmentation and variety; mainly verbal communication; and an unrelenting pace.

Another observation was that managers moved frequently between roles, switching from, say, reviewing financial results to negotiating prices with a customer. They were constantly receiving, reviewing and giving information, usually by telephone or in unscheduled meetings. They reacted immediately to live information by redirecting their attention to the most pressing issues, so that their days were largely unplanned, with frequent interruptions. They spent only a quarter of their time in scheduled meetings compared to Mintzberg's finding that managers in large organisations spent almost 60 per cent of their time in this way. Finally, the owners of these small businesses spent 8 per cent of their time in non-managerial activities – twice that of those in Mintzberg's study.

The research shows that the nature of managerial work in small growth-orientated businesses is in some ways similar to, and in others different from, that in large organisations. There is the same brevity and fragmentation, but more informal communication.

Source: O'Gorman *et al.* (2005).

Managers as networkers

Does the focus of a manager's influencing activities affect performance? Mintzberg's study gave no evidence on this point, but work by Luthans (1988) showed that the relative amount of time spent on specific roles did affect outcomes. The team observed 292 managers in four organisations for two weeks, recording their behaviours in four categories – communicating, 'traditional management', networking, and human resource management. They also distinguished between levels of 'success' (relatively rapid promotion) and 'effectiveness' (work-unit performance and subordinates' satisfaction). They concluded that *successful* managers spent much more time networking (socialising, politicking, interacting with outsiders) than the less successful. *Effective* managers spent most time on communication and human resource management.

Wolff and Moser (2009) confirmed the link between **networking** and career success, showing building, maintaining and using internal and external contacts was positively associated with current salary, and with salary growth. Good networks help entrepreneurs to secure resources, information and status – which then further extends their network. Effective networkers seek out useful contacts, and also look critically at their networks to ensure they all add value: they cut those that bring little value for the time they take.

Networking refers to behaviours that aim to build, maintain and use informal relationships (internal and external) that may help work-related activities.

1.6 Influencing through the tasks of managing

Management tasks are those of planning, organising, leading and controlling the use of resources to add value to them.

A second way in which managers influence others is when they manage the transformation of resources into more valuable outputs. Building on Figure 1.1, this involves the **management tasks** of planning, organising, leading and controlling the transformation process. The amount of each varies with the job and the person, and they perform them simultaneously, switching as required.

Figure 1.3 illustrates the elements of this definition. It expands the central 'transforming' circle of Figure 1.1 to show the tasks that together make up the transformation process. People draw inputs (resources) from the environment and transform them through the tasks of planning, organising, leading and controlling. This results in goods and services that they pass as output into the environment. The feedback loop indicates that this output is the source of future resources.

External environment

Organisations depend on the external environment for the tangible and intangible resources they need to do their work. So they depend on people in that environment being willing to buy or otherwise value their outputs. Commercial firms sell goods and services and use the revenue to buy resources. Public bodies depend on their sponsors being sufficiently satisfied with their performance to provide their budget. Most managers face the challenge of using natural resources not just efficiently, but sustainably. Part 2 of the book deals with the external environment.

Planning

Planning sets out the overall direction of the work. It includes forecasting future trends, assessing resources, and developing performance objectives. It means deciding on the scope of the business, the areas of work in which to engage, and how to allocate resources between

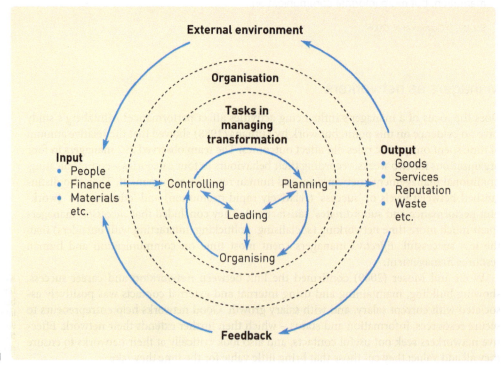

Figure 1.3 The tasks of managing

different projects or activities. Managers invest time and effort in developing a sense of direction for the organisation, or their part of it, and express these as goals. Part 3 deals with planning.

Management in practice   Planning major rail projects   www.networkrail.co.uk

More than most civil engineering projects, rail projects depend on extensive and detailed advance planning. In 2010 the UK government announced the preferred route for the first stage of a high speed West Coast railway line. The first stage will run from London to Birmingham, but construction is not expected to begin unto 2015 at the earliest, with completion about four years later. The Crossrail project in London (see Chapter 6 Case Study) also illustrates the scale and complexity of the planning required to build a large railway through (and below) the centre of London.

Source: Company website.

Organising

Organising moves abstract plans closer to reality by deciding how to allocate time and effort. It includes creating a structure for the enterprise, developing policies for HRM, deciding what technology people need, and how to encourage innovation. Part 4 deals with organising.

Management in practice   Chris Thompson, serial entrepreneur
                                      www.express-group.co.uk

Chris Thompson's grandfather was a shipyard worker on Tyneside and his father a draughtsman who set up Express Engineering, an engineering business in the 1970s. While working as an apprentice toolmaker in the company, Mr Thompson also sold jeans on a market stall, and turned oil drums into barbecues in his spare time. He took over Express Engineering in 1986, and since then has created more than 40 new businesses. He has sold some to management or third parties, while remaining closely involved with about 20 of them as an investor, director or chairman, many grouped under the brand name Express Group.

The companies are in manufacturing, product development, consultancy, training and property, with many customers in relatively resilient economic sectors such as oil and gas, aerospace and defence. A senior colleague from another company says of Mr Thompson:

> He is clear and decisive. He is very considered; doesn't jump to conclusions but makes decisions very quickly. He could have simply continued with the business his father started and been very successful: he is a great example, a great role model.

As well as being closely involved with about 20 of the companies he has founded, he also takes on public sector roles, notably as deputy chair of the regional development agency:

> I enjoy the good things in life, but I'm conscious of the disparity between the haves and the have-nots.

Source: From an article by Chris Tighe and Peter March, *Financial Times*, 17 June 2009, p.12.

Leading

Leading is the task of generating effort and commitment – influencing, motivating, and communicating – whether with individuals or in teams. It is directed at the tasks of planning, organising and controlling, so is in the middle of Figure 1.3. Part 5 deals with this topic.

Controlling

Control is the task of monitoring progress, comparing it with plan, and taking corrective action. Managers set a budget for a housing department, an outpatients' clinic, or for business travel. They ensure there is a system to collect information regularly on expenditure or performance – to check they are keeping to budget. If not, they decide how to bring actual costs into line with budget. Are the outcomes consistent with the objectives? If so, they can leave things alone. But if by Wednesday it is clear that staff will not meet the week's production target, the manager needs to act. They may deal with the deviation by a short-term response – authorising overtime. Control is equally important in creative organisations. Ed Catmull, co-founder of Pixar comments:

> Because we're a creative organisation, people [think that what we do can't be measured]. That's wrong. Most of our processes involve activities and deliverables that can be quantified. We keep track of the rates at which things happen, how often something had to be reworked, whether a piece of work was completely finished or not when it was sent to another department ... Data can show things in a neutral way, which can stimulate discussion. (Catmull, 2008, p. 72)

The discussion to which Catmull refers is the way to learn from experience. Good managers create and use opportunities to learn from what they are doing. Part 6 deals with control.

The tasks in practice

Managers typically switch between tasks many times a day. They deal with them intermittently and in parallel, touching on many different parts of the job, as this manager in a not-for-profit housing association explains:

> My role involves each of these functions. Planning is an important element as I am part of a team with a budget of £8 million to spend on promoting particular forms of housing. So planning where we will spend the money is very important. Organising and leading are important too, as staff have to be clear on which projects to take forward, clear on objectives and deadlines. Controlling is also there – I have to compare the actual money spent with the planned budget and take corrective action as necessary.

And a manager in a professional services firm:

> As a manager in a professional firm, each assignment involves all the elements to ensure we carry it out properly. I have to set clear objectives for the assignment, organise the necessary staff and information to perform the work, supervise staff and counsel them if necessary, and evaluate the results. All the roles interrelate and there are no clear stages for each one.

Activity 1.5 Gather evidence about the tasks of managing

Reflect on a time when you have been responsible for managing an activity.

- Do the four tasks of managing cover all of your work, or did you do things that are not included?
- Give an example of something which you did in each of the tasks.
- On reflection, were there any of these to which you should have given more time? Or less?
- If possible compare your results with other members of your course.

> **Case study** Ryanair – the case continues   www.ryanair.com

Top management is organised in a functional structure. Under Michael O'Leary as chief executive are two deputy chief executives who also hold the roles of chief operating officer and chief financial officer respectively. There are executives in charge of pilots, customer service, engineering, legal affairs, ground operations, and personnel/in-flight. The board of directors consists of the chief executive and eight non-executive directors, who are senior managers in other businesses.

Managers are responsible for delivering the strategy - of bringing the benefits of flying to as many people as possible. They control costs rigorously by:

- using a single aircraft type (Boeing 737-800 – most of which are under four years old) simplifies maintenance, training and crew scheduling;
- using secondary airports (away from major cities) with low landing charges, sometimes as little as £1 per passenger against £10 at a major airport; it also avoids costs caused by congestion;
- staff typically turning an aircraft round between flights in 25 minutes (older airlines take an hour) which allows aircraft to spend more time earning revenue (11 hours a day compared to 7 at British Airways);
- not assigning seats simplifies administration, and passengers arrive early to get their preferred seat;
- flying directly between cities avoids transferring passengers and baggage between flights, where mistakes and delays are common;
- cabin staff collecting rubbish from the cabin, saving the cost of separate cleaning crews.

Managers soon saw the potential of the internet, and in 2000 opened Ryanair.com to take bookings. Within a year it sold 75 per cent of seats online and now sells over 99 per cent in this way. It has tried to minimise staff costs by introducing productivity-based incentive payments – such as awarding a bonus to cabin staff based on their in-flight sales, and to pilots based on the number of hours they fly, within the legal limits. Over 91 per cent of flights arrived on time in 2011–12, helped by a daily conference call between the company and airport personnel at each base airport. These record the reasons for any flight or baggage delays, and aim to identify their root causes to prevent them happening again.

Sources: *Economist*, 20 July 2004; company website.

> **Case question 1.3**
> - Make notes showing examples of the tasks of management in the Ryanair case.

1.7 Influencing through shaping the context

A third way to influence others is by changing the context in which they work – the office layout, their reporting relationships, or the reward system. The context influences managers, and is a tool they use to influence others:

> It is impossible to understand human intentions by ignoring the settings in which they make sense. Such settings may be institutions, sets of practices, or some other contexts created by humans – contexts which have a history, within which both particular deeds and whole histories of individual actors can and have to be situated in order to be intelligible. (Czarniawska, 2004, p. 4)

Managers aim to create contexts that will support their objectives.

Dimensions of context

Internal context

Figures 1.1 and 1.3 showed the links between managers, their organisation and the external environment. Figure 1.4 enlarges the 'organisation' circle to show more fully the elements that make up the internal context within which managers work. Any organisation contains these elements – they represent the immediate context of the manager's work. As Apple grew into

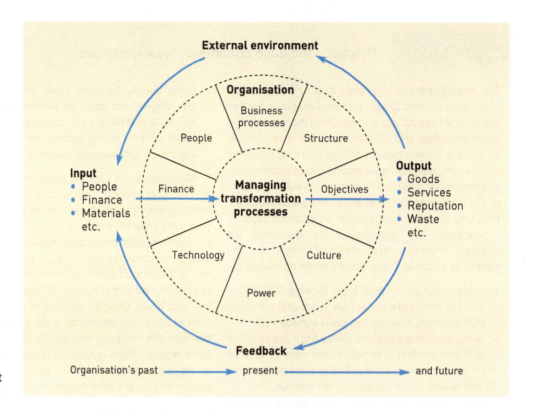

Figure 1.4 The internal and external context of management

a major business, the management team made decisions about structure, people, technology, business processes – and indeed to all the elements in the figure, which later chapters examine:

- **culture** (Chapter 3) – norms, beliefs and underlying values of a unit;
- **objectives** (Chapters 6 and 8) – a desired future state of an organisation or unit;
- **structure** (Chapter 10) – how tasks are divided and coordinated to meet objectives;
- **technology** (Chapter 12) – facilities and equipment to turn inputs into outputs;
- **power** (Chapter 14) – the amount and distribution of power with which to influence others;
- **people** (Chapter 15) – their knowledge, skills, attitudes and goals;
- **business processes** (Chapter 18) – activities to transform materials and information; and
- **finance** (Chapter 20) – the financial resources available.

Effective managers do not accept these as constraints or limitations – all can represent an opportunity as well as a threat. They also try to change the context to support their goals (Chapter 13).

Historical context

Managers work in the flow of history, as what people do now reflects past events and future uncertainties. Managers typically focus on current issues, ensuring that things run properly, and that the organisation works. At the same time, history influences them as the source of the structure and culture within which they work, affecting how people respond to proposals. People at all levels become attached to familiar practices, and may resist attempts to change them.

Effective managers also look to the future, questioning present systems and observing external changes. Are we wasting resources? What are others doing? The arrow at the foot of the figure represents the historical context.

External context

Chapter 3 shows that the external context includes an immediate competitive (micro) environment and a general (or macro) environment. These affect performance and part of the

Table 1.3 Examples of influencing others by managing tasks in each context

	Internal (organisational)	Micro (competitive)	Macro (general)
Planning	Clarifying the objectives of a business unit, and communicating them clearly to all staff	Reducing prices in the hope of discouraging a potential competitor from entering the market	Lobbying for a change in a trade agreement to make it easier to enter an overseas market
Organising	Changing the role of a business unit and ensuring staff understand and accept it	Creating a new division to meet a competitive challenge more robustly	Lobbying government to simplify planning laws to enable more rapid business development
Leading	Redesigning tasks and training staff to higher levels to improve motivation	Arranging for staff to visit customers so that they understand more fully what they need	Sending staff to work in an overseas subsidiary to raise awareness of cultural differences
Controlling	Ensuring the information system keeps an accurate output record	Implementing an information system directly linked to customers and suppliers	Lobbying for tighter procedures to ensure all countries abide by trade agreements

manager's work is to identify, and adapt to, external changes. Managers in the public sector are expected to deliver improved services with fewer resources, so they seek to influence people to change the internal context (such as how staff work) to meet external expectations. They also seek to influence those in the external context to secure more resources and/or lower their expectations.

Table 1.3 summarises the last two sections and illustrates how managers can influence others as they perform tasks affecting internal, micro and macro contexts.

Managers and their context

Managers use one of three theories (even if subconsciously) of the link between their context and their action – determinism, choice or interaction.

Determinism

This describes the assumption that factors in the external context determine an organisation's performance – micro and macro factors such as the industry a company is in, the amount of competition, or the country's laws and regulations. Managers adapt to external changes and have little independent influence on the direction of the business. On this view, the context is an independent variable – as in Figure 1.5(a).

Choice

An alternative assumption is that people influence events and shape their context. Those in powerful positions choose which businesses to enter or leave, and in which countries they will operate. Managers in major companies lobby to influence taxation, regulations and policy generally to serve their interests. On this view, the context is a dependent variable – shown in Figure 1.5(b).

Interaction

The interaction approach expresses the idea that people are influenced by, and themselves influence, the context. They interpret the existing context and act to change it to promote personal, local or organisational objectives. A manager may see a change in the company's external environment, and respond by advocating that it enters the market with a product to meet a perceived demand. Others interpret this proposal in the light of *their* perspective – competitors may lobby government to alter some regulations to protect them. All try to influence decisions

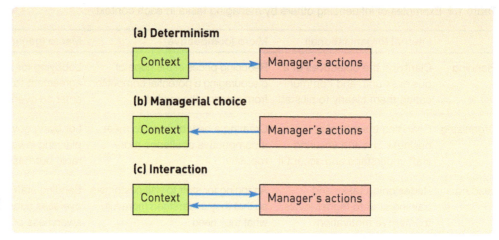

Figure 1.5
Alternative models of managers and their context

to suit their interests. The outcomes from these interactions affect the context (the company enters the market, or the regulations deter them) – which now provides the historical background to future action. The essential idea is that the relationship between manager and context works both ways – Figure 1.5(c). People shape the context, and the context shapes people.

Case study   Ryanair – the case continues   www.ryanair.com

According to statistics published by the International Air Transport Association, Ryanair carried over 76 million passengers on international scheduled flights in 2011 – ahead of Lufthansa (49 million), easyJet (42 million), Air France (32 million), Emirates (32 million) and British Airways (29 million). In that year it received less than one complaint for every 2000 passengers – an improvement on the previous year.

At the end of 2011 CEO Michael O'Leary said that he was planning to increase the number of passengers carried each year from the current 76 million to about 130 million by 2021. He sees particular growth opportunities in Eastern Europe and Scandinavia, and was confident the company would continue to increase market share on short European routes. To achieve this he would need to buy up to 300 more aircraft, and was discussing this with US, Chinese and Russian manufacturers.

In 2012 the company launched a third takeover bid for Aer Lingus: it already owns 29 per cent of the shares with the Irish government holding another 25 per cent. Previous bids failed after objections from the Irish government and the European Commission.

Source: *Financial Times*, 31 August 2012, p.17 and 20 March 2013, p.19.

Case questions 1.4

- Which aspects of the external general environment have affected the company (including some mentioned earlier)?
- How has the company affected these environments?
- In early 2013 the company was dealing with two strategic issues – the bid for Aer Lingus, and a decision on further aircraft purchases beyond the deal just announced. Visit the website or other news sources to discover the outcome on these issues, and what management lessons, if any, may be drawn from that.

1.8   Thinking critically

Managers continually receive data, information and knowledge – but cannot take it at face value. They must test it by questioning the underlying assumptions, relating them to context, considering alternatives, and recognising limitations. These are the skills of critical thinking.

Critical thinking

Brookfield (1987) stresses the benefits of thinking critically, in that it:

> involves our recognising the assumptions underlying our beliefs and behaviours. It means we can give justifications for our ideas and actions. Most important, perhaps, it means we try to judge the rationality of these justifications ... by comparing them to a range of varying interpretations and perspectives. (p. 13)

Critical thinking is positive activity that enables people to see more possibilities, rather than a single path. Critical thinkers 'are self-confident about their potential for changing aspects of their worlds, both as individuals and through collective action' (p. 5). He identifies four components of critical thinking.

Critical thinking identifies the assumptions behind ideas, relates them to their context, imagines alternatives and recognises limitations

Identifying and challenging assumptions

Critical thinkers look for the assumptions that underlie ideas, beliefs and values, and question their accuracy. They discard those that no longer seem valid in favour of more suitable ones. A manager who presents a well-supported challenge to a marketing idea that seems unsuitable to the business, or who questions the assumptions used to justify a new venture, is thinking critically.

Recognising the importance of context

Critical thinkers are aware that context influences thought and action. Thinking uncritically means assuming that ideas and methods that work in one context will work equally well in others. What we regard as an appropriate way to deal with staff reflects a specific culture: people in another culture – working in another place or at a different time – will have other expectations. Critical thinkers look for ideas and methods that seem suitable for the context.

Imagining and exploring alternatives

Critical thinkers develop the skill of imagining and exploring alternative ways of managing. They ask how others have dealt with a situation, and seek evidence about the effectiveness of different approaches. This makes them aware of realistic alternatives, and so increases the range of ideas which they can adapt and use.

Seeing limitations

Critical thinking alerts people to the limitations of knowledge and proposals. They recognise that because a practice works well in one situation it will not necessarily work in another. They are sceptical about research whose claims seem over-sold, asking about the sample or the analysis. They are open to new ideas, but only when supported by convincing evidence and reasoning.

> **Key ideas** — **Techniques to help develop your ability to think critically**
>
> 1 Identifying and challenging assumptions:
>   - Reflect on recent events which worked well or not-so-well; describing what happened and your reactions to it may help to identify assumptions that were confirmed or challenged by events.
>   - Do the same for an achievement of which you are most proud.
>   - Imagine you have decided to leave your job, and are advising on your replacement: list the qualities that person should have. That may indicate your assumptions about the nature of your job: are they correct?

2 **Recognising the importance of context:**
- Select a practice which people in your organisation take for granted; ask people in other organisations how they deal with the matter, and see if the differences relate to context.
- Repeat that with people who have worked in other countries.

3 **Imagining and exploring alternatives:**
- Brainstorming – try to think of as many solutions to a problem as you can in a short period, by temporarily suspending habitual judgements.
- Gather evidence about how other businesses deal with an aspect of management that interest you: the more alternatives you find, the easier it may become to think of alternatives that could work for you.

4 **Seeing limitations:**
- Acknowledge the limited evidence behind a theory or prescription.
- Ask if it has been tested in different settings or circumstances.

Source: Based on Brookfield (1987) and Thomas (2003), p. 7.

Thinking critically will deepen your understanding of management. It is not 'do-nothing' cynicism, 'treating everything and everyone with suspicion and doubt' (Thomas, 2003, p. 7). Critical thinking is part of a successful career, as it helps to ensure that proposals reflect reasonable assumptions, suit their context, take account of alternatives and acknowledge limitations.

Managing your studies

Studying management is itself a task to manage. Each chapter sets out some learning objectives. The text, including the activities and case questions, help you work towards these objectives and you can check your progress by using the review questions at the end of each chapter. The questions reflect objectives of varying levels of difficulty which Table 1.4

Table 1.4 Types of learning objective in the text

Type of objective	Typical words associated with each	Examples
Remember – retrieve relevant knowledge from memory	Recognise, recall	State or write the main elements and relationships in a theory
Understand – construct meaning from information	Interpret, give examples, summarise, compare, explain, contrast	Compare two theories of motivation; contrast two strategies, and explain which theory each reflects
Apply – use a procedure in a specified situation	Demonstrate, calculate, show, experiment, illustrate, modify	Use (named theory) to show the issues which managers in the case should consider
Analyse – break material into parts, showing relation to each other and to wider purpose	Classify, separate, order, organise, differentiate, infer, connect, compare, divide	Collect evidence to support or contradict (named theory); which theory is reflected in (example of practice)?
Evaluate – make judgements based on criteria and standards	Decide, compare, check, judge	Decide if the evidence presented supports the conclusion; should the company do A or B?
Create – put parts together into a coherent whole; reorganise elements	Plan, make, present, generate, produce, design, compose	Present a marketing plan for the company; design a project proposal

Source: Adapted from A Taxonomy for Learning, Teaching and Assessing: A Revision of Bloom's Taxonomy of Educational Objectives, Longman, New York (Anderson, L.W. and Krathwohl, D.R. 2001) p. 31, Table 3.3, Copyright © 2001 by Addison Wesley Longman, Inc., reproduced by permission of Pearson Education, Inc.

illustrates. Working on these will help develop your confidence to think critically in your studies and as a manager.

Studying is an opportunity to practise managing. You can plan what you want to achieve, organise the resources you need, generate personal commitment and check your progress. The book provides opportunities to improve your skills of literacy, reflection (analysing and evaluating evidence before acting), critical thinking, communicating, problem solving and teamwork.

The most accessible sources of ideas and theory are this book, (including the 'further reading' and websites mentioned), your lectures and tutorials. Draw on the experience of friends and relatives to help with some of the activities and questions. In your educational and social lives you experience organisations, and may help to manage them. Reflecting on these, to connect theory with practice, will support your studies.

1.9 Integrating themes

Entrepreneurship

Managers depend on others to get things done, and entrepreneurs must be able to build and use informal networks. Shaw (2006) studied six small advertising and design companies (less than ten employees), and showed (as have other studies) that informal networking is vital to entrepreneurs in this intensely competitive sector. She worked closely with the firms' owners and staff for 18 months to trace the pattern of their informal contacts, their focus, and why they used them.

The networks typically built upon the owners' personal networks, and those of their families and people they knew in non-competing firms. Most encouraged staff to use *their* personal networks to gather evidence about competitor moves or new entrants to the market. Such information (as well as that about legal, tax or financial matters) was the most common reason for the network contacts, as it was a significant addition to the resources available to these small firms – who rarely used official business support agencies. Their personal networks also generated new business. Finally, the study showed that entrepreneurs are selective – only networking with people they think can contribute directly, or indirectly by reputation and referral, to their client base and revenue.

Sustainability

Amory Lovins (Hawken *et al.*, 1999) is an influential advocate of running organisations sustainably, believing it is wrong to see this as increasing costs. Drawing on years of advisory experience at the Rocky Mountain Institute which he helped to found, he maintains that companies who achieve **sustainability** of performance – who make productive use not just of financial and physical resources, but also of human and natural ones – do well. They turn waste into profit – for example by taking a radical approach to energy efficiency in buildings, processes and vehicles, and by designing products and services to avoid waste.

Sustainability refers to economic activities that meet the needs of the present population while preserving the environment for the needs of future generations.

He acknowledges that 'turning waste into profit' does not happen easily – it needs thought and careful planning, and will change the way people throughout the organisation do things. Like any innovation, people have to focus on the problem to implement a workable solution. This is likely to involve new competences such as working on a whole system, rather than isolated parts; working with colleagues in other units; developing a culture of long-term thinking; and engaging with external stakeholders. These are all part of the work of managing in organisations.

Internationalisation

Developments in communications technology and changes in the regulations governing international trade have led to an increase the amount of trade which crosses national borders. Managing the international activities of an organisation has become a common feature of the work of many managers – whether working as an expatriate manager in another country or being part of an international team with colleagues from other countries.

The international dimension is a pervasive theme of management, with implications for each of the tasks of managing – how to lead in an international environment, and the implications of an increasingly dispersed business for planning, organising and controlling the organisation. Chapter 4 introduces these issues and this section at the end of each chapter links them to its theme.

Governance

High-profile corporate scandals and collapses have occurred despite the companies' annual reports giving the impression that all was well. There is much criticism of the pay and pensions of senior executives, especially in banks. These scandals have damaged investors and employees – and public confidence in the way managers were running these and other large companies.

Many questioned how such things could happen. Why could such apparently successful businesses get into such difficulties so quickly? Were there any warning signals that were ignored? What can be done to prevent similar events happening again? How can public confidence in these businesses be restored? These questions are all linked to **corporate governance:**

> **Corporate governance** is concerned with ensuring that internal controls adequately balance the needs of those with a financial interest in the organisation, and that these are balanced with the interests of other stakeholders.

a lack of effective corporate governance meant that such collapses could occur; good corporate governance can help prevent [them] happening again. (Mallin, 2013, p. 1)

Chapter 3 shows that governance is an essential part of management if it:

- ensures adequate systems of control to safeguard assets;
- prevents any individual from becoming too powerful;
- reviews relationships between managers, directors, shareholders and other stakeholders; and
- ensures transparency and accountability.

This theme continues in this section at the end of each chapter.

Summary

1 **Explain that the role of management is to add value to resources**
   - Managers create value by transforming inputs into outputs of greater value: they do this by developing competences within the organisation which, by constantly adding value (however measured) to resources is able to survive and prosper. The concept of creating value is subjective and open to different interpretations. Managers work in an infinite variety of settings, and Table 1.1 shows how each setting raises unique challenges.

2 **Give examples of management as a universal human activity and as a distinct role**
   - Management is an activity that everyone undertakes to some extent as they manage their daily lives. In another sense management is an activity within organisations, conducted in varying degrees by many people. It is not exclusive to those called

'managers'. People create the distinct role when they separate the work itself from the management of that work, and allocate the tasks to different people. The distinction between management and non-management work is fluid and the result of human action.

3 **Compare the roles of general, functional, line, staff and project managers, and entrepreneurs**
- General managers are responsible for a complete business or a unit within it. They depend on functional managers who can be either in charge of line departments meeting customer needs, such as manufacturing and sales, or in staff departments such as finance which provide advice or services to line managers. Project managers are in charge of temporary activities usually directed at implementing change. Entrepreneurs create new businesses, or new ventures in existing ones, to exploit opportunities they have seen.

4 **Explain how managers influence others to add value to resources through**
- The processes of managing. Rosemary Stewart drew attention to the fragmented and interrupted nature of management work, while Mintzberg identified ten management roles in three groups which he labelled informational, interpersonal and decisional. Luthans and more recently Moser have observed that successful managers were likely to be those who engaged in networking with people inside and outside of the organisation.
- The tasks (or content) of managing. Planning is the activity of developing the broad direction of an organisation's work, to meet customer expectations, taking into account internal capabilities. Organising is the activity of deciding how to deploy resources to meet plans, while leading seeks to ensure that people work with commitment to achieve plans. Control monitors activity against plans, so that people can adjust either if required.
- Contexts within which they and others work. The organisation's internal context consists of eight elements which help or hinder the manager – objectives, technology, business processes, finance, structure, culture, power, and people. The historical context also influences events, as does the external context of competitive and general environments.

5 **Explain the elements of critical thinking and use some techniques to develop this skill**
- Critical thinking is a positive approach to studying, as it encourages people to develop the skills of identifying and challenging assumptions; recognising the importance of context; imagining and exploring alternatives; and seeing the limitations of any idea or proposal.

6 **Integrating themes**

Each chapter ends by relating the topic to four themes of management:
- Entrepreneurship: Research by Shaw (2006) shows that entrepreneurs depend very heavily on a network of informal contacts to get things done.
- Sustainability: Advocates have abundant evidence that this approach to managing can reduce costs, not raise them – quite apart from the long term benefits.
- Internationalisation: This is a pervasive theme in discussing management, and affects each aspect of the role discussed in this chapter.
- Governance: Public criticism of corporate scandals and failures has increased interest in how managers are controlled in the interests of stakeholders – which affects all aspects of their work.

Test your understanding

1 How do non-commercial organisations add value to resources?
2 What is the difference between management as a general human activity and management as a specialised occupation? How has this division happened, and what are some of its effects?

3 What examples are there in the chapter of this boundary between 'management' and 'non-management' work being changed, and what were the effects?
4 Describe, with examples, the differences between general, functional, line, staff and project managers.
5 How does Mintzberg's theory of management roles complement that which identifies the tasks of management?
6 Give examples from your experience or observation of each of the four tasks of management.
7 What is the significance to someone starting a career in management of Luthans' theory about roles and performance?
8 How can thinking critically help managers do their job more effectively?
9 Review and revise the definition of management that you gave in Activity 1.1.

Think critically

Think about the way managers in a company with which you are familiar, go about their work. If you are a full time student, draw on jobs you have held or on the management of your studies. Review the material in the chapter, and make notes on these questions:

- What **assumptions** about the role of management appear to guide the way you, or others, manage? Are these assumptions supported by the evidence of recent events – have they worked, or not? Does your observation support, or contradict, Luthans' theory?
- What aspects of the historical or current **context** of the company appear to influence how you, and others, interpret the management role? Do people have different interpretations?
- Can you compare and contrast your role with that of colleagues on your course? Does this suggest **alternative** ways of constructing your role – where you focus time and energy?
- What **limitations** can you see in the theories and evidence presented in the chapter? For example, how valid is Mintzberg's theory (developed in large firms) for those managing a small business, or in the public sector?

Read more

Drucker, P. (1999), *Management Challenges for the 21st Century,* Butterworth/Heinemann, London.

> Worth reading as a collection of insightful observations from the enquiring mind of this great management theorist.

Hales, C. (2006), 'Moving down the line? The shifting boundary between middle and first-line management', *Journal of General Management*, vol. 32, no. 2, pp. 31–55.

> Reviews the growing pressure on managers as additional responsibilities are added to their role.

Handy, C. (1988), *Understanding Voluntary Organisations,* Penguin, Harmondsworth.

> A valuable perspective on management in the voluntary sector.

Hopkins, M. S. (2009), 'What Executives Don't Get About Sustainability', *MIT Sloan Management Review*, vol. 51, no. 1, pp. 35–40.

Brief introduction to sustainability from a manager's perspective, including an interview with one of the authors of *Natural Capitalism* (Hawken *et al.,* 1999).

Magretta, J. (2013), *What Management Is (How it works, and why it's everyone's business)*, Profile Books, London.

A new edition of this small book by a former editor at the *Harvard Business Review* offers a brief, readable and jargon-free account of the work of general management.

Go online

These websites have appeared in the chapter:

www.ryanair.com
www.uk.coop
www.johnlewispartnership.co.uk
www.circlepartnership.co.uk
www.suma.coop
www.bhf.org
www.davymarkham.com
www.nokia.com
www.scottgroupltd.com
www.networkrail.co.uk
www.express-group.co.uk

Visit two of the business sites in the list, or those of other organisations in which you are interested, and navigate to the pages dealing with recent news, press or investor relations.

- What are the main issues which the organisation appears to be facing?
- Compare and contrast the issues you identify on the two sites.
- What challenges may they imply for those working in, and managing, these organisations?

WHAT DO MARKETERS DO?

Objectives

After reading this chapter you should be able to:
- Describe the main roles marketers have
- Explain the responsibilities of various types of marketing manager
- Explain the core concepts of marketing
- Explain how marketing activities fit in with other business disciplines
- Describe the development of the marketing concept.

INTRODUCTION

This chapter is an introduction to the basic concepts of marketing, seen in terms of the roles that marketers carry out in their day-to-day jobs. Although marketers have many different job titles, what they have in common is the same orientation towards running the organisation; marketing is concerned with ensuring the closest possible fit between what the organisation does and what its customers need and want.

Electrolux

Electrolux is a long-established Swedish electrical goods manufacturer. The company prides itself on producing innovative products based on finding solutions for consumers. Often the company finds itself producing items that people were not aware they needed, but it does not seek to innovate for innovation's sake.

Understanding customers is therefore paramount for Electrolux. Aware that customers are the driving force of everything the company does, Electrolux know that they will only succeed in a cluttered market if they are able to offer real advantages that other manufacturers cannot match. Company representatives observe how people relate to their appliances and are aware of macro-trends in the market – for example, the move towards open-plan kitchen and dining areas, so that appliances are on show for guests and family.

Monitoring what competitors are doing is also important. The company watches what all the main competitors are doing, not for the purpose of copying them, but in order to find gaps in the market – areas where competitors are not meeting customer need.

Hans Stråbirg, President of the Electrolux Group

Watch the video clip, then try to answer the following questions. The answers are on the companion website.

Questions

1 How does Electrolux manage exchange?
2 What is the role of customer need in the Electrolux strategy?
3 How would a brand manager for Electrolux try to go about his or her job?

ABOUT MARKETING

Marketing is the term given to those activities which occur at the interface between the organisation and its customers. It comes from the original concept of a marketplace, where buyers and sellers would come together to conduct transactions (or exchanges) for their mutual benefit. The aim of marketing as a discipline is to ensure that customers will conduct exchanges with the marketer's organisation rather than with the other 'stallholders'. To do this effectively, marketers must provide those customers with what they want to buy, at prices which represent value for money.

This basic concept of managing exchange leads us on to the most important concept in marketing, that of customer centrality. Marketing, above all else, uses the customer (who is often also the consumer) and his or her needs as the starting point for all decisions. Of all the building blocks of marketing, in both theory and practice, this is far and away the most important: it is also often difficult to do because it involves thinking like someone else.

The two most widely used definitions of marketing are these:

Marketing is the management process which identifies, anticipates, and supplies customer requirements efficiently and profitably. (UK Chartered Institute of Marketing)

Marketing is the process of planning and executing the conception, pricing, promotion and distribution of ideas, goods and services to create exchange and satisfy individual and organisational objectives. (American Marketing Association 2004)

Both of these definitions have been criticised. The Chartered Institute of Marketing (CIM) definition has been criticised because it takes profit as being the only outcome of marketing, whereas marketing approaches and techniques are widely used by organisations such as charities and government departments that do not have profit as their goal. The American Marketing Association (AMA) definition has also been criticised for failing to take account of the increasing role of marketing in a broader social context, and for appearing to regard consumers as being passive in the process. The same criticism could equally be applied to the CIM definition. Interestingly, neither definition includes the word 'consumer'. This may be because there are many customers who buy the product, but do not themselves consume it (for example, a grocery supermarket buyer might buy thousands of cans of beans, but dislike beans himself). Equally, someone can be a consumer without actually making the buying decision – an example would be a child whose parents make most of the decisions about food, clothing, entertainment and so forth on behalf of the child.

To the non-marketer, marketing often carries negative connotations; there is a popular view that marketing is about persuading people to buy things they do not want, or about cheating people. In fact, marketing practitioners have the responsibility for ensuring that the customer has to come first in the firm's thinking, whereas other professionals might be more concerned with getting the balance sheet to look right or getting the production line running smoothly. Marketers are well aware that the average customer will not keep coming back to a firm that does not provide good products and services at an acceptable price, and without customers there is no business.

Competition in many markets is fierce. If there is room for four companies in a given market, there will be five companies, each trying to maximise their market share; the customer is king in that situation, and firms that ignore the customer's needs will go out of business. Marketers therefore focus their attention entirely on the customer, and put the customer at the centre of the business.

THE DEVELOPMENT OF THE MARKETING CONCEPT

The marketing concept is a fairly recent one, and has been preceded by other business philosophies. These philosophies have not necessarily come about in the straight progression implied by the following section: although at different times there may have been a general way in which business was conducted, there have certainly been considerable overlaps between the different philosophies, and many firms have not been part of this general trend.

Production orientation

During the nineteenth century it was often thought that people would buy anything, provided it was cheap enough. This belief had some truth in it, since the invention of the steam engine allowed very much cheaper mass-produced items to be made. If an item was on sale at around one-tenth the price of the hand-made equivalent, most customers were prepared to accept poorer quality or an article that didn't exactly fit their needs. The prevailing attitude among manufacturers was that getting production right was all that mattered; this is called **production orientation**. This paradigm usually prevails in market conditions under which demand greatly exceeds supply, and is therefore somewhat rare in the twenty-first century (although it does exist in some markets, for example in some Communist countries).

With rising affluence people are not prepared to accept standardised products, and global markets allow manufacturers to reap the benefits of mass production despite providing more specialised products; therefore the extra cost of having something that fits one's needs more exactly is not high enough to make much difference.

Product orientation

Because different people have different needs some manufacturers thought that an ideal product could be made, one that all (or most) customers would want. Engineers and designers developed comprehensively equipped products, with more and 'better' features, in an attempt to please everybody. This philosophy is known as **product orientation**.

Product orientation tends to lead to ever-more complex products at ever-increasing prices; customers are being asked to pay for features that they may not need, or that may even be regarded as drawbacks.

Sales orientation

As manufacturing capacity increases, supply will tend to outstrip demand. In this scenario, some manufacturers take the view that a 'born salesman' can sell anything to anybody and therefore enough salesmen could get rid of the surplus products, provided they are determined enough and don't take no for an answer. This is called *sales orientation*, and relies on the premise that the customers can be fooled, the customer will not mind being fooled and will let you do it again later, and that if there are problems with the product these can be glossed over by a fast-talking sales representative. Up until the early 1950s, therefore, personal selling and advertising were regarded as the most important (often the only) marketing activities.

Sales orientation takes the view that customers will not ordinarily buy enough of the firm's products to meet the firm's needs, and therefore they will need to be persuaded to buy more. Sales orientation is therefore concerned with the needs of the seller, not with the needs of the buyer (Levitt 1960). Essentially, what these businesses try to do is to produce a product with given characteristics, then change the consumers to fit it. This is, of course, extremely difficult to do in practice.

Selling orientation and the practice of selling are two different things – modern salespeople are usually concerned with establishing long-term relationships with customers who will come back and buy more (Singh and Koshy 2011). This is an important distinction that is often missed by marketing theorists; there is more on this later in the book (Chapter 9). In the meantime, though, selling skills are a necessary factor in successful marketing (Wachner *et al.* 2009, Troilo *et al.* 2009).

Customer orientation

Modern marketers take the view that the customers are intelligent enough to know what they need, can recognise value for money when they see it, and will not buy again from the firm if they do not get value for money. This is the basis of the *marketing concept*.

Putting the customer at the centre of all the organisation's activities is more easily said than done. The marketing concept affects all areas of the business, from production (where the engineers and designers have to produce items that meet customers' needs) through to after-sales services (where customer complaints need to be taken seriously). The marketing concept is hard to implement because, unlike the sales orientation approach which seeks to change the customers' behaviour to fit the organisation's aims, the marketing concept seeks to change the organisation's behaviour to fit one or more groups of customers who have similar needs. This means that marketers often meet resistance from within their own organisations.

At this point, it may be useful to remind ourselves of the distinction between customers and consumers. Customers are the people who buy the product; consumers are those who consume it. Customers could therefore be professional buyers who are purchasing supplies for a company, or possibly a parent buying toys for a child. The customer might also be the consumer, of course, but the consumer could equally be the recipient of a gift or the user of a service which is paid for by others.

Critical thinking

Many companies say that they are customer (or consumer) orientated, but how true is this? Do companies seriously expect us to believe that the customers come first when they reserve the best parking space for the managing director? Or that the customer comes first when they raise their prices? Or that the customer comes first when the offices close at weekends?

In fact, would it be fairer to say that we always consider the customer's needs, since this is the best way of getting their money off them?

Societal marketing

Societal marketing holds that marketers should take some responsibility for the needs of society at large, and for the sustainability of their production activities. This orientation moves the focus away from the immediate exchanges between an organisation and its customers, and even away from the relationship between the organisation and its consumers, and towards the long-term effects on society at large. This need not conflict with the immediate needs of the organisation's consumers: for example, Body Shop operates a highly successful consumer-orientated business while still promising (and delivering) low environmental impact.

Kotler *et al.* (2001) say that products can be classified according to their immediate satisfaction and their long-run consumer benefits. Figure 1.1 illustrates this. In the diagram, a product which has high long-term benefits and is also highly satisfying is classified as a desirable product. For example, a natural fruit juice which is high in vitamins and also tastes good might fit this category. A product which has long-term benefits but which is not immediately satisfying, for example a household smoke alarm, is a salutary product. Products which are bad for consumers in the long run, but which are immediately satisfying (such as alcohol, cigarettes and confectionery) are called pleasing products: research shows that people believe that 'unhealthy' foods taste better (Raghunathan *et al.* 2006). Finally, products which are neither good for consumers nor satisfying are called deficient products; examples might include ineffective slimming products, or exercise equipment which is poorly designed and causes injury. In theory, firms should aim to produce desirable products – but consumers often choose the pleasing products instead; for example, eating unhealthy foods when they feel unhappy (Garg *et al.* 2006).

Figure 1.1 Societal classification of new products

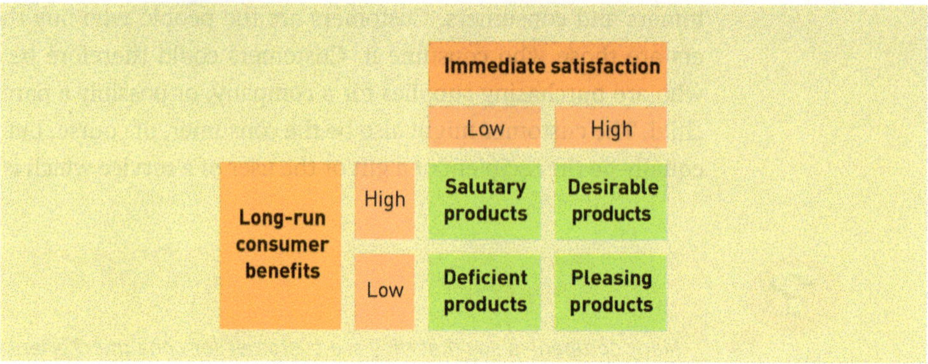

		Immediate satisfaction	
		Low	High
Long-run consumer benefits	High	Salutary products	Desirable products
	Low	Deficient products	Pleasing products

Source: Kotler, P., Armstrong, G., Saunders, J. and Wong, V., 2001, *Principles of Marketing*. Pearson Education Limited © 2001.

The societal marketing concept includes the marketing concept in that it recognises the needs of individual consumers, but it goes further in that it aims to improve the well-being of the wider society in which the firm operates. This means that the organisation takes on responsibility for good citizenship, rather than expecting consumers to understand or take account of the wider implications of their consumption behaviour. The problem is that firms need to balance three factors: customer needs, company profits (or other objectives) and the needs of society as a whole. Since competing companies may not be so concerned about society at large, it is not clear how societal marketing will contribute to creating competitive advantage; it is very clear how customer orientation helps firms to compete, however.

Ultimately, consumer orientation and societal marketing both seek to ensure that the organisation (whether a business or a non-profit organisation) should be looking to create greater value for customers, and thus meet the competition better (or even create competition in new markets).

Relationship marketing

During the 1990s, marketing thinking moved towards the **relationship marketing** concept. Traditional marketing has tended to concentrate on the single transaction with a short-term focus. Relationship marketing focuses on the 'lifetime' value of the customer. For example, a motor manufacturer might have one model aimed at young drivers, another aimed at families with children, and another aimed at middle-aged motorists. Each segment might be treated as a separate and unique entity. Under a relationship marketing paradigm, the organisation recognises that the young motorist will pass through each lifestyle stage in turn, and is then a customer for a different model each time. Relationship marketing aims to determine who will be (or could be) the most loyal customer throughout his or her life: marketers are responsible for establishing and maintaining these relationships.

In practice, relationship marketing has met with its greatest success in the business-to-business world. Companies which sell to other companies have generally been most proactive in establishing long-term cooperative relationships; for example, aircraft engine manufacturers such as Rolls-Royce and Pratt & Whitney need to establish close relationships with aircraft manufacturers such as Airbus Industrie and Boeing, since the designs of airframes and engines need to be coordinated. The ability to adapt the designs to meet the needs of the other company has obvious advantages in terms of cost savings and (eventually) greater profits, but it also has an advantage from the supplier's viewpoint in that close cooperation makes it harder for competitors to enter the market. Customers that have committed to a shared design process are unlikely to want to start the process all over again with another supplier. Creating this kind of loyalty has a significant effect on future revenues (Andreassen 1995).

The key elements in relationship marketing are the creation of customer loyalty (Ravald and Gronroos 1996), the establishment of a mutually rewarding connection, and a willingness to adapt behaviour to maintain the relationship (Takala and Uusitalo 1996).

Critical thinking

Do we really want to have a relationship with the companies which supply our needs? Of course politeness is one thing – but we aren't going to go on a long walking holiday with our bank, are we? Maybe the relationship is a bit one-sided: the company wants to lock us in to a long-term deal, and offers us all kinds of incentives to do so, whereas actually we would rather be free to choose between firms. We soon learn that threatening to leave means we get freebies, so the more they try to hang on to us, the more we take advantage!

Hardly the basis for a long-term relationship, is it?

There is more on relationship marketing throughout the book: it has become, like the Internet, central to marketing practice in recent years.

MARKETING AND OTHER BUSINESS DISCIPLINES

As the marketing concept has evolved from production orientation through to customer orientation, the role marketing occupies relative to other business functions has also evolved. Under a production-orientated regime, marketing usually occupies a departmental role; the marketing role is contained within a marketing department which carries out the communications functions of the firm.

Figure 1.2 shows the evolution of marketing's role within the organisation.

Figure 1.2 Evolution of marketing's role

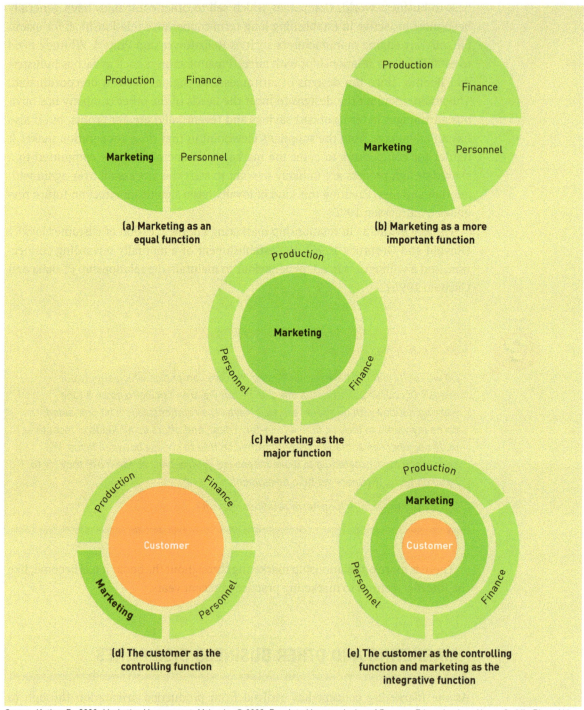

Source: Kotler, P., 2003, *Marketing Management*, 11th edn, © 2003. Reprinted by permission of Pearson Education Inc., Upper Saddle River, NJ.

If customers are central to the organisation's thinking, marketers act as the moderating group. Marketing can be seen in several ways, as follows:

- As a moderating force in the exchange process.
- As the driving philosophy of the business. Looked at in this way, everyone in the organisation becomes concerned primarily with adding value for the customer.
- A managerial function. This aspect of marketing means that marketers manage resources to obtain the most positive responses from customers.
- A dynamic operation, requiring analysis, planning and action. Because customers' needs, tastes and requirements change rapidly, marketing needs to change also. A product-orientated firm does not have this difficulty, since it seeks to change its customer base (either by persuading customers to buy, or by seeking out new customers) rather than change the product or the overall offer.
- A catalyst for change. Market-orientated firms need to change to meet customer need: marketers are at the forefront of these changes because they represent the customer.

Integration of different functions will almost always improve performance (Lyus et al. 2011), and in a customer-orientated firm it is the marketing people who are best placed to coordinate activities to maximise customer satisfaction. Bringing colleagues from other disciplines on board in developing a marketing orientation is as essential to this process as communicating with customers (Korhonen-Sande 2010).

MARKETING ON A DAY-TO-DAY BASIS

Marketers deal with the **marketing mix**, which was described by McCarthy (1960) as the four Ps of marketing. These are:

- *Product.* The product should fit the task the target consumers want it for, it should work, and it should be what the consumers expected to get.
- *Place.* The product should be available from wherever the firm's target group of customers find it easiest to shop. This may be a high street shop, it may be mail order through a catalogue or from a magazine coupon, or it may even be doorstep delivery.
- *Promotion.* Advertising, public relations, sales promotion, personal selling and all the other communications tools should put across the organisation's message in a way that fits what the particular group of consumers and customers would like to hear, whether it be informative or appealing to the emotions.

- *Price.* The product should always be seen as representing good value for money. This does not necessarily mean that it should be the cheapest available; one of the main tenets of the marketing concept is that customers are usually prepared to pay a little more for something that really works well for them.

The 4-P model has been useful when applied to the manufacture and marketing of physical products, but with the increase in services provision the model does not provide a full enough picture. In 1981 Booms and Bitner proposed a 7-P framework to include the following additional factors:

- *People.* Virtually all services are reliant on people to perform them, very often dealing directly with the consumer; for example, the waiters in restaurants form a crucial part of the total experience for the consumers. In effect, the waiter is part of the product the consumer is buying.
- *Process.* Since services are usually carried out with the consumer present, the process by which the service is delivered is, again, part of what the consumer is paying for. For example, there is a great deal of difference between a silver-service meal in an upmarket restaurant and a hamburger bought from a fast-food outlet. A consumer seeking a fast process will prefer the fast-food place, whereas a consumer seeking an evening out might prefer the slower process of the restaurant.
- *Physical evidence.* Almost all services contain some physical elements; for example, a restaurant meal is a physical thing, even if the bulk of the bill goes towards providing the intangible elements of the service (the decor, the atmosphere, the waiters, even the dishwashers). Likewise, a hairdressing salon provides a completed hairdo, and even an insurance company provides glossy documentation for the policies it issues.

In fact, virtually all products combine a physical product with a service element. In some cases, the service element is the main factor in distinguishing one product from another, especially in business-to-business markets (Raddats and Easingwood 2010).

Each of the above elements of the marketing mix will be dealt with in greater detail throughout the book, but it is important to recognise that the elements need to be combined as a mix. Like a recipe, one ingredient of the mix will not substitute for another, and each ingredient must be added in the right quantities at the right time if the mix is to prove successful in achieving consumer satisfaction. Each organisation will tend to have its own approach to the mix, and therefore no two firms will follow exactly the same marketing approach. This is one of the features that distinguishes marketing from the other business disciplines such as accountancy or company law. The marketing mix concept is also useful as a way of thinking about marketing, but in practice many marketing activities do not fall neatly within the boxes: there is considerable overlap. For example, a money-off special offer overlaps between pricing and sales promotion.

To illustrate how the marketing concept is implemented in practice, the next section looks at some of the jobs that marketers have.

MARKETING JOBS

In a sense, everybody in the organisation is responsible to some extent for ensuring that the consumers' needs are met. Clearly, though, some individuals will have greater responsibility than others for this; some of the job titles that marketers hold are shown in Table 1.1.

In market-orientated companies it is the customer who has the major say in what happens, and it is the marketing team that works within the company to ensure

Table 1.1 Marketing job titles and descriptions

Job title	Job description
Brand manager	Responsible for all the decisions concerning a particular brand. This concept was originally introduced at Mars; brand managers compete with each other as well as with other firms for market share in the chocolate bar market, even though they are all working for the same firm. This tends to result in greater efforts and greater corporate share all round.
Product manager	Responsible for all the decisions around a group of similar products within a firm. For example, a biscuit manufacturer might have one product manager in charge of chocolate-covered snack biscuits, and another in charge of savoury biscuits for cheese.
Sales manager	Responsible for controlling, training and motivating the salesforce and the sales back-up team. Sales managers often also have a role in credit control, since they are in the best position to know the individual customers and can give an opinion on the customer's creditworthiness or (as a last resort) on the least damaging way to get the customer to pay up.
Salesperson	Finds out what each customer needs, and tries to arrange for it to be delivered. Salespeople do this by selecting from the range of products that the company has on offer, and explaining those products in terms of how they will meet the client's needs.
Advertising manager	Controls media purchases, deals with advertising agencies, generally handles the flow of information to the company's customers and consumers.
Public relations manager	Monitors the company's public image and applies corrective measures if the company is acquiring a bad reputation. Organises events and activities that will put the company in a good light, and tries to ensure that the company behaves responsibly towards its wider publics.
Market research manager	Collects evidence about what it is that consumers really need, and what they would really like to buy. Sometimes this also includes monitoring competitors' activity so that the company can take action early to counteract it.
Webmaster	Controls the design and maintenance of the corporate website, including regular updates to reflect changes in the product range, and arranges the design of new promotions (for example, online games and viral marketing activities).

that everything is geared to the customer's (and consumer's) needs. Not all companies are market-orientated in the sense of putting customer satisfaction at the core of everything the business does; even some marketing managers see marketing as being purely a departmental responsibility rather than an organisational one (Hooley *et al.* 1990). In fact, everyone within the firm has some responsibility for ensuring customer satisfaction; those who have direct contact with the firm's customers have a particular role to play (for example, secretaries, delivery drivers, receptionists, telephonists and credit controllers).

The **marketing orientation** is adopted because it works better than any other orientation; customers are more likely to spend money on goods and services that meet their needs than on those that do not. In other words, looking after customers is good for business, and organisations which adopt a customer orientation are more likely to meet their objectives than those which do not. This applies even in non-profit organisations; charities, government departments and other organisations that offer benefits to 'customers' also function more effectively if they put their customers at the centre of everything they do (Modi and Mishra 2010).

KEY CONCEPTS IN MARKETING

Apart from customer centrality, there are several more key concepts which are the running themes of any marketing course or career. These will be dealt with in more detail later in the book, but they are as follows:

- *Managing exchange.* This goes further than promoting exchange through clever advertising and sales techniques: it also means ensuring that goods are where they should be when they should be, and ensuring that the products themselves are worthy of exchange. Viewing marketing as the management of the exchange process gives clear guidance to people working within the firm.
- *Segmentation and targeting.* This is the idea that people can be grouped according to their needs (i.e. there are groups of potential customers who are looking for the same type of product) and that we can, and should, devote our limited resources to meeting the needs of a few groups rather than trying to please everybody.
- *Positioning.* As marketers, we often seek to create an appropriate attitude towards our brands, and the firms for whom we work. This perception needs to be accurate, at least for our target customers, otherwise they will be disappointed and will not do business with us again. The position our brand occupies in the minds of the target group is therefore critical, and in this context the brand is the focusing device for all our planning – it is the lens through which our customers see us.

DEFINITIONS OF SOME MARKETING TERMS

Customers are the people or firms who buy products; *consumers* actually use the product, or consume it. Frequently customers are also consumers, so the terms might be used interchangeably, but often the person who buys a product is not the one who ultimately consumes it.

A **need** is a perceived lack of something. This implies that the individual not only does not have a particular item, but also is aware of not having it. This definition has nothing to do with necessity; human beings are complex, and have needs which go far beyond mere survival. In wealthy western countries, for example, most people eat for pleasure rather than from a fear that they might die without eating – the need for enjoyment comes long before there is a necessity for food.

A **want**, on the other hand, is a specific satisfier for a need. An individual might need food (hunger being awareness of the lack of food) and want (for example) a curry rather than a sandwich.

Wants become **demands** when the potential customer also has the means to pay for the product. Some marketers have made their fortunes from finding ways for people to pay for the products, rather than from merely producing the product. The demand for a given product is therefore a function of need, want and ability to pay.

A **product** is a bundle of benefits. This is a consumer-orientated view, because consumers will buy a product only if they feel it will be of benefit. Diners in a restaurant are not merely buying a full stomach; they are buying a pleasant evening out. Customers in a bar are not buying fizzy water with alcohol and flavourings in it; they are buying a social life. Here a distinction should be made between *physical goods* and *services*. For marketers, both of these are products, since they may well offer the same benefits to the consumer. An afternoon at a football match or a case of beer might serve the same morale-raising function for some men. Services and physical goods are difficult to distinguish between, because most services have a physical good attached to them and most physical goods have a service element attached to them. The usual definition of services says that they are mainly intangible, that production usually happens at the same time as consumption, that they are highly perishable, and that services cannot be owned (in the sense that there is no second-hand market for them).

Publics are any organisations or individuals that have actual or potential influence on the marketing organisation. This is an important definition for public relations practitioners, because they have the task of monitoring and adjusting the firm's activities relative to all the firm's publics, which can include government departments, competitors, outside pressure groups, employees, the local community and so forth.

Markets are all the actual and potential buyers of the firm's products. Few firms can capture 100% of the market for their products; marketers more commonly aim for whichever portions of the market the firm can best serve. The remainder of the customers would go to the competition, or just be people who never hear of the product and therefore do not buy it. Even giant firms such as Coca-Cola have less than half of the market for their product category. For this reason, marketers usually break down the overall market into *segments* (groups of customers with similar needs and characteristics) or even *niches* (very specific need and product categories).

Price is the amount of money for which a product is sold. *Value* is what the product is worth to the customer or consumer. The value is always higher than the price, or no business would result, but individual customers will make a judgement as to whether the product is good value or poor value. If the product is poor value, the customer will try to find alternatives; if the product is good value, the customer will remain loyal. The decision about value for money is, of course, subjective; what one customer considers a great bargain, another customer might see as a waste of good money.

MEETING MARKETING RESISTANCE

Most organisations still tend to see marketing as one function of the business, rather than seeing it as the whole purpose of the business. Marketing departments are frequently seen as vehicles for selling the company's products by whatever means present themselves, and marketers are often seen as wizards who can manipulate consumers into buying things they do not really want or need. This means that many marketers find that they meet resistance from within the firm when they try to introduce marketing thinking.

This is at least in part due to the fact that the practice of marketing is difficult. Adopting a marketing stance means trying to think like somebody else, and to anticipate somebody else's needs. It means trying to find out what people really need, and develop products that they will actually want. It means bending all the company's activities towards the customer. Inevitably there will be people within the firm who would rather not have to deal with these issues, and would have a quieter life if it were not for customers.

Table 1.2 shows some typical arguments encountered within firms, together with responses that the marketer could use.

Overcoming this type of resistance is not always easy because of the following factors:

- Lack of a leadership which is committed to the marketing concept.
- Lack of a suitable organisational infrastructure. For example, information about customers and consumers is a great deal more difficult to communicate throughout the firm if the firm's information technology systems are inadequate.
- Autocratic leadership style from senior management. In companies where the top managers believe that only their own ideas are right, the idea of changing the corporate direction to meet customer need better is less likely to take root.

Table 1.2 Reasons not to adopt a marketing philosophy

Source	Argument	Response
Production people	This is what we make efficiently. It's a good, well made product, and it's up to you to find people to sell it to.	You might like the product, but the customers may have other ideas. What we need to do is not just 'keep the punters happy' but *delight* our customers and ensure their loyalty in future.
Accountants and financial directors	The only sensible way to price is allocate all the costs, then add on our profit margin. That way we know for sure we can't lose money! Also, how about cutting out the middle man by selling direct to the retailers?	If you use cost-plus pricing, you will almost certainly either price the product lower than the consumers are prepared to pay, in which case you are giving away some of your profit, or you'll price it too high and nobody will buy the product. And that way you'll *really* lose some money! And cutting out the wholesalers means we'd have to deliver odd little amounts to every corner shop in the country, which would make our transport costs shoot up. Not to mention that the retailers won't take us seriously – we need the wholesalers' contacts!
Legal department	We have no legal obligation to do more than return people's money if things go wrong. Why go to the expense of sending somebody round to apologise?	With no customers, we have no business. We have all our eggs in one basket; we can't afford to upset any of them.
Board of Directors	Business is not so good, so everybody's budgets are being cut, including the marketing department. Sorry, you'll just have to manage with less.	If you cut the marketing budget, you cut the amount of business coming in. Our competition will seize the advantage, and we'll lose our customer base and market share – and we won't have the money coming in to get it back again, either.
Front-line staff	I'm paid to drive a truck, not chat up the customers. They're getting the stuff they've paid for, what more do they want?	Giving the customer good service means they're pleased to see you next time you call. It pays dividends directly to you because your job is more pleasant, but also it helps business and keeps you in a job.
Salesforce	You're paying me commission to get the sale, so getting the sale is all I'm interested in.	You can get sales once by deceit, but what happens when you go back? How much more could you sell if your customers know you're a good guy to do business with? And apart from all that, if you're doing your best for the customers, you can sleep at nights. Collaboration between sales and marketing is known to improve overall business performance (Le Meunier-Fitzhugh and Piercy 2007).

- Inherent mistrust of marketing by some individuals in positions of power.
- A preference for a production or sales focus (as seen in Table 1.2).
- A transactional approach to business, in which making each sale is seen as the appropriate focus rather than thinking in terms of encouraging customers to return.

In an ideal corporate situation, marketing would be seen as the coordinating function for every department. The marketing function would be supplying information about the customer base, there would be common control systems in place to ensure that each department contributes primarily to customer satisfaction, the business strategy would be based around customer need, and goals for the organisation would be realistic and aimed at customer satisfaction. In practice, most firms have some way to go in reaching this ideal.

QUOTATIONS ABOUT MARKETING

For companies to be successful, the management must put the customer first. Here are some quotations that illustrate this.

> **Probably the most important management fundamental that is being ignored today is staying close to the customer to satisfy his needs and anticipate his wants. In too many companies the customer has become a bloody nuisance whose unpredictable behaviour damages carefully-made strategic plans, whose activities mess up computer operations, and who stubbornly insists that purchased products should work.**
>
> (Lew Young, Editor-in-Chief of *Business Week*)

> **Marketing is so basic that it cannot be considered a separate function . . . It is the whole business seen from the point of view of its final result, that is, from the customer's point of view.**
>
> (Peter F. Drucker, 1973)

> **There is only one boss – the customer. And he can fire everybody in the company from the chairman on down, simply by spending his money somewhere else.**
>
> (Sam Walton, American founder of Wal-Mart Stores, the largest retail chain in the world)

And finally, Tom Watson of IBM was once at a meeting where customer complaints were being discussed. The complaints were categorised as engineering complaints, delivery complaints, servicing complaints, etc., perhaps ten categories in all. Finally Watson went to the front of the room, swept all the paper into one heap, and said 'There aren't any categories of problem here. There's just one problem. Some of us aren't paying enough attention to our customers.' And with that he swept out, leaving the executives wondering whether they would still have jobs in the morning. IBM salespeople are told to act at all times as if they were on the customer's payroll – which of course they are.

CASE STUDY 1 Waitrose

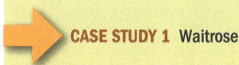

Waitrose is a UK supermarket chain operating mainly in England, with a few branches in Wales and Scotland. It is an unusual company because it is in fact a partnership between its employees. As part of the John Lewis Partnership, the chain is owned by the people who work there – which, as one might imagine, gives them a much greater commitment to the firm and its customers than might be the case elsewhere. Waitrose operates differently from other supermarket chains in other ways, too. For one thing, the stores do not compete on price. They do not claim to be cheaper than anywhere else, but they do claim to provide much higher quality products and a much better customer service: Waitrose customers are happy to pay a small premium to obtain these very important benefits.

For example, Waitrose staff will pack customers' groceries at the checkout and carry the bag to the customers' cars if necessary. Staff will accompany customers round the store if necessary, so that they can find products easily. A subsidiary, Waitrose Entertaining, will help plan and cater for important events such as weddings, birthdays and christenings, supplying canapés, buffets, drinks and glasses. Or, if you prefer, Waitrose will lend you glasses, fish kettles, and other items free of charge. Customers only pay for breakages, and there is no obligation to make any purchase at all (although few people would be cheeky enough to borrow without buying anything).

Another unique service is the Quick Check scan-as-you-shop system. Customers can, if they wish, use a hand-held scanner while they shop, packing the goods as they go. At the checkout, the customer simply downloads the scanner information and pays for the goods, without having to queue for a checkout operator or pack and repack the goods. This is a great saving in time for many people, but it also reduces the number of times that goods are packed and repacked, which helps to ensure that the goods reach the customer's home undamaged.

Customers can also order by telephone or on the Internet for home delivery, or even (unusually) visit the store in person, do the shopping, and leave the goods to be delivered later. The customer doesn't even need to go to the checkout for this service – he or she simply leaves the trolley at the customer service desk and goes home. Waitrose staff will scan the goods, pack them and arrange delivery. This service is obviously useful to people who are disabled, or who use public transport, or who perhaps walked to the store and have too much shopping to carry home.

Waitrose's only concession to the fixation on price that many customers have is to say that they offer 'Quality food, honestly priced'. The company's aim is to offer the convenience of a supermarket with the expertise of a small shop – no small feat, but possible, given modern communications technology.

Waitrose has certainly made a considerable success of the enterprise. The company has won several awards for customer service, and has been awarded the Royal Warrant, which makes them the official grocers to Her Majesty the Queen (and, incidentally, Prince Charles, the Prince of Wales). They were formerly grocers to Her Majesty the Queen Mother as well.

In 2011 Waitrose won the prestigious Customer Satisfaction Award from the Institute of Customer Service. Attention to customer needs, attention to the quality of the products on offer and, most especially, attention to the service being given to customers has been the foundation of Waitrose's success. No doubt there are other supermarkets which are bigger, and no doubt there are chains which are cheaper, but Waitrose has a solid base of customers who appreciate being treated as the most important element in the company's success.

Questions

1. Why shouldn't Waitrose compete on price as well?
2. Why does the company offer to lend people glasses and other equipment rather than steer them towards the company's catering side?
3. How might relationship marketing help the company?
4. Why might staff, who own the firm after all, pay so much attention to customer service?
5. Why is the Royal Warrant important to a firm like Waitrose?

SUMMARY

This chapter has been about the terms and concepts of marketing. Here are some key points from the chapter:

- Marketing is about understanding what the consumer needs and wants, and seeing that the company provides it.
- A need is a perceived lack; a want is a specific satisfier.
- Customers buy things; consumers use them.
- Price is what something costs; value is what it is worth.
- A product is a bundle of benefits; it is only worth what it will do for the consumer.
- Consumer (or customer) orientation is used because it is the most profitable in the long run.

CHAPTER QUESTIONS

1. In a situation where supply exceeds demand, which orientation would you expect most firms to have?
2. Why might a consumer feel that paying £150 for a pair of designer jeans represents good value for money?
3. What needs are met by buying fashionable clothes?
4. What needs might a mother meet by buying a child sweets?
5. Why should marketers always refer back to the consumer when making decisions?

Further reading

The Marketing Book edited by Michael Baker (London, Heinemann/Chartered Institute of Marketing, 1991) contains a very good chapter by Michael Baker himself on the history of the marketing concept.

Marketing: Concepts and Strategies, 4th edn by S. Dibb, L. Simkin, W. Pride and O.C. Ferrell (London, Houghton Mifflin, 2000) contains a realistic and interesting appendix on careers in marketing.

Principles of Marketing, 3rd edn by Frances Brassington and Stephen Pettitt (Harlow, Financial Times Prentice Hall, 2002) has a good overview of marketing's relationship with other business disciplines in Chapter 1.

References

Andreassen, T.W.: 'Small, high-cost countries' strategy for attracting MNCs' global investments', *International Journal of Public Sector Management,* **8** (3) (1995), pp. 110-18.

Booms, B.H. and Bitner, M.J.: 'Marketing strategies and organisation structures for service firms', in *Marketing of Services,* J. Donnelly and W.R. George, eds (Chicago, IL, American Marketing Association, 1981).

Drucker, P.F.: *Management: Tasks, Responsibilities, Practices* (New York, Harper & Row, 1973).

Garg, N., Wansink, B. and Inman, J.J.: 'The influence of incidental affect on consumers' food intake', *Journal of Marketing,* **71** (1) (2006), pp. 194-206.

Hooley, G.J., Lynch, James E., Shepherd, Jenny et al.: 'The marketing concept: putting theory into practice', *European Journal of Marketing,* **24** (9) (1990), pp. 7-23.

Korhonen-Sande, S.:'Micro-foundations of market orientation: influencing non-marketing managers' customer information processing', *Industrial Marketing Management,* **39** (4) (2010), pp. 661-71.

Kotler, P., Armstrong, G., Saunders, J. and Wong, V.: *Principles of Marketing* (Harlow, Financial Times Prentice Hall, 2001).

Le Meunier-Fitzhugh, K. and Piercy, N.F. 'Exploring collaboration between sales and marketing', *European Journal of Marketing,* **41** (7/8) (2007), pp. 939-55.

Levitt, T.: 'Marketing myopia', *Harvard Business Review* (July-August 1960), pp. 45-56.

Lyus, D., Rogers, B. and Simms, C.: 'The role of sales and marketing integration in improving strategic responsiveness to market change', *Journal of Database Marketing and Customer Strategy Management,* **18** (1) (2011), pp. 39-49.

McCarthy, E.J.: *Basic Marketing: A Managerial Approach,* 9th edn (Homewood, IL, Irwin, 1987; 1st edition 1960).

Modi, P. and Mishra, D.: 'Conceptualising market orientation in non-profit organizations: definition, performance, and preliminary construction of a scale', *Journal of Marketing Management,* **26** (5 & 6) (2010), pp. 548-69.

Raddats, C. and Easingwood, C.: 'Services growth options for B2B product-centric businesses', *Industrial Marketing Management,* **39** (8) (2010), pp. 1334-45.

Raghunathan, R., Naylor, R.W. and Hoyer, W.D.: 'The unhealthy = tasty intuition and its effects on taste inference, food enjoyment, and choice of food products', *Journal of Marketing,* **70** (4) (2006), pp. 170-84.

Ravald, A. and Gronroos, C.: 'The value concept and relationship marketing', *European Journal of Marketing,* **30** (2) (1996), pp. 10-30.

Singh, R. and Koshy, A.: 'Does salesperson's customer orientation create value in B2B relationships? Empirical evidence from India', *Industrial Marketing Management,* **40** (1) (2011), pp. 78-85.

Takala, T. and Uusitalo, O.: 'An alternative view of relationship marketing: a framework for ethical analysis', *European Journal of Marketing,* **30** (2) (1996), pp. 45-60.

Troilo, G., DeLuca, L.M. and Guenzi, P.: 'Dispersion of influence between marketing and sales: its effects on superior customer value and market performance', *Industrial Marketing Management,* **38** (8) (2009), pp. 872-82.

Wachner, T., Plouffe, C.R. and Gregoire, Y.: 'SOCO's impact on individual sales performance; the integration of selling skills as a missing link', *Industrial Marketing Management,* **38** (1) (2009), pp. 32-44.

THE MARKETING ENVIRONMENT

Objectives

After reading this chapter you should be able to:

- Recognise the main environmental factors affecting marketing decisions
- Formulate ways of coping with the marketing environment
- Recognise ways to exploit opportunities in the environment
- Understand the principles of marketing strategy
- Explain the strategic issues behind the formulation of marketing plans.

INTRODUCTION

No business operates in a vacuum; any organisation is surrounded by laws and liabilities, pressure groups and public bodies, customers and competitors. These are part of the marketing environment within which the organisation works, and since marketing is at the interface between the organisation and the outside world, dealing with this environment is a major part of the marketer's work.

This means that the marketing policy of a firm (or any organisation) should be viewed as operating within a complex and rapidly changing environment. These external factors must be monitored and responded to if the organisation is to meet its goals, and an understanding of the environment is (ultimately) the basis for all marketing strategy.

St Paul's Cathedral

St Paul's Cathedral is an icon of London. Built just after the Great Fire of London, it is a major tourist attraction based at the heart of London's financial district. At the same time it is a working church, with a congregation and regular religious services. Around 700,000 visitors a year visit St Paul's, about 75% of whom come from overseas, but it still needs £5.5 million a year to keep its doors open.

St Paul's, as a religious monument, is a non-profit organisation. It is primarily a place of worship, and the Dean and Chapter welcome anybody to come in, but equally the church needs contributions, so entrance charges are levied for visiting some parts of the building. This is regarded as a compromise between free access for Christian worshippers and others, and the need for finance. No one has to pay to come to a service, since this would conflict with the church's primary purpose, and some people object strongly to having to pay to go into a church.

Reconciling the needs of visitors and the needs of the church is only part of the problem – meeting the needs of people who may only be in London for a short visit while at the same time remaining competitive with other major attractions in London (of which there are many, spread out over a large city). The fact that the cathedral has been there for nearly 350 years is, paradoxically, not helpful – people can always come back next year, or in another 50 years, and the cathedral will still be there.

Canon Precentor Lucy Winkett

Watch the video clip, then try to answer the following questions. The answers are on the companion website.

Questions

1 How can St Paul's reconcile the conflict between the internal and external environments?
2 What micro-environmental factors most impact on St Paul's?
3 What macro-environmental factors most affect St Paul's?

THE MARKETING ENVIRONMENT

The marketing environment represents a complex array of threats and opportunities for the organisation, and can sometimes seem difficult to categorise. Generally speaking, the marketing environment can be divided into two areas: the **external environment** and the **internal environment**. The external environment is concerned with everything that happens outside the organisation, and the internal environment is concerned with those marketing factors that happen within the organisation. Often organisations concentrate far more attention on the external environment than on the internal environment, but both are of great importance.

There are two basic approaches to dealing with environmental forces: reactive and proactive. **Reactive management** regards environmental factors as being uncontrollable, and will therefore tend to adjust marketing plans to fit environmental changes. **Proactive management** looks for ways to change the organisation's environment in the belief that many, even most, environmental factors can be controlled, or at least influenced in some way (Kotler 1986).

THE EXTERNAL ENVIRONMENT

The external environment consists of two further divisions: factors close to the organisation (called the **micro-environment**) and those factors common to society as a whole (the **macro-environment**). Micro-environmental factors might include such things as the customer base, the location of the company's warehouses, or the existence of a local pressure group that is unsympathetic to the business. Some micro-environmental factors (for example, availability of skilled employees) overlap into the internal environment. The macro-environment might include such factors as government legislation, foreign competition, exchange rate fluctuations or even climatic changes.

The external environment is often not susceptible to direct control; the best that marketers can do is to influence some elements of it, and to react in the most appropriate ways to avoid the threats and exploit the opportunities it presents.

Situational analysis

Managers need to know where they are now if they are to be able to decide where they are going. This analysis will involve examining the internal state of health of the organisation, and the external environment within which the organisation operates.

At the simplest level, managers can use SWOT analysis to take stock of the firm's internal position: SWOT stands for Strengths, Weaknesses, Opportunities and Threats. Strengths and weaknesses are factors that are specific to the firm; opportunities

Table 2.1 Swot analysis

	Internal factors	External factors
Positive factors	*Strengths* What are we best at? What intellectual property do we own? What specific skills does the workforce have? What financial resources do we have? What connections and alliances do we have? What is our bargaining power with both suppliers and intermediaries?	*Opportunities* What changes in the external environment can we exploit? What weaknesses in our competitors can we attack? What new technology might become available to us? What new markets might be opening up to us?
Negative factors	*Weaknesses* What are we worst at doing? Is our intellectual property outdated? What training does our workforce lack? What is our financial position? What connections and alliances should we have, but don't?	*Threats* What might our competitors be able to do to hurt us? What new legislation might damage our interests? What social changes might threaten us? How will the economic (boom-and-bust) cycle affect us?

and threats arise from the external environment. These factors can be broken down further, as shown in Table 2.1.

The list in Table 2.1 is not, of course, comprehensive. Equally, a threat might be turned into an opportunity: a competitor's new technological breakthrough might lead us to consider a takeover bid, for example, or new legislation might provide a loophole which we can exploit while our competitors have to abide by the new rules.

STEP (Socio-cultural, Technological, Economic and Political) analysis is a useful way of looking at the external environment (it is also sometimes written as PEST). Table 2.2 shows some of the main changes that are occurring under each of those headings.

STEP and SWOT analyses are simply different ways of looking at the environment and at the firm's place in it. The external marketing environment is itself subdivided into micro- and macro-environments, as shown in Figure 2.1.

The micro-environment

The micro-environment is made up of those factors that impact closely on the organisation, and typically consists of the following elements:

- Competitors
- Customers
- Suppliers
- Intermediaries
- Micro-environment publics.

Table 2.2 Current environmental changes

	Example	Implications
Socio-cultural	Lifestyle expectations	As people have become more wealthy, they have come to expect more. In twenty-first century Britain, few people would consider living without a telephone, television, refrigerator, car, bank account or credit cards. In 1960, all these products were examples of things owned by only a minority of the population.
	Post-industrial society (Bell 1974)	As automation of manufacturing increases, more people work in service industries. Traditional class divisions are disappearing, with new ones rising to take their place; the growth of lifestyle analysis affects the way marketers portray their target consumers.
	Demography	A report prepared for the United Nations stated that, apart from 18 countries which are regarded as 'demographic outliers' (i.e. abnormal), every country in the world is experiencing the ageing of its population, as birth rates fall and life expectancy increases (Haishan et al. 2005). This has important implications for marketers, who may need to move from providing goods for children and young families towards providing for the elderly.
Technological	Information technology	Few serious marketers would consider not having a corporate website, yet only 10 years ago such websites were rare, and were often merely 'presence' sites which directed visitors to a telephone number or address.
	Space technology	Apart from the revolution in communications (telephone, Internet and television) that satellites have brought, there are increasing possibilities for new manufacturing techniques to be used in space. Virgin Galactic even offers space tourism, and this is likely to increase in future years as competitors enter the market. Also, the technology used for space exploration has resulted in spin-offs for terrestrial production of goods.
Economics	Boom-and-bust cycle	At approximately 8-year intervals most national economies go into recession. This means that the production of goods and services shrinks, jobs are lost and businesses become bankrupt. Purchase of major capital items such as new kitchens, houses, cars and washing machines slows down, and consumers become less willing to buy on credit as job security reduces. Occasionally, as in the 1930s, a full-scale depression is triggered when the economy enters a long-term downward trend. Triggers for recessions vary: the 2008–9 recession was caused by problems in the banking system, but others have been triggered by punitive increases in commodity prices, over-rapid expansion of small businesses and even crop failures.
	Micro-economics	Micro-economics is concerned with exchanges and competition. Competitive activities are very much the domain of the marketer.

Table 2.2 continued

	Example	Implications
Politics	Influence of political parties	Governments usually have policies concerning trade and industry: in part this is to ensure a growing economy and increased prosperity, in part it is to increase the number of jobs and thus improve the government's finances. Changes of government will often cause shifts in emphasis which might lead to disruption for individual firms.
	Legislation	Laws arise in two ways: government legislation (laws created by politicians) and case law, which is the law as interpreted by judges. Politicians can be influenced by petitions and by reasoned argument; this is called lobbying. Case law can be appealed by the parties to it, but is harder to influence. International law can sometimes have powerful influences on businesses, depending on where the firm is located. For example, European (EU) law must be passed through the national governments of the member states; changes during the 1990s mean that EU law supersedes national law and can therefore virtually be imposed on the member states. This makes it difficult to influence or control.

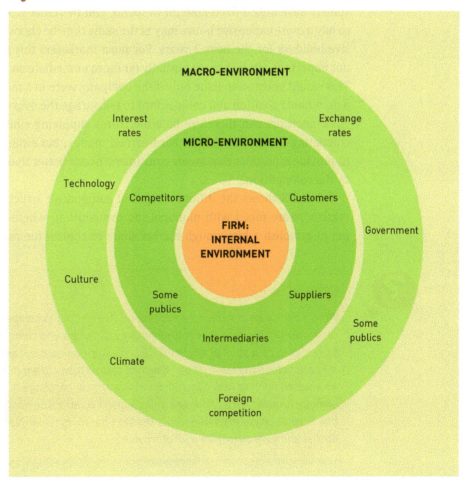

Figure 2.1 Micro- and macro-environment forces

Competitors

Frequently firms fail to recognise who their *competitors* are. It is not at all unusual for firms to define competition too narrowly, simply because they define their business too narrowly. For instance, if a bus company defines itself solely as being in the bus business, the management might reasonably define the competitors as being other bus companies. If, on the other hand, the company defines itself as being in the transportation business, the management will recognise the competition from railways, taxis and even bicycles.

In the early days of the Internet, many retailers did not recognise that online retailing represented competition. Now, many bricks-and-mortar retailers have their own websites so that customers can order directly: although the Internet is, for various reasons, unlikely to replace bricks-and-mortar retailers entirely, it does represent a threat.

When assessing competitive threat, marketing managers need to decide which competitors offer the closest substitutes *in terms of meeting the consumers' needs*. Grouping consumers with similar needs and characteristics is called **segmentation** (see Chapter 4). Since each segment has different needs, the threat from competition will come from different sources in each case.

At the extreme, all businesses compete with all others for consumers' money; consumers have only a fixed amount to spend, and therefore a consumer who chooses to buy a more expensive house may at the same time be choosing not to have expensive holidays for the next 2 years. For most marketers this type of competition is not important, since there are usually far more immediate competitors to deal with. This would become an issue only if the company were in a monopolistic (or at least a dominant) position and could afford to encourage the overall market to increase.

Competitors can therefore be either firms supplying similar products or firms competing for the consumer's hard-earned money, but either way marketers need to provide a product that meets consumers' needs better than the products offered by the competition.

Table 2.3 shows the different types of competitive structure. In practice, most marketers are faced with monopolistic competition, where each company is trying to establish a big enough market share to control the market, but has no real

Critical thinking

Wow! That's a lot of different competitors! If everybody is competing for customers' cash, how can we hope to identify who our customers and competitors are? Surely there has to be a point at which we say, 'These people are not our competitors, they are potentially our friends.' Which of course leads to another point – why do we keep on fighting with competitors instead of cooperating? After all, major motor manufacturers such as Ford and Volkswagen cooperate on designing new vehicles (the Ford Galaxy is the same car as the VW Sharan, for example), so why don't we all do that and save ourselves a lot of trouble?

Table 2.3 Competitive structures

Type of competitive structure	Explanation	Examples
Perfect competition	There is a large number of suppliers, no one of which is powerful enough to influence the supply level overall. Products are homogeneous – that is to say, they are virtually identical. Entry to the market is easy. Everybody in the market (both suppliers and consumers) has full knowledge of what everybody else is doing. There are few examples, and although economists sometimes use the perfect competition model for purposes of discussion, marketers will be very unlikely to be operating within this environment.	Unregulated agricultural markets. The international money markets.
Monopolistic competition	A situation where one major supplier has obtained a large share of the market by the use of a differentiated marketing approach, but competitors can still enter and try to carve out their own share of the market.	Coca-Cola and PepsiCo have a major share of the soft drinks industry, but other firms are not prevented from entering the market.
Oligopoly	A few companies control the market almost entirely. Typically this happens when costs of entry to the market are high; very often the size of the market is not great enough to repay the capital cost of entry for a new firm. Oligopolies are often investigated by government monopoly regulators, who exist to ensure that large firms do not abuse their power.	Commercial aircraft manufacture. The detergent industry. Oil extraction and refining.
Monopoly	Monopolies exist when a single firm has a product with no close substitutes. In practice, this situation is almost as rare as perfect competition; the few examples still permitted are the so-called 'natural monopolies' which would clearly not be efficient if effort were duplicated.	Electricity supply grids. Some countries' national rail networks.

prospect of becoming the sole supplier for the product category. The largest firm in such a market may find it more worthwhile to seek to increase the total market for the product category than to try for a bigger share of the existing market. This approach has the added advantage that it will not attract the attention of the government monopoly regulators.

Michael Porter's Five Forces model offers a useful approach to competitor analysis (Porter 1990). The five forces are as follows:

1. *The bargaining power of suppliers:* the greater this is, the stronger the competitive pressures.
2. *The bargaining power of customers:* again, the stronger this is, the more competitive the environment.

3. *The threat of new entrants:* if it is easy to enter a market, or if there is a likelihood that the market is becoming attractive to new players, the market will become competitive.
4. *The threat of substitute products and services:* this threat is often not seen until it is too late. New products may come along which meet the same need as the existing product, but in a different way: it is sometimes difficult to see this threat until it is too late.
5. *The rivalry among current competitors:* in some markets, competitors are careful not to compete too strongly for fear of losing out in the long run – such markets are oligopolistic (see Table 2.3). In other markets, competition is fierce.

The main strength of Porter's model is that it broadens the concept of competition and enables marketers to look at the wider picture. Correct identification of competitors is essential; in simple terms, a firm's competitors are any firms that seek to meet a similar need. This definition may be hard to apply in practice.

Customers

Customers may change their needs, or may even disappear altogether. Some years ago, the American company Johnson & Johnson became aware that much larger quantities of its baby shampoo and talcum powder were being sold than could possibly be accounted for by the number of babies in the country. Research discovered that many adults were using the products on themselves, so the company launched a promotion campaign based around the slogan, 'Are you still a Johnson's baby?' A new category of customer had become apparent, and the company was able to respond to this and capitalise on the changed environment. Clearly customers' needs are of paramount importance to marketers, and it is essential that new segments can be identified easily and accurately; however, it is also important to recognise that some segments may be disappearing, and to know when to switch the marketing effort to more lucrative segments.

Suppliers

Suppliers also form part of the micro-environment since they impact closely on the company. At first sight, suppliers would appear to be outside the scope of the marketing department, but in fact the firm relies heavily on the good will of its suppliers, and a good public relations exercise will always try to involve suppliers. A supplier can easily cause an adverse effect within a firm by supplying shoddy goods, or failing to meet delivery dates, and this will inevitably impact on the firm's customers. This is of greater importance for some firms than for others (retailers will be more concerned about suppliers than will government offices, for example) but most organisations need to monitor their suppliers and ensure that they are providing appropriate goods.

Current thinking in purchasing and supply is that the relationship between suppliers and their customers should be a close one, with frequent visits to each other's premises and a high level of information exchange. This is encompassed within the

logistics approach to supply, in which the firm is seen as a link in a system for providing the right goods and services in the right place at the right time; the system as a whole takes raw materials and moves and transforms them into goods that consumers need. This philosophy relies on the supplier and purchaser integrating their activities and developing a mutual understanding of each other's problems. It is also (from the supplier's viewpoint) an example of good relationship marketing – establishing a close, long-term relationship is likely to prove more efficient in the long run than continually seeking new customers as existing customers go elsewhere for their supplies.

Intermediaries

Intermediaries are the retailers, wholesalers, agents and others who distribute the firm's goods. Relationships with these intermediaries need to be good if the firm is to succeed in getting its goods to the final consumer successfully (this is part of the logistics approach). Intermediaries may also include marketing services providers such as research agencies, advertising agencies, distribution companies providing transport and warehousing, and exhibition organisers – in fact, any individuals or organisations that stand between the company and the consumer and help in getting the goods out. These relationships are, of course, of great importance to marketers, but intermediaries have their own businesses to run and are working to their own agendas. As with suppliers, it pays dividends to establish good relationships with intermediaries, mainly by sharing information and by maintaining good communication links (see Chapter 8).

Micro-environment publics

Finally, some of the firm's publics form part of the micro-environment. 'Publics' is a generic term encompassing all the groups that have actual or potential impact on the company. The range of publics can include financial publics, local publics, governmental publics, media publics, citizen action publics and many others. The marketing activity concerned with these publics is called (not surprisingly) public relations; there is more on this in Chapter 9.

Financial publics might include the banks and shareholders that control the firm's finances, and who can pressure the firm to behave in particular ways. These pressures can be strong, and can even threaten the firm's existence; firms are often compelled by their financial publics to do things they would otherwise prefer not to. It is to address this problem that glossy company reports are produced for shareholders, and positive information about the company is issued to banks and others.

Local publics consist mainly of the firm's neighbours. These local organisations and individuals may well pressure the company to take local actions, for example clean up pollution or sponsor local charities. Obtaining the goodwill of the local public will, of course, make it much easier for the company to live harmoniously with its neighbours and will reduce short-term local difficulties. For example, Body Shop expects its franchisees to participate in projects that will help the local community, whether by supervising a play area or by raising funds for a local charity. Employees participate in these projects on company time; the activities improve the image of the company and generate positive feelings about the store among local residents. There is a spin-off for the firm's staff, who feel that they are working for a caring company; Body Shop employees tend to be very positive about their employer.

Each of the elements in the micro-environment is small enough that the organisation at the centre should have influence over most of them, and be able to react effectively to the remainder.

The macro-environment

The macro-environment includes the major forces that act not only on the firm itself, but also on its competitors and on elements in the micro-environment. The macro-environment tends to be harder to influence than does the micro-environment, but this does not mean that firms must simply remain passive; the inability to control does not imply an inability to influence. Often the macro-environment can be influenced by good public relations activities (see Chapter 9).

The main elements of the macro-environment are:

- Demographic factors
- Economic factors
- Political factors
- Legal factors
- Socio-cultural factors
- Ecological and geographical factors
- Technological factors
- Macro-environment publics.

Demographic factors

Demographics is the study of population factors such as the proportion of the population who are of a given race, gender, age or occupation, and also of such general factors as population density, size of population and location. Demographic changes can have major effects on companies: the declining birth rate in most western countries has an obvious effect on sales of baby products, but also means that, without immigration, the working population would be shrinking and consequently there would be a shortage of people to become employees (Cruijsen *et al.* 2002). Likewise, changes in the ethnic composition of cities, or in the population concentration (for example, fewer people living in the centres of large cities) cause changes in the demand for local services and retailers, and (more subtly) changes in the type of goods and services demanded. There is more on this in Chapter 3.

Economic factors

Economic factors encompass such areas as the boom-and-bust cycle, and the growth in unemployment in some parts of the country as a result of the closing of traditional industries. Macro-economic factors deal with the management of demand in the economy; the main mechanisms that governments use for this are interest rate controls, taxation policy and government expenditure. If the government increases expenditure (or reduces taxation), there will be more money in the economy and demand will rise; if taxation is increased (or expenditure cut), there will be less money for consumers to spend, so demand will shrink. Rises in interest rates tend to reduce demand, as home loans become more expensive and credit card charges rise.

Micro-economic factors are to do with the way in which people spend their incomes. As incomes have risen over the past 40 years or so, the average standard of living has risen, and spending patterns have altered drastically. The proportion of income spent on food and housing has fallen (Office for National Statistics 2003) whereas the proportion spent on entertainment and clothing has risen. Information on the economy is widely publicised, and marketers make use of this information to predict what is likely to happen to their customers and to demand for their products.

Political factors

Political factors often impact on business: recent examples are the severe austerity measures imposed by many governments as a result of the financial crisis of 2008. Firms need to be able to respond to the prevailing political climate, and adjust the marketing policy accordingly. For example, British Telecom, Deutsche Telekom and Telstra of Australia have all had to make major readjustments to their marketing approaches since being privatised, and in particular since seeing an upswing in competitive levels. Almost all the firms' activities have been affected, from cutting the lead time between ordering and obtaining a new telephone through to price competition in response to competitors' cut-price long-distance and international calls.

Legal factors

Legal factors follow on from political factors, in that governments often pass laws which affect business. For example, Table 2.4 shows some of the legislation on marketing issues currently in force in various countries.

Sometimes judges decide cases in a way that reinterprets legislation, however, and this in itself can affect the business position. A further complication within Europe arises as a result of EU legislation, which takes precedence over national law, and which can seriously affect the way firms do business in Europe.

Case law and EU law are not dependent on the politics of the national governments, and are therefore less easy to predict. Clearly businesses must stay within the law, but it is increasingly difficult to be sure what the law says, and to know what changes in the law might be imminent.

For companies operating in global markets, legal issues can become a minefield: the fact that a product is legal in one country does not mean that it is, or even should be, in another. Product modifications required in different countries often mean that even a 'world' product has to be virtually reinvented each time it crosses borders,

Table 2.4 Examples of legislation affecting marketing

Country	Legislation
France	Food advertisers must include one of four 'healthy eating' messages (for example, 'for your health, avoid eating snacks between meals').
UK	Consumers can opt out of receiving mailings and cold telephone calls: firms that contact people who have opted out can be fined.
Sweden	Advertising of alcoholic drinks is forbidden on TV, except for low-alcohol beers. Companies have got round this by using the same branding for low-alcohol as for full-strength beers.
Germany	Advertising for war toys and games of chance are forbidden (Chee and Harris 1988). Advertising aimed at children is severely restricted.
Japan	All rooftop and flashing-light advertisements have been banned in Kyoto, in an attempt to preserve the city's unique heritage of ancient buildings.

but the problem goes further for marketers, since some marketing techniques which are perfectly normal and acceptable in some cultures are regarded as unacceptable or manipulative in others. For example, a home improvement salesman calling at someone's home in the United States of America would be likely to bring a small gift such as flowers or a cake, as one would if calling to visit a friend. In the UK, this would be regarded with some suspicion, and the Office of Fair Trading have ruled that it is an unfair practice.

Socio-cultural factors

Socio-cultural factors are those areas that involve the shared beliefs and attitudes of the population. People learn to behave in particular ways as a result of feedback from the rest of society; behaviour and attitudes that are regarded as inappropriate or rude are quickly modified, and also people develop expectations about how other people should behave. In the marketing context, people come to believe (for example) that shop assistants should be polite and helpful, that fast-food restaurants should be brightly lit and clean and that shops should have advertised items in stock. These beliefs are not laws of nature, but merely a consensus view of what *should* happen. There have certainly been many times (and many countries) where these standards have not applied.

These prevailing beliefs and attitudes change over a period of time owing to changes in the world environment, changes in ethnic mix and changes in technology. These changes usually happen over fairly long periods of time. Since 1970, in most western countries there has been a development towards a more diverse, individualistic society; a large increase in the number of couples living together without being married; and a marked increase in the acceptance (and frequency) of single-parent families (European Commission 2001).

Cultural changes over the same period include a major change in eating habits owing to an increase in tourism, migration and greater globalisation of food markets (Maucher 1993).

A very few cultural changes come about as the result of marketing activities: the popularity of social networking sites has created an entirely new way of making friends and relating to them, for example. In turn, these sites have opened up new opportunities for marketers: many firms have Facebook pages, and products can be promoted using 'word of mouse' facilitated by such sites: additionally, firms can use such sites as sources of information about customer attitudes and needs (Woodcock et al. 2011).

Ecological and geographical factors

Ecological and geographical factors have come to the forefront of thinking in the past 20 years or so. The increasing scarcity of raw materials, the problems of disposing of waste materials and the difficulty of finding appropriate locations for industrial complexes (particularly those with a major environmental impact) are all factors that are seriously affecting the business decision-making framework (see Chapter 12). In a marketing context, firms are having to take account of public views on these issues and are often subjected to pressure from organised groups as well as individuals, who often define themselves as 'green' consumers (Autio et al. 2009). Often the most effective way to deal with these issues is to begin by consulting the pressure groups concerned, so that disagreements can be resolved before the company has committed too many resources (see Chapter 9); firms adopting the societal marketing concept (see Chapter 1) would do this as a matter of course.

Technological factors

Technological advances in the past 40 years have been rapid, and have affected almost all areas of life. Whole new industries have appeared; for example, satellite TV stations, cable networks, the Internet, CD recordings and virtual reality and computer-aided design systems. All of these industries were unknown even 20 years ago. It seems likely that technological change will continue to increase, and that more new industries will appear in future. The corollary, of course, is that some old industries will disappear, or at the very least will face competition from entirely unexpected directions. Identifying these trends in advance is extremely difficult, but not impossible.

Clearly the Internet has had a tremendous impact on marketing. Nobody owns the Internet; it is a communications medium spread across thousands (even millions) of computers worldwide, which operates independently of the telephone companies that supply its cable connections, of the governments in whose countries it resides, and even of the computer owners in whose machines data are stored. The Internet therefore operates under its own rules; there is little or no international law to govern its use or abuse. From a marketing viewpoint, one major impact of the Internet is that it has placed market power even more firmly in the hands of consumers. People are able to compare prices and suppliers much more quickly, can comment to each other much more quickly about exceptionally good or exceptionally bad service, and can make themselves much better informed about products than before.

The rapid growth in virtual shopping (accessing catalogues on the Internet) means that consumers can buy goods anywhere in the world and have them shipped – or, in the case of computer software, simply downloaded – which means that global competition will reach unprecedented levels. Virtual shoppers are able to access high-quality pictures of products, holiday destinations and even pictures of restaurant food before committing to a purchase. Consumers can use bots which can be programmed to search the Internet on their behalf and find products that might be of interest. A correctly programmed bot acts exactly like the individual, knowing what the person likes or dislikes, and developments in the pipeline would enable the bot to negotiate prices on behalf of the individual.

There is more on Internet marketing throughout the book, particularly Chapter 12.

Macro-environment publics

The macro-environment also contains the remainder of the organisation's publics.

- *Governmental publics* are the local, national and international agencies that restrict the company's activities by passing legislation, setting interest rates, and fixing exchange rates. Governmental publics can be influenced by lobbying and by trade associations.

- *Media publics*. Press, television and radio services carry news, features and advertising that can aid the firm's marketing, or conversely can damage a firm's reputation. Public relations departments go to great lengths to ensure that positive images of the firm are conveyed to (and by) the media publics. For example, a company might issue a press release to publicise its sponsorship of a major sporting event. This could generate positive responses from the public, and a positive image of the company when the sporting event is broadcast.

- *Citizen action publics* are the pressure groups, such as Greenpeace or consumers' rights groups, who lobby manufacturers and others to improve life for the public at large. Some pressure groups are informally organised; recent years have seen an upsurge in local pressure groups and protesters, and there has been a surge in the number of websites which protest about company or government activities. Most major companies' websites are shadowed by anonymous counter-culture sites: these carry derogatory stories about the companies. Such sites are difficult to stop since the Internet is largely unregulated and the people posting stories on the sites can remain anonymous.

> **Critical thinking**
>
> Why do we worry about citizen action publics? If people want to complain about us, why not let them? After all, nobody really pays much attention to a few soreheads complaining – they usually don't have much credibility, and they certainly don't have much of a budget.
>
> In fact there may even be some advantages. If we look at the websites concerned, we might be able to gain some ideas for improving what we do, and meeting customer needs better – which, for marketers, is the name of the game. We could even go a step further, and invite such pressure groups to advise us in future, so that we can tailor what we do to meet their needs better.

THE INTERNATIONAL ENVIRONMENT

As business becomes increasingly global, marketers find themselves more and more in the position of doing business across cultural divides, and across national boundaries. International marketing differs from domestic marketing in the following ways:

- Cultural differences mean that communications tools will need to be adapted, and sometimes changed radically
- Market segmentation issues are likely to be more geographically based
- Remoteness of the markets makes monitoring and control more difficult
- Both physical distribution (logistics) and place decisions will be affected by infrastructure differences in some overseas markets.

International marketing is important because of the economic theory of **comparative advantage**. This theory states that each country has natural advantages over others in the production of certain goods, and therefore specialisation and the trading of surpluses will benefit everybody. For example, although it is possible to grow tomatoes under glass in the Netherlands, they can be grown more easily and cheaply in Spain, so it makes economic sense for the Dutch to buy Spanish tomatoes and sell Spain chemical products that are produced more readily in the Netherlands.

Comparative advantage does not explain all of the thrust behind internationalisation; Japanese, US and UK multinationals have all made major impacts in overseas markets without having an apparent natural advantage over their overseas competitors. In some cases this can be explained by economies of scale; in others by the development of expertise within the firms; in others the reasons are historical.

WORLD TRADE INITIATIVES

Marketing to an international audience will usually bring **economies of scale** in manufacture, research and development and marketing costs. Most governments encourage firms to market internationally because it brings in foreign exchange, which enables the country to buy in essential imports (for example, aluminium ore or oil), which are needed to support the national economy.

The downside of world trade is that it sometimes results in the export of cultural values as well as goods and services, so that traditional cultures become eroded. Evidence exists to show that Latin America and Africa have lost ground in terms of share of world markets owing to internationalisation (Preston 1993). Also, firms have sometimes over-reached themselves and diseconomies of scale have resulted.

In general, though, the accepted view is that world trade results in greater wealth and higher standards of living for most of the world's population; trade is therefore regarded as beneficial in terms of its economic benefits, and governments worldwide try to encourage it, within the limits of getting the best deal for their own countries. Table 2.5 shows some of the major initiatives undertaken in recent years to encourage world trade.

The thrust behind much government thinking worldwide is to reduce tariffs and increase trade, while at the same time establishing trading blocs which can stand up to each other. The dominance of the United States of America has clarified the thinking of smaller countries, and there is little doubt that the European Union, Mercosur and the Asia-Pacific Economic Forum will make significant contributions to world competition.

Most governments are in favour of **exporting** their own manufacturers' goods, but would prefer to restrict **importing** if possible: this is to protect the **balance of payments**. Having more foreign currency coming in than is going out (a positive balance of payments) allows the government to keep interest rates down and also helps keep inflation down (a fuller explanation of the mechanisms by which this happens is beyond the scope of this book; further reading is given at the end of the chapter). This means that negotiations about reducing tariff barriers tend to be long-drawn-out as each government seeks to open up markets abroad while keeping out foreign competition.

Developing countries frequently impose tariff barriers on importers to protect their fledgling industries; unfortunately, this often results in these industries becoming inefficient since they do not need to compete with more efficient overseas manufacturers (Preston 1993). For example, Venezuela adopted an import substitution strategy in 1983 which included multiple exchange rates: an official rate, a rate for debt payment, a rate for essential exports and a free market rate. Importers had to wait several months for foreign currency, only obtaining the balance after the goods had arrived. This was hardly efficient, nor did it help business confidence, but it did protect Venezuelan manufacturers. Unfortunately, the failure of Latin American and African countries to agree to reduce tariffs with other countries meant that their

Table 2.5 World trade initiatives

Name	Description
World Trade Organization	An ongoing set of international negotiations to reduce customs duties which act as a barrier to trade. Approximately 116 nations are involved in the talks, which were initiated after the Second World War under the title The General Agreement on Tariffs and Trade. Tariffs among industrialised nations have fallen from an average 40% in 1947 to approximately 5% at present.
European Union	This is a trading group of 27 countries that have eliminated customs duties between the member states. Border controls are minimal (and in some cases non-existent), and 17 of the member countries use the same currency (the euro). There are still many problems to be overcome in achieving greater unity, but the EU remains a major trading bloc.
North American Free Trade Agreement (NAFTA)	Creating a *customs union* between the USA, Canada and Mexico, this agreement cancelled most tariffs between the member states except for some agricultural products.
Mercosur	A customs union between the nations of South America, this has already resulted in passportless travel throughout the continent (citizens need only carry identity cards) and in removal of tariff barriers on most items.
Cairns Agreement (IMF)	This is an agreement on world agricultural production and prices; compliance with it has been patchy, but the signatories to the Agreement continue to negotiate.
Association of South-East Asian Nations (ASEAN)	ASEAN has grown dramatically in recent years until it now covers 10 member states, with several other countries having associate or candidate status. The member states have agreed to preferential tariffs between them, and to remove almost all tariffs by 2015. ASEAN members also pledge to assist each other in economic development, a policy which seems to be working since this part of the world has seen impressive growth in recent years.
International Monetary Fund (IMF)	The IMF acts as a stabilising influence on the world economy by injecting funds into national economies, on a loan basis, subject to special conditions regarding government economic policies. The IMF exists to turn round ailing economies.
World Bank	The World Bank exists to fund projects which reduce poverty in the Third World. It is owned and funded by major economies: the United States has the biggest share, then Japan, then Germany, then the UK, then France.

exports became priced out of the market; while other countries developed effective international trading systems, the Third World was left behind (Preston 1993).

Governments also influence or control *exchange rates*; this means that exporters lose some control over prices, as the government controls the rate at which one currency is exchanged for another. Having a low-value currency will encourage exports in the short run, but also raises the price of imports; this can result in increased costs, which raise the prices anyway. Having a strong currency, on the other hand, may make exporting difficult and will probably suck in imports as the imported goods become cheaper than home-produced ones.

Culture

Cultural differences encompass religion, language, institutions, beliefs and behaviours that are shared by the members of a society. It is as well for marketers to take the advice of natives of the countries in which they hope to do business, since other people's cultural differences are not always obvious.

Classic examples of errors arising from language differences abound. The General Motors Nova brand name translates as 'no go' in Spanish; Gerber means 'to throw up' in colloquial French, creating problems for the baby food manufacturer of the same name; and Irish Mist liqueur had to be renamed for the German market since 'mist' means 'excrement' in German. Many cultural problems are more subtle, and have to do with the way things are said rather than the actual words used. In Japanese, 'yes' can mean 'yes, I understand' but not necessarily 'yes, I agree'. Portuguese has a total of seven different words for 'you', depending on the status and number of people being addressed.

Body language is also not universal. The American sign for 'OK', with the thumb and forefinger making a circle, is a rude gesture in Brazil (equivalent to sticking up the index and middle finger in Britain, or the extended middle finger in the USA and most of Europe). Showing the soles of the feet is considered insulting in Thailand, and while Americans are usually very happy to hear about an individual's personal wealth and success, Australians are less likely to take kindly to somebody acting like a 'tall poppy' in this way.

Sometimes local superstitions affect buying behaviour. American high-rise hotels do not have a thirteenth floor – the floor numbers go directly from twelve to fourteen. In China, consumers do not like to buy products where the price ends in a four, because four is a number associated with death: Chinese people prefer to buy products whose prices end in eight, which is considered lucky and is associated with financial prosperity (Simmons and Schindler 2003).

In general, marketers need to be wary of **ethnocentrism**, which is the tendency to believe that one's own culture is the 'right' one and that everybody else's is at best a poor imitation (Shimp and Sharma 1987). This is not an easy task for managers: most managers tend to underestimate the differences between the overseas market and the home market (Pedersen and Petersen 2004). This can be due to the fact that we tend to judge other cultures from the perspective of our own culture – this is called self-referencing, and is clearly difficult to avoid.

It can be easier to aim for countries where there is some **psychological proximity**. These are countries with some cultural aspects in common. For example, English-speaking countries have psychological proximity with each other; Spain has psychological proximity with most of Latin America; and the former Communist countries of Eastern European are close. Within countries with large migrant populations there may be subcultures that give insights into overseas markets: Australia is well placed to take advantage of Far Eastern markets and Greek markets as well as other English-speaking markets, and Brazil has good links with Germany as well as with Portugal, Angola and Mozambique. In an interesting reversal, Ireland also has good contacts in many countries owing to the Irish diaspora of the past 200 years.

In most West African countries tribal loyalties cross national borders, so that people from the same tribe might inhabit different countries. In a sense, this is paralleled in the Basque country of France and Spain, and in the language divide in Belgium, where Flemish speakers feel closer to their Dutch neighbours than to their Walloon compatriots, and Walloons feel closer to the French than to their Flemish neighbours.

From a marketer's viewpoint, cultural differences are probably reducing as consumers become more globally minded: foreign travel, the widespread globalisation of the entertainment media, and existing availability of foreign products in most economies have all served to erode the world's cultural differences (Ohmae 1989). Increasingly, marketers are able to identify distinct subcultures that transcend national boundaries; for example, the world youth culture fuelled by media such as MTV (Steen 1995).

Political factors

The *political environment* of the target country will also affect the entry decision. Table 2.6 shows some of the issues.

Table 2.6 Political factors in international marketing

Political factor	Explanation and implications
Level of protectionism	Some governments need to protect their own industries from foreign competition, either because the country is trying to industrialise and the fledgling companies cannot compete (as in some developing nations) or because lack of investment has resulted in a run-down of industry (as in much of Eastern Europe). Sometimes this can be overcome by offering inward investment (to create jobs) or by agreeing to limit exports to the country until the new industries have caught up.
Degree of instability	Some countries are less politically stable than others, and may be subject to military takeover or civil war. Usually the exporter's government diplomatic service can advise on the level of risk attached to doing business in a particular country.
Relationship between the marketer's government and the foreign government	Sometimes disputes between governments can result in trade embargoes or other restrictions. Obviously this is particularly prevalent in the arms trade, but trade restrictions can be applied across the board to unfriendly countries. For example, the USA still has a trade ban with Cuba for many items; Greece and Turkey have restrictions on travel and trade; and trade restrictions exist between Zimbabwe and Britain.

Economic influences

The *economic environment* of the target country is more than the issue of whether the residents can afford to buy our goods. In some cases the level of **wealth concentration** is such that, although the average **per capita income** of the country is low, there is a large number of millionaires: India is an example of this, as is Brazil. Economic issues also encompass the public prosperity of the country: is there a well developed road system, for example? Are telecommunications facilities adequate? Is the population sufficiently well educated to be able to use the products effectively?

A crucial economic issue is that of foreign exchange availability. If the target country does not have a substantial export market for its own products, it will not be able to import foreign products because potential importers will not be able to pay for the goods in the appropriate currency. This has been a problem in some countries in the Third World and in some Communist countries, and there has as a result been a return to **barter** and **countertrading**. Countertrading is the export of goods on the condition that the firm will import an equal value of other goods from the same market, and in the international context can be complex: for example, a firm may export mining machinery to China, be paid in coal, and then need to sell the coal on the commodities market to obtain cash (a **buy-back** deal). These complex arrangements are becoming much rarer as the world moves towards freely exchangeable currencies: barter and countertrade are inherently inefficient.

The *demographic environment* includes such factors as family size, degree to which the country has a rural as opposed to an urban population, and the migration patterns that shape the population. Migration patterns can make marked changes to the structure of a country's consumption: consumption of Indonesian food in the Netherlands, of Thai food in Australia, of Indian food in the United Kingdom, and of Algerian food in France are all much greater than can be accounted for by the respective ethnic minorities in those countries (Paulson-Box 1994). Marketers have played a part in this culture-swapping process to the extent that segmentation by ethnicity is no longer possible for many products (Jamal 2003).

THE INTERNAL ENVIRONMENT

Internal publics are the employees of the company. Although employees are part of the internal environment rather than the external environment, activities directed at the external environment will often impinge on employee attitudes; likewise, employee attitudes frequently impinge on the external publics. Sometimes employees convey a negative image of the organisation they work for, and this is bound to have an effect on the perceptions of the wider public.

The organisation's internal environment is a microcosm of the external environment. All organisations have employees; they will develop a corporate culture with its own language, customs, traditions and hierarchy. Sub-groups and individuals within the firm will have political agendas; pressure groups form; and the organisation has its own laws and regulations.

From the viewpoint of a marketer, the internal environment is as important as the external one, since the organisational culture, rules, hierarchy and traditions will inevitably be a major component of the organisation's public face. The members of the organisation can give a positive or negative image of the firm after they leave work for the day and interact with their families and friends, and even while in work they will usually come into contact with some of the firm's external publics. Since the members of those external publics will regard such communications as being authoritative, the effect is likely to be stronger than anything the marketing department can produce in terms of paid communications. In other words, if the company's staff speak badly about the company to outsiders, the outsiders are far more likely to believe those comments than to believe the company's promotional campaigns.

The days are long gone when the loyalty of staff could be commanded, and giving orders was all that was necessary to ensure obedience. Employees expect to have a degree of autonomy in their daily tasks, and do not feel any particular obligation towards an employer simply by reason of being employed. The employees of the organisation therefore constitute a market in their own right; the firm needs their loyalty and commitment, in exchange for which the staff are offered pay and security. Internal marketing is the process of ensuring (as far as possible) that employees know and understand the firm's strategic policies, and should feel that putting these policies into practice will be in their own best interests.

As we saw in Chapter 1, marketing can be a unifying force within the firm, giving the lead to each separate organisational function and providing staff with a single direction. Equally, it can be seen as a manipulative force, seeking to persuade people to act in ways which do not come naturally.

There is more on handling internal relationships (together with some techniques for communicating with the internal environments) in Chapter 9.

CASE STUDY 2 Home insulation

Fuel poverty was first defined by Dr Brenda Boardman in 1991, in her book *Fuel Poverty* (Boardman 1991). In the UK, fuel poverty is defined as the state of affairs whereby a household has to spend more than 10% of its income on fuel to maintain an adequate level of warmth. Fuel poverty may therefore come about either through low income or through high heating bills: as fuel becomes more expensive, it seems inevitable that fuel poverty will worsen unless something drastic is done to correct the situation.

Social policy in the past has led to the UK government providing financial assistance in meeting fuel bills. Even now, people over 60 are paid a winter fuel allowance of £250 to help with bills: this is in response to a rise in deaths from hypothermia among the elderly during the 1980s. However, this policy runs counter to the UK's policy on cutting carbon emissions, under which the UK has committed to reducing carbon emissions by 60% by 2050, with substantial improvement to be gained by 2020.

Much of the fuel poverty in the UK has come about as a result of poorly insulated housing; poorer people tend to live in older Victorian houses which have solid walls, single-glazed windows and thin ceilings which allow heat to escape into the roof space. In addition, these properties are often rented, and landlords have no real incentive to invest in good insulation because they do not usually pay the heating bills.

The government response to this has been the creation of a system of grants for home insulation. Under the umbrella title 'Warm Front', grants are available for loft insulation and cavity wall insulation. The grants are available to all householders, whether they rent or own the home, provided they meet certain conditions mainly relating to income. The scheme was revised in April 2011 as a result of government spending cuts so that fewer people would qualify; of course, as the scheme progresses, fewer homes will need the work since more homes will have benefited from the insulation.

During the period when many individuals and homes qualified for the grants there was a boom in companies offering the insulation service. Since the market might disappear at any time (for example, if the government decide to scrap the scheme or all the homes are insulated up to the required standard) there was something of a gold-rush element in the approach to the market. This meant that householders often found themselves being telephoned by eager salespeople, and receiving mailshots and leaflets from home insulation companies. The somewhat aggressive approach to the market was caused by several factors. First, the knowledge that there was only a fairly small window of opportunity available for firms, since sooner or later all the homes would be insulated. Second, home insulation is something of a distress purchase – it is something that is easily put off and which is perceived as having a long-term rather than a short-term benefit. Third, many of the homes were rented, and householders often did not want the disruption of having the home insulated when their perception was that the landlord would be the main beneficiary (many tenants having forgotten that they were the ones paying the fuel bills). Fourth, there was a high level of ignorance about the Warm Front initiative. It had been poorly publicised by the government, who believed (not unnaturally) that the insulation contractors would publicise it for them.

All of these factors led to a high-pressure approach by firms, using every marketing tool they could manage. SMS messages to mobile telephones, cold-calling by telephone and indiscriminate mailings all contributed to the various campaigns. By their nature, such campaigns could not be targeted effectively; it was virtually impossible to know in advance which households would qualify for the grants, since there was no way of telling what the household income might be or what insulation was already in place.

As the market became saturated, some companies moved on to offer energy producing products such as solar panels: again, this is a government sponsored scheme which helps householders to install solar panels which generate electricity, the surpluses from which are fed back to the national grid. In some cases, householders could remove themselves altogether from the need to pay for electricity. Like the insulation grants, these schemes are relatively unknown to most people, and therefore need to be marketed aggressively – a situation which will, no doubt, engender a great deal of irritation among householders who are on the receiving end of telephone calls and mailings.

In the long run, there is little doubt that people will need to adopt energy saving and energy producing policies in individual households. In the meantime, suspicion and reluctance to change are likely to inhibit progress and lead to greater effort on the part of salespeople in breaking down resistance.

Questions

1 What was the role of government in developing the market for home insulation?
2 What social factors contributed to the process of developing the market?
3 Why might salespeople meet resistance to home insulation initiatives?
4 What technological developments are likely to contribute to the energy market?
5 Why has government policy changed towards energy consumption?

SUMMARY

The environment within which the marketing department is operating consists of both internal and external factors. Internal factors are what happens within the organisation; external factors are those operating outside the firm, and consist of the micro-environment and the macro-environment. Macro-environmental factors are largely uncontrollable by individual firms; in fact, it is difficult for marketers to have any influence on them, except in the case of very large firms or powerful trade organisations.

While it may be possible for the largest firms to influence the macro-environment by lobbying Parliament, or even by affecting the national culture directly, small and medium-sized firms cannot alone hope to make sufficient impact on the external environment to make any major changes. Therefore these marketers need to learn to work with, or around, the macro-environmental factors they find, rather than seek to make changes.

Since the marketing environment has profound effects on the organisation, marketing strategy begins with two main activities: analysis of the environment (perhaps by STEP analysis) to see what threats and opportunities exist, and analysis of the firm's position within that environment and within itself (perhaps by SWOT analysis).

Here are the key points from this chapter:

- Businesses and other organisations do not operate in a vacuum
- The micro-environment is easier to influence than the macro-environment, but both are impossible to control
- The business should be defined from the customer's viewpoint; this will help to identify a broader range of competitors
- Customers should be grouped into segments so that scarce resources can be targeted to the most profitable areas (see Chapter 4)
- Close relationships with suppliers and intermediaries will be helpful in influencing the environment
- Public relations is about creating favourable impressions with all the company's publics
- Case law and EU law can both affect businesses, and are harder to predict since they are independent of national government
- The socio-cultural environment changes, but slowly
- Technology changes rapidly and will continue to do so; this both creates and destroys opportunities for marketers
- Internal publics need special attention, since they are the 'front line' of the company's relationships with its environment.

CHAPTER QUESTIONS

1 Why is the external environment impossible to control?
2 What can SWOT analysis tell a firm about its environment?
3 Given that businesses are made up of people, how is it that the same people are included as part of the firm's internal environment?
4 What are the most important factors making up the micro-environment?
5 What are the main problems faced when dealing with the macro-environment?

Further reading

This is a somewhat narrow area, with few books dedicated solely to the marketing environment. Most marketing strategy books will go into greater detail than is the case here, but the only text which is dedicated to discussion of the marketing environment is Adrian Palmer and Bob Hartley's book, *The Business Environment* 5th edition (Maidenhead: McGraw-Hill, 2006).

References

Autio, M., Heiskanen, E., Heinonen, Visa: 'Narratives of "green" consumers – the antihero, the environmental hero and the anarchist', *Journal of Consumer Behaviour*, **8** (1) (2009), pp. 40–53.

Bell, D.: *The Coming of Post-industrial Society: A Venture in Social Forecasting* (London, Heinemann, 1974).

Boardman, B.: *Fuel poverty: from Cold Homes to Affordable Warmth* (London, Belhaven Press, 1991).

Chee, H. and Harris, R.: *Global Marketing Strategy* (London, Financial Times Pitman, 1988).

Cruijsen, H., Eding, H. and Gjatelma, T.: 'Demographic Consequences of Enlargement of the European Union with the 12 Candidate Countries'. Statistics Netherlands, Division of Social and Spatial Statistics, Project Group European Demography, January 2002.

European Commission: *The Social Situation in the European Union 2001* (Luxembourg, Office for Official Publications of the European Communities, 2001), pp. 201–17.

Haishan, Fu, Fuentes, Ricardo, Ghosh, Arunabha *et al.*: *Human Development Report: International Development at a Crossroads: Aid, Trade and Security in an Unequal World* (United Nations, 1 UN Plaza, New York, NY 10017, USA, 2005).

Jamal, A.: 'Marketing in a multicultural world: the interplay of marketing, ethnicity and consumption', *European Journal of Marketing*, **37** (11) (2003), pp. 1599–620.

Kotler, P.: 'Megamarketing', *Harvard Business Review* (March–April 1986), pp. 117–24.

Maucher, H.O.: 'The impact of the single European market on regional product and price differentiation – the example of the European food industry', in C. Halliburton and R. Hunerberg (eds) *European Marketing; Readings and Cases* (Wokingham, Addison Wesley, 1993).

Office for National Statistics: *Household Expenditure Survey*, 2003.

Ohmae, K.: 'Managing in a borderless world', *Harvard Business Review* (May–June 1989), pp. 152–61.

Paulson-Box, E.: 'Adoption of ethnic food: a dietary innovation in the UK', *Proceedings of the Marketing in Education Group Conference* (1994), p. 792.

Pedersen, T. and Petersen, B.: 'Learning about foreign markets: are entrant firms exposed to a "shock effect"?' *Journal of International Marketing*, **12** (1) (2004), pp. 103–23.

Porter, M.E.: 'How competitive forces shape strategy', *Harvard Business Review*, **57** (2) (1990), pp. 137–45.

Preston, J. (ed.): *International Business: Text and Cases* (London, Pitman Publishing, 1993), p. 31.

Shimp, T. and Sharma, S.: 'Consumer ethnocentrism; construction and validation of CETSCALE', *Journal of Marketing Research*, **24** (8) (August 1987), pp. 280–9.

Simmons, C.L. and Schindler, R.M.: 'Cultural superstitions and the price endings used in Chinese advertising', *Journal of International Marketing*, **11** (2) (2003), pp. 101–11.

Steen, J.: 'Now they're using suicide to sell jeans', *Sunday Express* (26 March 1995).

Woodcock, N., Green, A. and Starkey, M.: 'Social CRM as a business strategy', *Journal of Database Marketing and Customer Strategy Management*, **18** (1) (2011), pp. 50–64.

10

MARKETING PLANNING, IMPLEMENTATION AND CONTROL

Objectives

After reading this chapter you should be able to:

- Analyse the firm's current situation and develop a forward strategic plan
- Explain the difference between strategy and tactics
- Explain the main issues surrounding budgeting
- Describe the basic approaches to budgeting
- Set up systems for the monitoring and control of your plans
- Develop strategic approaches to integrating a firm's marketing activities.

INTRODUCTION

This chapter is about integrating and coordinating the firm's marketing efforts, producing marketing plans and ensuring that the plans are carried out in a cost-effective manner. In most cases, marketing planning takes place in the context of overall corporate strategy, which may or may not be market-orientated; in any event, marketers have to decide where the organisation's resources need to be directed to ensure customer satisfaction and maximise opportunities for exchange.

Marketing Planning, Implementation and Control 79

Indian tourism

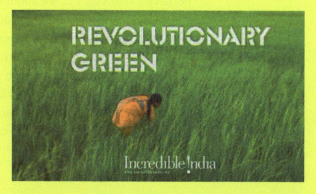

Marketing an entire country is not easy – there are too many factors to take into account. In the case of India, the Tourist Authority is dealing with an extremely diverse nation. India has everything – from beaches to ancient monuments, deserts to the highest mountains in the world, internationally famous cuisine to adventure trips in the jungle. The potential customers are also diverse; student backpackers on gap years, middle-aged tourists on world cruises, adventure seekers and sports enthusiasts, amateur historians, wildlife enthusiasts and beach-lovers all come to India. In recent years, as the Indian economy has taken off, more than 400,000 internal tourists travel to resorts and sites of interest in India every year.

Promoting this diversity led to the 2008 'Incredible India' campaign, which involved TV advertising on international cable channels such as CNN. This was coupled with poster advertising at major airports to appeal directly to regular travellers. The aim is to move Indian tourism upmarket; currently, the majority of tourists visiting India do so on a tight budget since it is one of the world's cheapest destinations. India is a very big country, well able to absorb and cater for much larger numbers of tourists; the difficulty lies in attracting wealthier tourists.

Sujata Thakur, Regional Director, Incredible India

Watch the video clip, then try to answer the following questions. The answers are on the companion website.

Questions

1 How would you measure the results of the Incredible India campaign?
2 What targets are the Tourist Authority setting – and how realistic are they?
3 How should the Tourist Authority plan for attracting a more upmarket group of tourists?

THE MARKETING PLANNING PROCESS

The basic process of planning is as shown in Figure 10.1. Strategic decisions concern the overall direction of the organisation. **Strategy** is about where we want to be; decisions on **tactics** are about how we are going to get there.

Strategic decisions tend to be difficult to reverse; they usually involve a rejection of other strategic options and they generally involve strong personal commitment on the part of the decision-maker. Tactical decisions are relatively easy to change, involve less commitment and can often run alongside other options. A comparison of strategic and tactical decisions is given in Table 10.1.

Strategy must be integrated across the whole range of marketing activities, it must be formulated in the light of good analysis of the environment and it must

Figure 10.1 The marketing planning process

Table 10.1 Comparison of strategic and tactical decisions

Strategic decisions	Tactical decisions
Concern overall direction	Concern methods of achievement
Difficult to reverse	Relatively easy to change
Involve rejection of alternatives	Allow combination of alternatives

include a feedback system so that the strategy can be adapted in the light of environmental changes. Strategy is influenced by organisational objectives and resources, competitor activities, the structure of the market itself and the firm's willingness to make changes and take risks.

From an overall strategic perspective, marketers need to decide on the following issues and formulate strategies for coping with them:

- Which market should the firm be in?
- What strengths and weaknesses is the firm bringing to the marketplace?
- Where does the firm intend to be in 5–30 years' time?
- What will the firm's competitors do in response to the market?
- Does the firm have sufficient resources to achieve the objectives decided upon?

The first stage in the planning process is to determine where the firm is now; this can be determined by carrying out a marketing audit.

THE MARKETING AUDIT

In marketing, strategic planning revolves around issues such as launching new products, changing brand names, deciding which segments to target and designing new promotional campaigns. The **marketing audit** is a review of the firm's current objectives, strategies, organisation, performance and activities, and its primary purpose is to pick out the firm's strengths and weaknesses so that managers can improve on them in future. It evaluates how effectively the organisation is performing its marketing tasks within the context of the seven Ps – products, price, place, promotion, people, processes and physical evidence (Band 1984).

The marketing audit is a snapshot of what is actually happening in the firm now. It should therefore be carried out on a fairly regular basis – within the limits of the amount of money that can be spared for the task and the amount of time that can be spared from doing the marketing tasks at hand.

Table 10.2 shows an overview of the scope of the marketing audit. Such an audit encompasses the SWOT and STEP analyses introduced in Chapter 2, but goes into considerably more detail. Once the exercise has been carried out, managers will have a very clear idea of what needs to be changed to meet the firm's objectives.

Table 10.2 The marketing audit

Main areas	Subsections	Issues to be addressed
Marketing environment audit *Macro-environmet*	Economic–demographic	Inflation, materials supply and shortages, unemployment, credit availability, forecast trends in population structure
	Technological	Changes in product and process technology, generic substitutes to replace products
	Political–legal	Proposed laws, national and local government actions
	Cultural	Attitude changes in the population as a whole, changes in lifestyles and values
	Ecological	Cost and availability of natural resources, public concerns about pollution and conservation
Task environment	Markets	Market size, growth, geographical distribution, profits; changes in market segment sizes and opportunities
	Customers	Attitudes towards the company and competitors, decision-making processes, evolving needs and wants
	Competitors	Objectives and strategies of competitors, identifying competitors, trends in future competition
	Distribution and dealers	Main trade channels, efficiency levels of trade channels
	Suppliers	Availability of key resources, trends in patterns of selling
	Facilitators and marketing firms	Cost and availability of transport, finance and warehousing; effectiveness of advertising (and other) agencies
	Publics	Opportunity areas, effectiveness of PR activities
Marketing strategy audit	Business mission	Clear focus, attainability
	Marketing objectives and goals	Corporate and marketing objectives clearly stated, appropriateness of marketing objectives
	Strategy	Core marketing strategy, budgeting of resources, allocation of resources
Marketing organisation audit	Formal structure	Seniority of marketing management, structure of responsibilities
	Functional efficiency	Communications systems, product management systems, training of personnel
	Interface efficiency	Connections between marketing and other business functions
Marketing systems audit	Marketing information system	Accuracy and sufficiency of information, generation and use of market research
	Marketing planning system	Effectiveness, forecasting, setting of targets
	Marketing control system	Control procedures, periodic analysis of profitability and costs
	New product development system	Gathering and screening of ideas, business analysis, pre-launch product and market testing

Table 10.2 continued

Main areas	Subsections	Issues to be addressed
Marketing productivity audits	Profitability analysis	Profitability of each product, market, territory and distribution channel. Entry and exit of segments
	Cost-effectiveness analysis	Costs and benefits of marketing activities
Marketing function audits	Products	Product portfolio; what to keep, what to drop, what to add, what to improve
	Price	Pricing objectives, policies and strategies. Customer attitudes. Price promotions
	Distribution	Adequacy of market coverage. Effectiveness of channel members. Switching channels
	Advertising, sales promotion, PR	Suitability of objectives. Effectiveness of execution format. Method of determining the budget. Media selection. Staffing levels and abilities
	Salesforce	Adequate size to achieve objectives. Territory organisation. Remuneration methods and levels. Morale. Setting quotas and targets

Source: Adapted from Kotler, P., 2003, *Marketing Management*, 11th edn, © 2003. Reprinted by permission of Pearson Education Inc., Upper Saddle River, N.J.

CORPORATE OBJECTIVES

Corporate objectives are the strategic statements of where the company wants to be. The objectives might be as follows:

- *Financial:* market share, sales, profit, return on investment, etc.
- *Philosophical:* perhaps a mission statement expressing the core values of the organisation.
- *Qualitative:* service levels, innovation, etc.

Corporate objectives often involve trade-offs, since all firms have limited resources and can concentrate on only one area at a time. In some cases the trade-offs involve diametrically opposed objectives. Weinberg (1969) proposed a set of eight trade-offs in setting objectives, as follows:

1 Short-term profit *v* long-term growth.
2 Profit margin *v* market positioning.
3 Direct sales effort *v* **market development**.
4 Penetrating existing markets *v* developing new ones.
5 Profit *v* non-profit goals.
6 Growth *v* stability.
7 Change *v* stability.
8 Low-risk *v* high-risk environments.

Table 10.3 Strategic alternatives

Strategic objective	Explanation
Backward integration	Taking control of suppliers, either by purchase or by merger
Forward integration	Taking control of customers (in industrial or commercial markets)
Horizontal integration	Taking control of competitors
Concentric diversification	Developing new products that fit well with the existing product range, but delivering them to new markets
Conglomerate diversification	Developing new products that are unrelated to the firm's existing technology. This is a high-risk strategy: see Chapter 6
Horizontal diversification	Introducing new products (unrelated to the present range) into existing markets. For example, Virgin markets everything from CDs to life insurance to the same target group of consumers

Setting the overall corporate objectives may indicate strategic sub-objectives; Table 10.3 contains some examples of strategic objectives.

As a general rule, most firms want to grow. Growth increases the firm's security in the market, it increases the power and influence of managers (not to mention their salaries) and it reduces costs. There are four main advantages to growth, as shown in Table 10.4.

Table 10.4 Advantages of growth

Advantage	Explanation
Protection against competition	If the firm becomes the largest in the industry, competitors find it harder to enter the market. Growing firms are able to apply more resources to the market and take away market share from their competitors, thus reducing the competitors' ability to compete effectively.
Improved economies of scale	Greater size means greater efficiency in the purchase of raw materials, use of employee skills and use of corporate resources. This eventually results in higher profit margins, and consequently a greater ability to survive if business worsens.
Better control of distribution networks	Growing firms are attractive to distributors and suppliers because they will provide more business in the future. This gives the firm a negotiating advantage.
More opportunities for career advancement	Managers and staff have better opportunities for promotion when working for a growing firm. This means greater motivation, which in turn means improved working practices.

Growth in growing markets is likely to happen in any case, even without any formal strategic attempts to encourage it; the key to success here lies in measuring whether the company is growing faster than the market, slower than the market or at the same pace as the market. Often firms that express their growth objectives in financial terms fail to notice that they are growing more slowly than the market and are thus (in effect) losing ground to competitors. Expressing growth targets in terms of market share will avoid this pitfall, although obviously a reliable measure of the overall size of the market needs to be available.

Once managers have a clear picture of where the company is and where they wish it to be, it is possible to move on to planning the tactics.

INTERNATIONALISATION STRATEGY

Although governments encourage firms to internationalise (and in particular to export), this is not in itself enough reason to seek markets overseas. Table 10.5 shows some of the other reasons that firms have for becoming international.

Table 10.5 Rationale for international marketing

Reason	Explanation
Small or saturated domestic markets	If the firm cannot expand any further in its domestic market, further growth can occur only by internationalising. In fact, most firms would go international long before the domestic market is saturated, if only because it would be easier to enter the overseas markets than to extract the last possible sales from the domestic market. Notably, the USA trades relatively little of its production; the home market is large enough that most firms do not need to consider exporting.
Economies of scale	For many industries, notably the electronics industry and the chemical industry, the cost of initiating a new product is so huge that it needs to be spread across a very large production run. Automation of production lines is making this more of an issue for more and more firms; recouping the capital cost of automation almost forces the firm into world markets.
International production	The capacity to source components and assemble finished products on a global scale means that the firm can take advantage of the most competitive prices worldwide. Shipping costs are relatively low compared with the savings made.
Customer relationships	Manufacturers who supply multinational firms must themselves be able to deliver worldwide and price in any currency to supply assembly plants in different countries.
Market diversification	The broader the range of markets served, the less likely that the firm will suffer if one market fails. For example, recessions do not usually happen in all countries at the same time; a truly multinational company will be able to make up losses in one market with gains in another. This was even true during the world financial crisis of 2008–2012: Australia, China, Brazil, Russia and many other countries continued to grow throughout the crisis.
International competitiveness	No firm is immune from competitors coming in from outside. If a firm is to remain viable in the long run, it may be forced to meet foreign competition on their own ground before having to meet them in the domestic market.

A further reason for internationalising is that the product life cycle will vary from one country to another. What is a mature product in one country may be at the introduction stage in another, so that the firm gains all the advantages of introducing new products to the market without the costs of research and development that would result from developing new products for the domestic market.

When dealing with foreign markets, marketers will meet barriers that would not be present in domestic markets. In addition, of course, marketers will sometimes find advantages that would not be present in the domestic market. Table 10.6 shows how internationalisation affects the seven Ps. The basic problem for companies who seek to internationalise is that nothing can be taken for granted in a foreign country. This places a heavy premium on forward planning.

Overall, a firm's internationalisation strategy decisions will depend on the following factors:

- The size of the firm in its domestic market
- The firm's strengths compared with overseas competitors

Table 10.6 Internationalisation and the 7-P framework

Element of the marketing mix	Effect in international markets
Product	Different cultural, climatic, technical or economic issues will affect product design. Modification of product policy ranges from the obvious issue of electricity supply to more subtle cultural differences (e.g. Americans prefer top-loading washing machines; Europeans prefer front-loaders).
Place	Distribution systems vary internationally. Germans have a much higher propensity to buy by mail order than do Italians; there are relatively few hypermarkets in Italy compared with Spain.
Promotion	Clearly, promotion issues are deeply affected by cultural differences. This is why advertisements shown on foreign TV stations often seem humorous.
Price	Pricing is usually done in the currency of the target country. This leads to problems with exchange-rate fluctuations, which can be overcome by buying or selling currency on the futures markets; most banks can arrange this.
People	Employing foreign sales staff, for example, can lead to problems in motivation and control.
Processes	In Brazil it is normal for patrons of bars and restaurants to pay the cashier for meals or drinks, receive a receipt, then order the items from the waiters. In Spain it is normal to pay for drinks only when leaving a bar. Processes do not necessarily cross national boundaries.
Physical evidence	For many years American banks have given free gifts to new depositors; merely handing over a cheque book and a deposit book would not be sufficient for a US customer.

- Management experience of dealing in other countries
- The firm's objectives for long-term growth

Having chosen a target country, the marketer is in a position to decide which market entry tactics are appropriate to the case. There are five basic strategies for entering foreign markets, as shown in Table 10.7.

Once the approach to the promotion and product development strategies has been decided, the firm needs to choose an entry strategy. The **stages of development** model suggests that firms seeking to internationalise go through a series of stages.

- *Exporting* implies the smallest commitment to the foreign market. Here the manufacturer sells the firm's products to a foreign importer, who then handles the marketing of the product. The advantage of this approach is that it involves the least cost; the disadvantage is that the exporting firm has little or no control over the way the product is marketed or used in the foreign market. This could lead to problems later on as the firm's reputation may be adversely affected. **Export agents** bring together buyers and sellers and are paid on commission; **export houses** buy goods for export to foreign countries. Sometimes foreign buyers will

Table 10.7 International market entry strategies

Strategy	Explanation
Keep product and promotion the same worldwide	The advantage of this is that it minimises entry costs. Coca-Cola often uses this approach, using basically the same advertising worldwide but translating any voiceovers into the local language. The major drawback of the approach is that it takes no account of local customs and attitudes, and tends to lead to a 'lowest common denominator' advertisement which can be understood by everybody and offends nobody.
Adapt promotion only	The product remains the same, but the promotion is adapted to local cultural norms. This is a fairly common approach, since it enables the marketing communications to reach the consumers more effectively while at the same time avoiding a redesign of the product itself.
Adapt product only	This is less common, but has been done by some detergent manufacturers to allow for differences in local water supplies and washing machines. Likewise, the supposedly 'global' Ford Focus is substantially modified for different markets to meet local emission standards and road safety laws.
Adapt both product and promotion	Sometimes it is necessary to adapt both the product and the promotion, as in the case of Cheer washing powder, a Procter & Gamble product marketed in Japan. Cheer was reformulated to allow for the extra fabric softeners the Japanese use, and the promotion emphasised that the powder worked well in cold water (since most Japanese wash clothes in cold water).
Invent new products	If the existing products cannot meet the conditions in the new market, a new product must be invented. For example, the clockwork radio was invented for use in countries where there is no mains power supply and batteries are difficult to obtain.

deal direct with companies, and some major stores (for example, Sears of the USA) maintain buying offices in foreign capitals.

- *Establishing a sales office* in the foreign market might be a next stage. This implies a greater financial commitment, but also gives more control. **Joint ventures** involve collaborating with a same-nationality firm that is already in the target market or with a foreign firm in its own country. A joint venture could involve a **piggy-backing** arrangement, under which one firm agrees to market the other firm's product alongside its own. This works best if the firms have complementary, non-competing products. For example, a cosmetics firm may agree to carry a perfumer's products. **Licensing** agreements allow a foreign manufacturer to use the firm's patents; for example, Pilkington licenses foreign glass manufacturers to use the float-glass technique. This is useful when the product itself is difficult to export owing to fragility or perishability, but it relies on the firm having good patents or other protection for its intellectual property. **Franchising** is similar; the franchisee agrees to run the business by a specific format. McDonald's hamburger restaurants are an example.

- *Overseas distribution* would involve establishing a warehousing and distribution network in the foreign country. This gives strong control over the marketing of the product, but still relies on importing from the home country.

- *Overseas manufacture* includes warehousing and distribution, but allows the firm to shorten the lines of supply and to adapt the product more easily for the overseas market. In some cases the manufacturing costs are lower in the foreign market, so there will be further economies made.

- Finally, the firm might become a true **multinational marketer**. The true multinational firm manufactures and markets in those countries that offer the best advantages. Although such a company may have originated in a particular country, it may well employ far more foreigners than it does its own nationals, and will think in global terms rather than national terms.

Broadly speaking, a firm can decide on a **globalisation** strategy, by which the company's products and attitudes are basically standardised throughout the world (examples are Coca-Cola and IBM), or a **customisation** strategy, where the company adapts its thinking and its marketing to each fresh market (examples are Sony and Nestlé). As global barriers to trade break down, more and more companies will be taking an international view of their marketing opportunities and will be seeking to do business across national borders and cultural differences.

An alternative view of internationalisation strategy is the **eclectic theory** proposed by Dunning (1993). Broadly, this theory supposes that the firm will look at its specific advantages over other firms both at home and overseas, and will plan its market entry strategies accordingly without necessarily going through a series of stages. For example, a firm with a strength in franchising is likely to use franchising as a market entry method into overseas markets, rather than begin by exporting, then setting up a salesforce, and so forth. The eclectic paradigm also has implications for production, since a true multinational will produce in whichever country offers the best advantages: Ford, for example, produces all the engines for its European cars in Wales, exporting them for assembly into car bodies in Germany, and perhaps later re-importing them back into the United Kingdom. Since transport costs are relatively low compared with the final price of the car, Ford deems it worthwhile to centralise production of the various components. In addition, the company can take advantage of government incentives to locate in high unemployment areas and can also use transfer pricing to minimise its tax liabilities.

Whether firms adopt the 'born global' approach of Dunning or the incremental approach does not appear to be dependent on the characteristics of the firms themselves. Most characteristics of 'born global' firms are shared with those taking an incremental approach, the difference between them depending on the attitudes of the managers rather than the nature of the firm (Chetty and Campbell-Hunt 2004).

In practice, of course, the Internet has made most firms global. Any firm with a website can be accessed from anywhere in the world, and in many cases orders for products can be placed on the website; whether delivery is achievable is, of course, another question.

TACTICAL PLANNING

Because marketers are usually looking for a competitive edge, they will usually try to offer their customers something that is unavailable elsewhere. In this respect, marketing differs from the other main business disciplines. If the legal directors were swapped over from one competing firm to another, they would have no trouble in carrying on with their jobs; the law remains the same for firms in the same industry. If the finance directors or the production managers were exchanged they would simply carry on working, because each industry operates with its own financial structure and production techniques. If the marketers were swapped, though, they would probably be completely lost for the first few weeks, because each would be addressing a different segment of the market, dealing with different distributors, different clients, different overall philosophies and different promotional campaigns.

For example, cosmetics are traditionally sold in pharmacies and department stores. Yet Avon Cosmetics has become one of the world's largest cosmetics companies by breaking the rules and selling the cosmetics door-to-door, training millions of women worldwide in sales techniques and then sending them out to sell to family, friends, neighbours, work colleagues and strangers. Even though the original door-to-door approach has been modified because of safety issues, the maverick approach still pays off.

There are three generic strategies (Porter 1980):

- **Cost leadership**, which is about keeping costs low enough to be able to maintain high profits even when competition is strong. There can only be one cost leader in the market, because only one firm can be the cheapest provider

- **Differentiation**, which means distinguishing the firm and its products from all competitors
- **Focus**, which is about concentrating on specific segments of the market.

Porter also identifies a fourth strategy, which is a strategy for failure: he says that a firm which tries to combine the above strategies will fail, because it is impossible to be the lowest cost provider while offering a range of products or while concentrating on a small part of the market, owing to the lack of economies of scale.

Competitive tactics will depend largely on the company's current product portfolio and on the activities of competitors. The Boston Group matrix (see Chapter 6) will help in making strategic decisions about which products to keep and which to discard, but the tactical problem still remains of approaching the appropriate markets.

Critical thinking

If Porter was right and there are only three strategies available, how do low-cost airlines figure in the equation? They all try to compete by being the cheapest, yet at the same time they differentiate by flying different routes. It could even be argued that, by flying into and out of obscure regional airports, they are operating on a focus basis.

Maybe they aren't as low-cost as they pretend to be – after all, such airlines should be looking for economies of scale, yet they do not own the largest, most economical aircraft.

The tactical possibilities in a marketing campaign are huge in number. Most of the tactics of marketing involve creativity on the part of practitioners, so it is virtually impossible to lay down any hard and fast rules about approaching different marketing problems. However, the following might prove to be useful guidelines:

- Try to do something that the competition has not thought of yet
- Always consult everybody who is involved in the day-to-day application of the plans. Salespeople in particular do not like to be told what to do by somebody back at Head Office
- Do not expect instant results from anything you do – but monitor the results anyway
- Ensure that the messages you give the consumers, the middle men, the suppliers and all your other publics are consistent
- Be prepared for a response from your competitors – try to anticipate what it might be when you are formulating your plans
- Communications tools cannot be used to achieve marketing objectives; they can only achieve communications objectives. Marketing objectives may well follow on from this, but this is not a good way to judge a communications medium.

Cost-effectiveness will always be an issue in promotional campaigns, and it is for this reason that there has been a growth in direct marketing worldwide (see Chapter 12). The accurate targeting of market segments made possible by computer technology has enabled marketers to refine the approach, and hence increase the response rate. Marketers now talk in terms of response rates from promotions, not in terms of contact numbers.

When considering tactical options it is useful to remember that marketers talk about mixes: the marketing mix, the promotional mix, and so forth. This implies that each area of marketing impinges on every other area and that decisions about (say) advertising tactics cannot be taken independently of decisions about pricing.

Having determined the details of what is to be done, the programme can be implemented. Sometimes the marketing managers will meet with resistance from colleagues from other disciplines (see Chapter 1) and sometimes the plan will need to be revised in the light of experience and later events. There will therefore need to be a degree of flexibility in the plan.

ORGANISATIONAL ALTERNATIVES

In general, there are five broad ways to organise marketing tasks, as shown in Table 10.8.

Table 10.8 Organisational alternatives

Alternative	Description
Functional organisation	Each marketing activity has a specialist in charge of it. This structure would have an advertising manager, a product development manager, a market research manager, and so forth.
Product organisation	Each manager is responsible for all the marketing decisions concerning a particular product. The firm may also employ specialists to advise and assist, but each product manager would have overall responsibility.
Regional organisation	This approach is usually used in international markets, but can also be used elsewhere. The regional managers are each responsible for all the marketing activities within their own geographical region.
Segmental organisation	Here each manager is responsible for a given market segment. For example, a glass manufacturer might have one manager in charge of marketing to the automotive industry, another for marketing to the building trade, another marketing to the bottling industry, and so forth. Each manager would thus be able to develop specialist knowledge of the customers' needs.
Matrix	Here there is joint decision-making between the specialist market researchers, sales managers, etc. and the product managers. No one manager is in overall control and decisions are made by balancing each person's role and demands. This method is surprisingly effective in decision-making since it pools the available expertise.

An extension of the matrix organisation structure is the **organismic** structure. Unlike the traditional **mechanistic (or bureaucratic)** pyramid, there is no clear 'boss'. Each individual contributes expertise (and effort) towards achieving the **corporate objectives**. The leader for each task is determined by the project being tackled at the time. This type of structure is typical of small consultancy firms who may be dealing with a wide range of disparate tasks, but can be found in larger organisations or departments of larger organisations. The main advantage of the organismic structure is that it is extremely flexible, which makes it a more appropriate structure for dealing with changing environments. On the other hand, there is some evidence that organismic structures may not be effective in relationship marketing, because of the difficulties inherent in maintaining relationships when people change roles frequently (Desmond 2004).

In smaller firms there may be no specific marketing department, and of course in some firms marketing is not very high on the agenda because the firm has little control over the variables of the marketing mix. Such firms may have a marketing department, but it may be concerned only with running the occasional advertisement and organising trade fairs.

PROMOTIONAL STRATEGIES

Formulating a promotional strategy is concerned with deciding overall aims and objectives. The aims of the promotion strategy can be selected from the following:

- *Category need* is the aim of persuading consumers that the product will meet a need. This can be difficult when the product is first introduced, particularly if it is a novel product.
- *Brand awareness* is the process of fixing the brand and its characteristics in the consumer's mind. The brand must be made to stand out from the competition and must be positioned accordingly.
- *Brand attitude* leads on from brand awareness. Here the marketer is trying to build a favourable attitude in the consumer's mind; merely being familiar with the brand is only part of the story. (See Chapter 3 for an overview of attitude.)
- *Brand purchase intention* is a positive conation on the part of the consumer. Here the marketer is suggesting that the consumer should 'get some today!'
- *Purchase facilitation* is the part of promotion geared to ensuring that the product is readily available, and the consumer knows where to go to get it.

The above five aims have been presented in sequence, but there is not always a necessity for a promotion strategy to follow exactly this order. Sometimes the earlier stages will already have been covered by other earlier marketers. For example, when Radion washing powder was launched in the United Kingdom the promotion strategy omitted the first stage and went straight to brand awareness. This was achieved by using Day-Glo billboard advertisements with the brand name in 1-metre high letters. Having established the brand name, the company could then go on to develop positive brand attitudes, but there was little need to tell the consumers where to buy the product, since they would naturally expect to buy washing powder in a supermarket. Unfortunately, although the brand was recognisable, the product features and benefits were not, and the brand was first withdrawn and then amalgamated into Unilever's better established brand, Surf, as Surf Fun Fresh.

Regarding distribution channels, marketers need to decide whether to adopt a push strategy or a pull strategy, or rather to decide what the balance will be between the two.

Push strategies

Push strategies involve promoting the product only to the next link down the distribution channel; this means selling hard to the wholesalers and letting the wholesalers in their turn sell hard to the retailers, who then push the product out to the consumers. This method has the advantage of being cheap and relatively straightforward, and could be justified on the grounds that each member of the distribution chain is most familiar with the ways of marketing to the next member down the chain. On the other hand, it really cannot be said to be consumer-orientated.

Pull strategies

Pull strategies involve focusing effort on the consumer, on the basis that an increase in consumer demand for the product will pull it through the distribution chain.

A push strategy emphasises personal selling and advertising aimed at the members of the distribution channel. A pull strategy is aimed at the final consumers and emphasises consumer advertising and strong merchandising. Most launch strategies would involve elements of both push and pull. For example, retailers tend to be positive about TV advertising and will stock a product if they know there is to be a TV campaign aimed at consumers. The retailers believe that the campaign will stimulate demand for the product, thus generating sales; it is equally possible that the act of displaying the product prominently is what generates the sales, however.

If the distribution channels are properly managed and are cooperating well (see Chapter 8), a pull strategy is indicated; in other words, greater effort can be devoted to stimulating consumer demand, since the other channel members are likely to cooperate anyway. If the channel is uncoordinated or is dominated by the wholesalers or retailers, a push strategy is more likely to work since the channel members will need to be convinced to carry the product line. Again, there will always be elements of both push and pull in any promotional strategy, because channel members and consumers both need to move up the hierarchy of communications effects.

From a tactical viewpoint, the promotional mix should be carefully monitored to ensure that the right things happen at the right times.

TACTICAL APPROACHES

In the real world, marketers will adopt a combination strategy for setting budgets using several of the methods outlined in Table 10.9. Even an objective and task approach might begin by looking at what the competition is spending (comparative parity approach), if only to determine what the likely spend would have to be to overcome clutter. Likewise, a marketer may be part-way through a campaign and be told by the finance department that no more money is available (or perhaps be told that more than anticipated is available) and will switch to an all-you-can-afford policy.

Setting the right objectives is an essential part of any planning. Without objectives, the organisation as a whole has no clear direction to follow – objectives are what hold organisation members together in achieving success. It is important to distinguish between aims and objectives. An aim is a general statement about the

Table 10.9 Advertising planning functions

Planning function	Explanation
Setting the budget	This can be done in four ways. First, the objective and task approach involves setting objectives and setting aside an appropriate amount of money to achieve the objectives. This method is difficult to apply because it is difficult to assess how much will be needed to achieve the objective. Second, the percentage of sales approach sets the budget as a percentage of sales. This is based on the false idea that sales create advertising and usually results in less being spent on advertising when sales fall, thus reducing sales further. Third, the competition matching approach means that the company spends the same as the competition: this means that the firm is allowing its budgets to be set by its enemies. Fourth, there is the arbitrary approach, whereby a senior executive (usually a finance director) simply says how much can be allowed within the firm's overall budgets. This does not take account of how the firm is to achieve the objectives.
Identifying the target	Deciding to whom the ad is to be directed. It is better to approach a small segment of the market than try to use a 'scattergun' approach on everybody (see Chapter 4).
Media planning	This is about deciding where the ads are going to appear. There are two main decision areas: the reach (number of potential consumers the ad reaches) and the frequency (number of times each consumer sees the ad) of coverage. The decision is frequently made on the basis of cost per thousand readers/viewers, but this does not take into account the impact of the ad or the degree to which people are able to skip past it.
Defining the objectives	Deciding what the ads are supposed to achieve. It is essential here to give the advertising agency a clear brief: 'We want to raise awareness of the product to 50% of the adult population' is a measurable objective. 'We want to increase sales as much as possible' is not measurable, so there is no way of knowing whether it has been achieved.
Creating the advertising platform	Deciding the basic issues and selling points that the advertising must convey. This clarifies the advertising agency briefing, or at least clarifies the thinking on producing the advertising materials.

type of things we want to do as an organisation; for example, 'We aim to be the best in our field'. This is not an objective, because there is no way of measuring whether we have achieved it – if only for the reason that we have not specified a timescale. An objective, on the other hand, is a statement of something that we can measure; for example, 'We intend to be the largest supplier in our industry within five years.'

Objectives need to be SMART; in other words:

- *Specific.* The objective needs to be stated precisely, with a clear boundary. Vague statements such as 'being the best' are fine as aims, but since they are likely to be defined differently by different people they are open to misinterpretation.
- *Measurable.* Planners need to have some way of knowing whether the objective has been reached, and if the objective has been missed they need to be able to say by how wide a margin. Many objectives will be expressed numerically (for example, 'We want this campaign to increase brand recognition to 40% of the population'), which is helpful in deciding how far the campaign met, or exceeded, expectations.
- *Achievable.* If the objective is unrealistic, staff will not 'buy into' it and will not try to achieve it. This is especially important when setting objectives for salespeople, since they can easily decide not to do more than the minimum needed to maintain their standard of living.
- *Realistic.* Planners need to take account of the marketing environment, particularly competitive responses. For the same reasons that an objective must be achievable, planners need to ensure that what they are proposing is realistic within the constraints of the business environment.
- *Time-bound.* Without a timescale, there is no way of measuring whether an objective has been missed. Rather like making a decision to lose weight or give up smoking, unless we say by what date we will do these things the resolution is meaningless. Obviously, if the objective is achieved the timescale is irrelevant, but business objectives should always include a timetable.

DECIDING THE TYPE OF CAMPAIGN

Whether this stage comes before or after the budget-setting will depend on whether the marketer is adopting an objective and task policy or not. In most cases, though, planning the campaign in detail will come after the budget is known and agreed upon; few companies give the marketing department a blank cheque for promotional spending. Campaigns can be carried out to achieve many objectives; a new product launch was used in the example given earlier, but in most cases the products will be in the maturity phase of the product life cycle (see Chapter 6).

- Image-building campaigns are designed to convey a particular status for the product and to emphasise ways in which it will complement the user's lifestyle. For example, Volvo promotes the reliability and engineering of the car rather

than its appearance, thus appealing to motorists who prefer a solid, reliable vehicle.
- **Product differentiation** campaigns aim to show how the product is better than the competitors' products by emphasising its differences. In most cases this will take the form of the **unique selling proposition,** or **USP** for short. The USP is the one feature of the product that most stands out as different from the competition, and is usually a feature that conveys unique benefits to the consumer. Mature products often differ only very slightly from each other in terms of performance, so a USP can sometimes be identified in terms of the packaging or distribution. Of course, the USP will only be effective if it means something to the consumer – otherwise it will not affect the buying decision.
- Positioning strategies are concerned with the way consumers perceive the product compared with their perceptions of the competition. For example, a retailer may claim 'lower prices than other shops' or a restaurant may want to appear more up-market than its rivals.
- **Direct response** campaigns seek an immediate response from the consumer in terms of purchase, or request for a brochure, or a visit to the shop. For example, a retailer might run a newspaper campaign that includes a money-off coupon. The aim of the campaign is to encourage consumers to visit the shop to redeem the coupon, and the retailer can easily judge the effectiveness of the campaign by the number of coupons redeemed.

PUTTING IT ALL TOGETHER

To make the best use of the promotional effort it is worth spending time planning how it will all fit together. The recipe will need to be adapted according to what the product is and how the company wants to promote it.

The elements that marketers need to consider are:

- Size of budget
- Size of individual order value
- Number of potential buyers
- Geodemographical spread of potential buyers
- Category of product (convenience, unsought, shopping, etc.)
- What it is the firm is trying to achieve.

It is impossible to achieve everything all at once, so marketers plan the campaign as an integrated package. For example, Table 10.10 shows a product launch strategy designed to maximise penetration of a new food product.

Carrying out this kind of planning needs the cooperation of all the members of the marketing team. It is no use having the PR people doing one thing and the salesforce doing something else that negates their efforts. If the campaign is to be

Table 10.10 Example of a promotional calendar

Month	Activity
May	Press release to the trade press and retailers.
June	Sales campaign to persuade retailers to stock the product. Aim is to get 50% of retailers stocking the product, so the salesforce tells them a big ad spend is forthcoming. Run teaser campaign.
July/August	Denouement of teaser campaign. Promotion staff appear in major retail outlets offering free samples. Press releases to cookery writers, possibly reports on daytime TV if product is newsworthy enough.
September/October	Once 50% retailer penetration has occurred, start TV campaign. Brief ad agency to obtain maximum awareness.
January/February	Begin new campaign to *inform*. Possibly use money-off sales promotion, linked promotions, etc. Review progress so far using market research. Possibly some press releases, if the product is innovative enough, to the business/cookery press.

effective, it is important that all the team members are involved in the discussions so that unrealistic demands are not made of the team members.

Although this section has used promotional campaigns as an example, the same principles apply to other marketing mix elements. New product development needs to have objectives in place, as does developing a new distribution network.

MONITORING AND EVALUATING MARKETING PERFORMANCE

Once the plan has been implemented, managers need to make sure it works in practice. Feedback is essential for monitoring performance, and (in an ideal world) no marketing activity would be undertaken without having a monitoring and evaluation system in place beforehand.

There are two basic groups of approaches for performance analysis:

- **Sales analysis** which looks at the income generated by the firm's activities
- **Marketing cost analysis**, which looks at the costs of generating the income.

Table 10.11 illustrates some sales analysis measures.

Considerable amounts of information will be needed if the firm is to make effective use of sales analysis to monitor activities. This may involve the firm in substantial market research expenditure since market research is the cornerstone of monitoring and evaluation (see Chapter 5).

Table 10.11 Methods of sales analysis

Analysis method	Explanation
Comparison with forecast sales	The firm compares the actual sales achieved against what was forecast for the period.
Comparison with competitor's sales	Provided the information is available, the firm can estimate the extent to which marketing activities have made inroads into the competitor's business. The problem here is proving that the difference has been caused by the high quality of the firm's marketing activities rather than by the ineptness of the competitor.
Comparison with industry sales	Examination of the firm's performance in terms of market share. This is commonly used in industries where a relatively small number of firms control the market; for example the car industry.
Cash volume sales analysis	Comparison of sales in terms of cash generated. This has the advantage that currency is common to both sales and costs; it has the disadvantage that price rises may cause the company to think it has done better than it has.
Unit sales analysis	Comparison of sales in terms of the number of units sold, or sometimes the number of sales transactions. This is a useful measure of salesforce activities but should not be taken in isolation; sometimes the figures can be distorted by increased sales of cheaper models.
Sales by geographic unit	Sales are broken down regionally so that the firm can tell whether one or two regions are accounting for most of the sales and whether some less productive regions are not worth what they cost to service.
Sales by product group or brand	This is particularly important for judging the product portfolio (see the BCG matrix in Chapter 6). This serves two purposes: it is possible to identify products that should be dropped from the range and it is also possible to identify products that are moving into the decline phase of the product life cycle and should therefore be revived.
Sales by type of customer	Can reveal, for example, that most effort is being expended on a group of customers who make relatively few purchases. May reveal that the firm's customers tend to be ageing, and may therefore be a declining group in years to come.

Evaluating customers is a particularly important exercise in a relationship marketing scenario. Estimating customer equity (the value of the customers) can be complex; it is a combination of deciding on the profitability of the customer (i.e. a comparison between cost of serving the customer and revenue which will result), lifetime value of the customer (how long the relationship is likely to last, coupled with frequency and quantity of purchase) and likely loyalty of the customer (if the customer is likely to defect to a competitor, the customer's value will be low). Once calculated, however, customer equity can be used to focus marketing efforts on the most valuable customers (Rust *et al.* 2004).

The other part of the picture is to examine the cost of achieving the objectives that have been specified. *Marketing cost analysis* is a set of techniques for breaking down the costs of the firm's activities and associating them with specific marketing objectives. Costs can be broken down (broadly) into:

- **Direct costs** such as salespersons' salaries, which can be directly attributable to a given activity
- **Traceable common costs** such as costs of advertising that can be traced back to specific products
- **Non-traceable common costs** such as the cost of PR or corporate advertising that cannot be allocated to any particular product range or brand.

The main problem with marketing cost analysis lies in organising the firm's accounting systems in such a way as to permit analysis. For example, payroll records may not be easily broken down by job function; it may be difficult to sort out which of the administration staff spend most of their time on marketing-related tasks, or even to find out what the pay bill is for the salesforce. Likewise, defining which jobs constitute marketing jobs and which do not also presents problems. Clearly, the cost of servicing customers in remote areas is a marketing cost – so should transportation costs be taken into account as well as the salesforce mileage costs? Also, if a given product is not performing well, should we be looking at the costs of production?

For the dyed-in-the-wool customer-orientated firm these answers are obvious, since all the activities of the firm are regarded as marketing activities. In other firms, not all managers agree with the basic premises on which marketing is based. At the very least, many people find it difficult to translate the theory into practice and to gear the organisation's activities towards a consumer orientation, as seen in Chapter 1.

FEEDBACK SYSTEMS

When a discrepancy appears between the expected performance and the actual performance, the marketing manager will need to take action. This will usually take the following sequence:

1 *Determine the reason for the discrepancy*. Was the original plan reasonable? Have the firm's competitors seized the initiative in some way so that the situation has changed? Is someone at fault?
2 *Feed these findings back to the staff concerned*. This can be in the form of a meeting to discuss the situation, or in the form of memos and reports.
3 *Develop a plan for correcting the situation*. This will probably involve the cooperation of all the staff concerned.

Feedback should be both frequent and concise, and any criticisms should be constructive; managers should never (for example) go to a sales meeting and offer only criticisms, since this sends the salesforce out with negative feelings about themselves and the company.

Marketing strategy and planning is much like any other planning exercise; it relies on good information, a clear idea of where the organisation is going and regular examination of both outcomes and methods to ensure that the plan is still on target.

CASE STUDY 10 Audi A3 TDI Green Diesel

The Audi A3 Green Diesel car is an exceptionally low-emission vehicle, but unlike most environmentally friendly cars it performs well – in fact, it has the sporty performance that Audi drivers expect, a streamlined appearance, it delivers 42 miles to the gallon and has 30% less carbon emissions than other cars in its class. The car won *Green Car Journal's* Car of the Year award, and Audi decided that this was an award worth cashing in on in the lucrative US market.

Diesel cars have never been as popular in the US as they are in Europe, partly because of much lower fuel prices which mean the cost savings for owners are less than is the case in Europe. Additionally, the incidence of 'environmental sceptics' is also higher than in the rest of the world – many Americans simply do not believe that the environment is deteriorating because of human activities. Audi therefore needed to make a strong impact, and decided to use the nation's most prestigious sporting event (the Superbowl) to publicise the car.

The company's aims were as follows:

1 Increase desire for the Audi brand.
2 Maximise the Superbowl as a media opportunity.
3 Drive Audi's image as a green, progressive leader.
4 Increase traffic both online and to dealerships.
5 Sell more cars, not only A3 and A3 Diesel, but across the Audi brand.

Many of the audience for the Superbowl (and for the Audi) are not especially environment-conscious and, indeed, many of them see environmentalists as spoil-sports or as 'thought police' who try to control other people. Audi therefore decided to satirise the environmental extremists in a humorous way by showing the car escaping from the clutches of the 'Green Police'. The 60-second ad showed a man being arrested for using plastic bags ('You picked the wrong day to mess with the environment, Plastic Boy'), homes being raided when people had thrown batteries into the bins, a couple being arrested for having the water in their jacuzzi at too high a temperature and a newsflash of a man being arrested for possession of an incandescent lightbulb. Meanwhile, at a Green Police checkpoint, the Audi is being allowed through because it meets the Green Police criteria. The soundtrack, from rock legend Cheap Trick, was a re-recording of their hit 'Dream Police'.

The ad cost $1.7m to make and $4.5m to air, so obviously the company was hoping for some fairly spectacular returns – additionally, the ad was downloaded to YouTube and the company also established a presence on Facebook and Twitter.

The advertisement is clearly intended as a spoof and is well produced and entertaining. Traditionally, Superbowl advertising has been intended to entertain but not promote, so Audi has certainly broken the mould in more ways than one. Previous 'eco-conscious' advertising has featured polar bears, children playing in the countryside and similar themes – using the idea of Green Police who have a role in punishing people was a major departure.

Integrating the overall campaign was a carefully planned exercise. In the period leading up to the Superbowl, the company introduced the Green Police theme and the Green Car of the Year award. The Green Police were introduced on Facebook and Twitter, and users were encouraged to comment on the characters. Interactive quizzes were set up online so that people could ask the Green Police for advice on becoming more eco-friendly, and the company posted on various blogs to generate debate. The company even reached out to Cheap Trick fans to introduce them to the Green Police.

During the game, Audi made maximum use of its slot in the fourth quarter of the game (a key spot for advertisers). The company promoted its website, on which it gave detailed information about the car (in other words, used a more factual approach as a follow-up to the emotive, entertaining approach of the advertisement itself). After the game, the ad reached number 2 in the Viral Video Chart, a measure of the extent to which the YouTube slot (as well as other online showings) was recommended by people to their friends.

The results? Brand awareness for Audi jumped from 3% to 76%, purchase consideration rose by 9%, and traffic to dealerships and online increased by 28%. In terms of sales, the luxury car market increased by 12.8% in 2010, but Audi sales increased by 22.9%, comfortably outstripping arch-rivals Mercedes and Lexus. Clearly, the effort was well worthwhile – and the Green Police have made their mark.

Questions

1 How did Audi coordinate its campaign?
2 Why was the Green Police approach so successful?
3 What type of strategy is Audi following?
4 How might Audi capitalise further on this approach?
5 How might Audi have set its objectives (as opposed to its aims)?

SUMMARY

This chapter has been about the ways in which marketers assemble the elements of marketing into a coherent whole.

Planning is not necessarily a tidy process; there will be many iterations of the plan, and much discussion. The difficulties of foretelling the future and of anticipating competitor response will always militate against a perfect planning scheme, yet the evidence is that companies that plan effectively tend to be more successful than those that do not; if we don't know where we are going, then any road will do to take us there.

Here are the key points from the chapter:

- Marketing is harder than not marketing, but it works better
- The marketing audit will tell us where we are now; we need to know this to plan our route to where we want to be
- Objectives are the route map to where we are going as a company, and they need to be specific, measurable, achievable, realistic and time-bound

- When considering tactics, be creative. Success in marketing lies in doing something the competitors are not doing
- Feedback is essential if the plan is to remain on course
- Plans need to be sufficiently flexible to allow for the unexpected.

CHAPTER QUESTIONS

1 What is the difference between strategy and tactics?

2 Who should be consulted when setting objectives?

3 Describe three main methods of sales analysis.

4 What is the purpose of integrating marketing tactics?

5 What organisational structures might a multinational computer manufacturer (e.g. IBM) use?

6 Compare Dunning's eclectic theory of internationalisation with the stages of development approach.

Further reading

Marketing Strategy and Competitive Positioning 5th edn, by Graham Hooley, Brigitte Nicolaud and Nigel Piercy (Financial Times/Prentice Hall, 2011). This book is written by some of the leading thinkers on marketing strategy and gives a comprehensive account of the development of a complete strategic plan.

Marketing Plans: How to Prepare Them, How to Use Them, by Malcolm McDonald and Hugh Wilson (John Wiley & Sons, 2011) gives a practically orientated approach to planning.

References

Band, William A.: 'A marketing audit provides an opportunity for improvement', *Sales and Marketing Management in Canada* (March 1984), pp. 24–6.

Chetty, C. and Campbell-Hunt, Colin: 'A strategic approach to internationalization: a traditional vs. a "born-global" approach', *Journal of International Marketing*, **12** (1) (2004), pp. 57–81.

Desmond, John: 'An evaluation of organizational control strategies for relationship marketing', *Journal of Marketing*, **20** (1) (February 2004), pp. 209–37.

Dunning, John H.: *The Globalisation of Business* (London, Routledge, 1993).

Kotler, Philip: *Marketing Management*, 11th edn (Pearson Education Inc., Upper Saddle River, NJ, 2003).

Porter, M.E.: *Competitive Strategy: Techniques for Analysing Industries and Competitors* (New York, Free Press, 1980).

Rust, Roland T., Lemon, Katherine N. and Zeithaml, Valeria A.: 'Return on marketing: using customer equity to focus marketing strength', *Journal of Marketing*, **68** (1) (January 2004), pp. 109–17.

Weinberg, R.: 'Developing marketing strategies for short term profits and long term growth', paper presented at the Advanced Management Research Inc. Seminar, New York (1969).

CONSUMER AND BUYER BEHAVIOUR

Objectives

After reading this chapter you should be able to:
- Explain how consumers make purchasing decisions
- Describe the differences between the ways in which professional buyers work and the ways consumers make decisions
- Explain how consumers develop a perceptual map of the product alternatives
- Develop ways of dealing with customer complaints.

INTRODUCTION

This chapter is about how buyers think and behave when making purchasing decisions. Buyers fall into two categories: *consumers*, who are buying for their own and for their family's consumption, and *industrial buyers*, who are buying for business use. In each case, the marketer is concerned with both the practical needs of the buyer or the buyer's organisation, and the emotional or personal needs of the individual.

Royal Enfield

Royal Enfield is an Indian-based manufacturer of motorcycles. The original Royal Enfield company was British, but the Indian side of the business was taken over after Indian independence in the late 1940s. The technology is basically unchanged since the 1950s, so the main appeal to a British customer base is that of nostalgia. This is different from the appeal in India, where the brand is regarded as an upmarket, large motorcycle. This has dramatic implications for the company's promotional policy.

Different policies have to be adopted for different countries in Europe: the bike's appeal cannot be solely based on price, even though it is a relatively cheap bike in Europe. Within Europe, the biggest markets are the UK and Germany, both well established biking nations, and Europe now accounts for 10% of sales. The company is well aware that it is competing with leisure products – nobody buys a Royal Enfield to commute. Typical buyers are likely to be men in their fifties who had motorbikes when they were young, and are reassured by the Enfield's old-fashioned appearance and basic technology.

The basic platform for Royal Enfield in the UK is the concept of 'true motorcycling'. The fun aspects are emphasised, and the 'back to one's youth' feel is foremost.

Ashish Joshi, Director, Royal Enfield Motorcycles Europe

Watch the video clip, then try to answer the following questions. The answers are on the companion website.

Questions

1. How does perception affect Royal Enfield's marketing?
2. What are the main drivers for Royal Enfield consumers in the UK?
3. What is the role of sociology theory in Royal Enfield's success in the UK as compared to India?

CONSUMER BEHAVIOUR

The consumer decision-making process follows the stages shown in Figure 3.1.

Problem recognition

Problem recognition arises when the consumer realises that there is a need for some item. This can come about through **assortment depletion** (where the consumer's stock of goods has been used up or worn out) or **assortment extension** (which is where the consumer feels the need to add some new item to the assortment of possessions). At this point the consumer has only decided to seek a solution to a problem, perhaps by buying a category of product. The needs felt can be categorised as either **utilitarian** (concerned with the functional attributes of the product) or **hedonic** (concerned with the pleasurable or aesthetic aspects of the product) (Holbrook and Hirschmann 1982). The current view is that there is a balance between the two types of need in most decisions (Engel *et al*. 1995).

An internal stimulus, or **drive**, comes about because there is a gap between the **actual** and **desired states**. For example, becoming hungry leads to a drive to find food; the hungrier the individual becomes, the greater the drive becomes, but once the hunger has been satisfied the individual can move on to satisfying other needs. For marketers, the actual state of the individual is usually not susceptible to influence, so much marketing activity is directed at influencing the desired state (e.g. 'Don't you deserve a better car?'). Thus drives are generated by encouraging a revision of the desired state. The higher the drive level (i.e. the greater the gap between actual and desired states), the more open the individual is to considering new ways

Figure 3.1 Consumer decision-making

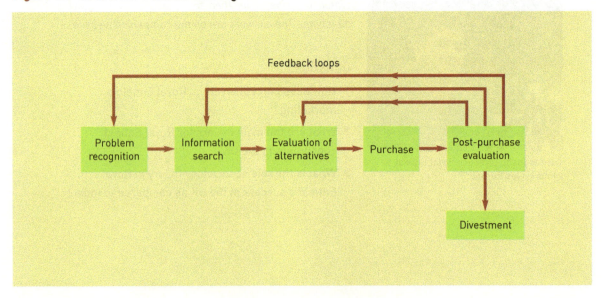

of satisfying the need – in simple terms, a starving man will try almost any kind of food.

It is, of course, stimulating and enjoyable to allow gaps to develop between the desired and actual states: working up a thirst before going for a drink makes the experience more pleasurable, for example. Each individual has an **optimal stimulation level** (OSL), which is the point at which the drive is enjoyable and challenging, without being uncomfortable. OSL is subjective; research shows that those with high OSLs like novelty and risk-taking, whereas those with low OSLs prefer the tried and tested. Those with high OSLs also tend to be younger (Raju 1980).

Drives lead on to **motivation**, which is the reason why people take action. The level of motivation will depend on the desirability of the end goal, and the ease of achieving the end goal; motivations are subjective, so it is difficult to infer motivation from behaviour. Few actions take place as a result of a single motivation, and sometimes a motivation may not even be apparent to the individual experiencing it; in other words, some motivations operate below the conscious level.

Information search

Having become motivated to seek a solution to the need problem, consumers engage in two forms of information search.

- The **internal search** involves remembering previous experiences of the product category and thinking about what he/she has heard about the product category
- The **external search** involves shopping around, reading manufacturers' literature and advertisements, and perhaps talking to friends about the proposed purchase.

For most purchases, the internal search is probably sufficient. For example, a consumer who needs to buy biscuits will easily remember what his or her favourite brand tastes like, and will also remember where they are on the supermarket shelf. When buying a new laptop, on the other hand, a fairly extensive information search might be carried out, reading manufacturers' brochures and looking around the electronics shops. The purpose of this exercise is to reduce risk; buying the wrong brand of biscuits involves very little risk, since the financial commitment is low, but buying the wrong laptop could prove to be an expensive mistake. For this reason many retailers offer a no-quibble return policy, since this helps to reduce the level of risk and make purchase more likely.

Evaluation of alternatives

Having found out about several competing brands, the consumer will *evaluate* the alternatives, based on the information collected or remembered. Too much choice leads to decision paralysis, in which the person finds it impossible to choose (Shankar *et al.* 2006), so in the first instance the individual will select a **consideration set**, which is the group of products that would most closely meet the need.

Typically a consumer will use **cut-offs** to establish a consideration set: these are the minimum and maximum acceptable values for the product characteristics. For example, a consumer will typically have a clear idea of the acceptable price range for the product. (This price range might have a minimum as well as a maximum; the individual may not want something that is perceived as being cheap and nasty.) **Signals** are important when making choices; a particular price tag, a brand name, even the retailer will have some effect on the consumer's perception of the product. Price is frequently used as an indicator of quality, for example, but this can be reduced in the presence of other signals. The purpose is to reduce confusion, which comes from three sources: similarity, information overload and ambiguity. Confusion and information overload leads to decision postponement, and also to loyalty behaviour – sticking with the tried and tested rather than risking a mistake with something new (Walsh *et al.* 2007, Wang 2006).

Occasionally the use of cut-offs eliminates all the possibilities from the consideration set, in which case the consumer will have to revise the rules. This can result in the creation of a hierarchy of rules. For marketers, the challenge is often to ensure that the product becomes a 'member' of the consideration set.

The decision-making process appears lengthy and complex as stated here, yet most of us make several purchasing decisions in a day without going through a lengthy decision-making process. This is because most of us use **heuristics**, or decision-making rules, for most purchases. These are simple 'if ... then' rules that reduce risk by using previous experience as a guide. For example, an international traveller in a strange city might have a heuristic of eating only in restaurants that are full of local people, on the grounds that the inhabitants of the city would know which are the best restaurants. Heuristics divide into three categories:

- *Search heuristics*, which are concerned with rules for finding out information
- *Evaluation heuristics*, which are about judging product offerings
- *Choice heuristics*, which are about evaluation of alternatives.

The decision-making process may contain a number of **interrupts** – points at which the search is temporarily suspended. Interrupts come in four categories:

- **Environmental stimuli**, which include in-store promotions (perhaps eye-catching posters for other products)
- **Affective states**, which include physiological needs (the sudden need to go to the toilet or to have a coffee)
- *Unexpected information*; for example, a change of layout in the shop or some change in the product attributes
- *Conflicts*, which occur when the consumer realises that the original decision-making plan cannot be followed, or an alternative plan appears that is not consistent with the original plan.

For example, an approach–approach conflict occurs when a second product is presented that would probably do the job just as well. This means that the consumer has to make a comparison, and the search pattern is temporarily suspended. An approach–avoidance conflict might arise when the consumer finds out that the product is much more expensive than expected; an avoidance–avoidance conflict might arise when the two alternatives are equally distasteful (an example might be the reluctance to spend money on new shoes while at the same time not wanting to be embarrassed by wearing old ones).

The effect of the interrupt will depend on the consumer's interpretation of the event. Sometimes the interrupt activates a new end goal (for example, a long shopping trip might be transformed into a search for somewhere to sit down and have a coffee), or perhaps a new choice heuristic might be activated (for example, meeting a friend who recommends a brand). Sometimes the interrupt is serious enough for the search to be abandoned altogether; here the strength of the interrupt is important. Clearly a sudden desire for a cup of tea will not permanently interrupt a search process, but the news that one has lost one's job very well might.

In most cases, consumers will resume the interrupted problem-solving process once the stimulus has been absorbed and accepted or rejected.

Purchase

The actual *purchase* comes next; the consumer will locate the required brand, and perhaps choose a retailer he or she has faith in, and will also select an appropriate payment method.

Post-purchase evaluation

Post-purchase evaluation refers to the way the consumer decides whether the product purchase has been a success or not. This process usually involves a comparison between what the consumer was expecting to get and what was actually purchased, although sometimes new information obtained after the purchase will also colour the consumer's thinking (Oliver 1980). In some cases, particularly in the virtual environment, the value obtained from the product can be manipulated by consumers after purchase; this means that the interpretation of value is subject to change (Harwood and Garry 2010).

Before the purchase, the consumer will have formed expectations of the product's capabilities in terms of:

- **Equitable performance** (what can be reasonably expected given the cost and effort of obtaining the product)
- **Ideal performance** (what the consumer hopes the product will do)
- **Expected performance** (which is what the product probably will do).

Sometimes this evaluation leads to **post-purchase dissonance**, when the product has not lived up to expectations, and sometimes to **post-purchase consonance**, when the product is as expected or better. In either event, the consumer will feed back this information into memory to inform the internal search for next time.

One of the more interesting aspects of dissonance is that there is evidence to show that a small discrepancy between expectation and outcome may provoke a bigger change in attitude than a large discrepancy. This is because a small discrepancy may force the consumer to confront the purchase behaviour without offering a ready explanation for it; for example, a general feeling of being unhappy with a new car might crystallise around its poor acceleration (a major problem), and the consumer might simply shrug and accept this as part of the deal. On the other hand, if the only immediately identifiable problem is that the car's ashtray is poorly positioned, this may lead the owner to look for other faults with the car (and, of course, find them).

Consumers will usually act to reduce post-purchase dissonance. There are four general approaches to doing this:

1 Ignore the dissonant information and concentrate on the positive aspects of the product.
2 Distort the dissonant information (perhaps by telling oneself that the product was, after all, the cheap version).
3 Play down the importance of the issue.
4 Change one's behaviour.

From a marketing viewpoint, it is generally better to ensure that the consumer has accurate information about the product beforehand so as to avoid post-purchase dissonance, but if it occurs then marketers need to reduce it in some way. People differ in their propensity to complain – complaints are more likely if the consumer is involved with the product and also acts on impulse; they are less likely if the consumer self-monitors, i.e. is very aware of his or her behaviour (Sharma *et al.* 2010b). Consumers express dissatisfaction in one of three ways:

- **Voice responses**, in which the customer comes back and complains. Older people in particular are often reluctant to take this route, which may mean that the supplier is unaware of dissatisfaction among customers (Grougiou and Pettigrew 2009). The possibility of a repeated violation of trust appears to be more important in voice responses than the magnitude of the violation (Sijun and Huff 2007), which has implications for complaint-handling
- **Private responses**, in which the consumer complains to friends. In some cultures this is more likely than voice responses (Ngai *et al.* 2007)
- **Third-party responses**, which may include complaints to consumer organisations, trade associations and TV consumer programmes, or even legal action (Singh 1988).

The most effective way of reducing post-purchase dissonance is to provide a product that meets the customer's expectations. This is partly a function for the manufacturer, but is also a problem for the retailer to address since it should be possible to ensure that the consumer's needs are fully understood before a recommendation about a product is made. As a fall-back position, though, every effort should be made to encourage the consumer to complain if things do not come up to expectations. This is why waiters always ask if the meal is all right, and why shops frequently have no-quibble money-back guarantees. Ferry companies and airlines provide customer comment slips, and some marketers even make follow-up telephone calls to consumers to check that the product is meeting expectations. There is more on these techniques in Chapter 5.

In business-to-business markets, where buyer–seller relationships are often long term, negative incidents can give rise to shifts in the relationship. Analysing these negative events can be very useful in assessing the relationship and making adjustments where necessary, so complaint handling serves an extremely useful function in relationship marketing (Strandvik and Holmlund 2008).

Research shows that the perceptions of employees about the shared values of the firm, and especially their view of how fair the firm is in its dealings, are reflected in the way in which they deal with customer complaints. This in turn is reflected in the ways in which customers perceive the complaint-handling process (Maxham and Netemeyer 2003).

It is important that dissatisfied customers are allowed to voice their complaint fully, and that the appropriate compensation is negotiated in the light of:

- The strength of the complaint
- The degree of blame attaching to the supplier, from the consumer's viewpoint
- The legal and moral relationship between the supplier and the consumer.

A consistent failure to solve problems raised by post-purchase dissonance will, ultimately, lead to irreparable damage to the firm's reputation. In the last analysis, it is almost always cheaper to keep an existing customer than it is to attract a new one, and therefore it makes sense for suppliers to give customers every chance to express problems with the service or product provision. Customer retention is, according to one research exercise, associated with complaint-handling procedures – and nothing else (Ang and Buttle 2006).

Critical thinking

It sounds as if we are going back to the idea that the customer is always right. What about people who deliberately find fault with everything, in the hope of winning some concession from the company? What about simple misunderstandings, where someone has bought a product and then decided it wasn't what they wanted after all? And what about the people who buy a new item of clothing, wear it to go out for the evening, then bring it back the next day?

Surely we aren't expected to put up with fraud, lies and stupidity! Or is that a small price to pay for looking after the genuine cases – after all, the customers may not always be right, but they are always the customers!

Divestment

Finally, the **divestment** stage refers to the way the individual disposes of the product after use. This could be as simple as throwing an empty food container into the bin, or it could be as complex as the trade-in of a second-hand car. This stage is of increasing importance to marketers, both in terms of green marketing (the environmental issues raised) and in terms of the possibility of making sales of new products (for example, on trade-in deals). There is more on divestment in Chapter 12, in relation to the environmental impact of the disposal of packaging and used products.

This model of the decision-making process appears somewhat long and involved, but in practice most purchasing decisions are habitual, and the process is carried out quickly and virtually automatically. Table 3.1 shows a comparison of a non-habitual purchase and a habitual purchase, showing how each stage in the decision-making model is carried out.

Table 3.1 Habitual v non-habitual purchase behaviour

Stage in the process	New DVD player	Can of tuna
Problem recognition	The old DVD player doesn't have a facility for recording DVDs, and for some reason it suddenly skips to another part of the movie.	We used the last can yesterday, and we're going to the supermarket tonight.
Information search	Ask a few friends, see what they've got. Go online to a comparison site. Visit some local electronics stores (predominantly an external search).	Remember the brand that we like (predominantly an internal search).
Evaluation of alternatives	Discuss the options with one's husband or wife. Perhaps ask a knowledgeable friend for advice.	Find the right one on the shelves. Perhaps look at a premium brand and compare it with the store's own brand.
Purchase	Return to the store or the website and make the purchase. Perhaps use a credit card to spread the cost.	Put the can in the basket and run it through the checkout with everything else. Possibly (if we're desperate for tuna) buy it from the corner shop.
Post-purchase evaluation	Try playing a movie. Judge the ease of use of the equipment and the quality of playback. Decide on aspects such as reliability as time goes on. File the information away, or pass it on to friends as necessary.	Eat the tuna. Was it up to the usual standard? If so, no further action. If not, perhaps go back to the shop and complain, or perhaps buy a different brand in future.
Divestment	When the DVD player becomes obsolete, sell it on eBay, give it to a friend or simply throw it away.	Throw the empty can into the bin or take it for recycling.

PERCEPTION

Human senses constantly feed information into the brain; the amount of stimulation this involves would seriously overload the individual's system if the information were not filtered in some way. People therefore quickly learn to abstract information from the environment; the noise from a railway line near a friend's home might seem obvious to you, but your host is probably unaware of it. In effect, the brain is automatically selecting what is relevant and what is not, and for this reason the information being used by the brain does not provide a complete view of the world.

The gaps in the world view thus created are filled in by the individual's imagination and experience. The cognitive map of the world is affected by the following factors:

- *Subjectivity:* the existing world view of the individual
- *Categorisation:* the pigeon-holing of information. This usually happens through a 'chunking' process, whereby information is grouped into associated items. For example, a particular tune might make someone recall a special evening out from some years ago
- *Selectivity:* the degree to which the individual's brain has selected from the environment. This is also a subjective phenomenon; some people are more selective than others
- *Expectation:* the process of interpreting later information in a specific way. For example, look at this series of letters and numbers:

$$\mathcal{A} \; \mathit{13} \; \mathcal{C} \; \mathcal{D} \; \mathcal{E} \; \mathcal{F} \; \mathcal{G} \; \mathit{5} \; \mathcal{J}$$
10 11 12 13 14 15 16

In fact, the number 13 appears in both series, but would be interpreted as a B in the series of letters because that is what the brain is being led to expect

- *Past experience:* this leads us to interpret information in the light of existing knowledge. This is also known as the **law of primacy**. The sound of sea birds might make us think of a day at the beach, but could in fact be part of an advertisement's soundtrack.

In practice, people develop a model of how the world works and make decisions based on the model. Since each individual's model differs slightly from every other individual's model, it is sometimes difficult for marketers to know how to approach a given person.

One of the problems for marketers is that the perception the consumers have of marketing communications may not be what was intended. For example, fast-paced advertisements on television attract people's attention involuntarily, but have little effect on people's voluntary attention, so the message is often lost. Furthermore, a fast pace focuses attention on the style of the advertisement at the expense of its message (Bolls *et al.* 2003). Likewise, people often 'straighten up' gay imagery in TV shows or advertising if they find it embarrassing – in other words, they reinterpret the imagery to find a different explanation (Borgerson *et al.* 2006).

INFLUENCES ON THE BUYING DECISION

The main influences on the buying decision are of three types:

- *Personal factors* are features of the consumer that affect the decision process
- *Psychological factors* are elements of the consumer's mental processes
- *Social factors* are those influences from friends and family that affect decision-making.

Personal factors are shown in Table 3.2.

Involvement can be a major factor in consumer decision-making. Consumers often form emotional attachments to products, and most people would be familiar with the feeling of having fallen in love with a product – even when the product itself is hopelessly impractical. Involvement can also operate at a cognitive level, though; the outcome of the purchase may have important practical consequences for the consumer. For example, a rock climber may feel highly involved in the purchase of a climbing rope, since the consequences of an error could be fatal. Whether this is a manifestation of a logical thought process regarding the risk to life and limb or whether it is an emotional process regarding a feeling of confidence about the product would be hard to determine. People also become involved with companies and become champions for them (Bhattacharya and Sen 2003). Customers are often swayed by their relationship with the people who work for the firms they buy

Table 3.2 Personal factors in the buying decision

Personal factor	Explanation
Demographic factors	Individual characteristics such as age, gender, ethnic origin, income, family life cycle and occupation. These are often used as the bases for segmentation (see Chapter 4).
Situational factors	Changes in the consumer's circumstances. For example, a pay rise might lead the consumer to think about buying a new car; conversely, being made redundant might cause the consumer to cancel an order for a new kitchen.
Level of involvement	Involvement concerns the degree of importance the consumer attaches to the product and purchasing decision. For example, one consumer may feel that buying the right brand of coffee is absolutely essential to the success of a dinner party, where another consumer might not feel that this matters at all. Involvement is about the emotional attachment the consumer has for the product.

from; research shows that the relationship with the dealer is more important than the price when buying a new car (Odekerken-Schroder *et al.* 2003).

Involvement can be extremely complex: a study carried out with members of a major art gallery in the UK found six characteristics of involvement in total. These were: (1) centrality and pleasure, (2) desire to learn, (3) escapism, both spiritual and creative, (4) sense of belonging and prestige, (5) physical involvement, and (6) drivers of involvement (Slater and Armstrong 2010). Obviously, people who have joined an art gallery, as opposed to simply visiting one, will have much higher involvement than most.

Psychological factors in the decision-making process are as shown in Table 3.3. Consumers' attitudes to products can be complex. They vary according to:

- **Valence** – whether the attitude is positive, negative or neutral
- **Extremity** – the strength of the attitude
- **Resistance** – the degree to which the attitude can be changed by outside influences
- **Persistence** – the degree to which the attitude erodes over time
- **Confidence** – the level at which the consumer believes the attitude is correct.

Table 3.3 Psychological factors in the buying decision

Psychological factor	Explanation
Perception	This is the way people build up a view of the world. Essentially, this process of selection or analysis means that each person has an incomplete picture of the world; the brain therefore fills in the gaps by a process of synthesis using hearsay, previous experience, imagination, etc. Marketers are able to fill some of the gaps through the communication process, but will come up against the problem of breaking through the selection and analysis process.
Motives	The internal force that encourages someone towards a particular course of action. Motivation is a vector; it has both intensity and direction.
Ability and knowledge	A consumer who is, for example, a beginner at playing the violin is unlikely to spend thousands of pounds on a Stradivarius. Ability therefore affects some buying decisions. Likewise, pre-existing knowledge of a product category or brand will also affect the way the consumer approaches the decision. Pre-existing knowledge is difficult for a marketer to break down; it is much better to try to add to the consumer's knowledge wherever possible.
Attitude	Attitude has three components: cognition, which is to do with conscious thought processes; affect, which is about the consumer's emotional attachment to the product; and conation, which is about planned courses of behaviour. For example, 'I love my Volkswagen (affect) because it's never let me down (cognition). I'll definitely buy another (conation)'. Conations are only intended actions – they do not always lead to action, since other factors might interrupt the process.
Personality	The traits and behaviours that make each person unique. Personalities change very slowly, if at all, and can be regarded as constant for the purposes of marketing. Typically marketers aim for specific personality types, such as the gregarious, the competitive, the outgoing or the sporty.

People who are particularly knowledgeable ('savvy' consumers) are usually competent in the use of technology, good at interpersonal networking both in person and online, marketing-literate, empowered by their own consumer effectiveness and know what to expect from firms (Macdonald and Uncles 2007). These personal characteristics make them efficient and effective at getting what they want from firms.

It should be noted that the conation component of attitude (see Table 3.3) is not necessarily consistent with subsequent behaviour; a consumer's intentions about future behaviour do not always materialise, if only because of the existence of interrupts. For example, an individual with a grievance against a bank may intend to move his/her account to a different bank, but find that the difficulties of switching the account would create too much paperwork to be worthwhile.

The traditional view of attitude is that affect towards an object is mediated by cognition; Zajonc and Markus (1985) challenged this view and asserted that affect can arise without prior cognition. In other words, it is possible to develop a 'gut feeling' about something without conscious evaluation.

Attitude contains elements of belief (knowledge of attributes) and opinion (statements about a product), but is neither. Belief is neutral, in that it does not imply attraction or repulsion, whereas attitude has direction; and, unlike opinion, attitudes do not need to be stated.

From the marketer's viewpoint, attitudes are important since they often precede behaviour. Clearly a positive attitude towards a firm and its products is more likely to lead to purchase of the firm's products than a negative attitude. There is, however, some evidence to show that people often behave first, then form attitudes afterwards (Fishbein 1972) and therefore some car manufacturers find that it is worthwhile to give special deals to car rental companies and driving schools so that consumers can try the vehicles before forming their attitudes. Trial is considerably more powerful than advertising in forming attitudes (Smith and Swinyard 1983).

Social factors

Social factors influence consumers through:

- **Normative compliance** – the pressure exerted on the individual to conform and comply
- **Value-expressive influence** – the need for psychological association with a particular group
- **Informational influence** – the need to seek information from a group about the product category being considered.

Of the three, normative compliance is probably the most powerful; this works because the individual finds that acting in one way leads to the approval of friends or family, whereas acting in a different way leads to the disapproval of friends and family. This process favours a particular type of behaviour as a result. Good moral behaviour is probably the result of normative compliance.

Peer-group pressure is an example of normative compliance. The individual's peer group (a group of equals) will expect a particular type of behaviour, including (probably) some purchase behaviour. For example, most cigarette smokers began to smoke as a result of pressure from their friends when they were young teenagers. The desire to be a fully accepted member of the group is far stronger than any health warnings.

The main source of these pressures is **reference groups**. These are the groups of friends, colleagues, relatives and others whose opinions the individual values. Table 3.4 gives a list of types of reference group. The groups are not mutually exclusive; a formal group can also be a secondary group, and so forth. Some researchers go so far as to identify reference groups as tribes, especially when the group

Table 3.4 Reference group influences

Reference group	Explanation
Primary groups	The people we see most often. Family, friends, close colleagues. A primary group is small enough to allow face-to-face contact on a regular, perhaps daily, basis. These groups have the strongest influence.
Secondary groups	People we see occasionally and with whom we have a shared interest; for example, the members of a golf club or a trade association. These groups sometimes have formal rules that members must adhere to in their business dealings or hobbies, and may also have informal traditions (e.g. particular clothing or equipment) that influence buying decisions.
Aspirational groups	The groups to which we wish we belonged. These groups can be very powerful in influencing behaviour because the individual has a strong drive towards joining; this is the source of value-expressive influences. These groups can be particularly influential in fashion purchases.
Dissociative groups	The groups with which the individual does not want to be associated. This makes the individual behave in ways opposite to those of the group; for example, somebody who does not wish to be thought of as a football hooligan might avoid going to football matches altogether.
Formal groups	Groups with a known, recorded membership list. Often these groups have fixed rules; a professional body will lay down a code of conduct, for example.
Informal groups	Less structured, and based on friendship. There are no formalities to joining; one merely has to fit in with the group's joint ideals.
Automatic groups	The groups we belong to by virtue of age, race, culture or education. These are groups that we do not join voluntarily, but they do influence our behaviour; for example, a woman of 45 will not choose clothes that make her look like 'mutton dressed as lamb'. Likewise, expatriates often find that they miss food from home or seek out culture-specific goods of other types.

focuses around a specific object such as a celebrity or a brand. In some cases, groups may arise through social networking sites, and thus be virtual groups: often these have tribal characteristics, since the networking site may be established around a celebrity, a brand or a specific hobby such as aviation or support for a sports team. Such tribes can become creative, and usually offer their members a strong feeling of belonging (Hamilton and Hewer 2010).

Roles

The **roles** we play are also important in decision-making. Each of us plays many different roles in the course of our lives (in fact, in the course of a day) and we buy products to aid us accordingly (Goffman 1969). Somebody who is to be best man at a wedding will choose a suitable suit, either to buy or to hire, to avoid looking ridiculous or otherwise spoiling the day. In terms of longer-lasting roles, the role of Father will dictate purchasing behaviour on behalf of children; the role of Lover may dictate buying flowers or wearing perfume; the role of Friend might mean buying a gift or a round of drinks; the role of Daughter might mean buying a Mother's Day present. In some immigrant families, parental roles involve negotiating cultural boundaries as well (Lindridge and Hogg 2006).

Family roles influence decision-making far beyond the normative compliance effects. Frequently, different members of the family take over the role of buyer for specific product categories; the husband may make the main decisions about the car and its accessories and servicing, while the wife makes the main decisions about the decor of the home. Recent research shows that some convenience foods can empower mothers to take control of their 'caretaker' role within the family, provided that marketers can remove the guilt feelings many women feel about using convenience foods (Carrigan and Szmigin 2006). Older children may decide on food, choosing the healthy or environmentally friendly alternatives, and often help their parents to learn about new products (Ekstrom 2007).

In terms of its functions as a reference group, the family differs from other groups in the following respects:

- Face-to-face contact on a daily basis
- *Shared consumption* of such items as food, housing, car, TV sets and other household durables
- *Subordination of individual needs* to the common welfare. There is never a solution that will suit everybody
- *Purchasing agents* will be designated to carry out the purchasing of some items. As the number of working parents grows, pre-teens and young teens are taking an ever-increasing role in family shopping.

Conflict resolution within the family decision-making unit is usually more important than it would be for an individual, since there are more people involved. Whereas an individual might have difficulty in choosing between two equally attractive holiday destinations, discussions about family holidays are inevitably much more difficult since each family member will have his or her own favourite idea on a holiday destination or activity. There is likely to be a degree of negotiation, and even small children quickly develop skills in negotiating, justifying the benefits of a particular choice, forming coalitions with other family members and compromising where necessary (Thomson *et al.* 2007).

Culture can have a marked effect: African cultures tend to be male-dominated, whereas European and North American cultures show a more egalitarian pattern of decision-making (Green *et al.* 1983). This may be because decision-making becomes more egalitarian when both partners earn money outside the home (Filiatrault and Brent Ritchie 1980).

Decision-making stage also affects the roles of the family in the decision; problem recognition may come from any family member, whereas information search and product evaluation may be undertaken by different members. For example, the father may notice that the teenage son needs new football boots, the son might ask around for types, and the mother might decide which type falls within the family's budget.

Four kinds of marital role specialisation have been identified:

- *Wife dominant*, where the wife has most say in the decision
- *Husband dominant*, where the husband plays the major role
- *Syncratic or democratic*, where the decision is arrived at jointly
- *Autonomic*, where the decision is made entirely independently of the partner (Davies and Rigaux 1974).

Marketers need to know which type of specialisation is most likely to occur in the target market, since this will affect the style and content of promotional messages; for example, some advertising in the UK has tended to portray men as being incompetent at household tasks, despite evidence that men are taking a more active role in housework (Dwek 1996).

In most industrialised countries the family is undergoing considerable changes because of the rising divorce rate and the increasing propensity for couples to live together without marrying. In the above role specialisations, the terms 'husband' and 'wife' apply equally to unmarried partners.

Children have an increasing role in purchasing decisions: 'pester power' often results in increased family purchases of particular brands of chocolate, pizza, burgers and snack foods (Dwek 1995). Consequently, marketers often try to reach children aged between 5 and 12 through the use of sponsorship of teaching materials, free samples and sponsorship of prizes in schools (Burke 1995). Some recent research indicates that children are well aware of the possible responses parents might make, and view this kind of activity as a game; children tend to regard this as good-natured rather than as a conflict (Lawlor and Prothero 2011).

Children sometimes have greater influence on the family purchasing decisions than do the parents themselves, for the following reasons:

- Often they do the shopping since both parents are out at work
- They watch more TV than do their parents, so they are more knowledgeable about products. Often older children (and female children) are more aware of these issues than are their parents (Nancarrow *et al.* 2011)
- They tend to be more attuned to consumer issues, and have the time to shop around for (for example) environmentally friendly products
- Parents are often concerned about the image the child presents; poor families, in particular, go to great lengths to ensure that their children are not embarrassed by poverty (Hamilton and Catterall 2006).

Purchasing behaviour is also affected by people's identity – in other words, their view of themselves. The more closely the purchasing behaviour fits with the person's identity, the more likely it is to occur; this is particularly important in non-profit marketing such as charitable donations or participation in voluntary work, where the exchange involves individuals and is often based on social exchanges (Arnett *et al.* 2003). For some women, buying things for a new baby reinforces their own role as mother; research shows that purchase of a pram carries a public signal meaning, a private signal meaning, an experiential meaning and a role embrace. Each of these aspects contributes to the mother's self-image (Thomsen and Sorensen 2006).

Interestingly, consumption behaviour has a role in binding families closer together. Apart from the obvious aspects of sharing some items, such as household equipment and family cars, older family members often pass down heirlooms to younger members. These goods are valued far beyond their usefulness or monetary value since they provide a link with older family members, helping to create and nurture a family identity (Curasi 2011).

IMPULSE BUYING

Impulse purchases are not based on any plan, and usually happen as the result of a sudden confrontation with a stimulus.

Pure impulse is based on the novelty of the product. Seeing something new may prompt the consumer to buy it just to try it. **Reminder impulse** acts when the consumer suddenly realises that something has been left off the shopping list. **Suggestion impulse** arises when confronted with a product that meets a previously unfelt need, and **planned impulse** occurs when the consumer has gone out to meet a specific need, but is prepared to be swayed by what is on special offer.

For example, someone may be on a shopping trip to buy a new jacket for a weekend dinner party. In the shop he notices a rack of bow ties, and buys one because he has never owned one before (pure impulse). Next he remembers that he has not got a suitable summer shirt, so he picks one up from the counter (reminder impulse), and near it he sees a rack of cotton trousers which are on offer (suggestion impulse). Finally, he sees a safari jacket which, although it is not the style he was thinking of, is actually ideal for the job so he buys it (planned impulse). Most shoppers are familiar with these situations, and, indeed, they commonly occur when browsing in supermarkets.

The purchase process itself is an important part of the benefits that consumers get from consumption; research has shown that satisfaction with the process relates to the desire to participate in future purchases (Tanner 1996). Typically, impulse buyers are also variety seekers; impulse buying often results from the desire to do something stimulating and interesting as an antidote to boredom (Sharma *et al.* 2010a).

Impulse buying has perhaps been made easier by the Internet. There is certainly evidence that people often act on impulse when browsing the websites of charities (Bennett 2009), and it seems likely that the ease of purchase on the Internet will foster impulsive behaviour.

INDUSTRIAL BUYER BEHAVIOUR

Industrial buyers differ from consumers in that they are (at least theoretically) more formalised in their buying behaviour. The major areas where organisational buying differs from consumer buying are as follows:

- Bigger order values in terms of finance and quantity
- Reciprocity; the firms may buy each other's products as part of a negotiated deal
- Fewer buyers, because there are fewer firms than there are individuals
- More people in the decision process
- Fewer sales in terms of the number of deals
- More complex techniques exist for buying and for negotiating.

Organisational buyers are buying to meet the organisation's needs, but it should also be remembered that they have their personal needs. These might be a need for *prestige*, a need for *career security,* for *friendship and social needs,* and other personal factors such as the satisfaction of driving a hard bargain, or the buyer's personality, attitudes and beliefs (Powers 1991). The astute marketer, and particularly the astute salesperson, will not ignore these personal needs of the buyers.

Critical thinking

Are professional buyers really so easily swayed by their personal needs? After all, they have their careers to think about – surely that implies a certain amount of care about how they behave, and showing favouritism to one supplier over another almost smacks of corruption!

Of course, we are all human – and we each bring our humanity to our working day, so maybe we shouldn't expect buyers to be any different from the rest of us.

Table 3.5 Industrial buyers' methods

Method	Explanation
Description	Managers within the organisation lay down exactly what is required and the buyer is given the brief of finding the best supplier. The buyer might, for example, be asked to find a supplier of steel bolts. He or she will then ask manufacturers to quote prices, and will make a judgement based on price and delivery reliability.
Inspection	This is commonly carried out for variable goods, such as second-hand plant and equipment. Car dealers will usually inspect the cars before buying, for example.
Sampling	Commonly used for agricultural products. A buyer might sample, say, wool from an Australian sheep-station and fix a price for it on the basis of its quality. Often these decisions will be made by reference to a very small sample, perhaps only a few strands of wool.
Negotiation	Typically used for one-off or greenfield purchase situations. This involves the greatest input in terms of both the buyer's skills and the salesperson's time, and it is likely that a number of people from the buying organisation will be involved.

Regarding the organisation's needs, however, the chief considerations of most buyers appear to revolve around quality, delivery, service and price (Green and Wind 1968). This often means that buyers will be working to a set of *specifications* about the products, and will probably use some or all of the formal techniques shown in Table 3.5.

The industrial purchase task might be a *new task,* in which case the buyer will need to adopt extensive problem-solving behaviour. The vendor has the opportunity of establishing a relationship which might last for many years, however. New-task situations will often involve the greatest amount of negotiation, since there is little (if any) previous experience to draw on.

Straight re-buy tasks are routine; the buyer is simply placing an order for the same products in the same quantities as last time. This requires very little thought or negotiation on the part of either buyer or seller. Often these deals are conducted over the telephone rather than spending time and money on a face-to-face meeting.

Modified re-buy involves some change in the purchase order; for example, a larger order value or a different delivery schedule. Sometimes the re-buy can be modified by the salesperson, for example by suggesting that the buyer orders a slightly larger value of goods than usual or by altering the delivery schedule in some way. In circumstances where the two firms have an ongoing relationship, buyers will often track the performance of their suppliers over a long period of time; buying firms that monitor their suppliers effectively can gain real competitive advantage, because they can control their supply of inputs much better (Bharadwaj 2004). Unfortunately, most firms appear reluctant to develop their suppliers (Wagner 2006).

Often the demand for industrial products will be dictated by factors outside the buying organisation's control. For example, **derived demand** occurs because the buyers are using the products either for resale or in making other products. The demand is therefore dictated by the demand for the end product. Frequently the demand for a component will be *inelastic*; for example, the price of wheel nuts will not affect the demand for them much, since they form only a tiny proportion of the price of a car, and also the car cannot be made without them. **Joint demand** occurs because the demand for one type of product dictates the demand for another. For instance, if the demand for guitars rises, so will the demand for guitar strings in the following months.

Fluctuating demand is more extreme in industrial markets because a small reduction in consumer demand for a product will lead to de-stocking by retailers and wholesalers, which causes a big reduction in demand from the manufacturers. A rise in consumer demand is likely to lead to re-stocking, which causes a bigger than expected rise in demand from the producers. In this way the fluctuations in demand for industrial products are more extreme than for consumer products.

Decision-making units

Industrial buying decisions are rarely made in isolation. Usually several people are involved in the process at different stages.

Gatekeepers such as secretaries and receptionists control the flow of information to the decision-makers. Often they will act as a barrier to salespeople, and see their role as being primarily to prevent interruptions to the decision-maker's work pattern.

Influencers are those individuals who 'have the ear' of the decision-makers. They could be people within the firm whom the decision-maker trusts, or they could be golf partners, spouses or even children.

Users are those who will actually use the product. For example, if the organisation is contemplating the purchase of a new computer system, the finance department and the IT department will clearly want to have some say in the decision.

Deciders are the ones who make the real decision. These are usually the hardest to influence, since they are usually the more senior people in the decision-making unit and are surrounded by gatekeepers. They are also sometimes hard to identify. They are not necessarily buyers, but they do hold the real power in the buying decision.

Buyers are the ones given the task of actually going through the process of buying. The buyers may be given a very specific brief by the decider, and may have very little room to negotiate except on areas such as price and delivery schedules.

Sometimes they are merely there to handle the mechanical aspects of getting tenders from possible suppliers.

Each of these people has an independent existence outside the organisation; each will bring their own personal needs and aspirations to their role. In some cases this will be a job-related need (for example, career progression or the need to appear professional); in other cases the individual may have personal needs, such as a need to exercise power or the hedonic need to drive a hard bargain. The need to impress others within the firm can be extremely powerful.

From the viewpoint of the industrial marketer, it is essential to get to the deciders in some way rather than wait for the buyers to make the first contact by issuing a tender. The reason for this is that a tender will usually be very specific, and the buyers will then be deciding on the basis of price. The only way to get the order in those circumstances is to be the cheapest, and this inevitably results in reduced profits. If the seller has managed to approach the decision-maker beforehand, the seller can persuade the decision-maker to include certain essential aspects of the product in the tender, and thus ensure that the tender contains specifications that are difficult or impossible for the competition to meet.

Webster and Wind (1972) theorised that four main forces determine organisational buyer behaviour: environmental forces (such as the state of the economy), organisational forces (for example, the size of the organisation and therefore its buying power), group forces (internal politics and the relative power of group members) and individual forces (the personality and preferences of the decision-maker). These forces combine in complex ways to influence the final decision.

This means that the role of the salesperson is crucial in industrial markets. Salespeople are able to identify potential customers and approach them with a solution for their specific problem; even in cases where the buyer is going to invite tenders from other firms, the salesperson can often ensure that the tender is drawn up in a way that excludes the competition. Salespeople, and in particular key-account salespeople, are crucially important in relationship marketing, since they negotiate the terms of the relationship and are the human face of the supplying corporation.

In the end, organisations do not make purchases. Individuals make purchases on behalf of organisations, and therefore salespeople are always dealing with human beings who have their own needs, failings, attitudes and blind spots. Purchasing decisions are not made entirely rationally; often the personal relationship between the representatives of the buying and selling companies has the biggest role in the purchase. Buyers will naturally prefer to deal with someone they know and trust (see the section on personal selling in Chapter 9).

CASE STUDY 3 Choosing a holiday

Forty years ago the majority of holidays were package deals. Ever since Butlins invented the all-inclusive holiday in the 1930s, there has been a demand for the kind of holiday where everything is arranged in advance, there are no surprises and no challenges, and the holidaymaker can simply enjoy the experience without having any stressful situations to deal with.

During the 1950s and 1960s, the air-inclusive package holiday grew in popularity. People could travel to foreign countries (mainly Spain, France and Italy in those days) and have everything organised for them, including the flight and the hotel, without having to speak the language or deal with travel arrangements. Also, such holidays were relatively cheap because they got around the stringent international flight restrictions that were then in force – scheduled flights were all operated by national flag-carrying airlines and were expensive, whereas chartered aircraft were exempt from the international agreements restricting destinations and charges.

However, as time went by several changes occurred in the marketplace. First, there were some high-profile bankruptcies of tour operators, with holidaymakers left stranded abroad, often with their hotels unpaid and the proprietors demanding money. This led to the establishment of a compensation and licensing system funded by the industry, which put costs up. Second, the European Union agreed an 'open skies' policy which did away with the old treaties and allowed low-cost airlines to start operations. Third, the Internet made it easy for people to book their own flights, transfers, hotels and so forth. Fourth, increased travel meant increased confidence among consumers, so that people felt happy to organise their own holidays. Fifth, an increasing mood of independent thinking, born from increasing wealth and universal education, meant people did not want to be regimented on holiday, or even be forced to stay in the same hotel for 2 weeks. Sixth, the wider availability of information about foreign countries (gleaned from television or from independent travel guides such as *Rough Guides* or *Lonely Planet*) encouraged people to travel 'off the beaten track' more. Finally, increased wealth meant that people were more prepared to take a risk, knowing that most problems could be overcome with a big cheque book.

Choosing a holiday has therefore become less a matter of selecting from a fixed menu of destinations, hotels and tour options, and more a process of deciding where one wants to go and what one wants to do there and then putting together the various elements of flight, hotels, local transport, tour bookings and so forth. This makes the decision process more complex, but at the same time it is more engaging and interesting for the person planning the trip – and the Internet makes the whole process relatively straightforward anyway, since airline websites offer hotels and car hire.

Whatever the reasons, holiday choices are much wider than they used to be, and holiday companies are struggling to keep up with the changed environment. Many former package tour operators now sell flights and hotels separately for those who prefer to make their own arrangements, and many more have found the new conditions too tough and have closed down. The new consumer empowerment may have proved too much for some firms, but it has transformed holiday choices forever.

Questions

1. What influence might family roles have on the buying process for a holiday?
2. How has demographic change affected the holiday market?
3. How might people evaluate the alternatives?
4. How might someone establish a consideration set when booking an independent holiday?
5. How has the information search become modified over the past 40 years, as far as holiday booking is concerned?

SUMMARY

In this chapter we have looked at how people behave when faced with buying decisions. We have looked at the decision-making process both for consumers and for organisational buyers, and at the influences and pressures on each group.

Here are the key points from this chapter:

- Consumers buy because they recognise either assortment depletion or assortment extension needs
- Complaints should be encouraged, because they give the opportunity to cure post-purchase dissonance and create loyal customers
- Individuals belong to several reference groups and are also influenced by groups to which they do not belong such as aspirational groups and dissociative groups
- Normative compliance is probably the most powerful factor in attitude formation and decision-making
- The family is probably the most powerful reference group
- Industrial buying is complex because of the number of people involved, and because of greater formality in the process
- Gatekeepers, users, influencers, deciders and buyers are all involved in organisational decision-making. They each have personal agendas, and none of them should be ignored if the deal is to go through
- The route to success in industrial marketing is to make sure the tender has something in it that the competition cannot match.

CHAPTER QUESTIONS

1 How do family members influence each other's buying behaviour?
2 What are the main differences between industrial buyers and consumers?
3 What is the difference between assortment depletion and assortment extension?
4 How can the use of choice heuristics reduce post-purchase dissonance?
5 How can a marketer use interrupts to influence consumer behaviour?

Further reading

Consumer Behavior: A European Perspective 4th edition by Michael R. Solomon, Gary Bamossy, Soren Askegaard, and Margaret K. Hogg (Harlow, FT Prentice Hall, 2009). This is a very comprehensive text adapted from an American book, covering all aspects of consumer behaviour.

Business Marketing Management: A Global Perspective by Jim Blythe and Alan Zimmerman (London, Thomson, 2005). This book provides an in-depth view of business-to-business marketing, taking a global perspective. It covers all aspects of marketing to other businesses, including buyer behaviour and strategic issues.

References

Ang, Lawrence and Buttle, Francis: 'Customer retention management processes', *European Journal of Marketing*, **40** (1/2) (2006), pp. 83–9.

Arnett, Dennis B., German, Steve D. and Hunt, Shelby D.: 'The identity salience model of relationship marketing success: the case of non-profit marketing', *Journal of Marketing*, **67** (April 2003), pp. 89–105.

Bennett, Roger: 'Impulsive donation decisions during online browsing of charity websites', *Journal of Consumer Behaviour*, **8** (2 and 3) (Mar–Jun 2009), pp. 116–34.

Bharadwaj, Neeraj: 'Investigating the decision criteria used in electronic components procurement', *Industrial Marketing Management*, **33** (4) (2004), pp. 317–23.

Bhattacharya, C.B. and Sen, Sankar: 'Consumer-company identification: a framework for understanding consumers' relationships with companies', *Journal of Marketing*, **67** (2) (April 2003), pp. 76–88.

Bolls, Paul D., Muehling, Darrel D. and Yoon, Kak: 'The effects of television commercial pacing on viewers' attention and memory', *Journal of Marketing Communications*, **9** (1) (March 2003), pp. 17–28.

Borgerson, Janet, Schroeder, Jonathan, Blomberg, Britta and Thorssen, Erica: 'The gay family in the ad: consumer responses to non-traditional families in marketing communication', *Journal of Marketing Management*, **22** (9) (2006), pp. 955–78.

Burke, J.: 'Food firms pester pupils for sales', *Sunday Times* (11 June 1995).

Carrigan, Marylyn and Szmigin, Isabelle: '"Mothers of invention": maternal empowerment and convenience consumption', *European Journal of Marketing*, **40** (9/10) (2006), pp. 1122–42.

Curasi, Carolyn F.: 'Intergenerational possession transfers and identity maintenance', *Journal of Consumer Behaviour*, **10** (2) (Mar/April 2011), pp. 111–18.

Davies, Harry L. and Rigaux, Benny P.: 'Perception of marital roles in decision processes', *Journal of Consumer Research*, **1** (June 1974), pp. 5–14.

Dwek, R.: 'In front of the children', *The Grocer*, **2** (December 1995), pp. 45–9.

Dwek, R.: 'Man trouble', *Marketing Business* (February 1996), p. 18.

Ekstrom, Karin M.: 'Parental consumer learning, or keeping up with the children', *Journal of Consumer Behaviour*, **6** (4) (2007), pp. 203–17.

Engel, James F., Blackwell, Roger D. and Miniard, Paul W.: *Consumer Behaviour*, 8th edn (Fort Worth, TX, Dryden Press, 1995).

Filiatrault, Pierre and Brent Ritchie, J.R.: 'Joint purchasing decisions; a comparison of influence structure in family and couple decision-making units', *Journal of Consumer Research*, **7** (September 1980), pp. 131–40.

Fishbein, Martin: 'The search for attitudinal-behavioural consistency', in Joel E. Cohen (ed.) *Behavioural Science Foundations of Consumer Behaviour* (New York, Free Press, 1972), pp. 257–67.

Goffman, Erving: *The Presentation of Self in Everyday Life* (Harmondsworth, Penguin, 1969).

Green, P., Robinson, P. and Wind, Y.: 'The determinants of vendor selection: the evaluation function approach', *Journal of Purchasing* (August 1968).

Green, Robert T., Leonardi, Jean-Paul, Chandon, Jean-Louis, Cunningham, Isabella C.M., Verhage, Bronis and Strazzieri, Alain: 'Societal development and family purchasing roles; a cross-national study', *Journal of Consumer Research*, **9** (March 1983), pp. 436–42.

Grougiou, Vassiliki, and Pettigrew, Simone: 'Seniors' attitudes to voicing complaints: a qualitative study', *Journal of Marketing Management*, **25** (9/10) (2009), pp. 987–1001.

Hamilton, Cathy and Catterall, Miriam: 'Consuming love in poor families: children's influence on consumption decisions', *Journal of Marketing Management*, **22** (9/10) (2006), pp. 1031–82.

Hamilton, Kathy, and Hewer, Paul: 'Tribal mattering spaces: social-networking sites, celebrity affiliations, and tribal innovations', *Journal of Marketing Management*, **26** (3 and 4) (2010), pp. 271–9.

Harwood, Tracy, and Garry, Tony: 'It's Mine! Participation and ownership within virtual co-creation environments', *Journal of Marketing Management*, **26** (3 and 4) (2010), pp. 290–301.

Holbrook, Morris P. and Hirschmann, Elizabeth C.: 'The experiential aspects of consumption; consumer fantasies, feelings and fun', *Journal of Consumer Research*, **9** (September 1982), pp. 132–40.

Lawlor, Margaret-Anne, and Prothero, Andrea: 'Pester power – a battle of wills between children and their parents', *Journal of Marketing Management*, **27** (5 and 6) (2011), pp. 561–81.

Lindridge, Andrew M. and Hogg, Margaret K.: 'Parental gate-keeping in diasporic Indian families: examining the intersection of culture, gender and consumption', *Journal of Marketing Management*, **22** (9/10) (2006), pp. 979–1008.

Macdonald, Emma K. and Uncles, Mark D.: 'Consumer savvy: conceptualization and measurement', *Journal of Marketing Management*, **23** (5/6) (2007), pp. 497–517.

Maxham, James G. III and Netemeyer, Richard G.: 'Firms reap what they sow: the effect of shared values and perceived organizational justice on customers' evaluation of complaint handling', *Journal of Marketing*, **67** (1) (January 2003), pp. 46–62.

Nancarrow, Clive, Tinson, Julie and Brace, Ian: 'Profiling key purchase influencers: those perceived as consumer savvy', *Journal of Consumer Behaviour*, **10** (2) (2011), pp. 102–10.

Ngai, Eric W.T., Heung, Vincent C., Wong, Y.H. and Chan, Fanny K.Y.: 'Consumer complaint behaviour of Asians and non-Asians about hotel services: an empirical analysis', *European Journal of Marketing*, **41** (11/12) (2007), pp. 1375–91.

Odekerken-Schroder, Gaby, Ouwersloot, Hans, Lemmink, Jos and Semeijn, Janjaap: 'Consumers' trade-off between relationship, service, package and price: an empirical study in the car industry', *European Journal of Marketing*, **37** (1) (2003), pp. 219–42.

Oliver, Richard L.: 'A cognitive model of the antecedents and consequences of satisfaction decisions', *Journal of Marketing Research*, **17** (November 1980), pp. 460–9.

Powers, T.L.: *Modern Business Marketing: A Strategic Planning Approach to Business and Industrial Markets* (St Paul, MN, West, 1991).

Raju, P.S.: 'Optimum stimulation level; its relationship to personality, demographics, and exploratory behaviour', *Journal of Consumer Research*, **7** (December 1980), pp. 272–82.

Shankar, Avi, Cherrier, Helene and Canniford, Robin: 'Consumer empowerment: a Foucauldian interpretation', *European Journal of Marketing*, **40** (9/10) (2006), pp. 1013–30.

Sharma, Piyush, Sivakumaran, Bharadwaj and Marshall, Roger: 'Exploring impulse buying and variety seeking by retail shoppers: towards a common conceptual framework', *Journal of Marketing Management*, **26** (5 and 6) (2010a), pp. 473–94.

Sharma, Piyush, Marshall, Roger, Reday, Peter Alan and Na, Woonbang: 'Complainers vs non-complainers: a multinational investigation of individual and situational influences on customer complaint behavior', *Journal of Marketing Management*, **26** (1 and 2) (2010b), pp. 163–80.

Sijun, Wang and Huff, Leonard C.: 'Exploring buyers' response to sellers' violation of trust', *European Journal of Marketing*, **41** (9/10) (2007), pp. 1033–52.

Singh, Jagdip: 'Consumer complaint intentions and behaviour: definitions and taxonomical issues', *Journal of Marketing*, **52** (January 1988), pp. 93–107.

Slater, Alex and Armstrong, Kate: 'Involvement, Tate, and me', *Journal of Marketing Management*, **26** (7&8) (2010), pp. 727–48.

Smith, Robert E. and Swinyard, William R.: 'Attitude-behaviour consistency; the impact of product trial versus advertising', *Journal of Marketing Research*, **20** (August 1983).

Strandvik, Tore and Holmlund, Maria: 'How to diagnose business-to-business relationships by mapping negative incidents', *Journal of Marketing Management*, **24** (3/4) (2008), pp. 351–81.

Tanner, J.F.: 'Buyer perceptions of the purchase process and its effect on customer satisfaction', *Industrial Marketing Management*, **25** (2) (March 1996), pp. 125–33.

Thomsen, Thyra Uth and Sorensen, Elin Brandi: 'The first four-wheeled status symbol: pram consumption as a vehicle for the construction of motherhood identity', *Journal of Marketing Management*, **22** (9/10) (2006), pp. 907–27.

Thomson, Elizabeth S., Laing, Angus W. and McKee, Lorna: 'Family purchase decision making: exploring child influence behavior', *Journal of Consumer Behaviour*, **6** (4) (2007), pp. 182–202.

Wagner, Stephan M.: 'Supplier development practices: an exploratory study', *European Journal of Marketing*, **40** (5/6) (2006), pp. 554–71.

Walsh, Gianfranco, Hennig-Thurau, Thorsten and Mitchell, Vincent-Wayne: 'Consumer confusion proneness: scale development, validation and application', *Journal of Marketing Management*, **23** (7/8) (2007), pp. 697–721.

Wang, Shih-Lun Alex: 'The effects of audience knowledge on message processing of editorial content', *Journal of Marketing Communications*, **12** (4) (2006), pp. 281–96.

Webster, F.E. and Wind, Y.: *Organisational Buying Behaviour* (Englewood Cliffs, NJ, Prentice Hall, 1972).

Zajonc, Robert B. and Markus, Hazel: 'Must all affect be mediated by cognition?' *Journal of Consumer Research*, **12** (December 1985), pp. 363–4.

4

SEGMENTATION, TARGETING AND POSITIONING

Objectives

After reading this chapter you should be able to:

- Describe the main methods of segmenting markets
- Explain how segmentation aids profitability
- Decide whether a given segment is sufficiently profitable to be worth targeting
- Explain the purpose of segmentation
- Develop ways of assessing the economic viability of segments
- Explain the growth of segmented markets
- Establish strategies for dealing with segmented markets
- Describe perceptual mapping
- Describe the main issues surrounding the positioning of brands.

INTRODUCTION

The segmentation concept was first developed by Smith (1957) and is concerned with grouping consumers in terms of their needs. The aim of segmentation is to identify a group of people who have a need or needs that can be met by a single product, in order to concentrate the marketing firm's efforts most effectively and economically. For example, if a manufacturer produces a standardised product by a mass production method, the firm would need to be sure that there are sufficient people with a need for the product to make the exercise worthwhile.

The assumptions underlying segmentation are:

- Not all buyers are alike
- Sub-groups of people with similar behaviour, backgrounds, values and needs can be identified
- The sub-groups will be smaller and more homogeneous than the market as a whole
- It is easier to satisfy a small group of similar customers than to try to satisfy large groups of dissimilar customers (Zikmund and D'Amico 1995).

Continued on p. 76

Birmingham

Marketing a whole city may seem like a tall order, but all cities need to attract industry, tourists and even residents, or it will die. The marketers involved are in a unique position because they do not own the brand – the brand is owned and developed by the people who live in the city.

Identifying appropriate market segments is far from easy: a city the size of Birmingham contains within it virtually all segments of both consumer and business markets. The aim of Birmingham's positioning is to place the city as a youthful, lively city, on the basis that nobody believes that they are old.

Repositioning Birmingham as an exciting city to visit means building on what was essentially an industrial past – removing the image of a grimy industrial town and replacing it with a vibrant city where many events happen is a challenge that the marketers seek to meet.

The marketers monitor the league tables published by tourism organisations, and carry out their own research to determine how many people visit, how much they spend, how long they stay and whether they intend to return. Monitoring the market is essential for future decision-making about promotion activities.

Neil Rami, Managing Director

Watch the video clip, then try to answer the following questions. The answers are on the companion website.

Questions

1 What segmentation bases are most appropriate for Birmingham?
2 What positioning problems are apparent for the city?
3 How should Birmingham target potential visitors?

Targeting is concerned with choosing at which segments to aim. Segmentation is essentially about dividing up the market; targeting is about the practicalities of doing business within the market. The two are clearly closely linked, since the segmentation process will usually provide information as to which segments are likely to prove most profitable or will help the firm to achieve its strategic objectives in other ways.

Positioning is concerned with the brand's relationship with other brands aimed at the same segment. Positioning is about the place the brand occupies in the minds of potential customers, relative to other brands.

REASONS FOR SEGMENTING MARKETS

Each consumer is an individual with individual needs and wants. On the face of it, this creates a major problem for marketers, since it would clearly be impossible to tailor-make or customise each product to the exact requirements of each individual.

Before the Industrial Revolution most products were individually made. This proved to be expensive and essentially inefficient once mass production techniques had come into being. Unfortunately, mass production (taken to the extreme) means a reduction in the available choice of product, since the best way to keep production costs low is to have long production runs, which means standardising the product. Every adaptation costs money in terms of retooling and repackaging the product. In some economies, particularly those in parts of Eastern Europe and in the Third World, there is not sufficient wealth or investment in industry to allow for the production of many different types of product. These economies still rely heavily on mass production and mass marketing.

Mass marketing (or undifferentiated marketing) in which a standard product is produced for all consumers will only be effective if the consumers concerned have little choice and do not already own a product that meets the main needs. For example, in 1930s Germany few families owned cars. Hitler promised the German people that every family would own a car, so Porsche was commissioned to develop the Volkswagen (literally 'people's car') as a basic vehicle which could be cheaply produced for the mass market. The car had few refinements: it even lacked a fuel gauge.

This approach is less effective in economies where most consumers already own the **core benefits** of the product. Once car ownership was widespread and the core benefit of personal transportation was owned by most families, consumers demanded choices in features and design of their vehicles. Segmentation deals with finding out how many people are likely to want each benefit, roughly how much they will be willing to pay for it, and where they would like to buy it from. In this way, the firm approaching a segmented market is able to offer more functional benefits and more attention to *hedonic needs*, i.e. the products are more fun (see Chapter 3).

To make these adaptations worthwhile, marketers need to be reasonably sure that there is a large enough market for the product to be viable economically. On the other hand, concentrating on a smaller segment means that economies can be made in the supplier's communications activities; rather than advertise to a mass market, for example, the marketer would be better off concentrating resources on producing an advertisement that is tailored to the target segment – an ad, in other words, designed for the ideal customer and no other.

The reason for this is that we are surrounded by advertising messages. Consequently, people learn to avoid advertisements, and particularly to avoid ones that are clearly never going to be of any interest. At the same time, consumers will go out of their way to find out about products they have some interest in, often by reading special interest magazines. Therefore an advertisement that is tailored to a specific group of consumers and that appears in a medium that those consumers use is likely to be far more effective than an untargeted advertisement in a general interest medium.

Companies that aim for small segments usually have much greater credibility with consumers, and can learn to provide exactly what most pleases those consumers. In recent years, the Internet has provided opportunities for companies to relate to customers as individuals, and to be able to use interactive communications as a method of developing a 'segment of one' (Bailey *et al.* 2009).

Overall, the main purpose of segmenting is to enable the company to concentrate its efforts on pleasing one group of people with similar needs, rather than trying to please everybody and probably ending up pleasing nobody. Table 4.1 shows the advantages of segmenting the market.

Table 4.1 Advantages of segmentation

Advantage	Explanation
Customer analysis	By segmenting, the firm can get to understand its best customers better.
Competitor analysis	It is much easier to recognise and combat competition when concentrating on one small part of the overall market.
Effective resource allocation	Companies' scarce resources can be concentrated more effectively on a few consumers, rather than spread thinly across the masses.
Strategic marketing planning	Planning becomes easier once the firm has a clear picture of its best customers.
Expanding the market	Good segmentation can increase the overall size of the market by bringing in new customers who fit the profile of the typical customer, but were previously unaware of the product.

It is useful to remember that segmentation is not only concerned with choosing the right customers – it also means deciding which customers cannot be served effectively. Sometimes this is because the firm lacks the resources and sometimes it is because some groups of customers are more trouble than they are worth. Rejecting some customers is called demarketing (Kotler and Levy 1971), and research conducted by Medway *et al.* (2011) showed that marketers responsible for managing places (for example, ancient monuments) use demarketing as a way of controlling sustainability of the place as well as controlling such factors as seasonality and crisis prevention.

SEGMENTATION VARIABLES

A segment must fulfil the following requirements if it is to be successfully exploited:

- *It must be measurable, or definable.* In other words, there must be some way of identifying the members of the segment and knowing how many of them there are.
- *It must be accessible.* This means it must be possible to communicate with the segment as a group, and to get the product to them as a group.
- *It must be substantial,* i.e. big enough to be worth aiming for.
- *It must be congruent,* that is to say the members must have a close agreement on their needs.
- *It must be stable.* The nature and membership of the segment must be reasonably constant.

The three key criteria are accessibility, substance and measurability (Kotler 1991), but it is important also to look at the causes underlying the segmentation (Engel *et al.* 1995). This enables the marketers to anticipate changes more easily and sometimes to verify that the segmentation base is correctly defined.

There are many bases for segmenting, but the following are the main ones:

- *Geographic.* Where the consumers live, the climate, the topology, etc. For example, cars in Brazil almost always have air conditioning but may not have heaters; cars in Sweden have headlights that stay on constantly because of the poor quality of the light for much of the year. Geographic segmentation is very commonly used in international marketing, but is equally useful within single nations.
- *Psychographic.* Based on the personality type of the individuals in the segment. For example, the home insurance market might segment into those who are afraid of crime, those who are afraid of natural disasters and those who are afraid of accidental damage to their property.
- *Behavioural.* This approach examines the benefits, usage situation, extent of use and loyalty. For example, the car market might segment into business users and private users. The private market might segment further to encompass those

who use their cars primarily for commuting, those who use their cars for hobbies such as surfing or camping and those who use the car for domestic duties such as shopping or taking children to school. The business market might segment into 'prestige' users such as managing directors and senior executives, or high mileage users such as salespeople.

- *Demographic.* Concerned with the structure of the population in terms of ages, lifestyles and economic factors. For example, the housing market can be divided into first-time buyers, families with children, older retired people and elderly people in sheltered accommodation; equally, the market could be segmented according to lifestyle, with some accommodation appealing to young professionals, some appealing to country lovers, and so forth.

Geographic segmentation

Geographic segmentation may be carried out for a number of reasons.

- The nature of the product may be such that it applies only to people living within a specific area or type of area. Clothing manufacturers know that they will sell more heavy-weather clothing in cold coastal areas than in warm inland areas.
- If the company's resources are limited, the firm may start out in a small area and later roll out the product nationally.
- It might be that the product itself does not travel well. This is true of sheet glass, wedding cakes and most personal services such as hairdressing.

Markets may be segmented geographically according to the type of housing in the area. Firms that supply products specifically aimed at elderly people may wish to locate (or at least concentrate their marketing efforts) in retirement areas. Products aimed at young people might be heavily marketed in university towns, and so forth.

Psychographic segmentation

Psychographic segmentation classifies consumers according to their personalities. Psychographic segmentation remains problematical because of the difficulties of measuring consumers' psychological traits on a large scale. This type of segmentation can therefore fail on the grounds of accessibility. For example, researchers might find out that there is a group of people who relate the brand of coffee that they buy to their self-esteem. The problem then is that there is no obvious medium in which to advertise this feature of the coffee – if there were a magazine called *Coffee Makes Me Feel Good* there would be no problem.

In recent years, the Internet has increased the number of possibilities for allowing people to self-define into segments: our coffee-drinkers might have a website dedicated to them, at relatively little cost, where they might be able to exchange views and ideas. Segmentation can therefore be conducted in reverse by seeing who visits the website.

Behavioural segmentation

Behavioural segmentation can be a useful and reliable way of segmenting. At its most obvious, if the firm is marketing to anglers they are not interested in how old the anglers are, what their views are on strong drink or where they live. All the firm cares about is that they go fishing and might therefore be customers for a new type of rod. Accessing the segment would be easily undertaken by advertising in angling magazines or by developing an attractive website (for example, one which offers useful tips on angling). At a deeper level the firm might be interested in such issues as where they buy their fishing tackle, how much they usually spend on a rod, what kind of fish they are after, and so forth, but this information is easily obtained through questionnaire-type surveys, or by running an online forum. *Lifestyle* analysis has been widely used for the past 30 years or so, and seeks to segment markets according to how consumers spend their time, what their beliefs are about themselves and about specific issues, and the relative importance of their various possessions (e.g. cars, clothes, homes). The attraction of this approach is that it takes account of a wide range of characteristics of the segment, encompassing some psychographic features and some behavioural features (Plummer 1974).

Demographic segmentation

Demographic segmentation is the most commonly used method of segmenting markets, probably because it is easy to pick up the relevant information from government statistics. Demographics is the study of how people differ in terms of factors such as age, occupation, salary and lifestyle stage.

Typically, demographic segmentation revolves around age. While this is relevant in many cases, it is often difficult to see the difference between, say, a 20-year-old's buying pattern and a 30-year-old's buying pattern. Equally, it cannot be said with much reliability that all 10-year-olds share the same tastes. There are undoubtedly 10-year-olds who would not want to visit Disneyland or Luna Park and 10-year-olds who would prefer duck á l'orange to a hamburger. Age is, of course, relevant but it should be included as part of a range of measures, not relied upon on its own.

Critical thinking

Can we really be pigeonholed this easily? Surely our behaviour cannot be entirely governed by our age, or our gender, or our religious beliefs! As we grow older, or change our jobs, or have children, or become better educated, do our basic likes and dislikes really change?

If you like chips, you like chips, and no amount of lottery wins will make you suddenly like caviar instead. But then again – how are our tastes determined in the first place? By our upbringing, our friends, our experiences – and these are governed by our age, our gender, our religious beliefs, our education, etc. etc.

Maybe we CAN be pigeonholed that easily!

As we saw in Chapter 2, demographic variables are shifting over time, as the birth rate falls and the average age of the population rises. In addition, the number of single-person households is rising as people marry later and divorce rates increase; in 2001, single-person households represented 30% of UK households (Office for National Statistics 2003). The implications of this one change for marketers are far-reaching. Here are some of the possibilities:

- Increase in sales of individual packs of food
- Increase in sales of recipe products and ready meals
- Decrease in sales of gardening equipment and children's items
- Increase in sales of mating-game items
- Decrease in family-sized cars, packs of breakfast cereal, cleaning products, etc.

In Australia, immigration from South-East Asia is causing major changes in eating habits, religious observances and the linguistic structure of the country. In some cases, marketing activities have themselves contributed to a cross-fertilisation of cultural behaviour, so that individuals from one ethnic group behave in ways more usually associated with another group. This culture swapping means that ethnic and racial segmentation is no longer possible in most cases (Jamal 2003, Lindridge 2010).

Overall, demographic change means that new segments are emerging, some of which offer greater opportunities to marketers than do the segments they replace. Marketers need to monitor these changes in the demography if they are to remain able to segment the market effectively.

Not all segmentation variables will be appropriate to all markets. A pizza company might segment a market geographically (locating in a town centre) but would not segment by religion; the situation would be reversed for a wholesale kosher butcher. This is despite the fact that both firms are in the food business. **Single-variable segmentation** is based on only one variable; for example, size of firm. This is the simplest way to segment, but is also the most inaccurate and would rarely be used in practice. To achieve **multivariable segmentation**, several characteristics are taken into account. The more characteristics that are used, the greater the accuracy and effectiveness, but the smaller the resulting markets.

In practice, segmentation is difficult to apply. Many managers have difficulty in interpreting segmentation solutions presented to them by researchers; some even confess to a lack of understanding of segmentation theory (Dolnicar and Lazarevski 2009).

SEGMENTING INDUSTRIAL MARKETS

Industrial or organisational markets can be, and are, segmented by marketers according to the following criteria:

- *Geographic location.* Probably the commonest method, since most organisational markets are serviced by salespeople, and geographical segmentation enables the salesperson to make best use of drive time. Often firms in the same industry will locate near each other, perhaps because of availability of raw materials, or for traditional reasons to do with availability of local skilled workers.

- *Type of organisation.* IBM segments its market according to the industry the customer is in. This means that some IBM salespeople specialise in banking, others in insurance, others perhaps in local government applications of the equipment.
- *Client company size.* Many companies have separate salesforces to deal with large accounts, and often such salespeople need to use special techniques for dealing at this level.
- *Product use.* Oil companies have separate strategies (and sometimes separate subsidiaries) for marketing household central heating oil, for the plastics industry, for petrochemicals and for automotive sales.
- Usage rate. Customers who use large quantities of a given product will expect (and get) different treatment from customers who buy only in small quantities. This is partly because their needs are different, and partly because the supplier will tend to value the large buyer over the small buyer.

Bonoma and Shapiro (1984) suggest a nested approach to organisational market segmentation. This approach entails starting with broad characteristics such as the type of industry and the size of the organisations in it, then narrowing the segment by working through operating variables (processes, product types, etc.), then looking at the purchasing approach of the organisations, followed by situational factors such as delivery lead times and order size, and finally looking at the individual types of buyer in each firm.

For example, a glass manufacturer might begin by segmenting according to type of industry (window glass for construction, toughened glass for cars or bottles and jars for food packaging). Within the food packaging market the industry might break down further to pickles and sauces, wines and beers, and soft drinks. The wine and beer bottle market may further break down into major brewers and bottlers who buy in large quantities, and small privately owned vineyards who buy on a once-a-year basis. Some of the brewers may buy by tender, some may prefer to use a regular supplier and some may have special requirements in terms of bottle shape or design.

As in consumer markets, it is not necessarily the case that buyers act from wholly rational motives (see Chapter 3), so it would be unreasonable not to include the buyers' personal characteristics in the segmentation plan somewhere. This is likely to be the province of the salesforce since they are dealing with the buyers on a day-to-day basis.

SEGMENTATION EFFECTIVENESS

If a segment is correctly identified, it should be possible for the marketer to meet the needs of the segment members much more effectively than their competitors can. The firm will be able to provide specialist products that are more nearly right for the consumers in the segment, and will be able to communicate better with them. From the consumer's viewpoint, this is worth paying an extra premium for. Rather than

Figure 4.1 Segmentation trade-offs

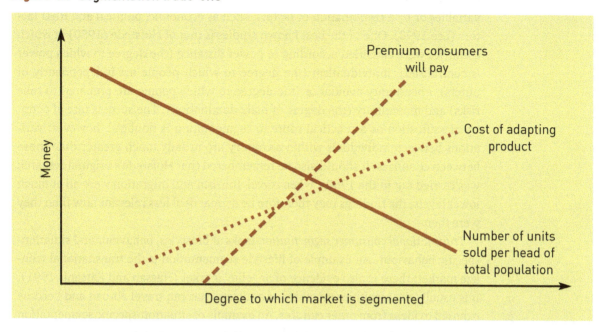

putting up with a product that does not quite fit the bill, the consumer will pay a little more for something that more closely approaches the ideal.

The segment will be profitable as long as the **premium** that the consumer will pay is greater than the cost to the manufacturer of making the modifications. There is therefore a trade-off; the finer-tuned the segmentation, the smaller the market but the greater the premium the target consumers will be prepared to pay. This is illustrated in Figure 4.1.

As the segmentation becomes narrower, fewer units will be sold, so the number of items sold as compared with the population at large will drop. This is partly offset by higher prices, but the profitability of the segment will begin only where the premium line and the cost line diverge. Where the costs of adaptation are higher than the premium, it is not worthwhile to make the adaptations; where the premium is higher than the cost, it may be worthwhile but the firm must still take account of the reduction in unit sales overall.

GLOBAL SEGMENTATION

Although cultural variance (and differences in consumer behaviour) are still major issues for international marketers (Hofstede 1994), transnational segments are still identifiable. The main bases for segmentation are:

- By country
- By individual characteristics (in much the same way as segmentation is handled within one's own country).

Countries can be grouped according to economic development criteria, by cultural variables or by a combination of factors, such as economic, political and R&D factors (Lee 1990). One of the best known studies is that of Hofstede (1980) in which countries were classified according to power distance (the degree to which power is centralised), individualism (the degree to which people act independently of others), uncertainty avoidance (the degree to which people are prepared to take risks) and masculinity (the degree of male domination). The success rate of country classification as a practical route to segmentation is doubtful, however; variations between individuals within a country are usually much greater than those between countries. It should also be remembered that Hofstede's original research was carried out in the 1960s, when travel, tourism and migration were all at much lower levels; the findings may therefore be a great deal less relevant now than they were then.

Transnational consumer segmentation looks at lifestyles, behaviour and situation-specific behaviour. An example of lifestyle segmentation is the transnational teenage market; there is also evidence of an 'elite' market (Hassan and Katsanis 1991). It is usually the wealthier members of a society that can travel abroad and become exposed to ideas from other cultures. An example of situation-specific segmentation is the attitudes to gift-giving, which seem to be common to many cultures (Beatty *et al*. 1991). More recent research has found transnational segments for dairy products, although the researchers found that some of the marketing communications needed to be adapted to address some aspects of the product, even when the consumers showed similar characteristics (Moskowitz *et al*. 2008).

The main difficulty with seeking transnational consumer segments lies in generating adequate research within the target countries.

TARGETING

Having divided the market into segments, managers must decide which segment will be the best to target, given the firm's overall objectives. Normally managers would choose the most profitable segment, but equally a firm may decide to aim for a particular segment of the market that is currently neglected, on the grounds that competitors are less likely to enter the market. The process of selecting a segment to aim for is called **targeting**. There are three basic strategic options open to marketers.

1 Concentrated marketing (single segment). This is also known as **niche marketing**; Pickfords heavy haulage and MTV follow this approach. The niche marketer concentrates on being the very best within a single tiny segment.

2 **Differentiated marketing** (multisegmented) means concentrating on two or more segments, offering a differentiated marketing mix for each. Holiday Inn aims to attract business travellers during the week but aims for the leisure market at the weekend and promotes to families. At the weekend, the hotels often have events for children and special room rates for families.

3 **Undifferentiated marketing** is about using a 'scattergun' approach. The producers who do this are usually offering a basic product that would be used by almost all age groups and lifestyles. For example, the market for petrol is largely undifferentiated. Although oil producers occasionally try to differentiate their products by the use of various additives and detergents, the use of petrol is much the same for everybody, and there would not appear to be any relationship between segmentation variables and petrol use. It would be difficult to imagine any real adaptation to the product that would meet people's needs sufficiently well to merit a premium price. Such examples of undifferentiated products are increasingly rare; even the producers of such basic commodities as salt and flour have made great strides forward in differentiating their products (i.e. meeting consumers' needs better).

The decision regarding which strategy to adopt will rest on the following three factors:

- The company's *resources*
- The product's features and benefits
- The characteristics of the segment(s).

Clearly, if resources are limited the company will tend to adopt a concentrated marketing approach. This approach is taken by Titleist, the golf supply company. Titleist supplies everything the golfer needs, from clubs to golfing clothes, rather than diversifying into a general sporting products market. This enables the firm to become very close to its market, and to understand the needs of golfers (and intermediaries such as club professionals) better than any other firm.

A higher level of resourcing coupled with a range of segments to approach will lead to a differentiated approach, and a simple made-for-everybody type product will lead to an undifferentiated approach. Table 4.2 shows this in action.

Table 4.2 Resourcing and degree of differentiation

		Type of product	
		High-differentiation consumers	Low-differentiation consumers
High-resource company	Mass market	Differentiated	Undifferentiated
	Specialist market	Differentiated	Concentrated
Low-resource company	Mass market	Concentrated	Differentiated (perhaps geographically)
	Specialist market	Concentrated	Concentrated

Table 4.3 Targeting decisions

Segment size	Profit per unit sold	Number of competitors	Strategic decision rationale
Large	Large	Large	A large market with large profits will attract competitors; prices will fall rapidly, and so will profits.
Large	Small	Large	This is a mature market. A new entrant would have to have something special to dominate the market: perhaps a much reduced cost base.
Small	Large	Large	A small segment with a high profit per unit and a large number of competitors can be captured entirely by a penetration pricing strategy.
Large	Large	Small	If the segment is both large and profitable, competitors will certainly enter the market. A skimming policy is best for this market; as competitors enter, it will be possible to reduce prices to compete effectively.
Large	Small	Small	This is a mature market, but should be low risk; the lack of competition means that it should be easy to capture a share, and the low profit margin will discourage others from entering.
Small	Small	Large	This is a dying market. Really not worth entering at all.
Small	Large	Small	This is a niche market. It should be possible to capture all of this market.
Small	Small	Small	This is clearly not a very profitable segment at all. Unless the firm has something very new to bring to the segment, this is probably not worth targeting.

Companies with a small resource base are often unable to make their voices heard in mass markets simply because they cannot afford the level of promotional spend. They therefore need to segment narrowly, perhaps by starting out in a small area of the country (geographical segmentation) and gradually spreading nationwide as resources become available.

Table 4.3 shows the decision matrix for choosing a segment to target. The marketing strategy should be tailored to fit the intended audience – this means that each of the seven Ps, and every element of the promotion mix, needs to be built around the segment.

Accurate targeting is best achieved by carrying out detailed market research into the needs and wants of the target group (see Chapter 5). In this way the company is able to decide what to offer the target audience to improve on the competitors' offering. Note that three factors are being taken into account here. First, what do the

Table 4.4 Market coverage strategies

Strategy	Explanation	Example
Product/market concentration	Niche marketing; the company takes over one small part of the market	Tie Rack, Sock Shop
Product specialisation	Firm produces a full line of a specific product type	Campbell's Soup
Market specialisation	Firm produces everything that a specific group of consumers needs	Titleist golf clubs, golf balls, tees, caddies
Selective specialisation	Firm enters selective niches that do not relate closely to each other, but are profitable	British Telecom sells telephone services to consumers and industry, but also owns satellite time, which it sells to TV broadcasters and others
Full coverage	Firm enters every possible segment of its potential market	Mitsubishi Industries, which produces everything from musical instruments to supertankers

consumers in the target segment need? Second, what is already available to them? Third, what can the firm offer that would be better than what is currently available? There is a danger in that companies can sometimes hinder their future targeting by placing too much emphasis on currently successful target market responses. This is especially prevalent in online and database marketing, where managers can end up focusing only on those people who were contacted in the first place; sometimes there are people in the target market who, for one reason or another, were not targeted in the particular mailing (Rhee and McIntyre 2009). This results in what is known as selection bias.

The five basic strategies of market coverage were outlined by Derek F. Abell in 1980. They are shown in Table 4.4.

Choosing the right market and then targeting it accurately are possibly the most important activities a marketer carries out. Choosing the wrong segment to target or, worse, not attempting to segment the market at all, leads to lost opportunities and wasted effort. Most firms find that Pareto's Law applies, and the firm obtains 80% of its profits from 20% of its customers – choosing the right group therefore becomes absolutely crucial to success.

Accessing the target market is another issue that deserves attention. For a segment to be viable, it needs to be accessible via some communications medium or another; the segment may comprise people who read a particular magazine or watch a particular TV station. If there is no way to reach the segment, it cannot become a target market. In some cases the segment is defined by the medium; for example, *Cosmopolitan* readers represent a group of independently minded women with career aspirations, usually with high disposable incomes or aspirations in that direction, and interests that are more likely to run to business issues than to knitting patterns. These women represent a valuable market segment in their own right, but can probably only be easily identified as a group because they read *Cosmopolitan*.

POSITIONING

Positioning has been defined as: 'The place a product occupies in a given market, as perceived by the relevant group of customers; that group of customers is known as the target segment of the market' (Wind 1984). Usually positioning refers to the place the product occupies in the consumer's **perceptual map** of the market: for instance, as a high-quality item or as a reliable one or perhaps as a cheap version. The product is positioned in the perceptual map alongside similar offerings; this is a result of the categorisation and chunking processes (see Chapter 3).

Consumers build up a position for a product based on what they expect and believe to be the most pertinent features of the product class. Marketers therefore need to find out first what the pertinent features of the products are in the target consumers' **perceptions**. The marketer can then adjust the mix of features and benefits, and the communications mix, to give the product its most effective position relative to the other brands in the market. Sometimes the positioning process is led by consumers, sometimes by marketers.

Research shows that consumers use a relatively short list of factors in determining the position of a product (Blankson and Kalafatis 2004). These are as follows.

- *Top-of-the-range.* This refers to the product which consumers believe to be the most expensive or 'the best'. In the UK, this is often called 'the Rolls-Royce of...' whichever product type is under discussion.
- *Service.* The service levels which surround the product can be an important factor.
- *Value for money.* This is the degree to which the product's benefits represent a fair exchange for the price being asked.
- *Reliability.* Products are often positioned as being more (or less) reliable than their competitors.
- *Attractiveness.* This can refer to factors other than appearance, but implies factors other than the purely practical, performance-related factors.
- *Country of origin.* Some countries have a reputation for producing the best examples of some categories of product. For example, German engineering is highly regarded whereas the French are known for their food and wine. Some countries have a correspondingly poor reputation, of course, and this can be difficult to overcome (Martin *et al.* 2011). Firms can use self-focused mental imagery to develop a better image for these countries' products.
- *Brand name.* Branding is a key issue in positioning, as it identifies the product and conveys an impression of its quality (see Chapter 6).

- *Selectivity.* The degree to which the consumer can distinguish between brands and select from the range is a factor in positioning.

Ultimately, product positioning depends on the attitudes of the particular target market, so the marketer must either take these attitudes as they are and tailor the product to fit those attitudes or they must seek to change the attitudes of the market. Usually it is easier and cheaper to change the product than it is to change the consumers, but sometimes the market's attitudes to the product are so negative that the manufacturer feels constrained to reposition the product. For example, Skoda cars had to fight hard to throw off the negative connotations of the vehicle's Eastern European origins. Not wishing to be classed with Ladas, Yugos and Polski Fiats and thus share the perception of poor workmanship and unreliability, Skoda made great efforts to emphasise Volkswagen's takeover of the company and to position the car next to VW in the consumer's mind.

Skoda has pointed out that, under the auspices of VW ownership, the company's quality control and engineering procedures have been greatly improved. Skoda was, in any case, the jewel in the crown of Eastern European car manufacture, so the firm has been able to demonstrate that the cars are made to a high standard.

To determine the product's position, research is carried out with the target group of consumers, and a perceptual map such as the one in Figure 4.2 will be produced.

From Figure 4.2 it can be seen that Brand B has the image of being both high price and high quality: this is probably the Rolls-Royce of the products (top-of-the-range factor). Brand D is perceived as being low price but low quality: this would be a cheap, everyday brand. Brand A has a problem: although tending towards a high

Figure 4.2 Perceptual mapping

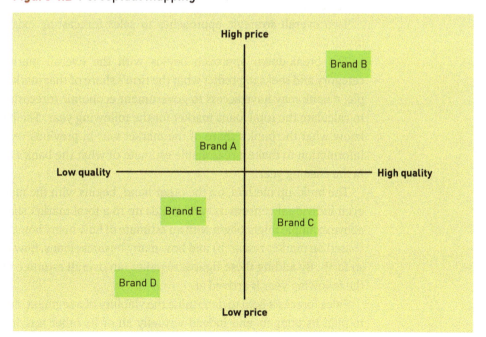

price, this product is perceived as being below-average quality. Sales are likely to be low, or will take place only when the consumer has no other choice available. Brand C, on the other hand, enjoys a low price and good quality, so is probably the top-selling brand (value-for-money factor).

It should be noted that these positions are based on average responses from consumers in the target groups. They are not objective, nor are they based on the firm's view of the quality of its products. For this reason, they can sometimes be changed by promotional efforts. Far more commonly, though, the firm will need to do something more practical about changing the product or changing its price to make the necessary changes.

In Figure 4.2, the products have been mapped against only two dimensions, but it is perfectly possible (perhaps even advisable) to map the product against more dimensions. This can be done on a computer using multidimensional mapping software.

One of the most useful tactical aspects of positioning maps is that they can be used to identify gaps in the market. Using Figure 4.2 as an example, there is clearly a gap next to Brand A and below Brand B for a medium-to-high quality product at a medium-to-high price. Currently this market seems to be dominated by lower-priced brands; a brand entering this market would need to be perceived as higher quality than Brand C, but at a lower price than Brand B.

SALES FORECASTING

Having segmented the market, targeted the appropriate segments and decided on a positioning strategy, the firm is in a better position to forecast the expected sales of the product.

Two overall strategic approaches to sales forecasting exist: **break-down** and **build-up**.

The break-down approach begins with the overall market for the product category and seeks to predict what the firm's share of that market will be. For example, a bank may have access to government economic forecasts which can be used to calculate the total loans market for the following year. The bank forecasters will know what the bank's share of the market was in previous years and can use this information to make a reasonable estimate of what the bank's total lending will be in the ensuing year.

The build-up method, on the other hand, begins with the market segments (and even individual consumers) and builds up to a total market share. The bank in the above example might begin with an estimate of how many home loans it might make (based on market research) and how many business loans, how many car loans, and so forth. By adding these figures together, an overall estimate of the total sales for the following year is arrived at.

Sales forecasts help to determine the viability of a segment, and also help the firm to plan its budgets and indeed virtually all of its other activities. Forecasting the future is always difficult; many firms rely on **executive judgement**, using the skill and experience of its senior people in deciding whether a product is a winner or not. Unfortunately, this approach can fail because the executives will favour a product that they would buy as private consumers, rather than a product that the target market segment would buy.

Through a **customer survey** firms are able to ask potential customers how much of a given product they are likely to buy within the next 12 months or so. These intent-to-buy studies work best for existing product categories; for a radically new product it is much more difficult, since only the most innovative of consumers will be able to say with any certainty that they would be prepared to buy the product early in its launch. The main drawback with this method is that customers may intend to purchase, but change their minds during the course of the year, perhaps owing to a competitor's actions. On the other hand, some customers who say in the survey that they will not buy may well do so if their circumstances change.

Other firms may use a **salesforce survey**, asking the salesforce how much of a given product they might expect to sell over the next 12 months. This has the advantage that the salespeople, unlike senior management, are usually close to the customer and are able to make judgements based on this. Also, salespeople will be wary about making rash forecasts that they might later be held to. On the other hand, salespeople generally like to be consulted about their own targets and quotas. A variation on the salesforce survey is the **distributor survey**, where the company's distributors are asked how much they expect to sell over a specific period. Since the distributors will be giving the total sales in the product category (e.g. supermarkets might be asked how much mineral water they expect to sell in the next 12 months), the company will then have to make a judgement regarding the amount of market share they might reasonably expect to capture.

The **Delphi technique** involves taking in the managers' and salespeople's forecasts, combining them centrally, then sending the aggregate forecast back to the individuals concerned for revision. This approach has proved popular with firms because it tends to produce a consensus of opinion to which all those concerned can adhere. A problem with using Delphi might be that individuals will only make forecasts that they are quite sure are achievable: in other words, they might underestimate the possible sales rather than risk being unable to hit targets.

Time-series analysis uses the company's past sales records to predict what will happen in the future. Although this can be quite accurate, it does not take account of the unexpected – a sudden entry by a competitor, a change in legislation or a change in the company's fortunes through takeover or merger. Few forecasting methods can take account of these factors, of course, and ultimately the company has to plan in some way. Time-series forecasters usually perform four types of analysis, as shown in Table 4.5 (Marino 1986). Having carried out each of these analyses, the forecaster is able to combine the results to develop the sales forecast.

Time-series analysis works best for well established products with fairly stable purchasing patterns. It is not suitable for new products or for products with erratic demand cycles.

Table 4.5 Time-series analysis

Type of analysis	Description
Trend analysis	Focuses on aggregate sales data collected over a long period to determine whether sales are rising, falling or staying level
Cycle analysis	Here the forecaster examines the sales figures from a number of years to see whether there is a cyclical pattern; perhaps a response to the economic boom-and-bust cycle. This method has been largely discredited for most markets, since the cycles do not follow a regular pattern
Seasonal analysis	Sales figures are analysed on a monthly or even weekly basis to see whether there is a seasonal cycle operating
Random factor analysis	In any analysis there will be figures that do not fit the pattern; random factor analysis seeks to attribute explanations for these abnormal findings. For example, a spell of unseasonal weather might have affected one month's figures

For new products, a **test marketing** exercise might be carried out. This involves making the product available in one geographical area for a period of time, and monitoring the actual sales of the product in the area. The key to success with test marketing lies in ensuring that the area chosen is an accurate representation of the country as a whole; if not, the predicted sales on national roll-out will not be as expected. The major drawback of test marketing is that it allows the firm's competitors to see the product and possibly develop their own version before the product goes national. For this reason, test marketing exercises are usually short.

CASE STUDY 4 Selling Ford

Ford Motor Company is probably one of the best known vehicle manufacturers in the world. The company is the fifth largest car manufacturer in the world and is the company that originally invented mass production in 1903. At first, all the cars were identical: Henry Ford, the company's founder, famously said that 'Any customer can have a car painted any colour that he wants so long as it is black'. However, it quickly became apparent that people were making changes to the cars – altering the engines to gain more power, cutting off the bodywork to make truck versions, altering the seating to gain more space, and so forth. This represented a possible loss of revenue to the company, so Ford decided to produce different models for different markets.

Today, that approach has become standard. Originally, Ford built different models in each national market (e.g. the Taunus in Germany, the Anglia and Cortina in Britain and, of course, entirely separate (and larger) cars for the US market). Eventually, Ford tried to create 'world' models but, with the exception of the Focus, these did not always do well – the Mondeo, which sold extremely well in Europe, did not do well in the US (marketed as the Contour) or in Australia, where it met with strong competition from the Falcon. Most of the 'world cars' have been developed in Europe, and therefore tend to suit European conditions.

Ford produce a full range of vehicles for each global market, however. Some are large family models (such as the Mondeo and the Galaxy), some are small economical cars (such as the Fiesta and the Ka) and some are luxury models (Ford owns Lincoln and has owned Volvo, Jaguar and Land Rover). Furthermore, the company produces light vans such as the Transit, sometimes called 'the people's van' because it is used by so many small enterprises and is hired by so many people for the purpose of moving furniture, collecting large items or going on camping trips.

Ford keeps a very careful eye on how the market is developing. With this in mind, the company has developed a number of vehicles designed to run on alternative fuels. In Brazil, the company has for many years offered cars which run on pure alcohol or on an alcohol petrol mix, since these fuels have been available there for many years. However, the company has added hybrid vehicles to the range and expects to be producing fully electrically powered vehicles during the next decade or so. The problem is the availability of charging stations for such vehicles; currently, they are too few and far between for the project to be viable.

In all, Ford offers an extremely wide range, aiming to fill every segment of its market. In this, they do moderately well; the problem lies in identifying the right segments.

Questions

1 How might Ford segment the market behaviourally?
2 What have been the problems with geographical segmentation?
3 How might Ford segment demographically?
4 How can global markets be targeted?
5 How is Ford positioning its brands?

SUMMARY

This chapter has been about ways of dividing markets up into manageable portions. Here are the key points from this chapter:

- There are few, if any, mass markets left untouched
- If most consumers already own the core benefits of a product, the market must be segmented if success is to follow, since there is otherwise no reason for consumers to switch brands
- Segments must be measurable, accessible, substantial and congruent
- The profitability of a segment is calculated as the number of people in the segment multiplied by the premium they are willing to pay

- The narrower the segment the fewer the customers, but the greater the satisfaction and the greater the premium they are willing to pay (provided the segment has been correctly identified)
- There are many ways to segment a market – in fact, as many ways as there are groups with congruent needs
- Targeting is concerned with selecting an appropriate segment or segments, and approaching it in a consistent and effective way
- Some segments are defined by the media used to target them
- Sales forecasting is difficult, but can most easily be accomplished where the product is a fairly standard item
- Forecasting is likely to be self-fulfilling if all the interested parties are involved in the process.

CHAPTER QUESTIONS

1 What might be the segmentation bases for the home computer market?
2 What sales forecasting approaches would be most suitable for the launch of a new family car?
3 When should an industrial market be segmented geographically?
4 When should a consumer market be segmented geographically?
5 How might a TV company assess the viability of a new drama series?

Further reading

Unlike consumer behaviour or marketing communications, there are relatively few texts that cover segmentation in any great detail.

Consumer Behaviour and Marketing Strategy, 8th edn, by J. Paul Peter and Jerry C. Olson (Chicago, IL, Irwin, 2007) has a good section on segmenting consumer markets in Chapter 16.

References

Abell, Derek F.: *Defining the Business: The Starting Point of Strategic Planning* (Englewood Cliffs, NJ, Prentice Hall, 1980).

Bailey, Christine, Baines, Paul, R., Wilson, Hugh and Clark, Moira: 'Segmentation and customer insight in contemporary services marketing practice: why grouping customers is no longer enough', *Journal of Marketing Management*, **25** (3 and 4) (2009), pp. 227–52.

Beatty, S.E., Kahle, L. and Homer, P.: 'Personal values and gift-giving behaviours: a study across cultures', *Journal of Business Research*, **22** (1991), pp. 149–57.

Blankson, Charles and Kalafatis, Stavros P.: 'The development and validation of a scale measuring consumer/customer derived generic typology of positioning strategies', *Journal of Marketing Management*, (1) **20** (February 2004), pp. 5–43.

Bonoma, T.V. and Shapiro, B.P.: 'How to segment industrial markets', *Harvard Business Review* (May/June 1984), pp. 104–10.

Dolnicar, Sara and Lazarevski, Katie: 'Methodological reasons for the theory/practice divide in market segmentation', *Journal of Marketing Management*, **25** (3 and 4) (2009), pp. 357–73.

Engel, J.F., Blackwell, R.D. and Miniard, P.W.: *Consumer Behaviour*, 8th edn (Fort Worth, TX, Dryden Press, 1995).

Hassan, S.S. and Katsanis, L.P.: 'Identification of global consumer segments: a behavioural framework', *Journal of International Consumer Marketing*, **3** (2) (1991), pp. 11–28.

Hofstede, G.: 'Management scientists are human', *Management Science*, **40** (1) (1994), pp. 4–13.

Hofstede, G.: *Culture's Consequences: International Differences in Work-Related Values* (Beverly Hills, Sage, 1980).

Jamal, Ahmed: 'Marketing in a multicultural world: the interplay of marketing, ethnicity and consumption', *European Journal of Marketing*, **37** (1) (2003), pp. 1599–620.

Kotler, P.: *Marketing Management*, 7th edn (Englewood Cliffs, NJ, Prentice Hall, 1991).

Kotler, Philip and Levy, Sidney: 'Demarketing, Yes, Demarketing', *Harvard Business Review*, (Nov–Dec 1971), pp. 71–80.

Lee, C.: 'Determinants of national innovativeness and international market segmentation', *International Marketing Review*, **7** (5) (1990), pp. 39–49.

Lindridge, Andrew: 'Are we fooling ourselves when we talk about ethnic homogeneity? The case of religion and ethnic subdividions among Indians living in Britain', *Journal of Marketing Management*, **26** (5 and 6) (2010), pp. 441–72.

Marino, Kenneth E.: *Forecasting Sales and Planning Profits* (Chicago, IL, Probus Publishing, 1986), p. 155.

Martin, Brett A.S., Lee, Michael, Shyue, Wai and Lacey, Charlotte: 'Countering negative country of origin effects using imagery processing', *Journal of Consumer Behaviour*, Mar/Apr, **10** (2) (2011), pp. 80–92.

Medway, Dominic, Warnaby, Gary and Dhami, Sheetal: 'Demarketing places: rationales and strategies', *Journal of Marketing Management*, **27** (1 and 2) (2011), pp. 124–42.

Moskowitz, Howard R., Beckley, Jacqueline H., Luckow, Tracy and Paulus, Klaus: 'Cross-national segmentation for a food product: defining them and a strategy for finding them in the absence of "mineable" databases', *Journal of Database Marketing & Customer Strategy Management*, June, **15** (3) (2008), pp. 191–206.

Office for National Statistics: Census 2001, www.statistics.gov.uk/cci/nugget.cisp?id=350, 2003.

Plummer, Joseph T.: 'The concept and application of life style segmentation', *Journal of Marketing* (January 1974), pp. 33–7.

Rhee, Eddie and McIntyre, Shelby: 'How current targeting can hinder targeting in the future and what to do about it', *Journal of Database Marketing and Customer Strategy Management*, Mar, **16** (1) (2009), pp. 15–28.

Smith, W.R.: 'Product differentiation and market segmentation as alternative marketing strategies', *Journal of Marketing* (21 July 1957).

Wind, Yoram: 'Going to market: new twists for some old tricks', *Wharton Magazine*, **4** (1984).

Zikmund, William G. and D'Amico, Michael: *Effective Marketing: Creating and Keeping Customers* (St Paul, MN, West, 1995), p. 232.

6

PRODUCTS, BRANDING AND PACKAGING

Objectives

After reading this chapter you should be able to:

- Describe the stages that a product goes through from introduction to obsolescence
- Assess products in a given range and decide which ones are worth keeping and which should be dropped from the range
- Decide on an appropriate policy for developing and introducing new products to the market
- Identify some of the risks inherent in new product development
- Understand what a marketer means by 'product'.

INTRODUCTION

This chapter is about developing new products and about product policy. The success of an organisation will depend, ultimately, on what bundles of benefits it offers to consumers; the decisions about what the firm should be offering need to be made in the light of the consumer's needs and wants.

There is a strong positive relationship between a firm's innovative activities and its ability to survive and prosper (Hart 1993), so many companies place a strong emphasis on developing new products to replace those which become obsolete or which are superseded by competitors' offerings.

Products, Branding and Packaging 153

Acme Whistles

Normally, whistles are not things that we think about a great deal. Yet a great many whistles are sold each day – some for sporting events, some for emergency purposes (whistles on lifejackets, for example) and some just for fun – no carnival would be complete without dancers blowing whistles!

Acme Whistles are the world leaders in making whistles. The company prides itself on the reliability of its products – each whistle is individually tested before it leaves the factory (by using an air line – the days of the company's founder blowing every whistle before it left are long gone). New products are developed at the rate of two a year – even whistles eventually date, since every product has its life cycle. New product development (NPD) also keeps the company ahead of its competitors. The company aims to develop patentable whistles as a way of protecting its intellectual property from competitors.

The company is well aware of the needs of its customers. For business-to-business customers, who may be adding the whistles to an existing product such as a fire safety kit, the company emphasises the reliability of the whistle, since this will reduce returns of faulty products. For consumer markets, the company produces a range of specialist whistles, such as the *Titanic* Mate's Whistle, a replica of the whistles the company made for the crew of the *Titanic*. Overall, the company has a surprisingly wide range of whistles!

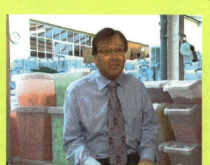

Simon Topman, Managing Director

Watch the video clip, then try to answer the following questions. The answers are on the companion website.

Questions

1 What is the significance of the company's brand?
2 What type of NPD strategy does Acme have?
3 Why does the company aim to produce two patentable new products a year?

DEFINING PRODUCTS

Marketers define a *product* as being a *bundle of benefits*. This means that the product is more than just the sum of its physical characteristics; it includes fringe elements such as the brand image, the way the product is packed and delivered, even the colour of the box it comes in. **Primary characteristics** are those core benefits of the product that it has in common with its competitors; **auxiliary characteristics** are the features and benefits that are unique to the product. For instance, consider the contrast between a pizza from a delivery service and a pizza from the supermarket freezer. The primary characteristics of each are the same: a dough base with tomato sauce and cheese on top, with other ingredients included. The primary benefit is that each provides a tasty and filling meal; it is the auxiliary characteristics that make the difference.

Apart from the differences in flavour, ingredients and so forth, the delivery service is more expensive (perhaps double the price of the supermarket version). The supermarket pizza can be kept in the freezer and heated when needed, and can even be 'customised' by adding extra cheese or other ingredients. On the other hand, the delivery service pizza includes the service element of delivery, and is already heated and ready to eat. Clearly the benefits are different and therefore a marketer would say that the products are different.

Marketers need to be aware of the ways in which the needs and wants of consumers are changing so that the benefits offered by the product range can be tailored to fit those needs and wants. This is the function of market research (see Chapter 5), but it is important to make good use of the information gathered to see which new products might be developed or which old products might be adapted, and also to see which products are nearing the end of their useful lives.

CLASSIFYING PRODUCTS

Products bought to satisfy personal and family needs are **consumer products**; products bought for the purposes of resale or to be used to make other products are **industrial products**. As in any other question of marketing, the subdivision of these broad categories into smaller, more convenient, categories is carried out by reference to the consumer or the customer. In the case of consumer goods, the classification will be as shown in Table 6.1.

Likewise, industrial products can be categorised according to the use the purchasers intend to make of them. Table 6.2 illustrates this. In some ways, industrial buying has parallels with consumer buying behaviour (see Chapter 3), so parallels can also be drawn with the types of product purchased. First, the company must

Table 6.1 Classification of consumer products

Classification	Explanation
Convenience products	*Cheap, frequently purchased items that do not require much thought or planning.* The consumer typically buys the same brand or goes to the same shop. Examples are newspapers, basic groceries and soft drinks. Normally, convenience products would be distributed through many retail outlets and the onus is on the producer to promote the products because the retailer will not expend much effort on such low-priced items.
Shopping products	*Products people shop around for.* Usually infrequently purchased items such as computers, cars, hi-fi systems or household appliances. From the manufacturer's viewpoint, such products require few retail outlets, but will require much more personal selling on the part of the retailer. Hence there is usually a high degree of cooperation between manufacturer and retailer in marketing the products.
Speciality products	*People plan the purchase of these products with great care, know exactly what they want and will accept no substitutes.* Here the consumer's efforts bend towards finding an outlet that can supply exactly the item needed: this accentuates the exclusivity of the product, so some marketers deliberately limit the number of outlets that are franchised to sell the products. An example of this is the American hair-product manufacturer Redken, which appoints a limited number of hair salons to carry its products.
Unsought products	*These products are not bought; they are sold.* Examples are life insurance, fitted kitchens and encyclopaedias. While most people would recognise the need for these items, it is rare for consumers to go out looking for them; far more commonly the products are sold either by salespeople or are bought as the result of a sudden change of circumstances (for example, most mortgage lenders require house buyers to take out life insurance).

develop a clear view of what the customer is buying. Levitt (1986) has suggested the following hierarchy of levels:

1 *Core or generic.* This is the basic physical product, or the minimum features that the customer would expect it to have. For example, a microwave oven would be expected to have a timer and a space inside to put the food, and would be expected to heat things up effectively.

2 *Expected.* This is the generic product plus some extra features that the customer would reasonably expect to see. In the microwave example, the customer would expect there to be an instruction book, a guarantee and some kind of servicing network in case of breakdowns.

3 *Augmented.* These are the factors that differentiate the product. For the microwave, this could be a sensor to say when the food is cooked, a defrost facility, free delivery or an after-sales call to check the product is functioning well. These are the features that make the customer buy one brand rather than another.

Table 6.2 Categorisation of industrial products

Categorisation	Explanation
Raw materials	*Basic products that will be transformed entirely into something else.* These are usually bought in large quantities and usually have a standardised quality range and prices; this makes it hard for the producer to differentiate the product from those of the competitors.
Major equipment	*The capital machinery and tools used for running the buyer's business.* These are equivalent to shopping goods; the purchasers spend considerable time and effort in choosing which to buy, and therefore there is considerable emphasis on personal selling and on product differentiation. After-sales service is also crucial to success in this market.
Accessory equipment	*Equipment used for the peripheral needs of the firm.* Examples are office equipment and health and safety equipment. Often these are distributed through many outlets and are more standardised than the major equipment items. This means there is more competition, but also a bigger market for such items as fire extinguishers or PCs.
Component parts	*Manufactured items which will be assembled into the finished product.* These are usually bought by negotiation or tender; often the purchaser has the most power in the relationship, as with car manufacturers.
Process materials	Rather more advanced than raw materials, process materials might be the special alloys used in aircraft construction, or specially tailored plastics. From a marketing viewpoint, process materials are similar to component parts, but with more opportunity for differentiation.
Consumable supplies	*Materials that are used by the purchasers but that do not become part of the finished product:* for example, industrial cleansing products. Consumable supplies are used for maintenance, repair and operation, so they are sometimes called MRO items.
Industrial services	*The intangible products used by firms:* for example, industrial cleaning services, accountancy and legal services, and some maintenance services. Some firms provide these for themselves; for others it is cheaper to buy in the services as needed (for instance, a ten-person light engineering firm would not need a full-time lawyer on the staff).

4 *Potential.* This is all the possible features and benefits that could be wanted by customers. It is unlikely that any product could have all the necessary features (and it would be too expensive to buy anyway), but this list still needs to be developed so that the company can produce different models of the product for different customer needs. If a microwave oven manufacturer knows who the end buyer of the microwave is, it would be possible to keep the customer informed of new models coming onto the market in, say, three years' time when the old microwave is beginning to show signs of wear. The idea behind this is to encourage the customer to remain loyal to the original manufacturer.

From the consumer's viewpoint, some of those benefits are essential requirements, others are less important but still good to have, while others are not really relevant. Each consumer will have a different view as to which benefit belongs to which category.

MANAGING THE PRODUCT RANGE

The **product life cycle (PLC)** is a useful concept to describe how products progress from introduction through to obsolescence. The theory is that products, like living things, have a natural life cycle beginning with introduction, going through a growth phase, reaching maturity, then going into decline and finally becoming obsolete. Figure 6.1 illustrates this in graphical form.

In the introduction phase, the product's sales grow slowly and the profit will be small or negative because of heavy promotion costs and production inefficiencies. If the product is very new, there will also be the need to persuade retailers and others to stock it.

In the growth stage, there will be a rapid increase in sales as the product becomes better known. At this stage profits begin to grow, but competition will also be entering the market so the producer may now need to think about adapting the product to meet the competitive threat.

In the maturity phase the product is well known and well established; at this point the promotional spend eases off and production economies of scale become established. By this time competitors will almost certainly have entered the market, so the firm will need to develop a new version of the product.

In the decline phase, the product is losing market share and profitability rapidly. At this stage the marketer must decide whether it is worthwhile supporting the product for a little longer or whether it should be allowed to disappear; supporting a product for which there is little natural demand is very unprofitable, but sometimes products can be revived and relaunched, perhaps in a different market.

The assumption is that all products exhibit this life cycle, but the timescale will vary from one product to the next. Some products, for example computer games,

Figure 6.1 Product life cycle

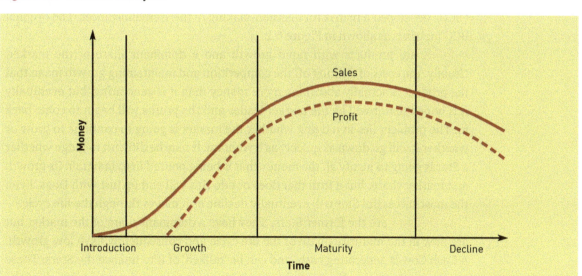

may go through the entire life cycle in a matter of months. Others, like pitta bread, have a life cycle measured in thousands of years, and may never become obsolete.

The PLC concept is a useful way of looking at product development but, like many simple theories, it has a number of flaws:

- The theory assumes that changes in consumer preference go only one way, and that there is no swing back to an earlier preference. Some clothing fashions return after a few years and some styles of music enjoy periodic revivals; also, some traditional products can suddenly become popular again, often following advertising campaigns based on nostalgia.
- The model assumes that nobody does anything to revive the product when it begins to decline or be superseded by other products. Most marketers would look at their declining products and decide whether a revival is possible, or worthwhile.
- The model looks at only one product, whereas most marketing managers have to balance the demands of many differing products and decide which ones are most likely to yield the best return on investment.

Note here that the PLC concept is useful to describe what is happening, but is not much use for predicting what is going to happen, since it is virtually impossible to tell how long the maturity phase will continue. This makes it difficult to use as a decision-making device; marketers are not easily able to tell which part of the PLC the product currently occupies. A temporary fall-off in sales might be caused by extraneous factors such as a recession or new competitive activity, without actually heralding the beginning of the decline phase.

Most firms produce several different products at the same time, and it is possible to superimpose the PLC diagrams for each product onto the graph to give a composite view of what is happening to the firm's product portfolio. This will give a long-term overview, but the problems of prediction still remain; for many managers, a 'snapshot' of what is happening now is more useful. The Boston Consulting Group (BCG) developed a matrix for decision-making in these circumstances. The original BCG matrix is as shown in Figure 6.2.

Stars are products with rapid growth and a dominant share of the market. Usually, the costs of fighting off the competition and maintaining growth mean that the product is actually absorbing more money than it is generating, but eventually it is hoped that it will be the market leader and the profits will begin to come back in. The problem lies in judging whether the market is going to continue to grow or whether it will go down as quickly as it went up. It may be difficult to judge whether a Star is going to justify all the money that is being poured in to maintain its growth and market share, but a firm that does not do this will end up just with Dogs. Even the most successful Star will eventually decline as it moves through the life cycle.

Cash Cows are the former Stars. They have a dominant share of the market but are now in the maturity phase of the life cycle and consequently have low growth. A Cash Cow is generating cash, and can be 'milked' of it to finance the Stars. These are the products that have steady year-in year-out sales and generate much of the

Figure 6.2 Boston Consulting Group matrix

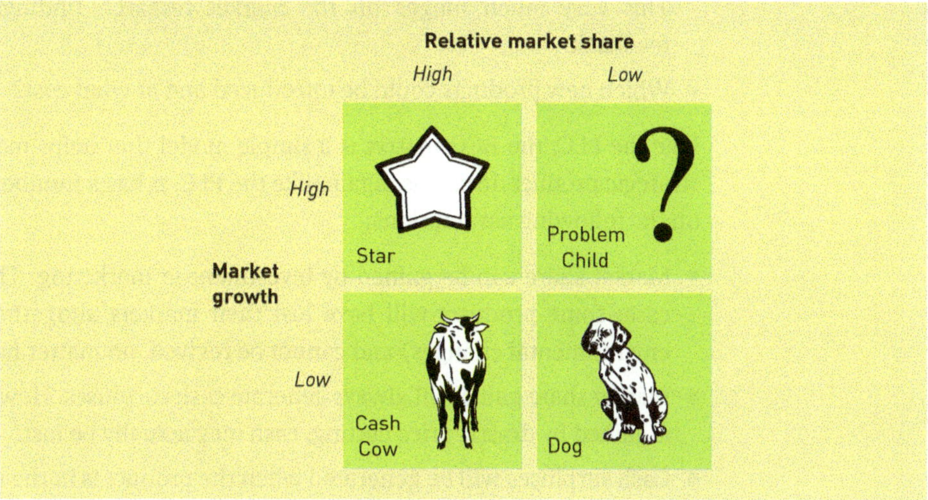

Source: Reprinted by permission of the Boston Consulting Group

firm's profits: examples might be the Big Mac hamburger, Coca-Cola and the Ford Mondeo.

Dogs have a low market share and low growth prospects. The argument here is not whether the product is profitable; it almost always is. The argument is about whether the firm could use its resources to make something that would be more profitable, and this is also almost always the case.

The **Problem Child** (also sometimes shown as a question mark) has a small share of a growth market and causes the marketer the most headaches since it is necessary to work out a way of building market share to turn the product into a Star. This means finding out why the share is so low and developing strategies to increase market share rapidly. The Problem Child could be backed with an even bigger promotion campaign or it could possibly be adapted in some way to fit the market better. Market research plays a crucial role in making these decisions; finding out how to adapt a product is a difficult area of research, but the potential rewards are huge, and adapting the product to meet people's needs better is almost always cheaper than increasing the advertising spend.

The policy decisions that arise from this view of the firm's product portfolio lie in the following areas:

- Which products should be dropped from the range entirely? This question not only hinges on how profitable the product itself is; sales of one product often indirectly generate sales of another, more profitable, product. For example, Black and Decker sell electric saws cheaply, but make their profit on sales of replacement saw blades.

- Which products should be backed with promotion campaigns? Backing the wrong product can be extremely expensive; advertising campaigns have no second-hand value, so if it does not work the money is lost forever.

- Which products could be adapted to fit the market better, and in what ways? This very much hinges on the market research findings and on customer feedback.
- Which new products could be introduced and at what cost?

Like the PLC, the BCG matrix is a simple model that helps marketers to approach strategic product decisions; again, like the PLC, it has a number of flaws. It is based on the following assumptions:

- Market share can be gained by investment in marketing. This is not always the case; some products will have lost their markets altogether (perhaps through environmental changes) and cannot be revived, no matter how much is invested.
- Market share gains will always generate cash surpluses. However, if market share is gained by drastic price cutting, cash may actually be lost.
- Cash surpluses will be generated when the product is in the maturity stage of the life cycle. This is not necessarily so; mature products may well be operating on such small margins because of competitive pressure that the profit generated is low.
- The best opportunity to build a dominant market position is during the growth phase. In most cases this would be true, but this does not take account of competition. A competitor's product might be growing even faster.

Barksdale and Harris (1982) proposed two additions to the BCG matrix. **War Horses** have high market share but the market has negative growth; the problem for management is to decide whether the product is in an irreversible decline or whether it can be revived, perhaps by repositioning into another market. **Dodos** have a low share of a negative growth market and are probably best discontinued (Figure 6.3).

The BCG matrix has proved a useful tool for analysing product portfolio decisions, but it is really only a snapshot of the current position with the products it describes. Since most markets are to a greater or lesser extent dynamic, the matrix should be used with a certain degree of caution.

Critical thinking

The BCG matrix is all very well, but how do we decide whether a market is 'high growth' or 'low growth?' Is 5% per annum high growth? It would be in the car industry – but not in mobile telephones. Likewise, what is a high market share? 5%? 50%? 2%? Any of these might be regarded as a respectable share in some markets.

Maybe we are back to executive judgement as the key factor in decisions – or maybe the BCG matrix just helps to focus our thinking!

The size of the product portfolio and the complexity of the products within it can have further effects on the firm's management. For example, it has been shown that manufacturing a wide range of products with many options makes it difficult for

Figure 6.3 Expanded Boston Consulting Group matrix

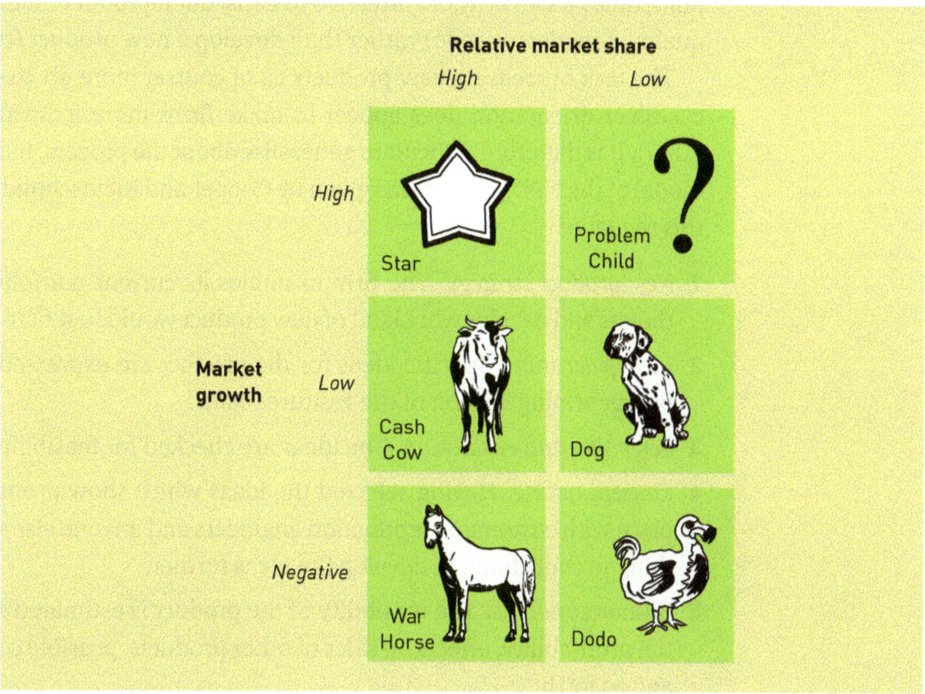

Source: Barksdale and Harris, 1982

the firm to use just-in-time purchasing techniques and complicates the firm's supply activities (Benwell 1996).

DEVELOPING BETTER PRODUCTS

There is often debate within firms as to what constitutes a 'better' product. For marketers, the definition must be 'a product that more closely meets our customers' needs than does the product it supersedes'. Engineers, accountants and managers may have differing definitions; there is, however, general agreement that firms must introduce new products if they are not to be left with a range of obsolete, dying products. **New product development (NPD)** is therefore a crucial area of marketing activity and a great deal has been published on the subject.

New product development

Venture teams or *project teams* develop new products or projects. Typically a venture team will be an interdisciplinary group, perhaps comprising engineers, research scientists, finance experts and marketers. Among other considerations, marketers need to take an overview of the product range to see how the proposed new products match up with existing products. Sometimes a new product can lead to cannibalism of old product lines (in other words, the company ends up competing with itself). Sometimes it can be more effective to carry out a product modification (in terms of quality, function or style) rather than develop a new product from scratch.

The task of creating new products is, of course, more art than science; however, customer orientation does appear to make firms more innovative (Tajeddini *et al.* 2006). It is therefore difficult to generalise about the process, but a frequently quoted model of the NPD process was given by Cooper and Kleinschmidt (1988) and follows this sequence:

1 *New product strategy.* The firm examines its current portfolio, opportunities and threats and decides what kind of new product would best fit in with future strategy.
2 *Idea generation.* Specific ideas for the product are expressed, perhaps through a brainstorming session of the venture team.
3 *Screening and evaluation.* The ideas are checked for feasibility and marketability.
4 *Concept testing.* Having selected the ideas which show promise, discussions take place with customers, production engineers and anyone else who may have something to contribute, to develop the ideas further.
5 *Business analysis.* The feasibility of the product is estimated in terms of its potential profitability, effects on sales of other products, possible competitive responses and so forth.
6 *Technical development.* The engineering aspects of the product are investigated and a prototype is developed. The final design of the product needs to reflect the results of the concept testing stage.
7 *Market testing.* Formal market research is carried out to assess the product's viability in the market.
8 *Commercialisation.* Assuming the market research is positive about the product, the firm puts it into production.

All of these stages are likely to be covered in one form or other, but in many cases the methods used are likely to be subjective or carried out ineffectively. This can often be a source of problems following the launch; for example, a proper market appraisal may not be carried out because the venture team fall in love with the project and champion it through the process. *Product champions* within firms often perform a valuable function in ensuring that the new product actually comes into existence rather than being sidelined by the routine tasks of making existing products; this is sometimes encouraged by firms, but is believed by some researchers to be a sign of a failed management who have abdicated their responsibility for keeping the firm up to date (Johne and Snelson 1990).

There are six broad types of innovation strategy:

1 *Offensive.* Pride in being the first. This is very much the strategy of firms such as Sony and 3M.
2 *Defensive.* 'Me-toos', copies of other companies' products, but slightly better.
3 *Imitative.* Straight copies of other companies' products.

4 *Dependent*. Led by bigger companies, perhaps customers or suppliers. For example, Microsoft produces new computer software, so it is dependent on new technology developed by computer chip manufacturers.

5 *Traditional*. Not really innovative at all; the firm is merely resurrecting old-fashioned designs.

6 *Opportunist*. Selling and marketing of inventions.

Launch decisions might revolve around areas such as test marketing (see Chapter 5); if the firm *test markets* the product (i.e. launches the product in a small geographical area to see whether it will be successful), this may save money on promotion but loses the advantage of surprise. On the other hand, if the firm goes for a national launch, this means committing large amounts of money and mistakes are much harder to correct afterwards. The process of launching in one area at a time is called *roll-out*. The promotion policy will be affected by the customer category the firm is aiming for: innovators, early adopters, early majority, late majority or laggards.

Whether to go ahead or not with a new product is a decision which revolves around five dimensions (Carbonell-Foulquie *et al.* 2004). These are as follows:

1 *Strategic fit*. The degree to which the new product fits in with the company's overall marketing strategy.

2 *Technical feasibility*. Whether an effective product can be made economically.

3 *Customer acceptance*. Whether customers like the product.

4 *Market opportunity*. The level of competition the firm might be expected to face and the current state of the external environment.

5 *Financial performance*. Whether the product will prove sufficiently profitable to be worth launching.

Of these, customer acceptance should be the most important consideration throughout the NPD process.

Success and failure in NPD

NPD is extremely risky; eight out of ten new products eventually fail (i.e. do not recover their development costs) and the remaining two out of ten thus have to fund all the others (Clancy and Shulman 1991). Great effort has been expended on trying to find better ways of forecasting a product's prospects in the market, with only limited results.

First of all, though, it is necessary to define what a new product is, and the researchers Calentone and Cooper (1981) have identified nine categories of new product, as shown in Table 6.3. The clusters were identified according to whether the product was new to the firm or new to the world, and whether there was a production or marketing *synergy* with the firm's existing products.

Success rates for each cluster were as laid out in Table 6.4. Data were obtained on 102 successes and 93 failures. Some 177 firms were surveyed, and there were 103 usable replies.

Table 6.3 New product clusters

Clusters	Description
Cluster 1 **The Better Mousetrap with No Synergy**	This is a product that, while being an improvement over existing offerings, does not fit in with the firm's existing product lines.
Cluster 2 **The Innovative Mousetrap that Really Wasn't Better**	This might be a product that, while being technically excellent, has no real advantage for the consumer over existing products.
Cluster 3 **The Close-to-Home Me-Too Product**	A copy of a competitor's offering. Not likely to be perceived as new by consumers.
Cluster 4 **The Innovative High-Tech Product**	A truly new-to-the-world product.
Cluster 5 **The Me-Too Product with No Technical/Production Synergy**	A copy of a competitor's product, but with no real connection with existing product lines.
Cluster 6 **The Old But Simple Money-Saver**	Not a new product at all, except to the firm producing it.
Cluster 7 **The Synergistic Product that was New to the Firm**	A product that fits the product line, but is new.
Cluster 8 **The Innovative Superior Product with No Synergy**	A product that does not fit the existing product line, but is new.
Cluster 9 **The Synergistic Close-to-Home Product**	A product line extension; perhaps a minor improvement over the firm's existing products.

Clusters 9, 8 and 6 were the most successful by far, perhaps indicating that the safest course is not to be too innovative. In recent years, many new products have been introduced which are reproductions of old designs: the Chrysler PT, Volkswagen Beetle and Mini Cooper are all examples from the motor industry, and there are many household appliances which have been designed with a 'retro' image. These products rely on the following factors for their success (Brown *et al.* 2003):

- *Allegory.* This is the brand 'story', the history of the original product
- *Aura.* This is the 'essence' of the brand, the mystique surrounding it
- *Arcadia.* This is the idealised community in which such products might be used. Based on nostalgia, Arcadia is the place people would like to return to (for example, the 1960s, when they owned their first VW Beetle)

Table 6.4 Success rates of new products

Cluster	Success ratio	% successes	% of cases
9 The Synergistic Close-to-Home Product	1.39	72	12.82
8 The Innovative Superior Product with No Synergy	1.35	70	10.26
6 The Old But Simple Money-Saver	1.35	70	10.26
7 The Synergistic Product that was New to the Firm	1.2	67	10.76
4 The Innovative High-Tech Product	1.23	64	14.35
3 The Close-to-Home Me-Too Product	1.08	56	8.20
1 The Better Mousetrap with No Synergy	0.69	36	7.17
5 The Me-Too Product with No Technical/Production Synergy	0.27	14	10.26
2 The Innovative Mousetrap that Really Wasn't Better	0.00	0	10.26

Source: Calentone and Cooper, 1981

- *Antinomy.* This is brand paradox. New technology is viewed as unstoppable and overpowering, yet at the same time is responsible for people's desire to return to a simpler, less high-tech past.

Although not all products in Cluster 6 are retro, the advent of a significant interest in retro styling has certainly changed the success rate of such products.

Cluster 8 contains the truly innovative, new-to-the-world product, but until it is actually launched it may be difficult to distinguish from Cluster 2, the Innovative Mousetrap that Really Wasn't Better. This category had no successes at all.

What the above research does not show is the degree to which new products are successful. The innovative, new-to-the-world product may carry the highest risks, but potentially it also carries the highest rewards if successful. The evidence is, therefore, that the safest route is to produce 'me-too' products (minor adaptations of existing market leaders), but that the much riskier route of producing real innovations (e.g. the Nintendo Wii) is the only way to become a world-leading company. Producing retro products may well be a useful strategy, combining the success factors of both approaches.

The research also does not consider what a firm might use as a measure of success. Is it profitability? Or is it market share? This will depend on the firm's overall strategy, which may or may not put profitability first. Research shows that the most commonly used measures of success in NPD are customer acceptance, customer satisfaction, product performance and quality (Huang et al. 2004).

Another aspect not addressed by the Calentone and Cooper research is that of the consumer's view of new products. Although a given product may be new to the firm, and may even involve a radical rethink of the company's production and marketing methods, consumers may not see the product as being significantly different from what is already available. If consumers do not see any advantage in using the new product, they will not buy it; this re-emphasises the importance of good market research and analysis.

Calentone and Cooper's research was borne out by research published in 2006, in which the authors found that incremental innovations (those which are a small improvement on existing products) carry the least risk for firms who are first to bring them to market. Discontinuous innovation (truly new-to-the-world products) carry the greatest risk for firms first into the market and for firms which follow later; in other words, being first to market only carries risks, not rewards (Min et al. 2006).

Overall, NPD is concerned with replacing the firm's existing product range with fresh products that come even closer to meeting customer needs. Firms that do not innovate will, eventually, lose market share to firms that do, since the competitor firms will be offering better products. This places a heavy premium on NPD. Having said that, new products do not sell themselves – unsurprisingly, firms which provide high levels of marketing and technological support for their new products experience greater financial rewards from their innovations (Sorescu et al. 2003). It is therefore no surprise that firms with a strong market orientation are more likely to be successful in launching new-to-the-world products (Augusto and Coelho 2009), nor that firms with strong customer relationship management also find it easier to innovate (Battor and Battor 2010).

DIFFUSION OF INNOVATION

New products are not immediately adopted by all consumers. Some consumers are driven to buy new products almost as soon as they become available, whereas others prefer to wait until the product has been around for a while before risking their hard-earned money on it. Innovations therefore take time to filter through the population: this process is called diffusion and is determined partly by the nature of consumers and partly by the nature of the innovation itself.

Everett M. Rogers (1962) classified consumers as follows:

- **Innovators**: those who like to be first to own the latest products. These consumers predominate at the beginning of the PLC
- **Early adopters**: those who are open to new ideas, but like to wait a while after initial launch. These consumers predominate during the growth phase of the PLC
- **Early majority**: those who buy once the product is thoroughly tried and tested. These consumers predominate in the early part of the maturity phase of the PLC
- **Late majority**: those who are suspicious of new things and wait until most other people already have one. These consumers predominate in the latter part of the maturity phase of the PLC
- **Laggards**: those who adopt new products only when it becomes absolutely necessary to do so. These consumers predominate in the decline phase of the PLC.

The process of diffusion of innovation is carried out through reference-group influence (see Chapter 3). Theories concerning the mechanisms for this have developed over the past 100 years, the three most important ones being trickle-down theory, two-step flow theory and multistage interaction theory.

Trickle-down theory says that the wealthy classes obtain information about new products and the poorer classes then imitate their 'betters' (Veblen 1899). This theory has been largely discredited in wealthy countries because new ideas are disseminated overnight by the mass media and copied by chain stores within days; for example, the dress worn by Kate Middleton when she married Prince William in 2011 was copied almost immediately by Chinese dressmakers in Suzhou (Moore 2011).

Critical thinking

Perhaps nowadays we don't blindly copy the doings of the aristocracy, or even the upper middle class, but does that mean we are entirely uninfluenced by our betters? We seem to have developed a new aristocracy, largely composed of entertainers such as footballers and singers, who set the fashions for us in many ways.

Even without celebrity endorsement, where such people are paid to say they use a particular brand of perfume or a particular set of golf clubs, we watch avidly to see what they are wearing, buying and doing. So maybe Veblen was stating a universal truth, back in 1899!

Two-step flow theory is similar, but this time it is 'influentials' rather than wealthy people who are the start of the adoption process (Lazarsfield *et al.* 1948). This has considerable basis in truth, but may be less true now than it was in the 1940s, when the theory was first developed; access to TV and other information media has proliferated, and information about innovation is disseminated much faster.

The multistage interaction model (Engel *et al.* 1995) recognises this and allows for the influence of the mass media. In this model the influentials emphasise or facilitate the information flow (perhaps by making recommendations to friends or acting as advisers). A more recent concept is that of the market maven: a maven is someone who knows a great deal about a product category (for example, someone who knows a lot about computer software) and is willing to share the knowledge. Mavens usually have confidence in their ability to acquire knowledge, and confidence that people will respond positively to their offers of help. Mavens are usually very strong influencers and are therefore an important group from a marketer's viewpoint (Clark *et al.* 2008).

Whether people are innovators, late adopters, laggards, etc. may depend on the degree to which they like to differentiate themselves from others. There is a conflict between wanting to be different and wanting to fit in with others, so adoption may relate to the individual's perception of the size of the group that uses the product already. If someone likes to be different, he or she might be attracted to a small group of users and would thus tend to be an innovator (Timmor and Katz-Navon 2008). On the other hand, the actual usefulness of the product is often decided by referring to internal factors, with little reference to social factors (Munnukka and Jarvi 2011).

Consumers often need considerable persuasion to change from their old product to a new one. This is because there is always a cost of some sort. For example, somebody buying a new car will lose money on trading in the old car (a *switching cost*), or perhaps somebody buying a new computer will also have to spend money on new software and spend time learning how to operate the new equipment (an *innovation cost*).

On the other hand there is strong evidence that newness as such is an important factor in the consumer's decision-making process (Haines 1966). In other words, people like new things, but there is a cost attached. Provided the new product offers real additional benefits over the old one (i.e. fits the consumer's needs better than the old product), the product will be adopted.

Consumers must first become aware of the new product, and then become persuaded that there is a real advantage in switching from their existing solution. A useful model of this adoption process is as follows:

- *Awareness.* This will often come about as a result of promotional activities by the firm.
- *Trial.* For a low-price item (e.g. a packet of biscuits) this may mean that the consumer will actually buy the product before trying it; for a major purchase, such as a car, the consumer will usually need to have a test-drive. Increasingly, supermarkets hold tasting sessions to allow customers to try new products.
- *Adoption.* This is the point at which the consumer decides to buy the product or make it part of the weekly shopping list.

Rogers (1962) identified the following perceived attributes of innovative products, by which consumers apparently judge the product during the decision-making process:

- **Relative advantage**. The degree to which the innovation is perceived as better than the idea it supersedes.

- **Compatibility**. Consistency with existing values, past experiences and needs of potential adopters.
- **Complexity**. Ideas that are easily understood are adopted more quickly.
- **Trialability**. Degree to which a product can be experimented with.
- **Observability**. The degree to which the results of an innovation are visible to others.

In some cases, the actual usefulness of the product is determined in part by the number of people who already own it. This is particularly true of innovations in communications technology: e-mail is of no use unless a large number of people use it, and the recent growth in social networking sites is only possible if a lot of people join the sites (Wang and Lo 2008).

Apart from the issue of adopting a product as it stands, there is the concept of **reinvention**. Sometimes users find new ways to use the product (not envisaged by the designers) and sometimes this leads to the creation of whole new markets. For example, in the 1930s it was discovered that baking soda is good for removing stale smells from refrigerators, a fact that was quickly seized on by baking soda manufacturers. Deodorising fridges is now a major part of the market for baking soda.

BRANDING

Many products are so similar to other manufacturers' products that consumers are entirely indifferent as to which one they will buy. For example, petrol is much the same whether it is sold by Shell, Esso, BP, Statoil, Elf or Repsol: such products are called commodity products because they are homogeneous commodities rather than distinct products with different benefits from the others on offer.

At first sight, water would come into the category of a commodity product. Yet any supermarket has a range of bottled waters, each with its own formulation and brand name, and each with its loyal consumers. In these cases the original commodity product (water) has been converted into a brand. Branding is a process of adding value to the product by use of its packaging, brand name, promotion and position in the minds of the consumers. Even non-profit-making firms are more successful if they are brand-oriented (Napoli 2006).

DeChernatony and McDonald (1998) offer the following definition of brand:

> A successful brand is an identifiable product, service, person or place, augmented in such a way that the buyer or user perceives relevant, unique added values which match their needs most closely. Furthermore, its success results from being able to sustain those added values in the face of competition.

This definition emphasises the increased value that accrues to the consumer by buying the established brand rather than a generic or commodity product. The values that are added may be in the area of reassurance of the brand's quality, they may be in the area of status (where the brand's image carries over to the consumer) or they may be in the area of convenience (making search behaviour easier).

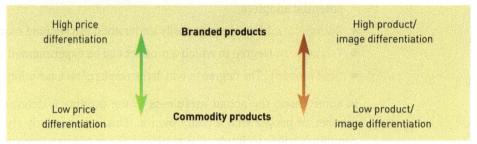

Figure 6.4 Commodity products v branded products

Figure 6.4 shows the relationship between commodity products and branded products in terms of image and price. Commodity products tend to be undifferentiated in price (for example, petrol tends to be much the same price in petrol stations within a given geographical area; a differential of even 10% would be very noticeable). They also tend to have a low degree of differentiation in the product characteristics and the image. Branded goods, on the other hand, score high on both factors; since they command a premium price, this is likely to lead to an increased profit, which strengthens the case for developing a strong brand.

Brand names

When a new product has been developed, the producer will usually give it a *brand name*. A brand name is a term, **symbol** or design that distinguishes one seller's product from its competitors. The strategic considerations for brand naming are as follows:

- *Marketing objectives.* The brand name should fit the overall marketing objectives of the firm: for example, a firm intending to enter the youth market will need to develop brand names that appeal to a young audience.
- *Brand audit.* An estimate of the internal and external forces such as critical success factor (also known as the unique selling proposition).
- *Brand objectives.* As with the marketing objectives, the overall intentions about the brand need to be specified.
- *Brand strategy alternatives.* The other ways of achieving the brand's objectives and the other factors involved in its success have a bearing on the choice of brand name.

Brand names can be protected in most countries by *registration*, but there is some protection for brands in that it is illegal to try to 'pass off' a product as being a branded one when it is not. For example, using a very similar brand name to a famous brand, or even using similar package design, could be regarded as passing off. This is a civil offence, not a criminal one, so it is up to the offended brand owner to take legal action.

Ries (1995) suggests that brand names should have some, or all, of the following characteristics:

- They should shock, i.e. catch the customer's attention. French Connection United Kingdom use their FCUK acronym for this purpose.
- They should be alliterative: this helps them to be memorable. For example, West'n'Welsh Windows is a more memorable name than BJ Double Glazing.
- They should connect to the product's positioning in the consumer's perceptual map. UK biscuit brand Hob Nobs conveys an image of a warm kitchen (the hob) with friendliness (hob-nobbing).
- They should link to a visual image: again, this helps the memorability. Timberland outdoor clothing conjures a visual image of mountain country.
- They should communicate something about the product or be capable of being used to communicate about the product. Duracell conveys the main advantage of the batteries – they are durable. Brand names in French are often perceived as being more hedonic (Salciuviene *et al.* 2010).
- They should encourage the development of a nickname (for example, Bud for Budweiser Beer).
- They should be telephone- and directory-friendly. Words often seem muffled on the telephone, so that 'Bud' becomes 'Mud'.

Brands and semiotics

Semiotics is the study of meaning, and is concerned with the symbolism conveyed by objects and words. Semiotics refers to systems of signs; the most obvious system is words, but other systems exist. For example, a film would use the sign systems of the spoken word, the gestures of the actors, the music of the soundtrack and the conventions of movie direction and production to generate an overall meaning. The overall meaning is generated as a result of an interaction between the sign system and the observer or reader; the viewer interprets the information in the light of existing knowledge and attitudes, later including it in an overall perceptual map of reality (see Chapter 3).

Brands are important symbols, often using more than one sign system to create meaning; the brand name, the logo, the colour and the design of the packaging all contribute. In terms of semiotics, brands have four levels:

1 *A utilitarian sign.* This is about the practical aspects of the product and includes meanings of reliability, effectiveness, fitness for purpose and so forth.
2 *A commercial sign.* This is about the exchange values of the product, perhaps conveying meanings about value for money or cost-effectiveness.
3 *A socio-cultural sign.* This is about the social effects of buying (or not buying) the product, with meanings about membership of aspirational groups or about

the fitness of the product for filling social roles. Research shows that even young children are affected by this – having the right brand of snack in the lunch-box was found to be extremely important for 8- to 11-year-olds (Roper and La Niece 2009).

4 *A sign about the mythical values of the product.* Myths are heroic stories about the product, many of which have little basis in fact; for example, the Harley Davidson motorcycle brand has a strong mythical value due (in part) to its starring role in the film *Easy Rider*.

Myths provide a conceptual framework through which the contradictions of life can be resolved, and brands can build on this. For example, modern industrial life is, presumably, the antithesis of frontier adventure. Yet the Harley Davidson, a product of twentieth-century industry, was used to represent the (probably mythical) freedom and adventure of the American West. Most powerful brands have at least some mythical connotations – in the United Kingdom, the Hovis bread brand has mythical connotations centred around corner bakery shops at the turn of the century; in Malaysia and Singapore Tiger Balm carries mythical connotations about ancient Chinese apothecaries; in Australia Vegemite carries mythical connotations about Australian family life that its main competitor, Promite, has never tapped into.

The association of different values with the brand name can be extremely useful when researching the acceptability of a brand's image. The importance that consumers place on these values can be researched using focus groups, with a subsequent analysis of the key signs contained within the brand, and consumers can be segmented according to their responsiveness to the particular signs contained within the brand and their relevance to the consumer's own internal values.

Research carried out by Gordon and Valentin (1996) into retail buying behaviour showed that different retail outlets convey different meanings to consumers in terms of a continuum from planned, routine shopping through to impulse buying. Each store type met the needs differently and conveyed different meanings in terms of appropriateness of behaviour. Convenience stores conveyed an image of disorder and feelings of guilt and confusion (perhaps associated with having forgotten to buy some items in the course of the regular weekly shop). Supermarkets represented planned shopping and conveyed an image of efficient domestic management and functionality. Petrol stations carried a dual meaning of planned purchase (for petrol) and impulse buying (in the shop). Business travellers seeking a break from work and pleasure travellers seeking to enhance the 'holiday' feeling both indulged in impulsive behaviour motivated by the need for a treat. Finally, off-licences legitimated the purchase of alcohol, allowing shoppers to buy drinks without the uneasy feeling that other shoppers might disapprove. Off-licences also provided an environment in which people felt able to experiment with new purchases.

These signs are relevant not only for the retailers themselves in terms of their own branding, but also for branded-goods manufacturers who need to decide which outlets are most appropriate for their brands and where in the store the brand should be located. For example, snack foods and chocolate are successfully sold in petrol stations, where travellers are often looking for a treat to break up a boring journey.

STRATEGIC ISSUES IN BRANDING

Adding value to the product by branding involves a great deal more than merely giving the product a catchy name. Branding is the culmination of a range of activities across the whole marketing mix, leading to a brand image that conveys a whole set of messages to the consumer (and, more importantly, to the consumer's friends and family) about quality, price, expected performance and status. For example, the Porsche brand name conveys an image of engineering excellence, reliability, sporty styling, high speed and high prices, and of wealth and success on the part of the owner. People do not buy Porsches simply as a means of transport.

Because branding involves all the elements of the marketing mix, it cannot be regarded simply as a tactical tool designed to differentiate the product on the supermarket shelves. Instead, it must be regarded as the focus for the marketing effort, as a way of directing the thought processes of the management towards producing consumer satisfaction. The brand acts as a common point of contact between the producer and the consumer, as shown in Figure 6.5.

As the figure shows, the consumer benefits from the brand in terms of knowing what the quality will be, knowing what the expected performance will be, gaining some self-image values (for example, a prestigious product conveys prestige to the consumer by association – conversely, a low-price product might enhance a consumer's sense of frugality and ability to find good value for money).

In many cases the core product has very little to differentiate it from other products, and the brand is really the only differentiating feature. A famous example is the rivalry between Pepsi Cola and Coca-Cola; in blind taste tests, most people prefer the flavour of Pepsi, but Coca-Cola outsells Pepsi in virtually every market. This apparent discrepancy can only be explained by the brand image which Coca-Cola has, and in taste tests where consumers are able to see the can the drink comes out of, Coca-Cola is the preferred brand.

Despite the apparently artificial nature of differentiation by branding, the benefits to the consumer are very real; experiments show that branded analgesics work better than generic analgesics at relieving pain, even though the chemical formula is identical. This is because of the psychosomatic power of the brand. Someone driving a prestige car gains very real benefits in terms of the respect and envy of others, even if the performance of the car is no better than that of its cheaper rival.

Brands can be looked at in a number of different ways. Table 6.5 shows eight different strategic functions of brands.

Branding clearly has advantages for the manufacturer and the retailer, since it helps to differentiate the product from the competitor's product. Economies of scale and scope are attributed to branding, and a brand with high sales will generate

Figure 6.5 Brands as a contact point

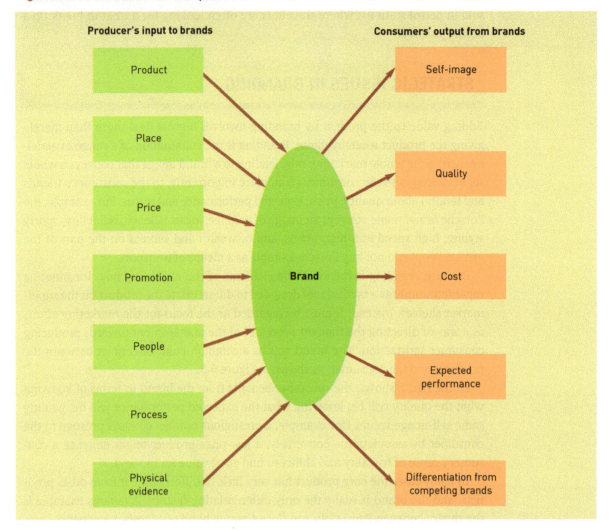

production economies. A successful brand also creates a *barrier to entry*, so that competitors find it harder to enter the market (Demsetz 1982). Brands also allow firms to compete other than on price, which clearly has advantages since the firm does not have to cut its profit margins to compete.

Furthermore, brands that are held in high esteem tend to be more consistent in their sales, riding over the ups and downs of the marketplace (Png and Reitman 1995). Not all brands are priced at a premium; many brands are competitively priced to take advantage of consistent sales.

Branding has advantages for the consumer; it is easy to recognise the product and easy to identify with it. Messages about the formulation and benefits are clearly conveyed, and in most cases the use of a particular brand says something about the consumer (for example, wearing designer clothes) (Bagwell and Bernheim 1996). Because most purchases involve only limited problem-solving behaviour, branding

Table 6.5 Strategic functions of brands

Function	Explanation
Brand as a sign of ownership	Brands were at one time a way of showing who had instigated the marketing activities for the brand. This was an attempt to protect the formulation of the product in cases where intellectual property protection was insufficient, and also to ensure that customers knew whether they were buying a manufacturer's brand or a retailer's brand.
Brand as a differentiating device	A strong brand undoubtedly does differentiate the product from similar products, but having a strong brand name is not enough. The product itself also needs to be different in some way; the brand image is the communicating device that conveys the difference to the consumer.
Brand as a functional device	Branding can be used to communicate functional capability. In other words, the brand conveys an image of its quality and expected performance to the consumer.
Brand as a symbolic device	The symbolism of some brands enables the consumer to say something about themselves. This is particularly apparent in the 'designer' clothes industry – a very ordinary T-shirt acquires added value because the name of the designer is printed on the front. If the consumers believe that the brand's value lies in its communication ability they will spend considerable time and effort in choosing the brand that conveys the appropriate image.
Brand as a risk reducer	Every purchase involves a degree of risk; the product might not perform as expected and if it fails to do so then the vendor might not be prepared to put matters right. Buying a strongly branded product offers the consumer a degree of reassurance about both the product and the producer. Astute marketers find out what types of risk are of most concern to the customers or consumers and develop a brand presentation which addresses those risks.
Brand as a shorthand device	Brands are used as a way of 'tagging' information about a product in the consumers' memories. This is particularly relevant when the brand is extended to other product categories, since the consumer's view of the parent brand is transferred to the new brand. For example, Virgin has successfully extended the brand image from CDs to retailing to airlines to financial services, all offering the same innovative approach and serving similar market segments.
Brand as a legal device	Brands give a certain amount of legal protection to the producer, since pack design and name can be protected where (often) the formulation of the product cannot. Strong branding offers some protection for the firm's intellectual property.
Brand as a strategic device	The assets constituting the brand can be identified and managed so that the brand maintains and builds on the added value that it represents.

helps to reduce the decision-making time and also the effort of evaluating competing products: brands do not necessarily need to have unique features for this to happen (Romaniuk and Gaillard 2007). Consumers who either do not want to spend time on an extended information search or do not have the expertise to do so can use the brand as an implicit guarantee of quality. These positive feelings about the brand are called consumer brand equity and can be affected by all aspects of the brand, including country of origin (Pappu *et al.* 2006).

In business-to-business markets, buyers may be prepared to pay a premium for a known brand, based on the following dimensions (Persson 2010):

1 *Brand familiarity*.
2 *Product solution*. This is the extent to which the product is known to provide a solution to the buyer's problems.
3 *Service associations*. This is the degree to which the buyer can see that there will be good after-sales services.
4 *Distribution associations*. This is the degree to which the deliveries will be reliable and effective.
5 *Relationship associations*. This is the degree to which the buyer has good working relationships with the supplier.
6 *Company associations*. These are the factors surrounding the supplying company's reputation.

Information storage and retrieval in humans are carried out by a process of 'chunking', or collecting information in substantial quantities and storing them under a single 'file name' (Buschke 1976). In effect, the brand name provides an informational chunk; the individual is able to summon up a huge amount of information from memory using the brand name as the trigger.

From a strategic viewpoint, the brand image provides a focus for the creative energies of the marketing team. Koestler (1964) suggested that creativity involves the bringing together of hitherto unrelated, yet familiar, objects to generate a creative insight. The difficulty for marketers is that product and brand development is often a team process and, as such, the team needs to keep a firm picture of what the product is intended to convey – the 'personality' of the product – if they are to maintain consistency in their creative activities. One way of doing this is to use a metaphor for the product. For example, the Honda Accord developers used the metaphor 'Rugby player in a dinner suit' to achieve product coherence across the team, even though the entire creative team consisted of hundreds of people, from automotive stylists through to ad designers (Clark and Fujimoto 1990).

Brand planning is important but time-consuming; often the job is given to a brand manager, many of whom are young and inexperienced. Developing the brand is a process of integrating a number of strands of business activity, so a clear idea of the brand image is essential, as is a long-term view. To see branding as merely being about design or advertising or naming is inadequate and short-sighted; successful brands are those that act as a lens through which the consumer sees the corporation and the product. Constant evaluation of the image seen through the lens is essential if the brand is to retain its status.

Occasionally products need to be rebranded, sometimes because of a bad association (for example, after the Zeebrugge ferry disaster the company rebranded itself from Townsend Thoresen to P&O Ferries), but more commonly because of a structural change in the firm, perhaps caused by a merger or a takeover (Muzellec and Lambkin 2006). Within the European Union, rebranding has often occurred in recent years to develop a Europe-wide identity (as in the case of Jif cleaners, which became Cif). Such rebranding needs to be handled carefully, and invariably involves added promotional expenditure to establish the new brand.

EXTENDING THE BRAND

A **brand extension** is another product in the company's range that uses a similar brand name. For example, Cherry Coke is a brand extension of the original Coca-Cola. Overall, **family branding** is where one brand name is used for a range of products, such as Heinz 57 Varieties, and **line family branding** is where a smaller group of brands carries a single identity.

In each case the aim is to convey a message of quality to the consumer by borrowing from the established reputation of the parent brand, and to appeal to the target market, who are already familiar with the parent brand. Properly carried out, the establishment of a brand is a long-term project, which can be expensive; this leads to an emphasis by some firms on brand extensions that are intended to maximise the return on the investment made in establishing the brand. In some cases, brands have been extended to the breaking point; relatively few brands (Virgin being one example) can be extended apparently indefinitely, and even as well-established a brand as Levi Strauss jeans could not extend itself to smart suits (the company's attempt to do so in the early 1980s turned to disaster). The most important driver for brand extension success is the fit between the present brand and the extension product (Volckner and Sattler 2006); Virgin's ability to extend relies on the brand's image as being original and fresh-thinking, coupled with a combination of solidity and practicality. Even so, the bad publicity which surrounded Virgin Trains at the beginning of the century is thought to have damaged the brand and the company has been forced to make major investments in their rolling stock to recover some of the lost ground.

Having a strong brand associated with a new product does affect consumer perceptions significantly; people will generally have a higher perception of a new product if it is associated with a well-known and trusted brand (Besharat 2010). Conversely, people will often look for other ways of confirming the quality of an unbranded item, and will even be prepared to pay a premium for such confirmation (Ubilava et al. 2011).

A more recent development has been **compositioning**, in which products are grouped under a brand name to create a composite value greater than that of the components (Ruttenberg et al. 1995). Joint marketing and distribution alliances come under this heading. The products concerned do not necessarily come from the same producer and may not even be in the same general category; for example, Disneyland has 'official airlines' or 'official ferry companies' to transport visitors to its theme parks. A further extension of this concept is **brand architecture** (Uncles et al. 1995), which is concerned with setting up 'partner' brands and creating a balance between branding at the product level and corporate or banner levels.

Within the international arena, firms have the opportunity to extend the brand across international frontiers. This raises fundamental strategic issues; for example, should the brand be globalised, with the firm offering a standard package throughout the world (as does Coca-Cola), or should the brand be adapted for each market (as does Heinz)? Some firms brand globally, but advertise locally (Sandler and Shani 1992), while others organise task groups to handle the brand on a global scale (Raffee and Kreutzer 1989).

RETAILERS' OWN-BRANDS

Retailer power has grown considerably over the past 30 years, with a proliferation of own-brand products. In the past, the retailer's own-brand products were usually of poorer quality than manufacturers' brands, but they are now often of equal or even superior quality. These brands now account for up to 60% of the sales in some major retail stores such as Tesco and Sainsbury in the United Kingdom, and Carrefour in France (slogan: *'Carrefour – c'est aussi une marque'*, which translates as 'Carrefour – it's also a brand') (Hankinson and Cowking 1997). For manufacturers this creates a problem of response; should the manufacturer try to invest in the firm's brands more heavily to overcome the retailer's brand, or should he or she capitulate entirely and produce on behalf of the retailer (Quelch and Harding 1995). Often manufacturers will become suppliers of retailer-brand products which compete with their own branded goods. Reasons for doing this are as follows:

- *Economies of scale.* The manufacturer may be able to buy raw materials in greater quantities or may be able to invest in more efficient production methods if the throughput of product is increased.
- *Utilise excess capacity.* Seasonality or production synergies may make production of own-brand products attractive in some cases.
- *Base for expansion.* Supplying a retailer with own-brand goods may lead to other opportunities to supply the retailer with other products in future.
- *No promotion costs.* The retailer bears all the investment in the brand (which is, of course, a brand extension of the retailer's trading name in any case).
- *No choice.* Some retailers (the UK's Marks & Spencer being an example) only trade in their own brands. Manufacturers who wish to trade with these retailers have no choice but to produce under the retailer's brand name.
- *To shut out the competition.* If the manufacturer does not produce goods under the retailer's brand name, another manufacturer will and will thus gain ground.

Manufacturers with very strong branding often refuse to produce own-brand goods, Kellogg's breakfast cereals being a notable example. If the brand is strong enough this allows the firm to promote on an 'accept no substitutes' platform.

In the past, own-brand products were cheap versions of the leading brands, but in more and more cases the retailers now have enough financial strength to fund the development of entirely new versions of products, some of which are superior to the proprietary brands and have achieved substantial market shares.

In many cases this is achieved by producing 'lookalike' branding, where the product looks very similar to the brand leader. In the United Kingdom this led to the formation of the British Producers and Brand Owners Group, which lobbied Parliament to regulate the visual and physical simulation of successful brands. In fact, research showed that few, if any, consumers accidentally pick up the wrong brand (Balabanis and Craven 1997), but some confusion is engendered. Retailers (perhaps disingenuously) claim that using similar packaging helps consumers identify products, whereas manufacturers claim that lookalikes give the impression that the products are identical. In other words, the confusion arises not at the level of picking up the wrong pack, but at the more subtle level of forming inaccurate beliefs about the lookalike's attributes based on the attributes of the leading brand (Foxman *et al*. 1992).

A further argument advanced by retailers is that strong manufacturers' brands have created generic product categories of their own – 'Gold Blend-type' instant coffees, for example. The retailers argue that products with similar quality and specifications should look as similar as possible to the brand that first created those values – an argument that is particularly annoying to manufacturers who have invested large sums of money in creating those brand values in the first place.

PACKAGING

Packaging of the product is equally part of the product, since the packaging can itself convey benefits. In fact, recent research shows that attractive packaging triggers areas of the brain which are normally associated with rewards, while unattractive packaging triggers activity in a different part of the brain, one which is usually associated with processing things such as unfair offers or disgusting pictures (Stoll *et al*. 2008).

The main purpose of packaging is to protect the contents from the outside environment and vice versa, but packaging also carries out the following functions:

- Informs customers
- Meets legal information requirements
- Sometimes aids the use of the product (e.g. ring pulls on drinks cans make it easier to open the can).

Packaging decisions might include such areas as **tamper resistance** (paper strips around caps to prevent bottles being opened while on supermarket shelves) and *customer usage* (e.g. the resealable nipples on mineral water bottles, making it easier to drink the water while participating in sports such as running or cycling). The protection of the environment has become important to consumers in recent years, so much packaging is either recyclable or biodegradable. Customer acceptability is of obvious importance; packaging must be hygienic and convenient for the consumer. Within the United Kingdom there has been a growing trend to develop packaging designs that can be legally protected under the 1994 Trade Marks Act; the purpose of this is to prevent imitators from making close copies of the packaging. In some cases the package design has been made expensive to copy, requiring retooling for unusual pack shapes, or expensive printing processes (Gander 1996). 'Me-too' packaging has become particularly common among supermarket own-brand versions of popular products, and there has been some debate about the ethics of this. In some countries these close copies infringe copyright or patent laws (Davies 1995).

Colour can also be important; for example, Heinz's use of a turquoise label for their baked beans tin emphasises the orange colour of the beans when the can is opened. Even the proportions of the package make a difference; the ratio of the sides of the package affect perception (Raghubir and Greenleaf 2006).

In recent years, because of the huge upsurge in world trade, it has also become necessary to consider the legal requirements of labelling, which differ from one country to the next; nutritional information may have to be in a different form for each country (for example, in the United States food has to be labelled with the amount of fat it contains expressed as a percentage of a 2000-calorie daily intake). In recent years there has been a requirement in many countries to label foods which contain genetically modified crops; this has created a major problem for global food corporations, since they may source ingredients from many places, as well as market-finished products globally (D'Souza *et al.* 2008).

Packaging can often be used for promotion of other products in the manufacturer's range (via recipe instructions, for example) or for joint promotions with non-competing companies. Interestingly, corporate brands on packaging seem to have little impact on the desirability of the product, whereas brand category dominance has a significant effect (LaForet 2011).

CASE STUDY 6 G24 Innovations

Global warming, dwindling resources and rising fuel costs have certainly raised interest in alternative energy sources in recent years. Solar power in particular has received a lot of interest – solar cells are not noisy like wind turbines, they are less obtrusive and they can often be used to power small appliances in locations away from mains power sources.

Into this market has stepped G24 Innovations. G24i is a company based in South Wales, founded by two Americans, Ed Stevenson and Bob Hertzberg. The technology they are applying is really futuristic; the company has acquired the rights to organic inks (developed by Michael Graetzel, a Swiss chemist) which generate electricity when exposed to sunlight. This means that the company can manufacture flexible solar panels – so flexible that they can be sewn onto the tops of shoulder bags and bicycle panniers.

The solar generators are manufactured as a continuous strip, kilometres long, which can be cut to any shape. The strips are not as flexible as cloth, but are certainly flexible enough to be moulded around unusual shapes, unlike traditional solar panels which are rigid and fairly thick.

Obviously the power generated in this way is very small, but it means that a customer can charge up a mobile telephone from a panel on a shoulder bag or recharge bicycle lights from a pannier's top. Hertzberg, a former politician from California, says that standby power is their 'killer app' – the application that will fuel the company's growth. Having electronic devices on standby uses up a surprising amount of power – around 8% of total power consumption – but using a solar panel to provide the standby power removes the problem. Hertzberg and Stevenson say that their solar panels have the potential to generate enough power to replace the giant Drax power station in Yorkshire, England. Drax, according to Stevenson and Hertzberg, is the biggest single source of pollution in Western Europe.

So far the company has produced a limited range of products using the technology. Solar-powered handbags and panniers are probably at the 'gimmick' end of the market, being a startling way of demonstrating the technology, but developments such as solar-powered computer keyboards and mice have real potential. Although the organic inks are less efficient than traditional rigid solar panels, they have the advantage (not being rigid) that they can easily be manufactured in a range of shapes and thus be incorporated into many products. Using ordinary room lighting, they can generate enough power to run a wireless keyboard or mouse.

This capability has led Texas Instruments to sign a one-year partnership agreement with G24i: Texas Instruments say that G24i's products are the most efficient for harvesting room light to power small equipment. G24i hopes to seal deals with other major electronics manufacturers to integrate the technology into their products and has several deals in the pipeline.

Other applications include products where using mains power or even batteries would be inconvenient; for example, smoke detectors. With one of G24i's solar strips wrapped round its base, there is no need to check and replace the batteries in a smoke detector. Electric clocks might be another example, or wireless doorbells – the possibilities are endless.

The company's production line is based in Cardiff, South Wales, but the founders continue to live in California, where they are well placed to negotiate with the industry. Day-to-day management of the company is handled by a UK-based team of executives, some of whom are American.

Clearly, there are many possible applications for solar-power units and the company is active in seeking out ways of exploiting the technology. However, in some ways this is a product in search of a market – the advantages over conventional solar panels are relatively few and must outweigh the increased efficiency of a conventional panel if the product is to sell. So far, the founders have burned through $120m and have a deal to raise another $40m – as Hertzberg said in an interview with *The Times*, 'We never thought it would be this expensive but the thing is, this stuff is really hard to get right' (*The Times*, 17 July 2011).

Questions

1. What type of innovation is this?
2. What type of innovation strategy do G24i appear to be following?
3. Currently the company does not have a product brand. How might branding help the company?
4. At what stage in the product life cycle are the solar panels?
5. In Calentone and Cooper's definitions, what type of product is this?

SUMMARY

This chapter has been about those decisions that are closest to the product. The main issues revolve around managing the product portfolio to ensure that the firm continues to offer relevant products to meet the needs of consumers, knowing when to drop a product from the mix and knowing when to introduce a new product.

Branding is concerned with communicating the unique selling proposition of the product to the consumers and is the focus of all the firm's marketing activities relating to the product. The brand is the 'personality' of the product, communicating subtle messages about quality and performance.

Here are the key points from this chapter:

- The product life cycle is a useful description, but not much help in prediction
- Products in the Star stage will cost more money to maintain than they bring in, but are an investment for the future
- Dogs may still be profitable, but are probably a poor use of resources and could be replaced by more profitable products
- War Horses and Dodos will eventually disappear unless they can be repositioned into new, growing markets
- Most products will decline and must be replaced eventually
- The safe route in NPD is the me-too; the high-growth route is innovation
- A product is a bundle of benefits, not merely the sum of its physical characteristics.

CHAPTER QUESTIONS

1 What are the stages of new product development?
2 Why should firms innovate?
3 How might a firm use reinvention when repositioning a product?
4 From the BCG matrix, which products would probably be bought by the late majority of adopters?
5 What disadvantages might family-line branding have over individual branding?

Further reading

Innovation Management and New Product Development **by Paul Trott** (Harlow, FT Prentice Hall, 2011) provides a detailed account of the new product development process and the management of the adoption process by customers.

Services Marketing: Concepts, Strategies and Cases **by K. Douglas Hoffman and John E.G. Bateson** (South Western Educational Publishing, 2010) has an excellent overview of service product marketing.

Building Strong Brands **by David A. Aaker** (Pocket Books, 2010) gives a good, practitioner-orientated guide to developing brands.

References

Augusto, Mario, and Coelho, Filipe: 'Market orientation and new-to-the-world products: exploring the moderating effects of innovativeness, competitive strength, and environmental forces'. *Industrial Marketing Management*, **38** (1) (2009), pp. 94–108.

Bagwell, L.S. and Bernheim, B.D.: 'Veblen effects in a theory of conspicuous consumption', *The American Economic Review*, **86** (1996), pp. 349–73.

Balabanis, G. and Craven, S.: 'Consumer confusion from own-brand lookalikes: an exploratory survey', *Journal of Marketing Management*, **13** (4) (May 1997), pp. 299–313.

Barksdale, H.C. and Harris, C.E.: 'Portfolio analysis and the PLC', *Long Range Planning*, **15** (6) (1982), pp. 74–83.

Battor, Moustafa, and Battor, Mohamed: 'The impact of customer relationship management capability on innovation and performance advantages: testing a mediated model', *Journal of Marketing Management*, **26** (9/10) (2010), pp. 842–57.

Benwell, M.: 'Scheduling stocks and storage space in a volatile market', *Logistics Information Management*, **9** (4) (1996), pp. 18–23.

Besharat, Ali: 'How co-branding versus brand extensions drive consumers' evaluations of new products: a brand equity approach', *Industrial Marketing Management*, **39** (8) (2010), pp. 1240–9.

Brown, Stephen, Sherry, John F. and Kozinetts, Robert V.: 'Teaching old brands new tricks: retro branding and the revival of brand meaning', *Journal of Marketing*, **67** (3) (July 2003), pp. 19–33.

Buschke, H.: 'Learning is organised by chunking', *Journal of Verbal Learning and Verbal Behaviour*, **15** (1976), pp. 313–24.

Calentone, Roger J. and Cooper, Robert G.: 'New product scenarios: prospects for success', *American Journal of Marketing*, **45** (Spring 1981), pp. 48–60.

Carbonell-Foulquie, Pilar, Munuera-Aleman, Jose L. and Rodriguez-Escudero, Ana I.: 'Criteria employed for go/no-go decisions when developing successful highly innovative products', *Industrial Marketing Management*, **33** (4) (April 2004), pp. 307–16.

Clancy, Kevin J. and Shulman, Robert S.: *The Marketing Revolution* (New York, Harper Business, 1991), p. 6.

Clark, K. and Fujimoto, T.: 'The power of product integrity', *Business Review* (November/December 1990), pp. 107–18.

Clark, Ronald A., Goldsmith, Ronald L. and Goldsmith, Elizabeth B.: 'Market mavenism and consumer self-confidence', *Journal of Consumer Behaviour*, (May/Jun) **7** (3) (2008), pp. 239–48.

Cooper, R.G. and Kleinschmidt, E.J.: 'An investigation into the new product process: steps, deficiencies and impact', *Journal of Product Innovation Management*, (June 1988), pp. 71–85.

Davies, I.: 'Look-alikes; fair or unfair competition?' *Journal of Brand Management* (October 1995), pp. 104–20.

DeChernatony, L. and McDonald, M.: *Creating Powerful Brands*, 2nd edn (Oxford, Butterworth Heinemann, 1998).

Demsetz, H.: 'Barriers to entry', *American Economic Review*, **72** (1982), pp. 47–57.

D'Souza, Clare, Rugimbana, Robert, Quazi, Ali and Nanere, Marthin G.: 'Investing in consumer confidence through genetically modified labeling: an evaluation of compliance options and their marketing challenges for Australian firms', *Journal of Marketing Management*, **24** (5/6) (2008), pp. 621–35.

Engel, James F., Blackwell, Roger D. and Miniard, Paul W.: *Consumer Behaviour*, 8th edn (Fort Worth, TX, Dryden Press, 1995).

Foxman, E.R., Berger, P.W. and Cote, J.A.: 'Consumer brand confusion: a conceptual framework', *Psychology and Marketing*, **19** (1992), pp. 123–41.

Gander, P.: 'Patently obvious', *Marketing Week* (28 June 1996), pp. 51–5.

Gordon, W. and Valentin, V.: 'Buying the brand at point of choice', *Journal of Brand Management*, **4** (1) (1996), pp. 35–44.

Haines, George H.: 'A study of why people purchase new products', *Proceedings of the American Marketing Association* (1966), pp. 685–97.

Hankinson, G. and Cowking, P.: 'Branding in practice: the profile and role of brand managers in the UK', *Journal of Marketing Management*, **13** (4) (May 1997), pp. 239–64.

Hart, Susan: 'Dimensions of success in new product development; an exploratory investigation', *Journal of Marketing Management*, **9** (1) (January 1993), pp. 23–42.

Huang, Xueli, Soutar, Geoffrey N. and Brown, Alan: 'Measuring new product success: an empirical investigation of Australian SMEs', *Industrial Marketing Management*, **33** (2) (February 2004), pp. 101–23.

Johne, A. and Snelson, P.: *Successful Product Development: Management Practices in American and British Firms* (Oxford, Basil Blackwell, 1990).

Koestler, A.: *The Act of Creation* (London, Pan Books Ltd, 1964).

LaForet, Sylvie: 'Brand names on packaging and their impact on purchase preference', *Journal of Consumer Behaviour*, (Jan/Feb) **10** (1) (2011), pp. 18–30.

Lazarsfield, Paul F., Bertelson Bernard R. and Gaudet, Hazel: *The People's Choice* (New York, Columbia University Press, 1948).

Levitt, T.: *The Marketing Imagination* (New York, The Free Press, 1986).

Min, Sungwook, Kauwani, Manohar U. and Robinson, William T.: 'Market pioneer and early follower survival risks: a contingency analysis of really new vs. incrementally new products', *Journal of Marketing*, **70** (1) (2006), pp. 15–33.

Moore, Malcolm: 'Royal wedding: Chinese tailors rush to copy Kate Middleton's dress', *Daily Telegraph*, 30 April 2011.

Munnukka, Juha, and Jarvi, Pentti: 'The value drivers of high-tech consumer products', *Journal of Marketing Management*, **27** (5/6) (2011), pp. 582–601.

Muzellec, Laurent and Lambkin, Mary: 'Corporate rebranding: destroying, transferring or creating brand equity?' *European Journal of Marketing*, **40** (7/8) (2006), pp. 803–24.

Napoli, Julie: 'The impact of non-profit brand orientation on organizational performance', *Journal of Marketing Management*, **22** (7/8) (2006), pp. 673–94.

Pappu, Ravi, Quester, Pascale and Cooksey, Ray W.: 'Consumer-based brand equity and country of origin relationships', *European Journal of Marketing*, **40** (5/6) (2006), pp. 696–717.

Persson, Niklas: 'An exploratory investigation of the elements of B2B brand image and its relationship to price premium', *Industrial Marketing Management*, **39** (8) (2010), pp. 1269–77.

Png, J.P. and Reitman, D.: 'Why are some products branded and others not?' *Journal of Law and Economics*, **38** (1995), pp. 207–24.

Quelch, J. and Harding, D.: 'Brands versus private labels: fighting to win', *Harvard Business Review* (January–February 1995), pp. 99–109.

Raffee, H. and Kreutzer, R.: 'Organisational dimensions of global marketing', *European Journal of Marketing*, **23** (5) (1989), pp. 43–57.

Raghubir, Priya and Greenleaf, Eric A.: 'Ratios in proportion: what should the shape of the package be?' *Journal of Marketing*, **70** (2) (2006), pp. 95–107.

Ries, A.: 'What's in a name?' *Sales and Marketing Management* (October 1995), pp. 36–7.

Rogers, Everett M.: *Diffusion of Innovations* (New York, Macmillan, 1962).

Romaniuk, Jenni and Gaillard, Elise: 'The relationship between unique brand associations, brand usage and brand performance: analysis across eight categories', *Journal of Marketing Management*, **23** (3/4) (2007), pp. 267–84.

Roper, Stuart, and LaNiece, Caroline: 'The importance of brands in the lunch-box choices of low-income British schoolchildren', *Journal of Consumer Behaviour*, (Mar-Jun), **8** (2/3) (2009), pp. 84–9.

Ruttenberg, A., Kavizky, A. and Oren, H.: 'Compositioning – the paradigm-shift beyond positioning', *Journal of Brand Management* (December 1995), pp. 169–79.

Salciuviene, Laura, Ghauri, Pervez N., Streder, Ruth Salomea, and De Mattod, Claudio: 'Do brand names in a foreign language lead to different brand perceptions?' *Journal of Marketing Management*, **26** (11/12) (2010), pp. 1037–56.

Sandler, D. and Shani, D.: 'Brand globally but advertise locally? An empirical investigation', *Marketing Review* (1992), pp. 18–31.

Sorescu, Alina B., Chandy, Rajesh K. and Prabhu, Jaideep C.: 'Sources and financial consequences of radical innovation: insights from pharmaceuticals', *Journal of Marketing*, **67** (4) (October 2003), pp. 82–102.

Stoll, Marco, Baecke, Sebastian, and Kenning, Peter: 'What they see is what they get? An fMRI study on neural correlates of attractive packaging', *Journal of Consumer Behaviour*, (Jul-Oct) **7** (4/5) (2008), pp. 342–59.

Tajeddini, Kayhan, Trueman, Myfanwy and Larsen, Gretchen: 'Examining the effect of marketing orientation on innovativeness', *Journal of Marketing Management*, **22** (5/6) (2006), pp. 529–51.

Timmor, Yaron, and Katz-Navon, Tal: 'Being the same and different: a model explaining new product adoption', *Journal of Consumer Behaviour*, (May/Jun) **7** (3) (2008), pp.249–62.

Ubilava, David, Foster, Kenneth A., Lusk, Jayson L. and Nilsson, Tomas: 'Differences in consumer preferences when facing branded versus non-branded choices', *Journal of Consumer Behaviour*, (Mar/Apr) **10** (2) (2011), pp. 61–70.

Uncles, M., Cocks, M. and Macrae, C.: 'Brand architecture: reconfiguring organisations for effective brand management', *Journal of Brand Management* (October 1995), pp. 81–92.

Veblen, T.: *The Theory of the Leisure Class* (New York, Macmillan, 1899).

Volckner, Franziska and Sattler, Henrik: 'Drivers of brand extension success', *Journal of Marketing*, **70** (2) (2006), pp. 18–34.

Wang, Chih-Chien, Lo, Shao-Kang, and Fang, Wenchang: 'Extemding the technology acceptance model to mobile telecommunication innovation: the existence of network externalities', *Journal of Consumer Behaviour*, **7** (2) (2008), pp. 101–10.

7

PRICING STRATEGIES

Objectives

After reading this chapter you should be able to:

- Explain the advantages and disadvantages of different pricing methods
- Calculate prices using different approaches
- Choose the correct pricing strategy to fit a firm's overall objectives
- Explain some of the economic theories underlying the marketer's view of price and value.

INTRODUCTION

Pricing may not be exciting, but it is one of the most important issues for marketers; it is crucial not only to the profit that is to be made, but also to the quantity of the products that will be sold. It touches on all the other elements of the marketing mix because it clarifies the offer of exchange being made – it is the signal to the customer of what we expect in exchange for what we are offering. This chapter examines the different ways of pricing that are used and offers some ideas on how to choose a pricing strategy.

Pricing Strategies

Tata

Tata is India's largest industrial company, generating more than 3% of the country's gross national product. The company's motor division manufactures trucks, buses, scooters and three-wheel motor rickshaws. India is a large country, but most people are poor – in fact, too poor to own cars at all.

Tata's promise was to build a car for 1 lakh rupees (a lakh is 100,000). This price equates to around £1500, a price which the company thought was realistic for many Indians (although still out of reach of the poorest, many of whom would struggle to afford a bicycle).

Most major car manufacturers thought that this target was entirely unrealistic, given the cost of raw materials: even with the low wage structure of India, producing even a very small car for £1500 seemed out of the question. No matter how basic, the task seemed impossible.

The Tata Nano was eventually unveiled and, true to his promise, Ratan Tata, the company's chairman, put the car on the market for 1 lakh. The car has a 600 cc engine, continuous transmission (no gearbox or clutch), no passenger mirror, no radio and only one windscreen wiper. The car meets all safety standards for India, but might need adapting for Europe or the United States – but it is still a remarkable feat of engineering.

Ratan Tata, Chairman

Watch the video clip, then try to answer the following questions. The answers are on the companion website.

Questions

1. What type of pricing is Tata using for the Nano?
2. What should be the company's pricing policy for Europe?
3. Should the car meet the European safety standards?
4. What are the drawbacks of charging such a low price?

ECONOMIC THEORIES OF PRICING AND VALUE

Classical economists assumed that prices would automatically be set by the laws of *supply and demand*. Figure 7.1 shows how this works.

As prices rise, more suppliers find it profitable to enter the market, but the demand for the product falls because fewer customers think the product is worth the money. Conversely, as prices fall there is more demand, but fewer suppliers feel it is worthwhile supplying the product so less is produced. Eventually a state of equilibrium is reached where the quantity produced is equal to the quantity consumed, and at that point the price will be fixed.

Unfortunately, this neat model has a number of drawbacks.

- The model assumes that customers know where they can buy the cheapest products (i.e. it assumes perfect knowledge of the market)
- Second, it assumes that all the suppliers are producing identical products, which is rarely the case
- Third, it assumes that price is the only issue that affects customer behaviour, which is clearly not true
- Fourth, it assumes that customers always behave completely rationally, which, again, is substantially not the case
- Fifth, there is an assumption that people will always buy more of a product if it is cheaper. This is not true of such products as wedding rings or artificial limbs
- Finally, the model assumes that the suppliers are in perfect competition – that none of them has the power to 'rig' the market and set the prices (see Chapter 2).

Figure 7.1 Supply and demand

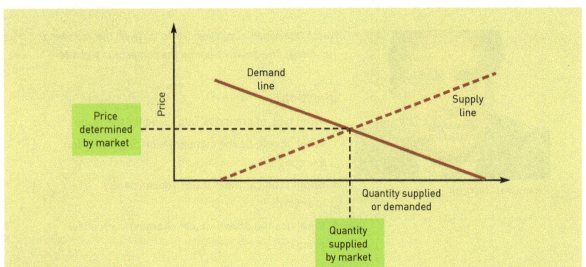

The model does, at least, take account of customers, and it was the pioneer economist Adam Smith who first said that 'the customer is king' (Smith 1776). Unfortunately, the shortcomings of the model mean that it has little practical use, no matter how helpful it is in understanding a principle. Economists have therefore added considerably to the theory.

Elasticity of demand

This concept states that different product categories will show different degrees of sensitivity to price change.

Figure 7.2(a) shows a product where the quantity sold is affected only slightly by price fluctuations, i.e. the demand is **inelastic**. An example of this is salt. Figure 7.2(b) shows a product where even a small difference in price leads to a very substantial shift in the quantity demanded, i.e. the demand is **elastic**. An example of this is borrowed money, e.g. mortgages, where even a small rise in interest rates appears to affect the propensity to borrow. Although these examples relate to consumers, the same is true for suppliers; in some cases suppliers can react very quickly to changes in the quantities demanded (for example, banking), whereas in other cases the suppliers need long lead times to change the production levels (for instance, farming).

The **price elasticity of demand** concept implies that there is no basis for defining products as necessities or luxuries. If a necessity is defined as something without which life cannot be sustained, then its demand curve would be entirely inelastic; whatever the price was, people would have to pay it. In practice, no such product exists.

Economic choice

Economists have demonstrated that there can never be enough resources in the world to satisfy everybody's wants, and therefore resources have to be allocated in

Figure 7.2 Price elasticity of demand

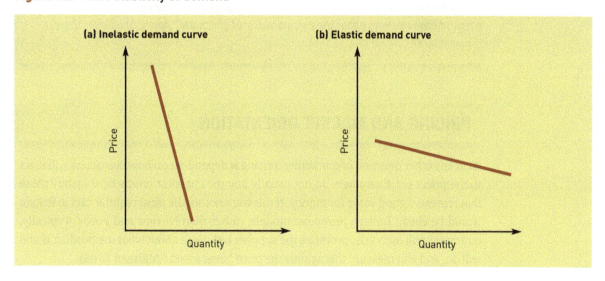

some way (which will probably mean an equality of dissatisfaction). Resources used for one purpose cannot, of course, be used for another; this is the concept of the **economic choice**.

For example, a clothing manufacturer has only a certain number of machinists who work a certain number of hours. This means that it may be possible to produce either 8000 shirts with the available resources or 4000 pairs of trousers. If the manufacturer has two orders, one for each type of product, he or she will have to choose which order to supply and disappoint the other customer.

From the customer's viewpoint, the economic choice means having to choose between going to the cinema or going to the pub; there may not be the time or the money to do both. Because of this, customers may also take into account the price of activities other than those the prospective supplier is providing; the pub, for example, may not be aware that the cinema is competition, and that a fall in the price of going to the cinema may affect the takings over the bar. In the UK in recent years, pubs have been closing down at an unprecedented rate, largely owing to the availability of cheap alcoholic drinks from supermarkets; many pubs have failed to recognise this as competition and counter it effectively.

Although the economists' view of pricing offers some interesting insights, there is little practical value in the theories offered because they do not take account of the consumer decision-making process (see Chapter 3). Consumers are not always rational; marketers are aware of this.

Critical thinking

Are we really that illogical when we buy things? It's a rather bleak comment on human beings – after all, we are the most intelligent creature so far discovered! If we don't use our brains to decide how to spend our hard-earned money, doesn't that imply that we don't use our brains much for anything else?

Of course, maybe we do think about things sometimes. If it's an important purchase or if we are short of money, we might make more effort – but who bothers to spend time thinking about the price of a bar of chocolate? Apart, of course, from marketers!

PRICING AND MARKET ORIENTATION

As in any other question of marketing, pricing is dependent on how customers will react to the prices set. Customers do not usually buy the cheapest products; they buy those that represent good value for money. If this were not so, the most popular cars in Britain would be cheap Eastern European models, rather than Nissans and Fords. Typically, customers will assess the promises the supplier has made about what the product is and will do, and will measure this against the price being asked (Zeithaml 1988).

This leaves the marketer with a problem. Marketers need to decide what price will be regarded by customers as good value for money, while still allowing the company to make a profit.

The main methods of pricing used by firms are cost-based, customer-based and competition-based.

Cost-based pricing

Cost-based methods are the least customer-orientated; two still used are **cost-plus pricing** and **mark-up pricing**.

Cost-plus pricing

Cost-plus pricing is commonly advocated by accountants and engineers, since it is simple to use and appears to guarantee that the company meets a predetermined profit target. The method works by calculating the cost of manufacturing the product, including distributed overhead costs and research and development costs, then adding on a fixed percentage profit to this figure to arrive at the price. Such a calculation might look like Table 7.1.

A variant of cost-plus pricing is absorption costing, which works by calculating the costs of each unit of production, including an allowance for overheads within the unit price. This allows the firm to calculate a break-even point at which further sales will be profitable.

On the face of it, this type of pricing seems logical and straightforward; unfortunately, it does not take account of how customers will react to the prices quoted. If customers take the view that the price does not represent value for money, they will not buy the product and the result will be that the company will have made 20,000 units of a product for which there will be no sales. Conversely, if customers take the view that the price is incredibly good value for money, the company may not have enough stocks on hand to meet demand and competitors will be able to enter the market easily (not to mention that the company could have charged more for the product and therefore made more money).

Table 7.1 Cost-plus pricing

Item	Cost per unit
Labour costs	£2.52
Raw materials	£4.32
Electricity	£0.27
Tooling costs (assuming production run of 20,000 units)	£1.78
Overheads	£3.43
Total production cost per unit	£12.32
Plus profit of 20%	£2.46
Net price	£14.78

Some government contracts are awarded on a cost-plus basis, but experience in the United States has shown that allowing cost-plus contracts to be granted will often result in the supplier inflating the costs to make an extra profit.

Mark-up pricing

Mark-up pricing is similar to cost-plus pricing, and is the method used by most retailers. Typically, a retailer will buy in stock and add on a fixed percentage to the bought-in price (a mark-up) to arrive at the **shelf price**. The level will vary from retailer to retailer, depending on the type of product; in some cases the mark-up will be 100% or more, in others it will be near zero (if the retailer feels that stocking the product will stimulate other sales). Usually there is a standard mark-up for each product category.

Here the difference needs to be shown between a **mark-up** and a **margin**. Mark-up is calculated on the price the retailer pays for the product; margin is calculated on the price the retailer sells for. This means that a 100% mark-up equals a 50% margin; a 25% mark-up equals a 20% margin (Table 7.2).

Retailers use this method because of the number of lines the shop may be carrying. For a hypermarket, this could be up to 20,000 separate lines, and it would clearly be impossible to carry out market research with the customers for every line. The buyers therefore use their training and knowledge of their customer base to determine which lines to stock and (to some extent) rely on the manufacturers to carry out formal market research and determine the recommended retail prices.

This method is identical to the cost-plus method except for two factors; first, the retailer is usually in close contact with the customers and can therefore develop a good 'feel' for what customers will be prepared to pay; second, retailers have ways of disposing of unsold stock. In some cases, this will mean discounting the stock back to cost and selling it in the January sales; in other cases, the retailer will have a sale-or-return agreement with the manufacturer so that unsold stock can be returned for credit. This is becoming increasingly common with major retailers such as Toys 'R' Us who have sufficient 'clout' in the market to enforce such agreements. In a sense, therefore, the retailer is carrying out market research by test-marketing the product; if the customers do not accept the product at the price offered, the retailer can drop the price to a point that will represent value for money or can return it to the manufacturer for credit.

Table 7.2 Mark-up *v* margin

Bought-in price	£4.00
Mark-up at 25% of £4.00	£1.00
Price on the shelf	£5.00
Margin of 20% of £5.00	£1.00
Bought-in price	£4.00

Customer-based pricing methods

The various approaches to *customer-based pricing* do not necessarily mean offering products at the lowest possible price, but they do take account of customer needs and wants.

Customary pricing

Customary pricing is customer-orientated in that it provides the customer with the product for the same price at which it has always been offered. An example is the price of a call from a coin-operated telephone box. Telephone companies need only reduce the time allowed for the call as costs rise. For some countries (e.g. Australia) this is problematical since local calls are allowed unlimited time, but for most European countries this is not the case.

The reason for using customary pricing is to avoid having to reset the call-boxes too often. Similar methods exist for taxis, some children's sweets and gas or electricity pre-payment meters. If this method were to be used for most products there would be a steady reduction in the firm's profits as the costs caught up with the selling price, so the method is not practical for every firm.

Demand pricing

Demand pricing is the most market-orientated method of pricing. Here, the marketer begins by assessing what the demand will be for the product at different price levels. This is usually done by asking the customers what they might expect to pay for the product and seeing how many choose each price level. This will lead to the development of the kind of chart shown in Table 7.3.

As the price rises, fewer customers are prepared to buy the product, as fewer will still see the product as good value for money. In the example given in Table 7.3, the fall-off is not linear, i.e. the number of units sold falls dramatically once the price goes above £5. This kind of calculation could be used to determine the stages of a skimming policy (see below) or it could be used to calculate the appropriate launch price of a product.

For demand pricing, the next stage is to calculate the costs of producing the product in the given quantities. Usually the cost of producing each item falls as more are made (i.e. if we make 50,000 units, each unit costs less than would be the case if

Table 7.3 Demand pricing

Price per unit	Number of customers who said they would buy at this price
£3 to £4	30,000
£4 to £5	25,000
£5 to £6	15,000
£6 to £7	5000

Table 7.4 Costings for demand pricing

Number of units	Unit cost (labour and materials)	Tooling-up and fixed costs	Net cost per unit
30,000	£1.20	£4000	£1.33
25,000	£1.32	£4000	£1.48
15,000	£1.54	£4000	£1.81
5000	£1.97	£4000	£2.77

we made only 1000 units). Given the costs of production, it is possible to select the price that will lead to a maximisation of profits. This is because there is a trade-off between quantity produced and quantity sold; as the firm lowers the selling price, the amount sold increases but the income generated decreases.

The calculations can become complex, but the end result is that the product is sold at a price that customers will accept and that will meet the company's profit targets. Table 7.4 shows an example of costings to match up with the above figures. The tooling-up cost is the amount it will cost the company to prepare for producing the item. This will be the same whether 1000 or 30,000 units are made.

Table 7.5 shows how much profit could be made at each price level. The price at which the product is sold will depend on the firm's overall objectives; these may not necessarily be to maximise profit on this one product, since the firm may have other products in the range or other long-term objectives that preclude maximising profits at present.

Based on these figures, *the most profitable* price will be £4.50. Other ways of calculating the price could easily lead to making a lower profit from this product. For instance, the price that would generate *the highest profit per unit* would be £6.50, but at this price they would sell only 5000 units and make £18,650. The price that would generate *the highest sales* would be £3.50, but this would (in effect) lose the firm almost £10,000 in terms of foregone profit.

A further useful concept is that of *contribution*. Contribution is calculated as the difference between the cost of manufacture and the price for which the product is sold – in other words, it does not take account of overheads. Sometimes a product

Table 7.5 Profitability at different price bands

Number of units sold	Net profit per unit	Total profit for production run	Percentage profit per unit
30,000	£2.17	£65,100	62
25,000	£3.02	£75,500	67
15,000	£3.61	£54,150	66
5000	£3.73	£18,650	57

is worth producing because it makes a significant extra contribution to the firm's profits without actually adding to the overheads. It is not difficult to imagine a situation where a product carries a low profit margin and is therefore unable to support a share of the overheads, but is still worth producing (perhaps because it supports sales of something else or is bought by our most loyal customers). A calculation which included an overall share of the overheads might not give a fair picture, since the contribution would be additional to existing turnover.

Demand pricing works by knowing what the customers are prepared to pay and what they will see as value for money.

Product-line pricing

Product-line pricing means setting prices within linked product groups. Often sales of one product will be directly linked to the sales of another, so that it is possible to sell one item at a low price to make a greater profit on the other one. Gillette sells its razors at a very low price, with the aim of making up the profit on sales of the blades. In the long run, this is a good strategy because it overcomes the initial resistance of consumers towards buying something untried, but allows the firm to show high profits for years to come (incidentally, this approach was first used by King C. Gillette, the inventor of the disposable safety razor blade).

Polaroid chose to sell its instant cameras very cheaply (almost for cost price) for the US market and to take their profit from selling the films for a much higher price. For Europe, the firm chose to sell both films and cameras for a medium level price and profit from sales of both. Eventually this led Kodak to enter the market with its own instant camera, but this was withdrawn from sale in the face of lawsuits from Polaroid for patent infringement.

Skimming

Skimming is the practice of starting out with a high price for a product, then reducing it progressively as sales level off. It relies on two main factors: first, that not all customers have the same perception of value for money and, second, that the company has a technological lead over the opposition which can be maintained for long enough to satisfy the market.

Skimming is usually carried out by firms which have developed a technically advanced product. Initially the firm will charge a high price for the product, and at this point only those who are prepared to pay a premium price for it will buy. Profit may not be high, because the number of units sold will be low and therefore the cost of production per unit will be high. Once the most innovative customers have bought and the competition is beginning to enter the market, the firm can drop the price and 'skim' the next layer of the market, at which point profits will begin to rise. Eventually, the product will be sold at a price that allows the firm only a minimum profit, at which point only replacement sales or sales to late adopters will be made.

The advantage of this method is that the cost of developing the product is returned fairly quickly, so that the product can later be sold near the marginal cost of production. This means that the competitors have difficulty entering the market at all, since their own development costs will have to be recovered in some other way.

Skimming is commonly used in consumer electronics markets. This is because firms frequently establish a technological lead over the competitors and can sometimes even protect their products by taking out patents, which take some time for competitors to overcome. An example of this is the MP3 player, which sold at a premium price when it was first launched. As competitors entered the market with cloned products, the price dropped dramatically. Research shows that customers are aware of skimming in electronics markets and are delaying purchases of new electronic devices until the prices drop. This may affect the way firms view skimming in the future.

Skimming requires careful judgement of what is happening in the marketplace, in terms both of observing customer behaviour and of observing competitive response. Market research is therefore basic to the success of a skimming policy, and very careful monitoring of sales is needed to know when to cut the price again.

Critical thinking

Skimming seems like a bit of a cheat. The firm makes the product for a low price, then sells it at a high price, knowing that the price is going to fall later. Isn't this a bit like cheating the first few customers by overcharging them?

Or maybe they are enjoying the fun of being the first to own the product and the firm is making them pay for the privilege. It seems an expensive bit of fun to have, though – and anyway, people know about skimming.

On the other hand, of course, firms are not in business for the fun of it. They are entitled to make a profit, and of course recover the rather expensive research and development costs they incur in producing new products for us!

Psychological pricing

Psychological pricing relies on emotional responses from the consumer. Higher prices are often used as an indicator of quality (Erickson and Johansson 1985), so some firms will use **prestige pricing**. This applies in many service industries, because consumers are often buying a promise; a service that does not have a high enough quality cannot be exchanged afterwards. Consumers' expectations of high-priced restaurants and hairdressers are clearly higher in terms of the quality of service provision; cutting prices in those industries does not necessarily lead to an increase in business. Interestingly, there is evidence that the price–quality relationship was affected considerably in Germany by the introduction of the euro. Prices previously expressed in Deutschmarks appeared higher than the new price in euros because there were approximately two euros to the Deutschmark – people's perception was that the price had 'halved' which lowered their expectations of quality (Molz and Gielnik 2006).

Odd–even pricing is the practice of ending prices with an odd number, for example £3.99 or $5.95 rather than £4 or $6. It appears that consumers tend to categorise these prices as '£3 and a bit' or '$5 and change' and thus perceive the price as being lower. The effect may also be due to an association with discounted or sale prices; researchers report that '99' endings on prices increase sales by around 8% (Schindler and Kirby 1997). Paradoxically, some recent research shows that people are more likely to try a new product for the first time if the price is a round number (Bray and Harris 2006).

This apparent discrepancy may be due to cultural differences. Research has shown that odd–even pricing does not necessarily work in all cultures (Suri *et al*. 2004). In Poland, for example, the effects are negligible. Odd–even pricing also has effects on perceptions of discounts during sales. Rounding the price to (say) £5 from £4.99 leads people to overvalue the size of the discount, which increases the perception of value for money (Gueguen and Legoherel 2004). Thus the positive effect on sales of using a 99-ending can be negated by the effect when the product is on offer in a sale.

Another effect of discounting can arise when retailers set upper or lower purchase requirements on discounted prices. A retailer offering a discount for buying more of a product (for example, 10% off for buying at least three items) leads people to want to buy more of the product than they had intended, whereas with a discount which has an upper limit (10% off, limited to two items per customer), people tend to want to buy less of the product than they had intended (Yoon and Vargas 2011). This response seems almost perverse, but it certainly shows which type of discount a retailer should use.

Second-market discounting

Second-market discounting is common in some service industries and in international markets. The brand is sold at one price in one market and at a lower price in another; for example, museums offer discounts to students, some restaurants offer discounts to elderly people on week-nights, and so forth. Often these discounts are offered to even out the **loading** on the firm; week-night discounts fill the restaurant on what would otherwise be a quiet night, so the firm makes more efficient use of the premises and staff.

In international markets, products might be discounted to meet local competition. For example, Honda motorcycles are up against strong local competition in India from Royal Enfield, so the price of their basic 100-cc motorcycle is around Rs39,000 (about £600). A similar Honda motorcycle in the UK costs around £2000. The specifications of the motorcycles do differ somewhat, and the import duty structures are different – however, it is difficult to see any difference that would account for a £1400 price differential.

Competitor-based pricing

Competitor-based pricing recognises the influence of competition in the marketplace. Strategically, the marketer must decide how close the competition is in providing for the consumers' needs; if the products are close, then prices will need to be similar to those of the competition. A **meet-the-competition strategy**

has the advantage of avoiding price wars and stimulating competition in other areas of marketing, thus maintaining profitability. An **undercut-the-competition strategy** is often the main plank in the firm's marketing strategy; it is particularly common among retailers, who have relatively little control over product features and benefits and often have little control over the promotion of the products they stock. Some multinational firms (particularly in electronics) have the capacity to undercut rivals since they are able to manufacture in low-wage areas of the world or are large enough to use widespread automation. There is a danger of starting price wars when using an undercutting policy (see penetration pricing below). Undercutting (and consequent price wars) may be becoming more common (Mitchell 1996).

Firms with large market shares often have enough control over their distribution systems and the production capacity within their industries to become **price leaders**. Typically, such firms can make price adjustments without starting price wars and can raise prices without losing substantial market share (see Chapter 2 for monopolistic competition) (Rich 1982). Sometimes these price leaders become sensitive to the price and profit needs of their competitors, in effect supporting them, because they do not wish to attract the attention of monopoly regulators by destroying the competition. Deliberate price fixing (managers colluding to set industry prices) is illegal in most countries.

Penetration pricing

Penetration pricing is used when the firm wants to capture a large part of the market quickly. It relies on the assumption that a lower price will be perceived as offering better value for money (which is, of course, often the case).

For penetration pricing to work, the company must have carried out thorough research to find out what the competitors are charging for the nearest similar product. The new product is then sold at a substantially lower price, even if this cuts profits below an acceptable level; the intention is to capture the market quickly before the competitors can react with even lower prices. The danger with this pricing method is that competitors may be able to sustain a price war for a long period and will eventually bankrupt the incoming firm. It is usually safer to compete on some other aspect of the offering, such as quality or delivery.

Predatory pricing

In some cases, prices are pitched below the cost of production. The purpose of this is to bankrupt the competition so that the new entrant can take over entirely; this practice is called **predatory pricing** and (at least in international markets) is illegal. Predatory pricing was successfully used by Japanese car manufacturers when entering European markets in the 1970s, and is commonly used by large firms who are entering new markets. For the strategy to be successful, it is necessary for the market to be dominated by firms that cannot sustain a long price war. It is worth doing if the company has no other competitive edge, but does have sufficient financial reserves to hold out for a long time. Naturally, this method is customer-orientated since it can work only by providing the customers with very much better value for money than they have been used to. The company will eventually raise prices again to recoup the lost profits once the market presence has been established, however.

The ultimate in predatory pricing is dumping. This is the practice of selling goods at prices below the cost of manufacture and was at one time commonly practised by Communist countries desperate for hard currency. Dumping is illegal under international trade rules, but is difficult to prove, and by the time the victim countries have been able to prove their case and have the practice stopped, it is usually too late.

Competitor-based pricing is still customer-orientated to an extent, since it takes as its starting point the prices that customers are currently prepared to pay.

SETTING PRICES

Price setting follows eight stages, as shown in Table 7.6.

Price setting can be complex if it is difficult to identify the closest competitors, but it should be borne in mind that no product is entirely without competition; there is almost always another way in which customers can meet the need supplied by the product. Also, different customers have different needs and therefore will have differing views on what constitutes value for money – this is why markets need to be segmented carefully to ensure that the right price is being charged in each segment. As in any question of marketing, it is wise to begin with the customer.

Table 7.6 Eight stages of price setting

Stage	Explanation
Development of pricing objectives	The pricing objectives derive from the organisation's overall objectives; does the firm seek to maximise market share or maximise profits?
Assessment of the target market's ability to purchase and evaluation of price	Buyers tend to be more sensitive to food prices in supermarkets than to drinks prices in clubs. Also, a buyer's income and availability of credit directly affect the ability to buy the product at all.
Determination of demand	For most products demand falls as price rises. This is not necessarily a straight-line relationship, nor is the line necessarily at 45 degrees; for some products even a small price rise results in a sharp fall in demand (e.g. petrol), whereas for other products (e.g. salt) even a large price rise hardly affects demand at all.
Analysis of demand, cost and profit relationships	The firm needs to analyse the costs of producing the item against the price that the market will bear, taking into account the profit needed. The cost calculation will include both the fixed costs and the unit costs for making a given quantity of the product; this quantity will be determined by the market and will relate to the selling price.

continued

Table 7.6 continued

Stage	Explanation
Evaluation of competitors' prices	This will involve a survey of the prices currently being charged, but will also have to consider the possible entry of new competitors. Prices may be pitched higher than those of competitors to give an impression of exclusivity or higher quality; this is common in the perfume market and in services such as restaurants and hairdressing.
Selection of a pricing policy	The pricing policy needs to be chosen from the list given in the early part of the chapter.
Development of a pricing method	Here the producer develops a simple mechanism for determining prices in the future. The simplest method is to use cost-plus or mark-up pricing; these do not take account of customers, however, so something a little more sophisticated should be used if possible.
Determining a specific price	If the previous steps have been carried out in a thorough manner, determining the actual price should be a simple matter.

Source: Adapted from Dibb et al. 1994.

CASE STUDY 7 Grey markets

A grey market is one in which goods are sold which, although not illegal, are distributed through channels the manufacturer did not intend, usually for lower prices. Grey markets have grown up because of differential pricing – the practice of pricing the same goods at different prices for different markets.

In 2002, Levi Strauss obtained an injunction against Tesco's supermarket in the UK preventing them from establishing a grey market for jeans. Tesco's had been importing Levi's jeans from Eastern Europe, where they were being sold at lower prices than could be obtained in the UK. Levi claimed that Tesco's were damaging their brand image by such drastic undercutting, and the judge agreed – meaning that Tesco's had to withdraw the product. This was, according to Tesco's spokespeople, a sad day for consumers.

A similar market was created for the Apple iPhone. Apple launched the phone in New York, amid a blaze of publicity, and planned on rolling out the launch across the world in easy stages. The aim was to ensure that the production could match the demand. This time, though, the price went up: middlemen bought up thousands of the phones and sold them at premium prices in other countries.

Sometimes the grey market is created because the manufacturer knows that the product cannot sell for the same price in markets where the incomes and wealth levels are very different. At other times, the market comes about because of limited supplies of the product. In still other cases, the market comes about because of rights restrictions. This is the case in the broadcasting market. For example, Sky Digital is a satellite service which is only available to subscribers in the UK and Ireland for copyright reasons. In countries where there is a large expatriate population of British and Irish people, cards for decoding Sky are widely used, even though this breaches Sky's agreements with its suppliers of programmes. Sky has the technology to disable the cards and does not condone their use, but it is extremely difficult to catch the people using the cards. Equally, Canadians who wish to access some American satellite services can buy 'bootleg' decoders.

The problem for producers is serious. A carefully laid strategic plan can be completely undermined by the grey marketers – and in some cases profits can be eaten away dramatically as products cannot be sold at the intended price. On the other hand, for consumers the grey market seems to be fairer. After all, why should someone have to pay more for goods simply because he or she lives in a particular place? Or be unable to buy something that other people are able to buy?

Questions

1 How might companies counteract the grey market?
2 What makes grey markets attractive to firms?
3 Why might consumers find that the grey market is not as beneficial as it at first appears?
4 What might be the role of governments in controlling grey markets?
5 What are the dangers for broadcasters should they simply ignore the grey market?

SUMMARY

Value for money is a subjective concept; each person has a differing view of what represents value for money, and this means that different market segments will have differing views on whether a given price is appropriate. Marketing is about encouraging trade so that customers and manufacturers can maximise the satisfaction gained from their activities; to this end, marketers always try to make exchanges easier and pleasanter for customers.

Here are the key points from this chapter:

- Prices, ultimately, are fixed by market forces, not by suppliers alone. Therefore suppliers would be ill-advised to ignore the customer
- There is no objective difference between necessities and luxuries; the distinction lies only in the mind of the customer
- Customers cannot spend the same money twice, so they are forced to make economic choices. A decision to do one thing implies a decision not to do another
- Customers have a broad and sometimes surprising range of choices when seeking to maximise utility
- Pricing can be cost-based, competition-based or customer-based; ultimately, though, consumers have the last word because they can simply spend their money elsewhere.

CHAPTER QUESTIONS

1 What is the difference between margin and mark-up?
2 When should a skimming policy be used?
3 How can penetration pricing be used in international markets?
4 Why should a firm be wary of cost-plus pricing?
5 How does customary pricing benefit the supplier?

Further reading

For a fairly readable text on the economic aspects of pricing, **Richard Lipsey and Alec Chrystal's** *Economics*, **12th edn** (Oxford, Oxford University Press, 2011) is worth looking at.

Len Rogers' *Pricing for Profit* (Oxford, Basil Blackwell, 1990) is a practitioner-style book which contains a very comprehensive 'how-to' guide to pricing.

References

Bray, Jeffrey Paul and Harris, Christine: 'The effect of 9-ending prices on retail sales: a quantitative UK-based field study', *Journal of Marketing Management*, 22 (5/6) (2006), pp. 601–7.

Dibb, S., Simkin, L., Pride, W. and Ferrell, O.C.: *Marketing; Concepts and Strategies*, 2nd edn (London, Houghton Mifflin, 1994).

Erickson, G.M. and Johansson, J.K.: 'The role of price in multi-attribute product evaluation', *Journal of Consumer Research*, 12 (1985), pp. 195–9.

Gueguen, Nicolas and Legoherel, Patrick: 'Numerical encoding and odd-ending prices: The effect of a contrast in discount perception', *European Journal of Marketing*, 38 (1) (2004), pp. 194–208.

Mitchell, A.: 'The price is right', *Marketing Business*, 50 (May 1996), pp. 32–4.

Molz, Gunter and Gielnik, Michael: 'Does the introduction of the Euro have an effect on subjective hypotheses about the price-quality relationship?' *Journal of Consumer Behaviour*, 5 (3) (2006), pp. 204–10.

Rich, Stuart A.: 'Price leaders: large, strong, but cautious about conspiracy', *Marketing News* (25 June 1982), p. 11.

Schindler, R.M. and Kirby, P.N.: 'Patterns of right-most digits used in advertised prices: implications for nine-ending effects', *Journal of Consumer Research* (September 1997), pp. 192–201.

Smith, Adam: *An Inquiry into The Wealth of Nations* (1776).

Suri, Rajneesh, Anderson, Rolph E. and Kotlov, Vassili: 'The use of 9-ending prices: contrasting the USA with Poland', *European Journal of Marketing*, 38 (1) (2004), pp. 56–72.

Yoon, Sukki, and Vargas, Patrick: 'More leads to "Want more" but "No less" leads to "Want less": Consumers' counterfactual thinking when faced with quantity restriction discounts', *Journal of Consumer Behaviour*, Mar/Apr, 10 (2) (2011), pp. 93–101.

Zeithaml, Valerie A.: 'Consumer perceptions of price, quality and value', *Journal of Marketing*, 52 (July 1988), pp. 2–22.

DISTRIBUTION

Objectives

After reading this chapter you should be able to:

- Understand the role of distribution as providing an integral part of the product's benefits
- Explain the way agents, wholesalers and retailers work in the distribution system
- Choose the best distribution channel for a given market segment and product
- Explain some of the challenges facing retailers
- Know what to expect of different types of wholesaler
- Understand the difference between logistics and distribution.

INTRODUCTION

Producing something that consumers would like to buy is only part of the story; people can only buy products that are available and easily obtained. In terms of the seven Ps, distribution is the means by which place is determined. Marketers therefore spend considerable effort on finding the right channels of distribution and on ensuring that the products reach consumers in the most efficient way.

In business-to-business marketing, distribution is often the real key to success. Business buyers may buy through agents or wholesalers rather than direct from producers, so that tapping into a good distribution network is the most important step a company can take.

Distribution

Friday's

Friday's is a family business in the egg-producing business. Although the company produces foods other than eggs, fresh egg production and selling is the core of the business. The company has grown from a small chicken farm: it produces 4 billion eggs a year, which is about 6% of the UK market. Sixty per cent of the eggs are produced intensively, but free-range and barn eggs are also sold. Most of the eggs are sold under the supermarkets' own brands: the company is happy to help the supermarkets to brand the eggs appropriately. About 40% of the free-range eggs produced in Europe are produced in the UK.

Eggs are labelled with the Red Lion mark, which indicates that the eggs are British and the chickens are vaccinated against diseases such as salmonella. The lion mark was originally used in the 1950s and 1960s but fell out of use. Consumer confidence was shaken in the 1980s by a salmonella scare, but the brand has now been re-established via a series of TV advertisements.

Friday's is a price taker rather than a price maker: either the supermarkets set the price or prices are set by supply and demand. Feed prices create a problem for producers – consumers have already moved away from organic eggs due to the cost and clearly supermarkets are driven by what consumers are prepared (or able) to pay.

Distribution is a problem with such a fragile and perishable commodity. Friday's seek to minimise the distance from farm to retailer, and are the only egg producer able to deliver local eggs in the south east of Britain.

David Friday, Managing Director

Watch the video clip, then try to answer the following questions. The answers are on the companion website.

Questions

1 What are the main logistical problems for Friday's?
2 Why do Friday's distribute mainly through supermarkets?
3 Why does the company produce a mix of free-range and intensively farmed eggs?

LOGISTICS v DISTRIBUTION

Physical distribution is concerned with the ways organisations position physical products at a point where it is most convenient for consumers to buy them. *Logistics* takes a wider view; originally based on military terminology, logistics is concerned with the process of moving raw materials through the production and distribution processes to the point at which the finished product is needed. This involves strategic decision-making about warehouse location, materials management, stock levels and information systems. Logistics is the area in which purchasing and marketing overlap.

In some ways the physical distribution of a product is part of the bundle of benefits that make up that product. For example, a jacket bought online offers convenience benefits which a chain-store jacket does not. Conversely, the chain-store purchase may include hedonic benefits (the fun of shopping around, the excitement of finding a real bargain), which the Internet retailer does not supply. Even when the actual jacket is identical, the benefits derived from the distribution method are different.

The purpose of any physical distribution method is to get the product from its point of production to the consumer efficiently and effectively. The product must arrive in good condition and fit the consumer's need for convenience, or cheapness, or choice, or whatever else the particular target market thinks is important. Thus, from a marketing viewpoint, the subject of distribution covers such areas as transportation methods, wholesaling, high street retailing, direct mail marketing and even farm-gate shops.

Physical distribution is to do with transportation methods; **distribution strategy** decisions are about which outlets should be used for the product.

Transportation methods

Transportation methods vary according to speed, cost and ability to handle the type of product concerned. As a general rule, the quicker the method the more expensive it is, but in some cases it may be cheaper to use a faster method because the firm's capital is tied up for less time. The same applies to perishable items.

The transportation method chosen for a particular product will depend on the factors listed in Table 8.1. In all these cases, there will be trade-offs involved. Greater customer service will almost always be more expensive; greater reliability may increase transit time, as will greater traceability because in most cases the product will need to be checked on and off the transport method chosen. As with any other aspect of marketing activity, the customer's overall needs must be taken into account, and the relative importance of those needs must be judged with some accuracy if the firm is to remain competitive.

Distribution channels

Transportation method is also affected by the **channel of distribution**, or marketing channel. Figure 8.1 shows some of the possible channels of distribution that a consumer product might go through.

Table 8.1 Choosing a transportation method

Factor	Explanation and examples
The physical characteristics of the product	If the product is fragile (e.g. sheet glass), distribution channels need to be short and handling minimised. For perishable goods (e.g. fruit), it may be cheaper to use **standby airfreight** than to ship by sea, because there will be less spoilage en route.
The methods used by the competition	It is often possible to gain a significant competitive edge by using a method which is out of the ordinary. For example, most inner-city courier companies use motorbikes to deliver urgent documents, but a few use bicycles. In heavy traffic bicycles are often quicker and can sometimes use routes that are not open to powered vehicles, so deliveries are quicker.
The costs of the various channels available	The cheapest is not always the best; for example, computer chips are light, but costly, and therefore it is cheaper to use airfreight than to tie up the company's capital in lengthy surface transportation.
The reliability of the channel	Emergency medical supplies must have 100% reliable transportation, as must cash deliveries.
The transit time	This also applies to fruit and computer chips.
Security	Highly valuable items may not be easily distributed through retailers. Direct delivery may work much better.
Traceability	The ease with which a shipment can be located or redirected. For example, oil tankers can be diverted to deliver to different refineries at relatively short notice. This allows the oil companies to meet demand in different countries.
The level of customer service required	Customers may need the product to be delivered in exact timings (for example, in just-in-time manufacturing). The Meals on Wheels service is another example; it is essential that deliveries are 100% reliable.

Source: Adapted from *The Management of Business Logistics*, 4th edn, by Coyle, Bardi and Langley. © 1988 South-Western, a part of Cengage Learning, Inc. Reproduced by permission. www.cengage.com/permissions

Products are rarely delivered directly from producer to consumer, but instead pass through the hands of wholesalers, agents, factors or other middle men. For example, it is hardly likely to be very efficient for a tuna importer to deliver directly to every small grocery business in the country. (It would be even less efficient to deliver to each consumer.) The importer will probably employ an **agent** (who will be working for several manufacturers) to take orders from wholesalers. The importer will bulk-deliver the tuna to the **wholesalers**, who will then break the delivery down to send out to the **retailers**. The wholesaler will either deliver to the retailers along with the products of many other importers and manufacturers or will offer a cash-and-carry service so that the retailers can make all their supply purchases in one trip. The net result is a great saving in time since the trucks are not going perhaps hundreds of miles with one case of tuna on board.

Figure 8.1 Channels of distribution

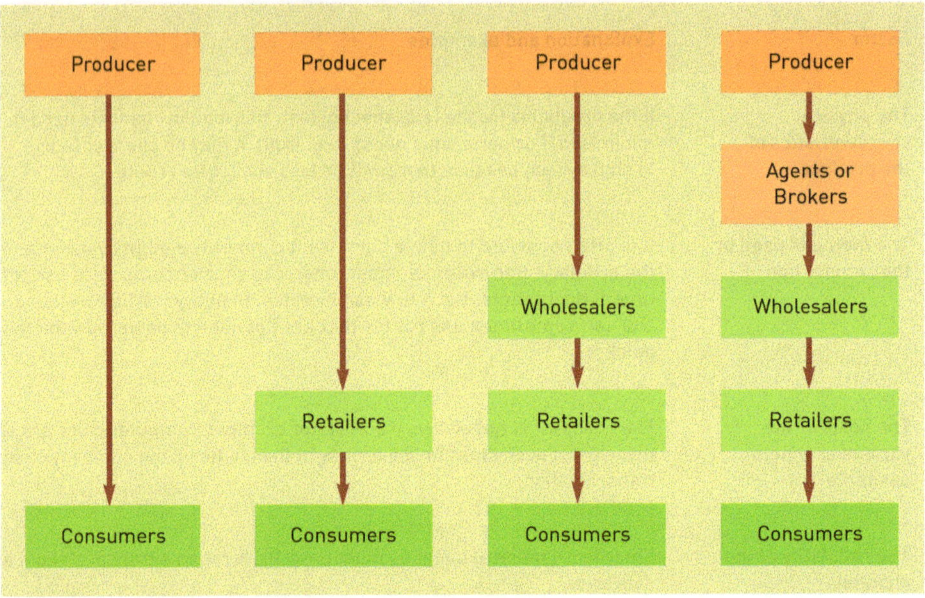

```
Producer          Producer          Producer          Producer
   │                 │                 │                 │
   │                 │                 │                 ▼
   │                 │                 │           Agents or
   │                 │                 │            Brokers
   │                 │                 │                 │
   │                 │                 ▼                 ▼
   │                 │           Wholesalers       Wholesalers
   │                 │                 │                 │
   │                 ▼                 ▼                 ▼
   │            Retailers         Retailers         Retailers
   │                 │                 │                 │
   ▼                 ▼                 ▼                 ▼
Consumers        Consumers         Consumers         Consumers
```

Source: Dibb et al. 1998

In fact, food frequently passes through lengthy and complex distribution systems. Each intermediary in the process performs a useful function, increasing the efficiency of the exchanges. Table 8.2 shows some of the functions carried out by intermediaries.

Table 8.2 Functions of channel members

Function	Explanation
Sorting out	Separating out heterogeneous deliveries into homogeneous ones. For example, sorting a tomato crop into those suitable for retail sale and those suitable only for juice production.
Accumulation	Aggregating small production batches into amounts big enough to be worth shipping. Forwarding agents will arrange for small exporters to share a container, for example.
Allocation	Breaking down large shipments into smaller amounts. A wholesaler receiving a truckload of baked beans will sell them on a case at a time. This is also called bulk breaking.
Assorting	Combining collections of products that will appeal to groups of buyers. For example, clothes shops stock clothes from many manufacturers; food cash-and-carry wholesalers will specialise in all the products needed by caterers and grocers, including shop signs and plastic knives and forks.

'Cutting out the middle man' is popularly supposed to be a way of buying things cheaper. In fact, for most products where agents and wholesalers are used, the savings made by greater efficiency more than cover the cost of the extra mark-up on the product. This means that cutting out the middle man is more likely to increase the cost of the product.

Critical thinking

If cutting out the middle man is such a bad idea, why do companies often advertise it as if it's an advantage? And if it reduces efficiency, why have so many developed interactive websites so that people can order online?

Is it actually cheaper to order online (taking account of delivery costs) or is it more about convenience? And how convenient is it, in fact, when one may have to visit several websites to buy items which are available in one convenient retail store – why not just stop on the way home from work and browse?

Perhaps it depends on one's personal circumstances!

Direct producer-to-consumer channels are typical of personal services such as hairdressing, where use of intermediaries would be impossible, and of major capital purchases such as houses or home improvements. This is because these products cannot be broken down into smaller units, or assorted, or accumulated. There is therefore no function for the middle men to fulfil.

If the distribution network is efficiently managed, goods come down the channel and information goes up. Retailers can feed back information about what consumers need, either *formally* (by carrying out a monitoring exercise and passing the information to the manufacturer or wholesaler) or *informally* (since retailers order only what is selling, producers can infer what is required by the consumers). A good salesperson will also act as an information channel and will find out from the retailers what they think consumers want, as well as convey information from the manufacturers to the retailer.

Major manufacturers often have several distribution channels, catering for different market segments. Food processing firms will usually have separate channels for caterers and for retailers, car manufacturers may deal directly with large fleet operators rather than operating through their retail dealer network and electronics manufacturers may have one channel for consumer products and another for defence products.

Table 8.3 shows the functions of some of the members of a channel of distribution.

Table 8.3 Categories of channel members

Channel member	Function
Agents	Agents usually act purely as a sales arm for the manufacturer, without actually buying the products. The agent never takes title to the goods; agency sales representatives call on major retailers and on wholesalers on behalf of a number of manufacturers, and take orders and arrange delivery. This saves the manufacturer the cost of operating a large salesforce to carry perhaps only a small product range.
Wholesalers	Wholesalers actually buy the goods from the manufacturers, often through an agent, then sell the goods on to the retailers or sometimes the final consumers.
Retailers	A retailer is any organisation that offers goods directly to consumers. This includes mail order companies, door-to-door salespeople and e-commerce organisations selling over the Internet.

WHOLESALERS

Wholesalers carry out the following functions:

- Negotiate with suppliers
- Some promotional activities: advertising, sales promotion, publicity, providing a salesforce
- Warehousing, storage and product handling
- Transport of local and sometimes long-distance shipments
- Inventory control
- Credit checking and credit control
- Pricing and collection of pricing information, particularly about competitors
- Channel of information up and down the distribution network, again particularly with regard to competitors' activities.

All of these functions would have to be carried out by each manufacturer individually if the wholesaler did not exist; by carrying them out on behalf of many manufacturers the wholesaler achieves economies of scale which more than cover the profit taken.

The wholesaler also provides services to the retailers, as follows:

- Information gathering and dissemination
- One-stop shopping for a wide range of products from a wide range of manufacturers

- Facilities for buying relatively small quantities
- Fast deliveries – often cash-and-carry
- Flexible ordering – can vary amounts as demand fluctuates.

Again, from the retailer's viewpoint it is much more convenient and cheaper to use a wholesaler. Only if the retailer is big enough to order economic quantities direct from the manufacturer will it be worthwhile to do so. For example, few hairdressers are big enough to order everything direct from the manufacturers, so a large part of a salon's stock-in-trade is bought from wholesalers.

There are many different types of wholesalers:

- **Merchant wholesalers** buy in goods and sell directly to the retailers, usually delivering the goods and having a salesforce calling on retailers in their area.
- **Full-service merchant wholesalers** provide a very wide range of marketing services for retailers, including shop design, sales promotion deals, advertising (sometimes nationally), coupon redemption, own-brand products and so forth. A good example is Spar, the grocery wholesaler, which supplies corner shops throughout the UK and parts of the rest of Europe. The shops carry the Spar logo and stock Spar's own-brand products, but each shop is individually owned and managed.
- **General-merchandise wholesalers** carry a wide product mix, but little depth, dealing mainly with small grocery shops and general stores. They operate as a one-stop shop for these retailers. Cash-and-carry warehouses are a good example.
- **Limited-line wholesalers** offer only a limited range of products, but stock them in depth. They are often found in industrial markets, selling specialist equipment (such as materials handling equipment) and offering expertise in the field.
- **Speciality line wholesalers** carry a very narrow range, for example concentrating on only one type of food (e.g. tea). They are typically found dealing in goods that require special knowledge of the buying, handling or marketing of the product category.
- **Rack jobbers** own and maintain their own stands or displays in retail outlets. Typical products might be cosmetics, tights or greetings cards. The retailer pays only for the goods sold, and usually does not take title to the goods – this can be a big saving in terms of capital and, since the rack jobber undertakes to check the stock and restock where necessary, the retailer also saves time.
- **Limited-service wholesalers** take title to goods, but often do not actually take delivery, store inventory or monitor demand. A typical example might be a coal wholesaler, who buys from a producer and arranges for the coal to be delivered direct to coal merchants, without the coal first being delivered to the wholesaler.
- **Cash-and-carry wholesalers** offer a way for wholesalers to supply small retailers at minimum cost. The cash-and-carry wholesaler operates like a giant supermarket; retailers call, select the cases of goods needed and pay at a

checkout, using their own transport to take the goods back to their shops. This is an extremely flexible and efficient system for both parties.

- **Drop shippers** (or *desk jobbers*) obtain orders from retailers and pass them on to manufacturers, buying the goods from the manufacturer and selling to the retailer without ever actually seeing the goods. The drop shipper provides the salesforce and takes on the credit risk on behalf of the manufacturer, but does not have the storage costs or the overheads of a merchant wholesaler.
- *Mail order wholesalers* use catalogues to sell to retailers and industrial users. This avoids the use of an expensive salesforce and works best for dealing with retailers in remote areas. Goods are despatched through the post or by commercial carriers; these wholesalers take title to the products.

To summarise, wholesalers perform a wide variety of functions, all aimed at making the exchange of goods easier and more efficient. This leaves the manufacturer free to concentrate resources on improving production efficiencies and the physical product offering, and retailers to concentrate on providing the most effective service for the consumer.

RETAILERS

Retailers deal with any sales that are for the customer's own use, or for the use of family and friends. In other words, any purchases that are not for business needs are the domain of the retailer.

Therefore, a retailer is not necessarily a high street shop or a market trader; mail order catalogues, TV phone-in lines, online retailers such as Amazon and even door-to-door salesmen are all retailers. Tupper Corporation (which sells Tupperware on the party plan) is as much a retailer as Aldi, Makro or Coles, even though the product is sold in the customer's own home.

Traditionally most retail outlets have been in city centres or suburban high streets. Partly this was for convenience, so that shoppers had a central area to visit for all their shopping requirements, and partly it was due to planning regulations which zoned most retail shops in traditional retail areas, away from industrial parks and housing estates.

More recently, out-of-town hypermarkets and shopping parks have been growing up. This is in response to the following factors:

- Greater car ownership means an increase in **outshopping** (shopping outside the area where the consumer lives)
- High city-centre rents and property taxes make out-of-town sites more attractive for retailers
- Town planners have used retail parks as a way of regenerating decaying industrial sites on the edges of towns.

Such out-of-town sites have not necessarily damaged all town-centre retailers, although there has been a shift in the composition of city-centre retail districts. For example, food retailers have largely gone from central sites in major cities, except for delicatessens and speciality food outlets. In the United Kingdom, supermarket chain Tesco has begun to reverse this trend, with the establishment of Tesco Metro stores in city centres. These stores carry a limited range of products, usually in smaller pack sizes, and aim at office workers shopping in their lunch hours or convenience shopping.

Here are some descriptions of different types of retail outlet:

- **Convenience stores**, or corner shops, offer a range of grocery and household items. These local shops often open until late at night. They are usually family-run, often belong to a trading group such as Spar, Circle K or 7-Eleven, and cater for last-minute and emergency purchases. In recent years, the Circle K and 7-Eleven franchises have expanded internationally from the United States and are making inroads into the late-night shopping market. Convenience stores have been under threat from supermarkets as later opening has become more common, and as the laws on Sunday trading in many countries have been relaxed.
- **Supermarkets** are large self-service shops which rely on selling at low prices. Typically they are well laid-out, bright, professionally run shops carrying a wide range of goods.
- **Hypermarkets** are even bigger supermarkets, usually in an out-of-town or edge-of-town location. A typical hypermarket would carry perhaps 20,000 lines. The true hypermarket sells everything from food to TV sets.
- **Department stores** are located in city centres and sell everything; each department has its own buyers and functions as a separate profit centre. Examples are Harrods of London, El Corte Ingles in Spain and Clery's in Dublin. Within department stores, some functions are given over to **concessionaires**, who pay a rental per square foot plus a percentage of turnover to set up a store-within-a-store. Miss Selfridge, Brides and Principles all operate in this way within department stores. The trend is towards allowing more concessionaires and around 70% of Debenham's floor space is allocated this way.
- **Variety stores** offer a more limited range of goods, perhaps specialising in clothes (e.g. Primark) or in books and stationery (e.g. WH Smith).
- **Discounters** (sometimes called baby sharks) are grocery outlets offering a minimum range of goods at very low prices. Often the decor is basic, the displays almost non-existent and the general ambience one of pile-it-high-and-sell-it-cheap. German retailers Lidl and Aldi are examples of this approach; such stores typically carry only 700 lines or so.
- **Niche marketers** stock a very limited range of products, but in great depth. Examples are Sock Shop and Tie Rack. They frequently occupy tiny shops (even kiosks at railway stations) but offer every possible type of product within their

very narrow spectrum. Niche marketers were the success story of the 1980s but declined somewhat during the 1990s.

- **Discount sheds** are out-of-town DIY and hardware stores. They are usually businesses requiring large display areas, but with per-square-metre turnovers and profits that do not justify city-centre rents. Service levels are minimal, the stores are cheaply constructed and basic in terms of decor and ambience, and everything is geared towards minimising the overhead.
- **Catalogue showrooms** have minimal or non-existent displays and are really an extension of the mail order catalogue. Customers buy in the same way as they would by mail order, by filling in a form, and the goods are brought out from a warehouse at the rear of the store. These outlets usually have sophisticated electronic inventory control.
- **Non-store retailing** includes door-to-door selling, vending machines, telemarketing (selling goods by telephone), mail order and catalogue retailing. **Telemarketing** may be inbound or outbound; inbound means that customers telephone the retailer to place an order, whereas outbound means the retailer telephones potential customers to ask them to buy. Outbound telemarketing has grown in the UK in recent years; it is often used to make appointments for sales representatives to call, for products such as fitted kitchens or double glazing, and is also used for direct selling of some items which are then delivered by mail. In general, it is unpopular with customers and in both the USA and the UK systems have been set up to allow people to be removed from the lists of telesales companies. In the UK, the system is the Telephone Preference Service (TPS); firms that continue to call after someone has registered with the TPS can be fined, although in practice this is rare. The TPS has no power to prevent people being telephoned from outside the UK, nor does it have any power to curb companies with whom the person has an existing relationship; for example, the individual's bank or electricity supply company.

E-commerce refers to retailing over the Internet. In its early days, e-commerce was dominated by business-to-business marketing, but dot.com firms such as Amazon.com, Lastminute.com and Priceline.com quickly made inroads into consumer markets. The growth of such firms is limited mainly by the growth in Internet users; as more people go online, the potential market increases and is likely to do so for the foreseeable future. The other main limiting factor is the degree to which people enjoy the process of shopping – factors such as a social experience outside the home, the pleasure of bargaining, diversion and sensory stimulation are all likely to ensure that people will continue to enjoy visiting traditional retail stores. Traditional retailers have not been slow to respond to the perceived threat, however; many retailers now offer an Internet service, with free delivery. The Internet is more likely to be used when the customer has high levels of experience with the product and the Internet, and a low perceived risk; conventional retailers or call centres are more likely to be used when the customer has low experience levels and high perceived risk (Rhee 2010).

Because consumer needs change rapidly, there are fashions in retailing (the rise and fall of niche marketing demonstrates this). Being responsive to consumer needs is, of course, important to all marketers, but retailers are at the 'sharp end' of this process and need to be able to adapt quickly to changing trends. The following factors have been identified as being crucial to retail success:

- *Location.* Being where the consumer can easily find the shop – in other words, where the customers would expect such a shop to be. A shoe shop would typically be in a high street or city-centre location, whereas a furniture warehouse would typically be out of town.
- *Buying the right goods in the right quantities* to be able to supply what the consumer wants to buy.
- *Offering the right level of service.* If the service level is less than the customer expects, he/she will be dissatisfied and will shop elsewhere. If the service level is too high, the costs increase and the customer may become suspicious that the prices are higher than they need be. Discount stores are expected to have low service levels and consumers respond to that by believing that the prices are therefore lower.
- *Store image.* If the shop and its goods are upmarket, so must be the image in the consumer's mind. As with any other aspect of the product, the benefits must be as expected or post-purchase dissonance will follow. Trust in the store extends to trust in the store's own-brand goods (see Chapter 6); conversely, mistrust will reduce intention to buy the retailer's own brands (LaForet 2008).
- *Atmospherics.* These are the physical elements of the shop design that encourage purchase. Use of the right colours, lighting, piped music and even odours can greatly affect purchasing behaviour (Bitner 1992). For example, playing slow-tempo music to a supermarket queue makes people feel more relaxed and satisfied and also makes the waiting time seem shorter; however, music played when the supermarket is overcrowded can make people irritable (Oakes and North 2008).
- *Product mix.* The retailer must decide which products will appeal to his/her customers. Sometimes this results in the shop moving away from its original product range into totally unrelated areas.

Recent trends in retail include the greater use of EPOS (electronic point-of-sale) equipment and laser scanners to speed checkout queues through (and, incidentally, to save staffing costs), and the increasing use of **loyalty cards**. These cards give the customer extra discounts based on the amount spent at the store over a given period. The initial intention is to encourage customers to buy at the same store all the time to obtain the discounts, and in this sense the cards are really just another sales promotion. This type of loyalty programme, involving economic benefits, does have a positive effect on customer retention. The schemes also tend to help in terms of increasing the retailer's share of the customers (Verhoef 2003).

There is a further possibility inherent in EPOS technology, however. It is now possible to keep a record of each customer's buying habits and to establish the purchasing pattern, based on the EPOS records. Theoretically, this would mean that customers could be reminded at the checkout that they are running low on certain items, since the supermarket computer would know how frequently those items are usually bought. The phrase Domesday marketing has been coined by Professor Martin Evans to describe this; whether it could be seen as a useful service for consumers or as an unwarranted invasion of privacy remains a topic for discussion (Evans 1994). Loyal customers tend to be attracted to store brands during promotional periods, presumably because they trust the store (Rajagopal 2008).

EPOS systems in the UK were redesigned in 2004 to allow for the introduction of chip-and-pin credit cards, which require customers to enter a personal identity number (PIN) rather than sign a receipt. These have been used in France and Spain for many years to reduce credit card fraud and reduce time spent at the checkouts, and UK cards can now be used in those countries.

Perception is important in the retail environment. Store atmospherics have already been mentioned, but people also like to be able to touch products, open the boxes and see what they are buying. This can cause problems, since people will tend to open the box to examine the product but then take an unopened box to the checkout. The opened box will probably not sell until it is the last one, since people tend to believe that the product is contaminated and no longer new if other people have handled it. This phenomenon is known as shop soiling, but is explained by anthropologists in terms of magic; the 'contaminated' product has had part of the essence of the other shopper transferred to it (Argo *et al.* 2006).

SELECTING CHANNELS

Choosing a channel involves a number of considerations. These are as follows:

- Whether to use a single channel, or several channels
- Location of customers
- Compatibility of the channels with the firm
- Nature of the goods
- Geographic, environmental and terrain decisions
- Storage and distribution issues
- Import and export costs.

Above all, of course, the firm must begin by considering the customers' needs. Having said that, the needs of channel members will also be involved, since they are unlikely to cooperate if their needs are not considered.

Using a single channel clearly provides the channel members with the security of knowing that they will not be competing with other firms carrying the same product line. Some retailers insist on being given exclusive rights to the products they carry, so that they can make 'price promises' without fear of consumers actually being able to buy the identical product anywhere else, whether at a lower price or not. On the other hand, the needs of consumers are best met by having the product widely available.

Location of customers influences the channel as well as the physical distribution. Some channels might be unavailable in some countries – for example, distribution via the Internet is not viable in many African countries because few people are online and the road infrastructure makes delivery difficult.

Channels need to be compatible with the firm's capability and size; small manufacturers can become overwhelmed by dealing with large retailers, for example.

The nature of the goods determines which type of retailer would be best. Sometimes firms have obtained a competitive advantage by using unusual routes to market – jewellery firms have distributed through hairdressing salons, for example.

Geographic and environmental (in the sense of business environment) considerations can render some routes unviable. For example, mail order in the United States became popular with people living in remote regions during the nineteenth century (a geographical consideration). Such people were unable to reach major stores easily and local stores were unable to carry all the products people might need. Mail order grew in Germany for a different reason; at one time, the business environment required retail stores to close at 5 pm and prohibited weekend opening except for one Saturday a month. This meant that most working people had serious difficulty in getting to shops, and mail order became a favourite way of buying almost everything.

Storage and distribution costs, particularly for overseas markets, may mean that a wholesaler becomes necessary simply because of the need to make few large deliveries rather than many small ones. Likewise, if storage is expensive, an on-demand service such as that supplied by motor factors to small garages might be necessary.

Import and export costs, especially duties and tariffs, might mean that a local agent (or even a local assembly plant) might need to be used. Shipping costs are likely to make it more efficient to fill a shipping container rather than send small quantities at a time, but the nature of the product needs to be considered – perishable or expensive products might need to be sent immediately, rather than waiting until there are enough to fill a container.

MANAGING DISTRIBUTION CHANNELS

Channels can be led by any of the channel members, whether they are producers, wholesalers or retailers, provided that the member concerned has **channel power**. This power comes from seven sources, as shown in Table 8.4 (Michman and Sibley 1980).

Channel cooperation is an essential part of the effective functioning of channels. Since each member relies on every other member for the free exchange of goods

Table 8.4 Sources of channel power

Economic sources of power	Non-economic sources of power	Other factors
Control of resources. The degree to which the channel member has the power to direct goods, services or finance within the channel	Reward power. The ability to provide financial benefits or otherwise favour channel members	Level of power. This derives from the economic and non-economic sources of power
Size of company. The bigger the firm compared with other channel members, the greater the overall economic power	Expert power. This arises when the leader has special expertise which the other channel members need	Dependency of other channel members
Referent power emerges when channel members try to emulate the leader		Willingness to lead. Clearly some firms with potential for channel leadership prefer not to have the responsibility or are unable to exercise the potential for other reasons
Legitimate power arises from a superior–subordinate relationship. For example, if a retailer holds a substantial shareholding in a wholesaler, it has legitimate power over the wholesaler		
Coercive power exists when one channel member has the power to punish another		

down the channel, it is in the members' interests to look after each other to some extent. Channel cooperation can be improved in the following ways:

- The channel members can agree on target markets, so that each member can best direct effort towards meeting the common goal.
- The tasks each member should carry out can be defined. This avoids duplication of effort or giving the final consumer conflicting messages.

A further development is **co-marketing**, which implies a partnership between manufacturers, intermediaries and retailers. This level of cooperation involves pooling of market information and full agreement on strategic issues (Marx 1995).

Channel conflict arises because each member wants to maximise its own profits or power. Conflicts also arise because of frustrated expectations; each member expects the other members to act in particular ways, and sometimes these expectations are unfulfilled. For example, a retailer may expect a wholesaler to maintain large enough stocks to cover an unexpected rise in demand for a given product, whereas the wholesaler may expect the manufacturers to be able to increase production rapidly to cover such eventualities.

An example of channel conflict occurred when EuroDisney (now Disneyland Paris) first opened. The company bypassed travel agents and tried to market directly to the public via TV commercials. Unfortunately, this did not work because European audiences were not used to the idea of booking directly (and also were not as familiar with the Disney concept as American audiences), so few bookings resulted. At the same time Disney alienated the travel agents and has had to expend considerable time and money in wooing them back again. This is a general problem for companies seeking to use multiple channels of distribution; if the company decides to deal direct with the public via its website or uses several different routes, existing channel members may feel that the relationship is being undermined. This does not mean that using multiple channels is impossible; it simply means that marketers need to be cautious not to damage the interests of existing channel members. In general, there is unlikely to be a problem if the new channels approach a segment of the market which the existing channels do not reach.

Channel management can be carried out by cooperation and negotiation (often with one member leading the discussions) or it can be carried out by the most powerful member laying down rules that weaker members have to follow. Table 8.5 shows some of the methods which can be used to control channels. Most attempts to control distribution by the use of power are likely to be looked on unfavourably by the courts, but of course the abuse of power would have to be fairly extreme before a channel member would be likely to sue.

Critical thinking

If controlling the channel is regarded as unfair, how about buyers who specify particular ways in which potential suppliers can approach them? Is it unreasonable to ask for salespeople to call on a particular day or only by appointment? Clearly not. But then, would it be unreasonable to expect suppliers to draw up detailed reports on their ability to meet delivery schedules and quality standards? Hmmm . . . Perhaps. Would it be unreasonable to expect suppliers to provide copies of their accounts and allow the customer's auditors to check on the supplier's financial stability and probity? Well, maybe not. Would it be reasonable to use knowledge of a supplier's financial difficulties to force through lower prices? Maybe, maybe not.

Business isn't exactly a coffee morning, but there are ethical and practical issues at stake. Knowing where to draw the line might not be so easy.

Sometimes the simplest way to control a distribution channel is to buy out the channel members. Buying out members across a given level (for example, a wholesaler buying out other wholesalers to build a national network) is called **horizontal integration**; buying out members above or below in the distribution chain (for example, a retailer buying out a wholesaler) is **vertical integration**. An example of extreme vertical integration is the major oil companies, which extract crude oil, refine it, ship it and ultimately sell it retail through petrol stations. At the extremes,

Table 8.5 Channel management techniques

Technique	Explanation	Legal position
Refusal to deal	One member refuses to do business with one or more other members; for example, hairdressing wholesalers sometimes refuse to supply mobile hairdressers on the grounds that this is unfair competition for salons.	In most countries suppliers do not have to supply anybody with whom they do not wish to deal. However, grounds may exist for a lawsuit if the refusal to deal is a punishment for not going along with an anti-competitive ruling by a supplier or is an attempt to prevent the channel member from dealing with a third party with whom the manufacturer is in dispute.
Tying contracts	The supplier (sometimes a franchiser) demands that the channel member carries other products as well as the main one. If the franchiser insists that all the products are carried, this is called *full-line forcing*.	Most of these contracts are illegal, but are accepted if the supplier alone can supply goods of a given quality or if the purchaser is free to carry competing products as well. Sometimes they are accepted when a company has just entered the market.
Exclusive dealing	A manufacturer might prevent a wholesaler from carrying competitors' products or a retailer might insist that no other retailer be supplied with the same products. This is often used by retailers to ensure that their 'price guarantees' can be honoured – obviously consumers will not be able to find the same product at a lower price locally if the retailer has prevented the manufacturer from supplying anybody else.	Usually these are legal provided they do not result in a monopoly position in a local area; in other words, provided the consumer has access to similar products, there will not be a problem.
Restricted sales territories	Intermediaries are prevented from selling outside a given area. The intermediaries are often in favour of this idea because it prevents competition within their own area.	Courts have conflicting views about this practice. On the one hand, these deals can help weaker distributors and can also increase competition where local dealers carry different brands; on the other hand, there is clearly a restraint of trade involved.

this type of integration may attract the attention of government monopoly regulation agencies, since the integration may cause a restriction of competition.

Producers need to ensure that the distributors of their products are of the right type. The image of a retailer can damage (or enhance) the image of the products sold (and vice versa). Producers need not necessarily sell through the most prestigious retailer, and in fact this would be counter-productive for many cheap, everyday items. Likewise, a prestigious product should not be sold through a down-market retail outlet.

In the long run, establishing good relationships between channel members will improve overall profitability for all members. As the relationship between members of the distribution channel becomes closer, power and conflict still remain important, but they are expressed in other ways and the negotiations for their resolution change in nature (Gadde 2004).

EFFICIENT CONSUMER RESPONSE

Efficient consumer response (ECR) seeks to integrate the activities of manufacturers and retailers using computer technology; the expected result is a more responsive stocking system for the retailer, which in turn benefits the manufacturer. Some of the features of ECR are as follows:

- *Continuous replenishment* under which the supplier plans production using data generated by the retailer.
- *Cross-docking* attempts to coordinate the arrival of suppliers' and retailers' trucks at the distribution centres so that goods move from one truck to the other without going into stock. Although transport efficiency falls because a supermarket truck collecting (say) greengrocery might have to wait for several suppliers' trucks to arrive, the overall speed of delivery of products improves, which can be crucial when dealing with fresh foods.
- *Roll-cage sequencing* allows storage of products by category at the warehouse; although this adds to the labour time at the warehouse, it greatly reduces labour time at the retail store.

The main problem with ECR is that it relies on complete cooperation between supplier and retailer. In any channel of distribution where the power base is unequal, this is less likely to happen; despite the overall savings for the channel as a whole, self-interest on the part of channel members may lead to less than perfect cooperation.

CASE STUDY 8 Davies Turner

Davies Turner is a freight-forwarding company based in London and Manchester. It is the largest freight-forwarding company in Britain, sending goods all over the world via land, sea and air. The company was founded in 1870 by Alfred Davies, in partnership with his father in law; their major innovation was to combine a number of shipments into one bill of lading, thus saving a great deal of the administrative charges imposed by shipping companies.

This idea of consolidating shipments grew; in the 1890s the company developed the idea of reuseable lift vans, the precursor to modern containers. By 1914, the company had its own fleet of motorised trucks, giving them a major advantage over other companies who were still using horse-drawn wagons for road freight. In 1950, when London's Heathrow Airport opened, Davies Turner developed an air freight division; in 1960 the company operated the first TIR services to the Continent, using trailers which had been sealed by Customs officers and which were transported on the first roll-on-roll-off ferries.

The company now has over 750 employees and a turnover of £145m per annum. It offers a complete freight service – everything from grouping small shipments into one large shipment through to booking the lorries, ships, aircraft space and warehouse space to accommodate shipments. The company will organise all the necessary paperwork and clearances, will track shipments (and, in fact, has a page on the website where customers can track their own shipments) and will arrange insurance. For air freight, Davies Turner has its own in-house security X-ray equipment so that all freight leaving the warehouses is acceptable to the airlines without delaying the shipment.

Davies Turner operates a fleet of vehicles for local collections and deliveries, but relies heavily on its relationships with local freight companies throughout the world as well as with shipping companies and airlines. Davies Turner is in the business of organising the logistics – not in the business of actually running a shipping line or a fleet of heavy goods vehicles. As a result, the company can offer a specialist service which covers almost any kind of freight, almost anywhere, whether it is fresh fruit or fashion garments, heavy machinery or ladies' watches, vehicle parts or excess luggage. The measure of the company's versatility lies in its specialist departments – there is a department dedicated to shipping live fish and reptiles, one dedicated to fine wine, one dedicated to fashion, and so forth.

Broadly, Davies Turner will move anything, anywhere, by any means. A truly versatile company!

Questions

1 Why is there the need to be so versatile?
2 What is the advantage of working through other companies rather than owning one's own transport fleet?
3 Why would a major company use Davies Turner rather than having its own department for freight-forwarding?
4 Why is there the need for someone to handle the paperwork?
5 What might be the drawbacks of using Davies Turner from the viewpoint of a manufacturer?

SUMMARY

This chapter has been about getting the goods to the consumer in the most efficient and effective way possible.

Here are the key points from this chapter:

- Distribution forms part of the product because it has benefits attached to it
- The faster the transport, the more expensive in upfront costs but the greater the savings in terms of wastage and in capital tied up
- Transport methods must consider the needs of the end user of the product
- Cutting out the middle man is likely to increase costs in the long run, not decrease them
- Retailing includes every transaction in which the purchase is to be used by the buyer personally or for family use
- Retailing is not necessarily confined to high street shops.

CHAPTER QUESTIONS

1 Under what circumstances might air freight be cheaper than surface transport?
2 How might wholesalers improve the strength of their position with retailers?
3 Why might a wholesaler be prepared to accept a restricted-territory sales agreement?
4 When should a manufacturer consider dealing direct with retailers?
5 When should a manufacturer consider dealing direct with the public?

Further reading

Marketing Channels: A Management View, 8th edn, by **Bert Rosenbloom** (South-Western, 2012). A readable text, with a practically orientated view of how to deal with distribution issues.

Logistics and Supply Chain Management by **Martin Christopher** (Harlow, FT Prentice Hall 2010) gives a good readable overview of logistics problems, though not really from a marketing perspective as such.

References

Argo, Jennifer J., Dahl, Darren W. and Morales, Andrea C.: 'Consumer contamination: how consumers react to products touched by others', *Journal of Marketing*, **70** (2) (2006), pp. 81–94.

Bitner, Mary Jo: 'Servicescapes: the impact of physical surroundings on customers and employees', *Journal of Marketing* (April 1992), pp. 57–71.

Coyle, J., Bardi, E. and Langley C.: *The Management of Business Logistics* (St Paul, MN, West, 1988).

Dibb, S., Simkin, L., Pride, W. and Ferrell, O.C.: *Marketing: Concepts and Strategies* (London, Houghton Mifflin, 1998).

Evans, Martin: 'Domesday marketing', *Journal of Marketing Management*, **10** (5) (1994), pp. 409–31.

Gadde, Lars-Erik: 'Activity co-ordination and resource combining in distribution networks: implications for relationship involvement and the relationship atmosphere', *Journal of Marketing Management*, **20** (1) (2004), pp. 157–84.

LaForet, Sylvie: 'Retail brand extension – perceived fit, risks and trust', *Journal of Consumer Behaviour*, (May/Jun) **7** (3) (2008), pp. 189–209.

Marx, W.: 'The co-marketing revolution', *Industry Week* (2 October 1995), pp. 77–9.

Michman, R.D. and Sibley, S.D.: *Marketing Channels and Strategies*, 2nd edn (Worthington, OH, Publishing Horizons Inc., 1980).

Oakes, Steve, and North, Adrian C.: 'Using music to influence cognitive and affective responses in queues of low and high crowd density', *Journal of Marketing Management*, **24** (5/6), pp. 589–602.

Rajagopal: 'Point-of-sales promotions and buying stimulation in retail stores', *Journal of Database Marketing and Customer Strategy Management*, (Dec) **15** (4) (2008), pp. 249–66.

Rhee, Eddie: 'Multi-channel management in direct marketing retailing: Traditional call centre versus Internet channel', *Journal of Database Marketing and Customer Strategy Management*, (June) **17** (2) (2010), pp. 70–7.

Verhoef, Peter C.: 'Understanding the effect of customer relationship management efforts on customer retention and customer share development', *Journal of Marketing*, **67** (4) (October 2003), pp. 30–45.

MARKETING COMMUNICATIONS AND PROMOTIONAL TOOLS

Objectives

After reading this chapter you should be able to

- Explain how marketing communications operate
- Plan a promotional campaign
- Explain how the elements of the promotional mix fit together to create a total package
- Select suitable promotional tools for achieving a given objective
- Understand what public relations (PR) will do for you and what it will not do
- Explain the main pitfalls of defensive PR
- Plan a media event
- Understand the problems facing a PR executive or agent
- Formulate a suitable PR policy for a given set of circumstances
- Formulate a brief for an advertising agency
- Explain the main criteria for writing advertising copy
- Understand what personal selling is intended to achieve for the firm
- Outline the main features of sales management
- Explain the role of word-of-mouth communication
- Explain how sponsorship helps in building a positive corporate image.

INTRODUCTION

This chapter is about communicating the organisation's messages to the public. The tools of communication (advertising, personal selling, PR and sales promotions) are the most visible aspects of marketing, so non-marketers tend to think they represent the whole of marketing.

Communication requires the active participation of both the sender and the receiver, so the messages not only have to contain the information the organisation wishes to convey but must also be sufficiently interesting to the consumers (or the organisation's other publics) for them to pay attention to it.

Voluntary Service Overseas

VSO is a voluntary organisation which sends skilled volunteers overseas to help with projects in the Third World. The volunteers are usually people with significant experience in industry or education who are prepared to work for up to two years in another country. Volunteers are paid at local rates. Often this is well below their previous salaries, but the typical volunteer is someone who has had a successful career and now wants to put something back.

Volunteers find the whole process very rewarding – but the professionals still need to be recruited and there are many needs that volunteers have. VSO, like most charities, has a relatively small budget for marketing, so the organisation has to get the most from its funding by careful targeting. Professional needs are very diverse – some go for the experience of living abroad, some get a warm glow of satisfaction, some go for the professional challenge, but clearly none of them do it for the money!

Obviously VSO needs cash donations as well as volunteers; the volunteers still need to be sent overseas, and even at Third World rates they still need to be paid.

Vicky Starnes, Head of Marketing

Watch the video clip, then try to answer the following questions. The answers are on the companion website.

Questions

1 Which communications tools are most appropriate for VSO?
2 What is the role of public relations in VSO's work?
3 How might VSO use database marketing?

MARKETING COMMUNICATIONS THEORY

Communication is one of the most human of activities. The exchange of thoughts that characterises communication is carried out by conversation (still the most popular form of entertainment in the world), by the written word (letters, books, magazines and newspapers) and by pictures (cartoons, television and film).

Communication has been defined as a transactional process between two or more parties whereby meaning is exchanged through the intentional use of **symbols** (Engel *et al*. 1994). The key elements here are that the communication is intentional (a deliberate effort is made to bring about a response), it is a transaction (the participants are all involved in the process) and it is symbolic (words, pictures, music and other sensory stimulants are used to convey thoughts). Since human beings are not telepathic, all communication needs the original concepts to be translated into symbols that convey the required meaning.

This means that the individual or firm issuing the communication must first reduce the concepts to a set of symbols which can be passed on to the recipient of the message; the recipient must decode the symbols to get the original message. Thus the participants in the process must share a common view of what the symbols involved actually mean. In fact, the parties must share a common field of experience. This is illustrated in Figure 9.1.

The sender's field of experience must overlap with the receiver's field of experience, at least to the extent of having a common language. The overlap is likely to be much more complex and subtle in most marketing communications; **advertisements** typically use references from popular culture such as TV shows, from proverbs and common sayings, and will often make puns or use half-statements which the audience is able to complete because it is aware of the cultural referents involved. This is why foreign TV adverts often seem unintentionally humorous or even incomprehensible.

Figure 9.1 Model of the communication process

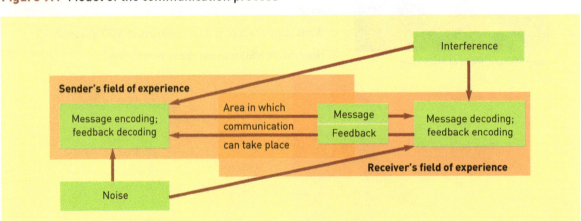

Figure 9.2 Redundancy in communication

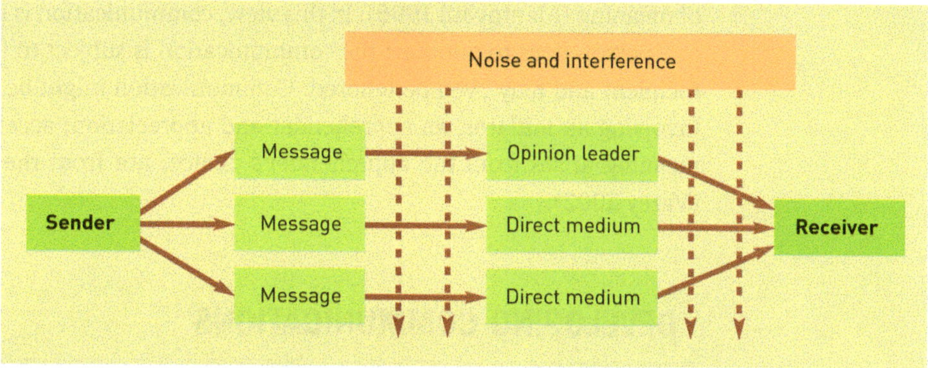

![Figure 9.2 diagram: Sender sends three Messages through Opinion leader, Direct medium, Direct medium to Receiver, with Noise and interference affecting all channels]

Noise is the surrounding distraction present during the communications process and varies from children playing during the commercial break through to arresting headlines in a magazine. **Interference** is deliberate attempts to distract the audience's attention with intelligent communications. For example, a car driver may be distracted away from a radio ad by another car cutting in (noise) or by seeing an interesting billboard (interference). For most marketing purposes, the difference is academic.

The above model is essentially a one-step model of communication. This is rather oversimplified; communications do not necessarily occur in a single step in this way. In most cases, the message reaches the receiver via several routes. Sending the same message by more than one route is called **redundancy**, and is a good way of ensuring that the message gets through. Figure 9.2 shows this diagrammatically.

In the diagram, the sender sends almost identical messages via different routes. The effect of noise and interference is to distort the message, and the opinion leader will moderate the message, but by using three different routes the meaning of the message is more likely to get through. This is the rationale behind the integration of marketing communications.

Critical thinking

When messages are sent by different routes, the medium must surely affect the message. After all, a news story written for a tabloid newspaper comes across very differently from the same story printed in a respectable broadsheet. And that's a comparison between two newspapers! How different the story would be if it were to be broadcast on TV or read over the radio!

Yet we're being asked to believe that an advertisement can be designed which will convey the same message, even though it is sent through several different media. How is that going to be accomplished?

An alternative view of communication is that it is concerned with the co-creation of meaning (Mantovani 1996). In this view, communication is not something which one person does to another; the communication is subject to interpretation by the recipient and may even be ignored. Communication might be better thought of as involving an initiator, an apprehender and appreciation; acceptance of a common meaning arises from the apprehender's choice, not from the initiator's intention (Varey 2002).

DEVELOPING COMMUNICATIONS

Developing effective marketing communications follows a six-stage process, as follows:

1 *Identify the target audience*. In other words, decide who the message should get to.
2 *Determine the response sought*. What would the marketer like members of the audience to do after they get the message?
3 *Choose the message*. Write the copy, or produce an appropriate image.
4 *Choose the channel*. Decide which newspaper, TV station or radio station the audience uses.
5 *Select the source's attributes*. Decide what it is about the product or company that needs to be communicated.
6 *Collect feedback*. For example, carry out market research to find out how successful the message was.

Communication is always expensive; full-page advertisements in Sunday colour supplements can cost upwards of £11,000 per insertion; a 30-second TV ad at peak time can cost £30,000 per station. It is therefore worthwhile spending time and effort in ensuring that the message is comprehensible by the target audience. Communications often follow the **AIDA** approach:

>   **A**ttention
>   **I**nterest
>   **D**esire
>   **A**ction.

This implies that marketers must first get the customer's *attention*. Clearly, if the receiver is not 'switched on' the message will not get through. Second, the marketer must make the message *interesting*, or the receiver will not pay attention to it. This should, if the message is good, lead to a *desire* for the product on the part of the receiver, who will then take *action*. Although this is a simplistic model in some ways, it is a useful guide to promotional planning; however, it is very difficult to get all four of these elements into one communication. For this reason, marketers usually use a mixture of approaches for different elements, called the promotional mix.

THE PROMOTIONAL MIX

The basic promotional mix consists of advertising, sales promotion, personal selling and public relations (PR). When the concept of the promotional mix was first developed, these were the only elements available to marketers, but in the past 40 years more promotional methods have appeared which do not easily fit within these four categories. For example, a logo on a T-shirt might be considered as advertising or as public relations. For the purposes of this book, however, the original four components are still considered to be the main tools available to marketers.

The important word here is 'mix'. The promotional mix is like a recipe, in which the ingredients must be added at the right times and in the right quantities for the promotion to be effective. Figure 9.3 shows how the mix operates. Messages from the company about its products and itself are transmitted via the elements of the promotional mix to the consumers, employees, pressure groups and other publics. Because each of these groups is receiving the messages from more than one transmitter, the elements of the mix also feed into each other so that the messages do not conflict.

The elements of the promotional mix are not interchangeable, any more than ingredients in a recipe are interchangeable; a task that calls for personal selling cannot be carried out by advertising, nor can public relations tasks be carried out by using sales promotions. Promotion is all about getting the message across to the customer (and the consumer) in the most effective way, and the choice of method will depend on the message, the receiver and the desired effect.

Figure 9.3 The promotional mix

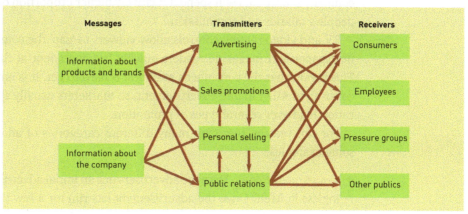

MANAGING ADVERTISING

Advertising is defined as 'a paid message inserted in a medium'. This definition can be broken down as follows:

- *Paid:* news about a company or its products is not necessarily advertising; sometimes a medium (television, radio, newspaper or magazine) will carry a message about a company in the form of a news item, but this is not advertising unless the space is paid for.
- *Message:* there must be some kind of communication intention in an advertisement, however obscure.
- *In a medium:* the message must appear in a newspaper, magazine, billboard or broadcast medium. Leaflets through doors, company names printed on T-shirts and telephone selling are not necessarily advertising (but they are promotion).

Most advertising works below the conscious level. People are often familiar with a brand name and even know a lot about the product without being able to remember where they saw the product advertised. Advertising is a *non-personal* communication in that it has to speak to a large number of people, so the message has to be clear for the whole of the target audience to understand. Research by Farris and Buzzell (1979) indicated that the proportion of promotional spending devoted to advertising is higher under the following conditions:

- The product is standardised rather than produced to order
- There are many end users (for example, most households)
- The typical purchase amount is small
- Sales are made through channel intermediaries (such as retail shops) rather than direct to users.

For example, a company selling detergents will spend the largest proportion of its promotional budget on advertising, probably on TV and in the press, whereas a company selling cars will spend a relatively higher proportion of its money on salespeople's salaries and commission.

TV and video remote controls allow viewers to 'zap' the commercial breaks, and newspaper and magazine readers quickly become adept at flipping past the ads. This means that the consumer's attention is hard to get. It is not usually possible to cover all of AIDA in one advertisement, so marketers usually spread the communication load over several types of promotion.

For this reason, there are many different categories of ad campaign. Here are some examples:

- **Teaser campaigns**. Here the advertiser runs an initial advertisement that is meaningless in itself. Once the advertisement has run for a few weeks, the advertiser runs a second ad which explains the first one. The first ad is intended to attract attention by being mysterious. An example is the campaign run by modu, the mobile phone brand, in January 2008. A video was placed on YouTube showing people going about their normal day's activities, making calls, driving, preparing for work in the morning, and so forth without any explanation of what modu is or does. The video clip was engaging and entertaining, but the product was not featured – just the brand name at the end of the clip. Eventually the actual nature of the product was revealed, during February of that year.

- **Lifestyle campaigns**. These associate the product with a desirable lifestyle. Many perfume ads have taken this approach, showing women leading interesting or exciting lives. Lifestyle campaigns are mainly about positioning the product in the consumer's mind and linking it to an aspirational group (see Chapter 3).

- **Rational campaigns** appeal to the consumer's cognition. These advertisements are heavy on facts and seek to persuade by rational argument. Often an authoritative figure (a doctor, dentist or scientist) appears in the ad to lend greater weight to the arguments. Typically, this style is used for medicated shampoos, acne creams and over-the-counter medicines.

Advertising is mainly about getting the consumer's attention and arousing interest (the A and I of AIDA). To stimulate desire and action, marketers often link a special offer (sales promotion) to the advertisement.

Advertising is always culturally based. This means that an advertisement shown in one country, or aimed at a particular audience, is unlikely to work for consumers in other countries, or for a different audience. Research into standardisation of advertising shows that relatively few firms use an entirely standardised approach (Harris 1996). Of 38 multinational companies surveyed, 26 said that they used standard advertisements, but only four of these were completely standardised; the others varied from limited standardisation (perhaps only a corporate logo in common) through limited standardisation of the key executional elements to standard execution with some modifications. Even though the sample of firms is relatively small, it appears likely that the majority of multinationals would adapt their approaches to fit the markets they are targeting.

Advertising can often be over-used because firms place greater faith in it than is perhaps justified. There is an underlying assumption that a bigger advertising spend will inevitably lead to a greater sales volume. Table 9.1 contains a checklist for making decisions about advertising.

Of course, the checklist in Table 9.1 should also include a monitoring and review procedure to ensure that the advertising has achieved its objectives.

Advertising can be used for the following purposes:

- *To help the salesforce to open sales*. For example, an advertisement may contain a reply coupon for a brochure, which the salesperson can follow up.
- *To stimulate demand for the product category*. This is used by institutions, or firms that have a large market share; for example, the UK Meat and Livestock Commission advertises British meat on behalf of farmers and butchers.

Table 9.1 Advertising decision-making checklist

Question	Explanation
Does the product possess unique, important features?	Homogeneous products such as salt, petrol and cigarettes require considerably more advertising effort than differentiated products such as cars or holiday resorts. The product must not only be different, but the consumers must believe that those differences are important.
Are hidden qualities important to buyers?	If the product can be judged by looking at it or trying it out, advertising has less of a role to play than if there are features that are not apparent to the naked eye. For instance, the Pentium computer chip has been successfully advertised because it would not be immediately apparent to a computer purchaser that the machine has one.
Is the general demand trend for the product favourable?	If the product category is in decline, advertising will be less effective than if the category is generally increasing its sales.
Is the market potential for the product adequate?	Advertising will work only when there are enough actual or potential users of the product in the market. This is because advertising is a mass medium; much of the spend is wasted on advertising to people who will not be interested anyway.
Is the competitive environment favourable?	A small firm would have great difficulty competing with a large firm in terms of getting the message through. Advertising will not be sufficient when competing against a company with a large market share and correspondingly large budget.
Are general economic conditions favourable for marketing the product?	It is much easier to promote in times of rising prosperity, particularly for durable goods such as videos, cars, computers and household appliances. Such products are difficult to advertise successfully during a recession.
Is the organisation able and willing to spend the money required to launch an advertising campaign?	As a rule of thumb, if the organisation seeks to achieve a 20% market share, it must be willing to spend at least 20% of the total advertising spend of the industry on capturing that market. In other words, if the industry as a whole spends £5 million per annum on advertising, the company must be prepared to commit at least £1 million to the campaign.
Does the firm possess sufficient marketing expertise to market the product?	The company will need to coordinate all its activities, not just expect the advertisements to produce business. Not all firms possess this capability.

Source: Adapted from Patti 1977.

- *To promote specific brands.* This accounts for most advertising activity.
- *To counteract competitors' promotional activities.* Often used to counteract a possible loss in market share owing to a new competitor entering the market.
- *To suggest new ways to use the product.* Knorr hired chef Marco Pierre White to demonstrate the use of their stock cubes as an 'instant marinade' for chicken, mixing the cube with olive oil rather than water.
- *To remind consumers about the product.* For example, advertisements for traditional Christmas foods are run during December.

- *To reinforce consumers' good feelings about the product.* For example, chocolate advertising typically emphasises the 'reward' and 'pleasure' aspects of eating chocolate.
- *To support the value of the company's shares.* There is evidence that advertising expenditure helps reduce the risk of a fall in share values (McAlister *et al.* 2007).

Advertising can also be used to improve awareness of the company itself. This type of advertising is called **institutional advertising** and is commonly carried out by very large firms such as BP or Ford. It is almost a **public relations** activity, but the media space is paid for. Most advertising is **product advertising**, which means that the products are the main part of the advertisement.

Since advertising is a paid-for medium, there will be a budgetary constraint on the management as well as a creative constraint. The advertising manager must therefore carry out the planning functions shown in Table 9.2.

Table 9.2 Advertising planning functions

Planning function	Explanation
Setting the budget	This can be done in four ways. First, the objective and task approach involves setting *objectives*, and setting aside an appropriate amount of money to achieve the objectives. This method is difficult to apply because it is difficult to assess how much will be needed to achieve the objective. Second, the *percentage of sales* approach sets the budget as a percentage of sales. This is based on the false idea that sales create advertising and usually results in less being spent on advertising when sales fall, thus reducing sales further. Third, the *competition matching approach* means that the company spends the same as the competition; this means that the firm is allowing its budgets to be set by its enemies. Fourth, there is the *arbitrary* approach whereby a senior executive (usually a finance director) simply says how much can be allowed within the firm's overall budgets. This does not take account of how the firm is to achieve the objectives.
Identifying the target	Deciding to whom the ad is to be directed. It is better to approach a small segment of the market than try to use a 'scattergun' approach on everybody (see Chapter 4).
Media planning	This is about deciding where the ads are going to appear. There are two main decision areas: the **reach** (number of potential consumers the ad reaches) and the **frequency** (number of times each consumer sees the ad) of coverage. The decision is frequently made on the basis of cost per thousand readers/viewers, but this does not take into account the impact of the ad or the degree to which people are able to skip past it.
Defining the objectives	Deciding what the ads are supposed to achieve. It is essential here to give the advertising agency a clear brief: 'We want to raise awareness of the product to 50% of the adult population' is a measurable objective. 'We want to increase sales as much as possible' is not measurable, so there is no way of knowing whether it has been achieved.
Creating the advertising platform	Deciding the basic issues and selling points that the advertising must convey. This clarifies the advertising agency briefing or at least clarifies the thinking on producing the advertising materials.

Following on from the planning stage, the advertisements themselves will need to be produced. Some firms do this themselves, but most large firms will use specialist advertising agencies. Ad agencies are paid via discounts from the media so, provided that the advertising budget is big enough to interest an agency, their services cost the advertiser nothing. Typical agency discount is 15%.

Producing advertisements

Advertisements contain three key elements: the brand itself, the pictorial element and the text. The pictorial element is superior for capturing attention, regardless of the size of the ad or the picture. The text element captures attention proportional to its size and the brand element transfers attention to the other elements (Pieters and Wedel 2004).

When writing advertising **copy** the primary rule is to keep it short and simple. This is because people will not normally read a lengthy advertisement. Equally, the headline of the advertisement is important because people frequently read only the headline, quickly skipping on as they realise it is an advertisement. Declining literacy skills also play a role – many people are actually unable to read and understand a long and complicated message.

For example, Figures 9.4 and 9.5 show two fictitious advertisements for a surfboard. The first is written factually, the second is written as an advertisement. The first ad clearly contains more information and is really much more use to the consumer, but the second ad is much more likely to be read and acted upon because it has a more lively **execution format**. What the **copywriter** wants the consumers to do is go to the surfboard retailer and look at the SurfKing (this could be linked with

Figure 9.4 Factual advertisement for a surfboard

Figure 9.5 Simpler advertisement for a surfboard

a sales promotion). There is no need to tell the readers everything in one advertisement. A surprising number of advertisements are written in the first style because the advertisers are trying to communicate everything about the product to the consumer without having first ensured that people will read the advertisement.

Artwork should be eye-catching and relevant to the purpose. It is usually a good idea to include a picture of the product where this is possible, since it aids recognition when the consumer sees the product on the supermarket shelf. Much artwork is available off-the-shelf for smaller businesses, either from computer clipart folders or from books of non-copyright artwork.

Memory is stimulated by emotion-arousing advertisements, but it appears that women are more affected by this factor than are men (Baird *et al.* 2007). The reasons for this are obscure. Creating annoying or irritating copy or using several variants of a slogan also helps to fix an advertisement in people's memories as well as helping in matching the slogan to the brand (Rosengren and Dahlen 2006).

Assessing advertising effectiveness

Four elements appear to be important in the effectiveness of advertising:

- Awareness
- Liking
- Interest
- Enjoyment.

There is a high correlation between brand loyalty and **brand awareness** (Stapel 1990); likeability appears to be the single best predictor of sales effectiveness since likeability scales predict 97% of sales successes (Biel 1989), interest clearly relates to likeability (Stapel 1991) and enjoyment appears to be a good indicator in advertising pre-tests (Brown 1991). People's responses to advertising can be positive or negative; recent research shows that people who complain about advertising fall into four groups, as follows (Volkov *et al.* 2006):

1 *Advertising aficionados*. These people believe that, in general, advertising is a good thing, paints a fair picture and is a good source of information.
2 *Consumer activist*. These people are on a mission to protect other people and will complain to the manufacturer or through the press.
3 *Advertising moral guardians*. These people believe advertising is creating a materialist society and that it appeals to people's baser instincts.
4 *Advertising seeker*. This type of person watches a lot of TV advertising and enjoys it as entertainment.

Clearly, people will complain about advertising which offends them; in the UK, such complaints are regulated by the Advertising Standards Authority (see Chapter 12).

It is worthwhile making some efforts to find out whether the advertising has been effective in achieving the objectives laid down. This is much easier if clear objectives were set in the first place, of course, and if the advertising agency was given a clear brief.

Advertising effectiveness can be assessed by market research, by returned coupons and (sometimes) by increased sales. The last method is somewhat risky, however, since there may be many other factors that could have increased the sales of the product. Table 9.3 shows some common techniques for evaluating advertising effectiveness.

Table 9.3 Advertising effectiveness

Technique	Description and explanation
Pre-tests	These are evaluations of the advertising before it is released. Pre-tests are sometimes carried out using focus groups (see Chapter 5).
Coupon returns or enquiries	The advertiser counts up the number of enquiries received during each phase of an advertising campaign. This allows the marketing management to judge which advertisements are working best, provided the coupons have an identifying code on them.
Post-campaign tests (post-tests)	The particular testing method used will depend largely on the objectives of the campaign. Communications objectives (product awareness, attitude change, brand awareness) might be determined through surveys; sales objectives might be measured according to changes in sales that can be attributed to the campaign. This is difficult to do because of other factors (changes in economic conditions, for example) that might distort the findings.
Recognition tests and recall tests	In recognition tests, consumers are shown the advertisement and asked if they recognise it. They are then asked how much of it they actually recall. In an unaided recall test the consumer is asked which advertisements he or she remembers seeing recently; in an aided recall test the consumer is shown a group of advertisements (without being told which is the one the researcher is interested in) and is asked which ones he or she has seen recently.

Obviously, it is important to distinguish between remembering the advertisement and remembering the product. Research shows that humour in advertising frequently results in people remembering the advert but failing to remember the product (Hansen *et al.* 2009).

SALES PROMOTION

Sales promotions are short-term activities designed to generate a temporary increase in sales of the products.

Sales promotion has many guises, from money-off promotions to free travel opportunities. The purpose of sales promotion is to create a temporary increase in sales by bringing purchasing decisions forward and adding some immediacy to the decision-making process. Sales promotions have four characteristics, as follows (D'Astous and Landreville 2003):

1 *Attractiveness*. This is the degree to which the customer perceives the promotion as being desirable.
2 *Fit to product category*. A promotion which has no relationship with the product is less likely to appeal to customers.
3 *Reception delay*. If the promotional gift or discount will not arrive for some time, it is less attractive.
4 *Value*. High-value promotions work better than low-value ones, but it is the value as perceived by the customer which is important.

These characteristics interact with each other, so that an unattractive offer may still work if it is a good fit with the product category (for example).

Table 9.4 shows some of the techniques of sales promotion, and when they should be used to greatest effect.

Sales promotion will often be useful for low-value items and is most effective when used as part of an integrated promotion campaign. This is because advertising and PR build sales in the long term, whereas sales promotion and personal selling tend to be better for making quick increases in sales. The combination of the two leads to the **ratchet effect**: sales get a quick boost from sales promotions, then build gradually over the life of an ad campaign (Moran 1978).

Care needs to be taken with sales promotions. First, a sales promotion that is repeated too often can become part of the consumer's expectations; for example, UK furniture retailer Court's had a near-permanent 'sale' on, with large discounts: eventually, customers would not buy anything unless it was heavily discounted and eventually the company went bankrupt.

Second, brand switching as a result of a sales promotion is usually temporary, so it is unlikely that long-term business will be built by a short-term sales promotion.

Third, the promotion will benefit consumers who would have bought the product anyway, so a proportion of the spend will have been effectively wasted (though this

Table 9.4 Sales promotion techniques

Sales promotion technique	When to use to best effect
Free 'taster' samples in supermarkets	When a new product has been launched on the market. This technique works by allowing the consumer to experience the product first-hand and also places the consumer under a small obligation to buy the product. The technique is effective but expensive (Rajagopal 2008).
Money-off vouchers in press advertisements	This has the advantage that the company can check the effectiveness of the advertising by checking which vouchers came from which publications. It tends to lead to short-term brand switching; when the offer ends, consumers frequently revert to their usual brand.
Two-for-the-price-of-one	May encourage short-term brand switching. Appeals to the price-sensitive consumer, who will switch to the next cheap offer next time. Can be useful for rewarding and encouraging existing customers.
Piggy-backing with another product; e.g. putting a free jar of coffee whitener onto a jar of instant coffee	Good for encouraging purchasers of the coffee to try the whitener. Can be very successful in building brand penetration, since the consumer's loyalty is to the coffee, not to the whitener. Will not usually encourage brand switching between the 'free sample' brand and its competitors. Can also use vouchers on the backs of labels of other products (see co-marketing in Chapter 8).
Instant-lottery or scratchcards	Commonly used in petrol stations. The intention is to develop a habit among motorists of stopping at the particular petrol station. In the United Kingdom, for legal reasons, these promotions cannot require a purchase to be made or be linked to spending a specific amount, but few people would have the courage to ask for a card without buying anything.
Free gift with each purchase	Often used for children's cereals. Can be good for encouraging brand switching and is more likely to lead to permanent adoption of the brand because consumers do not usually switch brands when buying for children. This is because the children are not price-sensitive and will want their favourite brand.

is true of most promotional tools). Good targeting can help overcome this, but care should be taken that existing customers do not feel that they have been unfairly dealt with because they did not receive the promotional offer.

Fourth, discounting on price can seriously damage brand values because the product becomes perceived as being cut-price. Since price is widely used as a signal for quality, the potential for damage is obvious.

Sales promotions can be carried out from manufacturer to intermediary (*trade promotions*), from retailer to consumer (*retailer promotions*) or direct from the manufacturer to the consumer (*manufacturer promotions*).

Trade promotions can be used for the following purposes:

- *To increase stock levels.* The more stock the intermediary holds, the more commitment there will be to selling the stock and the less space there is for competitors' stock. (See push strategies in Chapter 10.)

- *To gain more or better shelf space.* The more eye-catching the position of the product in the retail shop, the more likely it is to sell.
- *To launch a new product.* New products always carry an element of risk for retailers as well as manufacturers (see Chapter 6). This means that the manufacturer may need to give the retailer an extra incentive to stock the product at all.
- *To even out fluctuating sales.* Seasonal offers may be used to encourage retailers to stock the products during slack periods. For example, the toy industry sells 80% of its production over the Christmas period, so it is common for firms to offer extra incentives to retailers to stock up during the rest of the year.
- *To counter the competition.* Aggressive sales promotion can sometimes force a competitor off the retailer's shelves, or at least cause the retailer to drive a harder bargain with a competitor.

Retailer promotions are used for the following purposes:

- *To increase store traffic.* Almost any kind of sales promotion will increase the number of people who come into the shop, but retailers commonly have special events or seasonal sales.
- *To increase frequency and amount of purchase.* This is probably the commonest use of sales promotions; examples are two-for-one offers, buy-one-get-discount-off-another-product, and so forth.
- *To increase store loyalty.* Loyalty cards are the main example of this (although these have other uses – see Chapter 8). Using the loyalty card enables the customer to build up points, which can be redeemed against products.
- *To increase own-brand sales.* Most large retailers have their own brands, which often have larger profit margins than the equivalent national brands. Own-brands sometimes suffer from a perception of lower quality, and therefore increased sales promotion effort may need to be made. In fact, own-brands help to increase sales of manufacturers' brands but, since heavy own-brand consumers contribute less to the retailer's overall profits (because they spend less overall, being bargain hunters), retailers might do better to encourage sales of manufacturers' brands as a way of encouraging bigger-spending customers (Ailawadi and Bari 2004).
- *To even out busy periods.* Seasonal sales are the obvious examples, but some retailers also promote at busy times to ensure a larger share of the market.

Manufacturer promotions are carried out for the following reasons:

- *To encourage trial.* When launching a new product the manufacturer may send out free samples to households or may give away samples with an existing product. (See Chapter 10 for pull strategies.)
- *To expand usage.* Sales promotion can be used to encourage reinvention of the product for other uses (see Chapter 6).
- To attract new customers.

- *Trade up.* Sales promotions can encourage customers to buy the larger pack or more expensive version of the product.
- *Load up.* Encouraging customers to stock up on a product (perhaps to collect coupons) effectively blocks out the competition for a period.
- To generate a mailing list for direct marketing purposes (for example, by running an on-pack competition).
- *To enhance brand values* by (for example) running some type of **self-liquidating offer**. For example, a promotion offering a discounted wristwatch that carries the brand logo might encourage sales of the product as well as ensuring that the brand remains in the forefront of the consumer's attention.

Often, the gains made from sales promotions are only temporary, but in many cases this is acceptable since a temporary shift in demand is all that is required to meet the firm's immediate need. Also, much sales promotion activity is carried out with the intention of spoiling a competitor's campaign; using sales promotion to respond to a competitive threat, particularly by offering a price incentive, can be very fast and effective.

MANAGING PERSONAL SELLING

Selling is probably the most powerful marketing tool the firm has. A salesperson sitting in front of a prospect, discussing the customer's needs and explaining directly how the product will benefit him or her, is more likely to get the business than any advertising, PR or sales promotion technique available. Unfortunately, selling is also the most expensive promotional tool for the firm; on average, a sales representative on the road will cost a firm around £60,000 p.a. and will probably call on only 1600 prospects or so in that time, at best. Selling is therefore used only for high-order-value or highly technical products that need a lengthy decision-making procedure.

Some retail shop assistants are trained in selling techniques, in particular in shops where the customer needs advice, such as electrical goods outlets or shoe shops. In these cases the retailer may spend considerable time and effort in training salespeople both in the technicalities of the product range and in selling techniques. Selling is learned – there is no such thing as a 'born' salesperson, although (as is true of any skill) some people have a greater aptitude for selling than do others.

Salespeople fall into four categories:

- **Order takers**, who collect orders for goods from customers who have already decided to buy
- **Order getters**, who find solutions for new and existing customers and persuade them to buy
- **Missionaries**, who seek out new customers and prepare them to buy
- Support staff such as technical salespeople who demonstrate technical products and persuade users to adopt them.

What the firm expects of its salespeople is that they will close business by persuading customers to buy the firm's products rather than a competitor's products. The firm wants its salespeople to be able to explain the benefits of the products in terms of the customer's needs, then ask for the order – in some industries (though by no means the majority), this results in a better than 50% success rate, which is, of course, vastly greater than the best advertising responses.

Salespeople have a bad reputation, largely undeserved, for being pushy and manipulative. In practice, successful salespeople know that they are as much there to help the customer as to help the firm achieve its sales objectives. It is a common saying among salespeople that it is easier to get another company than it is to get new customers, so salespeople find it pays to look after the customer's interests. Many salespeople regard themselves as managers of the firm's relationships with the customers; however, some will inevitably develop inappropriate attitudes to their role and may need some careful management or retraining (Davies *et al.* 2010).

Good salespeople begin by finding out the customer's needs, and go on to decide which of the company's products will best meet those needs. The next stage is to give an explanation of the product's benefits to the customer, connecting these to the customer's needs. Finally, the salesperson closes the deal by asking for the order. The process is the same as that conducted by marketers generally, except that the salesperson is dealing on a one-to-one basis rather than with a mass market. In this sense, selling can be seen as micro-marketing.

This means that the customer can 'pick the brains' of the salesperson, who presumably has superior knowledge of the products that are available. This can cut a lot of the effort out of the search for the most suitable product and the salesperson can also help people through the decision-making barrier. Experienced salespeople often say that the hardest part of the job is to get a decision, not necessarily to get a sale.

The salesperson therefore combines knowledge of the product (obtained beforehand) with knowledge of the customer's needs (obtained during the presentation) and knowledge of sales techniques (which are aids to decision-making) to help the customer arrive at a decision.

MANAGING THE SALESFORCE

Possibly the most expensive marketing tool the company has, the salesforce is in some ways the hardest to control. This is because it is composed of independently minded people who each have their own ideas on how the job should be done, and who are working away from the office and out of sight of the sales managers.

Sales managers are responsible for recruitment, training, motivation, controlling and evaluating salesforce activities, and managing sales territories.

Recruitment

Recruitment is complicated by the fact that there is no generally applicable set of personality traits that go to make up the ideal salesperson. This is because the sales task varies greatly from one firm to another, and the sales manager will need to draw up a specific set of desirable traits for the task in hand. This will involve analysing the company's successful salespeople and also the less successful ones to find out what the differences are between them.

Some companies take the view that almost anybody can be trained to sell, and therefore the selection procedures are somewhat limited, or even non-existent; other companies are extremely selective and subject potential recruits to a rigorous selection procedure. Sources of potential recruits are advertising, employment agencies, recommendations from existing sales staff, colleges and universities, and internal appointments from other departments.

Training

Training can be long or short, depending on the product and the market. Table 9.5 illustrates the dimensions of the problem. The role the salesperson is required to take on will also affect the length of training: *missionary salespeople* will take longer to train than order takers, and *closers* will take longer than *telephone canvassers*.

Typically, training falls into two sections: *classroom training*, in which the recruits are taught about the company and the products and may be given some grounding in sales techniques; and *field training*, which is an ongoing training programme carried out in front of real customers in the field. Field training is often the province of the sales managers, but classroom training can be carried out by other company personnel (in some cases, in larger firms, there will be specialists who do nothing else but train salespeople).

Table 9.5 Factors relating to length of training of sales staff

Factors indicating long training	Factors indicating short training
Complex, technical products	Simple products
Industrial markets with professional buyers	Household, consumer markets
High order values (from the customer's viewpoint)	Low order values
High recruitment costs	Low recruitment costs
Inexperienced recruits – for example, recruited direct from university	Experienced recruits from the same industry

People tend to learn best by performing the task, so most sales training programmes involve substantial field training, either by sending out rookies (trainees) with experienced salespeople or by the 'in-at-the-deep-end' approach of sending rookies out on their own fairly early in their careers. The latter method is indicated if there are plenty of possible customers for the product; the view is that a few mistakes (lost sales) will not matter. In industrial selling, though, it is often the case that there are very few possible customers and therefore the loss of even one or two could be serious. In these circumstances it would be better to give rookies a long period of working alongside more experienced salespeople.

Sales team learning is impacted by their perceptions of the organisation's readiness to change. Salespeople working for an organisation which has demonstrated the ability to adapt to new conditions are more willing to spend time learning new techniques and new products than they would be in organisations which rarely move with the times (Ranganjaran *et al.* 2004).

Ultimately, of course, salespeople will lose more sales than they get. In most industries, fewer than half the presentations given result in a sale; a typical proportion would be one in three.

Payment

Payment for salespeople traditionally has a commission element, but it is perfectly feasible to use a *straight salary* method, or a *commission-only* method. Although it is commonly supposed that a commission-only salesperson will be highly motivated to work hard, since otherwise he or she will not earn any money, this is not necessarily the case. Salespeople who are paid solely by commission will sometimes decide that they have earned enough for this month and will give themselves a holiday; the company has very little moral power to compel them to work since there is no basic salary being paid. Conversely, a salesperson who is paid a salary only may feel obligated to work to justify the salary.

Herzberg (1966) said that the payment method must be seen to be fair if demotivation is to be avoided; the payment method is not in itself a good motivator. Salespeople are out on the road for most of their working lives and do not see what other salespeople are doing – whether they are competent at the job, whether they are getting some kind of unfair advantage, even whether they are working at all. In these circumstances a commission system does at least reassure the salesperson that extra effort brings extra rewards. Table 9.6 shows the trade-offs between commission-only and salary-only; of course, most firms have a mixture of salary and commission.

Salespeople tend to judge whether their pay is fair or not by looking at factors other than the actual money (Ramaswamy and Singh 2003). They tend to look at such factors as the fairness of their supervision, trust between themselves and the sales manager, and interactional fairness (negotiation and explanation). This is perhaps not surprising; the implication is that people only become concerned about their salary levels if they feel they are being unfairly dealt with or are unhappy in the job.

Table 9.6 Trade-offs in salespeople's pay packages

Mainly salary	Mainly commission
Where order values are high	Where order values are low
Where the sales cycle is long	Where the sales cycle is short
Where staff turnover is low	Where staff turnover is high
Where sales staff are carefully selected against narrow criteria	Where selection criteria for staff are broad
For new staff or staff who have to develop new territories	For situations where aggressive selling is indicated (e.g. selling unsought goods)
Where sales territories are seriously unequal in terms of sales potential	Where sales territories are substantially the same

Motivation

Motivation, perhaps surprisingly, tends to come from sources other than payment. The classic view of motivation was proposed by Abraham Maslow (1954). Maslow's Hierarchy of Need theory postulates that people will fulfil the needs at the lower end of a pyramid (survival needs and security needs) before they move on to addressing needs at the upper end (such as belonging needs, esteem needs and self-actualisation needs). Thus, once a salesperson has assured his or her basic survival needs, these cease to be motivators; the individual will then be moving on to esteem needs or belonging needs. For this reason sales managers usually have a battery of motivational devices for which salespeople can aim.

For rookies (new salespeople), the award of a company tie might address the need to belong; for more senior salespeople, membership of a Millionaire's Club (salespeople who have sold more than a million pounds' worth of product) might address esteem needs. Many sales managers offer prizes for salespeople's spouses or partners. This can be a powerful incentive since salespeople often work unusual hours and thus have disrupted home lives; the spouse or partner is sometimes neglected in favour of the job, so a prize aimed at them can help assuage the salesperson's natural feelings of guilt.

There is some evidence to suggest that salespeople perform better if they are allowed to manage themselves within a team environment. Control of teamwork facilitates performance on the team level; performance at the individual level is influenced more by control of selling skills (Lambe *et al.* 2009).

Sales territory management

Sales territory management involves ensuring that the salesforce have a reasonably equal chance of making sales. Clearly a home-improvement salesperson in a major city will have an easier task than one in a rural area, simply because of the shorter distances between **prospects**; such a salesperson would spend more time in presentations and less time driving. On the other hand, the city salesperson would probably face more competition and might also have to cover poorer homes who would be less likely to spend much money on improvements.

Territories can be divided *geographically* or by *industry*; IBM divides territories by industry, for example, so that salespeople get to know the problems and needs of the specific industry for which they have responsibility. IBM salespeople might be given responsibility for banks, insurance companies or local government departments. This sometimes means that salespeople have greater distances to travel to present IBM products, but are more able to make sensible recommendations and give useful advice. Geographical territories are more common, since they minimise travel time and maximise selling time.

It is virtually impossible to create exactly equal territories. Thus it is important to discuss decisions with salespeople to ensure that people feel they are being treated fairly. For example, some salespeople may be quite happy to accept a rural territory because they like to live and work in the country, even if it means earning less.

MANAGING PR

PR, or public relations, is about creating favourable images of the company or organisation in the minds of consumers. PR officers and marketers often have differing viewpoints: PR people tend to see their role as being about image-building with everybody who has anything at all to do with the firm, whereas marketers are concerned mainly with customers and consumers. There is therefore a lack of fit between the information-processing requirements of marketers and PR people (Cornelissen and Harris 2004).

PR is defined as 'the planned and sustained effort to establish and maintain goodwill and mutual understanding between an organisation and its publics: customers, employees, shareholders, trade bodies, suppliers, Government officials, and society in general' (Institute of Public Relations 1984). PR managers have the task of coordinating all the activities that make up the public face of the organisation, and will have some or all of the following activities to handle:

- Organising press conferences
- Staff training workshops
- Events such as annual dinners
- Handling incoming criticisms or complaints

- Grooming senior management for the press or for TV appearances
- Internal marketing; setting the organisation's culture towards a customer orientation.

The basic routes by which PR operates are word-of-mouth, press and TV news stories, and personal recommendation. The aim is to put the firm and its products into people's minds and conversations in a positive way. PR is not advertising; advertising is aimed at generating specific behaviour (usually a purchase), whereas PR is aimed at creating a good impression.

Here are some examples of good PR activities:

- A press release saying that a company has developed a way of recycling garbage from landfills to produce plastics
- The company sponsors a major charitable or sporting event (e.g. the London Marathon or a famine-relief project)
- An announcement that one of the firm's senior executives has been seconded to a major government job-creation programme
- Body Shop requires all their franchise operations to run projects to benefit their local communities. This gives a positive image of the company to the community and also gives the staff pride in working for a caring firm. Such initiatives are not always exportable, however; McDonald's ran into difficulties in Norway when they tried to establish a Ronald McDonald house, with strong resistance from political parties, academics and others (Bronn 2006)
- McDonald's counters the negative publicity from environmental pressure groups by running litter patrols outside the restaurants.

These examples have in common that they are newsworthy and interesting, that they put the companies concerned in a good light, and that they encourage people to talk about the companies in a positive way.

Public relations and staff

PR is largely concerned with creating favourable impressions in people's minds. It is rarely, if ever, connected with directly bringing in business, and in this respect it differs from the other tools in the promotional mix. Although most of the time and for most activities PR will be the responsibility of a press agent or PR officer, PR is the responsibility of everybody who comes into contact with people outside the organisation. This will include the 'front-liners', the people whose day-to-day work brings them into contact with outsiders. For example:

- Receptionists
- Telephonists
- Truck drivers
- Warehouse staff
- Serving staff in the canteen.

This is apart from the marketing staff, such as salespeople, who come into contact with outsiders. In a sense, everybody in the organisation must take some responsibility for PR since everybody in the organisation goes home after work (and discusses their company with their friends).

In this context, a bad approach to PR (but one that is all too common) is to hire somebody with a nice smile and a friendly voice to sit by the telephone to handle complaints and smooth over any problems that arise. This is a *fire-fighting* or **reactive** approach.

A good PR approach is to make all the staff feel positive about the company. This is done by ensuring that everybody knows what the organisation is doing, what the policies are and what the company's overall aims are, in simple language. Most people would like to think that they are working for a good, responsible, successful organisation; it is part of the job of PR to ensure that this is communicated to staff. This is sometimes done by using a slogan or company motto to sum up the company's main aim. Some examples are given in Table 9.7.

Internal PR uses staff newsletters, staff training programmes and staff social events to convey a positive image. Intranet-enabled PR can include e-mailing staff about corporate developments, forums and blogs to encourage discussion of issues of interest, and there is also the capacity for direct contact with senior management. Such systems can be abused, but in most cases they are a force for good in helping to develop the corporate culture.

Because most of the front-liners are working away from the company's headquarters, the PR process has to be handled by persuasion, not by command. It would be impossible for the PR staff to be everywhere at once, following people around to ensure that they say and do the 'right' things.

Table 9.7 Examples of company slogans

Example	Explanation
We're Number Two, So We Try Harder (Avis)	This communicates to staff that the company is among the biggest, but that their efforts to 'try harder' are recognised and appreciated. It also conveys a valuable image to the customers. This slogan has become so well-known that Avis have now reduced it to 'We try harder'.
Créateur des Automobiles (Renault)	The literal translation of this French phrase, Creator of Automobiles, may not mean much, but the French phrase conveys an image of care and artistry – the cars are created, not manufactured.
Putting the Community First (Barnet Council)	Like many local government organisations, Barnet wants to reassure residents that they come first in its thinking. This slogan emphasises the community and implies that there is neighbourliness and solidarity within Barnet.

PR has a role in conciliation and internal arbitration, although much of this will be handled by human resources departments. Because internal conflict can lead to bad feeling towards the organisation, part of the PR role is to provide a clear lead in terms of corporate culture.

Public relations and the press

Usually, PR communicates through the news media. Newspapers and magazines earn their money mainly through paid advertising, but they attract readers by having stimulating articles about topics of interest to the readership.

Press releases

PR often involves creating a news story or event that brings the product or company to the public attention. A news story is more likely to be read than an advertisement and is also more likely to be believed. A press release differs from advertising in that the message is not paid for directly; the newspaper or magazine prints the story as news, and of course is able to slant the story in any way it wishes. PR people are often ex-journalists who have some contacts with the news media, and who know how to create a story that will be printed in the way the company wants it to be done. Newspaper editors are wary of thinly disguised advertisements and will only print items that are really newsworthy.

Good press releases can be much more effective than advertising for the following reasons:

- The press coverage is free, so there is better use of the promotional budget
- The message carries greater credibility because it is in the editorial part of the paper
- The message is more likely to be read, because while readers tend to skip past the advertisements, their purpose in buying the paper is to read the news stories.

Table 9.8 shows the criteria under which the press stories must be produced if they are to be published.

The news media will, of course, reserve the right to alter stories, add to them, comment on them or otherwise change them around to suit their own purposes. For example, a press agent's great little story on the launch of Britain's most powerful sports car may become part of an article on dangerous driving. There is really very little the firm can do about this.

For this reason, a large part of the PR manager's job lies in cultivating good relationships with the media. Sometimes this will involve business entertaining, but more often it will involve making the journalists' lives as easy as possible. A well written press release will often be inserted in the paper exactly as it stands, because the editorial staff are too busy to waste time rewriting something that is already perfectly acceptable.

The journals and newspapers gain as well. Normally editors have to pay for editorial, either paying freelance writers to produce articles or paying the salaries of journalists to come up with interesting stories. A good press release can go in with

Table 9.8 Criteria for successful press releases

Criterion	Example
Stories must be newsworthy, i.e. of interest to the reader	Articles about your new lower prices are not newsworthy; articles about opening a new factory creating 200 jobs are.
Stories must not be merely thinly disguised advertisements	A story saying your new car is the best on the market at only £7999 will not go in. A story saying your new car won the East African Safari Rally probably would.
Stories must fit the editorial style of the magazine or paper to which they are being sent	An article sent to the *Financial Times* about your sponsored fishing competition will not be printed; an article about the company's takeover of a competitor will.

little or no editing, and no legwork on the part of journalists, so it fills space with minimal cost to the paper.

Media events

Often companies will lay on a **media event**, a launch ceremony for a new product or to announce some change in company policy. Usually this will involve inviting journalists from the appropriate media, providing a free lunch with plenty of free drinks and inviting questions about the new development in a formal press conference. This kind of event has only a limited success, however, unless the groundwork for it has been very thoroughly laid.

Journalists tend to be suspicious of media events, sometimes feeling that the organisers are trying to buy them off with a buffet and a glass of wine. This means they may not respond positively to the message the PR people are trying to convey, and may write a critical article rather than the positive one that was hoped for.

To minimise the chance of this happening, media events should follow these basic rules:

- Do not call a media event or press conference unless you are announcing something that the press will find interesting
- Check that there are no negative connotations in what you are announcing
- Ensure that you have some of the company's senior executives there to talk to the press, not just the PR people
- Only invite journalists with whom you feel you have a good working relationship
- Do not be too lavish with the refreshments
- Ensure that your senior executives (in fact, anybody who is going to speak to the press) have had some training in doing this. This is particularly important for TV
- Be prepared to answer all questions truthfully. Journalists are trained to spot lies and evasions.

Journalists much prefer to be able to talk directly to genuine corporate executives rather than being allowed only to talk to the PR department; however, care should be exercised in ensuring that the executives spoken to are able to handle this type of questioning. It is also a good idea to have a press office that can handle queries from journalists promptly, honestly and enthusiastically and can arrange interviews with senior personnel if necessary.

PR and the Internet

It goes without saying that a good, interactive website is an essential component for effective PR. Most people considering doing business with a company will want to check the website first, if only to find out what the company can offer. Since people will probably check several websites, the PR people need to ensure that the company's website presents a fair but positive image of the company.

A good corporate website will include the following features:

- *Company history.* The background to the company's foundation and development is an important factor for people in deciding how solid the firm is
- *Mission or vision statement.* This tells prospective customers what the company is all about; in other words, its guiding philosophy
- *Profiles of senior management.* This puts a human face on the company. For example, Waterstone's bookshop website has a section where senior managers talk about their favourite books
- *Any sponsorship or charitable activities undertaken by the firm.* Apart from the opportunity to increase the effectiveness of those activities, their inclusion on the website shows that the company takes its corporate responsibilities seriously
- *A contact point for comments about the company or its products.* This should be an e-mail address, but a telephone number should also be included since a lack of a contact point may make it seem that the company has something to hide or is not prepared to speak to its customers
- *A press page.* This should include latest press releases and contact details for the press officer or PR manager.

All of the above features should be included purely from a PR perspective. Obviously the website will also have sections aimed at increasing business; for example, product descriptions and pictures, contact details for salespeople and retailers and possibly online ordering facilities.

PR and other publics

PR involves dealing with the company's other **publics**, apart from the consumers. These are typically the following groups:

- Shareholders, for whom the company will produce end-of-year reports, special privileges and so forth

- Government departments, with whom the company will liaise about planned legislation or other government activities
- The workforce
- External pressure groups such as environmentalists or lobbyists.

Pressure groups can cause problems for companies by producing adverse publicity, by picketing company plants or by encouraging boycotting of company products. This can usually be dealt with most effectively by counter-publicity.

Sometimes adverse publicity from pressure groups is dealt with by advertising. For example, McDonald's was attacked by environmental groups for indirectly encouraging the destruction of rainforests for the purpose of producing cheap beef. McDonald's responded with a series of full-page press adverts proving that beef for their hamburgers comes only from sources in the countries where it is eaten and is not imported from the Third World.

Usually a journalist who is offered a story from a pressure group will respond by trying to get the other side of the story from the firm. This is partly for legal reasons, since newspapers can be sued for libel if they print stories that turn out to be untrue, but it is also because most journalists want to ensure the accuracy and fairness of their stories. This means that a firm's press office, a PR manager or even a senior executive may be asked for comment with little or no prior warning. It is therefore advisable to be as prepared as possible beforehand and to answer as fully as possible in the event of being asked questions. However, it is better to delay comment than to say something that will make matters worse.

In these circumstances, it is better to use a phrase such as 'I'm sorry, I'll have to look into that and get back to you later' than to use the standard 'No comment'. The former phrase at least gives the impression that you are trying to help, whereas 'No comment' gives the impression that you are trying to hide something.

Defensive PR

Defensive PR is about responding to attacks from outside the firm and counteracting them as they arise. The attacks might come from pressure groups, from investigative reporters or from members of parliament. The safest way to handle this type of attack is to begin by trying to understand the enemy and, to this end, the following questions should be asked:

- Are they justified in their criticism?
- What facts do they have at their disposal?
- Who are they trying to influence?
- How are they trying to do it?

If the pressure group is justified in its criticisms, it may be necessary to help them to effect the changes in the organisation to quell the criticism. Otherwise the problem will simply continue. Good PR people will always respond in some way; however, as anyone who watches investigative reporters on TV will know, the company managers and directors who flee with a hasty 'No comment' always look guilty, whereas the ones who are prepared to be interviewed always appear honest (until the reporter produces the irrefutable evidence, of course).

During such a crisis, the news media can greatly increase the negative effects on the brand image, as compared with the effects that would occur purely through consumers' direct experience (Yannopoulou *et al.* 2011).

Another aspect of defensive PR is crisis management. Some industries (for example airlines) are more prone to crises than others, but any company can be subject to bad publicity of one sort or another. A good approach to handling crises is to be prepared beforehand by establishing a crisis team who are able to speak authoritatively to the media in the event of a problem arising. The crisis team should meet regularly and should consider hypothetical cases and their responses to them. They should also ensure that they are immediately available in the event of a crisis occurring.

Proactive PR

Proactive PR means setting out deliberately to influence opinion, without waiting for an attack from outside. Here the manager will decide on the following:

- Whom to influence
- What to influence them about
- How to influence them
- How to marshal the arguments carefully to maximise the impact.

Overall, it is probably better to be proactive rather than defensive (or reactive) because that way the PR office is in control of the process and is better prepared. If the firm is planning on dumping toxic waste in a beauty spot, for example, it is better to contact Greenpeace beforehand and get its opinion rather than suffer the inevitable protests afterwards and take a chance on being able to patch up any problems.

What PR will do

Good PR will achieve the following outcomes for the firm:

- Help to build a positive image
- Counter bad publicity
- Improve employee motivation
- Improve the effectiveness of both advertising and the salesforce.

On the other hand, here are some of the things that PR will *not* do for the firm:

- Directly increase sales
- Cover up something adverse to the company
- Replace other promotional activities.

Ultimately, PR works best as part of a planned and integrated programme of promotional activities which includes advertising, sales promotion and personal selling. It works worst when used only occasionally and in isolation.

Word-of-mouth

Word-of-mouth is probably the most powerful communication medium in existence and can be used by marketers to good effect. The reasons for the power of word-of-mouth are as follows:

- It is interactive, involving a discussion between the parties. This forces the recipient to think about the communication. The problem for marketers is that the interaction takes place between parties who are not usually under the control of the firm
- It allows for feedback and confirmation of the messages
- The source, being a disinterested friend or acquaintance, carries a lot more credibility than any marketer-generated communications.

People often discuss products and services; they like to talk about their own recent purchases, to advise people considering a purchase, to show friends and family their latest acquisitions and even to discuss controversial or interesting marketing communications. The problem for marketers is that people will talk about products and companies whether the firm likes it or not, and there is very little that firms can do to control the process. Word-of-mouth communications can therefore be positive or negative, and it often appears that bad news travels twice as fast as good news, so that much word-of-mouth is negative. Interestingly, some word-of-mouth is more effective before the initiator of it has experienced the product; there is evidence that word-of-mouth is at its most active before a movie is released, rather than afterwards (Yong 2006). The richness of the message and the degree of implied or explicit advocacy of the product are key themes in the success of positive word-of-mouth (Mazzarol *et al.* 2007).

Table 9.9 shows some of the ways that marketers can increase positive word-of-mouth. Part of the problem for the marketer lies in identifying the opinion leaders in a given market. Journalists, influential individuals and organisations in industry, and some prominent TV pundits are obviously easy to identify, but among the general public it usually takes careful research to identify the people who are likely to be opinion leaders regarding a particular product. The main characteristics of influentials are shown in Table 9.10.

Much word-of-mouth communication is, unfortunately, negative. Some authorities state that dissatisfied customers tell three times as many people about the product than do satisfied customers; if true, this means that preventing negative word-of-mouth is actually a more pressing problem for marketers than is generating positive word-of-mouth. Complaint handling is therefore a key issue (see Chapter 3).

The electronic version of word-of-mouth, word-of-mouse, has become vastly more important with the advent of social networking sites. Astute marketers have tapped into this; many corporations now have pages on Facebook, and the use of free games on corporate websites has encouraged people to e-mail their friends with links to the site. There is more on social networking in Chapter 12.

Table 9.9 Ways to encourage positive word-of-mouth

Method	Explanation and examples
Press releases	A press release with a good, newsworthy story will usually stimulate discussion, particularly if it is linked to another promotion. For example, a press release announcing a sports competition for school squash players will generate word-of-mouth among squash players.
Bring-a-friend schemes	In these schemes an existing customer is invited to recruit a friend in exchange for a small reward. In some cases, the reward is given to the friend rather than to the introducer – some people feel uncomfortable about accepting a reward for 'selling' to a friend. For example, a health club might have special 'bring a friend' days when the friend is allowed to use all the facilities free for a day. This gives the member a chance to show off his or her club, and encourages the friend to join.
Awards and certificates	Trophies and certificates are sometimes displayed, and often talked about. For example, Laphroaig Whisky distillery has a Friends of Laphroaig club, in which the members (regular drinkers of the whisky) are given a square foot of land on the island of Islay and a certificate of ownership. The proud owners of this little piece of Scotland frequently mention it to their friends, especially when offering them a glass of the whisky itself. The distillers also occasionally invite the Friends of Laphroaig to nominate a friend to receive a free miniature of the whisky, on the grounds that the 'Friend' could be sure of a 'dram' when calling on the 'friend'.
T-shirts	Promotional clothing often excites comment from friends: designer labels, names of bands, names of tourist destinations and names of concert venues all provoke comment from friends and acquaintances.
Viral marketing	Some websites include games, jokes or interesting images which visitors are invited to 'e-mail to a friend'. In most cases, the web link would only be sent on to those friends the original visitor thinks might be interested in the product category. Note: this is entirely different from the unsolicited e-mails called spam which are sent out indiscriminately.

Table 9.10 Characteristics of influentials

Characteristic	Description of influential
Demographics	Wide differences according to product category. For fashions and film-going, young women dominate. For self-medication, women with children are most influential. Generally, demography shows low correlation and is not a good predictor.
Social activity	Influencers and opinion leaders are usually gregarious.
General attitudes	Generally innovative and positive towards new products.
Personality and lifestyle	Low correlation of personality with opinion leadership. Lifestyle tends to be more fashion conscious, more socially active, more independent.
Product-related	Influencers are more interested in the specific product area than are others. They are active searchers and information gatherers, especially from the mass media.

People who are knowledgeable about products and like to advise other people are called mavens. They often have a higher need for variety than opinion leaders and are often less involved with the product categories; however, both groups have high levels of satisfaction with the products they use and recommend (Stokburger-Sauer and Hoyer 2009).

Sponsorship

Sponsorship of the arts or of sporting events is an increasingly popular way of generating positive feelings about firms. Sponsorship has been defined as 'An investment, in cash or kind, in an activity in return for access to the exploitable commercial potential associated with this activity' (Meenaghan 1991).

Sponsorship in the United Kingdom grew from £4 million in 1970 (Buckley 1980) to £35 million by 1980 (Mintel 1990) and £400 million by 1993 (Mintel 1993). Much of this increase in expenditure came about because tobacco firms are severely restricted in what they are allowed to advertise and where they are allowed to advertise it; thus sponsorship of Formula One racing and of horse racing and cricket matches by tobacco firms became commonplace. This source of sponsorship has now ceased, because tobacco firms are no longer allowed to sponsor events; in some cases this has forced events to cut back or even disappear altogether.

Companies sponsor for a variety of different reasons, as Table 9.11 shows (Zafer Erdogan and Kitchen 1998).

Sponsorship attempts to link beliefs about the sponsoring organisation or brand and connect them to an event or organisation that is highly valued by target consumers (Zafer Erdogan and Kitchen 1998). The success of a sports team has a significant effect on fans' purchase of sponsors' products (Lings and Owen 2007), so it is worthwhile spending some time choosing the correct team to back – it is also worthwhile being loyal to a team, as audiences become increasingly aware of the

Table 9.11 Reasons for sponsorship

Objectives	% Agreement	Rank
Press coverage/exposure/opportunity	84.6	1
TV coverage/exposure/opportunity	78.5	2
Promote brand awareness	78.4	3
Promote corporate image	77.0	4
Radio coverage/exposure/opportunity	72.3	5
Increase sales	63.1	6
Enhance community relations	55.4	7
Entertain clients	43.1	8
Benefit employees	36.9	9
Match competition	30.8	10
Fad/fashion	26.2	11

sponsor's brand the longer the sponsorship continues (Mason and Cochetel 2006; Lacey *et al.* 2007). Sponsoring rival teams is a mistake; although it might seem as if the company is hedging its bets, supporters of each team resent support of the rivals, thus cancelling out any goodwill engendered by support for their own team (Davies *et al.* 2006).

Sponsorship is not adequate as a stand-alone policy. Although firms can run perfectly adequate PR campaigns without advertising, sponsorship will not work effectively unless the sponsoring firm is prepared and able to publicise the link. Some researchers estimate that two to three times the cost of sponsorship needs to be spent on advertising if the exercise is to be effective (Heffler 1994). In most cases it is necessary to spell out the reasons for the firm's sponsorship of the event to make the link clear to the audience; merely saying 'Official snack of the Triathlon' is insufficient. Since the audience is usually interested in anything about the event, it is quite possible to go into a brief explanation of the reasoning behind the sponsorship; for example, to say 'Our snack gives energy – and that's what every triathlete needs more than anything. That's why we sponsor the Triathlon.'

The evidence is that consumers do feel at least some gratitude towards the sponsors of their favourite events; whether this is gratitude *per se* or whether it is affective linking is hard to say, and the answer to that question may not be of much practical importance anyway (Crimmins and Horn 1996). There are certainly spin-offs for the internal PR of the firm; most employees like to feel that they are working for a caring organisation, and sponsorship money also (on occasion) leads to free tickets or price reductions for staff of the sponsoring organisation.

Sponsorship appears to work best when there is some existing link between the sponsoring company and the event itself. In other words, a company that manufactures fishing equipment would be more successful sponsoring a fishing competition than it would in sponsoring a painting competition. More subtly, a bank would be better off sponsoring a middle-class, 'respectable' arts event such as an opera rather than an open-air rock concert. The following criteria apply when considering sponsorship (Heffler 1994):

- The sponsorship must be economically viable; it should be cost-effective, in other words
- The event or organisation being sponsored should be consistent with the brand image and overall marketing communications plans
- It should offer a strong possibility of reaching the desired target audience
- Care should be taken if the event has been sponsored before; the audience may confuse the sponsors and you may be benefiting the earlier sponsor.

Occasionally a competitor will try to divert the audience's attention to themselves by implying that they are sponsoring the event; this is called ambushing (Bayless 1988). For example, during the 2010 World Cup it was common for firms to use World Cup events in their advertising or sales promotions without actually sponsoring anything to do with the event itself.

Another risk in sponsoring an individual (say, a sportsperson) is that there may be a negative incident such as a drugs conviction. Brand managers may respond to these events in many different ways, depending on attribution of blame, societal norms, zone of tolerance and perceived severity of the event (Westberg *et al.* 2011). If a cultural event has been sponsored for some time, ending the relationship can be difficult for the staff who have been involved in the sponsorship programme – in some cases they may try to continue with relationships established with the other organisation during the sponsorship period despite management attempts to prevent this (Ryan and Blois 2010).

Critical thinking

If it's so easy to ambush an event, why would anybody pay to be a sponsor? After all, ambushing is easy – all the firm has to do is put 'Olympic-Size Offers!' on its publicity to cash in on the Olympic Games, or 'Marathon Guarantees!' to ride piggy-back on the London Marathon.

On the other hand, maybe supporters and fans of these events can see through that kind of ploy – and react accordingly. Being exposed as a bit of a liar is hardly good for the corporate image.

Sponsorship is likely to grow in importance in the foreseeable future. More credible than advertising, it is often cheaper and has important effects on both brand and corporate image; given the restrictions being imposed on advertising, sponsorship has much to offer.

INTEGRATING THE PROMOTIONAL MIX

Communication does not necessarily create all its impact at once. A series of communications will move the recipient up a 'ladder' of effects, as shown in Figure 9.6. At the bottom of the ladder are those consumers who are completely unaware of the product in question; at the top of the ladder are those who actually purchase the product.

Given the differing nature of the consumer's involvement at each stage of the hierarchy, it is clear that no single communication method will work at every stage. Equally, not every consumer will be at the same stage at the same time; therefore it follows that several different communications approaches will need to run at once if the communications package is to work effectively.

- In the early stages of a product launch, moving consumers from *brand ignorance* to *brand awareness* will be largely the province of advertising. At first, the marketer needs to get the consumers' attention and prepare them for the more detailed information which is to follow. A teaser campaign is almost entirely concerned with creating awareness.

Figure 9.6 The hierarchy of communications effects

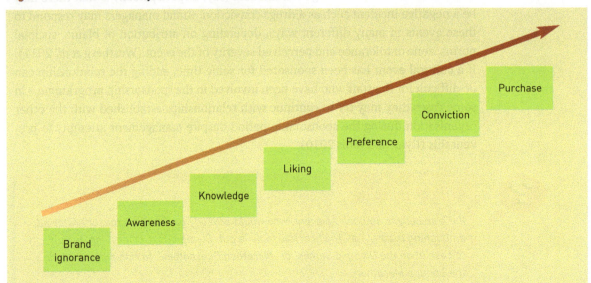

- Having made the target audience aware of the product, the next stage is to build *knowledge*. Again, mass advertising will play a major role, but if the product is complex it may be necessary to use **mailshots** or other more personal communications. This is because the emphasis is on providing information about the product: what it is, what it does, how it works and even that it works at all. In some cases an element of prior knowledge can be assumed; for example, most people would already know that fluoride is a good thing to have in toothpaste, not quite so many would know that it helps prevent tooth decay and very few would know how it works.
- *Liking* for the product might come from trying it (perhaps through a sales promotion), from reading positive news stories about it (PR) or from persuasive advertising. Liking is an attitude towards a product, and therefore has elements of affect, cognition and conation (see Chapter 3).
- *Preference* for the product implies comparison with other brands, so is very much concerned with positioning. An important point to note is that preference will come about only if the product matches up to (or exceeds) the claims made for it in the earlier advertising; if the claims made were inaccurate, unrealistic or simply misunderstood, the consumer will be disappointed and will not buy the product again. Also, preference implies that the consumer will need to have sufficient knowledge of the pros and cons of other brands; salespeople will play a role in this part of the process if the product is a high-value one, since they will often be able to point out the drawbacks of competing brands.
- **Conviction** may come about only after several trials of the product (if it is a fast-moving consumer good) or after a lengthy discussion with a salesperson if the product is a high-value or high-involvement item. **Adoption** is the final stage of the process, when the consumer builds the product into his or her daily life.

There is likely to be some 'slippage' because it is not possible to expose all the target audience to the communication at the same time. Also, some consumers will already know more than others about the product category. Marketers will need to overlap the promotional effort to give maximum coverage.

One of the problems with the hierarchy of communications effects is that it implies that the process is invariably linear. This is not necessarily the case; an individual can become aware of a product and form an instant liking for it without having detailed knowledge of the product. Equally, it is perfectly possible for a consumer to buy a product on impulse and form an opinion about it afterwards.

Having said that, the hierarchy of effects model is helpful in planning communications campaigns, since different communications methods and styles can be used according to the consumer's level on the hierarchy. For example, when a new product is introduced (or a product is introduced into a new market), few of the target audience will know anything about it.

CASE STUDY 9 British Gas

During the Industrial Revolution, the discovery of coal gas revolutionised energy distribution in towns and cities throughout Britain. The gas, extracted by heating coal, could be piped to homes and businesses to be used for lighting, cooking and heating; the residue from the manufacturing process, coke, could be burned as an almost smokeless fuel with very few harmful emissions. Initially, coal gas (or town gas, as it was commonly known) was produced by local town councils or by private companies, each operating only within its local area. This system worked well, since the technology did not exist at the time to pump the gas over long distances; making gas-tight pipework was prohibitively expensive since it had to be made of lead. However, following on from the Second World War, gas production and distribution had been so badly damaged by bombing that the local gas producers were unable to repair the damage and thus the country's entire gas industry was nationalised. The country was divided up into twelve regions, each with its own Gas Board, each under independent management.

During the 1960s the gas boards diversified, opening up high street showrooms to promote the use of gas for all household energy needs. At the same time, the other great nationalised energy business, the Electricity Board, was also promoting the use of its fuel. However, in the mid-1960s large reserves of natural gas were discovered under the North Sea and the decision was made to convert the entire country to natural gas. Over the following 10 years, new gas mains were laid throughout the country and a gas national grid was developed to move gas to where it was needed.

During the 1980s British Gas was privatised, with shares being sold largely to the general public. Following this, the energy industry was deregulated, allowing any competent company to enter the market and thus opening up real competition for the first time. This meant that British Gas had to compete directly with the electricity companies, but could sell electricity as well as gas. Deregulation led to a wide range of companies entering the market and thus to cut-throat competition; householders found that salespeople were appearing on the doorstep looking to persuade them to switch suppliers and there were many instances of sharp practice by these salespeople – forging signatures on documents was far from unknown, and many people were surprised to find themselves being telephoned by their supplier asking why they were defecting to the opposition. This kind of behaviour tended to bring the industry into disrepute and major efforts were made to clean up the marketing effort.

Nowadays, British Gas offers a wide range of services. In common with other energy suppliers, the company offers a range of energy-saving devices. It also offers a maintenance service for gas-fired central heating systems, mainly through a monthly insurance payment. The company sells central heating systems and replacement boilers, but no longer operates high street retail outlets for appliances; these are catered for more effectively through more general retailers, who are able to offer dual-fuel devices (for example, cookers with electric ovens and gas hobs) which were formerly unavailable owing to the monopoly positions of the gas and electricity suppliers.

For British Gas, the main marketing problem lies in creating a unique selling proposition. Gas is gas is gas – the specifications of the core product cannot be altered, and in any case the gas is supplied through the same grid whichever company markets it, i.e. British Gas has to pay wholesale prices for the gas it puts into the grid, and receives the retail price from its consumers – there is no way of identifying which exact molecules of gas are which once it enters the pipeline. In common with other suppliers, British Gas has to be creative in its pricing structure – offering people fixed prices for a given period, offering special tariffs for high users, and so forth. In terms of electricity supplies, there is slightly more scope; some suppliers offer sustainably sourced power from wind farms or hydroelectric dams, some specialise in nuclear power sources, and so forth – but again, the actual electrons are pretty much identical.

This being the case, British Gas relies heavily on its peripheral services and has developed a strong position in the servicing, maintenance and fitting area. Although there are many small local gas fitters who will service central heating boilers, British Gas has by far the largest share of the market. The company also has an extensive training programme, helped by the fact that UK law prevents anyone who is not a qualified gas fitter from servicing boilers or any other gas appliances. Similar rules do not as yet apply to electrical work, although there are moves to introduce such regulations. Engineers who service the boilers are in a strong position to recommend new boilers when necessary – the life of a boiler can be as short as 10–12 years, and engineers are able to recommend boilers which are more reliable or better suited to the circumstances of the householder. It is obviously in the interests of British Gas to recommend reliable boilers, since the service contracts operate on a fixed monthly subscription rather than a per-call basis.

There are clearly some threats on the horizon, however. North Sea Gas is running out; the UK is no longer self-sufficient in gas but has to rely on imports from Russia and elsewhere. Gas prices are rising rapidly, and consequently people are beginning to shift to other fuels – wood-burning stoves are gaining a new popularity since they are more environmentally sustainable and also many people are able to obtain wood at a low cost, or even free. The cost advantage gas used to have over electric heating has also been eroded, as more electricity is generated from wind farms and nuclear power. Recent changes in the tax regime for gas producers have meant that some very large gas fields have become uneconomic and have been closed. On the other hand, new gas fields may be discovered at any time.

For the time being, British Gas seems to be holding its own against competition, insecure supplies and legislative changes. Whether the company can continue to reinvent itself as the environment around it shifts is another matter.

Questions

1. How might British Gas use PR to counter the bad publicity surrounding doorstep selling?
2. How might British Gas use innovative communications methods to create a USP?
3. How might British Gas counter the threat from alternative fuels?
4. What might be the role of sales promotion for British Gas?
5. How could the personal selling process be managed better?

SUMMARY

This chapter has been about the ways companies communicate with their publics. In it, we have looked at the main promotional tools that marketers have at their disposal, and at the strengths and weaknesses of each of those tools.

Here are the key points from this chapter:

- Communications work best when there is feedback
- It is essential for the sender of the message to have a common field of experience with the receiver
- The AIDA model can rarely be achieved with one form of communication
- The promotional mix is a recipe; the ingredients are not interchangeable
- Publicity and PR are probably the most cost-effective promotional tools you have available
- The media are interested only in newsworthy items, not in thinly disguised advertisements. PR works best when used as part of an integrated programme of activities
- PR requires a long-term commitment to cultivating the media
- It is advisable to invest in training anybody who may have to deal with the press, and even more so with TV
- PR will only help publicise your good points; it will not give you what you have not got
- Advertising is not the only way to increase sales, and may not even be the best way
- Advertising needs to be planned and targeted to the right segment to avoid wasting money and effort on people who will not buy the product
- People will not read long-winded advertisements
- Artwork is more memorable than copy
- Selling is about meeting the customer's needs with a suitable product from the range
- Selling is learned, not somehow magically inborn
- Sponsorship tends to have strong positive effects on both brand and corporate images.

CHAPTER QUESTIONS

1 How can sales promotions help a company's production planning process?

2 What are the main advantages of PR over advertising?

3 'The aim of marketing must be to make selling superfluous.' Discuss.

4 Which part of the AIDA model does personal selling best achieve?

5 What is the purpose of sponsorship?

Further reading

Marketing Communications: Interactivity, Communities and Content, 5th edn by Chris Fill (Harlow, FT Prentice Hall, 2009) gives a very good, readable overview of marketing communications. Chris Fill is a Senior Examiner for the Chartered Institute of Marketing, and the book certainly covers all the necessary ground.

Marketing Communications, 3rd edn by Jim Blythe (Harlow, Financial Times Prentice Hall, 2005) offers a more in-depth look at marketing communications theory and practice than is possible in this chapter.

How I Raised Myself from Failure to Success in Selling by Frank Bettger (London, Cedar Press, 1990; 1st edn, World's Work 1947). Anecdotes of a highly successful American salesman. This book is out of print at present, but if you can find a copy in a library or second-hand bookshop it makes riveting bedtime reading. A real classic!

References

Ailawadi, Kusum L. and Harlam, Bari: 'An empirical analysis of the determinants of retail margins: the role of store brand share', *Journal of Marketing,* **68** (1) (January 2004), pp. 147–55.

Baird, Thomas R., Wahlers, Russel G. and Cooper, Crystal K.: 'Non-recognition of print advertising: emotional arousal and gender effects', *Journal of Marketing Communications,* **13** (1) (2007), pp. 39–57.

Bayless, A.: 'Ambush marketing is becoming a popular event at Olympic Games', *Wall Street Journal* (8 February 1988).

Biel, A.: 'Love the advertisement, buy the product?' *ADMAP* (October 1989).

Bronn, Peggy Simcic: 'Building corporate brands through community involvement: is it exportable? The case of the Ronald McDonald House in Norway', *Journal of Marketing Communication,* **12** (4) (2006), pp. 309–20.

Brown, G.: 'Modelling advertising awareness', *ADMAP* (April 1991).

Buckley, D.: 'Who pays the piper?' *Practice Review* (Spring 1980).

Cornelissen, Joep P. and Harris, Phil: 'Interdependencies between marketing and public relations disciplines as correlates of communication organization', *Journal of Marketing,* **20** (1) (February 2004), pp. 237–65.

Crimmins, J. and Horn, M.: 'Sponsorship: from management ego trip to marketing success', *Journal of Advertising Research,* **36** (4) (July/August 1996), pp. 11–21.

D'Astous, Alain and Landreville, Valerie: 'An experimental investigation of factors affecting consumers' perceptions of sales promotions', *European Journal of Marketing,* **37** (11) (2003), pp. 1746–61.

Davies, Fiona, Veloutsou, Cleopatra and Costa, Andrew: 'Investigating the influences of a joint sponsorship of rival teams on supporter attitudes and brand preferences', *Journal of Marketing Communications,* **12** (1) (2006), pp. 31–48.

Davies, Iain A., Ryals, Lynette J. and Holt, Sue: 'Relationship management: a sales role, or a state of mind? An investigation of functions and attitudes across a business-to-business sales force', *Industrial Marketing Management* **39** (7) (October 2010), pp. 1049–62.

Engel, James F., Warshaw, Martin R. and Kinnear, Thomas C.: *Promotional Strategy* (Chicago, Irwin, 1994).

Farris, P.W. and Buzzell, R.D.: 'Why advertising and promotional costs vary: some cross-sectional analyses', *Journal of Marketing* (Fall, 1979).

Hansen, Jochim, Strick, Madelijn, van Baaren, Rick B., Hooghuis, Mirjam and Wigboldus, Daniel H.: 'Exploring memory for product names advertised with humour', *Journal of Consumer Behaviour*, 8 (2/3) (Mar-Jun 2009), pp. 135-48.

Harris, Greg: 'International advertising: developmental and implementational issues', *Journal of Marketing Management*, 12 (1996), pp. 551-60.

Heffler, Mava: 'Making sure sponsorship meets all the parameters', *Brandweek* (May 1994), p. 16.

Herzberg, F.: *Work and Nature of Man* (London, William Collins, 1966).

Institute of Public Relations: *Public Relations Practice: Its Roles and Parameters* (London, The Institute of Public Relations, 1984).

Lacey, Russel, Sneath, Julie Z., Finney, Zachary R. and Close, Angeline G.: 'The impact of repeat attendance on event sponsorship effects', *Journal of Marketing Communications*, 13 (4) (2007), pp. 243-55.

Lambe, C. Jay, Webb, Kevin L. and Ishida, Chiharu: 'Self-managing selling teams and team performance: The complementary role of empowerment and control', *Industrial Marketing Management*, 38 (1) (January 2009), pp. 5-16.

Lings, Ian N. and Owen, Kate M.: 'Buying a sponsor's brand: the role of affective commitment to the sponsored team', *Journal of Marketing Management*, 23 (5/6) (2007), pp. 483-96.

Mantovani, G.: *New Communication Environments: From Everyday to Virtual* (London, Taylor & Francis, 1996).

Maslow, Abraham: *Motivation and Personality* (New York, Harper and Row, 1954).

Mason, Roger B. and Cochetel, Fabrice: 'Residual brand awareness following the termination of a long-term event sponsorship and the appointment of a new sponsor', *Journal of Marketing Communications*, 12 (2) (2006), pp. 125-44.

Mazzarol, Tim, Sweeney, Gillian C. and Soutar, Geoffrey N.: 'Conceptualising word-of-mouth activities, triggers and conditions: an exploratory study', *European Journal of Marketing*, 41 (11/12) (2007), pp. 1475-94.

McAlister, Leigh, Srinavasan, Raji and Kim, Minching: 'Advertising, research and development, and systematic risk of the firm', *Journal of Marketing*, 71 (1) (2007), pp. 35-45.

Meenaghan, J.A.: 'The role of sponsorship in the marketing communication mix', *International Journal of Advertising*, 10 (1) (1991), pp. 35-47.

Mintel: *Special Report on Sponsorship* (London, Mintel, 1990).

Mintel: *Special Report on Sponsorship* (London, Mintel, 1993).

Moran, W.T.: 'Insights from pricing research' in E.B. Bailey (ed.), *Pricing Practices and Strategies* (New York, The Conference Board, 1978), pp. 7 and 13.

Patti, Charles H.: 'Evaluating the role of advertising', *Journal of Advertising* (Fall, 1977), pp. 32-3.

Pieters, Rik and Wedel, Michel: 'Attention capture and transfer in advertising: brand, pictorial and text-size effects', *Journal of Marketing*, 68 (2) (April 2004), pp 36-50.

Rajagopal: 'Outsourcing salespeople in building arousal towards retail buying', *Journal of Database Marketing and Customer Strategy Management*, 15 (2) (2008), pp.106-18.

Ramaswamy, Sridhar N. and Singh, Jagdip: 'Antecedents and consequences of merit pay fairness for industrial salespeople', *Journal of Marketing*, **67** (4) (October 2003), pp. 46–66.

Ranganjaran, Deva, Chonko, Lawrence B., Jones, Eli and Roberts, James A.: 'Organisational variables, sales force perceptions of readiness for change, learning and performance among boundary-spanning teams: a conceptual framework and propositions for research', *Industrial Marketing Management*, **33** (4) (2004), pp. 289–305.

Rosengren, Sara and Dahlen, Micael: 'Brand-slogan matching in a cluttered environment', *Journal of Marketing Communication*, **12** (4) (2006), pp. 263–79.

Ryan, Annemarie and Blois, Keith: 'The emotional dimension of organizational work when cultural sponsorship relationships are dissolved', *Journal of Marketing Management*, **26** (7&8) (2010), pp. 612–34.

Stapel, J.: 'Monitoring advertising performance', *ADMAP* (July/August 1990).

Stapel, J.: 'Like the advertisement but does it interest me?' *ADMAP* (April 1991).

Stokburger-Sauer, Nicola E and Hoyer, Wayne D.: 'Consumer advisers revisited: What drives those with market mavenism and opinion leadership and why?' *Journal of Consumer Behaviour*, **8** (2/3) (Mar–Jun 2009), pp.100–15.

Varey, Richard: *Marketing Communications: A Critical Introduction* (London, Routledge, 2002).

Volkov, Michael, Harker, Michael and Harker, Debra: 'People who complain about advertising: the aficionados, guardians, activists and seekers', *Journal of Marketing Management*, **22** (3/4) (2006), pp. 379–405.

Westberg, Kate, Stavros, Constantino and Wilson, Bradley: 'The impact of degenerative episodes on the sponsorship B2B relationship: Implications for brand management', *Industrial Marketing Management*, **40** (4) (May 2011), pp. 603–11.

Yannopoulou, Natalia, Koronis, Epaminondas and Elliott, Richard: 'Media amplification of a brand crisis and its effect on brand trust', *Journal of Marketing Management*, **27** (5&6) (2011), pp. 530–46.

Yong, Liu: 'Word of mouth for movies: its dynamics and impact on box-office revenue', *Journal of Marketing*, **70** (3) (2006), pp. 74–9.

Zafer Erdogan, B. and Kitchen, P.J.: 'The interaction between advertising and sponsorship: uneasy alliance or strategic symbiosis?' *Proceedings of the 3rd Annual Conference of the Global Institute for Corporate and Marketing Communications*, Strathclyde Graduate Business School, 1998.

SERVICES MARKETING

Objectives

After reading this chapter you should be able to:

- Explain the role of people, process and physical evidence in service provision
- Describe how empowerment of employees can enhance service provision and improve complaint handling
- Explain the role of risk on consumer decision-making about services
- Describe ways of improving customer loyalty in services
- Appreciate the importance of services in the economy
- Show how to motivate employees in service industries
- Describe the consumer decision process as it applies to service products.

INTRODUCTION

In recent years services markets have reached greater prominence in industrialised countries. In part this is because of increased automation, which has meant that physical products are cheaper and easier to produce with fewer employees, and in part it is because there is a limit to how many physical products an individual might want to own. Service industries employ a far higher proportion of the workforce than does manufacturing, and services markets account for a far higher proportion of GDP than manufacturing.

Services Marketing

IKEA

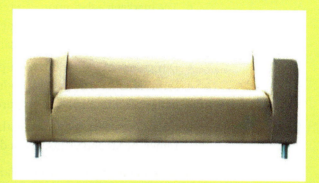

IKEA is a huge, and hugely successful, furniture retailer. The stores are huge too, and are incredibly popular; some stores in the UK attract more visitors than any tourist attraction or theme park in the country. The company's innovative designs are built around low prices – IKEA say they design the price tag first.

Scandinavian design is world famous, and the furniture is designed to be easy to transport and assemble. The store image is much the same throughout the world, but of course the cultures of the host countries are very different and, like most service industries, the company's staff are at the heart of the shopping experience for customers. Transferring the culture across borders and maintaining a level of consistency between stores is in part a matter of transferring Swedish culture across borders. The company's founder, Ingvar Kamprad, is still in evidence in the company even though he is now officially retired. His ideas about how people can and should work together are very much in evidence. The company believes that people want to share the IKEA culture, in which staff are referred to as co-workers and are empowered to provide solutions for customers who have problems.

IKEA is almost surprised by its own success. Suddenly becoming a world citizen, rather than just a Swedish furniture shop, is something the company is still coming to terms with.

Josephine Rydberg-Dumont, President, IKEA Sweden

Watch the video clip, then try to answer the following questions. The answers are on the companion website.

Questions

1. What is the importance of staff empowerment for IKEA?
2. What problems might arise from running a global service company for consumers?
3. How does IKEA add value to the basic physical product?

SERVICES v PHYSICAL PRODUCTS

For many marketers, the difference between services marketing and the marketing of physical goods is negligible. This is for the following reasons:

- The marketer's definition of a product as being a bundle of benefits. An individual seeking to be cheered up may achieve this by going to a good movie (a service) or by buying a new shirt (a physical product). The benefit is basically the same.
- Difficulties of definition. Most physical goods contain a service aspect and most services contain a physical product. In other words, most products lie somewhere along a continuum between purely service and purely physical products.
- Consumer orientation means that we should be looking at what the consumer thinks, needs and wants, not at defining our product in terms of its characteristics.

Some authors go even further: Vargo and Lusch (2004) postulate that all products are actually providing a service – a customer buying an electric drill is not buying a drill, nor even buying holes, but is buying a hole-drilling service which is co-created in the interaction between the customer and the physical product. This perspective, called service-dominant logic, has received increased interest in recent years and may well become the dominant view of how marketing works.

Having said that, there are clearly products where the service element is the major part of the cost of the product; for example, a restaurant meal. Here the cost of the raw materials (the ingredients of the food served) is only a tiny part of the overall cost of the meal. A gourmet dinner costing a week's wages may have been made from ingredients costing a tenth of the final bill; the diner is paying for the skill of the chef, the time and efforts of the waiters, and the pleasure of dining in luxurious surroundings (not to mention not having to do the washing-up). The main differences between service products and physical goods are shown in Table 11.1.

Successful brands in service industries have the following characteristics (DeChernatony and Cottam 2006):

- The companies concerned have a holistic, consistent and integrated approach to branding
- They focus on excellent customer service
- They have an ethos which challenges the norm; in other words, they do things differently from competitors
- They are responsive to change
- They have a high level of brand literacy; in other words, they understand how branding works
- There is synergy between the brand and the corporate culture.

Brand strength in service industries is linked to four factors: first, investment in marketing communications; second, contributing to the wider community; third, improving internal communication; and fourth, improving service quality (Gray 2006).

Table 11.1 Factors distinguishing services from physical products

Factor	Explanation and examples
Services are intangible	An insurance policy is more than the paper it is written on; the key benefit (peace of mind) cannot be touched.
Production and consumption often occur at virtually the same time	A stage play is acted out at the same time as the consumer enjoys the performance. Of course, the consumer also enjoys remembering the play and discussing it with friends for some time afterwards, so consumption does continue.
Services are perishable	An airline seat is extremely perishable; once the aeroplane takes off, the seat cannot be sold. Services cannot be produced in advance and stockpiled.
Services cannot be tried out before buying	It is not usually possible to try out a haircut before agreeing to have it done, nor will restaurants allow customers to eat the meal before committing to ordering and paying for it.
Services are variable, even from the same supplier	Sometimes the chef has a bad day or the waiter is in a bad mood; on the other hand, sometimes the hairdresser has a flash of inspiration that transforms the client's appearance.

These factors affect staff working in the industries as much as they affect consumers and other stakeholders.

SERVICES AND CONSUMER BEHAVIOUR

From the consumer's viewpoint, the risk attached to buying a service will inevitably be higher than is the risk of buying a physical product. Physical products are easily returned if they fail to satisfy; it is impossible to return a poor haircut and, unless the standard is very poor, it may even be difficult to avoid paying for it. Even a minor defect in a personal stereo can justify returning the item; an uncomfortable tram ride with a rude conductor will not result in a refund of the fare.

The result of this is that consumers are likely to spend more time on information-gathering and will rely more heavily on word-of-mouth recommendations than they would when buying a physical product. For professional services, the consumer is likely to examine the credentials and experience of the service provider. For example, a consumer looking for a doctor may want to know what experience and qualifications the doctor has to treat a particular complaint; few car buyers would be interested in the qualifications and experience of Ford's chief design engineer.

Service purchasing follows a slightly different sequence from purchase of a physical good, as shown in Figure 11.1. For a physical product, the experience of using the product (and consequently its evaluation) mainly occurs after purchase,

Figure 11.1 Service purchasing sequence compared with physical product purchasing sequence

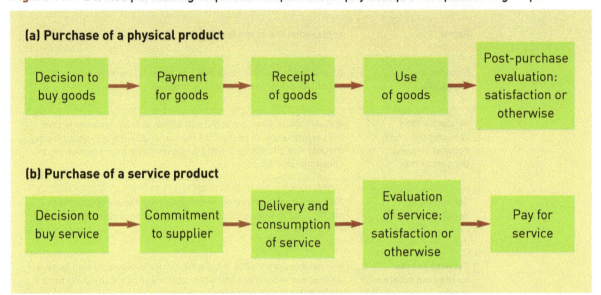

in some cases over a period of years after purchase. For a service product, the consumption experience happens immediately, as does virtually all of the evaluation – one decides whether a meal was enjoyable while enjoying it, and one either enjoys a flight or one does not. Some post-purchase evaluation may happen through discussion or second thoughts for products such as hairstyles but, in the main, services are evaluated immediately. Equally, some services are paid for in advance (transport, for example), but many are paid for after evaluation. This creates a risk for the supplier.

In most cases, customer satisfaction has traditionally been measured immediately during or after the provision of the service, since the memory of being satisfied tends to decline over time. However, satisfaction is a poor predictor of future purchase intention. There is some evidence to show that people who still express satisfaction with a service some time after it was provided are much more likely to recommend the service or to purchase again (Koenig-Lewis and Palmer 2008).

Most of the risk attached to buying a physical product is limited to the purchase price (though no doubt there will be exceptions to this general rule). Services carry additional risks.

- *Consequential losses* arise when a service goes wrong and causes a loss to the customer. For example, a poorly handled legal case could result in the loss of thousands of pounds or even loss of liberty in a criminal case. Service providers are usually careful to explain the risks beforehand, use disclaimers in contracts and carry professional liability insurance. Consumers can sue for consequential losses.
- *Purchase price risk* is the possible loss of the purchase price when the consumer buys a service that does not work. The usual consumer response is to refuse to pay for the service, so it is advisable for the supplier to check during the service process that everything is satisfactory. This is why waiters will check that the

food is satisfactory during a meal out, and why service stations call customers when they find something serious is wrong with the car. Checking during the service provision not only makes it easier to correct problems early, it also makes it harder for customers to claim that the service went wrong to avoid paying.

- *Misunderstanding* is common in service provision because of inability to try out services (trialability). Particularly in professional services, the provider may feel that the customer would not understand the finer details of what is being done and may therefore not bother to explain properly. This can easily result in post-purchase dissonance and refusal to pay.

Because consumers are buying a promise, they are more likely to use indirect measures of quality such as price. Diners tend to assume that more expensive restaurants will provide better food and/or service, that expensive hairdressers will provide better hairdos and that expensive lawyers are more likely to win cases. Long-established firms tend to be trusted more than new firms, the assumption being that they must be good to have survived (Desai *et al.* 2008).

Having made a purchasing decision, the consumer is more likely to become *involved* with the service provider. Consumers therefore tend to have favourite restaurants, hairdressers and family solicitors with whom the relationship might continue for a lifetime. Customers are reluctant to switch bank accounts, even when problems have become apparent; even though customers will readily change brands of canned tuna to save a few pence, they will still buy the tuna from the same supermarket as usual. This is because the customer knows where everything is kept in the supermarket, understands the store's policy on returned goods, knows which credit cards are acceptable and perhaps even knows some of the staff on the tills.

Obviously things can go wrong, and people will complain. Complaints about physical products are usually resolved fairly easily; a simple replacement of the faulty product will usually be sufficient, but it is always better to go a step further and provide some further recompense if possible. Services often require a more complex and extended complaint handling procedure.

Services fall into the following categories for the purpose of correcting complaints:

- Services where it is appropriate to offer a repeat service or a voucher. Examples are dry cleaners, domestic appliance repairers and takeaway food outlets
- Services where giving the money back will usually be sufficient. Examples are retail shops, cinemas and theatres and video rental companies
- Services where consequential losses may have to be compensated for. Examples are medical services, solicitors and hairdressers.

The above categories are not necessarily comprehensive nor exclusive; sometimes it may be necessary to give back the consumer's money and also make some other redress.

People who complain have the following expectations of service employees (Gruber *et al.* 2006):

1 Positive non-verbal signals.

2 Sufficient product and process knowledge to handle the complaint.

3 Sufficient authority to resolve the issue (see the section on empowerment below).
4 That the employee should try hard to resolve the problem.
5 For the employee to take the complaint seriously.

PROVIDING SERVICES

In services markets there is more emphasis on Booms and Bitner's additional three Ps: people, process and physical evidence (see Chapter 1) (Booms and Bitner 1981). Because most services involve direct contact between the producer and the consumer, the attitude and behaviour of the *people* involved are an integral part of the product; a hairdresser's personality affects trade in a way that the personality of a production-line worker does not.

Since the consumer is usually present during all or part of the *process* of providing the service, process becomes as important as outcomes in a service market. Online check-in systems used by low-cost airlines greatly ease the service for people travelling with hand baggage only; conversely, some of these airlines do not allow the booking of seats, so there is often an unpleasant rush for good seats when the aircraft boards. These factors affect people's choice of airline in future.

Physical evidence gives the consumer something to refer to and to show other people if necessary. Since service products are usually intangible, the consumer of (say) an insurance policy will need some written evidence of its existence to feel confident in the product. Physical evidence may not be as important as people; a study of Irish theme pubs showed that patrons and employees are at least as important as the rather expensive and contrived décor of the pub (Munoz *et al.* 2006).

In many ways services can be marketed in similar ways to physical products. In most cases there is no clear demarcation between physical products and services, so the techniques for marketing them will not differ greatly. However, the additional three Ps do require some changes in the way the firm operates, as the following sections show.

People

Employees can be categorised into four groups in terms of their contact with customers (Judd 1987).

1 **Contactors**. These people have frequent and regular contact with customers. Usually they are directly involved with marketing, as salespeople, call centre operators and customer service people. They may need to be trained in customer relations because they are dealing with customers on a day-to-day basis, and they should be recruited on the basis of their social skills as well as on their business skills. They should also be the kind of people who enjoy dealing with customers – not always an easy task – and they should be genuinely interested in customers, not just trained to smile at everyone. In fact, some research shows that smiling

has little or no effect on customers, probably because they believe the smiles to be false (Hennig-Thurau *et al.* 2006).

2 **Modifiers**. These people have no direct marketing role, but they deal with customers regularly. They are receptionists, truck drivers, switchboard operators and (sometimes) warehouse personnel or progress chasers. Modifiers need good social skills and training and monitoring of performance regarding their customer contacts; they should be given a clear view of the organisation's marketing strategy and be aware of their own role within it.

3 **Influencers**. These people deal with some elements of the marketing mix, but have little or no contact with customers. In a service firm, influencers are in a distinct minority, whereas in a physical product company they may well represent the majority of staff. An example of an influencer in a service company might be a solicitor's clerk, who rarely meets clients but whose effectiveness at the task will affect the service level the customer receives. Many back-room staff in financial services also fall into this category.

4 **Isolateds**. Isolateds have no customer contact and very little to do with conventional marketing functions. Again, these people are rare in service industries, although in large financial services companies there may well be a number of people (such as canteen staff, cleaners, and so forth) who fall into this category. Although they need to be alerted to the idea that their efforts are important in supporting the other staff, they do not need any specific training for dealing with customers. In essence, their role is to create the right conditions under which the customer-focused staff can do their jobs.

Figure 11.2 displays this graphically.

Of course, everyone goes home at the end of the day and talks to family and friends about the firm and, as such, everyone in the firm bears some responsibility for the corporate image and for marketing (see Chapter 9). Creating shared values

Figure 11.2 Employees and customers

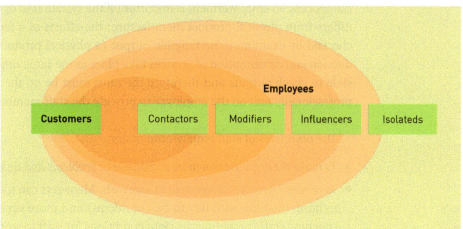

and especially creating a feeling of corporate justice (that one is working for a fair-minded company) affects how employees deal with customers; the brand image of the firm also affects employees' desire to work for the company (Knox and Freeman 2006). This in turn affects customers' perception of the organisation (Maxham and Netemeyer 2003).

Critical thinking

So if we're all marketers now, where does that leave the marketing department? Are they out of work all of a sudden? The rest of the organisation don't expect the marketers to sweep the floor, make the product and do the accounts – so surely marketers can't expect everybody else to do the marketers' work for them.

Or maybe that's what marketers are for, to create the right conditions for people to say good things about the company – and thus improve the interface between the company and its customers.

In practice, no matter how hard companies try to deliver the perfect service, the natural variability of employee performance will mean that there will always be some occasions on which the service falls below standard. This means that firms need to concentrate on recovering from service mistakes when they do occur (Rasmusson 1997). The first step in this is to empower front-line employees.

Empowerment means giving employees the authority to sort out problems without having to refer to management. This implies making employees responsible for their own actions and, more importantly, makes them responsible for controlling the service delivery. The purpose of empowering employees is to ensure that problems are dealt with as they arise, without the customer (who is already irritated by the problem) having to wait for a decision from senior management. Because service provision is carried out largely by people who are dealing with customers on a one-to-one basis, managers cannot be expected to supervise every aspect of the process, so empowerment is important if the system is to operate smoothly. This differs from physical product manufacture; the efforts of a factory worker can be checked by examining the tangible output (a physical product), but because production and consumption of services take place at the same time, it is often not possible to check outputs and therefore the onus must be on the staff member to act professionally and on the employer to provide the staff member with the authority to do so.

The objectives of staff empowerment are:

- *To make the organisation more responsive to problems* and deal with them faster.
- *To remove levels of management to save costs.* Managers can spend less time on firefighting (dealing with day-to-day problems) and more time on supporting and coaching staff (providing the right conditions for staff to work effectively).

- *To create employee networks.* If employees work more closely together and develop social links, this will encourage collaboration, teamwork and horizontal communication. This tends to improve employee motivation.

In most cases, staff prefer to be empowered since otherwise they can feel like unimportant functionaries in a large corporate machine. Being part of a small, empowered team is a strong motivator because it makes the workplace more manageable, putting everything on a human scale. Empowerment is not always a good thing, however, especially if it is poorly managed. The following problems can arise:

- Some people are risk-averse and would prefer not to accept the responsibility that empowerment implies. Sometimes managers can give extra support to these staff and may be able to offer additional motivation.
- A culture of blame can develop in which staff are blamed for wrong decisions. If staff make mistakes, this should be seen as a learning experience, not an occasion for punishment. The occasional wrong decision is much better than a situation where staff are afraid to make any decisions at all.
- Empowerment should not be taken back as soon as any important or interesting decisions have to be made. This is extremely demotivating for staff.
- Employees can become afraid of making wrong decisions because the boundaries are not clear. Clear guidelines need to be given, but without having too many rigid rules; it is impossible to anticipate every possible situation, so fixed regulations are counter-productive.
- Communication can sometimes be poor within the group. Whether the communication fails between management and employees, or between employees, failure to communicate means that customer problems can be dealt with in wildly different ways, leading to further customer dissatisfaction.

Murphy (2001) warns that empowerment can become a negative factor for some employees, who feel that management is abnegating responsibility and expecting employees to carry out extra tasks for which they are not being paid. Employees who become alienated (for whatever reason) may act in ways which are detrimental to the firm or to customer relations. For example, an alienated employee might neglect a customer who is regarded as a nuisance, or be over-generous to a favourite customer. Figure 11.3 shows some of the trade-offs in staff empowerment.

Successful empowerment of staff can be achieved by following these policies:

- Empowerment needs to be kept in mind when selecting, training, motivating and coaching employees
- Employees need to be given clear guidelines without being straitjacketed by rules which cannot, in any case, be designed to cover every eventuality
- A team approach needs to be cultivated, since support of other team members offers reassurance. Often, an empowered employee will need to ask for a second opinion on a course of action – this is likely to be much more easily available from a colleague than from management

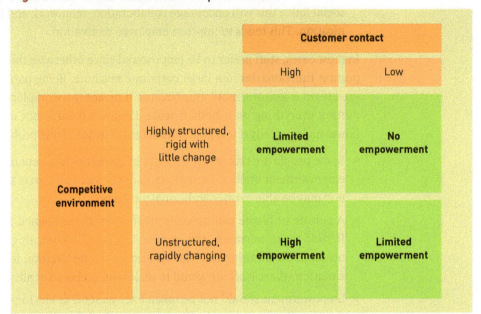

Figure 11.3 Trade-offs in staff empowerment

- Employees should be rewarded appropriately for the extra responsibility that empowerment brings
- There should not be a culture of blame. Mistakes are an opportunity to learn
- Power is not being devolved from management to employees – rather, employees are being asked to use their initiative.

Team building is an important management role, whether in service industries or not. Effort on the part of employees is driven by their personal needs, not the needs of the organisation – the need for personal development, the need to belong to a group, the need for promotion, and so forth (Cummings 1981). Successful teams should be allowed to develop shared objectives, preferably agreed within the group rather than imposed by management. Belbin (1981) suggests that teams should be allowed to perform the following tasks between them:

- Create useful ideas
- Analyse problems effectively
- Get things done
- Communicate effectively
- Have leadership qualities
- Evaluate problems and options logically
- Handle technical aspects of the job
- Control their work
- Report back effectively, either verbally or in writing.

Handy (1989) further suggested that leaders (managers) should be able to shape and share a vision which gives point to the work of others. This may be a difficult ideal to live up to.

Because people are an expensive part of any business, and even more so in the case of services, in recent years many service companies have tried to reduce the input of people, particularly for routine tasks which can be handled by computer; for example, booking hotel rooms or flights. There is evidence that, although personal service in hotels is still important for assessment of satisfaction, self-service technology for many hotel services may actually help customers in establishing relationships with hotels (Beatson et al. 2006).

In international service markets, cultural differences are often more apparent because of the 'people' element. For example, in fast food outlets the quality of the food affects buying intentions in Australia, China, Germany, Morocco and the United States, but not in the Netherlands and Sweden, where the surroundings are more important (Harris 1996).

Process

A process is a series of actions taken to convert inputs to something of greater value (Finlay 2000). In services, the process by which the product is developed and delivered should always add greater value, otherwise it is neither efficient nor effective. For example, a chef might take flour, eggs, apples, butter, and so forth, and create an apple pie, thus adding to the value of the ingredients. A master chef could take the same ingredients and create a work of art; a bad chef might take the same ingredients, which are already valuable, and end up with an inedible mess.

Every process combines the following basic resources:

- *Basic assets.* These include plant and equipment, cash in hand, work in progress, building, fixtures and fittings, and so forth (the tangible assets of the firm). Intangible assets include goodwill (which is an accountancy term for most intangible assets) and the reputation of the company and its brands.
- *Explicit knowledge.* This is knowledge which can be recorded, either in writing or otherwise. It includes intellectual property such as patents, market research information, customer databases, and so forth.
- *Tacit knowledge.* This is knowledge which employees have in their heads, rather than written down. In service industries, this would include specific training (such as being a qualified hairdresser or chef) and, of course, experience built up over a number of years. In some cases, this tacit knowledge makes a key employee difficult to replace; a lawyer specialising in Lithuanian business law, for example, might be virtually irreplaceable.
- *Procedure.* This is the mechanism by which all the other resources are brought together to create a value proposition for customers.

In services markets, customers can sometimes be seen as co-producers of the product. For example, a bar relies on having the right type of customer to create an appealing ambience and a theatre relies on having an audience to respond to the show. Without the other customers, the experience can seem bleak and uninteresting. At the extreme, a nightclub is an example of a service where the main product is the other customers – people go to nightclubs largely to meet members of the opposite sex. The same is true of dating services.

Service processes fall into three categories:

1 *Before-sales service processes*. These would include helpful staff, ready access to information and ensuring the availability of people to carry out the service.
2 *During-sales processes*. This is the actual provision of the service.
3 *After-sales processes*. Courtesy calls, prompt attention to complaints and careful record-keeping for future encounters are useful processes.

Because all these processes involve human interaction, they all provide opportunities to improve customer loyalty. There is a trade-off here between service level and cost; the level of service needs to be fixed at a point which provides value for money for the target audience, some of whom may be happy to pay more for a first-class service, while others might not be prepared to pay much at all and are happy with a basic service. Some firms (such as low-cost airlines) have created competitive advantage by reducing the service level to an absolute minimum, but being extremely cheap; other firms have built their success on luxurious service (for example, the Orient Express). The important point for the firm is to set the right level of service for the desired audience – too high, and the costs will price the service out of reach of the target audience; too low, and people will simply go elsewhere.

Some service processes are complex (for example, airlines). Several hundred different tasks need to be undertaken, and dozens of separate service processes need to be coordinated before the aircraft even takes off – quite apart from the services which are needed once the flight leaves. First, a travel agent needs to sell the ticket to ensure that the passenger is on the right aircraft at the right time, and leaves from the right airport. Second, the aircraft needs to be correctly serviced and fuelled by ground crews. Third, food and drink needs to be prepared for the passengers and delivered to the aircraft by yet another service company. Fourth, airports at either end of the journey need to be prepared to handle the aircraft on departure and arrival, and several air traffic control and advice agencies in different countries need to become involved. Fifth, passenger entertainment services, such as in-flight movies, music and games, need to be provided, and sixth, many service companies at the airports need to become involved in the process. In fact, almost every type of company, from Hollywood film studios to airport bookstalls, becomes involved in the process one way or another.

On the other hand, a flight is not a divergent service. The experience is much the same for all passengers, except for the differences between first class, business class and economy: the meals are the same, the flight attendants treat everyone the same and, of course, the start point and finish point of the flight is the same for everyone. Even the safety announcements are identical.

Hairdressing is a service which displays exactly the opposite characteristics. In most salons, only one or two people will deal with the client, and few (if any) other companies are involved. The process is therefore not complex. On the other hand, it is highly divergent – each person should leave the salon with a different hairstyle, produced to suit the individual's physical features and personal tastes. This variability of outcome does mean that things go wrong more often in hairdressing salons than they do on aircraft, of course.

The divergence and complexity of a service process can be adjusted to establish a competitive position, with the following consequences:

- Reducing divergence will reduce costs, improve productivity and make distribution easier. Fast-food restaurants offer limited menus of standardised food at low cost, for example.
- Increased divergence will offer more possibilities for customisation, greater flexibility and (usually) premium pricing. High divergency is what distinguishes *à la carte* restaurants, hairdressers and bespoke tailors.
- Reduced complexity means offering the core benefits of the product and not much else.
- Increased complexity increases customer choice by widening the range of products and the range of features on offer.

Process often becomes the main differentiator between services. Often the core product is the same from several suppliers – for example, air travel – but the process may be more or less straightforward, more or less efficient and more or less variable.

Physical evidence

Because services are often largely intangible, people often have little lasting evidence that the service ever took place; perhaps more importantly, there is very little evidence on which to base judgements about the quality of the service prior to actually committing to purchasing it. In some cases, physical evidence might be needed to demonstrate to others that the service has happened – a certificate from a training course, an insurance policy document or a medical certificate might all be needed for this purpose. Sometimes physical evidence acts as a reminder of the service; souvenirs from a holiday, a menu from a restaurant, a travel kit from an airline or even a simple business card might bring back happy memories or provide the means for repeating the experience.

As a way of assessing the likely quality of a service beforehand, aspects such as the décor of a bank, the menu in the window of a restaurant or the cleanliness of a supermarket all help. In some cases the service will have a substantial physical component anyway – restaurant meals fall into this category and, to an extent, hairdressing does as well. In both cases the physical element will not last long, but it is at least possible to observe other customers enjoying the physical aspects and thus be able to judge the probable quality of the service.

There are four generic ways to add value through physical evidence, as follows:

1. *Create physical evidence which increases loyalty.* Loyalty cards and frequent-flyer cards are typical of this, as are 'collectables' such as vouchers or ornaments. Some airline loyalty schemes include baggage tags which let the baggage handlers know they are dealing with an important suitcase; this probably has more effect on the customer than on the baggage handlers, of course.
2. *Use physical evidence which enhances the brand image.* Insurance companies convey a solid, respectable image by producing smart, glossy policy documents; low-cost airlines convey their thrifty image by requiring passengers to print off their own tickets on ordinary paper, or by having no tickets at all. Most airlines now allow online check-in, which means that customers choose their seats and print their own boarding cards as well.
3. *Use physical evidence which has an intrinsic value of its own.* This is common in the financial services sector; insurance companies give away carriage clocks, pen sets, DVD players, and so forth to new customers. Obviously, very few people would take out an insurance policy just to be given a clock, but the clock does serve as a useful reminder of the policy's existence.
4. *Create physical evidence which leads to further sales.* This could include reminder cards sent out when the next service is due (many garages do this), a desk calendar or wall calendar (often supplied by take-away food suppliers), or notepads and pens (hotels supply these). Such reminders are helpful to consumers, but may also generate new sales because the service provider's telephone number is convenient to hand when the need arises.

Physical evidence will not substitute for a poor service, of course. The core of a service will always be the intangibles, but it is important to remember that almost all products have both tangible and intangible elements; the intangibles are often as important as the tangibles.

Service quality

Under this regime, service quality can be defined as the ability of the organisation to meet or exceed customer expectations. The relationship marketer therefore needs to monitor the quality of the firm's output against two criteria: the customer's expectations and the firm's actual output. Parasuraman *et al.* (1985) developed a model of service quality which is reproduced in Figure 11.4.

The model shows various gaps in the understanding of service quality. These are as follows:

- Gap 1: difference between actual customer expectations and management perceptions of customer expectations.
- Gap 2: difference between management perceptions of customer expectations and service quality specifications.

Figure 11.4 Service quality model

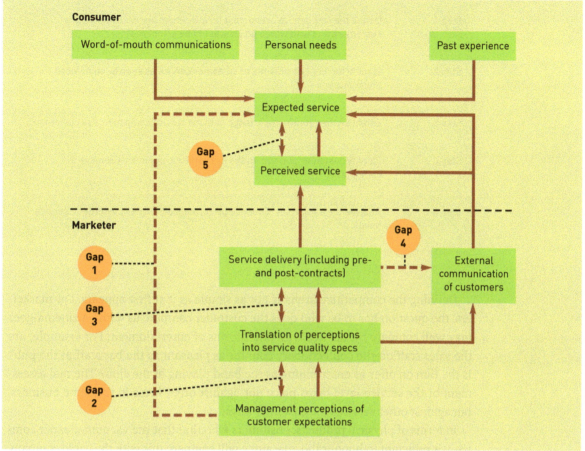

Source: Parasuraman *et al.* 1985. Reprinted with permission from the American Marketing Association.

- Gap 3: difference between service quality specifications and the service actually delivered.
- Gap 4: difference between service delivery and what is communicated about the service to customers.
- Gap 5: difference between customer expectations and perceptions of what is actually received. This gap is influenced by the other four.

To close these gaps, marketers need to adopt a range of quality control procedures.

Benchmarking is the process of comparing everything the company does with the same activities carried out by competitors, and seeking to match the best of the competitors in each activity. For example, a manufacturer might decide which competitor is best at engineering, and seek to match that, while at the same time matching another competitor which is best at delivery reliability. By doing this, firms end up as 'the best of the best'. **Service-quality benchmarking** takes this a step further; the comparison is made with both competitors and non-competitors. Christopher *et al.* (1991) have drawn up a five-stage approach to service benchmarking, as shown in Table 11.2.

Table 11.2 Five stages for service benchmarking

Step 1	Define the competitive arena; that is, with whom are we compared by customers and with whom do we want to be compared?
Step 2	Identify the key components of customer service as seen by customers themselves.
Step 3	Establish the relative importance of those service components to customers.
Step 4	Identify customer position on the key service components relative to competition.
Step 5	Analyse the data to see if service performance matches customers' service needs.

Source: Christopher et al. 1991

Defining the competitive arena is not as simple as it at first appears. For marketers, the question has to be who does the customer compare us with? A cinema-goer may well compare the service with other forms of entertainment. For example, are the sales staff on the confectionery counter as pleasant as the bar staff at the pub? Is the film on offer as entertaining as the band playing at the club? The real assessment of the service level takes place not against other firms in the same business, but against other services the customer buys.

In terms of physical products, customers who find that the vacuum-cleaner company is reluctant to honour the guarantee will compare this with the cable company that sent somebody round immediately to fix a problem, or with the car company that lent them a car to get around in while their own was being repaired under the warranty. Having had a good service from the TV company or car company tends to reduce the risk for the consumer and therefore increases the chances of a repeat purchase from the same company.

Regarding the key components of customer service, this again is too often left to executive judgement without reference to the customers. For example, a computer purchaser may regard on-site maintenance as being far more important than online assistance. A car owner whose car is in for servicing may regard the availability of a lift to the train station as being more important than the speed of servicing of the car.

Following on from establishing the key components, it is essential to establish the relative importance. This is simply because it is almost impossible, in a world with limited resources, to provide every customer with everything he or she wants. The firm therefore needs to concentrate on providing the most important aspects first.

Having found out where we want to be, we now need to find out where we are by establishing our position on service provision as compared with the competition. Again, we need to be careful who we are defining as competition and also be aware of the possibilities of comparing ourselves with firms who are not direct competition but who have something to teach us about service levels. This process is part of the marketing audit discussed in Chapter 10.

This leaves the firm in a position to compare its service provision with the service priorities of its customers.

LOYALTY IN SERVICES

Many service industries engender strong customer loyalty, in particular personal services such as hairdressing and beauty therapy, food and beverage services such as pubs and restaurants, and some technical services such as car maintenance and building. Banks generate a spurious loyalty; people only remain loyal because switching banks is time-consuming and risky, and also people often suppose that a long-term relationship with a bank will lead to special treatment in case they need an unexpected overdraft or loan.

Critical thinking

If a customer remains loyal, do we really need to know the reason why? If they stay loyal because they love us, that's great of course, but if they stay loyal because it's too much hassle to switch to someone else, does it really matter?

We don't need to love our banks, surely. Provided they look after the money and don't charge too much, what else do we want? Of course, if another bank made it easy to switch, that might be different!

Other services do not engender loyalty in themselves. Taxis and buses are examples; although people often use the same taxi firm when ordering a cab from home, they are unlikely to do so when arriving at a railway station or airport. It would be extremely rare for someone to use the same taxi driver on a regular basis, except in rural areas where there are few choices.

Generating loyalty carries distinct benefits for any organisation. There are six main benefits, as follows:

1 *Increased purchases* (Reichheld and Sasser 1990). Customers tend to increase their purchases when dealing with a firm with which they have a relationship. Naturally, people are prepared to spend money with firms they know and trust.
2 *Lower cost.* Attracting new customers is almost always more expensive than retaining existing ones, although there are exceptions to this general rule.
3 *Lifetime value of a customer increases.* Lifetime value is a key concept in relationship marketing; the value of a customer is measured by how much he or she will spend in a lifetime, rather than in a single transaction.

4 *Sustainable competitive advantage.* The intangible aspects of a service are often difficult to copy; a particular hairstylist or chef may be unique. By definition, loyal customers are difficult for competitors to lure away (Roberts *et al.* 2003).

5 *Word-of-mouth.* Because services are intangible and often difficult to judge in advance, word-of-mouth plays a much stronger role than is the case for physical products. People rely heavily on the recommendations of friends when choosing a restaurant, a hairdresser or a builder, and loyal customers are more likely to make those recommendations. Decisions about life insurance are based first on previous experience and second on personal recommendation (Devlin 2007). Published performance and cost are of much less importance.

6 *Employee satisfaction.* Staff often prefer to work for a firm with a loyal customer base, since they have to deal directly with the customers. Dealing with strangers is stressful, whereas dealing with familiar customers is more likely to involve being praised. Regular complaints will demoralise staff very rapidly.

Lowering the rate of customer churn will cause a substantial rise in overall profits (Reichheld and Sasser 1990). Part of the process involves ensuring that complaints are handled properly, since the variability of services can lead to a higher rate of complaint and a more difficult process of resolution.

Customer loyalty in service industries appears to be related positively to technical service quality, functional service quality and customer education (Bell and Eisingerich 2007). This means that the loyalty function is not only related to quality of service, but also to customer characteristics; interestingly, the same authors found that customer expertise, i.e. skill and knowledge of the market, was not negatively related to loyalty, as had been expected. The assumption was that expert customers would be more likely to shop around for the best deals, but this turned out not to be the case. Price is generally not an issue – regular brand 'switchers' turn out to be more price-sensitive than loyal 'stayers' (Leong and Qing 2006).

Online supermarkets are a recent phenomenon in the UK, so relatively little research has been carried out into them and their customers. Research into customer loyalty appears to show that people are attracted by price promotions and speed of delivery rather than by price; also, people tend to be loyal to the online supermarket rather than to the brand of the product they are buying (Cui and Wang 2010).

Loyalty is easily lost, however. For example, airlines frequently overbook aircraft by as much as 10% to ensure full use of the aircraft; no-shows and last-minute cancellations usually take care of the surplus, and economy passengers can be upgraded into business class (or even first class) in the event that economy class is overbooked. Sometimes business or first class are overbooked or the aircraft is completely full, in which case some passengers might be downgraded or refused boarding. In those circumstances, airlines which downgrade passengers or are unable to carry them almost always lose the customer; upgrading, on the other hand, only creates marginally greater loyalty (Wangenheim and Bayon 2007).

In business-to-business markets loyalty can be very strong, since relationships between suppliers and customers can last for many years or even decades.

Consequently, a customer who switches to another supplier may well be indirect when asked for reasons. In some cases, customers who are perfectly satisfied with their existing suppliers may defect anyway – and may be reluctant to admit that they have defected because the new supplier is cheaper (Naumann *et al.* 2010).

CASE STUDY 11 Ocado

There are many grocery supermarkets in the UK, and indeed several large chains – Tesco's, ASDA, Morrison's, Sainsbury's, Waitrose, and so forth. All of these offer an online ordering and delivery service as well as their bricks-and-mortar presence on the high street and in the out-of-town retail parks. However, since June 2001 a new force has appeared – Ocado.

Ocado is a dedicated online grocery supplier. The company has no shops at all, and instead operates entirely through delivery. Initially, the company only operated around the Hemel Hempstead and Hatfield areas, north of London, but within six months the company had expanded its delivery range to include North London. Within the first 12 months of operations, deliveries increased from 100,000 households to 2.2 million households, and the company began expanding on a 'hub and spoke' basis nationally. Currently Ocado can service 70% of UK households, following the opening of its new centre at Avonmouth, near Bristol, in the west of England.

Orders are picked and packed in Ocado distribution centres by staff working in separate sections. Crates move automatically around the centre, so that staff do not have to leave their own sections to find goods; each customer's crate is automatically tracked and guided. Staff are monitored carefully – even the delivery vans have close-circuit TV cameras to check on the drivers, to ensure that goods reach the customers in perfect condition.

Ocado pride themselves on using the available technology to its fullest extent to provide exemplary customer service. The company website is constantly evolving and even has the capacity to remind customers of regularly purchased items which they may have forgotten. There is an iPhone app, recently extended to Android, so that customers can order even when they do not have access to a computer, and the software systems ensure that better than 95% of deliveries happen on time or early. Ocado appears on Twitter and Facebook, and there is a corporate blog which enables people to find out what the company is doing or has planned for the future.

The company offers around 21,000 SKUs (stock-keeping units; in other words, products), which compares favourably with large supermarkets: 7000 SKUs are pegged to Tesco prices and the company offers a small range of Ocado own brands. Interestingly, Ocado have concluded an agreement with Waitrose which means that most of its range of products is sourced from Waitrose's buying centre, including Waitrose own-brands – this is particularly beneficial because Waitrose position their brand on high quality rather than on price, whereas Tesco position mainly on price.

Ocado's green credentials are impressive. Because the company has no stores, it has no open fridges or freezers and has very little carbon footprint (despite the fleet of delivery vehicles). The company points out that supermarkets also have warehouses and then deliver to stores to which customers often drive – Ocado's deliveries go directly from the warehouse to the customer's home so that the carbon footprint is overall less than would be created by a customer walking to the local supermarket. The company also supports Meat Free Monday, a campaign to encourage people to consume less meat (owing to its environmental impact).

The company's rapid growth seems likely to continue – the pressure on people's working lives and the increasing interest in environmentally friendly initiatives are bound to be drivers for the company's future success. As more and more people regard online shopping as the natural and obvious way to buy, Ocado is well placed to compete against mainstream supermarkets.

Questions

1 What is the importance of process for Ocado?
2 Why should the company be more successful than its bricks-and-mortar competitors, in the light of the fact that those competitors offer their own delivery services?
3 What is the role of benchmarking for Ocado?
4 What is the purpose of using social networking sites like Facebook?
5 How does Ocado minimise divergence?

SUMMARY

Services are the major part of most economies in the industrialised world. Service provision relies on all elements of the marketing mix, but people, process and physical evidence become more important in service marketing than in physical product marketing.

Companies in service industries therefore rely heavily on staff, most (though not all) of whom are in the front line of dealing with customers on a day-to-day basis. Therefore, motivating and looking after staff becomes of even greater importance than would be the case in physical product marketing.

The key points from this chapter are as follows:

- All products have some element of service and some element of physical product
- From the consumer's viewpoint, buying a service is riskier than buying a physical product
- Front-line employees should be empowered to deal with problems as they arise
- Employees need to feel that they are working for a good company
- Loyalty is more common in services as a way of reducing risk
- Word-of-mouth is important in services, again to reduce risk
- Physical evidence can be used to create more business
- Process can be complex or simple, divergent or standard; each of these has implications for marketing.

CHAPTER QUESTIONS

1 How might complaint handling be improved in the airline business?
2 What problems might arise from reducing staff levels in the hotel trade?

3 What are the implications of divergency and complexity in the fast-food business?

4 How does staff empowerment help in recruitment?

5 What mechanisms account for complaint behaviour in services?

Further reading

Principles of Services Marketing, 6th edn, by Adrian Palmer (Maidenhead, McGraw-Hill, 2011) is a well established, readable and comprehensive textbook. Now in its sixth edition, this book has become established as the leading text in the field.

Services Marketing, 6th edn, by Valerie Zeithaml, Mary Jo Bitner and Dwayne D. Gremler (New York, McGraw-Hill, 2012) is an American text with a good pedigree. Zeithaml and Bitner almost invented services marketing between them, so the text is certainly definitive, but of course uses American examples and contexts which are not always familiar to non-Americans.

References

Beatson, Amanda, Coote, Leonard V. and Rudd, John M.: 'Determining consumer satisfaction and commitment through self-service technology and personal service usage', *Journal of Marketing Management*, 22 (7/8) (2006), pp. 853–82.

Belbin, R.M.: *Management Teams: Why They Succeed or Fail* (London, Heinemann, 1981).

Bell, Simon and Eisingerich, Andreas B.: 'The paradox of customer education, customer expertise and loyalty in the financial services industry', *European Journal of Marketing*, 41 (5/6) (2007), pp. 466–86.

Booms, B.H. and Bitner, M.J.: 'Marketing strategies and organisation structures for service firms', in *Marketing of Services*, J. Donnelly and W.R. George, eds (Chicago, IL, American Marketing Association, 1981).

Christopher, M., Ballantyne, D. and Payne, A.: *Relationship Marketing* (Oxford, Butterworth-Heinemann, 1991).

Cui, Geng and Wang, Yanan: 'Consumers' SKU choice in an online supermarket: a latent class approach', *Journal of Marketing Management*, 26 (5/6) (2010), pp. 495–514.

Cummings, T.G.: 'Designing effective work groups', in *Handbook of Organisational Design*, P.C. Nystrom and W.H. Starbuck, eds (Oxford, Oxford University Press, 1981).

DeChernatony, Leslie and Cottam, Susan: 'Internal brand factors driving successful financial services brands', *European Journal of Marketing*, 40 (5/6) (2006), pp. 611–33.

Desai, Preyas S., Kalra, Ajay and Murthi, B.P.S.: 'When old is gold: the role of business longevity in risky situations', *Journal of Marketing*, 72 (1) (2008), pp. 95–107.

Devlin, James F.: 'Complex services and choice criteria: an example from the life assurance market', *Journal of Marketing Management*, 23 (7/8) (2007), pp. 631–50.

Finlay, P.: *Strategic Management: An Introduction to Business and Corporate Strategy* (Harlow, Financial Times Prentice Hall, 2000).

Gray, Brandan J.: 'Benchmarking services branding practices', *Journal of Marketing Management*, 22 (7/8) (2006), pp. 717–58.

Gruber, Thorstein, Szmigin, Isabelle and Voss, Roediger: 'The desired qualities of customer contact employees in complaint-handling encounters', *Journal of Marketing Management*, 22 (5/6) (2006), pp. 619–42.

Handy, C.: *The Age of Unreason* (London, Hutchinson, 1989).

Harris, Greg: 'International advertising: developmental and implementational issues', *Journal of Marketing Management*, **12** (1996), pp. 551–60.

Hennig-Thurau, Thorsten, Groth, Markus, Paul, Michael and Gremler, Dwayne D.: 'Are all smiles created equal? How emotional contingence and emotional labour affect service relationships', *Journal of Marketing*, **70** (3) (2006), pp. 58–73.

Judd, V.C.: 'Differentiate with the fifth P', *Industrial Marketing Management*, **16** (1987), pp. 241–7.

Knox, Simon and Freeman, Cheryl: 'Measuring and managing employer brand image in the service industry', *Journal of Marketing Management*, **22** (7/8) (2006), pp. 695–716.

Koenig-Lewis, Nicole and Palmer, Adrian: 'Experiential values over time – a comparison of measures of satisfaction and emotion', *Journal of Marketing Management*, **24** (1/2) (2008), pp. 69–85.

Leong, Yow Peng and Qing, Wang: 'Impact of relationship marketing tactics (RMTs) on switchers and stayers in a competitive service industry', *Journal of Marketing Management*, **22** (1/2) (2006), pp. 25–59.

Maxham III, James G. and Netemeyer, Richard G.: 'Firms reap what they sow: the effect of shared values and perceived organisational justice on customers' evaluation of complaint handling', *Journal of Marketing*, **67** (1) (January 2003), pp. 46–62.

Munoz, Caroline L., Wood, Natalie T. and Solomon, Michael R.: 'Real or blarney? A cross-cultural investigation of the perceived authenticity of Irish pubs', *Journal of Consumer Behaviour*, **5** (3) (2006), pp. 222–34.

Murphy, J.A.: *The Lifebelt: The Definitive Guide to Managing Customer Retention* (Chichester, John Wiley, 2001).

Naumann, Earl, Haverila, Matti, Khan, M. Sajid and Williams, Paul: 'Understanding the causes of defection among satisfied B2B service customers', *Journal of Marketing Management*, **26** (9/10) (2010), pp. 878–900.

Parasuraman, A., Zeithaml, V.A. and Berry, L.L.: 'A conceptual model of service quality and its implications for future research', *Journal of Marketing*, **49** (Fall 1985).

Rasmusson, E.: 'Winning back angry customers', *Sales and Marketing Management* (October 1997), p. 131.

Reichheld, F.F. and Sasser, W.E. Jr: 'Zero defections, quality comes to services', *Harvard Business Review*, (Sept–Oct 1990), pp. 105–11.

Roberts, K., Varki, S. and Brodie, R.: 'Measuring the quality of relationships in consumer services: an empirical study', *European Journal of Marketing*, **37** (1/2) (2003), pp. 169–96.

Vargo, Stephen L. and Lusch, Robert F.: 'Evolving to a new dominant logic for marketing', *Journal of Marketing*, **68** (January 2004), pp. 1–17.

Wangenheim, Florian and Bayon, Tomas: 'Behavioural consequences of overbooking service capacity', *Journal of Marketing*, **71** (4) (2007), pp. 36–47.

12

SUSTAINABLE MARKETING

Objectives

After reading this chapter you should be able to:
- Explain the role of quality in building long-term relationships
- Describe how relationship marketing builds long-term profitability
- Formulate strategies for developing customer loyalty
- Establish quality procedures within organisations
- Describe the basis for societal marketing
- Develop strategies for assessing responsibility towards stakeholders
- Establish ethical guidelines
- Take an ethical approach to marketing strategy decisions.

INTRODUCTION

During the first years of the twenty-first century, marketing thinking has been undergoing some radical changes. Much marketing thinking in the past has concentrated on the single transaction between producer and customer, on the assumption that customers who like the product will continue to buy and that no one else has any right to an input into the exchange. This approach, while laudable, ignores the fact that some customers are more valuable than others, that some customers can become very loyal indeed and that marketers should also take into consideration the needs and attitudes of other stakeholders in society at large.

At the same time, new communications media (the Internet, cellular telephones, short message systems (texting), and so forth) have made previous marketing communications strategies almost obsolete. Falling birth rates and increased competition through globalisation have meant that consumers are fewer and more firms are chasing them; also, rapidly rising prosperity levels mean that the rewards for firms which get it right are much greater than ever before.

This chapter is about creating long-term relationships with customers – selling 'products that don't come back to customers that do' (Baker 1991). It is about ensuring that the marketing-orientated firm is sustainable in the long run, both in terms of use of finite resources and also in terms of ethical behaviour towards society at large. Finally, it is about the successful exploitation of new technology in a rapidly changing world.

Land Rover

Land Rover originally started up just after the Second World War, producing utility vehicles for farmers and others who needed off-road capacity. The cars were built mainly from aluminium, because it was widely available at the time, rather than steel, which was in short supply. The vehicles were a huge success and became iconic. The company, originally part of the Rover Cars group, has continued in business even though Rover has now disappeared.

The original utility vehicle has been considerably updated. Modern Land Rovers are luxury four-by-fours, owned by the wealthy rather than the working farmer. Land Rover is now positioned as a premium brand; the TV advertising, using the strapline 'Go Beyond', shows how the car can be used in cities as well as off-road in harsh conditions.

Environmentalism represents something of a threat to the four-by-four market; gas-guzzling four-wheel drives, many of which are only used to go to the cash point or deliver children to school, are coming under fire from many critics. Land Rover meet these criticisms by contributing to carbon offset schemes and by reducing the company's carbon footprint.

Phil Popham, Global Managing Director

Watch the video clip, then try to answer the following questions. The answers are on the companion website.

Questions

1 How might Land Rover respond to the criticisms of environmentalists?

2 How might Land Rover establish a relationship with its end consumers?

3 What threats are apparent from globalisation for Land Rover?

RELATIONSHIP v TRADITIONAL MARKETING

Traditional marketing is concerned with the exchanges between organisations and their customers. The emphasis has always been on producing products that will satisfy customer needs and the focus has tended to be on the single transaction. This has led to an over-emphasis on acquiring new customers at the expense of ensuring that the firm keeps its old ones. Most of the marketing transactions in a traditional firm are undertaken anonymously and the customer is reduced from being an individual person, with needs and wants and problems, to being a member of a market segment.

Relationship marketing, on the other hand, looks at the customer as an individual and tries to establish a relationship. Relationship marketing is concerned with the lifetime value of the customer. For example, over the course of a lifetime's motoring, a motorist might own 30 or more cars. This represents a total expenditure of perhaps hundreds of thousands of pounds on cars, yet car manufacturers and dealers rarely keep in touch with their customers in any organised way. The focus is on the single transaction, that of buying one (and only one) car at a time. A relationship marketing approach would seek to look at the customer in terms of his or her total value to the company over (potentially) 30 or 40 years.

This orientation values the loyal customer ahead of the one-off big deal and gives the firm more chance of maintaining its customer base in the long run. Figure 12.1 illustrates how the concepts of customer service, quality and marketing come together to establish a relationship marketing orientation.

The key to relationship marketing is understanding that customers are buying a bundle of benefits, some of which include such factors as product reliability and an efficient service from the company with which they are dealing. Increasingly, customers expect suppliers to value their custom; during the nineteenth century, every shopper would expect the shopkeepers to know them by name, to be respectful and polite, to anticipate their needs and to arrange delivery or otherwise show that they regarded the customer as important to the firm. As firms have grown bigger, this level of personal attention has largely disappeared. Economic forces have removed the old systems from grocery shops, so that customers are now expected to find the goods themselves, carry them to the checkout, pay for them and carry them home. Many supermarkets now have self-service checkouts, so that a customer can go through the entire shopping experience without having any contact with the store's employees.

This increasingly impersonal and functional view of marketing is now being questioned, and relationship marketing seeks to address this issue by encouraging firms to treat customers as individuals, with individual needs and aspirations. This goes beyond the 'have a nice day' approach of the fast-food restaurant, replacing it with a genuine interest and concern for the customer.

Figure 12.1 Relationship marketing, quality and service

Source: Christopher et al. 1991

Critical thinking

This idea of being looked after on a personal basis looks really good on paper. Having the shop assistants smile at us, having somebody thinking about our every need, having them wish us to come back soon – it's like having an extra mother, but better!

Do we really want all this attention, though? Wouldn't it be better if everything just worked properly first time, without all the soft soap? Or maybe we expect things to work as well! We're just getting spoiled rotten!

In fact, business relationships do not divide entirely into **transaction** or relationship marketing – relationships develop, and can range from a single exchange through to a fully developed cooperative system. Table 12.1 shows the comparison between traditional, or transaction, marketing and relationship marketing.

Table 12.1 Transaction v relationship marketing

Transaction marketing	Relationship marketing
Focus on single sale	Focus on customer retention
Orientation on product features	Orientation on product benefits
Short timescale	Long timescale
Little emphasis on customer service	High emphasis on customer service
Limited customer commitment	High customer commitment
Moderate customer contact	High customer contact
Quality is the concern of the production department	Quality is the concern of all

Source: Christopher et al. 1991

Although many firms have adopted the relationship approach, most firms still keep to the traditional view. This tends to lead to the following bad practices:

- A reactive approach to customer complaints
- A failure to recognise the needs of long-term customers
- Greater expenditure on promotion than is necessary owing to the emphasis on acquiring new customers
- Inner conflict within departments as production people expect marketers to sell the goods, and marketers expect production people to handle quality issues.

As customer expectations rise, and more particularly as customers become longer lived, there is likely to be an increasing emphasis on establishing relationships. This is because the value to the firm of the customer's continued custom is greater, and the customer knows this and expects better treatment in return.

Relationship marketing has been most apparent in business-to-business markets, possibly because business needs do not change much over a period of time, whereas consumer needs change as people grow older, pass through different life stages and become wealthier or poorer. The view has been expressed that products are not bundles of benefits, but are instead relational processes (Tuli *et al.* 2007). There is some logic behind this, at least in business-to-business markets; each benefit is a step in strengthening the relationship.

Some fallacies of relationship marketing and the concept of customer retention have been discovered by recent research, as follows (East *et al.* 2006):

- The evidence is that in many consumer markets long-term customers are no more valuable than short-term ones. The key factor is the relative costs of acquisition

Figure 12.2 Dependence between suppliers and customers in business-to-business markets

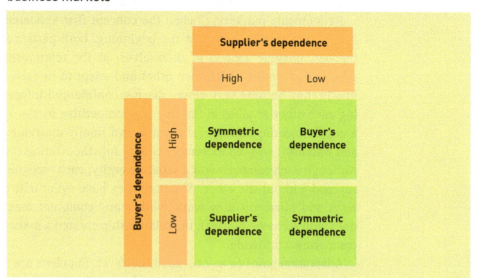

and retention – if acquisition is cheap and retention expensive, long-term customers will be less profitable.
- It is often difficult to influence long-tenure customers.
- Customer satisfaction does not lead to retention, but it does lead to increased acquisition through word-of-mouth.

Roemer (2006) has outlined a model for assessing the impact of dependence on customer lifetime value. This model also offers some insight into the power split between customer and supplier in business-to-business markets; the model is shown in Figure 12.2.

The figure shows that, if each company has high dependence on the other, dependence is symmetrical and the relationship should last; if, on the other hand, either party has the upper hand, the relationship becomes asymmetrical and is less likely to last. The concept of reciprocity is crucial here – that the parties to the relationship do not harm each other, that if harm does occur the other party does not retaliate, and the party causing harm makes some kind of reparation (Pervan et al. 2009).

One of the key concepts in relationship marketing is that of customer intimacy. This means getting close enough to the customer to be able to understand his or her needs almost before he or she does – being able to think like the customer is a key skill in establishing and maintaining the relationship. Research shows that there is a strong positive relationship between marketing orientation and customer intimacy (Tuominen et al. 2004). This means that companies which adopt a marketing orientation will usually try to get as close as possible to their customers. For small firms, customer relationship management is performed much more easily nowadays because of the availability of the Internet and e-communications generally (Harrigan et al. 2011). For example, corporate blogs (weblogs in which corporate news is disseminated) can be very powerful in building and maintaining relationships with customers (Ahuja and Medury 2010).

Relationship marketing, when the concept first appeared, was compared to a courtship (Levitt 1986). At the beginning, both parties are keen to present the best possible aspects of themselves; as the relationship progresses, they seek to know more about each other and adapt to fit each other's needs, until finally they become very close, sharing confidential information, and regarding each other as allies in fighting the competitive battle. This is equivalent to a couple meeting, dating for a while and finally marrying. For example, IBM and Microsoft worked extremely closely together during the 1980s and 1990s. Although each company was a separate entity, each recognised that it could not succeed without the other. Although they have eventually gone their separate ways and Microsoft now works with many computer manufacturers (as IBM does with software houses), the relationship created a massive increase in home computing worldwide.

Adaptation tends to be one-sided, however. Suppliers are much more likely to adapt their business approach than are buyers, for the following reasons (Brennan et al. 2003):

- *Relative power.* Buyers are usually in a position of power, especially in business-to-business markets, since they can always spend their money elsewhere.
- *Buyer support.* Buying companies will often help suppliers to make the necessary changes. For example, a motor manufacturer might supply design services to a component supplier to ensure that the components are produced to the right specification.
- *Managerial preference for a more or less relational exchange.* Suppliers typically want to get close to their customers to ensure a continuation of orders. The pressure is not as great for buyers to get close to suppliers (although there are advantages to doing so, and some buying firms actively seek long-term relationships).

Figure 12.3 shows the forces which combine to create pressure on companies to adapt. In the figure, the supplying firm is pressured by managerial preference, by a need to exclude its competitors from supplying the buying firm and by a need to guarantee a future stream of orders from the buying firm. The supplier and the buyer might both be affected by their relative power – although power is usually with the buying firm, there are cases where suppliers have the upper hand. For example, the American hair products firm Redken will only supply hairdressers who can demonstrate a high level of technical competence – Redken's products and reputation make them a desirable company to buy from, but Redken protect their brand by only supplying salons with whom they have a close relationship, even extending to training the hairstylists in the use of Redken products.

In some cases the relationship goes beyond a simple one-to-one arrangement. Relationships may extend to whole groups, or networks, and the companies involved

Figure 12.3 Pressures to adapt in developing relationships

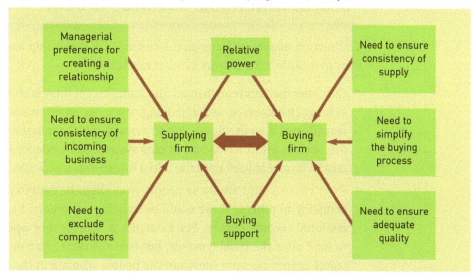

may need to balance a whole set of relationships rather than just one. Key network management has three basic elements (Ojasalo 2004):

1 *Identify a key network.* Choosing which is most important of the many networks in which a firm is involved is the starting point for network management.
2 *Develop a strategy for managing actors within the key network.* Each separate member of the network has separate needs, and will respond to different management tactics.
3 *Develop and apply operational level networks for managing actors.* Putting the strategies into effect means developing separate tactics for each strategy and each member of the network.

Creating value through closer relationships also means bringing weaker relationships into the portfolio (Johnson and Selnes 2004). Companies need to be aware that customers with whom they have a weak relationship should be encouraged, and efforts need to be made to strengthen the relationships. For example, firms offering products with low economies of scale (such as personal services or professional services such as accountancy and law) need to build closer relationships to create value – they are unlikely to be able to increase value by reducing prices because there is little room for manoeuvre in the cost structure and relatively little to be gained by an increase in business. A lawyer who is already fully booked can increase value for clients by improving the closeness of the relationship, and can raise his or her fees accordingly. Cutting prices for clients would add value for the client, but the lawyer would make less money because there is only a certain amount of working time available, and hiring more help would not make the situation much better. A good relationship is a better predictor of buying behaviour than is service quality (Roberts *et al.* 2003), but it is service quality which builds the relationship in the first place.

PEOPLE WITH WHOM BUSINESS IS DONE

Transaction marketers focus on the customer. Relationship marketers broaden the view to include other players in other markets.

- Customer markets remain much the same, except there is an emphasis on keeping existing customers as well as gaining new ones. Some retailers have membership fees (Costco is an example); customers who pay the initial fee can buy goods at a discount, in effect a two-part pricing system. The evidence is that such schemes ensure loyalty at least until the initial investment is recouped (Dick 1995).
- *Referral markets* are those people who might be expected to recommend the company to others. These could be existing customers, but could also be professional recommenders. For example, a holiday tour operator clearly needs to look after the holidaymaker; but tour operators also need to look after the travel agents, because these are the people who are in the best position to recommend the holidays to customers. In service industries this is common; in physical product manufacturing industries it is less so. Manufacturers are less likely to spend time and effort on establishing a good relationship with their retailers.
- *Supplier markets* are those people who provide raw materials and components for the company. A view has grown up that these suppliers are part of the team, and the traditional somewhat adversarial relationship is being replaced by the logistics paradigm of cooperation towards a common goal (see Chapter 8). Previously the emphasis has been on getting the lowest possible price from the suppliers, but this has now shifted towards other goals, such as reliability of delivery, zero-fault quality control procedures and cooperation in design and production.
- *Employee markets* refer to the need to recruit and train appropriately talented and motivated staff. Despite high unemployment rates in some areas, there is still an acute shortage of enthusiastic and skilled people to work in industry. Even when suitable employees have been found, firms need to ensure that they are market-orientated and understand the company's aims and objectives.
- *Influence markets* comprise those individuals who might have influence on the firm's activities. They include government departments, financial institutions, pressure groups, and so forth. Although the traditional marketers address these influence groups through PR activities, relationship marketing goes further than this. While PR concentrates on building a favourable image of the company by providing information, relationship marketing examines ways of meeting the needs of those institutions and individuals and helping them achieve their own aims (see Chapter 9).
- *Internal marketing* is concerned with ensuring that everybody inside the firm is not only aware of the company's policies, but is also enthusiastic and supportive

of them. This means more than simply informing staff of the policies; staff must feel that their own needs are being met, beyond the salary cheque at the end of the month. A prime example of this is Body Shop, which requires staff to participate in local community ventures. It is difficult to find Body Shop staff who are unenthusiastic about working for the company. All of them know what the aims of the firm are; all of them feel motivated and keen to participate in those aims. Strangely, Body Shop founder Anita Roddick was fond of saying that she did not believe in marketing – yet she was consummately good at doing it.

Internal marketing is not generally a separate activity, carried out in isolation. It is built into quality programmes, customer service programmes and ad hoc activities throughout the normal working lives of the staff.

DEVELOPING A RELATIONSHIP MARKETING APPROACH

Quality

Quality is the relationship between what customers expect and what they get. If a customer's expectations of a product are disappointed, his or her perception will be that the product is poor quality. If, on the other hand, the product exceeds expectations, the perception will be that the product is high quality.

Much of this is bound up in what customers perceive as value for money. The aim of the relationship marketer is not simply to satisfy the customer, or even to please the customer, but to delight the customer.

It follows from this that quality is not an absolute. It is only relevant to what the customer feels; what is good quality to one person may not be to another, simply because both are beginning with different expectations. For this reason, service support is critical to relationship marketing because it is during the pre-sale and after-sale support that the customers are approached as individuals. It is at this time that the customer's perception of quality can be addressed, either by ensuring that the expectations of the product are realistic (pre-sale) or by correcting any faults or errors after-sale.

In former years, quality has been seen as very much the province of the production department. This has led to the *product concept*, which holds that the company need only produce the best-quality product on the market and the customers will flock in. In fact, this is not true – even Rolls-Royce have gone through bankruptcy by following this precept. Under a relationship marketing ethos, quality becomes the integrating concept between production orientation and marketing orientation.

Total quality management

The basis of the **total quality management** (TQM) approach is to ensure that the firm does the right things at every stage of the production process in the expectation that this will result in a high-quality outcome at the end. The problem with this approach is that it does not take account of the customer's expectations and perceptions, but instead relies on the management's preconceptions of what constitutes good manufacturing practice. There is also some difficulty in judging the level at which the quality of the product should be pitched. Probably the main contribution that TQM has made is in reducing defects (the zero-defects target), which will, by reducing wastage, reduce costs.

Managing the relationship

Ultimately, the purpose of the relationship marketing philosophy is to ensure that customers come back, and keep coming back. Developing loyalty is an ongoing process; early on in the relationship, loyalty is a function of perceived value, but as the relationship progresses affective (emotional) factors become more important (Johnson *et al.* 2006).

Here are some examples of managing the relationship to generate loyalty.

Supermarket loyalty cards

These loyalty cards are in use throughout the world as supermarkets try to reward customers who use the store regularly. Previously, many shoppers would buy from whichever supermarket they happened to be passing, but the loyalty schemes have encouraged people to shop at the same supermarket every time and establish a shopping pattern. The next stage of the procedure is to use the EPOS (electronic point-of-sale) equipment to track the customer's spending patterns and thus be in a position to advise shoppers about their individual needs. For example, it is possible with current technology to be able to advise a shopper that he or she has forgotten the tomato ketchup. (The EPOS system knows how often this customer buys ketchup and knows what brand and size the customer favours.) Whether this is seen as a wonderful service for the customer or as an unwarranted invasion of privacy has been the subject of considerable debate (Evans 1994). In practice, legislation has been passed in the UK that makes it harder for supermarkets to use information in this way, since it would involve divulging personal information to junior store staff, but some online supermarkets such as Ocado offer the service routinely.

Critical thinking

OK, stores don't do it, but wouldn't it be marvellous? Just think if the store knew you so well that they could tell exactly when you were going to run out of sugar and make sure to remind you next time you're in the store! Maybe we could get to the point where you just telephone the store and tell them you're coming and they have everything ready for you when you arrive! What a time-saver!

Hands up anybody who finds that scary ...

Customer care

The UK's Nationwide Building Society has a commitment to customer care. It has declared that it will not follow the lead of other building societies and become a bank, since this would mean paying dividends to shareholders rather than offering benefits to customers. The intention is to retain the existing customers as customers rather than encouraging them to become shareholders in a new institution.

Frequent flyer programmes

Frequent flyer programmes on airlines offer regular users of the airlines the opportunity to have free flights or major discounts on travel. The frequent flyer programmes are usually extended to partner airlines: United Airlines of the United States has formed the Star Alliance with Thai Air, Lufthansa, Aloha Airlines in Hawaii, BMI in the UK and a large number of other airlines throughout the world. Frequent flyer points can be earned by travelling with any of these airlines, and can be exchanged with any of them. Thus a regular transatlantic flyer can use the points to travel with BMI to Frankfurt, for example. Frequent flyer members receive newsletters and some special treatment on the aeroplanes themselves – this encourages loyalty.

Museum or theatre season tickets

The museum uses the names and addresses of its season ticket holders to promote forthcoming attractions. By mailing people who are already known to be interested in the museum's activities, the management ensures a much higher response rate than would be the case if a 'scattergun' approach were adopted. Mailings to already interested parties are not expensive, even compared with placing advertisements in local newspapers. An example is Sydney Symphony Orchestra's 'Friends of the SSO' scheme: members are entitled to attend selected rehearsals, buy tickets at a discount and be invited to special events.

Direct marketing

This is a rapidly growing area in marketing, as computer technology is becoming more refined. The growth in **databases** (computer-based files on customers) has allowed firms to keep ever more accurate information about their customers' buying habits. The capacity for exchanging databases between firms gives a potential for building very detailed profiles of each individual in the country.

In practice, this is still some way off, but in the meantime the detailed information available enables companies, and in particular database brokers, to develop extremely accurate segmentation of markets. Because most of the relevant information about the customers concerned is on file, mailing list brokers are able to offer very specific mailings to companies. Ultimately, this will mean that customers will no longer receive junk mail – they will instead only be sent information that is of direct, immediate interest. Theoretically it should be possible to approach customers with a purchase suggestion almost at the point when they are considering the purchase. Database marketing was a major growth area in the 1990s and will probably continue to grow in this century; because the database allows the firm to retain and access large amounts of information about its customers, database marketing has become strongly associated with relationship marketing. In the nineteenth century, each shopkeeper knew his regular customers personally; for a modern supermarket to do this a computer is required.

An important point to bear in mind about relationship marketing is that many of the techniques used to generate loyalty are expensive and require considerable commitment; overall, the result for the firm is a steadier and more secure market, but relationship marketing is not necessarily a cheap option. There is evidence that satisfaction leads to loyalty, which in turn leads to profitability, but the relationship is non-linear (Helgesen 2006). Firms may need to be cautious before deciding to try to retain every customer.

Firms also need to remember that, whatever happens, some customers will leave; acquisition is therefore still important, yet less than half of all companies have a formal customer acquisition plan (Ang and Buttle 2006). Having a budget specifically for customer acquisition appears to be the key to success. Also, customers who have left (defected) can often be won back, because they do at least have some positive information about the brand, whereas new customers have only neutral information (Bogomolova and Romaniuk 2010).

INTERNET MARKETING

Nobody owns the Internet; it is a communications medium spread across thousands (even millions) of computers worldwide, which operates independently of the telephone companies that supply its cable connections, of the governments in whose countries it resides, and even of the computer owners in whose machines data are stored. The Internet therefore operates under its own rules; there is little or no international law to govern its use (or abuse). This means that consumers have the power to communicate bad experiences with companies very quickly – most major companies' websites are shadowed by anonymous counter-culture sites known as McNitemares, after the McSpotlight site which shadows McDonald's and which carries derogatory stories about McDonald's products and restaurants. Few companies are adequately prepared for this type of attack (Conway *et al.* 2007) and there is, in fact, a battle for supremacy going on between consumers and suppliers, with no clear winner in sight yet (Denegri-Knott 2006).

This type of website plays a major role in PR and news gathering. Environmental pressure groups, charitable organisations, self-help groups and others have all used websites to raise the profile of their causes, and some have had remarkable successes as a result. All in all, the consumer has most of the real power on the Internet. Online virtual communities, established through chatrooms and forums, replace some sources of information (such as salespeople and mailings), but have yet to replace the main sources of information (such as advertisements and brochures)

(Jepsen 2006). Communication via such forums and via e-mail is known as word-of-mouse, and the evidence is that opinion leaders are most effective when they post information about their own experiences (Huang 2010).

In recent years, online communities have developed around some brands. For example, Harley Davidson has an online membership forum. Online communities are valuable to companies in the following ways (Kim *et al.* 2008):

1 Building brand awareness and image.
2 Providing access to the voice of loyal consumers.
3 Increasing supplier commitment.
4 Generating revenue from new and existing customers.

The same research showed that online community members tended to have stronger brand commitment than non-members, whether they are active users of the brand or not. Often people use these online communities to enhance their personal identities or to feel close to others with similar interests and needs (O'Sullivan 2010).

Internet marketing has the characteristics outlined in Table 12.2.

Electronic business activities, or e-commerce, have tended to be adopted in stages by small firms. Five factors appear to influence the adoption of e-commerce: the support of top management, management understanding of the potential benefits, the presence of IT skills within the firm, the availability of consultancy and prioritisation of e-commerce (Wilson *et al.* 2008).

Table 12.2 Characteristics of the Internet as a marketing tool

Characteristic	Explanation
Communication style	The style is interactive and is either synchronous (happens immediately) or asynchronous (there are significant time delays between message and response).
Social presence	The feeling that the communications are taking place at a personal level. Internet communications have relatively high social presence if they are synchronous, particularly as the recipient is usually within his or her home environment when the communication takes place.
Consumer control of contact	Because the consumers are able to control the time and place at which they access the information, they are more willing to participate in the process of getting information from a machine. Most websites are interactive so that customers can control the information-gathering (and buying) process.
Consumer control of content	If the consumers can control the content of the message to some extent, the communication becomes truly interactive. For example, a consumer accessing a website can use a hyperlink to move to another page or can skip past information. An e-mail address allows customers to ask specific questions and thus tailor the communications.

Website design

Below is a checklist for establishing a successful website:

- The objectives for establishing the site must be clear from the outset.
- The site itself should be informative rather than persuasive, since it is a sought communication – people do not go online to be sold to.
- Graphics should be kept simple if possible; not everyone has a broadband connection and many people have slow connections or slow computers.
- The impact of the communication should not depend entirely on the graphics; people using a dial-up connection might find the download to be too expensive. This is not a problem in the United States or Australia, where telephone calls are free or are fixed price no matter what the duration of the call.
- The site must be integrated with other communications; cross-marketing will encourage subscribers to visit the site.
- The site should be set up to gather information from those who visit it, either through requesting contact details from visitors or through downloading a tracking cookie (a piece of software which records and feeds back customer activity) onto the visitor's computer.
- The site should encourage interactivity by the use of offers, competitions, sales promotions and other incentives; people prefer interactive communications in general (Vlasic and Kesic 2007).
- Hyperlinks need to be fast, so that users can access the information they really need quickly.

The Internet can be a useful tool for increasing customer intimacy. Because of the social presence effect, customers feel more comfortable in divulging information and feel closer to the website owner. There are five dimensions of service quality on the Internet (Jayawardene 2004):

1. *Access*. The website should be easy to access, quick to download and simple to understand.
2. *Website interface*. This should be informative, easy to navigate and engaging for the individual.
3. *Trust*. Establishing trust is particularly important, since ordering goods over the Internet involves divulging credit card details. Although security is constantly being tightened, fraudsters are also becoming more adept at breaching security.
4. *Attention*. Websites should attract attention and should also show that attention has been paid to customer needs.
5. *Credibility*. Exaggerated claims, small print and unverifiable statements are likely to detract from the overall credibility of the site.

Security is a key issue in adoption of Internet purchasing by consumers. Many people are put off buying online because of the perceived risk, and this can be even more apparent in the international context. The effects are strongest if the website is located in a country where the rule of law is weak, but also people from countries with a strong national identity give a great deal of weight to cultural similarities between the website and their own culture (Steenkamp and Geyskens 2006). The same research showed that people from individualistic cultures such as the UK and United States give greater weight to privacy, security and customisation options than do people from collectivist cultures. In general, people tend to prefer websites which are linked to their local culture (Singh *et al.* 2006).

People enjoy sensory stimuli from online retailers as much as they do from bricks-and-mortar retailers (Parsons and Conroy 2006). This means that good graphics, perhaps with an element of humour attached, will go down well with online consumers. People become frustrated and leave the website early if information is inaccurate, poorly presented, insufficient or of doubtful credibility (Grant *et al.* 2007). Using an avatar (a cartoon character which guides the individual through the site) leads to higher satisfaction with the retailer, a more positive attitude towards the product and greater purchase intention (Holzwarth *et al.* 2006). This is probably because of the perception of friendliness that avatars engender, leading to increased pleasure and arousal (Wang *et al.* 2007). Trust is clearly an issue – if people trust the website, this will overcome the potential risk of buying online (Buttner and Goritz 2008).

In an analysis of the factors influencing the extent to which people visit a given website, Wolk and Theysohn (2007) discovered the following:

- The number of visitors to a site is influenced by the quality of the offering, the level of interactivity, the accessibility and the relevance of the site to the individual.
- The number of page views (i.e. the length of time the individual stays on the site) is influenced by credibility, interactivity, personalisation and navigation issues.
- Credibility, branding and visibility also influence traffic levels.
- Accessibility, in itself, is not enough to ensure success since it reduces the number of page views per visitor, despite attracting more visitors. In other words, the number of hits on a page is not the main criterion for measuring success.

Future developments

Current thinking is that the effect of increased use of the Internet for marketing purposes has led to a new environment for marketing. The speed of information flow within firms, especially those operating globally, has offered greater possibilities for real-time negotiations between firms. The rapid growth in virtual shopping (accessing catalogues on the Internet) means that consumers can buy goods anywhere in the world and have them shipped – or, in the case of computer software, simply downloaded – which means that global competition has reached unprecedented levels, particularly among small firms which have, until now, been unable to access global markets. Many of these firms use the Internet to create closer collaboration with other firms as well as to create greater value for customers (Bell and Loane 2010). Virtual shoppers are able to access high-quality pictures of products, holiday destinations and even pictures of restaurant food before committing to a purchase. A recent development is the use of bots, which can be programmed to search the Internet on behalf of an individual and find products which might be of interest. A correctly programmed bot acts exactly like the individual, knowing what the person likes or dislikes, and developments in the pipeline will enable the bot to negotiate prices on behalf of the individual.

Online consumers can be seen as co-creators of brand value (Christodoulides *et al.* 2006). The brand value of an online retailer has five dimensions:

1 *Emotional connection*. Because the buying situation is usually taking place within the customer's home environment, there is an emotional element involved, and the brand should reflect this.
2 *Online experience*. This is a quality of both the retailer and the consumer – a consumer with very little online experience might have entirely different feelings about a website than would a more experienced online shopper.
3 *Responsive service nature*. If the service is poor or unresponsive, the brand will suffer.
4 *Trust*. Online consumers need to feel trusted and need to feel that the website is trustworthy.
5 *Fulfilment*. The delivery of the order, or the successful outcome of the sale, is a strong indicator of brand quality.

It is of course important to remember that Internet users are still individuals; currently, segmenting the market is difficult because the Internet and its users have gone through so much change in recent years: fifteen years ago, only real computer enthusiasts and a few scientists used the Internet, ten years ago its users were limited to the educated and wealthy, now the Internet is used by everyone. A suggested segmentation was proposed in 2007; the researchers categorised Internet users as risk-averse doubters, open-minded online shoppers and reserved information seekers. The doubters would be unlikely to have much to do with the Internet and could be called laggards, the online shoppers are clearly heavy Internet users and the information seekers use the Internet to find out about products, but then buy from traditional bricks-and-mortar retailers (Barnes *et al.* 2007).

Permission marketing

Permission marketing is the process by which consumers give a company permission to e-mail information about new products and special offers. A core principle of permission marketing is the shift in power from the marketer to the consumer (Kent and

Brandal 2003, Cross 2003). Dufrene *et al.* (2005) suggest that a key benefit of permission marketing for consumers is that they can be in control over what they receive.

Webcasting is the automatic delivery of items of interest direct to the individual's PC and is one form of permission marketing. Webcasting involves the subscriber in stating in advance what type of information he or she is interested in and having this automatically delivered by the webcaster, thus avoiding the time and effort spent in searching the Internet using a search engine. This type of permission marketing became extremely popular in the early part of the century, but recently there have been signs of a fall in interest on the part of consumers.

Consumer fatigue (the fall in interest caused by over-use of communications) has been growing with regard to permission-based e-mails (Eccles 2006, Nussey 2004). This may be because communication is still one-way, with the 'power' resting with the marketer; permission marketing is simply a gate that consumers can choose to open or not, but once the gate is opened consumers suffer the same intrusiveness that they used to experience from spam (Smith and Wood, 2004).

The average consumer received six marketing e-mails a day in 2004 (Duffy 2006) and this figure continues to grow; 63% of UK consumers now delete e-mail advertising without reading it, while 56% believe they receive too many e-mail marketing messages, therefore making it harder for marketers to 'cut through bloated inboxes' (Brookes 2005). Several writers also cite the frequency of mailings as a major concern for consumers (Quiris 2003, Nussey 2004).

Self-selection of messages is dependent on level of involvement, and since the Internet represents sought communication, the messages should be informative rather than persuasive. The Internet is not merely a simulation of the real world, it is an alternative to it in which consumers can have the illusion of being present in a computer-mediated environment (Hoffman and Novak 1996). Consumers have a role in creating the communications themselves; bulletin boards attract users, and the success of the board attracts more users and adds credibility to the site. This means that more consumers will see the marketer's messages.

Using the internet for research

Bulletin boards of newsgroups allow marketers to monitor the success of word-of-mouth campaigns and can also be directly useful in market research; Internet users' comments are often useful in assessing consumer attitudes. However, research shows that using the Internet for market research purposes is risky; although a large number of people respond to surveys, the proportion of respondents is less than 4% of the population. There is evidence that the remaining 96% differ from these respondents in some important ways (Grandcolas *et al.* 2003). The reasons for this may be as follows:

- Some people are better at using the Internet.
- Respondents may be faster typists and therefore need to dedicate less time to answering surveys.

- Respondents may have more time; for example, they may be retired or unemployed people who can spend time on surveys rather than people who use the Internet for work purposes and have deadlines to meet.
- Respondents may have unmetered Internet access. People with broadband provision or who do not pay for the Internet connection by the minute (i.e. are using a dial-up connection with unlimited time) may be more prepared to stay online to complete a questionnaire.

These differences may or may not be crucial, depending on what is being researched. Checking whether respondents differ from non-respondents is, of course, difficult simply because non-respondents (by definition) withhold the information.

Other research possibilities inherent in the Internet include virtual focus groups and rapid concept testing of new products.

Although much of the interest in the Internet has focused on business-to-consumer marketing, the medium has proved most useful in the business-to-business context. Full participation in e-marketing management of supply chains requires firms to integrate their internal and external supply chain activities and share strategic information with the other members of the supply chain (Eng 2004). This is most easily accomplished by the use of the Internet, allowing other members of the supply chain to access confidential parts of the company's website by using a password. Using technology to mediate the relationship between supplier and purchaser has been shown to have a significant positive effect on buyers' future intention to buy – in other words, buyers like to buy from suppliers who have an effective website (McDonald and Smith 2004). This may be because the website offers possibilities for fast after-sales service, particularly in the computer software industry, where online troubleshooting is used to correct errors in the software. This is often the main use that software companies have for their websites (Moen et al. 2003).

Integrating the company's database with its Internet activities can be used to provide one-to-one customer relationship management (O'Leary et al. 2004). For example, returning visitors to the website can be greeted by name, their details can be kept on the database so that there is no need to re-enter (for example) address and credit card details and the customer's preferences can be noted. This is achieved by the use of cookies (small programs downloaded onto the customer's computer). Ultimately, a profile of the customer's likes and dislikes can be built up, allowing the supplying company to target special offers and promotions much more accurately.

A further use of the Internet is to use internal networks within the firm to replace or supplement internal communications such as staff newsletters. This can have a stronger effect than paper versions, because it is rather harder to ignore; the staff member is generally more likely to read an e-mail than to open a staff newsletter, and the e-mail version is also quicker and cheaper to produce and distribute. In most organisations, paper memos and newsletters have virtually disappeared, although some people still print off e-mails.

MARKETING ETHICS

Ethics are the principles that define right and wrong. In most cases marketers do not become enmeshed in the deeper recesses of philosophy, but instead rely on the moral rules which are part of the corporate culture. Research shows that most business people have separate sets of morals for work and for home (Fraedrich 1988). For example, much of the jargon of marketing is warfare-based (counterattacks, offensive product launches, etc.) and of course 'all's fair in love and war'; soldiers may kill or maim the enemy, but would not do so in civilian life. Having said that, while the moral code of a company may not be the same as the moral code of its employees and managers, there will be less dissonance among the staff if the firm conforms reasonably closely to a code of ethics.

- *Products* should be honestly made and described; commercial pressures may tempt companies to use cheaper raw materials or to use new additives to make the product perform differently. The ethical issue arises when customers are not informed of such changes.
- *Promotions* can involve deceptive or misleading advertising, manipulative sales methods, and even bribery in selling situations. While a certain amount of advertising 'puff' is acceptable and even expected, it is clearly not acceptable to tell outright lies or even to use misleading phrases. For example, salespeople often face ethical conflicts; perhaps a salesperson is faced with correcting a customer's mistaken belief about a product, and thus losing the business, or allowing the customer to continue with the false belief right up to the point of taking delivery of the goods. Once a salesperson has deceived a customer it becomes increasingly difficult to tell the truth later, and eventually the customer will discover the truth anyway. At that point the business will be lost, probably for ever.
- *Pricing* raises ethical issues in the areas of price fixing, predatory pricing (pricing below the cost of production to bankrupt competitors) and not revealing the full cost of purchase. For example, some high street chains of opticians fail to mention that the prices displayed are for spectacle frames only – the lenses are extra.
- *Distribution ethics* involves abuse of power in channel management (see Chapter 8) and failure to pay for goods within the specified credit terms. Some stores (for example, Toys 'R' Us) operate no-quibble sale-or-return contracts which mean that manufacturers have to accept damaged goods back, even when there is no fault in the manufacture; this has been seen as unethical by some smaller manufacturers, who have little negotiating power and few choices of outlet for their products.

Establishing a code of ethics within an organisation should not be left to chance. It is better to have a code of practice, and monitor the code in practice, so that employees and others know exactly what the firm is doing about its ethical responsibilities. As with any other question of marketing, the decision as to what the code should contain can be made by reference to the firm's customers and consumers – what would these people regard as ethical behaviour?

The recent phenomenon of the ethical consumer has caused many firms to rethink their policies. Shoppers often consider global and local decisions in choosing where to shop (for example, choosing to support a small independent butcher rather than buying meat in a supermarket, or avoiding foreign-owned store chains), and may consider where the products have come from and whether human or animal rights have been compromised (Megicks *et al.* 2008). Many consumers recognise that this is not an easy task, but ethically conscious consumers will make an effort to buy locally, perhaps from farmers' markets, as often as they are able (McEachern *et al.* 2010).

Valor (2007) has identified three key factors in ethical consumption: should (ethical obligation), want (conflicting identities) and can (personal action to change). The concept of 'should' is based on individual conscience, of a moral sense of what is the right thing to do. 'Want' is based on the conflict between acting in an unethical but desirable way (in this case buying clothes which have been made by low-paid workers) and doing the right thing. 'Can' is based on what the consumer actually has the power to do to change things – in some cases, there may be no ethical choices available. Personality variables which may have an effect are extroversion, agreeableness and conscientiousness, all of which have a positive impact on the tendency to act ethically (Fraj and Martinez 2006).

Ultimately, of course, people working within the firm have to be able to live with their consciences; establishing a code of ethical conduct will help them to do so.

GLOBALISATION

Globalisation is a business philosophy under which firms regard the entire planet as their marketplace and source of supply. The truly global firm identifies competitors, suppliers, customers, employees, threats and opportunities throughout the world regardless of national boundaries.

The main drivers for globalisation are as follows:

- Increasing economies of scale and scope for firms in the market
- Convergence of consumer tastes and preferences
- Rapidly improving communications, in terms of both telecommunications and transport systems
- Increased political acceptance of global trading
- The continuing growth of large firms, coupled with limits imposed by national monopoly regulators on domestic growth.

Table 12.3 Stages in globalisation

Stage	Explanation
Ethnocentrism	Home-country orientation. The foreign market is seen as secondary, perhaps as a place to dispose of excess production. The assumption is that the foreign market is basically the same as the domestic market, so marketing strategies are hardly adapted at all for the overseas market.
Polycentrism	A polycentric firm only identifies the differences in each market. The firm treats each market as being unique, with its own marketing strategies; the products are modified to suit the local market, and tactical issues such as price and promotion are decided locally.
Geocentrism	The firm sees the world as a single market and seeks to identify market segments within that market. This results in developing uniform policies for approaching the segments that have been identified, so that promotions and products are similar across the globe.

Firms going global move through three stages:

- Ethnocentrism
- Polycentrism
- Geocentrism.

These stages are shown in Table 12.3.

Obviously it is not always possible to take a completely global view. Even firms such as McDonald's have to adapt their product somewhat for local markets. For example, in India McDonald's burgers are made from mutton since the cow is sacred to Hindus; in Japan the company offers teriyaki burgers; in Russia the main beverage offered is tea rather than coffee. Most firms appear to take a 'glocal' approach, adapting their communications and products somewhat to take account of local variations; this appears to be true even for Internet communications; in other words, even the corporate website will be adapted (Halliburton and Ziegfeld 2009).

In fact, although there is a concentration of interest on business-to-consumer markets, the bulk of global marketing is conducted within the business-to-business area. The practical, economic considerations of industrial buyers are likely to be the same whatever their cultural backgrounds; a Japanese steel buyer will source from whichever country offers the best deal, as would a steel buyer in New York or Buenos Aires. Buyers may be affected by the nationality of the supplying firm, because countries acquire reputations which affect the reputations of their companies. If both the supplier and the purchaser are global, a further problem arises. Because there are several decision-makers involved in industrial buying and they may be scattered across several countries, each buyer is subject to a separate set of cultural influences. This situation requires considerable negotiation and adaptation of both the product and the business methods to achieve agreement.

Globalisation is important for all firms, even those who are not themselves planning to expand into the international arena; those firms will still be affected directly or indirectly by foreign competition and by the growing strength of domestic competitors who have themselves expanded overseas.

An objection to globalisation is the erosion of cultural values. Major firms are often accused of forcing cultural changes on the population; this is called McDonaldisation, a reference to the well-known McDonald's practice of standardising the product worldwide. For example, there has been an overall growth in tobacco smoking worldwide in recent years as the tobacco companies have targeted Third World countries, in effect exporting the vices of the industrial world.

A further criticism is that global companies do not have any allegiance to individual countries, and therefore have no compunction about causing environmental damage or economic disruption in supplier countries. For example, farmers in Africa are encouraged to grow cash crops to supply global corporations, while neglecting to grow sufficient crops to feed the local population.

Anti-globalisation campaigns were a feature of twenty-first century business for the first few years of the century, but they did not have much impact on the way firms do business. In the last analysis, consumers indicate their support (or lack of support) for companies by the way they spend their money. If people in, say, France decide that they would rather have a quick snack at McDonald's than take their traditional two-hour lunch break, they will do so – and in practice McDonald's has many home-grown imitators in France, including Quick and Buffalo Grill.

MARKETING STRATEGY REVISITED

In previous chapters, strategy has been discussed in terms of knowing where the firm is now, and knowing where it is going. Tactical decisions have been illustrated, describing methods of achieving the destination.

In the broader contexts examined in this chapter, marketing strategy needs also to take account of the long-term sustainability of the company. Although it has been a general rule in the past that companies cannot stand still, there may in future be pressures requiring a company to mark time, so that 'reaching a destination' becomes 'remaining where we are'. Analysis therefore needs to go beyond the SWOT and STEP analyses described in Chapters 2 and 10, and include further analysis to take account of societal marketing (see Chapter 1). Tactically, marketers must take account of ethical thinking; the route to achieving the company's objectives needs to be an ethical one if the objective is to be reached. For example, there is some evidence that companies which reduce excess supply of products, reduce 'reverse supply' (where products have to be returned), and which have effective internal marketing within the supply chain tend to be more profitable and have stronger competitive advantage (Sharma *et al.* 2010).

Strategies for dealing with issues of societal marketing are as follows:

- **Reaction strategy** means ignoring a problem unless somebody complains. When the problem becomes known, the business managers usually deny responsibility, resolve the problem and clear up any consequential losses, and carry on as usual.
- **Defence strategy** seeks to wriggle out of any problems. The firm might lobby politicians to avoid adverse legislation, or change the way the business is run to avoid complying with regulations. For example, some shipping companies respond to safety regulations by registering the vessels in countries that have few regulations, such as Liberia and Panama.
- **Accommodation strategy** involves accepting responsibility for the firm's actions and accommodating the views of the **stakeholders**. A business might take action if it feels that a pressure group or government legislation is about to force an issue.
- **Proactive strategy** involves regularly examining the company's activities in the light of ethical and societal responsibilities, and repairing any failings or shortcomings without waiting for outside groups to notice the problem. This strategy requires the greatest effort (and cost) to the firm, but also ensures the maximum return in terms of maintaining a caring reputation.

THE TWENTY-FIRST CENTURY MARKETPLACE

According to Schultz and Schultz (1998) marketing has gone through two distinct phases since 1950, and is about to enter a third. In the 1950s and 1960s markets were dominated by manufacturers, who used market research to find out what consumers wanted and used intensive promotional campaigns to control markets or at least have the strongest influence in them. During the 1970s and 1980s retailers began to dominate because they were closest to the market. They have been able to determine which products are offered to consumers and which are not. The third phase, brought about by the increasing use of IT by consumers, is consumer domination of the marketplace.

In the fifteen years since Schultz and Schultz published their prophetic view of marketing, much of what they predicted has happened. The Internet has become almost universal in the wealthy countries of Europe and the Americas, and even in less-favoured countries the advent of Internet cafés means that a large proportion of the world's population are able to carry out information searches and shop online. This represents a dramatic shift of power towards consumers.

As consumers become more powerful in the relationship, the role of marketing is shifting from a strategic function to a tactical one. The model of marketing as a patriarchal function has been breaking down for some time now, in the face of unpredictable consumer responses, fragmentation of societies and increasing individualism. Consumers are impatient with the concept of the powerful, all-knowing marketers providing them with what the research says is best for them. This means that market research findings no longer act as truly effective predictors in many cases, and marketers are therefore left to respond as effectively as they can to consumer demands as expressed through interactive media.

Of course, the traditional manufacturer domination will continue in some markets and the retailer domination of major store chains will also continue, but the increasing ability of consumers to make their purchases almost anywhere in the world and to access information from almost anywhere will increase the pressure on marketers to integrate their activities to maximise effectiveness and efficiency. This set of circumstances will lead to a change in the way that marketing operates.

Firms go through four levels of marketing integration, as shown in Table 12.4. Evidence for this change manifests itself mainly on the Internet, where reverse-auction sites are springing up almost daily; sites such as Oltiby.com allow consumers to bid for manufactured products. Once the bids are in, the manufacturers are invited to supply products at the heavily discounted prices that the consumers have said

Table 12.4 Stages of integration of marketing communications

Stage	Explanation
Level 1 Tactical coordination	The 1980s and 1990s saw a massive increase in the available tools for communicating with consumers; level 1 response is to create 'one sight, one sound' by consolidating communications planning. Often this leads to the formation of teams of specialists from different areas of expertise to increase synergy and cross-fertilisation of ideas.
Level 2 Redefining the scope of marketing	Rather than viewing marketing as a series of outbound activities, the firm begins to consider all the points at which the consumer and the brand are in contact. One of the most important results of level 2 thinking has been the inclusion of employees both as targets for marketing communications and as communicators in their own right. Internal marketing thus becomes one of the driving forces of level 2 thinking.
Level 3 Application of IT	IT is both driving the changes in marketing and providing the solutions. The key ingredient in level 3 thinking is the use of databases to capture individual transactions. This enables the firm to move away from marketing to the average customer at the middle of a segment and to market to groups of individuals instead.
Level 4 Strategic and financial integration	Two issues are paramount: the ability to measure the return on customer investment and the ability to use marketing to drive organisational and strategic directions. Rather than measuring (for example) extra sales resulting from an advertising campaign, the firm would now measure the returns from a specific group of customers against the costs associated with all the marketing efforts directed at that group. Under this approach, financial directors would have sufficient information to be able to compare investment in communicating with a particular group of customers with, for example, investing in new manufacturing facilities.

they are prepared to pay. This type of consumer power is likely to become more prevalent as the century unfolds.

Overall, marketing in the twenty-first century presents many new challenges. Shrinking markets, green issues, runaway advances in communications technology and rapidly changing public attitudes towards consumption and communication predicate major changes not only in marketing techniques but also in corporate strategy. The role of marketing is still, at the end of the day, to meet customers' needs in the most effective, efficient and sustainable way possible for as long as it is possible to do so. Marketers will need to re-examine their models of marketing strategy many times; in an era where change is the only constant, marketing cannot afford to stand still. Ultimately, the firms who take the greatest care of their customers' interests are the ones most likely to maintain their competitive edge in a cut-throat world.

CASE STUDY 12 Mothercare

Mothercare is a UK retailer which specialises in everything for the mother-to-be and her baby. The Mothercare Group includes the Early Learning Centre, which specialises in educational toys, primarily for the 0–6-years age group. Mothercare is iconic in Britain – virtually every child in Britain will have had some, if not all, of its needs met from the store, and the majority of pregnant women have become familiar with its stores.

The company began as a purely mail order business in 1962, but quickly moved to a High Street format. Currently, the company has over 1000 stores worldwide, but still maintains its mail order roots by having a very active Internet presence. The online business is quite remarkable in its range – for example, the company offers over 350 types of pushchair and 300 types of car seat online. The growth strategy of the group is based on four factors: first, maximising the marketing synergies from its acquisition of the Early Learning Centres in 2007; second, restructuring the combined Mothercare and Early Learning Centre property portfolio; third, continuing the rapid growth of Direct (the online service); and fourth, driving the international reach of Mothercare and the Early Learning Centre.

Direct is clearly a major contributor to the corporate strategy, since Mothercare already has expertise going back 50 years in mail order; moving to online ordering is not a great leap for the company, since the fulfilment of orders is old technology for them. The company is moving much more towards its own brands, with Mothercare and Early Learning brands dominating the growth strategy. Currently, the major part of both ranges is available online, with free standard delivery on all orders over £50 (which probably means virtually all orders). The Blooming Marvellous Collection of maternity wear (acquired when Mothercare bought out a competitor) offers stylish clothes for expectant mothers – all available online.

Perhaps one of Mothercare's most interesting developments is Gurgle.com. A pun on the search engine Google, Gurgle.com is a social networking site for new mothers. Mothers and mothers-to-be are able to post queries on site and get advice from each other – often this is easier and less threatening than consulting, for example, health professionals. Discussion topics range from babies' medical problems through to whether to have another baby, to what the mothers miss most about life before having a baby – the topics are entirely up to the mothers. The site accepts advertising from various companies which supply baby goods, but the advertising is low-key and unobtrusive. The site also contains a lot of advice and information from professionals. The site has hyperlinks to the Mothercare and Early Learning sites, but there is no pressure – mothers can visit the site without feeling pressured. The whole tone of the site is cheerful – there are even baby photographs of the management team, with brief histories of quirky things from their pasts.

Gurgle.com provides huge advantages for Mothercare. Apart from the obvious marketing benefit of driving business to the Mothercare website, Gurgle.com provides an immediate insight into what the mothers are most interested in, and which problems they regard as the most serious. This enables Mothercare's buyers to anticipate what the market needs and act accordingly. Also, mothers posting on the forums will flag up problems with products, both those from Mothercare and those of competitors, thus providing a broader overview of the marketplace than might otherwise be obtained.

Mothercare has managed to carve out a niche in the market by developing a reputation for quality and reliability. The brand is very widely trusted, and the company now has the advantage that grandmothers-to-be (and even a few great-grandmothers-to-be) are recommending their daughters to use the store. The firm's willingness to move with the times while providing a traditional set of values is the key to its success.

Questions

1 Why should Mothercare have both online and bricks-and-mortar retailing?
2 How might the company make further use of Gurgle.com?
3 How does Mothercare maintain its closeness to its customers, considering that child-rearing is a relatively short period of most people's lives?
4 What are the advantages to mothers of using Gurgle.com?
5 What synergies with Early Learning Centres might exist for Mothercare?

SUMMARY

In this chapter we have looked at current issues in marketing: the ways in which companies try to establish long-term relationships with their customers, ethical issues and Internet marketing.

Here are the key points from this chapter:

- Relationship marketing suggests that manufacturers should try to develop the same closeness to the customer that service industries have
- Traditional marketing is concerned with single transactions; relationship marketing is concerned with long-term business
- It is cheaper to keep existing customers than to find new ones
- Quality is the relationship between expectations and results

- Benchmarking may make a firm the best of the best, but it is likely in the long run to stifle innovation
- Companies that fail to establish a good relationship with their customers will lose out to firms that do
- Responsible ethical approaches are likely to be directly beneficial to the firm in the long run; unethical approaches may be beneficial in the short run, but affect survival prospects in the long term
- The Internet is not without its problems, but Internet marketing is likely to continue to grow in future.

CHAPTER QUESTIONS

1 What are the potential problems with relationship marketing?

2 How would you go about establishing a code of ethics?

3 Why might transaction marketing be less effective than relationship marketing in the long run for, say, a car manufacturer?

4 What reasons might a firm have for consulting environmentalists about strategy?

5 What are the key issues in establishing a website?

Further reading

Good Business: Your World Needs You by Steve Hilton and Giles Gibbons (London, Texere Publishing, 2002) offers a view of how ethically run businesses can actually be more profitable than those run on purely self-centred lines. It is a cheerfully optimistic book, positive about the capitalist system, and offers plentiful advice on how to make it even better.

E-Marketing, 6th edn, by Judy Strauss, Adel el-Ansary and Raymond Frost (Harlow, Pearson, 2011) is structured like an introductory marketing text, but covers all the topics from an e-marketing perspective. It is thus currently the most comprehensive available book on Internet marketing. Obviously, it is likely to date quickly – new editions will replace this one fairly regularly!

Customer Relationship Management, 2nd edn, by Francis Buttle (Oxford, Butterworth–Heinemann, 2008). This book looks at customer relationship management as the core activity of the business, and gives a comprehensive overview of what information technology will (and will not) do in helping to manage customer relations, retention and development.

An alternative view is provided in *Why CRM Doesn't Work: How to Win by Letting Customers Manage the Relationship,* by Seth Godin and Frederick Newell (London, Kogan Page, 2003). Godin and Newell argue that trying to manage the relationship fails because the customer is not empowered – letting the customers manage the relationship is actually more successful.

References

Ahuja, Vandana, and Medury, Yajulu: 'Corporate blogs as e-CRM tools – building consumer engagement through content management', *Journal of Database Marketing and Customer Strategy Management,* 17 (2) (June 2010), pp. 91–105.

Ang, Lawrence and Buttle, Francis: 'Managing for successful customer acquisition: an exploration', *Journal of Marketing Management*, **22** (3/4) (2006), pp. 295-317.

Baker, M.J.: *Marketing: An Introductory Text*, 5th edn (Basingstoke, Macmillan, 1991).

Barnes, Stuart, Bauer, Hans H., Neumann, Marcus M. and Huber, Frank: 'Segmenting cyberspace: a customer typology for the Internet', *European Journal of Marketing*, **41** (1/2) (2007), pp. 71-93.

Bell, Jim and Loane, Sharon: 'New-wave global firms: Web 2.0 and SME internationalisation', *Journal of Marketing Management*, **26** (3/4) (2010), pp. 213-19.

Bogomolova, Svetlana and Romaniuk, Jenni: 'Brand equity of defectors and never boughts in a business financial market', *Industrial Marketing Management*, **39** (8) (Nov 2010), pp. 1261-8.

Brennan, Ross D., Turnbull, Peter W. and Wilson, David T.: 'Dyadic adaptation in business-to-business markets', *European Journal of Marketing*, **37** (11) (2003), pp. 1636-8.

Brookes, G.: 'Online: overcrowded inbox', *Marketing*, 13 July 2005.

Buttner, Oliver B. and Goritz, Anja S.: 'Perceived trustworthiness of online shops', *Journal of Consumer Behaviour*, **7** (1) (Jan/Feb 2008), pp. 35-50.

Christodoulides, George, DeChernatony, Leslie, Furrier, Olivier, Shiu, Eric and Abimbola, Temi: 'Conceptualising and measuring the equity of online brands', *Journal of Marketing Management*, **22** (7/8) (2006), pp. 799-825.

Christopher, M., Ballantyne, D. and Payne, A.: *Relationship Marketing* (Oxford, Butterworth-Heinemann, 1991).

Conway, Tony, Ward, Mike, Lewis, Gerard and Bernhardt, Anke: 'Internet crisis potential: the importance of a strategic approach to marketing communication', *Journal of Marketing Communication*, **13** (3) (2007), pp. 213-28.

Cross, R.: 'Permission marketing', *Admap*, **440** (June 2003), pp. 30-3.

Denegri-Knott, Janice: 'Consumers behaving badly: deviation or innovation? Power struggles on the Web', *Journal of Consumer Behaviour*, **5** (1) (2006), pp. 82-94.

Dick, A.S.: 'Using membership fees to increase customer loyalty', *Journal of Product and Brand Management*, **4** (5) (1995), pp. 65-8.

Duffy, P.: 'How to grow and enhance your customer email database', *Brand Republic*, 3 February 2006.

Dufrene, D., Engelland, B., Lehman, C. and Pearson, R.: 'Changes in consumer attitudes resulting from participation in a permission e-mail campaign', *Journal of Current Issues and Research in Advertising*, **27** (1) (2005), pp. 65-77.

East, Robert, Hammond, Kathy and Gendall, Philip: 'Fact and fallacy in retention marketing', *Journal of Marketing Management*, **22** (2006), pp. 5-23.

Eccles, M.: 'Email marketing growing, along with consumers fatigue', *Brand Republic*, 20 January 2006.

Eng, Teck-Yong: 'The role of e-marketplaces in supply chain management', *Industrial Marketing Management*, **33** (2) (February 2004), pp. 97-105.

Evans, M.J.: 'Domesday marketing?' *Journal of Marketing Management*, **10** (5) (1994), pp. 409-31.

Fraedrich, John: 'Philosophy type interaction in the ethical decision making process of retailers', PhD Dissertation (Texas, A&M University, 1988).

Fraj, Elena and Martinez, Eva: 'Influence of personality on ecological consumer behavior', *Journal of Consumer Behaviour*, **5** (3) (2006), pp. 167-181.

Grandcolas, Ursula, Rettie, Ruth and Marusenko, Kira: 'Web survey bias: sample or mode effect?' *Journal of Marketing Management*, **19** (2003), pp. 501–61.

Grant, Robert, Clarke, Rodney J. and Kyriazis, Elias: 'A review of factors affecting online consumer search behavior from an information value perspective', *Journal of Marketing Management*, **23** (5/6) (2007), pp. 519–33.

Halliburton, Chris and Zeigfeld, Agnes: 'How do major European companies communicate their corporate identity across countries? An empirical investigation of corporate internet communications', *Journal of Marketing Management*, **25** (9/10) (2009), pp. 909–25.

Harrigan, Paul, Ramsey, Elaine and Ibbotson, Patrick: 'Critical factors underpinning the e-CRM activities of SMEs', *Journal of Marketing Management*, **27** (5/6) (2011), pp. 503–29.

Helgesen, Oyvind: 'Are loyal customers profitable? Customer satisfaction, customer (action) loyalty, and customer profitability at the individual level', *Journal of Marketing Management*, **22** (3/4) (2006), pp. 245–66.

Hoffman, D. and Novak, T.: 'A new marketing paradigm for electronic commerce', *The Information Society*, **13** (1) (1996).

Holzwarth, Martin, Janiszewski, Chris and Neumann, Marcus M.: 'The influence of avatars on online consumer shopping behavior', *Journal of Marketing*, **70** (4) (2006), pp. 19–36.

Huang, Lei: 'Social contagion effects in experiential information exchange on bulletin board systems', *Journal of Marketing Management*, **26** (3/4) (2010), pp. 197–212.

Jayawardene, Chanaka: 'Management of service quality in Internet banking: the development of an instrument', *Journal of Marketing*, **20** (1) (February 2004), pp. 185–207.

Jepsen, Anna Lund: 'Information search in virtual communities: is it replacing use of off-line communication?' *Journal of Marketing Communications*, **12** (4) (2006), pp. 247–61.

Johnson, Michael D. and Selnes, Fred: 'Customer portfolio management: towards a dynamic theory of exchange relationships', *Journal of Marketing*, **68** (2) (April 2004), pp. 1–16.

Johnson, Michael D., Herrman, Andreas and Huber, Frank: 'The evaluation of loyalty intentions', *Journal of Marketing*, **70** (2) (2006), pp. 122–32.

Kent, R. and Brandal, H.: 'Improving email response in a permission marketing context', *International Journal of Market Research*, **45** (4) (2003), pp. 489–503.

Kim, Jae Wook, Choi, Jiho, Qualls, William and Han, Kyesook: 'It takes a marketplace community to raise brand commitment: the role of online communities', *Journal of Marketing Management*, **24** (3/4) (2008), pp. 409–31.

Levitt, T.: *The Marketing Imagination* (New York, Free Press, 1986).

McDonald, Jason B. and Smith, Kirk: 'The effects of technology-mediated communication on industrial buyer behaviour', *Industrial Marketing Management*, **33** (2) (2004), pp. 107–16.

McEachern, Morven, G., Warnaby, Gary, Carrigan, Marylyn and Szmigin, Isabelle: 'Thinking locally, acting locally? Conscious consumers and farmers' markets', *Journal of Marketing Management*, **26** (5/6) (2010), pp. 395–412.

Megicks, Phil, Memery, Juliet and Williams, Jasmine: 'Influences on ethical and socially responsible shopping: evidence from the UK grocery sector', *Journal of Marketing Management*, **24** (5/6) (2008), pp. 637–59.

Moen, Oysten, Endresen, Iver and Gavlen, Morten: 'Executive insights: use of the Internet in international marketing: a case study of small computer firms', *Journal of International Marketing*, **11** (4) (2003), pp. 129–49.

Nussey, B.: 'The quiet email revolution', *iUniverse* (Inc, New York, 2004).

O'Leary, Chris, Rao, Saly and Perry, Chad: 'Improving customer relationship management through database/Internet marketing: a theory-building action research project', *European Journal of Marketing*, **38** (3/4) (2004), pp. 338–54.

O'Sullivan, Terry: 'Dangling conversations: Web-forum use by a symphony orchestra's audience members', *Journal of Marketing Management*, **26** (7/8) (2010), pp. 656–70.

Ojasalo, Jukka: 'Key network management', *Industrial Marketing Management*, **33** (3) (2004), pp. 195–205.

Parsons, Andrew and Conroy, Denise: 'Sensory stimuli and e-tailers', *Journal of Consumer Behaviour*, **5** (1) (2006), pp. 69–81.

Pervan, Simon J., Bove, Liliana L. and Johnson, Lester W.: 'Reciprocity as a key stabilizing norm of interpersonal marketing relationships: scale development and validation', *Industrial Marketing Management*, **38** (1) (Jan 2009), pp. 60–70.

Quiris: *How Email Practices Can Win or Lose Long-term Business: A View from the Inbox* (Quiris, Westminster, 2003).

Roberts, Keith, Varki, Sajeev and Brodie, Rod: 'Measuring the quality of relationships in consumer services: an empirical study', *European Journal of Marketing*, **37** (1) (2003), pp. 169–96.

Roemer, Ellen: 'The impact of dependence on the assessment of customer lifetime values in buyer–seller relationships', *Journal of Marketing Management*, **22** (2006), pp. 89–109.

Schultz, D.E. and Schultz, H.E.: 'Transitioning marketing communications into the twenty-first century', *Journal of Marketing Communications*, **4** (1) (1998), pp. 9–26.

Sharma, Arun, Iyer, Gopalakrishna R., Mehrotra, Anuj and Krishnan, R.: 'Sustainability and business-to-business marketing: a framework and implications', *Industrial Marketing Management*, **39** (2) (Feb 2010), pp. 330–41.

Singh, Nitish, Rassott, Georg, Zhao, Hongzhin and Bouftor, Paul D.: 'A cross-cultural analysis of German, Chinese and Indian consumers' perception of website adaptation', *Journal of Consumer Behaviour*, **5** (1) (2006), pp. 56–68.

Smith, J. and Wood, C. 'Opt-in is just a start', *Direct*, **16** (4) (2004), p. 39.

Steenkamp, Jan-Benedict E.M. and Geyskens, Inge: 'How country characteristics affect the perceived value of websites', *Journal of Marketing*, **70** (3) (2006), pp. 136–50.

Tuli, Kapil R., Kohli, Ajay K. and Bharadwaj, Sundar G.: 'Rethinking customer solutions: from product bundles to relational processes', *Journal of Marketing*, **71** (3) (2007), pp. 1–17.

Tuominen, Matti, Rajalo, Arto and Möller, Kristian: 'Market-driving versus market-driven: divergent roles of market orientation in business relationships', *Industrial Marketing Management*, **33** (3) (2004), pp. 207–17.

Valor, Carmen: 'The influence of information about labour abuses on consumer choice of clothes: a grounded theory approach', *Journal of Marketing Management*, **23** (7/8) (2007), pp. 675–95.

Vlasic, Goran and Kesic, Tanja: 'Analysis of consumers' attitudes towards interactivity and relationship personalization as contemporary developments in interactive marketing communications', *Journal of Marketing Communications*, **13** (2) (2007), pp. 109–29.

Wang, Liz C., Wagner, Judy A. and Wakefield, Kirk: 'Can a retail website be social?' *Journal of Marketing*, **71** (3) (2007), pp. 143–57.

Wilson, Hugh, Daniel, Elizabeth and Davies, Iain A.: 'The diffusion of e-commerce in UK SMEs', *Journal of Marketing Management*, **24** (5/6) (2008), pp. 489–516.

Wolk, Agnieszka and Theysohn, Sven: 'Factors influencing website traffic in the paid content market', *Journal of Marketing Management*, **23** (7/8) (2007), pp. 769–96.

CHAPTER 2
MODELS OF MANAGEMENT

Aim

To present the main theoretical perspectives on management and to show how they relate to each other.

Objectives

By the end of your work on this chapter you should be able to outline the concepts below in your own terms and:

1. Explain the value of models of management, and compare unitary, pluralist and critical perspectives
2. State the structure of the competing values framework and evaluate its contribution to our understanding of management
3. Summarise the rational goal, internal process, human relations and open systems models and evaluate what each can contribute to a manager's understanding of their role
4. Use the model to classify the dominant form in two or more business units, and to gather evidence about the way this affects the roles of managing in those units
5. Show how ideas from the chapter add to your understanding of the integrating themes

Key terms

This chapter introduces the following ideas:

model (or theory)	open system
metaphor	system boundary
scientific management	feedback
operational research	subsystem
bureaucracy	socio-technical system
administrative management	contingency approach
human relations approach	complexity theory
system	non-linear system

Each is a term defined within the text, as well as in the glossary at the end of the book.

Case study: innocent drinks www.innocentdrinks.com

Richard Reed, Jon Wright and Adam Balon founded innocent drinks in 1998, having been friends since they met at Cambridge University in 1991. The business was successful, and in 2013 the founders sold most of their remaining shares to Coca-Cola for an undisclosed amount, but which observers estimated to be about £100 million. They stressed the sale would not affect the character of the company, as Coca-Cola had four years previously bought a small stake in the company to help finance expansion.

After they graduated, Reed worked in advertising, while Balon and Wright worked in (different) management consultancies. They often joked about starting a company together, considering several ideas before deciding on 'smoothies' – which they built into one of the UK's most successful entrepreneurial ventures of recent years.

Smoothies are blends of fruit that include the fruit's pulp and sometimes contain dairy products such as yoghurt. They tend to be thicker and fresher than ordinary juice. Some are made to order at juice bars and similar small outlets, but the trio decided to focus on pre-packaged smoothies sold mainly through supermarkets, and to offer a premium range. These contain no water or added sugar and cost more than the standard product.

Any new business requires capital and must also be assured of further cash for expansion. This is a challenge, as by definition the product is usually unknown, and the business has no record to show whether the promoters can make a profit. If investors doubt that they will get their money back, they will not lend it. Even if the initial plan succeeds, growth will require more finds – launching a new product or entering a new geographical market inevitably drains cash before it becomes profitable. The founders eventually persuaded Maurice Pinto, a private investor, to put in £235,000 in return for a 20 per cent share.

The company succeeded and, as sales grew, Pinto advised the founders to consider expanding in Europe and/or extending the product ranges. They initially started selling the core range in continental Europe and by early 2013 were active in 15 countries. They also diversified the product range. The table summarises the growth of the company.

The founders knew that their success would depend on the quality and commitment of their staff, including professional managers from other companies. Reed says:

Press Association Images/Edmund TeraKopian

	1999	2012
Number of employees	3	175
Number of recipes on sale	3	24
Market share	0%	62%
Turnover	£0	£165 million
Number of retailers	1 (on first day)	Over 11,000
Number of smoothies sold	24 (on first day)	2 million a week

> We've always set out to attract people who are entrepreneurial – we want them to stay and be entrepreneurial with innocent. But the inevitable result is that some want to go and do their own thing by setting up their own new businesses. We help and support them with whatever we can. (Quoted in *Director*, June 2011.)

The founders believe they are enlightened employers who look after staff well. All receive shares in the business which means they share in profits.

Sources: Based on material from 'innocent drinks', a case prepared by William Sahlman (2004), Harvard Business School, Case No. 9-805-031; Germain and Reed (2009); company website.

Case questions 2.1

Visit the website and check on the latest news about developments in the company.

- In what ways are managers at innocent adding value to the resources they use?
- As well as raising finance, what other issues would they need to decide once they had entered their chosen market?

2.1 Introduction

The story of innocent drinks illustrates three themes that run through this book. First, they were entrepreneurs who used their energies to create a new business – which would only survive if it offered something valuable to customers. Second, their personal values meant they wanted to leave the world a better place – such as by enabling staff to enjoy working there (and supporting some to become entrepreneurs themselves), treating suppliers fairly, and using sustainable production methods. Third, while based in the UK, they manage internationally – bringing materials from around the world, turning them into products, and selling these throughout Europe.

To achieve this they created an organisation through which to run the business – reliably securing resources, turning them into products which customers value, and so receiving revenues for the business to survive and grow. Most managers cope with similar issues. All need to recruit willing and capable people – at Apple to develop innovative software, at Tesco to work in their stores – and ensure that their work creates value. Many share the innocent drinks team's commitment to responsible business practice: the Co-op makes a point of working to clear ethical principles throughout their business, and still making healthy profits. Sustainability is now on the agenda of most management teams, as is the move to an international economy.

All managers, like those at innocent drinks, search for ways to manage their enterprises to add value. They make assumptions about the best way to do things – and through trial and error develop methods for their circumstances. No approach will suit all conditions – managers need to draw critically and selectively on several perspectives.

The next section introduces the idea of management models, and why they are useful. Section 2.3 presents the competing values framework – a way of seeing the contrasts and complementarities between four theoretical perspectives – and the following sections outline the ideas within each.

2.2 Why study models of management?

A **model (or theory)** represents a complex phenomenon by identifying the major elements and relationships.

A **model (or theory)** represents a more complex reality. Focussing on the essential elements and their relationship helps to understand that complexity, and how change may affect it. Most management problems can only be dealt with by using ideas from several models, as no one model offers a complete solution. Those managing a globally competitive business require flexibility, quality and low-cost production. Managers at Ford or DaimlerChrysler want models of the production process that help them to organise it efficiently from a technical perspective. Managers at GlaxoSmithKline want models that help them manage research programmes to create new pharmaceuticals at an acceptable cost. The management task is to convert ideas into a solution that is acceptable in their situation.

Managers act in accordance with their model (or theory) of the task, and the more accurate their model is (about, for example, how best to motivate talented scientists to deliver research that supports the company's strategy) the more likely they are to perform well. Good models save time and effort – they help us to identify the likely variables in a situation quickly, and to act more confidently. Knowing the models available help us to focus on the most likely factors, based on the models' underlying evidence. Pfeffer and Sutton (2006) suggest why people frequently ignore such evidence: see Key ideas.

> **Key ideas** — Pfeffer and Sutton on why managers ignore evidence
>
> In a paper making the case for evidence-based management Pfeffer and Sutton (2006) observe that experienced managers frequently ignore new evidence relevant to a decision and suggest that they:
>
> - trust personal experience more than they trust research;
> - prefer to use a method or solution which has worked before;
> - are susceptible to consultants who vigorously promote their solutions;
> - rely on dogma and myth – even when there is no evidence to support their value;
> - uncritically imitate practices that appear to have worked well for famous companies.
>
> Their paper outlines the benefits of basing practice on sound evidence – similar to the ideas of critical thinking presented in Chapter 1.
>
> Source: Pfeffer and Sutton (2006).

Models identify the variables

Models aim to identify the main variables in a situation, and the relationships between them: the more accurately they do so, the more useful they are. Since every situation is unique, some experienced managers doubt the value of theory. Magretta's answer is that:

> without a theory of some sort it's hard to make sense of what's happening in the world around you. If you want to know whether you work for a well-managed organization – as opposed to whether you like your boss – you need a working theory of management. (Magretta, 2002, p. 10)

We all use theory, acting on (perhaps implicit) assumptions about the relationships between cause and effect. Good theories help to identify variables and relationships, providing a mental toolkit to deal consciously with a situation. The perspective we take reflects our assumptions as we interpret, organise and makes sense of events – see Alan Fox in Key ideas.

> **Key ideas** — Alan Fox and a manager's frame of reference
>
> Alan Fox (1974) distinguished between unitary, pluralist or radical perspectives on the relationship between managers and employees. Which assumption a manager holds affects how they do their job. Fox suggested that those who take:
>
> - **a unitary perspective** believe that organisations aim to develop rational ways of achieving common interests. Managerial work arises from a technical division of labour, and managers work to achieve objectives shared by all members.
> - **a pluralist perspective** believe that the division of labour in modern organisations creates groups with different interests. Some conflict over ends and/or means is inevitable, and managerial work involves gaining sufficient consent to meet all interests to a mutually acceptable extent.
> - **a radical perspective** challenge both unitary and pluralist models, believing that they ignore how the horizontal and vertical division of labour sustains unequal social relations within capitalist society. As long as these exist managers and employees will be in conflict.
>
> Source: Fox (1974).

As managers influence others to add value they use their mental model of the situation to decide where to focus effort. Figure 2.1 develops Figure 1.3 (the internal context within

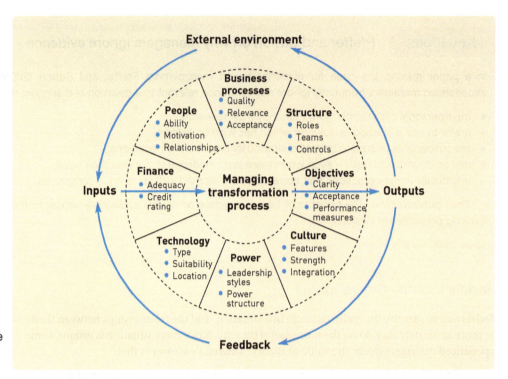

Figure 2.1 Some variables within the internal context of management

which managers work) to show some variables within each element: 'structure' could include more specific variables such as roles, teams, or control systems. In 2012 Willie Walsh, chief executive of British Airways, was continuing with one of his objectives (set by his predecessor) to raise operating profits to 10 per cent of sales. Figure 2.1 suggests ways of meeting this:

- **objectives** – retaining a reputation for premium travel (a different market than Ryanair);
- **people** – continuing to reduce the number of employees;
- **technology** – reducing BA's capacity at London City and basing more flights at Heathrow;
- **business processes** – negotiating new working practices with cabin staff.

In each area there are theories about the variables and their relationships – and about which changes will add most value. A change in one element affects others – reducing staff risks hindering the aim of providing a premium service. Any change would depend on available *finance* – and on the chief executive's *power* to get things done. External events (Chapter 3) such as rising fuel prices or changes in economic conditions shape all of these internal factors.

Managers need to influence people to add value: people who are aware, thinking beings, with unique experiences, interests and objectives. This affects what information they attend to, the significance they attach to it and how they act. There is an example in Chapter 3 of a retail business in which senior managers, store managers and shop-floor staff attached different meanings to the culture in which they worked. People interpret information subjectively, which makes it hard to predict how they will react: the MIP feature illustrates two managers' contrasting assumptions about how to deal with subordinates.

Management in practice — Practice reflects managers' theories

These examples illustrate contrasting theories about motivation.

- **Motivating managers:** Tim O'Toole, became chief executive of London Underground in 2003 (in 2013 he was chief executive of FirstGroup) and put in a new management structure – appointing a general manager for each line to improve accountability.

> Now there's a human being who is judged on how that line is performing and I want them to feel that kind of intense anxiety in the stomach that comes when there's a stalled train and they realise that it's their stalled train.
>
> Source: From an article by Simon London, *Financial Times*, 20 February 2004.
>
> - **Supporting staff:** John Timpson, chairman of the shoe repair and key cutting chain, believes the most important people in the company are those who cut customers' keys and re-heel their shoes:
>
> You come back for the service you get from the people in the shops. They are the stars ... we need to do everything to help them to look after you as well as possible. [A bonus based on shop takings] is fundamental to the service culture I want. It creates the adrenalin. That is the reason why people are keen to serve you if you go into one of our shops. And why they don't take long lunch breaks.
>
> Source: *Financial Times*, 3 August 2006.

Case questions 2.2
- Give examples of the variables in Figure 2.1 which innocent will be dealing with as it extends the product range.
- Which of the variables may have had a particularly strong influence on performance?

Models illuminate the manager's context

In 1974, the *New York Times* reported that sales of Peter Drucker's latest book, *Management: Tasks, Responsibilities, Practices* (Drucker, 1974) had overtaken those of Alex Comfort's illustrated primer *The Joy of Sex*. For one brief moment, management was the hottest topic of all. Only Drucker could have achieved this. 'No other person has had the impact on the practice of management that he did,' according to one of today's leading authorities, C.K. Pralahad. (From an article by Stefan Stern in the *Financial Times*, 24 November 2009.)

Stern was writing on the occasion of a conference to celebrate the hundredth anniversary of Drucker's birth, and to debate his significance and continued relevance. In many books and presentations Drucker aroused the enthusiasm of generations of managers, not least by putting complex ideas into an accessible form. For example, he advised managers to focus relentlessly on their purpose by remembering 'the five most important questions you will ever ask': What is our business? Who is our customer? What does the customer value? What are our results? What is our plan?

Managers have long valued such clear guidance but also find that, as Drucker acknowledged, they need to interpret these questions, and the answers they develop, in the light of their unique circumstances. Thousands of books offer advice to managers: these are only useful if the manager understands (has a good model of) his or her context, and uses ideas in a way which reflects that.

A **metaphor** is an image used to signify the essential characteristics of a phenomenon.

Key ideas — Gareth Morgan's images of organisation

Since organisations are complex creations we need to see them from several viewpoints: each will illuminate one aspect – while obscuring others. Gareth Morgan (1997) shows how alternative mental images and **metaphors** can represent organisations. Metaphors are a way of thinking, by attaching labels to represent an image of the object. They can help understanding, but can distort understanding if we use the wrong image. Morgan explores eight ways of seeing organisations:

- **Machines** – mechanical thinking and the rise of the bureaucracies.
- **Organisms** – recognising how the environment affects their health.
- **Brains** – an information-processing, learning perspective.
- **Cultures** – a focus on beliefs and values.
- **Political systems** – a view on conflicts and power.
- **Psychic prisons** – how people can become trapped by habitual ways of thinking.
- **Flux and transformation** – a focus on change and renewal.
- **Instruments of domination** – over members, nations and environments.

Critical thinking helps improve mental models

The ideas on critical thinking in Chapter 1 suggest that working effectively depends on being able and willing to test the validity of any theory, and to revise it in the light of experience by:

- identifying and challenging assumptions;
- recognising the importance of context;
- imagining and exploring alternatives;
- seeing limitations.

As you work through this chapter, there will be opportunities to practise these components of critical thinking.

2.3 The competing values framework

Quinn *et al.* (2003) believe that successive models of management (which they group according to four underlying philosophies – 'rational goal', 'internal process', 'human relations' and 'open systems') complement, rather than contradict, each other. They are all:

> symptoms of a larger problem – the need to achieve organizational effectiveness in a highly dynamic environment. In such a complex and fast-changing world, simple solutions become suspect ... Sometimes we needed stability, sometimes we needed change. Often we needed both at the same time. (p. 11)

While each adds to our knowledge, none is sufficient. The 'competing values' framework integrates them by highlighting their underlying values – see Figure 2.2.

The vertical axis represents the tension between flexibility and control. Managers seek flexibility to cope with rapid change. Others try to increase control – apparently the opposite of flexibility. The horizontal axis distinguishes an internal focus from an external one. Some managers focus on internal issues, while others focus on the world outside. Most models of management correspond to the values of one of the four segments.

The labels within the circle indicate the criteria of effectiveness which are the focus of models in that segment, shown around the outside. The human relations model, upper left in the figure, stresses the human criteria of commitment, participation and openness. The open systems model (upper right) stresses criteria of innovation, adaptation and growth. The rational goal model in the lower right focuses on productivity, direction and goal clarity. The internal process model stresses stability, documentation and control, within a hierarchical structure. Finally, the outer ring indicates the values associated with each model – the dominant value in the rational goal model is that of maximising output, while in human relations it is developing people. Successive sections of the chapter outline theories corresponding with each segment.

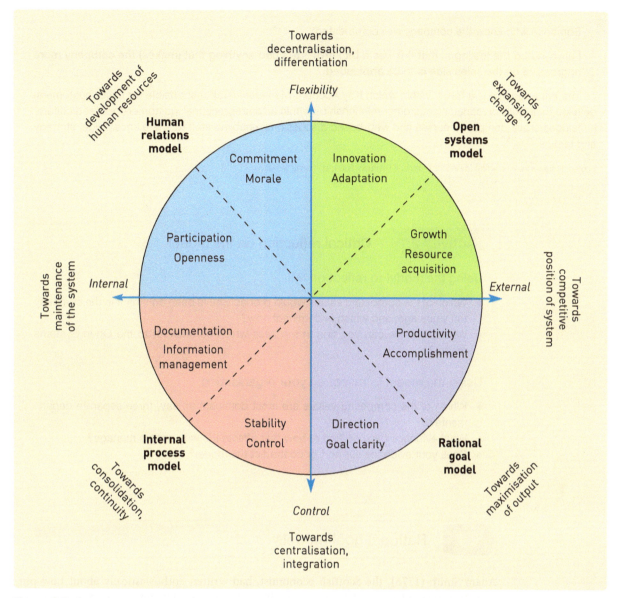

Figure 2.2 Competing values framework
Source: Quinn et al. (2003), p. 13.

Management in practice
Competing values at IMI? www.imiplc.com

When Martin Lamb took control of IMI (a UK engineering group which in 2013 employed 15,700 staff in 75 countries) he introduced significant changes to make the company profitable. He decided to concentrate the business on five sectors of engineering, each associated with high-value products and a strong chance of growth in the next few years. He moved much manufacturing to low-cost countries, encouraged close links with key customers and aimed to boost innovation. Mr Lamb says:

> This is a fundamental transition, aimed at moving IMI away from an old-established manufacturing enterprise to a company focussed on product development and applications of knowledge.

Someone who knew the company well commented:

I always had the feeling ... that IMI was a bit introverted and anything that (makes) the company more aggressive on the sales side is to be applauded.

The IMI Academy is a forum within which Key Account Managers (staff responsible for major customers) develop their skills of managing customer relationships within an entrepreneurial, customer-focussed culture. It includes cross-company courses and web-based discussions, enabling staff to share knowledge, strategy and tactics.

Source: Extracts from an article in *Financial Times*, 4 February 2004; company website.

Activity 2.1 Critical reflection on the model

Using the model to reflect on IMI

- Which of the competing values would probably have been dominant in the company ten years ago, and which is dominant now?
- What practices can you find in the case which correspond to the Open Systems model?

Using the model to reflect on your organisation

- Which of the competing values are most dominant in, say, three separate departments?
- What evidence can you find of how that affects the way people manage?
- Does your evidence support or contradict the model?

2.4 Rational goal models

Adam Smith (1776), the Scottish economist, had written enthusiastically about how pin manufacturers in Glasgow had broken a job previously done by one man into several small steps. A single worker now performed one of these steps repetitively, and this specialisation greatly increased their output. Smith believed this was one of the main ways in which the new industrial system was increasing the wealth of the country.

The availability of powered machinery during the Industrial Revolution enabled business owners to transform manufacturing and mining processes. These technical innovations encouraged, but were not the only reason for, the growth of the factory system. The earlier 'putting-out' system of manufacture, in which people worked at home on materials supplied and collected by entrepreneurs, allowed them great freedom over hours, pace and methods of work: those supplying the materials had little control over the quantity and quality of output. Entrepreneurs with capital found they could secure more control if they built a factory and brought workers into it. Having all workers on a single site meant that:

> coercive authority could be more easily applied, including systems of fines, supervision ... the paraphernalia of bells and clocks, and incentive payments. The employer could dictate the general conditions of work, time and space; including the division of labour, overall organisational layout and design, rules governing movement, shouting, singing and other forms of disobedience. (Thompson and McHugh, 2002, p. 22)

This still left entrepreneurs across Europe and later the United States with the problem of how to manage these new factories. Although domestic and export demand for manufactured goods was high, so was the risk of business failure. Similar problems still arise in rapidly growing manufacturing economies – see Management in practice.

> **Management in practice**   **Pressure at Foxconn**   www.foxconn.com
>
> In September 2012 Foxconn Technology Group's plant in Taiyuan, China, was the setting for one of China's worst incidents of labour unrest in years. Forty people were arrested after a riot by more than 2000 workers. The company is the largest private employer in China, with more than 1 million workers, making products for Apple, including most of the iPhones and iPads. A professor from the school of social sciences at Nanjing University said:
>
> > The nature of the Foxconn worker's job – the pressure, the monotony, the tediousness – has not changed. Therefore it is unavoidable that [despite the company awarding pay rises to the staff] incidents like this happen from time to time.
>
> Such is the pressure on the company to meet demand that it planned to increase the workforce at its Zengzhou iPhone factory from 150,000 in July 2012 to 250,000 by October.
>
> Sources: *Financial Times*, 25 and 26 September 2012.

> **Key ideas**   **Charles Babbage**
>
> Charles Babbage supported and developed Adam Smith's observations. He was an English mathematician better known as the inventor of the first calculating engine. During his work on that project he visited many workshops and factories in England and on the Continent. He then published his reflections on 'the many curious processes and interesting facts' that had come to his attention (Babbage, 1835). He believed that 'perhaps the most important principle on which the economy of a manufacture depends is the division of labour amongst the persons who perform the work' (p. 169).
>
> Babbage also observed that employers in the mining industry had applied the idea to what he called 'mental labour':
>
> > Great improvements have resulted ... from the judicious distribution of duties ... amongst those responsible for the whole system of the mine and its government'. (p. 202)
>
> He also recommended that managers should know the precise expense of every stage in production. Factories should also be large enough to secure the economies made possible by the division of labour and the new machinery.
>
> Source: Babbage (1835).

Frederick Taylor

The fullest answer to the problems of factory organisation came in the work of Frederick W. Taylor (1856–1915), always associated with the ideas of **scientific management**. An American mechanical engineer, Taylor focussed on the relationship between the worker and machine-based production systems:

> the principal object of management should be to secure the maximum prosperity for the employer, coupled with the maximum prosperity for each employee. The words 'maximum

Scientific management: the school of management called 'scientific' attempted to create a science of factory production.

prosperity' mean the development of every branch of the business to its highest state of excellence, so that the prosperity may be permanent.' (Taylor, 1917, p. 9)

He believed the way to achieve this was to ensure that each worker reached their state of maximum efficiency, so that each was doing 'the highest grade of work for which his natural abilities fit him' (p. 9). This would follow from detailed control of the process, which would become the managers' primary responsibility: they should concentrate on understanding the production systems, and use this to specify every aspect of the operation. In terms of Morgan's images, the appropriate image would be the machine. Taylor advocated five principles:

- use scientific methods to determine the one best way of doing a task, rather than rely on traditional methods;
- select the best person to do the job so defined, by ensuring they had suitable physical and mental qualities;
- train, teach and develop the worker to follow the defined procedures precisely;
- provide financial incentives to ensure workers follow the prescribed method; and
- move responsibility for planning and organising from the worker to the manager.

Taylor's underlying philosophy was that scientific analysis and fact, not guesswork, should inform management. Like Smith and Babbage before him, he believed that efficiency rose if tasks were routine and predictable. He advocated techniques such as time and motion study, standard tools and individual incentives. Breaking work into small, specific tasks would increase control. Specialist managerial staff would design these tasks and organise the workers:

> The work of every workman is fully planned out by the management at least one day in advance, and each man receives in most cases complete written instructions, describing in detail the task which he is to accomplish, as well as the means to be used in doing the work ... This task specifies not only what is to be done but how it is to be done and the exact time allowed for doing it. (Taylor, 1917, p. 39)

Taylor also influenced the development of administrative systems such as record keeping and stock control to support manufacturing.

Management in practice **Using work study in the 1990s**

Oswald Jones recalls his experience as a work study engineer in the 1990s, where he and his colleagues were deeply committed to the principles of scientific management:

> Jobs were designed to be done in a mechanical fashion by removing opportunities for worker discretion. This had dual benefits: very simple jobs could be measured accurately (so causing less disputes) and meant that operators were much more interchangeable which was an important feature in improving efficiency levels. (Jones, 2000, p. 647)

Source: Jones (2000).

Managers in many industrial economies adopted Taylor's ideas: Henry Ford was an enthusiastic advocate. When he introduced the assembly line in 1914 the time taken to assemble a car fell from over 700 hours to 93 minutes. Ford also developed systems of materials flow and plant layout, a significant contribution to scientific management (Biggs, 1996; Williams *et al.*, 1992).

Increased productivity often came at human cost – more from the way managers implemented them than from the ideas themselves. Trade unions believed Taylor's methods increased unemployment and many people find that working on an assembly line is boring.

Nevertheless, many modern industrial plants around the world use these ideas today, especially those making clothing and consumer electronic goods, like mobile phones.

> **Management in practice**   **Ford's Highland Park plant**
>
> Ford's plant at Highland Park, completed in 1914, introduced predictability and order 'that eliminates all questions of how work is to be done, who will do it, and when it will be done. The rational factory, then, is a factory that runs like a machine' **(Biggs, 1996, p. 6)**. Biggs provides abundant evidence of the effects of applying rational production methods:
>
> > The advances made in Ford's New Shop allowed the engineers to control work better. The most obvious and startling change in the entire factory was, of course, the constant movement, and the speed of that movement, not only the speed of the assembly line, but the speed of every moving person or object in the plant. When workers moved from one place to another, they were instructed to move fast. Labourers who moved parts were ordered to go faster. And everyone on a moving line worked as fast as the line dictated. Not only were workers expected to produce at a certain rate in order to earn a day's wages but they also had no choice but to work at the pace dictated by the machine. By 1914 the company employed supervisors called pushers (not the materials handlers) to 'push' the men to work faster.
> >
> > The 1914 jobs of most Ford workers bore little resemblance to what they had been just four years earlier, and few liked the transformation ... As early as 1912, job restructuring sought an 'exceptionally specialised division of labour [to bring] the human element into [the] condition of performing automatically with machine-like regularity and speed'. (Biggs, 1996, p. 132)

Frank and Lillian Gilbreth

Frank and Lillian Gilbreth (1868–1924 and 1878–1972) worked as a husband and wife team advocating scientific management. Frank Gilbreth had been a bricklayer, and knew why work was slow and output unpredictable. He filmed men laying bricks and used this to set out the most economical movements for each task. He specified exactly what the employer should provide, such as trestles at the right height and materials at the right time. Supplies of mortar and bricks (arranged the right way up) should arrive at a time which did not interrupt work. An influential book (Gilbreth, 1911) gave precise guidance on how to reduce unnecessary actions (from 18 to 5), and hence fatigue. The rules and charts would help apprentices:

> (They) will enable the apprentice to earn large wages immediately, because he has ... a series of instructions that show each and every motion in the proper sequence. They eliminate the 'wrong' way [and] all experimenting. (Quoted in Spriegel and Myers, 1953, p. 57)

Lillian Gilbreth focussed on the psychological aspects of management and workers' welfare, believing that scientific management, properly applied, would enable individuals to reach their potential. Through careful development of systems, careful selection, clearly planned training and proper equipment, workers would build their self-respect and pride. In *The Psychology of Management* (1914) she wrote that if workers did something well, and that was made public, they would develop pride in their work and in themselves. She believed workers had enquiring minds, and that management should explain the reasons for work processes:

> Unless the man knows why he is doing the thing, his judgment will never reinforce his work ... His work will not enlist his zeal unless he knows exactly why he is made to work in the particular manner prescribed. (Quoted in Spriegel and Myers, 1953, p. 431)

> **Activity 2.2 What assumptions did they make?**
>
> What assumptions did Frederick Taylor and Lillian Gilbreth make about the interests and abilities of industrial workers?

Operational research

Operational research is a scientific method of providing (managers) with a quantitative basis for decisions regarding the operations under their control.

Another practice within the rational goal model is **operational research** (OR). This originated in the early 1940s, when the UK War Department faced severe management problems – such as the most effective distribution of radar-linked anti-aircraft gun emplacements, or the safest speed at which convoys of merchant ships should cross the Atlantic (see Kirby (2003) for a non-technical introduction to the topic). To solve these it formed operational research (OR) teams, with expertise from scientific disciplines such as mathematics and physics. These produced significant results: Kirby points out that while at the start of the London Blitz 20,000 rounds of ammunition were fired for each enemy aircraft destroyed:

> by the summer of 1941 the number had fallen ... to 4,000 as a result of the operational research (teams) improving the accuracy of radar-based gun-laying. (Kirby 2003, p. 94)

After the war, managers in industry and government saw that operational research techniques could also help to run complex civil organisations. The scale and complexity of business was increasing, and required new techniques to analyse the many interrelated variables. Mathematical models could help, and computers supported increasingly sophisticated models. In the 1950s the steel industry needed to cut the cost of importing iron ore: staff used OR techniques to analyse the most efficient procedures for shipping, unloading and transferring it to steelworks.

The method is widely used in both business and public sectors, where it helps planning in areas as diverse as maintenance, cash flow, inventory and staff scheduling in call centres (e.g. Taylor, 2008). Willoughby and Zappe (2006) illustrate how a university used OR techniques to allocate students to seminar groups.

OR cannot take into account human and social uncertainties, and the assumptions built into the models may be invalid, especially if they involve political interests. The technique clearly contributes to the analysis of management problems, but is only part of the solution.

Current status

Table 2.1 summarises principles common to rational goal models and their modern application.

Table 2.1 Modern applications of the rational goal model

Principles of the rational goal model	Modern applications
Systematic work methods	Work study and process engineering departments develop precise specifications for processes
Detailed division of labour	Where staff focus on one type of work or customer in manufacturing or service operations
Centralised planning and control	Modern information systems increase the scope for central control of worldwide operations
Low-involvement employment relationship	Using temporary staff as required, rather than permanent employees

Examples of aspects of the rational goal approaches are common in manufacturing and service organisations – but note that a company will often use just one of the principles that suits their business. The Management in practice feature gives an example from a very successful service business with highly committed and involved members of staff – which wishes to give the same high-quality experience wherever the customer is. They use the principle of systematic work methods to achieve this.

> **Management in practice**   **Making a sandwich at Pret A Manger**   www.pret.com
>
> It is very important to make sure the same standards are adhered to in every single shop, whether you're in Crown Passage in London, Sauchiehall Street in Glasgow, or in New York. The way we do that is very, very detailed training. So for example how to make an egg mayonnaise sandwich is all written down on a card that has to be followed, and that is absolutely non-negotiable.
>
> When somebody joins Pret they have a ten-day training plan, and on every single day there is a list of things that they have to be shown, from how to spread the filling of a sandwich right to the edges (that is key to us), how to cut a sandwich from corner to corner, how to make sure that the sandwiches look great in the box and on the shelves. So every single detail is covered. At the end of that ten days the new team member has to pass a quiz, it's called the big scary quiz, it is quite big and it is quite scary, and they have to achieve 90 per cent on that to progress.
>
> Source: Interview with a senior manager at the company.

The methods are widely used in the mass production industries of newly industrialised economies such as China and Malaysia. Gamble *et al.* (2004) found that in such plants:

> Work organisation tended to be fragmented (on Taylorist lines) and routinised, with considerable surveillance and control over production volumes and quality. (p. 403)

Human resource management policies were consistent with this approach – the recruitment of operators in Chinese electronics plants was:

> often of young workers, generally female and from rural areas. One firm said its operators had to be 'young farmers within cycling distance of the factory, with good eyesight. Education is not important'. (p. 404)

> **Activity 2.3**   **Finding current examples**
>
> Try to find an original example of work that has been designed on rational goal principles. There are examples in office and service areas as well as in factories. Compare your examples with those of colleagues.

2.5 Internal process models

Max Weber

Max Weber (1864–1920) was a German social historian who noted that as societies became more complex, they concentrated responsibility for core activities in large administrative units. These government departments and large industrial or transport businesses were

Bureaucracy is a system in which people are expected to follow precisely defined rules and procedures rather than to use personal judgement.

hard to manage, a problem which those in charge solved by creating systems ('institutionalising the management process') – rules and regulations, hierarchy, precise division of labour, detailed procedures. Weber observed that **bureaucracy** brought routine to office operations just as machines had to production.

See Key ideas for the characteristics of bureaucratic management.

Key ideas — The characteristics of bureaucratic management

- **Rules and regulations:** The formal guidelines that define and control the behaviour of employees. Following these ensures uniform procedures and operations, regardless of an individual's wishes. They enable top managers to coordinate middle managers and, through them, first-line managers and employees. Managers leave, so rules bring stability.
- **Impersonality:** Rules lead to impersonality, which protects employees from the whims of managers. Although the term has negative connotations, Weber believed it ensured fairness, by evaluating subordinates objectively on performance rather than subjectively on personal considerations. It limits favouritism.
- **Division of labour:** Managers and employees work on specialised tasks, with the benefits originally noted by Adam Smith – such as that jobs are easier to learn.
- **Hierarchy:** Weber advocated a clear hierarchy in which jobs were ranked by the amount of authority to make decisions. Each lower position is under the control of a higher position.
- **Authority:** A system of rules, impersonality, division of labour and hierarchy forms an authority structure – the right to make decisions of varying importance at different levels.
- **Rationality:** This refers to using the most efficient means to achieve objectives. Managers should run their organisations logically and 'scientifically' so that all decisions help to achieve the objectives.

Activity 2.4 — Bureaucratic management in education?

Reflect on your role as a student and how rules have affected the experience. Try to identify one example of your own to add to those below or that illustrates the point specifically within your institution:

- Rules and regulations – the number of courses you need to pass for a degree.
- Impersonality – admission criteria, emphasising exam performance, not friendship.
- Division of labour – chemists not teaching management, and vice versa.
- Hierarchical structure – to whom your lecturer reports, and to whom they report.
- Authority structure – who decides whether to recruit an additional lecturer.
- Rationality – appointing new staff to departments that have the highest ratio of students to staff.

Compare your examples with those of other students and consider the effects of these features of bureaucracy on the institution and its students.

Weber was aware that, as well as creating bureaucratic structures, managers were using scientific management techniques to control production and impose discipline on factory work. The two systems complemented each other. Formal structures of management centralise power, and hierarchical organisation aids functional specialisation. Fragmenting tasks, imposing close discipline on employees and minimising their discretion ensures controlled, predictable performance (Thompson and McHugh, 2002).

Weber stressed the importance of a career structure clearly linked to a person's position. This allowed them to move up the hierarchy in a predictable and open way, which would increase their commitment. Rules about selection and promotion brought fairness when it was common practice to give preference to friends and family. He also believed that officials should work within a framework of rules – the right to give instructions derived from someone's position in the hierarchy. This worked well in large organisations such as government departments and banks. While recognising the material benefits of these methods, Weber saw their costs:

> Bureaucratic rationalisation instigates a system of control that traps the individual within an 'iron cage' of subjugation and constraint ... For Weber, it is instrumental rationality, accompanied by the rise of measurement and quantification, regulations and procedures, accounting, efficiency that entraps us all in a world of ever-increasing material standards, but vanishing magic, fantasy, meaning and emotion. (Gabriel, 2005, p. 11)

Activity 2.5   Gathering evidence on bureaucracy

Rules often receive bad publicity, and we are all sometimes frustrated by rules that seem obstructive. To evaluate bureaucracy, collect some evidence. Think of a job that you or a friend has held, or of the place in which you work.

- Do the supervisors appear to operate within a framework of rules, or do they do as they wish? What are the effects?
- Do clear rules guide selection and promotion procedures? What are the effects?
- As a customer of an organisation, how have rules and regulations affected your experience?
- Check what you have found, preferably combining it with that prepared by others on your course. Does the evidence support the advantages, or the disadvantages, of bureaucracy?

Henri Fayol

Managers were also able to draw on Henri Fayol's ideas of **administrative management**. While Taylor focussed on production systems, Fayol (1841–1925) devised principles that would apply to the whole organisation. He was an engineer who, in 1860, joined Commentry–Fourchambault et Decazeville, a coal mining and iron foundry company. He earned rapid promotion and was managing director from 1888 until 1918, when he retired – widely seen as one of France's most successful managers (Parker and Ritson, 2005). Throughout his career he kept diaries and notes which he used in retirement to stimulate debate about management. His book *Administration, industrielle et générale* became available in English in 1949 (Fayol, 1949).

Administrative management is the use of institutions and order rather than relying on personal qualities to get things done.

Fayol credited his success to the methods he used, not to his personal qualities. He believed that managers should use the principles in the Key ideas box. The term 'principles' did not imply they were rigid or absolute:

> It is all a question of proportion ... allowance must be made for different changing circumstances ... the principles are flexible and capable of adaptation to every need; it is a matter of knowing how to make use of them, which is a difficult art requiring intelligence, experience, decision and proportion. (Fayol, 1949, p. 14)

In using terms like 'changing circumstances' and 'adaptation to every need', Fayol anticipated the contingency theories which were developed in the 1960s (see Chapter 10). He was an early advocate of management education:

> Elementary in the primary schools, somewhat wider in the post-primary schools, and quite advanced in higher education establishments. (Fayol, 1949, p. 16)

> **Key ideas** — **Fayol's principles of management**
>
> 1. **Division of work:** If people specialise, they improve their skill and accuracy, which increases output. However, 'it has its limits which experience teaches us may not be exceeded.'
> 2. **Authority and responsibility:** The right to give orders derived from a manager's official authority or their personal authority. 'Wherever authority is exercised, responsibility arises.'
> 3. **Discipline:** 'Essential for the smooth running of business … without discipline no enterprise could prosper.'
> 4. **Unity of command:** 'For any action whatsoever, an employee should receive orders from one superior only' – to avoid conflicting instructions and resulting confusion.
> 5. **Unity of direction:** 'One head and one plan for a group of activities having the same objective … essential to unity of action, co-ordination of strength and focussing of effort.'
> 6. **Subordination of individual interest to general interest:** 'The interests of one employee or group of employees should not prevail over that of the concern.'
> 7. **Remuneration of personnel:** 'Should be fair and, as far as possible, afford satisfaction both to personnel and firm.'
> 8. **Centralisation:** 'The question of centralisation or decentralisation is a simple question of proportion … [the] share of initiative to be left to [subordinates] depends on the character of the manager, the reliability of the subordinates and the condition of the business. The degree of centralisation must vary according to different cases.'
> 9. **Scalar chain:** 'The chain of superiors from the ultimate authority to the lowest ranks … is at times disastrously lengthy in large concerns, especially governmental ones.' If a speedy decision was needed people at the same level of the chain should communicate directly. 'It provides for the usual exercise of some measure of initiative at all levels of authority.'
> 10. **Order:** Materials should be in the right place to avoid loss, and the posts essential for the smooth running of the business filled by capable people.
> 11. **Equity:** Managers should be both friendly and fair to their subordinates – 'equity requires much good sense, experience and good nature'.
> 12. **Stability of tenure of personnel:** A high employee turnover is not efficient – 'Instability of tenure is at one and the same time cause and effect of bad running.'
> 13. **Initiative:** 'The initiative of all represents a great source of strength for businesses … and … it is essential to encourage and develop this capacity to the full. The manager must … sacrifice some personal vanity to grant this satisfaction to subordinates … a manager able to do so is infinitely superior to one who cannot.'
> 14. **Esprit de corps:** 'Harmony, union among the personnel of a concern is a great strength in that concern. Effort, then, should be made to establish it.' Fayol suggested doing so by avoiding unnecessary conflict, and using verbal rather than written communication when appropriate.
>
> Source: Fayol (1949).

Current status

Table 2.2 summarises some principles common to the internal process models of management and indicates their modern application.

'Bureaucracy' has critics, who believe it stifles creativity, fosters dissatisfaction and hinders motivation. Others credit it with bringing fairness and certainty to the workplace, where it clarifies roles and responsibilities, makes work effective – and so helps motivation. Adler and Borys (1996) sought to reconcile this by distinguishing between bureaucracy which is:

- enabling – designed to enable employees to master their tasks; and that which is
- coercive – designed to force employees into effort and compliance.

They studied one aspect of bureaucracy – workflow formalisation (the extent to which an employee's tasks are governed by written rules etc) – in companies like Ford, Toyota and

Table 2.2 Examples of modern applications of the internal process model

Some principles of the internal process model	Modern applications
Rules and regulations	All organisations have these, covering areas such as expenditure, safety, recruitment and confidentiality
Impersonality	Appraisal processes based on objective criteria or team assessments, not personal preference
Division of labour	Setting narrow limits to employees' areas of responsibility – found in many organisations
Hierarchical structure	Most company organisation charts show managers in a hierarchy – with subordinates below them
Authority structure	Holders of a particular post have authority over matters relating to that post, but not over other matters
Centralisation	Organisations balance central control of (say) finance or online services with local control of (say) pricing or recruitment
Initiative	Current practice in many firms to increase the responsibility of operating staff
Rationality	Managers are expected to assess issues on the basis of evidence, not personal preference

Xerox. They concluded that if employees helped to design and implement a procedure, they were likely to accept it, knowing it would help them work effectively. 'Enabling bureaucracy' had a positive effect on motivation, while imposed rules ('coercive bureaucracy') had a negative effect.

Bureaucratic methods are widely used (Walton, 2005) especially in the public sector, and in commercial businesses with geographically dispersed outlets – like hotels, stores and banks. Customers expect a predictable service wherever they are, so management design centrally-controlled procedures and manuals - how to recruit and train staff, what the premises must look like and how to treat customers. If managers work in situations that require a degree of change and innovation that even an enabling bureaucracy will have trouble delivering, they need other models.

Case study: innocent – the case continues   www.innocentdrinks.com

Another early decision (after finance) was how to set up the roles to build the business. Reed, from advertising, took care of marketing. Balon, who had been selling Virgin Cola, took on sales, while Wright (who had studied manufacturing engineering) was in charge of operations. They agreed that rather than have one chief executive all three would jointly lead the company.

They had assumed they would build a factory but soon realised that it would be smarter to work with a manufacturing partner:

- their own factory would cost millions of pounds to establish and maintain;
- they had no experience of manufacturing;
- it would distract them from the core tasks of growing the business and building the brand; and
- it would make them less flexible to changes in packaging requirements.

Although there were no UK manufacturers able to make the fresh smoothies the team wanted, they found one who wished to diversify his market. They got on well and he agreed to become a supplier, enabling the company to increase sales rapidly with little capital.

Despite the fun image, they run the business very firmly and everyone must pull their weight. A core value is that products and production methods are as environmentally sustainable as possible – requiring growers and processing plants around the world to follow specified procedures. Fruit comes from thousands of farms, and the company tries to ensure they are certified by independent environmental and social organisations who certify their agricultural practices and treatment of staff: innocent only buy bananas from plantations with a Rainforest Alliance certificate.

To reduce the carbon footprint they process fruit near the farms, to avoid transporting waste material to the UK. Packaging is designed for low environmental impact, and all cartons use cardboard from sources certified by the Forestry Stewardship Council (FSC).

Sources: Based on material from 'innocent drinks', a case prepared by William Sahlman (2004), Harvard Business School, Case No. 9-805-031; Germain and Reed (2009); company website.

Case question 2.3

- What examples can you see in the case so far of elements of the 'competing values' framework?

2.6 Human relations models

In the early twentieth century, several writers such as Follett and Mayo recognised the limitations of the scientific management perspective as a complete answer.

Mary Parker Follett

Mary Parker Follett (1868–1933) graduated with distinction from Radcliffe College (now part of Harvard University) in 1898, having studied economics, law and philosophy. She took up social work and quickly acquired a reputation as an imaginative and effective professional. She realised the creativity of the group process, and the potential it offered for truly democratic government – which people themselves would have to create.

She advocated replacing bureaucratic institutions by networks in which people themselves analysed their problems and implemented their solutions. True democracy depended on tapping the potential of all members of society by enabling individuals to work in groups to solve a problem and accept personal responsibility for the result. Modern-day community enterprises and tenants' groups are examples of these ideas in action.

Key ideas — Mary Parker Follett on groups

Follett saw the group as an intermediate institution between the solitary individual and the abstract society, and argued that it was through the institution of the group that people organised co-operative action. In 1926 she wrote:

> Early psychology was based on the study of the individual; early sociology was based on the study of society. But there is no such thing as the 'individual', there is no such thing as 'society'; there is only the group and the group-unit – the social individual. Social psychology must begin with an intensive study of the group, of the selective processes which go on within it, the differentiated reactions, the likenesses and the unlikenesses, and the spiritual energy which unites them.

Source: Graham (1995), p. 230.

In the 1920s, leading industrialists invited Follett to investigate business problems. She again advocated the self-governing principle that would support the growth of individuals and their groups. Conflict was inevitable if people brought valuable differences of view to a problem: the group must resolve the conflict to create what she called an integrative unity of members.

She acknowledged that organisations had to optimise production, but did not accept that the strict division of labour was the right way to achieve this (Follett, 1920), as it devalued human creativity. The human side should not be separated from the mechanical side, as the two are bound together. She believed that people, whether managers or workers, behave as they do because of the reciprocal responses in their relationship. If managers tell people to behave as if they are extensions of a machine, they will do so. She implied that effective managers would not manipulate their subordinates, but train them to use power responsibly:

> managers should give workers a chance to grow capacity or power for themselves.

Graham (1995) provides an excellent review of Follett's work.

Elton Mayo

Elton Mayo (1880–1949) was an Australian who taught logic, psychology and ethics at the University of Queensland. In 1922 he moved to the United States, and in 1926 became Professor of Industrial Research at Harvard Business School, applying psychological methods to industry. He was a good speaker, and his ideas aroused wide interest in academic and business communities (Smith, 1998).

In 1924 managers of the Western Electric Company initiated experiments at their Hawthorne plant in Chicago to discover the effect on output of changing the physical environment. The first experiment studied the effect of lighting. The researchers established a control and an experimental group, varied the light level and measured the output. As light rose, so did output. More surprisingly, as light fell, output continued to rise: it also rose in the control group, where conditions had not changed. The team concluded that changing physical conditions had little effect, so set up a more comprehensive experiment to identify other factors.

They assembled a small number of workers in a separate room and altered variables in turn, including working hours, length of breaks and providing refreshments. The experienced workers were assembling small components for telephone equipment. A supervisor was in charge and an observer recorded how workers reacted to the changes. The researchers took care to prevent external factors disrupting the effects of the variables – for example by explaining what was happening, ensuring workers understood what they should do and listening to their views.

They also varied conditions every two or three weeks, while the supervisor measured output regularly. This showed a gradual, if erratic, increase – even when the researchers returned conditions to those at an earlier stage, as Figure 2.3 shows.

Activity 2.6 Explaining the trend

- Describe the pattern shown in Figure 2.3. Compare in particular the output in periods 7, 10 and 13. Before reading on, how would you explain this?

In 1928, the company invited Mayo to present the research to a wider audience (Smith, 1998; Roethlisberger and Dickson, 1939; Mayo, 1949). They concluded from the relay-assembly test room experiments that the increase in output was not related to the physical changes, but to changes in the social situation:

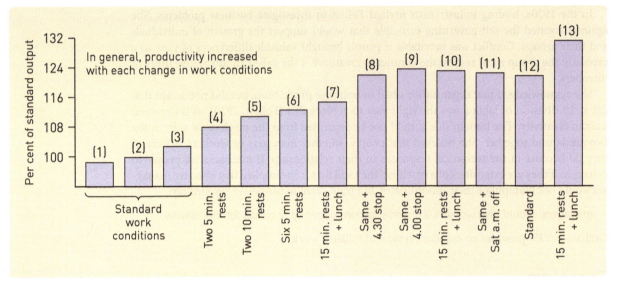

Figure 2.3 The relay assembly test room – average hourly output per week (as percentage of standard) in successive experimental periods
Source: Based on data from Roethlisberger and Dickson (1939). From *Behaviour in Organisations*, 6th edn, Greenberg and Baron, © 1997. Reprinted by permission of Pearson Education, Inc. Upper Saddle River, NJ.

the major experimental change was introduced when those in charge sought to hold the situation humanly steady (in the interests of critical changes to be introduced) by getting the co-operation of the workers. What actually happened was that 6 individuals became a team and the team gave itself wholeheartedly and spontaneously to co-operation in the environment. (Mayo, 1949, p. 64)

The group felt special: managers asked for their views, were involved with them, paid attention to them and they had the chance to influence some aspects of the work.

The research team also observed another part of the factory, the bank-wiring room, which revealed a different aspect of group working. Workers were paid according to a piece-rate system, in which management pays workers a set amount for each piece they produce. This reflects the assumption that financial incentives will encourage effort, yet the researchers observed that employees regularly produced less than they could have done. They had developed a sense of a normal rate of output, and ensured that all adhered to this, believing that if they produced, and earned, too much, management would reduce the piece-rate. Group members exercised sanctions against colleagues who worked too hard (or too slowly), until they conformed. Members who did too much were 'rate-busters' while those who did too little were 'chisellers'. Anyone who told the supervisor was a 'squealer'. Sanctions included being 'binged' – tapped on the shoulder to let them know that what they were doing was wrong. Managers had little or no control over these groups.

Finally, the research team conducted an extensive interview programme. They began by asking employees about the working environment and how they felt about their job, and then some questions about their life in general. The responses showed many close links between work and domestic life – work affected people's home life more than expected, and domestic circumstances affected their feelings about work. This implied that supervisors needed to think of a subordinate as a complete person, not just as a worker.

> **Activity 2.7** **A comparison with Taylor**
>
> Compare this evidence with Frederick Taylor's belief that piece-rates would be an incentive to individuals to raise their performance. What may explain the difference?

Mayo's reflections on the Hawthorne studies drew attention to aspects of human behaviour that practitioners of scientific management had neglected. He introduced the idea of 'social man', in contrast to the 'economic man' at the centre of earlier theories. While financial rewards would influence the latter, group relationships and loyalties would influence the former. On financial incentives, Mayo wrote:

> Man's desire to be continuously associated in work with his fellows is a strong, if not the strongest, human characteristic. Any disregard of it by management or any ill-advised attempt to defeat this human impulse leads instantly to some form of defeat for management itself. In [a study] the efficiency experts had assumed the primacy of financial incentive; in this they were wrong; not until the conditions of working group formation were satisfied did the financial incentives come into operation. (Mayo, 1949, p. 99)

People had social needs that they sought to satisfy – and how they did so may support or oppose management interests.

Analysis of the data by Greenwood *et al.* (1983) suggested the team had underestimated the influence of financial incentives: being in the experimental group in itself increased a worker's income. Despite possible inaccurate interpretations, the findings stimulated interest in social factors in the workplace. Scientific management stressed the technical aspects of work. The Hawthorne studies implied that management should give at least as much attention to human factors, leading to the **human relations approach**. Advocates of this believe that employees will work better if managers are interested in their well-being and supervise them humanely.

Human relations approach is a school of management which emphasises the importance of social processes at work.

Key ideas   Peters and Waterman – *In Search of Excellence*

In 1982 Peters and Waterman published their best-selling book *In Search of Excellence*. As management consultants with McKinsey & Co., they wanted to understand the success of what they regarded as 43 excellently managed US companies. One conclusion was that they had a distinctive set of philosophies about human nature and the way that people interact in organisations. They did not see people as rational beings, motivated by fear and willing to accept a low-involvement employment relationship. Instead, the excellent companies regarded people as emotional, intuitive and creative social beings who like to celebrate victories and value self-control – but who also need the security and meaning of achieving goals through organisations. From this, Peters and Waterman deduced some general rules for treating workers with dignity and respect, to ensure that people did quality work in an increasingly uncertain environment.

Peters and Waterman had a significant influence on management thinking: they believed that management had relied too much on rational goal models, at the expense of more intuitive and human perspectives. They developed the ideas associated with the human relations models and introduced the idea of company culture.

Source: Peters and Waterman (1982).

Current status

The Hawthorne studies have been controversial, and the interpretations questioned. Also, the idea of social man is itself now seen as an incomplete picture of people at work. Providing good supervision and decent working environments may increase satisfaction, but not necessarily productivity. The influences on performance are certainly more complex than Taylor assumed – and also more than the additional factors which Mayo identified.

Other writers have followed and developed Mayo's emphasis on human factors. McGregor (1960), Maslow (1970) and Alderfer (1972) have suggested ways of integrating human needs with those of the organisation as expressed by management. Some of this reflected a human relations concern for employees' well-being. A much stronger influence was the changing external environments of organisations, which have become less predictable. This encouraged scholars to develop open systems models.

2.7 Open systems models

The open systems approach builds on earlier work in general systems theory, and is widely used to help understand management and organisational issues. The basic idea is to think of the organisation not as a **system**, but as an **open system**.

The open systems approach draws attention to the links between the internal parts of a system, and to the links between the whole system and the outside world. The system is separated from its environment by the **system boundary**. An open system imports resources such as energy and materials which are transformed within the system, and leave as goods and services. The open systems view emphasises that organisations depend on their environment for resources. Figure 2.4 (based on Figure 1.1) presents a simple model of this.

The figure shows input and output processes, transformation processes and feedback loops. The organisation must satisfy those in the wider environment well enough to ensure that they continue to provide resources. The management task is to sustain those links. **Feedback** refers to information about the performance of the system. It may be deliberate, through customer surveys, or unplanned, such as losing business to a competitor. Feedback can prompt remedial action.

Another idea is **subsystems**. A course is a subsystem within a department or faculty, the faculty is a subsystem of a university, the university is a subsystem of the higher education system. This in turn is part of the whole education system. A course itself has several systems – one for quality assurance, one for enrolling students, one for teaching, another for assessment. In terms of Figure 2.1, each organisational element is itself a subsystem – there is a technical subsystem, a people subsystem, a finance sub-system and so on, as Figure 2.5 shows.

These subsystems interact with each other, and how well people manage these links affects the functioning of the whole: when a university significantly increases the number of students admitted to a popular course, this affects many parts of the system – such as accommodation (*technology*), teaching resources (*people*), and examinations (*business processes*).

> A **system** is a set of interrelated parts designed to achieve a purpose.
>
> An **open system** is one that interacts with its environment.
>
> A **system boundary** separates the system from its environment.
>
> **Feedback (systems theory)** refers to the provision of information about the effects of an activity.
>
> **Subsystems** are the separate but related parts that make up the total system.

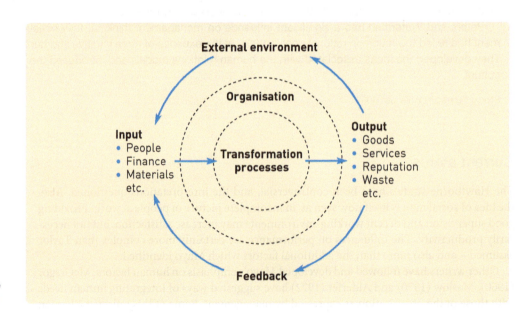

Figure 2.4 The systems model

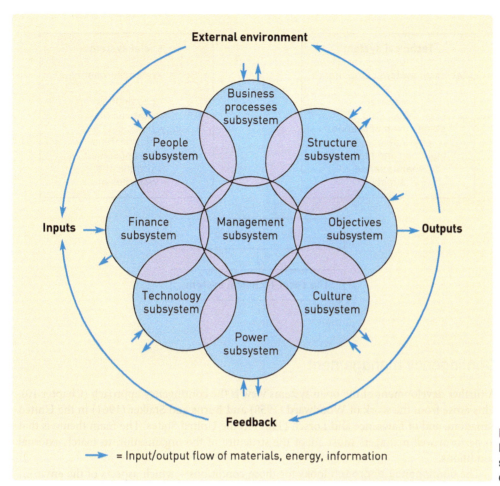

Figure 2.5
Interacting subsystems in organisations

A systems approach emphasises the links between systems, and reminds managers that a change in one will have consequences for others. For example, Danny Potter, managing director of Inamo (www.inamo-restaurant.com), a London restaurant where customers place their order directly to the kitchen from an interactive ordering system on their table, explains:

> I think the greatest challenge that we faced is communicating our ideas down through the business about what we're trying to achieve. There is a big overlap between essentially the computer software side and the actual restaurant side, to unite those in a way that people [new staff, suppliers etc.] understand has proven rather tricky.

Socio-technical systems

An important variant of systems theory is the idea of the **socio-technical system**. The approach developed from the work of Eric Trist and Ken Bamforth (1951) at the Tavistock Institute in London. Their most prominent study was of an attempt in the coal industry to mechanise the mining system. Introducing assembly line methods at the coalface had severe consequences for the social system formed under the old pattern of working. The technological system destroyed the social system: the solution was to reconcile the needs of both.

This and similar studies showed the benefits of seeing a work system as combining a material technology (tools, machinery, techniques) and a social organisation (people, relationships, constitutional arrangements). Figure 2.6 shows that an organisation has technical and social systems: it is a socio-technical system, implying that practitioners should aim to integrate both systems (Mumford, 2006).

A **socio-technical system** is one in which outcomes depend on the interaction of both the technical and social subsystems.

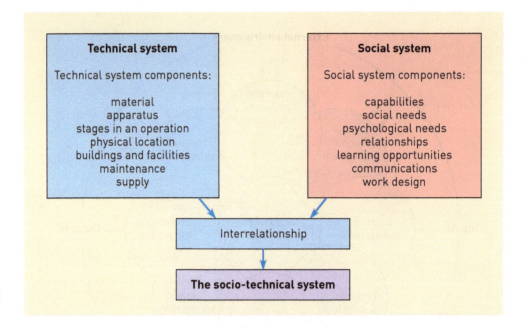

Figure 2.6 The organisation as a socio-technical system

Contingency management

A further development of the open systems view is the contingency approach (Chapter 10). This arose from the work of Woodward (1958) and Burns and Stalker (1961) in the United Kingdom, and of Lawrence and Lorsch (1967) in the United States. The main theme is that to perform well managers must adapt the structure of the organisation to match external conditions.

The **contingency approach** looks for those conditions – which aspects of the environment should managers take into account in shaping their organisation – see the Management in practice feature.

Contingency approaches to organisational structure are those based on the idea that the performance of an organisation depends on having a structure that is appropriate to its environment.

Management in practice Hong Kong firms adapt to the environment in China

Child et al. (2003) studied the experience of Hong Kong companies managing affiliated companies in China, predicting that successful firms would be those that adapted their management practices to suit those conditions. Because the business environment at the time was uncertain and difficult for foreign companies, they proposed that a key aspect of management practice in these circumstances would be the extent to which affiliated companies are controlled by, and integrated with, the parent company.

Their results supported this – in this transitional economy successful firms kept their mainland affiliates under close supervision, maintained frequent contact and allowed them little power to make decisions.

Source: Child et al. (2003).

As the environment becomes more complex managers can use contingency perspectives to examine what structure best meets the needs of the business. Contingency theorists emphasise creating organisations that can cope with uncertainty and change, using the values of the open systems model: they also recognise that some functions need to work in a stable and predictable way, using the values of the internal process model.

Complexity theory

A popular theme in management thinking is that of managing complexity, which arises from feedback between the parts of linked systems. People in organisations, both as individuals and as members of a web of working relationships, react to an event or an attempt to influence them. That reaction leads to a further response – setting off a complex feedback process. Figure 2.7 illustrates this for three individuals, X, Y and Z.

If we look at the situation in Figure 2.7 from the perspective of X, then X is in an environment made up of Y and Z. X discovers what Y and Z are doing, chooses how to respond and then acts. That action has consequences for Y and Z, which they discover. This leads them to choose a response, which has consequences that X then discovers, and acts on. This continues indefinitely. Every act by X feeds back to have an impact on the next acts of Y and Z – and the same is true of Y and Z. Successive interactions create a feedback system – and the sequence shown for the individuals in the figure also occurs between organisations. These then make up complex systems:

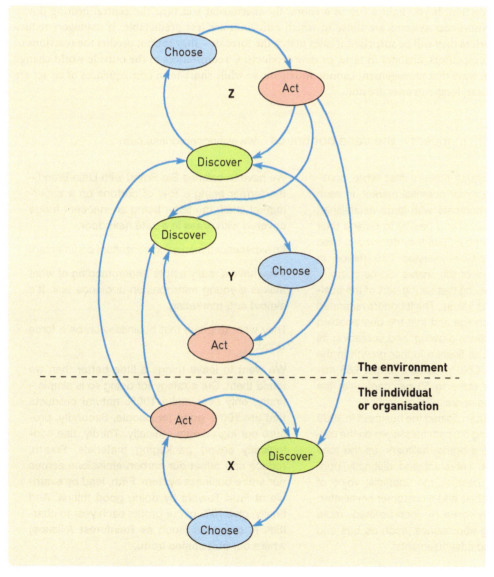

Figure 2.7
Feedback in non-linear systems
Source: Parker and Stacey (1994).

In contrast to simple systems, such as the pendulum, which have a small number of well-understood components, or complicated systems, such as a Boeing jet, which have many components that interact through predefined coordination rules...complex systems typically have many components that can autonomously interact through emergent rules. (Amaral and Uzzi, 2007, p. 1033)

In management, complex systems arise whenever agents (people, organisations or communities) act on the (limited) information available to them without knowing how these actions may affect other (possibly distant) agents, nor how the action of those agents may affect them. There is no central control system to coordinate their actions, so the separate agents organise themselves spontaneously, creating new structures and new behaviours as they respond to themselves and their environment: in other words, they change themselves. **Complexity theory** tries to understand how these complex, changing (dynamic) systems learn and adapt from their internal experiences and from their interactions with similar systems.

These ideas on self-organising systems have implications for management, especially for how they cope with change and innovation. The challenging management skill is to balance extremes. If an organisation is too stable it will stifle innovation, but if it is too unstable it will disintegrate.

This way of thinking about organisations sometimes uses the terms 'linear' and **'non-linear' systems**. 'Linear' describes a system in which an action leads to a predictable reaction. If you light a fire in a room, the thermostat will turn the central heating down. Non-linear systems are those in which outcomes are less predictable. If managers reduce prices they will be surprised if sales match the forecast – they cannot predict the reactions of competitors, changes in taste, or new products. Circumstances in the outside world change in ways that management cannot anticipate, so while short-term consequences of an act are clear, long-run ones are not.

> **Complexity theory** is concerned with complex dynamic systems that have the capacity to organise themselves spontaneously.

> **Non-linear systems** are those in which small changes are amplified through many interactions with other variables so that the eventual effect is unpredictable.

Case study — innocent – the case continues   www.innocentdrinks.com

Reed and his colleagues realised that while continental Europe was a major potential market, in each country they would compete with large established companies, who could spend heavily to defend their position. So in September 2008 they decided to raise more finance: Coca-Cola invested £30 million in return for 20 per cent of the shares. Some customers complained, believing that selling part of the business ran counter to its values. The founders reiterated that they remain in charge and that the deal enabled the company to continue growing, and spreading its values. In April 2010 to finance further growth in the product range Coca-Cola invested a further £65 million, increasing their stake to 58 per cent, with the founders still retaining operational control.

A friend, Dan Germain, joined the business in 1999 and suggested printing off-beat messages on the cartons, which became a brand 'hallmark' as the tone was offbeat, honest, irreverent and distinctly non-corporate. Germain became the unofficial voice of the brand – writing labels and a customer newsletter.

As the company grew it incorporated more traditional marketing approaches, such as bus and London Underground advertisements:

We have to balance Big Brand with Little Brand – the former being a row of cartons on a supermarket shelf, the latter being an innocent fridge covered with grass in a café next door.

An experienced marketing consultant commented:

They have a really astute understanding of what makes a young metropolitan audience tick. It's almost anti-marketing.

They want to prove that business can be a force for good:

We want to leave things a little better than we found them. Our strategy for doing so is simple – firstly, only ever make 100% natural products that are 100% good for people. Secondly, procure our ingredients ethically. Thirdly, use ecologically sound packaging materials. Fourth, reduce and offset our carbon emissions across our entire business system. Fifth, lead by example at Fruit Towers by doing good things. And finally, give 10% of our profits each year to charities in countries (such as Rainforest Alliance) where our fruit comes from.

innocent staff constantly communicate with customers – thousands of whom have signed up to receive a weekly email. As one observer noted:

> Consumers are looking for businesses to trust, and they want to reward that trustworthiness. innocent is a model of the values all businesses should aspire to.

Sources: Based on material from 'innocent drinks', a case prepared by William Sahlman (2004), Harvard Business School, Case No. 9-805-031; Germain and Reed (2009); company website.

Case questions 2.4
- In what ways will further growth pose new problems for the company, especially in Europe?
- What, if any, further elements of the competing values framework can you see in the case?
- What management challenges may arise if a company embodies several competing values?

2.8 Integrating themes

Entrepreneurship

From the perspective of the competing values model, entrepreneurs starting a new business are likely to take an open systems view, and focus on innovation, adaptation, growth and resource acquisition – though as the business develops the other parts of the model are likely to become significant too. They need to develop practices which help them do that: Genius, in the Management in practice feature, is an example of how one company did this.

Management in practice — genius www.geniusglutenfree.com

Lucinda Bruce-Gardyne created Genius in 2009 to supply gluten-free bread to the growing number of people who have an allergy to gluten (a substance present in wheat). She had been a cookery writer, and when her son was found to be gluten intolerant she began baking gluten-free loaves at home, and was considering setting up as a small business to supply local shops in Edinburgh where she lived. This changed when Sir Bill Gemmell, who suffered from the same condition, received one of her loaves by chance. He was himself an entrepreneur, having founded Cairn Energy some years before, and was so impressed by the loaf that he offered his services, and financial backing, to help Ms Bruce-Gardyne to create a much larger enterprise than she had planned.

By 2012 Genius had achieved an annual turnover of £15 million and was growing at 14 per cent a year with shelf space in the big UK supermarkets and a deal to supply Starbucks with gluten-free bread in the UK. Ms Bruce-Gardyne's 'model' for the success of her business:

- **Find a backer who shares the vision**, as in having a backer who was deeply familiar with the needs of the customers.
- **Surround yourself with the skills you lack**, so you can focus on where you can add value – in this case on product development and quality control.
- **Use social media to connect with customers**, and to become aware quickly of any snags with the product.
- **Listen and learn**, but stick to your instincts of what is right.

Source: *Financial Times*, 11 January 2012, p.14.

Successful entrepreneurs develop their models to suit their situations, and through experience and exchanging idea with others, evolve an approach which works for them.

Sustainability

Current attention to sustainability is an example of the values associated with the open systems model – recognising, in this case, that human and natural systems interact with each other in complex and often unpredictable ways. Senge *at al.* (2008) present a valuable explanation of the idea that not only do businesses have a duty to society to act sustainably, but that it is their business interest to do so. Reducing a company's carbon footprint not only reduces environmental damage but also reduces costs and makes the business more efficient.

In 2002 General Electric began making alternative energy technologies (such as de-salination systems) when oil was $25 dollars a barrel. As oil prices have risen to several times that amount, the company is reaping large profits as demand for non-oil energy systems has risen sharply. Customers too played a role – the authors quote the GE chief executive:

> When society changes its mind, you better be in front of it and not behind it, and this is an issue on which society has changed its mind. As CEO, my job is to get out in front of it, or you're going to get ploughed under.

Governments and other institutions are developing policies to try to limit the damage which human activity does to the planet. This work tends to reflect values of order, regulation and control – values associated with the internal process model. Distinct sets of people are working on the same problem, sustainability, from two distinct perspectives: how they reconcile these two approaches will have significant effects on progress towards a more sustainable economy.

Internationalisation

The theories outlined here were developed when most business was conducted within national boundaries, although of course with substantial foreign trade in certain products and services. Hofstede's (1991) widely-read study of differences in national cultures exemplifies the growth in awareness not only of differences in national cultures, but in the possible implications of these differences for those managing internationally. There is much more about national cultures in Chapter 4, but the point to make here is that theories relating to international management are still evolving and in particular there is still great uncertainty about whether, and in what ways, management models differ between countries.

Taras *et al.* (2011) review hundreds of empirical studies of culture, and conclude that while there are indeed observable differences in national culture, the evidence is unclear about their effect on management processes. They cite the example of a large US company which decided to expand the business in Europe, mainly by buying established companies. While theories of cultural difference imply that in such circumstances the acquiring firm should take account of local practices, the company did the opposite – rapidly imposing US practices and ways of working upon their (new) European employees. Cultural theorists would have predicted a disastrous outcome – but Taras *et al.* (2011) claim the venture succeeded – possibly beyond expectations. They contrast this with Walmart which went on a similar route to expansion – which was not a success.

Their paper uses this conflicting evidence to elaborate on the complexities of putting into practice the models of national culture, and how evolving practice is itself refining the models.

Governance

Theories of corporate governance, like those of management, continue to evolve in response to evidence that current arrangements are no longer suitable for the job. Pfeffer and Sutton (2006) present the case for basing management actions on substantiated theories and relevant evidence. They acknowledge the difficulties of putting that into practice, in part because evidence-based management depends on being willing to put aside conventional ways of working.

Nevertheless they identify practices which could help those responsible for corporate governance to foster an evidence-based approach:

> If you ask for evidence of efficacy every time a change is proposed, people will sit up and take notice. If you take the time to parse the logic behind that evidence, people will become more disciplined in their own thinking. If you treat the organization like an unfinished prototype and encourage trial programs, pilot studies, and experimentation - and reward learning from these activities, even when something new fails – your organization will begin to develop its own evidence base. And if you keep learning while acting on the best knowledge you have and expect your people to do the same – if you have what has been called 'the attitude of wisdom' – then your company can profit from evidence-based management. (p. 70)

Such an approach would bring substantial change to the way in which many organisations operate.

Summary

1 **Explain the value of models of management, and compare unitary, pluralist and critical perspectives**
   - Models represent more complex realities, help to understand complexity and offer a range of perspectives on the topic. Their predictive effect is limited by the fact that people interpret information subjectively in deciding how to act.
   - A unitary perspective emphasises the common purpose of organisational members, while the pluralist draws attention to competing interest groups. Those who take a critical perspective believe that organisations reflect deep divisions in society, and that attempts to integrate interests through negotiation ignore persistent differences in the distribution of power.

2 **State the structure of the competing values framework and evaluate its contribution to our understanding of management**
   - A way of integrating the otherwise confusing range of theories of management. Organisations experience tensions between control and flexibility and between an external and an internal focus. Placing these on two axes allows theories to be allocated to one of four types – rational goal, internal process, human relations and open systems.

3 **Summarise the rational goal, internal process, human relations and open systems models and evaluate what each can contribution to a managers understanding of their role**
   - Rational goal (Taylor, the Gilbreths and operational research):
     - clear direction leads to productive outcomes, with an emphasis on rational analysis and measurement.
   - Internal process (Weber, Fayol):
     - routine leads to stability, so an emphasis on defining responsibility, documentation and defined administrative processes.
   - Human relations (Follett, Mayo):
     - people are motivated by social needs, and managers who recognise these will secure commitment. Practices include considerate supervision, participation and seeking consensus.
   - Open systems (socio-technical, contingency and chaos):
     - Continual innovation secures external support, achieved by creative problem solving.

These theories have contributed to the management agendas in these ways:

- Rational goal – through techniques like time and motion study, work measurement and a variety of techniques for planning operations; also the narrow specification of duties, and the separation of management and non-management work.
- Internal process – clear targets and measurement systems, and the creation of clear management and reporting structures. Making decisions objectively on the basis of rules and procedures, rather than on favouritism or family connections.
- Human relations – considerate supervision, consultation and participation in decisions affecting people.
- Open systems – understanding external factors and being able and willing to respond to them through individual and organisational flexibility especially in uncertain, complex conditions characterised by the idea of non-linear systems, which are strongly influenced by other systems. This means that actions lead to unexpected consequences.

4 **Use the model to classify the dominant form in two or more business units, and to gather evidence about the way this affects the roles of managing in those units**

- You can achieve this objective by asking people (perhaps others on your course) to identify which of the four cultural types in the Competing Values Framework most closely correspond to the unit in which they work. Ask them to note ways in which that cultural type affects their way of working. Compare the answers in a systematic way, and review the results.

5 **Show how ideas from the chapter add to your understanding of the integrating themes**

- Entrepreneurship is inherently associated with the open systems model, but within that those starting a new business need to create a model of management that is suitable for them.
- Increased attention to sustainability is an example of the values associated with the open systems model, while attempts to regulate and control activities is perhaps associated with internal process values
- The alternative models in the competing values framework remind us that values that shape management practice in one country do not necessarily have the same influence in others.
- Pfeffer and Sutton's ideas on evidence-based management offer a model which those seeking more effective governance and control could use – challenging managers to back up ideas with more rigorous evidence and analysis to reduce risk

Test your understanding

1. Name three ways in which theoretical models help the study of management.
2. What are the assumptions of the unitary, pluralist and critical perspectives?
3. Name at least four of Morgan's organisational images and give an original example of each.
4. Draw the two axes of the competing values framework, and then place the theories outlined in this chapter in the most appropriate sector.
5. List Taylor's five principles of scientific management and evaluate their use in examples of your choice.
6. What was the particular contribution that Lillian Gilbreth made concerning how workers' mental capacities should be treated?
7. What did Follett consider to be the value of groups in a community?
8. Compare Taylor's assumptions about people with those of Mayo. Evaluate the accuracy of these views by reference to an organisation of your choice.

9 Compare the conclusions reached by the Hawthorne experimenters in the relay assembly test room with those in the bank wiring room.
10 Is an open system harder to manage than a closed system, and if so, why?
11 How does uncertainty affect organisations and how do non-linear perspectives help to understand this?
12 Summarise an idea from the chapter that adds to your understanding of the integrating themes.

Think critically

Think about the way your company, or one with which you are familiar, approaches the task of management, and the theories that seem to lie behind the way people manage themselves and others. Review the material in the chapter, and perhaps visit some of the websites identified. Then make notes on these questions:

- What **assumptions** about the nature of management appear to guide what people do? Do they reflect rational goal, internal process, human relations or open systems perspectives? Or several? Do the assumptions reflect a unitary or pluralist perspective, and if so, why?
- What factors such as the history or current **context** of the company appear to have influenced the prevailing view? Does the approach appear to be right for the company, its employees, and other stakeholders? Do people question those assumptions?
- Have people put forward **alternative** ways of managing the business, or part of it, based on evidence about other companies? Does the competing values model suggest other approaches to managing, in addition to the current pattern? How might others react to such alternatives?
- What **limitations** can you see in the theories and evidence presented in the chapter? For example, how valid might the human relations models be in a manufacturing firm in a country with abundant supplies of cheap labour, competing to attract overseas investment? Will open systems models be useful to those managing a public bureaucracy?

Read more

Biggs, L. (1996), *The Rational Factory*, The Johns Hopkins University Press, Baltimore, MD.

A short and clear overview of the development of production systems from the eighteenth to the early twentieth centuries in a range of industries, including much detail on Ford's Highland Park plant.

Drucker, P. (1954), *The Practice of Management*, Harper, New York.

Still the classic introduction to general management.

Fayol, H. (1949), *General and Industrial Management*, Pitman, London.

The original works of these writers are short and lucid. Taylor (1917) contains illuminating detail that brings the ideas to life, and Fayol's (1949) surviving ideas came from only two short chapters, which again are worth reading in the original.

Gamble, J., Morris, J. and Wilkinson, B. (2004), 'Mass production is alive and well: the future of work and organisation in east Asia', *International Journal of Human Resource Management*, vol. 15, no. 2, pp. 397–409.

Graham, P. (1995), *Mary Parker Follett: Prophet of management,* Harvard Business School Press, Boston, MA.

> The contribution of Mary Parker Follett has been rather ignored, perhaps overshadowed by Mayo's Hawthorne studies – or perhaps it was because she was a woman. This book gives a full appreciation of her work.

Leahy, T. (2012), *Management in 10 Words*, Random House, London.

> A thoughtful reflection on modern management by the former CEO of Tesco.

Smith, J.H. (1998), 'The Enduring Legacy of Elton Mayo', *Human Relations*, vol. 51, no. 3, pp. 221–49.

Taylor, F.W. (1917), *The Principles of Scientific Management*, Harper, New York.

Walton, E.J. (2005), 'The Persistence of Bureaucracy: A Meta-analysis of Weber's Model of Bureaucratic Control', *Organisation Studies*, vol. 26, no. 4, pp. 569–600.

> Three papers which show the continued use of early theories of management.

Go online

These websites have appeared in the chapter:

> www.innocentdrinks.com
> www.imiplc.com
> www.foxconn.com
> www.pret.com
> www.geniusglutenfree.com

Visit two of the business sites in the list, or those of other organisations in which you are interested, and navigate to the pages dealing with recent news, press or investor relations.

- What are the main issues which the organisation appears to be facing?
- Compare and contrast the issues you identify on the two sites.
- What models of management may be relevant for those working in, and managing, these organisations?

PART 1 CASE
APPLE INC.
www.apple.com

The company

In 2012 Apple sold 125 million iPhones, a 73 per cent increase on the previous year; it also sold 58 million iPads, up 80 per cent on 2011. It received revenue of $80 billion and $32 billion respectively from these two products, together accounting for about 70 per cent of total sales that year of over $156 billion. In the intensely competitive market for computer electronics, Apple had had a good year – though in the management commentary with the financial results it cautioned investors about the difficulties that it was likely to face in maintaining that rate of growth.

The company began in 1976, designing and making personal computers. At the time these were a novelty: most computers then were 'mainframe' machines, operated by companies and public bodies. By 2013 the company's product range included the Apple Mac personal computer, iTunes (launched in 2001), iPod digital music player (also 2001), iPhone (the company's first move into mobile phones – 2007), MacBook (2008) and iPad tablet (2010). The iPhone success was especially significant as it showed the ability of a computer maker to succeed in the mobile phone sector. The attractive design enabled the company quickly to become the leading player in the industry, helped by the thousands of applications available for the iPhone through the online Apple Store – which competitors like Nokia and Motorola could not match.

When the late Steve Jobs and Steve Wozniak set up the business in 1976, they invested $1300 each. They secured more funds from private investors, and by 1980 required more funds to finance the rapid growth – which they raised by selling 4.6 million shares in the company to the public, for $22 each. In early 2013 these were trading on the New York Stock Exchange at about $527. A measure of the value it was adding to resources is the operating profit margin – broadly the difference between its expenditure and income. In 2012 this was over 43 per cent, helped by strong sales of the iPhone and the declining cost of producing each one as sales increased. The table shows some measures of performance in the two most recent financial years.

Getty Images

Measures of a performance to 30 September in each year

	2012	2011
Total net sales ($m)	156,508	108,249
Cost of sales ($m)	87,846	64,431
Gross margin ($m)	68,662	43,818
Gross margin% of sales	43.9	40.5
Net income before tax ($m)	55,763	34,205
Net income after tax ($m)	41,733	25,922
Earnings per share ($)	44.64	28.05
Dividend per share	2.65	0.00

Source: Apple Inc. *Annual Report* filed with the United States Securities and Exchange Commission.

Managing to add value
Management style

Steve Jobs typified the distinctive business environment of 'Silicon Valley' – the area in California where many of the world's leading electronic businesses have their headquarters. Even as Apple grew, Jobs worked hard to create a corporate culture characterised by an intense work ethic and casual dress code. Michael

355

Moritz, who observed Jobs for many years noted in his biography, published before Jobs' death:

> Steve is a founder of the company [and the best founders] are unstoppable, irrepressible forces of nature ... Steve has always possessed the soul of the questioning poet – someone a little removed from the rest of us who, from an early age, beat his own path. [He has a sharp] sense of the aesthetic – that influence is still apparent in all Apple products and advertising. Jobs' critics will say he can be wilfull, obdurate, irascible, temperamental and stubborn [which is true, but he is also a perfectionist]. There is also ... an insistent, persuasive and mesmerising salesman. (Moritz, 2009, pp. 13–14)

In 1983 Jobs was chairman and Mike Markkula, who had joined the company at the start, was chief executive. Markkula had never intended to stay as CEO, and now wished to leave. The Board of Directors (including Jobs) decided to appoint John Sculley, an executive from Pepsi-Cola, to the post. The two men frequently disagreed and in 1985 Jobs (then aged 30) left the company. Apple did not perform well under Sculley, and in 1997 the Board persuaded Jobs to return to the company, soon appointing him as CEO.

He began to rebuild Apple by an insistent focus on a limited product range – cutting costs, staff and undistinguished products. The focus was the iMac – an immediate success since it delivered what consumers wanted by combining compelling designs with cutting edge technology. Apple again became known for sleek design and an elegant user interface. He also hired new senior managers with whom he had worked, skilled in software, hardware, retail and manufacturing. They included Jonathan Ive, a respected designer and Tim Cook who joined in 1999 and became chief executive when Jobs died.

Jobs insisted that a named individual be responsible for every task, however large or small: 'at Apple you can figure out exactly who is responsible'. This principle is enshrined in a company acronym – the DRI – which stands for Directly Responsible Individual: this is the person who is called to account if anything goes wrong:

> The DRI is a powerful management tool, enshrined as Apple corporate best practice, passed on by word of mouth to new generations of employees. Any effective meeting at Apple will have an action list – next to it will be the DRI. (Lashinsky, 2012, pp. 67–68)

Functional structure

Apple is organised by function, so people are hired and promoted for their ability in that function, not for their general management skills. Steve Jobs explained:

> [As companies grow large, they] lose their vision. They insert lots of layers of middle management between the people running the company and the people doing the work. They no longer have an inherent feel or passion about the products. The creative people, who are the ones who care passionately, have to persuade five layers of management to do what they know is the right thing to do (quoted in Lashinsky, 2012, p. 71).

When Jobs returned to Apple he found it had become like the companies he disparaged – good technical people had moved into general management roles.

> What was wrong with Apple wasn't individual contributors ... we had to get rid of about four thousand middle managers. (Lashinsky, 2012, p. 71)

At the top of the company is the CEO (since 2012, Tim Cooke), supported by the executive team, whose purpose is to coordinate the business and set the tone for the company. It comprises the head of each function directly involved in Apple products – marketing, hardware and software engineering, operations, retail stores, Internet services, and design – together with heads of finance and legal. The team meets weekly to review the company's product plans – which it does in great detail. Teams throughout the company prepare material for their respective bosses to inform the presentation by their functional head:

> Everybody is working towards these Monday presentations [says a former Apple designer] There is executive review of every significant project. (Lashinsky, 2012, p. 71)

Product innovation

Jobs continually stressed the significance of products rather than profit – believing that if management focussed on providing high quality, innovative products, profit would follow (Isaacson, 2011). He believed that

> putting products ahead of profit was the quality ... responsible for the success that made it the world's most valuable technology company, with a stock market value (in late 2011) two–thirds higher than its nearest competitor, Microsoft. (*Financial Times,* 25 October 2011, p. 18)

Apple engineers focus obsessively on the minutest details of how the customer will experience the product – including the box it arrives in, being the last thing the customer will see before the product:

> Obsessing over details and bringing a Buddhist level of focus to a narrow assortment of offerings sets Apple apart from its competitors ... good

design subliminally telegraphs to consumers that the manufacturer cares about them. This, in turn, creates a bond between brand and consumer. The genesis of most Apple products is simply Apple's desire to make them. Not focus groups. Not reader surveys. Not a competitive analysis ... The iPhone is a classic case in point. Prior to the device's introduction, Apple executive's typically hated their smartphones. 'That's why we decided to do our own' said Jobs. (Lashinsky 2012, pp. 53–4)

This involved analysing the other products and adapting ideas from them to create the distinctive iPhone. Moritz (2009) writes:

> Jobs' achievement ... was to ensure that a technology company employing tens of thousands of people could make and sell millions of immensely complicated yet exquisite products that were powerful and reliable, while also containing a lightness of being ... [the achievement] is to steer, coax, nudge, prod, cajole, inspire, berate, organise and praise – on weekdays and at weekends – the thousands of people all around the world required to produce something that drops into pockets and handbags or ... rests on a lap or sits on a desk. (pp. 339–40)

The key to Apple's design philosophy is that design is where products start. Competitors marvel at the prominence of Apple's industrial designers (led by Briton Jonathan Ive). Most companies make all their plans, all their marketing, all their positioning, and then they hand it down the designer ... the process is reversed at Apple, where everyone else in the organisation needs to conform to the designer's vision.

Secrecy

As well as investing heavily in R&D, the company is intensely secretive and protective of its intellectual property (IP) – the ideas and designs behind the products. Most companies protect these from outsiders, but Apple also has high internal secrecy. Staff do not discuss projects outside their immediate team, and new recruits are briefed on the strict security regime, including the penalty for revealing Apple secrets, intentionally or unintentionally: swift termination (Lashinsky, 2012, p. 36). When Apple launches a product, the secrecy creates curiosity and extensive media coverage – without heavy advertising.

It also helps to retain the 'start-up' mentality which the company values. As engineers work in isolated small teams they have little chance to contact those outside their team:

> By selectively keeping employees from concerning themselves with colleagues elsewhere in a giant company, Apple creates the illusion that [they] work for a start-up. (Lashinsky, 2012, p. 73)

Small teams have long been integral to the Apple way of working, and frequently major projects are assigned to *very* small teams – two engineers wrote the vast amount of code required for a feature of the iPad, which many companies would give to a team of ten. Small teams help foster the start-up mentality.

Tight control

The company uses an 'integrated model', in the sense that it controls the hardware and software components in its devices, as well as the services on which they rely. Jobs believed that integration is the only way to make 'perfect' products. As they design hardware and software, staff aim to give users an exceptionally good experience of the compatibility between all Apple devices and the applications that run on them.

Once the design is under way, the rest of the company moves in, especially the engineering and supply-chain teams, working to the Apple New Product Process. This details each stage in a product's creation, prescribes who touches it, assigns functional responsibilities, and shows when assignments will be completed (Lashinsky, 2012, p. 56).

The emphasis on control was extended when the company launched the Apple stores. This was unusual as manufacturers rarely become successful retailers. The Apple network of dealers and Apple Stores ensures that the image of the brand is closely dovetailed with the products themselves. The App Store has exceeded expectations, with thousands of software developers offering their products on the site.

Collaboration

While internally Apple displays tight control and secrecy, it is the hub of a creative network. It excels at co-operating with partners and rivals when this will benefit customers – an early example being when Jobs saw the value of 'mouse' technology in another company's product, which his engineers then incorporated into the first Macs. The company recognised that in the rapidly developing mobile phone industry, Apple could never generate consistently strong products and services on its own, so encouraged independent developers to build applications for the iPhone. These sell through the App Store, earning revenue for both the developer and Apple, while the huge range of apps available reinforces the iPhone's appeal to customers.

It also collaborates in manufacturing, which it has outsourced to overseas suppliers, especially Foxconn, an immense Chinese supplier which meets most of Apple's requirements. Apple has suffered negative publicity after reports that some Foxconn plants used underage labour, enforce excessive overtime and have inadequate safety standards. Apple has attempted to enforce higher standards but in doing so costs are bound to increase. It has tried to assure critics that it monitors supplier performance closely, and acts swiftly when it finds violation of its required labour standards.

Aspects of Apple's context

Apple has succeeded by offering products which appeal to consumers in previously separate industries. Its continued success will depend on how well it can do this, especially as current and new competitors are developing rival products.

Before Apple launched the iPhone the mobile phone industry was dominated by Nokia, with Sony Ericsson and Motorola having smaller but still significant shares of the market. Apple's success with the iPhone has been challenged by devices using Google's Android software, notably Samsung and its Galaxy range. In 2012 Samsung had about 33 per cent of the global smartphone market and Apple 16 per cent: the rest of the market was fragmented among many companies.

Apple's launch of the iPad helped to transform personal computing – one estimate was that tablets would take almost a fifth of the global PC market by 2013 (data quoted in *Financial Times*, 31 May 2011, p. 21). By late 2012 Apple's share of the global tablet market had fallen from two-thirds to half since the middle of the year. Many lower-priced competitors such as Samsung and Amazon had entered the market.

China is Apple's second largest market after the US, and in 2012 some investors were worrying that Apple was losing position there, as consumers can obtain other companies' rapidly improving devices much more cheaply – such as Samsung and Huawei.

Apple has also been successful in encouraging developers to work on apps they can sell through the App store. This strength can also be weakness, as developers can choose to work for other companies, if they appear to be gaining ground, or moving ahead of Apple.

With many innovative companies competing strongly, each vigorously defends its patents. Apple is involved in many disputes in which it accuses others of stealing its intellectual property, especially Samsung which it regards as an especially serious competitor.

Many observers believe that so-called 'cloud computing' will become a significant feature of the industry, allowing, for example, iPhone users to float their music and apps on to an iPad or a TV and then back again. Jobs stressed the urgency of the company transitioning towards being a cloud-services company – where it faces severe competition from Google, Microsoft and Amazon.

Current management dilemmas

In 2013 Apple was facing several issues to ensure that it retained its prominent position in the computing and telecommunications industry, especially that of ensuring that it continued the flow of innovations that its loyal customers and investors expected.

Strategic direction

A threat to the company's dominance could come from strong competitors such as Google and Microsoft, both of whom were targeting segments of Apple's market with new products. By 2012, half of the company's sales income came from the iPhone. Apple appeared to some to be becoming a handset company, which is fickle and subject to sudden changes of fashion.

It is considering offering more services (such as cloud computing) but as a hardware and software company, can it be equally successful in services?

Apple's shareholders have become used to high growth so they, and financial journalists, may have unrealistic expectations. They could begin to demand higher dividend payments, which would mean less money available to invest in the R&D essential for new products.

Innovation

In 2012 about $80 billion of Apple's revenue came from the iPhone, and another $30 billion from the iPad – neither of which existed five years ago. This remarkable achievement serves as a reminder of the need to keep investing heavily in new products – able to earn equally large revenues in just a few years.

An opportunity the company has been publicising since 2011 is 'cloud computing', which would enable users to integrate all the information they have on their several Apple devices to be seamlessly integrated and accessed at any time, often on other devices. This would enhance the user's experience, and also make it less likely that they would move to a rival device, since that would reduce easy access to their data. Apple may not have as strong a position in that market as companies that were created as services companies, like Google or Amazon

Management

One issue has been to reassure the market that it did not depend on the presence of Steve Jobs. During Jobs' last illness the company appointed Tim Cook, who had worked in Apple for 13 years, to be the new chief executive. He had worked very closely with Jobs for the whole of that time, and had a deep understanding of the values and methods which lay behind the company's success.

In 2012 Cooke appointed Jonathan Ive, the company's hardware designer to be head of software as well. He became responsible for all the company's user interfaces, giving him final say in the design and 'feel' of products and services. This perhaps recreated the dominant role which Steve Jobs played in this regard, ensuring the deep integration typical of Apple products.

Sources: Moritz (2009); *Economist*, 1 October 2009; Lashinsky (2012); Isaacson (2011); *Financial Times*, 27 August 2012, 31 October 2012, 21 December 2012.

Part case questions

(a) Relating to Chapters 1 and 2

1. Refer to Table 1.1, and the 'unique' challenges listed in the right-hand column. Identify examples of these challenges which Apple faced, as it evolved from 'business start-up' to 'international business'.
2. Refer to Table 1.2, and the 'Activity' suggested alongside each role. Identify as many examples as you can of managers in Apple having to perform these roles.
3. What examples of 'specialisation between areas of management' (Section 1.4) does the case mention?
4. What examples can you find in the case of Apple's management influencing people by shaping the contexts in which they work? (Section 1.7)
5. Which values and assumptions appear to be reflected in the company's practices? (Section 2.2)
6. What examples can you find in the case of Apple's management practices corresponding to one or more of the models in the 'competing values' framework. Which of these appears to dominate? (Section 2.3 and rest of Chapter 2)

(b) Relating to the company

1. Visit the company's website (and especially its latest Annual Report), and make notes about how, if at all, the dilemmas identified in the case are still current, and how the company has dealt with them.
2. What has been its relative market share of smartphones and tablets in the most recent trading period? Which competitors have gained and lost share? Access this information from the websites of *Economist*, *Financial Times* or *BBC News* (Business and Technology pages).
3. What new issues appear to be facing the company that were not mentioned in the case?
4. Can you trace how one or more aspects of the history of the company as outlined in the case has helped or hindered it in dealing with a current issue?
5. For any one of those issues it faces, how do you think it should deal with it? Build your answer by referring to one or more features of the company's history outlined in the case.

PART 1
EMPLOYABILITY SKILLS – PREPARING FOR THE WORLD OF WORK

To help you develop useful skills, this section includes tasks which relate the themes covered in the Part to six employability skills (sometimes called capabilities and attributes) which many employers value. The layout will help you to articulate these skills to employers and prepare for the recruitment processes you will encounter in application forms, interviews and assessment centres.

Task 1.1 Business awareness

If a potential employer asks you to attend an assessment centre or a competency-based interview, they may ask you to present or discuss a current business topic to demonstrate your business awareness. To help you to prepare for this, write an individual or group report on ONE of these topics and present it to an audience. Aim to present your ideas in a 750-word report and/or ten PowerPoint slides at most.

1 Using data from one or more websites or printed sources, outline significant recent developments in Apple, especially regarding their:
   - product range;
   - notable innovations;
   - significant moves by competitors; and
   - relations with shareholders and other stakeholders.

   Include a summary of commentators' views on Apple's recent progress.

2 Gather information on the interaction between Apple and their competitive environment in the consumer electronics industry, including specific examples of new challengers, or new moves by established competitors. What generally relevant lessons can you draw about competition in this sector? Use Section 3.4 (Chapter 3) to structure your answer.

3 Choose another company that interests you – and which you may be considering as a career option.
   - Gather information from the website and other sources about its structure and operations.
   - What unique challenges does it face? (use Table 1.1 as a starting point)
   - Look for clues suggesting which (possibly more than one) of the 'competing values' may be most dominant in the organisation. (Section 2.3).
   - In what ways, if any, have governments and politics influenced the business?
   - To what extent is it an international business?

When you have completed the task, write a short paragraph giving examples of the skills (such as in information gathering, analysis and presentation) you have developed while doing it. You can transfer a brief note of this to the Table at Task 1.7.

Task 1.2 Solving problems

Reflect on the way that you handled Task 1.1, and identify problems which you encountered in preparing your report, and how you dealt with them. For example:

1. How did you identify the relevant facts which you needed for your report?
2. Were there alternative sources you could have used, and if so, how did you decide between them? Were there significant gaps in the data, and how did you overcome this?
3. What alternative courses of action did you consider at various stages of your work?
4. How did you select and implement one of these alternatives?
5. How did you evaluate the outcomes, and what lessons did you draw from the way you dealt with the problem?

When you have completed the task, write a short paragraph giving examples of the problem solving skills (such as finding and accessing information sources, deciding which to use, and evaluation) you have developed from this task. You can transfer a brief note of this to the Table at Task 1.7.

Task 1.3 Thinking critically

Reflect on the way that you handled Task 1.1, and identify how you exercised the skills of thinking critically (Chapter 1, Section 1.8). For example:

1. Did you spend time identifying and challenging the assumptions implied in the reports or commentaries you read? Summarise what you found then, or do it now.
2. Did you consider the extent to which they took account of the effects of the context in which managers are operating? Summarise what you found then, or do it now.
3. How far did they, or you, go in imagining and exploring alternative ways of dealing with the issue?
4. Did you spend time outlining the limitations of ideas or proposals which you thought of putting forward?

When you have completed the task, write a short paragraph, giving examples of the thinking skills you have developed (such as identifying assumptions, seeing the effects of context, identifying alternative routes and their limitations) from this task. You can transfer a brief note of this to the Table at Task 1.7.

Task 1.4 Team working

Chapter 17 includes ideas on team working. This activity helps you develop those skills by reflecting on how the team worked during Task 1.1.

Use the scales below to rate the way your team worked on this task – circle the number that best reflects your opinion of the discussion.

1. How effectively did the group obtain and use necessary information?

1	2	3	4	5	6	7
Badly						Well

2 To what extent was the group's organisation suitable for the task?

1	2	3	4	5	6	7
Unsuitable						Suitable

3 To what extent did members really listen to each other?

1	2	3	4	5	6	7
Not at all						All the time

4 How fully were members involved in decision taking?

1	2	3	4	5	6	7
Low involvement						High involvement

5 To what extent did you enjoy working with this group?

1	2	3	4	5	6	7
Not at all						Very much

6 How did team members use their time?

1	2	3	4	5	6	7
Badly						Well

Write down three specific practices which members of the team could use in the next task they work on. If possible, compare your results and suggestions with other members of the team, and agree on specific practices which would help the team work better.

When you have completed the task, write a short paragraph giving examples of the team working skills (such as observing a group to identify good and bad practices, evaluating how a team made decisions, and making practical suggestions to improve performance) you have developed from this task. You can transfer a brief note of this to the Table at Task 1.7.

Task 1.5 Communicating

Chapter 16 includes ideas on communicating. This activity helps you to learn more about the skill by reflecting on how the team communicated during Task 1.1. For example:

1 What did people do or say that helped or hindered communication within the group?
2 What communication practices did you use to present your report to your chosen audience?
3 How did you choose them, and were they satisfactory for the circumstances?
4 What were the main barriers to communication which the group experienced?
5 What would you do differently to improve communication in a similar task?

Present a verbal summary of your report to a fellow student, and help each other to improve your work.

When you have completed the task, write a short paragraph giving examples of the communicating skills (such as observing communication to identify good and bad practices, evaluating how a team communicated, and making practical suggestions to improve performance) you have developed from this task. You can transfer a brief note of this to the Table at Task 1.7.

Task 1.6 Self-management

This activity helps you to learn more about managing yourself, so that you can present convincing evidence to employers showing, amongst other things, your willingness to learn, your ability to manage and plan learning, workloads and commitments, and that you have a well-developed level of self-awareness and self-reliance. You need to show that you are able to accept responsibility, manage time, and use feedback to learn.

Reflect on the way that you handled Task 1.1, and identify how you exercised skills of self management. For example:

1. Did you spend time planning the time you would spend on each part of the task?
2. Did this include balancing the commitments of team members across the work, so that all were fully occupied, and that no-one was under-used?
3. Can you identify examples when you used time well, and times when you wasted it? Who did what to improve the way you used time?
4. Were there examples of team members taking responsibility for an area of the work, and so helping to move the task forward?
5. Did you spend time reviewing how the group performed? If so, what lessons were you able to draw on each of the questions above, which you could use in future tasks?

When you have completed the task, write a short paragraph giving examples of the self management skills (such as managing time, balancing commitments, and giving constructive feedback) you have developed from this task. You can transfer a brief note of this to the Table at Task 1.7.

Task 1.7 Recording your employability skills

To conclude your work on this Part, use the summary paragraphs above to record the employability skills you have developed during your work on these tasks, and in other activities. Use the format of the table below to create an electronic record that you can use to combine the list of skills you have developed in this Part, with those in other Parts.

Most of your learning about each skill will probably come from the task associated with it – but you may also gain insights in other ways – include those as well.

Template for laying out record of employability skills developed in this Part

Skills/Task	Task 1.1	Task 1.2	Task 1.3	Task 1.4	Task 1.5	Task 1.6	Other sources of skills
Business awareness							
Solving problems							
Thinking critically							
Team working							
Communicating							
Self-management							

To make the most of your opportunities to develop employability skills as you do your academic work, you need to reflect regularly on your learning, and to record the results. This helps you to fill any gaps, and provides specific evidence of your employability skills.

4 The political environment

Ian Worthington

Politics is a universal activity which affects the business world in a variety of ways. Understanding political systems, institutions and processes provides a greater insight into business decisions and into the complexities of the business environment. Given the increasing globalisation of markets, this environment has an international as well as a domestic element and the two are closely interrelated. Appreciating some of the key aspects of this environment and its impact on business organisations is vital for students of business and managers alike.

Learning outcomes

Having read this chapter you should be able to:

- explain the political context within which business operates
- demonstrate the relevance of political values to the organisation of business activity
- identify and discuss key political institutions and processes at a variety of spatial levels
- illustrate how business organisations can influence, as well as be influenced by, the political environment

Key terms

Authoritarianism
Backbench MPs
Bureaucrats
Cabinet
Checks and balances
Civil servants
Coalition government
Constitution
Council of Ministers
Decisions
Democracy
Direct (or pure) democracy
Directives
Directorates-General
Electoral system
European Commission
European Council
European Court of Justice
European Parliament
Federal system of government

First-past-the-post system
Government
Government departments
House of Commons
House of Lords
Judiciary
Legislature
Lobbies
Manifesto
MEPs
Ministers
MPs
Parliament
Parliamentary system of government
Plebiscites
Political accountability
Political executive
Political parties
Political sovereignty

Politics
Presidential system of government
Pressure groups
Prime Minister
Professional lobbyist
Proportional representation
Qualified majority vote (qmv)
Recommendations and opinions
Referendums
Regulations
Representative government
Secretary of State
Separation of powers
Sovereignty
Supreme Court
The Council of the European Union
Unitary system of government

Introduction

In February 2013, the US and European Union announced a plan to open up negotiations on establishing a transatlantic free trade pact aimed at eliminating or minimising barriers to trade across all key industries from agriculture and pharmaceuticals to vehicles, services and investment. Faced with the growing influence of China in the global trading environment and the impact of the global recession in many of the world's leading economies, the proposed trade agreement was seen as a way of boosting economic performance in the participant countries and of circumventing the long-running stalemate in the Doha round of the world trade talks. Despite widespread support from political and business leaders on both sides of the Atlantic, it is accepted that establishing such a comprehensive trade pact will not be easy and will be affected by a variety of economic and political factors, including national interests and the electoral cycle (e.g. European elections in 2014). The expectation is that any agreement will take at least two years to negotiate and will require some concessions by both parties if the anticipated economic and commercial benefits are to be achieved.

What this simple example reminds us is that business activity takes place not only within but also across state boundaries and frequently involves governments, whether directly or indirectly, in shaping the business environment. Consequently the political and economic arrangements within the state in which a business is located and/or with which it is trading can have a fundamental impact on its operations – even to the extent of determining whether it is willing, or in some cases able, to trade at all. It is this politico-economic context within which businesses function and the philosophical foundations on which it is based that are the focus of this and the following chapter.

As a prelude to a detailed analysis of the political environment, it is necessary to make a number of general observations regarding political change and uncertainty and the impact on business activity. First, the nature of a country's political system – including its governmental institutions – tends to reflect certain underlying social values and philosophies which help to determine how decisions are made, including decisions about the allocation of resources. Thus, while governments may come and go, the values on which their decisions are based tend to be more enduring and as a result disputes normally centre around 'means' (e.g. sources of revenue) rather than 'ends' (e.g. controlling inflation). While this gives a certain degree of stability to the business environment, this stability cannot be taken for granted, as events in eastern Europe and the Middle East have readily demonstrated. In short, the political environment of business is a dynamic environment, containing elements of both continuity and change, and students and practitioners of business alike need to be constantly aware of developments in this area if they are to gain a greater insight into the background of business decision-making.

Second, changes in the political environment also emanate from a country's institutional arrangements. The tendency in democratic states, for example, to have regular elections, competing political parties offering alternative policies and a system of pressure groups helps to generate a degree of discontinuity, which renders predictions about the future more uncertain. For a business, such uncertainty can create not only opportunities but also a degree of risk which will often be an important influence on its decisions. Moreover, given that perceptions of such risks (or opportunities) are also normally reflected in the attitudes and behaviour of a country's financial and other markets, this represents a further variable that at times can be critical for an organisation's future prospects. For many businesses, taking steps to maximise opportunities (or to minimise risk) may ultimately make the difference between short-term failure and long-term survival.

Third, it is important to emphasise that political influences are not restricted to national boundaries – a point emphasised by the opening paragraph to this chapter and by the increasing importance of international and supranational groupings such as the G8 nations, the European Union and the World Trade Organisation, all of which are discussed below. These external politico-economic influences form part of the environment in which a country's governmental institutions take decisions, and their impact on domestic policy and on business activity can often be fundamental. No discussion of the business environment would be complete without an analysis of their role and impact, particularly in shaping international political and economic relationships.

Fourth, the precise impact of political factors on a business tends to vary to some degree according to the type of organisation involved. Multinational corporations – operating on a global scale – will be more concerned with questions such as the stability of overseas political regimes than will the small local firm operating in a localised market, where the primary concern will be with local market conditions. That said, there will undoubtedly be occasions when even locally based enterprises will be affected either directly or indirectly by political developments in other parts of the globe – as in the case of an interruption in supplies or the cancellation of a foreign order in which a small business is involved as a subcontractor. In short, while some broad generalisations can be made about the impact of global (or domestic) political developments on an individual organisation, each case is to some extent unique in both space and time, and observers of the business scene need to be cautious and open-minded in their analysis if they are to avoid the twin dangers of oversimplification and empiricism.

Finally, it needs to be recognised that businesses are not merely reactive to changes in the political environment, they can also help to shape the political context in which they operate and can influence government decision-makers, often in a way that is beneficial to their own perceived needs. One of the hallmarks of **democracy** is the right of individuals and groups to seek to influence government, and businesses – both individually and collectively – have been active in this sphere for centuries. It would be a mistake to underestimate their impact on government policy or on the shaping of values in the established capitalist nations of western Europe and elsewhere.

Political systems

The nature of political activity

All social situations at certain times require decisions to be made between alternative courses of action. Parents may disagree with their offspring about the kind of clothes they wear or how late they stay out at night or how long they grow their hair. Students may challenge lecturers about a particular perspective on an issue or when they should submit a piece of work. The members of the board of directors of a company may have different views about future investment or diversification or the location of a new factory. In all these cases, some solution needs to be found, even if the eventual decision is to do nothing. It is the processes involved in arriving at a solution to a problem, where a conflict of opinion occurs, that are the very essence of political activity.

Politics, in short, is concerned with those processes that help to determine how conflicts are contained, modified, postponed or settled, and as such can be seen as a universal social activity. Hence, individuals often talk of 'office politics' or the 'politics of the board room' or the 'mediating role' played by a parent in the event of a family dispute. For most individuals, however, the term 'politics' tends to be associated with activities at state level, where the resolution of conflict often involves large numbers of people and may even involve individuals in other states. Political activity at this level is clearly qualitatively different from the other social situations mentioned, and given the scale and complexity of the modern state, the problems requiring solutions can often be acute and chronic. Solving those problems tends to be seen, at least in part, as the function of government.

Government as a process is concerned with the pursuit and exercise of power – the power to make decisions which affect the lives of substantial numbers of people, be it at local, regional, national or even international level. Government may also refer to the institutions through which power tends to be formally and legitimately exercised, whether they be cabinets, parliaments, councils, committees or congresses. Whereas the pursuit and exercise of power tends to be an enduring feature of any society, governments are normally transitory, comprising those individuals and/or groups who, at a particular time, have the responsibility for controlling the state, including making laws for 'the good of society'. How governments exercise their power and the ideological foundations on which this is based helps to indicate the nature of the political system and its likely approaches to the resolution of conflicts.

Authoritarian political systems

Broadly speaking, political systems can be seen to range across two extremes, on the one hand authoritarian and on the other democratic. In an **authoritarian** political system the disposition is to settle conflicts through the enforcement of rules, regulations and orders by an established authority. This authority may be an individual (e.g. a monarch or other powerful individual) or a group of individuals (e.g. a political party or military junta) which may have assumed political power in a variety of ways (e.g. by birth, election or coup). Once in power, the individual or group will tend to act so as to limit the degree of participation by others in the process of decision-making, even to the extent of monopolising the process altogether and permitting no opposition to occur. Where this is the case, a society is often described as being 'totalitarian' and is perhaps best exemplified by Nazi Germany and Stalinist Russia.

Democratic political systems

In contrast, in a democratic political system, the assumption is that as far as possible conflicts should be resolved by rational discussions between the various parties concerned, with the final solution being accepted voluntarily by all participants, even if they disagree. At one extreme, such consultation may involve all individuals, who have – in theory at least – equal influence over the final outcome (e.g. as in **referendums** or **plebiscites**).

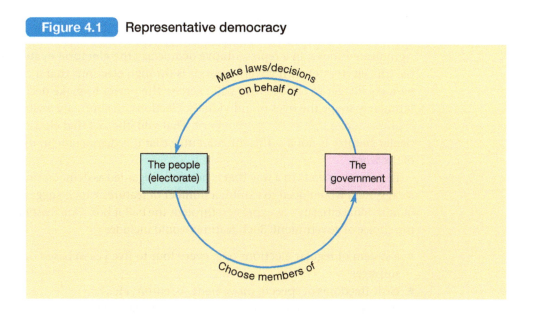

Figure 4.1   Representative democracy

Given the scale and complexity of modern states, however, such examples of **direct (or pure) democracy** tend to be rare and it is invariably the case that the democratic solution to conflict resolution is achieved 'indirectly' through a system of political representation and responsibility. Under such a system, the wishes and views of individuals are said to be represented in an established authority (e.g. a government) that has normally been chosen by the people and is accountable (responsible) to them at regular intervals through a variety of mechanisms, including regular and free elections (see Figure 4.1). Implicit in this, of course, is the requirement that individuals are able to change this authority and select another individual or group to represent them. Monopolisation of political power by any one individual or group can only occur, therefore, with the expressed consent of the people.

Government in democratic states

Democratic institutions and processes

Democracy means far more than just popular government or a system of regular elections; the democratic approach to government implies the existence of a complex array of institutions and processes through which the wishes of the people are articulated and carried out. While the specific institutional arrangements tend to vary between states, countries that are held to be democratic invariably have a political system which comprises four common and interlocking elements: an electoral system, a party system, a representative assembly and a system for the articulation of sectional interests. The generic roles of these major building blocks of democratic government are discussed below. Location-specific information on how the system operates in a national (i.e. United Kingdom) and a supranational (i.e. European Union) context can be found in the appendices to this chapter. Non-UK readers are encouraged to substitute their own political arrangements for those described in the appendices.

The electoral system

As indicated above, in a representative democracy the **electoral system** links the people (the electorate) with government; it is through elections that a country's citizens periodically get to choose who will exercise the power to make decisions which will ultimately shape the lives of individuals. Elections, in short, are a vital ingredient of a **representative system of government**. That said, the fact that elections exist in a particular country is not a sufficient guarantee that it is democratic in the accepted sense of the word.

In order to operate in a way that is normally regarded as democratic, a country's electoral system would need to exhibit a number of features which suggest that the wishes of individual citizens – as expressed through the ballot box – are reasonably reflected in the choice of government. Such features would include:

- a system of regular elections (e.g. every four to five years) based on universal adult suffrage;
- basic freedoms of speech, movement, assembly, etc.;
- freedom from coercion and the absence of illegal electoral practices;
- a secret ballot;
- free media.

Where conditions such as these are absent or are not fully operational, there will always be a suspicion that the electoral outcome may not be a true reflection of the wishes of the people. The act of voting, in other words, needs to be accompanied by a set of legal prescriptions that provides some kind of guarantee that an election to choose part, if not all, of the government is both free and fair.

To be democratic the electoral system must not only be transparent, it must also ensure that the wishes of the majority – as expressed through the number of votes cast – are reflected in the final result. In a **first-past-the-post system** (e.g. in most current UK elections) a simple majority is sufficient to ensure victory; as a consequence some winning candidates may be elected with fewer than half of the votes cast. Where a system of **proportional representation** operates (e.g. in many other European countries) a redistribution of votes occurs when there is no outright winner, resulting in a final decision that can be said to more closely represent the wishes of the whole electorate. While the intricacies of different electoral systems are beyond the scope of this book, it is worth observing that the voting system a country uses can have important ramifications for the government elected to office. On the whole, a plurality or first-past-the-post system of voting usually – though not inevitably (e.g. the 2010 election in the UK) – results in majority government, with a single party dominating the organs of decision-making and able to pursue its legislative programme relatively free from constraint by the losing side(s). In contrast, where a proportional representation system is used, the result is often a **coalition government** made up of different parties, some of which may hold significantly or even radically different views from the largest party within the coalition. In effect, coalition government is predominantly a matter of negotiation, accommodation and compromise, an exercise in consensus building and persuasion, as commonly found in most types of organisational setting, including the business world.

The party system

While it is possible to have democratic government in a one-party state, democracy is normally taken to imply that citizens get to choose between alternative candidates when casting their vote at an election. Invariably such candidates tend to represent different political parties and to this extent a vote for a specific candidate can be said to equate to a vote for the party that he or she represents and which is ultimately hoping to form the government.

The existence of political parties, which compete for office at election time, is clearly a convenient – if sometimes questionable – means of organising a system of representative democracy; hence the universality of party systems in democratic states and the relative lack of candidates standing with no party tag at governmental elections at all spatial levels. Parties not only help to choose most of the candidates who compete in these elections, they usually also support and sustain them (e.g. financially) before, during and after the election campaign and help to organise a system of (largely unpaid) volunteers to work to get them elected, as well as providing candidates with a platform of policies on which to stand for office. Whereas some of these activities tend to be the responsibility of the party at national level, others are undertaken at a regional and/or local level, often in the constituency (i.e. geographical area) that a candidate represents. Since questions of organisation, policy-making and finance are central to the operation and success of a political party in modern democratic states, party structures have tended to become complex, bureaucratic, multi-layered and increasingly professionalised. As in other types of organisational framework, they also provide an arena in which a substantial degree of in-fighting occurs between individuals of different temperaments, views and ambitions who are seeking to push the party in a particular direction.

From the electors' point of view, one of the primary benefits of the party system is that it provides a means of selecting political leaders and the kind of policies they are likely to pursue if the party achieves political office. Describing candidates by a party label (e.g. Democratic, Republican, Socialist, Conservative, Liberal, etc.) allows voters to choose those candidates whose views most closely represent their own, given that parties normally have an identifiable policy stance and produce some form of statement (or manifesto) outlining their policy preferences during an election campaign. Thus, while an individual elector is unlikely to agree with every single policy or proposed piece of legislation that a party puts forward in its attempts to gain office, he/she is at least able to express a preference between alternative approaches to government at the ballot box. To that extent it can be argued that there is likely to be a degree of congruence between the legislative programme of the party democratically elected to form the government and the wishes of the people who elected it, albeit that in some cases the government may have received less than 50 per cent of the popular vote.

It is worth remembering that party labels are not always a good guide to the policy or legislative preferences of individual candidates, since someone described as a 'Democrat' or 'Liberal' in one part of a country may hold radically different views on a range of issues from others of the same title elected to constituencies in other areas. If anything, identifying election candidates in party political terms gives voters a broad indication of the underlying values and beliefs to which an individual subscribes:

parties in practice are always destined to be (sometimes fragile) coalitions of groups and individuals representing a range of opinions and preferences under a party banner.

A representative assembly

As previously indicated, one of the key features of democratic government is the existence of a representative decision-making body, a group of individuals chosen by a country's citizens to help make important decisions on their behalf. In the same way that shareholders in a public company elect directors to guide the organisation and to represent their interest, voters at election time choose individuals they wish to represent them in government in the various organs of decision-making and policy implementation (see below). While not everyone chosen by the electorate becomes part of the small group of key decision-makers (the government or **political executive**), all normally have some kind of role to play in the decision-making process and usually get an opportunity to scrutinise policy and legislative proposals put forward by the governing element and to vote upon them. The fact that the electorate periodically has the opportunity to express its opinion on the performance of the incumbent decision-makers – and where necessary to replace them – provides for a degree of **political accountability**, a central tenet of a democratic system of government.

As more than two centuries of political theory have demonstrated, the concept of representation can have at least two meanings: decision-makers may represent the views of their constituents in the literal sense that they articulate them in or to government, or they may simply represent them in so far as they have been elected by a majority (simple or otherwise) of voters to be the representative of a geographical area. In practice, both these interpretations of representation can be seen to operate at different times, according to the predispositions of individual decision-makers and the influences emanating from the prevailing political culture in a country, region or area. For example, in a system of government where national political parties are relatively weak and where an individual's success in elections depends very much on supporting policies that are consistent with those of significant elements in one's electorate (e.g. in the United States), representation tends to be seen in the more literal sense of supporting local views and preferences. In contrast, where there is a strong party system and where individuals are held to be elected on the basis of party affiliation (e.g. the United Kingdom), elected representatives are generally expected to be loyal to the party in a policy sense, even if on occasion this results in a conflict with the views of the majority of one's constituents.

In modern democratic states the model of representative decision-making usually operates at all spatial levels. In Europe, for example, voters not only elect their own national governments but also choose decision-makers at a local and/or regional level and many European citizens are also able to vote in elections for pan-European institutions (i.e. for the European Parliament – see Appendix 4.3). One of the consequences of this arrangement is that sometimes the party (or parties) elected to office at national level may be different from that (or those) in power locally, regionally and/or supranationally. Where this occurs, clashes between decision-makers representing different geographical areas tend to be inevitable and can give rise to problems of decision-making and policy implementation, thus potentially disrupting the programme on which a government has been elected to office.

In this context a useful distinction can be drawn between a **federal** and a **unitary system of government**. In the former, **sovereignty** (i.e. the legitimate power to make decisions) is divided between two levels of government (e.g. national and local/regional), each with independent powers that are usually laid down in a written constitution which is interpreted by the courts. Thus, in the United States, education is in the hands of the elected government at state (i.e. subnational) level, while defence and foreign affairs are federal (i.e. national) governmental responsibilities. In Germany, the federal government similarly has exclusive jurisdiction over foreign and defence policy and environmental protection, while the Länder (states) control such areas as education and the police.

In contrast, under a unitary system ultimate authority rests with the national government and any powers granted to subnational levels by the central sovereign authority can ultimately be rescinded, including the right of government at subnational level to exist. Under such an arrangement – particularly where it is written down in the form of a **constitution** – government at national level clearly holds the whip hand and would normally expect its view to prevail where a dispute over an issue or policy occurs between it and a subnational authority. That said, decision-makers in democratic states at all levels and under different governmental systems have, on the whole, a tendency to settle such conflicts through negotiation, bargaining and compromise rather than by exerting their power and authority, although this might be used on occasions. This predisposition goes some way to explaining why in democratic systems of government, the policies and legislative programmes of elected governments are much more likely to be incremental than they are to be radical.

mini case   Brought to book

Politicians can have a significant impact on business activity at both the macro and micro levels. In addition to making decisions on how the economy should be managed overall, elected representatives can make or propose changes to regulations and legislation which affect how businesses operate, what they can and cannot do, and how they treat their employees, customers, suppliers and so on.

An illustration of how the political environment can potentially shape a firm's operations can be seen in the decision made by French MPs in October 2013 to support a bill to curb the discounting power of the globally influential company Amazon. Concerned that small, independent bookstores were facing unfair competition from the US giant, MPs from across all parties voted for a measure aimed at preventing Amazon from combining free delivery with 5 per cent discounts on books. Since 1981, France has had a law that establishes fixed book prices so that customers effectively pay the same for a book however or from wherever it is purchased, with extensive discounting banned. French legislators believe that small bookstores should be treated as a 'cultural exception' and should, if necessary, be protected from the kind of experiences suffered by UK independent book retailers when fixed prices were abandoned back in the 1990s.

A system for articulating sectional interests

Elections and a party system provide one way in which the views of an individual can be represented in government; an alternative is via **pressure group** activity. Like competing political parties, the existence of pressure groups is usually regarded as an important indicator of a democratic system of government. For many citizens in democratic countries, joining such a group is seen as a much more effective way of influencing government than through the party system.

Whereas political parties seek influence by formally contesting political office, pressure groups seek to influence government in other ways, although this distinction is increasingly becoming blurred. In essence, pressure groups (or **lobbies**) are collections of like-minded people who have voluntarily joined together to try to influence government thinking and behaviour and to represent the interests of their members. Nowadays, many of these groups are highly organised and are powerful bodies, supported by substantial funding and formidable research facilities. Such groups (frequently referred to as non-governmental or civic society organisations) provide a vehicle through which a collective and non-party political view can be articulated in decision-making circles; as such they can be said to operate as a kind of safety valve within a democratic system of government.

Traditionally in pressure group literature, a distinction tends to be drawn between groups which represent 'somebody' and those that represent 'something'. The former are usually referred to as 'interest groups' or 'protective groups' and would include groups representing a particular section of the community, such as trade unions or professional associations. The latter tend to be known as 'cause groups' or 'issue groups', as exemplified by Greenpeace, Amnesty International and the various animal rights groups. In practice, of course, it is often difficult to make such a clear-cut distinction, given that some interest groups such as trade unions often associate themselves with particular causes and may campaign vigorously alongside other groups in support of or against the issue concerned.

Most large pressure groups have websites offering useful information. Greenpeace, for example, can be accessed at *www.greenpeace.org*

From a governmental point of view the existence of structures for articulating sectional interests is seen as an aid to efficient and representative decision-making. Pressure groups not only provide government with detailed information on specific areas of everyday activity without which rational decision-making would be difficult, they also fulfil a number of other important functions in a democratic system. These would include:

- helping to defend minority interests;
- assisting in the implementation of government policy and legislation;
- providing for continuity in communication and consultation between the governors and the governed between elections.

The successful introduction of reforms in a country's health service, for example, is dependent upon support from the various arms of the medical profession and from organisations representing the different interests of health service workers. Similarly, the effectiveness of government economic policies, and their subsequent impact on the business community, will be conditioned at least in part by the reactions of groups representing large employers, small and medium enterprises, workers, financial interests, etc., as well as by individual entrepreneurs and consumers.

This relative interdependence between government and pressure groups under a democratic system is exemplified by the practice of prior consultation; this is the arrangement whereby the elected government actively seeks the views of interested parties during the policy and/or legislative process. Such consultation may be 'formal' (e.g. where a group has representation on an advisory or executive body or where it is invited to offer its views on a proposal) or 'informal' (e.g. off-the-record meetings between representatives of the group and the government) or a mixture of the two; it may also involve a group in hiring the services of a **professional lobbyist** – often a former politician or bureaucrat familiar with the structure of decision-making in government and with access to key decision-makers (see the case study at the end of this chapter). Groups that are regularly consulted and whose opinion is readily sought by government may acquire 'insider status' and may even be incorporated into the formal decision-making process – prizes that are highly valued since they imply that the group has a legitimate right to be consulted by government prior to deciding on a particular course of action or inaction. In comparison, 'outsider groups' often find it difficult to make their voice heard in decision-making circles and for this reason may be forced to resort to different forms of direct action in order to publicise their views in the wider community in the hope of gaining influence through public sympathy and support.

As this discussion of 'insider' and 'outsider' groups illustrates, pressure groups can use a variety of methods to attract support for their cause or to protect and promote the interests of their members. These range from direct lobbying of government to marches, strikes, disruption and other forms of demonstrative action designed to attract media and hence public attention – although frequently such action can have an adverse effect. In addition, some of the larger and better-resourced groups may employ experts to advise on policy issues and/or establish their own research facilities to provide information to strengthen their case (e.g. Greenpeace).

What method(s) a group employs and where it seeks to bring its influence to bear tends to vary from issue to issue and group to group, and generally reflects not only differences in group status and resources but also the structure of decision-making within the policy community concerned. In the United States, for instance, direct lobbying of Congressmen/women is a common tactic used by pressure groups, given the relative weakness of the party system and the tendency for an individual's electoral fortunes to be tied up with the views of key groups in the constituency. In the United Kingdom, the pressures of party discipline, the domination of the executive branch of government and the influence of senior civil servants tend to make direct appeals to key actors in government a more effective method of achieving political influence than operating at constituency level.

As a final comment it is worth recalling that decisions in a democracy may be made locally, nationally, supranationally or internationally and often require cooperation between different levels of government and/or between different agencies and arms of government at both the formulation and the implementation stages. Accordingly, pressure groups are increasingly to be found operating at the interface between the institutions of government and across the whole range of spatial levels from the local to the global. Given the large number of pressure points where vested interests can bring their influence to bear, it tends to be easier for a group to prevent or limit government action than to persuade decision-makers to change the direction of policy. To this extent policy formulation and implementation in democratic states is perhaps best portrayed as the 'art of the possible' rather than the 'science of the desirable'.

The three branches or functions of government

In a broad sense the process of governing involves three major activities: making decisions, putting them into effect and adjudicating over them in the event of dispute or non-compliance. Each of these functions or branches of government, as they operate at a national level, is discussed in turn below. A similar form of analysis could, if necessary, be applied at other spatial levels.

The legislative function

Governing, as we have seen, is about making decisions which affect the lives of large numbers of people. Some of these decisions require new laws or changes to existing laws to bring them into effect so that the individuals and/or groups to whom they apply become aware of the government's wishes and requirements. In a democratic system of government this formal power to make the law (i.e. to legislate) is vested in a legislative body (the **legislature**) which is elected either wholly or partly by the people. As indicated above, this process of choosing a representative decision-making body by popular election is a central feature of the democratic approach to government.

Leaving aside for one moment the relative power of the legislative and executive branches of government, it is possible to identify a number of common features that apply to legislatures and the legislative function in most, if not all, democratic states. These include the following:

A bicameral legislature, that is, a legislature with two chambers: an upper house and a lower house, each with specific powers and roles in the legislative process. In most countries each chamber comprises representatives chosen by a separate electoral process and hence may be dominated by the same party or different parties or by no single party, depending on the electoral outcome. For a legislative proposal to be accepted, the consent of both chambers is normally required. This is one of the many **checks and balances** normally found in democratic systems of government (see below).

A multi-stage legislative process, involving the drafting of a legislative proposal, its discussion and consideration, and where necessary amendment, further debate and consideration and ultimate acceptance or rejection by either or both legislative chambers. Debates on the general principles of a proposed piece of legislation would normally involve all members of each chamber, whereas detailed discussion tends to take place in smaller groups or committees.

An executive-led process, that is, one in which most major legislative proposals emanate from the executive branch of government. In a **presidential system of government** (e.g. the USA), the chief executive (the president) is normally elected separately by the people and is not part of the legislature (in other words, there is a **separation of powers**). In a **parliamentary system of government** (e.g. the UK), members of the executive may also be members of the legislative body and hence may be in a position to control the legislative process.

Opportunities for legislative initiatives by ordinary representatives, that is, arangements that permit ordinary members of the legislative assembly to propose new laws or changes to existing laws. In practice such opportunities tend to be limited and dependent to a large degree for their success on a positive response from the political executive.

Opportunities to criticise and censure the government and, in some cases, remove it from office (e.g. through impeachment) – this is a vital function within a democratic system of government in that it forces decision-makers to defend their proposals, explain the logic of their actions and account for any mistakes they may have made. Opposition parties play an important role in this context within the legislative body and through media coverage can attack the government and articulate alternative views to the wider public. Specialist and standing committees for scrutinising legislation and the day-to-day work of the executive branch of government also usually exist in democratic regimes.

Control of the purse strings, that is, the power to grant or deny government the money required to carry out its policies and legislative programme. In theory this is a formidable power, given that no government can operate without funds. In practice the power of the legislature to deny funding to a democratically elected government may be more apparent than real and, where necessary, compromise tends to occur between the executive and legislative branches of government.

mini case: The power of the purse

In 2013 the Republican-led US House of Representatives used its constitutional power to impose an annual borrowing limit on the US Treasury aimed at reducing the size of the country's budget deficit. In what was widely seen as an attempt to derail President Obama's healthcare reforms, the House set a debt ceiling limit that would be insufficient to cover the President's budgetary requirements, including the interest on public borrowings that were becoming due for repayment. The threat that the USA would become technically bankrupt during October of that year – with potentially serious consequences for the recovery of the global economy – set alarm bells ringing in financial markets and led to calls from international bodies including the IMF for urgent action to find a way around the impasse that had developed between the White House and Congress.

Pending a solution to the crisis, the US government laid off hundreds of thousands of federal employees, a decision which affected not only the provision of public services but also many of the businesses dependent on the spending of the state and its employees. In Washington, for example, a wide range of smaller businesses – including hairdressers, taxi firms, cafes and restaurants – experienced a sudden loss of trade as their pool of regular customers declined substantially. For these business owners, the threat of a prolonged period of declining revenues was far more important than esoteric discussions about the appropriate level at which to set the country's debt ceiling.

Since a great deal of media coverage of the issue at the time understandably focused on the partisan roots of the problem and on possible compromises, it is easy to forget that both action and inaction by political decision-makers almost invariably has consequences for a country's citizens and its businesses. As the next chapter demonstrates, decisions on taxing and spending by government have a major impact on the economy at both the macro and micro levels; spending and income are after all opposite sides of the same coin.

As will be evident from the comments above, legislating is a complex and time-consuming process, offering numerous opportunities for individuals and groups both within and outside the legislative body (e.g. pressure groups) to delay and disrupt the passage of legislation. While no government can guarantee to achieve all its legislative aims, there is a cultural expectation in a democracy that, as far as possible, promises made before an election will be put into effect at the earliest opportunity by the democratically elected government. Such an expectation usually provides the incumbent administration with a powerful argument for legislative support on the occasions when it is confronted with intransigence within the legislative assembly or with hostility from outside sectional interests.

The executive function

Governing is not only about making decisions, it is also about ensuring that these decisions are put into effect in order to achieve the government's objectives. Implementing governmental decisions is the responsibility of the executive branch of government.

In modern states the term 'the executive' refers to that relatively small group of individuals chosen to decide on policy and to oversee its implementation; some of these individuals will hold political office, others will be career administrators and advisers, although some of the latter may also be political appointees. Together they are part of a complex political and administrative structure designed to carry out the essential work of government and to ensure that those responsible for policy-making and implementation are ultimately accountable for their actions.

The policy-making aspect of the executive function is normally the responsibility of a small political executive chosen (wholly or in part) by popular election. Under a presidential system of government, the chief executive or president is usually chosen by separate election for a given period of office and becomes both the nominal and political head of state. He/she subsequently appoints individuals to head the various government departments/ministries/bureaux which are responsible for shaping and implementing government policy. Neither the president nor the heads of departments normally sit in the legislative assembly, although there are sometimes exceptions to this rule (e.g. the Vice-President in the United States).

In contrast, in a parliamentary system the roles of head of state and head of government are separated, with the former usually largely ceremonial and carried out by either a president (e.g. Germany, India) or a monarch (e.g. UK, Japan). The head of government (e.g. prime minister), while officially appointed by the head of state, is an elected politician, invariably the head of the party victorious in a general election or at least seen to be capable of forming a government, possibly in coalition with other parties. Once appointed, the head of government chooses other individuals to head the different government departments/ministries and to be part of a collective decision-making body (e.g. a **Cabinet**) which meets to sanction policy proposals put forward through a system of executive committees and subcommittees (e.g. Cabinet committees). These individuals, along with the head of government, are not only part of the executive machinery of the state but also usually members of the legislative assembly and both 'individually' and 'collectively' responsible to the legislature for the work of government.

The day-to-day administration of government policy is largely carried out by non-elected government officials (sometimes referred to as **civil servants** or **bureaucrats**), who work for the most part in complex, bureaucratic organisations within the state bureaucracy. Apart from their role in implementing public policy, government officials help to advise **ministers** on the different policy options and on the political and administrative aspects of particular courses of action. Needless to say, this gives them a potentially critical role in shaping government policy, a role which has been substantially enhanced over the years by the practice of granting officials a significant degree of discretion in deciding on the details of particular policies and/or on how they should be administered.

Whereas politicians in the executive branch of government tend to be transitory figures – who come and go at the whim of the head of government or of the electorate – most, if not all, officials are permanent, professional appointees who may serve a variety of governments of different political complexions and preferences during a long career in public administration. Whatever government is in power, officials are generally expected to operate in a non-partisan (i.e. neutral) way when advising their political masters and when overseeing the implementation of government policy. Their loyalty in short is to the current administration in office, a principle which helps to ensure a smooth transition of government and to guarantee that the upheaval caused by a general election does not prevent the business of the state from being carried out as usual.

The judicial function

Governing is not just about making and implementing laws, it is also about ensuring that they are applied and enforced. The latter is essentially the role of the third arm of government, namely the judiciary and the system of courts. Like political institutions, legal structures and processes tend to a degree to be country specific and vary according to a number of influences, including history, culture and politics. For example, while some states have a relatively unified legal system, others organised on a federal basis usually have a system of parallel courts adjudicating on federal and state/provincial law, with a Supreme Court arbitrating in the event of a dispute. In some countries a proportion of the judges may be directly or indirectly elected by the public, in others they may be appointed by government and/or co-opted by fellow judges. Business students should make themselves familiar with the legal arrangements within their own country (see, for example, Chapter 8, which contains information on the legal system in England and Wales). In this section we look briefly at the judicial function as related to the concept of democracy.

Whereas in totalitarian systems of government the judiciary is essentially the servant of the ruling élite (e.g. the 'party'), in a democracy it is an accepted principle that there should be a separation between the judicial function and the other two branches of government in order to protect the citizen from a too-powerful state. This notion of an impartial and independent judiciary, free to challenge the government and to review its decisions, is regarded as one of the hallmarks of a democratic system of government, a further manifestation of the doctrine of the separation of powers.

In practice, of course, notions of judicial independence and role within the democratic political process tend to be the subject of a certain amount of debate, particularly in countries where senior appointments to the judiciary appear to be in the gift of politicians (e.g. Supreme Court judges in the United States are nominated by the President with the consent of the Senate) or where individuals with judicial powers also have an executive and/or legislative role (e.g. the Home Secretary in Britain). Equally there are questions over the degree to which the courts should have the power to review the constitutionality of decisions made by a democratically elected government. In the United States, for example, the Supreme Court has a long-established right to declare a law void if it conflicts with its own interpretation of the American constitution. In Britain, the legal sovereignty of Parliament and the absence of a codified written constitution push the judiciary towards trying to interpret the intentions of the framers of government legislation and any legal decision unwelcomed by the government can be reversed by further legislation. That said, it is interesting to note that in recent years there has been an increased willingness on the part of the British judiciary to review administrative decisions, particularly those made by ministers.

Other aspects, too, call into question how far in modern democratic states there is a total separation between the different arms of government (e.g. increasing use of administrative courts/tribunals) and whether it makes sense to rigidly distinguish between rule making and rule adjudication. Certainly some of the past judgments by the United States Supreme Court (e.g. in the area of civil rights) demonstrate that the courts can be influential in shaping decisions on major issues of policy and suggest that the judiciary are susceptible to influences from their own values or to general societal pressures. In short, it seems fair to suggest that under current legal arrangements, legal adjudication is not far removed from the world of politics; arguably we may like to perpetuate the myth of an entirely separate and independent judiciary since this is a necessary aspect of the stability of many existing political systems.

Checks and balances in democracies

As will be evident from the analysis above, democracy implies the existence of a system of checks and balances, arrangements which serve to curb government action and restrict its influence on the day-to-day lives of its citizens. These restraints on the actions of the state at national level can be divided into two main types: political and social/economic.

Political checks and balances emanate primarily from three main sources:

- the separation of powers – particularly the notion that the three arms of government are in separate hands and that decisions require the concurrence of all branches of government;
- a bicameral legislature – with legislation having to be accepted by both houses and subject to scrutiny and amendment by opposition parties;
- the territorial division of powers – whether under a federal arrangement or through the devolution of power to regional bodies and/or local authorities. Supranationalism is a further development.

The point is not that these arrangements necessarily exist in their most complete form in democratic states but that – however imperfect in practice – their existence helps to provide time for reflection and delay in the decision-making process and to encourage consultation, negotiation and consensus building, the essence of the democratic approach to conflict resolution.

The notion of social and economic checks and balances refers to those countervailing pressures on the activities of the state and its agencies that derive from the existence of non-state structures and processes which affect the lives of individuals and which ultimately restrict the scope of government influence. These include private business organisations, professional associations, promotional bodies, churches and other groups which help to shape our economic, social and moral environment. As subsequent chapters will demonstrate, the bulk of economic decisions in democratic states are not taken by the government but by private individuals and organisations (i.e. firms) interacting through a market system. This acts as a kind of check and balance on the free activity of the public sector and is a fundamental characteristic of democratic government.

A model of the policy process

It is appropriate to conclude this examination of the political environment with a brief discussion of the process of governmental decision-making in democratic systems. Here, the basic model of the organisation in its environment introduced in Chapter 1 serves as a useful analytical tool (see Figure 4.2). Governments, like firms, are organisations which transform inputs into output and they do so in an environment largely the same as that which confronts other types of enterprise. Like other organisations, government is a user of resources, especially land, labour, capital, finance and expertise, but in addition all governments face political demands and supports when considering their policy options.

As indicated above, political demands – including those directly or indirectly impinging on business activity – become translated into action through a variety of mechanisms, including the electoral system, party activity, pressure group influence and political communication; hence a government is always keen to point out that electoral victory implies that it has a mandate for its policies. The supports of the political system are those customs, conventions, rules, assumptions and sentiments that provide a basis for the existence of the political community and its constituent parts and thus give legitimacy to the actions and existence of the incumbent government. In democratic systems, the belief in democratic principles, and the doctrines and practices emanating from that belief, are seen as central to the activities of government and its agencies.

The outputs of the political system vary considerably and range from public goods and services (e.g. healthcare) – provided predominantly from money raised through taxation – to rules and regulations (e.g. legislation, administrative procedures, directives) and transfer payments (i.e. where the government acts as a reallocator of resources, as in the case of the provision of state benefits). Taken together, the nature, range and extent of government output not only tend to make government the single biggest business in a state, they also influence the environment in which other businesses operate and increasingly in which other governments make decisions.

Figure 4.2 Government and its environment

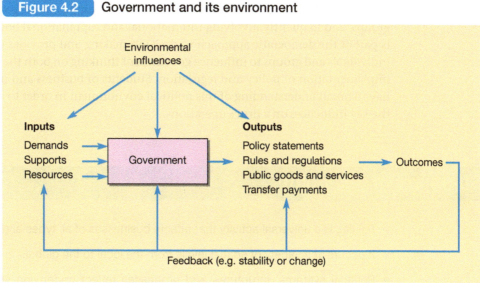

As far as governmental decision-making is concerned, this is clearly a highly complex process which in practice does not replicate the simple sequence of events suggested by the model. Certainly governments require 'means' (inputs) to achieve 'ends' (outputs), but the outputs of the political system normally emerge only after a complex, varied and ongoing process involving a wide range of individuals, groups and agencies. To add further confusion, those involved in the process tend to vary according to the decision under discussion as well as over time, making analysis fraught with difficulties. One possible solution may be to distinguish between the early development of a policy proposal ('initiation') and its subsequent 'formulation' and 'implementation', in the hope that a discernible 'policy community' can be identified at each stage. But even this approach involves a degree of guesswork and arbitrary decision-making, not least because of the difficulty of distinguishing precisely between the different stages of policy-making and of discerning the influence of individuals and groups at each phase of the process.

Notwithstanding these difficulties, it is important for students of business and for businesses themselves to have some understanding of the structure of decision-making, and of the underlying values and beliefs that tend to shape governmental action, if they are to appreciate (and possibly influence) the political environment in which they exist. Studies of political systems, institutions and processes help to provide insight into how and why government decisions are made, who is important in shaping those decisions and how influence can be brought to bear on the decision-making process. As an increasing number of individuals and groups recognise, knowledge of this kind can prove a valuable organisational resource that on occasions is of no less significance than the other inputs into the productive process.

Synopsis

Laws and policies that influence business activity are made by politicians and bureaucrats, operating at a variety of spatial levels. In democracies, decisions by governmental policy-makers emanate from a complex process of discussion and negotiation involving a range of formal and informal institutions, including political parties and pressure groups, and frequently involving international and supranational bodies. This process is part of the democratic approach to decision-making and provides opportunities for individuals and groups to influence government thinking on both the formulation and implementation of policy and legislation. Students of business and managers need to have a broad understanding of this political environment in order to appreciate one of the key influences on a firm's operations.

Summary of key points

- Politics is a universal activity that affects businesses of all types and sizes.
- It occurs at a variety of spatial levels from the local to the global.
- Political systems, structures and processes reflect underlying social values and philosophies and these influence the ways in which major decisions are taken.

- In any democratic system of government the key political institutions are likely to include an electoral system, a party system, a representative decision-making assembly and a system for articulating sectional interests.
- The three key functions of government are legislative, executive and judicial.
- While political institutions, practices and processes tend to vary between countries, democratic government is typified by a system of representative democracy and by political, social and economic checks and balances which act as a constraint on the actions of government.
- Such checks and balances in the system include the activities of pressure groups, which seek to influence government through a variety of means, and which often play a key role in policy formulation and implementation.
- Business organisations and the bodies that represent them are key pressure groups in democratic societies and an important part of the external environment in which government and its agencies operate.

Appendix 4.1 A democratic political system in action: UK national government

As far as the United Kingdom is concerned, the four interrelated elements of a democratic system of government are illustrated in Figure 4.3.

Through a system of regular elections, British citizens (the electorate) vote for candidates of competing political parties who are seeking to form the national government (or to be members of the devolved assemblies in Northern Ireland, Scotland or Wales). (Note that a referendum on Scottish independence to be held in September 2014 may result in an independent Scottish Parliament.) Successful candidates at the national elections become Members of Parliament (MPs) and the party with the largest

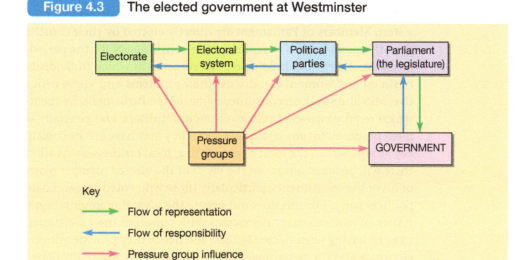

Figure 4.3 The elected government at Westminster

number of MPs is invited by the monarch to form a government, with individuals within the government being allocated specific responsibilities for particular areas of work. The work of government is scrutinised by Parliament (see below), which acts as the people's representative between elections, thereby providing for a measure of public accountability. Equally, between (or during) elections individuals are free to seek to influence government by joining pressure groups or other types of organisation (e.g. political parties) and by making their views known to their elected representatives. The media is free and therefore able to scrutinise the government's performance and to inform the public about political developments.

> **web link**
>
> For information on the political arrangements in Northern Ireland, Scotland and Wales, see, for example, www.nidirect.gov.uk; www.niassembly.gov.uk; www.scottish.parliament.uk; www.scotland.gov.uk; www.assemblywales.org; wales.gov.uk

The legislative branch of government at national level

As indicated above, a directly elected legislature – representative of the people and responsible for making laws – is an important component of a democratic system of government. In the United Kingdom as a whole this function is carried out by **Parliament**, which comprises a non-elected upper chamber (the **House of Lords**) and an elected lower chamber (the **House of Commons**) whose members (currently 650 **MPs**) are elected by universal suffrage by the majority of citizens aged 18 and over. While it is true to say that the Lords retains some important powers, including the power to delay and scrutinise government legislation, the House of Commons remains the most important part of the UK legislature, particularly since it contains key members of the political executive, including the Prime Minister and most of the Cabinet. For this reason the discussion below focuses on the role of the House of Commons.

> **web link**
>
> Website addresses for the UK Parliament include www.publications.parliament.uk and www.parliament.uk

Political representation and responsibility are achieved in a number of ways. For a start, Members of Parliament are directly elected by their constituents and one of the MP's main roles is to represent the constituency for the period between general elections. Apart from holding regular surgeries at which individuals (including businessmen and women) can discuss their problems and views with their representative, MPs also speak on constituency matters in Parliament, frequently raise questions which require answers from government ministers, and generally scrutinise government proposals for any potential effects they may have on the constituency, including key groups within the local electorate (e.g. local businesses). As alluded to previously, there will be occasions when the views of the elected member may differ from those of his or her constituents, particularly those who voted for candidates of an opposing political party, but this does not negate the idea of representation under the British system of parliamentary democracy. MPs represent their constituents first and foremost by having been elected *by them* and hence they provide a direct link between the electorate and the government of the day, which is essentially drawn from the senior members of the majority party in Parliament. In the event of a coalition government (e.g. the UK after the 2010 election), the government will contain representatives of those parties making up the coalition.

Parliament also provides opportunities for the people's representatives to scrutinise and, where necessary, to criticise and challenge the decisions of government. In addition to such parliamentary mechanisms as question time and the adjournment debate, Parliament provides for a system of select committees of **backbench MPs** whose primary role is to scrutinise the work of government departments and other state agencies. Such committees – chaired by both government and opposition backbenchers – are able to question ministers and civil servants, call for departmental papers, cross-examine experts from outside government, and generally investigate the work of the executive, prior to reporting to Parliament on their findings. In bringing their views before Parliament and the public generally (especially through the media), select committees provide a check on government activity and hence form one of the strands by which governments remain answerable to the electorate in the period between elections.

Another significant strand is provided by the opposition, which represents not only an alternative choice of government but also a means of scrutinising and criticising the work of the incumbent administration. Fundamental to this role is the ability of opposition MPs to publicise the decisions of government and to present alternative views to the public via party political broadcasts or promotional literature or debates in parliament, or by general media coverage. Such free and open discussion of issues and policies is a necessary condition for democracy and is an important element in the political education of the nation. Even where governments have large majorities, the role of opposition parties remains a vital component of democracy and helps to provide a curb on unlimited government action.

Turning to its role as a legislative body, there is little doubt that the UK Parliament is largely a legitimising institution, giving formal authority to the wishes of the majority party or coalition. Through its control of the process of legislation, the parliamentary timetable, the flow of information and the votes of its members, the government is able to ensure that its legislative proposals not only come before Parliament but also are almost invariably accepted, even if some delay occurs from time to time in enacting the government's programme, particularly in the event of coalition government where a degree of compromise is often necessary. Opportunities for individual MPs to sponsor legislation (e.g. through private members' bills) are few and far between and the outcome of such proposals depends ultimately on government support (or reluctant acquiescence) if the legislation is to get through its various stages in Parliament. Not surprisingly, this effective stranglehold by the government on the legislative process has led some commentators to talk of an 'elective dictatorship' and to question the true extent of democratic decision-making, particularly when modern governments are invariably elected by less than 50 per cent of the electorate.

The executive branch of government

Putting laws and policies into effect is formally the work of the executive. In the UK this role is carried out by a wide variety of institutions and agencies that is part of the machinery of government. These include the Cabinet, government departments, local authorities, nationalised industries and a large number of other non-departmental public bodies or quasi-autonomous national government agencies, often referred to as 'quangos'.[1] In the discussion below we focus initially on the key institutions at central level since these are fundamental to the process of decision-making in Britain. Discussion of some of the other agencies can be found in subsequent sections of this chapter.

Information on non-departmental public bodies (NDPBs) is available via the Cabinet Office website at *www.gov.uk/government/organisations/cabinet-office*

Under the British system of government, the core of the executive is the Cabinet, headed by the **Prime Minister**, an office of crucial importance given the absence of an elected head of state with effective political powers. British Prime Ministers not only have a number of significant political roles – including leader of the governing party, head of the government and head of the Cabinet – but also have traditionally held a formidable array of political powers, including the power to:

- choose members of the Cabinet;
- choose other non-Cabinet ministers;
- promote, demote or dismiss ministers;
- appoint individuals to chair Cabinet committees;
- appoint top civil servants and oversee the operation of the civil service;
- confer certain appointments and titles; and
- determine the date of the general election within the five-year term of office.

This latter power no longer exists following the decision (in 2011) to institute a system of five-year fixed-term parliaments.

While the existence of such rights and responsibilities does not infer that Prime Ministers will inevitably be all-powerful, it is clear that holders of the office have a key role to play in the decision-making process and much will depend upon how an individual interprets that role, upon their personality and upon the constraints they face (both 'real' and 'imagined') in carrying it out. As the Conservative Prime Minister Mrs Thatcher (1979–90) found to her cost, retaining the office of Prime Minister is dependent not only on the electorate but also on maintaining the support and confidence of parliamentary colleagues in the period between elections. In the event of a coalition government, a Prime Minister also has to take account of the wishes of the other party leaders in the coalition and may involve them in some of the decisions outlined below.

As head of the Cabinet the Prime Minister chairs the committee of senior ministers that is the overall directing force – or board of management – within British central government. Comprising about 20 to 25 ministers who have been appointed by the Prime Minister to head the various government departments (or to fulfil some other important functions), the Cabinet is responsible for directing and coordinating the work of the whole executive machine. Its functions include:

- making decisions on the nature and direction of government policy, including public expenditure, economic policy, defence, foreign relations, industrial policy, and so on;
- overseeing and coordinating the administration of government;

- arbitrating in the event of disputes between ministers or departments;
- discussing, deciding and generally directing the government's legislative programme, including laws relating to business.

A large part of this work, of course, is carried out using a system of committees and subcommittees, comprised of individuals chosen by the Prime Minister (including the chairperson) and supported by a small but powerful secretariat, headed by the Cabinet secretary (a civil servant). Apart from providing an opportunity for more detailed discussions of issues and policies prior to full consideration by the Cabinet, the committee system has the advantage of allowing non-members of the Cabinet (including non-Cabinet ministers and civil servants) to participate in discussions in which they may have an interest. In this way, the system helps to provide a mechanism for communication and coordination between government departments and serves as a training ground for junior ministers, many of whom will subsequently achieve full Cabinet responsibilities. An illustrative list of selected Cabinet committees in July 2013 is shown in Table 4.1.

Table 4.1 Selected Cabinet committees, 2013

Committee name
Coalition Committee
Home Affairs Committee
Economic Affairs Committee
Public Expenditure Committee
Parliamentary Business and Legislation Committee
Banking Reform Committee

Source: Cabinet Office.

Much of the day-to-day work of central government is carried out in vast and complex administrative structures called government departments – a selected list of which is shown in Table 4.2. Working together with a substantial number of executive agencies and other public bodies, **government departments** are usually headed by a Cabinet minister (normally called a **Secretary of State**) and include other ministers outside the Cabinet (e.g. Ministers of State, Parliamentary Under Secretaries of State) who have been appointed by the Prime Minister and who may include individuals drawn from the world of business. Together these ministers constitute the political executive. As the head of a department, the Secretary of State has ultimate responsibility for its work and is answerable to Parliament through the various mechanisms referred to above.[2] In addition, he or she is expected to give overall direction to the work of the department – within the policy of the government as a whole – and to represent its interest in the Cabinet (e.g. over the size and use of its budget), in Parliament (e.g. in steering through legislation) and in the outside world (e.g. in the media). Large areas of this work are delegated to the Ministers of State who assume responsibility for specific areas of departmental work and they in turn will tend to delegate some duties to the department's junior ministers. Such an arrangement not only ensures coverage of the different aspects of a department's responsibilities, it also provides invaluable experience and training for ambitious young MPs appointed to a ministerial post.

Table 4.2 Key government departments, September 2013

Cabinet Office
HM Treasury
Foreign and Commonwealth Office
Business, Innovation and Skills
Communities and Local Government
Energy and Climate Change
Home Office
Environment, Food and Rural Affairs
Defence
Health
Work and Pensions
Culture, Media and Sport

> **web link**
>
> Each government department has its own website with lots of useful material. Examples of current addresses include:
> www.gov.uk/government/organisations/department-for-business-innovation-skills, www.defra.gov.uk, www.gov.uk/government/organisations/hm-treasury

Ministers are assisted in their work by permanent officials, known as **civil servants**, many of whom have spent a large part of their working lives in the government machine and hence are familiar with how it works and how to manipulate it in order to achieve particular objectives. Whereas ministers are politicians, civil servants are administrators vested formally with the task of carrying out the policies of the incumbent government, irrespective of their own political views and preferences. Perhaps not surprisingly, as key advisers to ministers on policy formulation and implementation, senior civil servants can exercise considerable influence over the nature and shape of government policy and legislation.[3] For this reason, individuals or groups seeking to shape government thinking on an issue or piece of legislation frequently 'target' senior departmental officials in the hope of gaining influence in the policy process.

This potential for influence by senior civil servants is, of course, enhanced by the scope and complexities of modern government and by the fact that government ministers have a wide range of non-departmental as well as departmental responsibilities (e.g. as constituency MPs). Ministers consequently rely heavily on their officials for information and advice and civil servants are normally entrusted, under ministers, with the conduct of the whole gamut of government activities, including filling in the details of some legislation. Added to this, the need for policy coordination between departments requires regular meetings between senior officials, in groups that mirror the meetings of Cabinet subcommittees. Since these meetings of officials help to provide the groundwork and briefing papers for future discussions by ministers, they permit civil servants to influence the course of events, especially when a particular line or policy option is agreed by the senior officials in a number of departments.

It is perhaps worth noting at this point that, however pervasive its influence, the civil service is not the only source of policy advice for governments. Apart from traditional bureaucratic channels, ministers often turn to specially appointed bodies for help and guidance in making policy choices. Some of these sources are permanent (or relatively permanent) and include the various executive and advisory bodies set up by past and present governments to assist in the policy process in specific functional areas (e.g. Natural Environment Research Council). Others are temporary, having been specially constituted by government to consider a particular problem and to report on their findings prior to going out of existence (e.g. public inquiries, Royal Commissions). While the appointment of these advisory sources does not oblige the government to follow their advice, they can be regarded as useful sources of information, ideas and advice from outside the formal bureaucratic machine. Moreover, the fact that they tend to have a membership representing a wide cross-section of interests (including representatives of particular pressure groups, industrialists, trade unionists, MPs, academics and others drawn from the list of 'the great and the good') helps to widen the scope of consultation and thus to enhance the democratic process.

The last generation has also seen governments turning increasingly to special advisers and policy planning units for help with policy development. Whereas advisers are individuals appointed by ministers (including the Prime Minister), usually from outside the civil service, policy planning units and/or research units are groups of individuals generally recruited from and located within the government machine, with the aim of providing a range of policy and programme advice to both policy-makers and administrators. Often comprised of young and highly qualified individuals seconded to a unit from a wide range of occupational categories and disciplines (including statisticians, social scientists, economists and general administrators), policy units are a valuable source of information and advice, and their operation at both central and local government level provides policy-makers with detailed research and analysis with which to support their policy judgements.

A further important development has been the increased use of 'focus groups', collections of individual citizens consulted by government on policy proposals prior to legislation and/or implementation. In canvassing the views of individuals affected by government policy, government hopes to improve the policy process in a wide range of areas, including the delivery of public services where there has been a programme to provide round-the-clock availability and (ultimately) complete electronic access. While some see citizens' panels or focus groups as nothing more than a gimmick, others regard their use as a move towards a more modern and democratic form of government with increased levels of public accountability and access to information.

The judicial branch of government

The third arm of government, the judiciary – comprising the judges and the courts – is formally separate from and independent of Parliament and the government, despite the fact that until recently the head of the judiciary, the Lord Chancellor, was both a member of the government and a member of the House of Lords, where he or she presided as Speaker. In essence the role of the judiciary is to put into effect the laws enacted by Parliament and to keep the government within the limits of its powers as laid down in statutes and in common law, as interpreted by the judiciary. Since 1973, it has also been responsible for interpreting European Union law. Given the complexities of the legal system and its relevance to the world of business, it is important to examine this aspect of government in more detail. This is undertaken in Chapter 8.

Appendix 4.2 Subnational government: UK local authorities

Democratic government occurs at subnational as well as national level and takes a wide variety of forms. In addition to the local branches of central government departments and public utilities, many states have local agencies for the administration of justice, local special-purpose authorities (e.g. in the health service) and a system of regional and/or local government, whether under a federal or a unitary arrangement. Such decentralisation and deconcentration of political authority is generally seen as beneficial, since it brings the formulation and administration of policy 'nearer to the people' and is said to provide for decisions that are more sensitive to local needs and aspirations. It can, however, raise the question as to the degree of autonomy of local agencies within a centralised system of government, a controversial and perennial source of debate and dispute in many parts of the world, as recent history has demonstrated.

Within the United Kingdom as a whole, political power is devolved at two main levels: regionally and locally. Scotland, Wales and Northern Ireland have their own directly elected regional assemblies (the Scottish Parliament; the National Assembly for Wales; the Northern Ireland Assembly) and systems of executive government (the Scottish Executive; the Welsh Assembly Government; the Northern Ireland Executive), each with differing levels of devolved authority. The future referendum on independence in Scotland may result in a change in the current system. In England (outside of London), regional government does not currently exist, although voluntary regional chambers or assemblies were set up in the English regions to perform a number of core functions relating to regional issues such as housing development, planning, transport and strategic development. These have now been abolished.

Local government – the focus of this section – has a considerable historical pedigree and remains a key element of the country's system of institutionalised democracy and a major actor in the national as well as the local economy. Given its impact in the business environment, it deserves special attention.

As one form of local administration, local government has a number of distinctive features. For a start it involves self-government by the people of the locality as well as for them, with local authorities exercising considerable discretion in the ways they apply national laws within their areas. In addition, local decision-makers (councillors) are elected to oversee multi-purpose authorities, financed by revenue raised predominantly from local sources – although the proportion from central government has risen in recent years. In short, each local authority constitutes a miniature political and administrative system: each has the institutions and processes of government – including an electoral system, a legislative body (the council), appointed officials (local government officers), party activity, and conflict between individuals and groups within the local community over the allocation of resources and the enforcement of values.

Figure 4.4 illustrates this parallel between the basic operation of government at central and local level. The electorate in each local constituency (district, county, unitary, metropolitan district) periodically choose between candidates who are mostly representing the same parties as those found at national level and the successful candidates

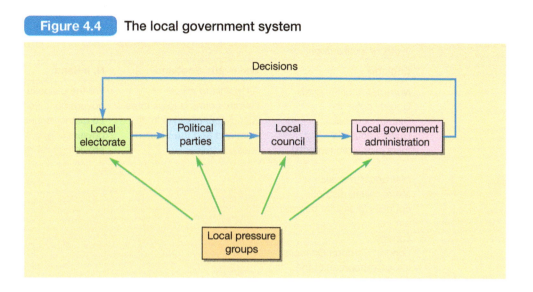

Figure 4.4 The local government system

in the election are elected to represent their constituency in the deliberating body (the council). Senior members of this body are chosen to serve on the various committees and subcommittees, with the leading party on the council having an in-built majority in the committee system, where most decisions have traditionally been made prior to being sanctioned (or not) by the full council. Since the passage of the Local Government Act (2000), councils have been allowed to adopt one of three broad categories of constitution which provide for a separate executive. These three categories are (1) a directly elected mayor with a Cabinet selected by the mayor, (2) a Cabinet either elected by the council or appointed by its leader, and (3) a directly elected mayor and council manager.

For the most part, senior councillors are the political heads of the various local authority departments and agencies (e.g. housing, social services, education and so on) that are responsible for providing those services within the local community which national laws require or, in some cases (e.g. sports centres), do not forbid. Much of this work is carried out by local officials who are appointed by the local authority to administer local services and to advise councillors on policy matters. As the local equivalent of civil servants, local government officers exercise considerable influence over the formulation as well as the implementation of local decisions. For this reason, they too tend to be targeted by local pressure groups which operate at all levels and stages of the political process in their attempts to influence local decision-making.

The current structure of local government in the United Kingdom is illustrated in Table 4.3. In England, outside the metropolitan areas, most 'shire' counties have a two-tier structure of county councils and district, borough or city councils, with the former providing the larger services (e.g. education and social services) while the latter have responsibility for a range of other services (such as housing, leisure, refuse collection and local planning). Elsewhere (e.g. Avon, Cleveland, Humberside, Isle of Wight) 'unitary authorities' have either taken over the functions of the former county and district councils or operate alongside them as all-purpose authorities (e.g. Leicester, York). In the metropolitan areas (including London) the single tier of district councils (or London borough councils) remains unchanged from previous years.

Table 4.3 The structure of UK local government, 2013

Types of local authority		
England	**Wales and Scotland**	**N. Ireland**
Non-metropolitan areas County councils District councils Unitary councils (plus joint arrangements)	*All mainland areas* Unitary councils (plus three island councils in Orkney, Shetland and the Western Isles)	For the purpose of local government Northern Ireland has 26 district councils with limited powers (e.g. collecting rubbish and providing leisure facilities)
Metropolitan areas Metropolitan district councils (plus joint boards)		
London London Borough Councils (plus Corporation of the City of London and joint boards)		

Following legislation in 1994, the two-tier structure in Wales and Scotland was abolished and was replaced (on 1 April 1996) with single-tier, all-purpose, unitary authorities, which have inherited the majority of the functions of the previous councils. In Northern Ireland the system of single-tier district councils remains, although these authorities still have limited responsibility for service provision.

Appendix 4.3 Supranational government: the European Union

Decisions and law affecting business activity are increasingly being made at supranational as well as national and subnational levels. Nowhere is this more evident than in western Europe, where the influence of the European Union is profound. As a significant part of the political environment of the major world economies, the EU deserves special consideration, particularly since its decisions often have global as well as regional consequences – affecting not only firms within its member states but also businesses and governments trading with these states, both directly and indirectly. The following analysis concentrates on the political institutions of the European Union and their relative importance in the process of decision-making.[4] The economic significance of the EU within the international marketplace is discussed in Chapter 16.

The EU's official website, called 'Europa', can be accessed at *europa.eu*
This provides links to lots of other useful sites.

The European Parliament

The **European Parliament** is a directly elected body, at the time of writing constituting 766 members (**MEPs**), with each member state's representation being roughly equivalent to the size of its population. The United Kingdom, for example, has

73 MEPs, elected at five-yearly intervals by UK citizens using a regional list system of proportional representation introduced for the June 1999 European elections.[5] Since voting under a proportional system enhances the prospects of representation by smaller political parties, the European Parliament contains members representing a diversity of political parties who sit in political groups with similar affiliations. Table 4.4 shows, for example, the number of MEPs by broad affiliation as they stood following the 2014 elections. The next elections are due to be held in 2014.

Table 4.4 MEPs by broad affiliation, 2014 election

Political group	Seats
EPP	273
S&D	196
ALDE	83
GREENS/EFA	57
ECR	57
GUE/NGL	35
EFD	31
NI	33
Total	765

Key
EPP: Group of the European People's Party (Christian Democrats)
S&D: Group of the Progressive Alliance of Socialists and Democrats in the European Parliament
ALDE: Group of the Alliance of Liberals and Democrats for Europe
GREENS/EFA: Group of the Greens/European Free Alliance
ECR: European Conservatives and Reformists Group
GUE/NGL: Confederal Group of the European United Left/Nordic Green Left
EFD: Europe of Freedom and Democracy group
NI: Non-attached Members
Source: www.europarl.europa.eu

For information on the European Parliament see www.europarl.europa.eu

The importance of party affiliation is emphasised by the fact that Parliament's organisation is deliberately biased in favour of multinational groupings, with recognition of a political grouping entitling the group to offices, funding, representation on committees and influence in debates and legislation. In order to decide its attitude to an issue or policy proposal coming before the Parliament or one of its committees, a group would normally meet for several days in the week before each session and the issue would be discussed and an agreed line would be decided. As in the case of national parliaments, the attitudes of the political groups have a significant impact on the discussions and decisions within the European Parliament, both in committee and when the House is in full session. Given the number of party groups, however, and the fact that no single group tends to have an absolute majority – unlike in some national parliaments – there is often a need for a group to try to build a coalition of support if it is to achieve its objectives in Parliament. Understandably – and perhaps inevitably – decisions by the European Parliament thus tend to involve compromise between individuals and groups, with the final outcome frequently being a course of action that is acceptable to a majority.

In terms of its role and methods of operation, the European Parliament essentially mirrors national parliaments. Under an elected president who is responsible for directing Parliament's activities and representing it externally and with other EU institutions, much of its detailed work is handled by specialist committees, meeting mostly in Brussels, which report on and offer recommendations to full sessions of the House, which take place in Strasbourg. Membership of each committee is broadly representative of the strengths of the party groupings and the chairmen and women of the permanent committees tend to be influential figures in their own right. In addition to drawing up legislative proposals and carrying out detailed examination and amendment of draft laws, the committees discuss issues (e.g. women's rights, consumer protection, employment), question officials, hold public hearings at which experts and representatives of specialist organisations give evidence, and generally offer their opinion and advice on issues of concern to the EU. As in the case of national parliaments, detailed discussion in committee prior to debate and decision by the full house provides Parliament with an effective means of carrying out its duties and serves as a mechanism for scrutinising the work of both the Council and the Commission.

With regard to its functions, these predominantly fall into five main areas:

Legislation. The Parliament's formal approval is required on most proposals before they can be adopted by the Council of Ministers (see below), i.e. the vast majority of European laws are adopted jointly by the European Parliament and the Council. Under the Lisbon Treaty (2009), the range of issues covered by the co-decision procedure has increased.

The budget. Along with the Council of Ministers, the Parliament acts as the Community's 'budgetary authority' and can reject the Council's draft budget and may modify expenditure proposals on 'non-compulsory' items. It can question the Commission's management of the budget and call in the Court of Auditors.

Supervision. The Parliament supervises the Commission, which it has the power to dismiss by a vote of censure and whose work it scrutinises using a variety of mechanisms. Under the Maastricht Treaty (1992) it has the right to be consulted on the appointment of a new Commission and can veto its appointment. The power of democratic supervision has been extended to other EU institutions, including the Council of Ministers.

Initiative. This includes debates on important regional and international issues and demands for changes to existing policies and/or legislation. Parliament must also approve applications from countries wishing to join the EU.

Relations with national parliaments. The European Parliament holds regular meetings with member states' national parliaments.

In the legislative field, authority traditionally rested with the Council of Ministers and the Commission, and Parliament's role was largely to sanction proposals put before it. Changes under the Single European Act (1986), the Maastricht Treaty (1992), the Amsterdam Treaty (1997), the Nice Treaty (2001) and the Lisbon Treaty (2009) have, however, helped to strengthen Parliament's position by establishing and subsequently extending new procedures for 'assent', 'cooperating' and 'co-decision', now known as the 'Ordinary legislative procedure'. Thus:

- In certain fields an absolute majority of the European Parliament must vote to approve laws before they are passed (e.g. foreign treaties, accession treaties, the Common Agricultural Policy).
- In specified areas Parliament now has a second reading of proposals and its rejection of such proposals can be overturned only by a unanimous decision of the Council of Ministers (e.g. Single Market laws, trans-European networks).

- Parliament can also reject certain legislation by an absolute majority vote if, after the second reading of a proposal and subsequent conciliation, the Council and Parliament are unable to agree (e.g. education and training, health, consumer protection).

The Lisbon Treaty also gave Parliament the power to appoint the President of the European Commission.

The Council of the European Union (the Council of Ministers)

The Council of the European Union (the Council of Ministers) – the Union's ultimate decision-making body – comprises one minister from each of the member states, with participants on the Council varying according to the issue under discussion (e.g. agricultural issues are discussed by Ministers of Agriculture from each state). Meetings of the Council, which are mainly held in Brussels, are chaired predominantly by the minister from the country holding the presidency, which currently rotates on a six-monthly basis (e.g. Greece and Italy held the presidency in 2014). Along with the meetings of ministers are regular meetings of officials (Council Working Groups), together with the work of the Committee of Permanent Representatives of the Member States (COREPER), whose task is to coordinate the groundwork for Union decisions undertaken by the numerous meetings of senior officials. In addition, the Council is serviced by a general secretariat, also based in Brussels.

> **web link**
> The Council of Ministers' website is at www.consilium.europa.eu
> Information is also available through the EU's main website at europa.eu

The role of the Council of Ministers is to make major policy decisions and to respond to legislative proposals put forward mainly by the Commission. Its key roles are to pass EU laws, coordinate EU economic policy, approve the EU budget, sign international agreements and develop EU foreign and defence policies. Major EU decisions require unanimity in the Council, but increasingly, many decisions (especially after the Amsterdam and Nice Treaties) are now being taken by a qualified majority vote (qmv). Member states have weighted votes in the Council that are roughly proportional to their relative population sizes, with the total number of votes being 352 at the time of writing. A qualified majority is reached if two conditions are met: 1) a majority of member states approve (in some cases a two-thirds majority is needed); 2) a minimum of 260 votes is cast in favour of the proposal. In addition, a member state can ask for confirmation that the votes in favour represent at least 62 per cent of the total population of the EU. If not, the decision will not be adopted. From 2014 the system is to be changed so that a proposal will require support by both a majority of countries and a majority (at least 65 per cent) of the total EU population.

While the 'right of initiative' under the Treaties rests with the Commission, the power of decision essentially lies with the Council, which may adopt Commission proposals as drafted, amend them, reject them, or simply take no decision, having consulted the European Parliament and normally a number of other bodies.

If adopted, Council of Ministers' decisions have the force of law and are described as regulations, directives, decisions, or recommendations and opinions. **Regulations** apply directly to all member states and do not have to be confirmed by national parliaments to have binding legal effect. **Directives** lay down compulsory objectives, but leave it to member states to translate them into national legislation. **Decisions** are binding on those states, companies or individuals to which they are addressed, while **recommendations and opinions** have no binding force but merely state the view of the institution that issues them.

The Council's power to pass a law – even if the European Parliament disagrees with it – was reduced under the Maastricht Treaty. In specified policy areas, joint approval is now necessary and MEPs have an effective veto if the two sides cannot reach agreement following conciliation. Moreover, following Maastricht a Committee of the Regions has been established to advise the Commission and the Council on issues concerning the European regions – a development which should help to ensure a stronger regional voice at European level. That said, it is still the case that the Council remains responsible for setting general policy within the EU and relies on the Commission to take decisions on the detailed application of legislation or to adapt legislative details to meet changing circumstances. To this extent – and given the Commission's other responsibilities – the ultimate influence over EU decisions is, to say the very least, open to question, as is often the case at national level.

The European Council

The work of the 'specialist' councils within the Council of Ministers (e.g. Agriculture, Economics and Finance, Employment and Social Affairs) is coordinated by the General Affairs Council, comprising the Foreign Ministers of the member states. This Council is also responsible for preparing for the meetings of the **European Council**, which occur around four times each year. The European Council is attended by the heads of government/state of each member state, the EU's representative for foreign affairs, the President of the Commission and the European Council President, and its work invariably attracts substantial media coverage. Under the chairmanship of its permanent President, the European Council's role is to discuss important policy issues affecting the EU and to set the EU's general political direction and priorities. These so-called 'summits' of heads of governments can have a profound effect on the development of the Union and its institutions.

> **web link** Information on the European Council is available via the Council of Ministers' website. See above.

The European Commission

The **European Commission**, which has its headquarters in Brussels and Luxembourg, is the EU's bureaucratic arm, currently comprising 28 Commissioners (one from each member state), nominated by their respective governments, and a staff of about 23,000 permanent civil servants drawn from all member states. Headed by a President, and organised into **Directorates-General**, each with a Commissioner responsible for its work, the European Commission's role is essentially that of initiator, supervisor and executive. More specifically its tasks are:

- to act as guardian of the Treaties so as to ensure that EU rules and principles are respected and implemented;
- to propose policies and legislation for the European Parliament and Council of Ministers to discuss and, if appropriate, adopt or amend;
- to implement EU policies and supervise the day-to-day running of these policies, including managing the funds that account for most of the EU budget (e.g. EAGGF, ERDF, ECSC);[6]
- to represent the EU internationally (e.g. in the World Trade Organisation).

You can find further information on the Commission at *ec.europa.eu*

In carrying out these duties, the Commissioners are required to act in the interests of the EU as a whole and may not receive instructions from any national government or from any other body (Article 157 of the Treaty of Rome). Moreover, while each Commissioner is responsible for formulating proposals within his or her area of responsibility, the final decision is taken on a collegiate basis and the work is subject to the supervision of the European Parliament. As mentioned above, Parliament is the only body that can force the Commission to resign collectively; interestingly, it has no authority over individual Commissioners, although its endorsement is needed when the President of the Commission and the other Commissioners are appointed.

Much of the undoubted power and influence of the Commission stems from its central involvement in the legislative process. Proposals for consideration by the Council and the Parliament are initially drafted by the Commission, usually following consultation with the Economic and Social Committee (representing the interests of employers, trade unions, farmers, consumers, etc.) and other advisory bodies as appropriate. Moreover, EU Treaties specifically give the Commission the power to make regulations, issue directives, take decisions, make recommendations and deliver opinions, as well as to implement policies based on either Council decisions or Treaty provisions. Thus, while legislative power in the EU in general rests with the Council of Ministers and the EU Parliament, the Commission is also able to legislate in order to implement earlier Council regulations, particularly where technical or routine matters are concerned – a situation that has parallels in the operation of government at national level.

Further powers with regard to specific sectors (e.g. coal and steel) or particular aspects of EU work (e.g. the budget, international agreements) serve to enhance the Commission's influence and to confirm its position as the 'driving force' of the Union. Perhaps understandably, pressure groups seeking to influence the policy process within the European Union regard the Commission as an important institution to target, together with Parliament and the Council of Ministers. Future changes in the relationship between these three institutions will undoubtedly have an effect not only on the legislative process but also on the practice of lobbying within the EU context.

The European Court of Justice

The European Court of Justice, which sits in Luxembourg, comprises twenty-eight judges, who are appointed for a six-year period by consent of the member states, and eight advocates-general. The Court's role is:

- to pass judgment, at the request of a national court, on the interpretation or validity of points of EU law;
- to quash, at the request of an EU institution, government or individual, any measures adopted by the Commission, the Council or national governments which are judged to be incompatible with the existing treaties;
- to consider actions brought by individuals, companies or organisations against EU decisions or actions.

The Court can also be invited to offer an opinion, which then becomes binding, on agreements the EU proposes to undertake with third countries.

Three aspects of its work are particularly worthy of note:

- Individuals as well as member states can bring cases to the Court, and its judgments and interpretations apply to all (i.e. EU institutions, member states, national courts and private citizens) and are backed by a system of penalties for non-compliance.
- Its rulings on matters of European law, which has primacy over national law, are final and its decisions are binding on member countries.
- The Court has tended to follow the principle that EU Treaties should be interpreted with a degree of flexibility so as to take account of changing conditions and circumstances. This has permitted the Community to legislate in areas where there are no specific Treaty provisions, such as the fight against pollution.

> **web link**
> The Court of Justice website can be accessed at *curia.europa.eu*. See also *europa.eu* for general information.

case study — The business of lobbying

A key characteristic of a democratic political system is the right of individuals, groups and organisations to seek to influence government thinking and behaviour. For a business wishing to have its voice heard in official circles, a variety of approaches is possible, ranging from direct appeals to decision-makers to joint action with other firms via an industry body, trade association or a business representative organisation (see Chapter 13). A firm may even consider hiring the services of a professional lobby organisation to act on its behalf.

Professional lobby organisations are essentially businesses that have been specifically set up to influence others on behalf of their clients. Where government decisions are concerned, the complexities of modern political and administrative structures provide numerous opportunities and points of access for professional lobbyists, who often have extensive knowledge of the decision-making process and of the individuals to approach on a given issue. In order to bring influence to bear in the places and institutions where important decisions are made, many lobbying firms have established a presence in major centres of power, including Washington, Brussels and London, often employing hundreds of permanent staff whose job is to lobby for or against a particular policy or piece of legislation according to the needs of their client.

A recent example of how businesses can use the services of professional lobbyists is the case of the EU's Tobacco Products Directive. Concerned over the health implications of smoking for EU citizens, EU member state governments agreed in June 2012 to a proposal that would require mandatory text and picture health warnings covering 75 per cent of the front and back of cigarette packets and to ban the sale of flavoured cigarettes that particularly appeal to younger smokers. A draft directive setting out these requirements was then sent to the European Parliament for a decision on whether to move forward on the issue or to allow time for further amendments.

To protect their interests, the major tobacco companies responded by launching an intense lobbying campaign aimed at potentially sympathetic MEPs whom they hoped would help to persuade others to oppose the suggested measures. Some estimates suggest that Philip Morris International – the makers of the brand Marlboro – alone spent more than €1 million wooing elected representatives to water down the proposals, reputedly employing over 150 staff and consultants during the process prior to the vote in the European Parliament. According to the Corporate Europe Observatory, which monitors the use of corporate lobbying in the EU, the tobacco industry has about 100 full-time lobbyists based in Brussels, with an annual budget of more than €5 million. Given this resource, it is not surprising to learn that a report in *Reuters* on 4 October 2013 claimed that EU officials were concerned that lobbying activity by the industry was threatening to derail the proposed anti-smoking legislation.

When the issue was finally discussed in the Parliament after some delay, the original proposals regarding both the sale and promotion of cigarettes within the EU were considerably scaled back. MEPs rejected the plan to ban 'slim' cigarettes and opted for menthol-flavoured products to be phased out over eight rather than three years as had been proposed. They also agreed to reduce health warnings from 75 per cent to 65 per cent of the packet, the latter evidently having been put forward as a compromise by the industry. Following subsequent negotiations between the Council of the EU and the EP, a revised directive was put forward which included the provision that member states retain the right to introduce more stringent measures, including plain packaging. Differences between the original scheme agreed by EU governments and the new revised plans would need to be resolved ahead of the May 2014 elections for the European Parliament before the directive could come into effect. No doubt the battle is still far from over.

Case study questions

1 Why do governments frequently express concern over the activities of professional lobby organisations?

2 Why do some businesses and industries choose to use such organisations?

Review and discussion questions

1 To what extent do you think a change of government in your country would affect the business community?

2 Many top civil servants take directorships in large companies on retirement from government. Why should companies be keen to recruit retired bureaucrats?

3 How far is the enlargement of the European Union likely to benefit UK businesses?

4 In what ways could a business organisation seek to influence central government decision-makers on issues in which it has an interest (e.g. taxes on company profits or the level of interest rates)?

Assignments

1 You are employed as a research assistant by a group representing the interests of small and medium-sized enterprises (e.g. a Chamber of Commerce). Using contemporary source material (e.g. the internet, manifestos, etc.), produce a draft report highlighting current government policy for the SME sector.

2 Imagine you are employed as a political lobbyist, with a special interest in conservation issues. You have been approached by a local conservation group, which is concerned about government plans to build a bypass round a village in its area. The government's proposals for the road would cause significant damage to a Site of Special Scientific Interest (SSSI) and the group is determined to oppose the plans. Your brief is to draft an 'action plan' for the group, indicating what forms of pressure group activity you would recommend, in what sequence and using which channels of potential influence.

Notes and references

1 See, for example, Barker, A., *Quangos in Britain,* Macmillan, 1982; Ridley, F. F. and Wilson, D. (eds), *The Quango Debate,* Oxford University Press/Hansard Society, 1995; Pollitt, C. and Talbot, C., *Unbundled Government,* Routledge, 2004.

2 Individual ministerial responsibility should not be confused with collective Cabinet responsibility, both of which apply to Ministers of the Crown.

3 Senior civil servants who are in a position to influence policy are sometimes called 'mandarins', a term that applies to a very small percentage of the civil service. Most civil servants are engaged in more routine administrative work, including providing services directly to the public (e.g. paying benefits and pensions).

4 There are numerous books on the EU. Students can also gain information by contacting EU institutions directly, particularly through their national offices, or by accessing the numerous websites.

5 The UK's continued membership of the EU is somewhat uncertain following the proposal – by the majority party in the current government – to hold an in/out referendum in 2017, assuming it is returned to office in the 2015 general election. The result of the Scottish referendum on independence could also complicate the picture further.

6 European Agriculture Guarantee and Guidance Fund (EAGGF); European Regional Development Fund (ERDF); European Coal and Steel Community (ECSC). See Chapter 13 for a further discussion of EU structural funds.

Further reading

Cocker, P. and Jones, A., *Contemporary British Politics and Government,* 4th edition, Liverpool Academic Press/Cambridge Media Group, 2014 (forthcoming).

Coen, D. and Richardson, J., *Lobbying the European Union: Institutions, Actors and Issues,* Oxford University Press, 2009.

Hix, S., *The Political System of the European Union,* 2nd edition, Palgrave Macmillan, 2005.

Kavanagh, D. and Moran, M., *Politics UK,* Pearson Education, 2007.

Leach, R., Coxall, W. and Robins, L., *British Politics,* Palgrave Macmillan, 2011.

Massey, A. and Pyper, R., *Public Management and Modernisation in Britain,* Palgrave Macmillan, 2005.

Moran, M., *Politics and Governance in the UK,* 2nd edition, Palgrave Macmillan, 2011.

Peterson, J. and Shackleton, M. (eds), *The Institutions of the European Union,* 3rd edition, Oxford University Press, 2012.

Wilson, D. and Game, C., *Local Government in the United Kingdom,* Palgrave Macmillan, 2011.

**Web links and further questions are available on the website at:
www.pearsoned.co.uk/worthington**

Leach, R., Coxall, W. and Robins, L., British Politics, Palgrave Macmillan, 2011.

Massey, A. and Pyper, R., Public Management and Modernisation in Britain, Palgrave Macmillan, 2005.

Moran, M., Politics and Governance in the UK, 2nd edition, Palgrave Macmillan, 2011.

Peterson, J. and Shackleton, M. (eds), The Institutions of the European Union, 3rd edition, Oxford University Press, 2012.

Wilson, D. and Game, C., Local Government in the United Kingdom, Palgrave Macmillan, 2011.

5 The macroeconomic environment

Ian Worthington

Business organisations operate in an economic environment which shapes, and is shaped by, their activities. In market-based economies this environment comprises variables that are dynamic, interactive and mobile and which, in part, are affected by government in pursuit of its various roles in the economy. As a vital component in the macroeconomy, government exercises a significant degree of influence over the flow of income and hence over the level and pattern of output by the public and private sectors. Other key influences include a country's financial institutions and the international economic organisations and groupings to which it belongs or subscribes.

Learning outcomes

Having read this chapter you should be able to:

- compare alternative economic systems and their underlying principles and discuss the problems of transition from a centrally planned to a market-based economy
- illustrate flows of income, output and expenditure in a market economy and account for changes in the level and pattern of economic activity
- analyse the role of government in the macroeconomy, including government macroeconomic policies and the objectives on which they are based
- explain the role of financial institutions
- identify the key international economic institutions and organisations that influence the business environment in open, market economies

Key terms

Accelerator effect
Aggregate monetary demand
Balance of payments
Capital market
Capitalist economy
Central bank
Centrally planned economy
Circular flow of income model
Consumer Price Index (CPI)
Consumer sovereignty
Credit rating agency
Crowding out
Cyclical unemployment
Deindustrialisation
Direct controls
Direct taxation
Economic growth
Economic scarcity
Economics
European Central Bank (ECB)

Exchange rate
Factory gate prices
Financial intermediaries
Fiscal policy
Free-market economy
Full employment
Government spending
Gross domestic product
Headline inflation
Income flows
Indirect taxation
Inflation
Injections
Interest rates
Leakages
Macroeconomic analysis
Macroeconomic environment
Microeconomic analysis
Monetary aggregates
Monetary policies

Money market
Money stock
Multiplier effect
National debt
Opportunity cost
Public sector net borrowing
Quantitative easing (QE)
Real cost
Real flows
Real interest rates
Real national income
Recession
Retail Price Index (RPI)
State bank
Stock exchange
Structural unemployment
Technological unemployment
Underlying rate of inflation
Wages/prices inflationary spiral
Withdrawals

Introduction

In April 2013, Japan's central bank announced its intention to embark on a huge programme of quantitative easing (see the case study at the end of this chapter) aimed at boosting the Japanese economy and ridding it of the deflation that had haunted the country for more than a decade. The plan was for the Bank of Japan to create new money and use it to buy trillions of yen worth of government bonds each month in the hope of increasing the overall level of demand, thereby pushing up both prices and wages. Part of a set of new macroeconomic policies known as 'Abenomics' – after Japan's new Prime Minister, Shinzo Abe – the scheme to effectively double the country's money supply had the support of the Bank of Japan, the Ministry of Finance and the private sector, which saw it as a means of persuading individuals to spend rather than hoard cash. Similar schemes in other countries, including the USA and the UK, represent one form of interventionary approach by governmental policy-makers aimed at steering the economy along a particular path thought to be beneficial for consumers and businesses alike.

What this simple example is designed to demonstrate is the intimate relationship between business activity and the wider economic context in which it takes place, and a glance at any quality newspaper will provide a range of similar illustrations of this interface between business and **economics**. What is important at this point is not to understand the complexities of global economic forces or their effect on businesses but to appreciate in broad terms the importance of the **macroeconomic environment** for business organisations and, in particular, the degree of compatibility between the preoccupations of the entrepreneur and those of the economist. To the economist, for example, a recession is generally marked by falling demand, rising unemployment, a slowing down in economic growth and a fall in investment. To the firm, it usually implies a loss of orders, a likely reduction in the workforce, a decline in output (or a growth in stocks) and a general reluctance to invest in capital equipment and/or new projects.

Much of the detailed discussion of the economic aspects of business can be found in Parts Three and Four. In this chapter we concentrate on the broader question of the economic structure and processes of a market-based economy and on the macroeconomic influences affecting and being affected by business activity in this type of economic system. As suggested in the previous chapter, an understanding of the overall economic context within which businesses operate – including its core values and principles – is central to any meaningful analysis of the business environment.

Three further points are worth highlighting at this juncture. First, business activity not only is shaped by the economic context in which it takes place but helps to shape that context; consequently the success or otherwise of government economic policy depends to some degree on the reactions of both the firms and the markets (e.g. the stock market) that are affected by government decisions. Second, economic influences operate at a variety of spatial levels, as illustrated by the opening paragraph, and governments can sometimes find that circumstances largely or totally beyond their control can affect businesses, either favourably or adversely. Third, the economic (and for that matter, political) influence of industry and commerce can be considerable and this ensures that business organisations – both individually and collectively – usually constitute one of the chief pressure groups in democratic states. This political and economic relationship between government and business is discussed more fully in Chapter 13.

Economic systems

The concept of economic scarcity

Like politics, the term 'economic' tends to be used in a variety of ways and contexts to describe certain aspects of human behaviour, ranging from activities such as producing, distributing and consuming, to the idea of frugality in the use of a resource (e.g. being 'economical' with the truth). Modern definitions stress how such behaviour, and the institutions in which it takes place (e.g. households, firms, governments, banks), are concerned with the satisfaction of human needs and wants through the transformation of resources into goods and services which are consumed by society. These processes are said to take place under conditions of **economic scarcity**.

The economist's idea of 'scarcity' centres on the relationship between a society's needs and wants and the resources available to satisfy them, the argument being that whereas needs and wants tend to be unlimited, the resources that can be used to meet those needs and wants are finite such that no society at any time has the capacity to provide for all its actual or potential requirements. The assumption here is that both individual and collective needs and wants consistently outstrip the means available to satisfy them, as exemplified, for instance, by the inability of governments to provide instant health care, the best roads, education, defence, railways and so on at a time and place and of a quality convenient to the user. This being the case, 'choices' have to be made by both individuals and society concerning priorities in the use of resources, and every choice inevitably involves a 'sacrifice' (i.e. forgoing an alternative). Economists describe this sacrifice as the **opportunity cost** or **real cost** of the decision that is taken (e.g. every pound spent on the health service is a pound not spent on some other public service) and it is one faced by individuals, organisations (including firms), governments and society alike.

From a societal point of view the existence of economic scarcity poses three serious problems concerning the use of resources:

1. What to use the available resources for. That is, what goods and services should be produced (or not produced) with the resources (sometimes described as the 'guns v. butter' argument)?
2. How best to use those resources. For example, in what combinations, using what techniques and what methods?
3. How best to distribute the goods and services produced with them. That is, who gets what, how much and on what basis?

In practice, of course, these problems tend to be solved in a variety of ways, including barter (voluntary, bilateral exchange), price signals and the market, queuing and rationing, government instruction and corruption (e.g. resources allocated in exchange for personal favours), and examples of each of these solutions can be found in most, if not all, societies, at all times. Normally, however, one or other main approach to resource allocation tends to predominate and this allows analytical distinctions to be made between different types of economic system, one important distinction being between those economies that are centrally planned and those that operate predominantly through market forces where prices form the integrating mechanism. Understanding this distinction is fundamental to an examination of the way in which business is conducted and represents the foundation on which much of the subsequent analysis is built.

The centrally planned economy

In this type of economic system – associated with the post-Second World War socialist economies of eastern Europe, China, Cuba and elsewhere – most of the key decisions on production are taken by a central planning authority, normally the state and its agencies. Under this arrangement, the state typically:

- owns and/or controls the main economic resources;
- establishes priorities in the use of those resources;
- sets output targets for businesses which are largely under state ownership and/or control;
- directs resources in an effort to achieve these predetermined targets; and
- seeks to coordinate production in such a way as to ensure consistency between output and input demands.

The fact that an economy is centrally planned does not necessarily imply that all economic decisions are taken at central level; in many cases decision-making may be devolved to subordinate agencies, including local committees and enterprises. Ultimately, however, these agencies are responsible to the centre and it is the latter which retains overall control of the economy and directs the use of scarce productive resources.

The problem of coordinating inputs and output in a modern planned economy is, of course, a daunting task and one which invariably involves an array of state planners and a central plan or blueprint normally covering a number of years (e.g. a five-year plan). Under such a plan, the state planners establish annual output targets for each sector of the economy and for each enterprise within the sector, identify the inputs of materials, labour and capital needed to achieve the set targets and allocate resources accordingly. Given that the outputs of some industries (e.g. agricultural machinery) are the inputs of others (e.g. collective farms), it is not difficult to see how the overall effectiveness of the plan would depend in part on a high degree of cooperation and coordination between sectors and enterprises, as well as on good judgement, good decisions and a considerable element of good luck. The available evidence from planned economies suggests that none of these can be taken for granted and each is often in short supply.

Even in the most centralised of economies, state planning does not normally extend to telling individuals what they must buy in shops or how to use their labour, although an element of state direction at times may exist (e.g. conscription of the armed forces). Instead, it tends to condition *what* is available for purchase and the *prices* at which exchange takes place, and both of these are essentially the outcome of political choices, rather than a reflection of consumer demands. All too often consumers tend to be faced by queues and 'black markets' for some consumer products and overproduction of others, as state enterprises strive to meet targets frequently unrelated to the needs and wants of consumers. By the same token, businesses that make losses do not have to close down, as the state would normally make additional funds available to cover any difference between sales revenue and costs. This being the case, the emphasis at firm level tends to be more on meeting targets than on achieving efficiency in the use of resources and hence a considerable degree of duplication and wastage tends to occur.

Given such an environment, the traditional entrepreneurial skills of efficient resource management, price setting and risk taking have little, if any, scope for development and managers behave essentially as technicians and bureaucrats, administering decisions largely made elsewhere. Firms, in effect, are mainly servants of the state and their activities are conditioned by social and political considerations, rather than by the needs of the market – although some market activity normally occurs in planned economies (especially in agriculture and a number of private services). Accordingly, businesses and their employees are not fully sensitised to the needs of the consumer and as a result quality and choice (where they exist) may suffer, particularly where incentives to improved efficiency and performance are negligible. Equally, the system tends to encourage bribery and corruption and the development of a substantial black market, with differences in income, status and political influence being important determinants of individual consumption and of living standards.

The free-market economy

The **free-market economy** (or **capitalist economy**) stands in direct contrast to the centrally planned system. Whereas in the latter the state controls most economic decisions, in the former the key economic agencies are private individuals (sometimes called 'households') and firms, and these interact in free markets, through a system of prices, to determine the allocation of resources.

The key features of this type of economic system are as follows:

- Resources are in private ownership and the individuals owning them are free to use them as they wish.
- Firms, also in private ownership, are equally able to make decisions on production, free from state interference.
- No blueprint (or master plan) exists to direct production and consumption.
- Decisions on resource allocation are the result of a decentralised system of markets and prices, in which the decisions of millions of consumers and hundreds of thousands of firms are automatically coordinated.
- The consumer is deemed to be sovereign, i.e. dictates the pattern of supply and hence the pattern of resource allocation.

In short, the three problems of what to produce, how to produce and how to distribute are solved by market forces.

Figure 5.1 illustrates the basic operation of a market economy. Individuals are owners of resources (e.g. labour) and consumers of products; firms are users of resources and producers of products. What products are produced – and hence how resources are used – depends on consumers, who indicate their demands by purchasing (i.e. paying the price) or not purchasing, and this acts as a signal to producers to acquire the resources necessary (i.e. pay the price) to meet the preferences of consumers. If consumer demands change, for whatever reason, this will cause an automatic reallocation of resources, as firms respond to the new market conditions. Equally, competition between producers seeking to gain or retain customers is said to guarantee that resources are used efficiently and to ensure that the most appropriate production methods (i.e. how to produce) are employed in the pursuit of profits.

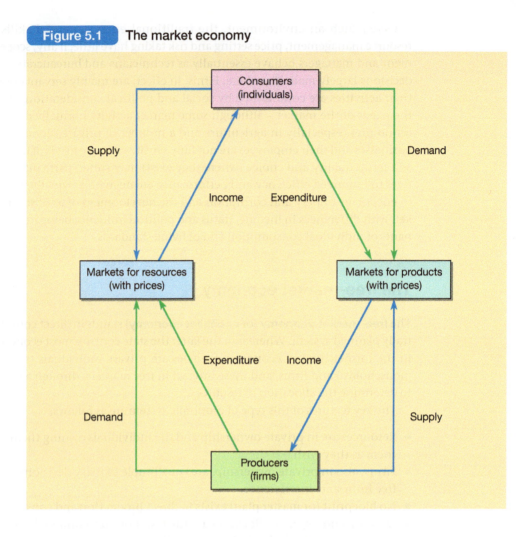

Figure 5.1 The market economy

The distribution of output is also determined by market forces, in this case operating in the markets for productive services. Individuals supplying a resource (e.g. labour) receive an income (i.e. a price) from the firms using that resource and this allows them to purchase goods and services in the markets for products, which in turn provides an income for firms that can be spent on the purchase of further resources (see below). Should the demand for a particular type of productive resource increase – say, as a result of an increase in the demand for the product produced by that resource – the price paid to the provider of the resource will tend to rise and hence, other things being equal, allow more output to be purchased. Concomitantly, it is also likely to result in a shift of resources from uses which are relatively less lucrative to those which are relatively more rewarding.

This matching of supply and demand through prices in markets is described in detail in Chapter 14 and the analysis can also be applied to the market for foreign currencies (see Chapter 16). In practice, of course, no economy operates entirely in the manner suggested above; after all, firms are influenced by costs and supply decisions as well as by demand and generally seek to shape that demand, as well as simply responding to it. Nor for that matter is a market-based economy devoid of government involvement in the process of resource allocation, as evidenced by the existence of a public sector responsible for substantial levels of consumption and output and for helping to shape the conditions under which the private sector operates. In short, any study of the market economy needs to incorporate the role of government and to examine, in particular, its influence on the activities of both firms and households. Such an analysis can be found in the later sections of this chapter.

Economies in transition

Most of the world's economies operate under a predominantly market-based system and the **centrally planned economy** in its original form is now largely a rare phenomenon. Three decades of reform have seen the old planned systems in eastern Europe and elsewhere gradually giving way to the march of free enterprise, with some former communist states (e.g. Czech Republic) now members of the European Union (see Chapter 16), while others – including Russia, China and Cuba – have gradually been experimenting with schemes aimed at developing an entrepreneurial culture and introducing capitalist market principles. Allowing business start-ups and expansion, deregulating some markets, partial privatisation of industries and sectors and encouraging foreign investment are just some of the ways in which this economic transition has been taking place.

For states anxious to move from an entrenched system of state planning to a market-based economic system, the obstacles can be formidable and can help to slow down the progress of economic (and political) reform. For example, among the problems faced by eastern European countries in the transitionary phase were:

- the need to create a legal and commercial framework to support the change to a market economy (e.g. company laws, laws on property rights, competition, external trade, the development of an appropriate accounting system);
- the need to establish different forms of free enterprise and to develop financial institutions capable of providing risk and venture capital, at commercial rates of return;
- the need to develop truly competitive markets, free from state control and protection;
- the need to liberalise labour markets and to develop entrepreneurial skills in a workforce traditionally demotivated by the old bureaucratic system;
- the need to allow prices to move to levels determined by market forces, rather than by political decision;
- the need to achieve macroeconomic stability as markets become more open, both internally and externally;
- the need to reduce the burden of international debt;
- the need to attract substantial overseas investment to assist in the rebuilding of the collapsed old socialist economies.

Meeting these requirements was not made any easier by economic collapse and the perceived need on the part of some reformers to bring about rapid economic change whatever the consequences. In Russia, in particular, widespread bribery, corruption and criminal activity have continued to undermine an economy struggling with economic and political instability that appears endemic and on occasions this has had a negative impact on foreign investment. We should not be surprised if the moves to restructure state economies prove a long and painful process for some countries in the coming years.

Politico-economic synthesis

The economic problem of resource allocation, described above, clearly has a political dimension, given its focus on the ownership, control and use of wealth-producing assets within society. This allows links to be made between a country's chosen economic system and its political regime. A useful way of representing possible relationships is illustrated in Figure 5.2. As suggested in Chapter 4, political systems can be characterised as ranging from democratic to authoritarian, depending on the degree of public involvement in decision-making processes. Similarly, economic systems can be seen to range from free market to planned, according to the level of state intervention in the process of resource allocation. This two-dimensional model thus provides for four major combinations of politico-economic systems, ranging from democratic–free-market on the one hand (quadrant 1) to authoritarian–planned on the other (quadrant 3).

In applying this model to specific cases, it is clear that free-market approaches to resource allocation have predominantly been associated with democratic states. Such a link is not surprising. Democracy, after all, includes the notion of individuals being able to express their preferences through the ballot box and having the opportunity to replace one government with another at periodic intervals. In free markets, similar processes are at work, with individuals effectively 'voting' for goods and services through the price system and their expressed preferences being reflected in the pattern of resource allocation.

A link between authoritarian regimes and planned economic systems can equally be rationalised, in that government control over the political system is considerably facilitated if it also directs the economy through the ownership and/or control of the means of production, distribution and exchange. In effect, the relative absence of democratic mechanisms, such as free elections and choice between alternative forms of

Figure 5.2 Politico-economic systems

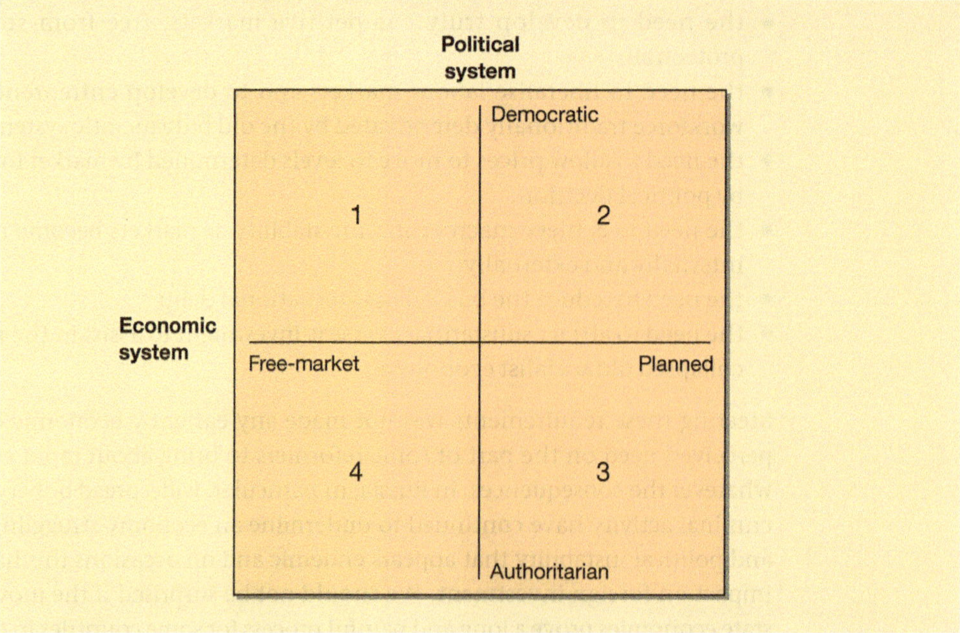

government, is echoed in the economic sphere by the inability of individuals to exercise any real influence over resource allocation. At the extreme, this could involve a government ban on any forms of free enterprise and total government control of the pattern of output and consumption in an economy which is devoid of effective **consumer sovereignty**.

Naturally the true picture is much more complicated than suggested by this simple dichotomy. Some authoritarian states, for instance, have predominantly capitalist economic systems (quadrant 4), while some democratic countries have a substantial degree of government intervention (i.e. moving them towards quadrant 2), either by choice or from necessity (e.g. wartime). Added to this, even in states where the political or economic system appears to be the same, considerable differences can occur at an operational and/or institutional level and this gives each country a degree of uniqueness not adequately portrayed by the model. That said, it is still the case that the basic congruity between democracy and free-market systems represents a powerful and pervasive influence in the business environment of the world's principal democratic states. The process of economic reform – as in eastern Europe – accordingly tends to be accompanied by corresponding pressures for political change and these are often resisted by regimes not prepared to give up their political and economic powers and their élite status.

The macroeconomy

Levels of analysis

As indicated above, economics is concerned with the study of how society deals with the problem of scarcity and the resultant problems of what to produce, how to produce and how to distribute. Within this broad framework the economist typically distinguishes between two types of analysis:

1 **Microeconomic analysis**, which is concerned with the study of economic decision-taking by both individuals and firms.
2 **Macroeconomic analysis**, which is concerned with interactions in the economy as a whole (i.e. with economic aggregates).

The microeconomic approach is exemplified by the analysis of markets and prices undertaken in Chapter 14, which shows how individual consumers in a market might be affected by a price change. This analysis could be extended to an investigation of how the total market might respond to a movement in the price, or how a firm's (or market's) decisions on supply are affected by changes in wage rates or production techniques or some other factor. Note that in these examples, the focus of attention is on decision-taking by individuals and firms in a single industry, while interactions between this industry and the rest of the economy are ignored; this is what economists call a 'partial analysis'.

In the real world all sectors of the economy are interrelated to some degree. A pay award, for example, in a particular industry (or in a single firm) may set a new pay norm that workers in other industries take up and these pay increases may subsequently influence employment, production and consumer demand in the economy as a whole, which could also have repercussions on the demand for a given product. Sometimes such repercussions may be relatively minor and so effectively can be ignored. In such situations the basic microeconomic approach remains valid.

The macroeconomics perspective recognises the interdependent nature of markets and therefore studies interactions in the economy as a whole, dealing with such questions as the overall level of employment, the rate of inflation, the percentage growth of output in the economy and many other economy-wide aggregates – exemplified by the analysis of international trade in Chapter 16 and by the macroeconomic model discussed below. It is worth noting that while the distinction between the micro and macro approaches remains useful for analytical purposes, in many instances the two become intertwined. For example, the reference at the start of this chapter to Japan's manipulation of the monetary base to overcome deflation in the economy is clearly a macroeconomic proposition. The idea that this approach will encourage households to spend rather than hoard cash leans heavily on microeconomic analysis, including notions of consumer preferences and anticipated price rises. Given that macroeconomic phenomena are the result of aggregating the behaviour of individual firms and consumers, this is obviously a common situation and one that is useful to bear in mind in any study of either the firm or the economy as a whole.

The 'flows' of economic activity

Economic activity can be portrayed as a flow of economic resources into firms (i.e. productive organisations) which are used to produce output for consumption, and a corresponding flow of payments from firms to the providers of those resources who use them primarily to purchase the goods and services produced. These flows of resources, production, income and expenditure accordingly represent the fundamental activities of an economy at work. Figure 5.3 illustrates the flow of resources and of goods and services in the economy – what economists describe as **real flows**.

In effect, firms use economic resources to produce goods and services, which are consumed by private individuals (private domestic consumption) or government (government

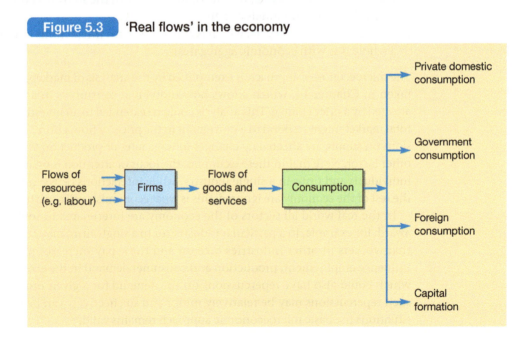

Figure 5.3 'Real flows' in the economy

consumption) or by overseas purchasers (foreign consumption) or by other firms (capital formation). This consumption gives rise to a flow of expenditures that represents an income for firms, which they use to purchase further resources in order to produce further output for consumption. This flow of income and expenditures is shown in Figure 5.4.

The interrelationship between **income flows** and real flows can be seen by combining the two figures into one, which for the sake of simplification assumes only two groups operate in the economy: firms as producers and users of resources, and private individuals as consumers and providers of those resources (see Figure 5.5). Real flows are shown by the arrows moving in an anti-clockwise direction, income flows by the arrows flowing in a clockwise direction.

Despite a degree of oversimplification, the model of the economy illustrated in Figure 5.5 is a useful analytical tool, which highlights some vital aspects of economic activity of direct relevance to the study of business. The model shows that:

1 Income flows around the economy, passing from households to firms and back to households and on to firms and so on, with these income flows having corresponding real flows of resources, goods and services.
2 What constitutes an income to one group (e.g. firms) represents an expenditure to another (e.g. households), indicating that income generation in the economy is related to spending on consumption of goods and services and on resources (e.g. the use of labour).
3 The output of firms must be related to expenditure by households on goods and services, which in turn is related to the income the latter receive from supplying resources.
4 The use of resources (including the number of jobs created in the economy) must also be related to expenditure by households on consumption, given that resources are used to produce output for sale to households.
5 Levels of income, output, expenditure and employment in the economy are, in effect, interrelated.

Figure 5.4 Income flows in the economy

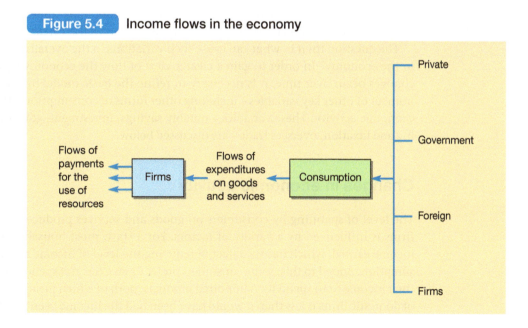

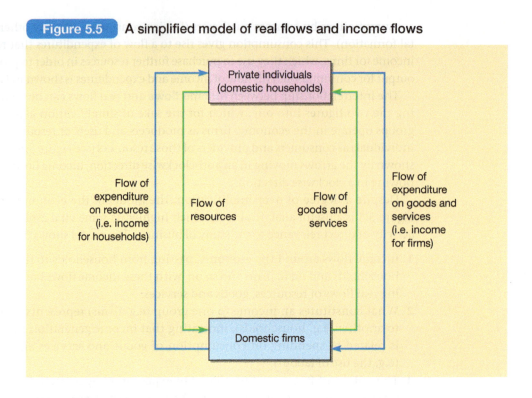

Figure 5.5 A simplified model of real flows and income flows

From the point of view of firms, it is clear from the model that their fortunes are intimately connected with the spending decisions of households and any changes in the level of spending can have repercussions for business activity at the micro as well as at the macro level. In a recession, an overall fall in demand can cause some businesses to close down while others experience a reduction in turnover and may be forced to make some staff redundant and/or delay investment decisions. As unemployment grows and investment is postponed or cancelled, demand may fall further and this will have a negative impact on many businesses. Once the economy gradually recovers and business confidence returns, many firms generally find the order book improves and this can have a positive effect on investment and employment as well as on turnover and profits.

The question then is, what can cause such variations in the overall level of spending in the economy? In order to gain a clearer view of how the economy works and why changes occur over time, it is necessary to refine the basic model by incorporating a number of other key variables – including other forms of consumption – that influence economic activity. These variables – notably savings, investment, government spending and taxation, overseas trade – are discussed below.

Changes in economic activity

The level of spending by consumers on goods and services produced by indigenous firms is influenced by a variety of factors. For a start, most households pay tax on income earned, which has the effect of reducing the level of income available for consumption. Added to this, some consumers prefer to save (i.e. not spend) a proportion of their income or to spend it on imported products, both of which mean that the income of domestic firms is less than it would have been had the income been spent with them.

Figure 5.6 The circular flow of income with 'leakages'

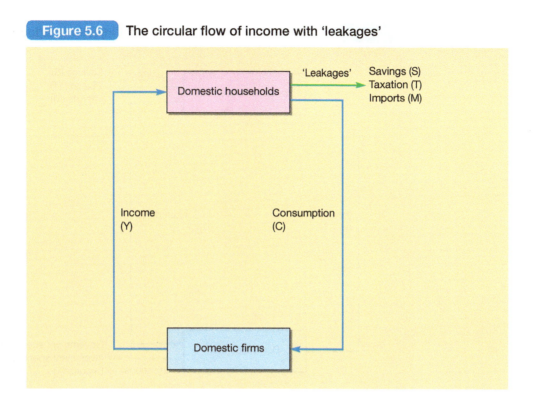

Circumstances such as these represent what economists call a **leakage** (or **withdrawal**) from the **circular flow of income** and help to explain why the revenue of businesses can fluctuate over time (see Figure 5.6).

At the same time as such 'leakages' are occurring, additional forms of spending in the economy are helping to boost the potential income of domestic firms. Savings by some consumers may be borrowed by firms to spend on investment in capital equipment or plant or premises (known as investment spending) and this generates income for firms producing capital goods. Similarly, governments use taxation to spend on the provision of public goods and services (public or government expenditure) and overseas buyers purchase products produced by indigenous firms (export spending). Together, these additional forms of spending represent an **injection** of income into the circular flow (see Figure 5.7).

While the revised model of the economy illustrated in Figure 5.7 is still highly simplified (e.g. consumers also borrow savings to spend on consumption or imports; firms also save and buy imports; governments also invest in capital projects), it demonstrates quite clearly that fluctuations in the level of economic activity are the result of changes in a number of variables, many of which are outside the control of firms or governments. Some of these changes are autonomous (i.e. spontaneous), as in the case of an increased demand for imports, while others may be deliberate or overt, as when the government decides to increase its own spending or to reduce taxation in order to stimulate demand. Equally, from time to time an economy may be subject to 'external shocks', such as the onset of recession among its principal trading partners or a significant price rise in a key commodity (e.g. oil price rises in 2007–8), which can have an important effect on internal income flows. Taken together, these and other changes help to explain why demand for goods and services constantly fluctuates and why changes occur not only

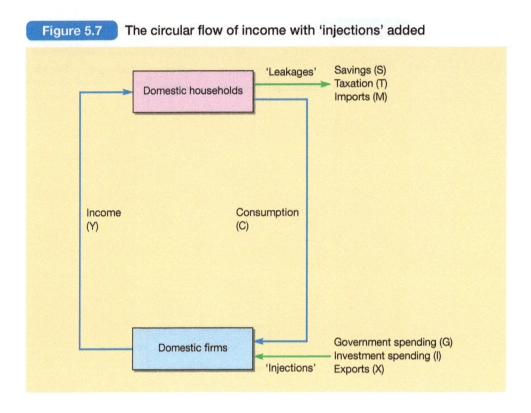

Figure 5.7 The circular flow of income with 'injections' added

in an economy's capacity to produce output but also in its structure and performance over time.

It is important to recognise that where changes in spending do occur, these invariably have consequences for the economy that go beyond the initial 'injection' or 'withdrawal' of income. For example, a decision by government to increase spending on infrastructure would benefit the firms involved in the various projects and some of the additional income they receive would undoubtedly be spent on hiring labour. The additional workers employed would have more income to spend on consumption and this would boost the income for firms producing consumer goods, which in turn might hire more staff, generating further consumption and so on. In short, the initial increase in spending by government will have additional effects on income and spending in the economy, as the extra spending circulates from households to firms and back again. Economists refer to this as the **multiplier effect** to emphasise the reverberative consequences of any increase or decrease in spending by consumers, firms, governments or overseas buyers.

Multiple increases in income and consumption can also give rise to an **accelerator effect**, which is the term used to describe a change in investment spending by firms as a result of a change in consumer spending. In the example above it is possible that the increase in consumption caused by the increase in government spending might persuade some firms to invest in more stock and capital equipment to meet increased consumer demands. Demand for capital goods would therefore rise, and this could cause further increases in the demand for industrial products (e.g. components, machinery) and also for consumer goods, as firms seek to increase their output to meet the changing market conditions. Should consumer spending fall, a reverse accelerator may occur and the same would apply to the multiplier as the reduction in consumption reverberates through the economy and causes further cuts in both consumption and investment. As the late Peter Donaldson has suggested, everything in the economy affects everything else; the economy is dynamic, interactive and mobile and is far more complex than implied by the model used in the analysis above.[1]

Government and the macroeconomy: objectives

Notwithstanding the complexities of the real economy, the link between business activity and spending is clear to see. This spending, as indicated above, comes from consumers, firms, governments and external sources and collectively can be said to represent total demand in the economy for goods and services. Economists frequently indicate this with the following notation:

Aggregate monetary demand = Consumer spending + Investment spending
+ Government spending + Export spending
− Import spending

or $\qquad$ AMD = C + I + G + X − M

Within this equation, consumer spending (C) is regarded as by far the most important factor in determining the level of total demand.

While economists might disagree about what are the most significant influences on the component elements of AMD, it is widely accepted that governments have a crucial role to play in shaping demand, not only in their own sector but also on the market side of the economy. Government policies on spending and taxation, or on interest rates, clearly have both a direct and indirect influence on the behaviour of individuals and firms, which can affect both the demand and supply sides of the economy in a variety of ways. Underlying these policies is a number of key objectives pursued by government as a prerequisite to a healthy economy and which help to guide the choice of policy options. Understanding the broad choice of policies available to government, and the objectives associated with them, is of prime importance to students of the business environment.

Most governments appear to have a number of key economic objectives, the most important of which are normally the control of inflation, the pursuit of economic growth, a reduction in unemployment, the achievement of an acceptable balance of payments situation, controlling public (i.e. government) borrowing, and a relatively stable exchange rate.

Controlling inflation

Inflation is usually defined as an upward and persistent movement in the general level of prices over a given period of time; it can also be characterised as a fall in the value of money. For governments of all political complexions, reducing such movements to a minimum is seen as a primary economic objective (e.g. under the **Consumer Price Index** the UK government's declared inflation target is 2 per cent).

Monitoring trends in periodic price movements tends to take a number of forms. In the UK these have included:

1. The use of a **Retail Price Index (RPI)**, which measures how an average family's spending on goods and services is affected by price changes. The RPI has traditionally been the measure used for **headline inflation** in the UK and includes mortgage interest payments.
2. An examination of the **underlying rate of inflation**, which excludes the effects of mortgage payments (known as RPIX in the UK).
3. Measuring **factory gate prices**, to indicate likely future changes in consumer prices.
4. Comparing domestic inflation rates with those of the United Kingdom's chief overseas competitors, as an indication of the international competitiveness of UK firms.

With regard to the latter, the UK now uses a new measure of inflation known as the Consumer Price Index (CPI) to allow for a more direct comparison of the inflation rate in the UK with that of the rest of Europe. The CPI excludes a number of items that have historically been part of the RPIX, especially items relating to housing costs (e.g. mortgage interest payments and council tax).

In addition, changes in **monetary aggregates**, which measure the amount of money (and therefore potential spending power) in circulation in the economy, and movements of exchange rates (especially a depreciating currency – see Chapter 16) are also seen as a guide to possible future price increases, as their effects work through the economy.

Explanations as to why prices tend to rise over time vary considerably, but broadly speaking fall into two main categories. Supply-siders tend to focus on rising production costs – particularly wages, energy and imported materials – as a major reason for inflation, with firms passing on increased costs to the consumer in the form of higher wholesale and/or retail prices. Demand-siders, in contrast, tend to emphasise the importance of excessive demand in the economy, brought about, for example, by tax cuts, cheaper borrowing or excessive government spending, which encourages firms to take advantage of the consumer's willingness to spend money by increasing their prices. Where indigenous firms are unable to satisfy all the additional demand, the tendency is for imports to increase. This may not only cause further price rises, particularly if imported goods are more expensive or if exchange rate movements become unfavourable, but also can herald a deteriorating balance of payments situation and difficult trading conditions for domestic businesses.

Government concern with inflation – which crosses both party and state boundaries – reflects the fact that rising price levels can have serious consequences for the economy in general and for businesses in particular, especially if a country's domestic inflation rates are significantly higher than those of its main competitors. In markets where price is an important determinant of demand, rising prices may result in some businesses losing sales, and this can affect turnover and may ultimately affect employment if firms reduce their labour force in order to reduce their costs. Added to this, the uncertainty caused by a difficult trading environment may make some businesses unwilling to invest in new plant and equipment, particularly if interest rates are high and if inflation looks unlikely to fall for some time. Such a response, while understandable, is unlikely to improve a firm's future competitiveness or its ability to exploit any possible increases in demand as market conditions change.

Rising prices may also affect businesses by encouraging employees to seek higher wages in order to maintain or increase their living standards. Where firms agree to such wage increases, the temptation, of course, is to pass this on to the consumer in the form of a price rise, especially if demand looks unlikely to be affected to any great extent. Should this process occur generally in the economy, the result may be a **wages/prices inflationary spiral**, in which wage increases push up prices which push up wage increases which further push up prices and so on. From an international competitive point of view, such an occurrence, if allowed to continue unchecked, could be disastrous for both firms and the economy. Thankfully, such a situation tends to be relatively uncommon in most economies, but, as recent problems in Zimbabwe have illustrated, hyperinflation can have disastrous consequences for a country's economy and its population (in mid-2008, for example, annual inflation in Zimbabwe was estimated at around 40 million per cent!).

Economic growth

Growth is an objective shared by governments and organisations alike. For governments, the aim is usually to achieve steady and sustained levels of non-inflationary growth, preferably led by exports (i.e. export-led growth), with growth being indicated by annual increases in **real national income** or **gross domestic product** (where 'real' = allowing for inflation and 'gross domestic product (GDP)' = the economy's annual output of goods and services measured in monetary terms).[2] To compensate for changes in the size of the population, growth rates tend to be expressed in terms of real national income per capita (i.e. real GDP divided by population).

Exactly what constitutes desirable levels of growth is difficult to say, except in very broad terms. If given a choice, governments would basically prefer:

- steady levels of real growth (e.g. 3–4 per cent p.a.), rather than annual increases in output which vary widely over the business cycle;
- growth rates higher than those of one's chief competitors; and
- growth based on investment in technology and on increased export sales, rather than on excessive government spending or current consumption.

It is worth remembering that, when measured on a monthly or quarterly basis, increases in output can occur at a declining rate and GDP growth can become negative. In the United Kingdom, a **recession** is said to exist following two consecutive quarters of negative GDP.

From a business point of view, the fact that increases in output are related to increases in consumption suggests that **economic growth** is good for business prospects and hence for investment and employment, and by and large this is the case. The rising living standards normally associated with such growth may, however, encourage increased consumption of imported goods and services at the expense of indigenous producers, to a point where some domestic firms are forced out of business and the economy's manufacturing base becomes significantly reduced (often called **deindustrialisation**). Equally, if increased consumption is based largely on excessive state spending, the potential gains for businesses may be offset by the need to increase interest rates to fund that spending (where government borrowing is involved) and by the tendency of government demands for funding to **crowd out** the private sector's search for investment capital. In such cases, the short-term benefits from government-induced consumption may be more than offset by the medium- and long-term problems for the economy that are likely to arise.

Where growth prospects for the economy look good, business confidence tends to increase and, as indicated above, this is often reflected in increased levels of investment and stock holding and ultimately in levels of employment. In Britain, for example, the monthly and quarterly surveys by the Confederation of British Industry (CBI) provide evidence of how output, investment and stock levels change at different points of the business cycle and these are generally seen as a good indication of future business trends, as interpreted by entrepreneurs. Other indicators – including the state of the housing market and construction generally – help to provide a guide to the current and future state of the economy, including its prospects for growth in the short and medium term.

 The CBI's website address is *www.cbi.org.uk*

Reducing unemployment

In most democratic states the goal of **full employment** is no longer part of the political agenda; instead government pronouncements on employment tend to focus on job creation and maintenance and on developing the skills appropriate to future demands. The consensus seems to be that in technologically advanced market-based economies, some unemployment is inevitable and that the basic aim should be to reduce unemployment to a level that is both politically and socially acceptable.

As with growth and inflation, unemployment levels tend to be measured at regular intervals (e.g. monthly, quarterly, annually), with the figures being adjusted to take into account seasonal influences (e.g. school-leavers entering the job market). Official statistics usually provide information on trends in long-term unemployment, areas of skill shortage and international comparisons, as well as sectoral changes within the economy. All of these indicators provide clues to the current state of the economy and to the prospects for businesses in the coming months and years, but need to be used with care. Unemployment, for example, tends to continue rising for a time even when a recession is over; equally, it is not uncommon for government definitions of unemployment to change or for international unemployment data to be based on different criteria.

The broader social and economic consequences of high levels of unemployment are well documented: it is a waste of resources; it puts pressure on the public services and on the Exchequer (e.g. by reducing tax yields and increasing public expenditure on welfare provision); it is frequently linked with growing social and health problems. Its implication for businesses, however, tends to be less clear-cut. On the one hand, a high level of unemployment implies a pool of labour available for firms seeking workers (though not necessarily with the right skills), generally at wage levels lower than when a shortage of labour occurs. On the other hand, it can also give rise to a fall in overall demand for goods and services, which could exacerbate any existing deflationary forces in the economy, causing further unemployment and with it further reductions in demand. Where this occurs, economists tend to describe it as **cyclical unemployment** (i.e. caused by a general deficiency in demand) in order to differentiate it from unemployment caused by a deficiency in demand for the goods produced by a particular industry (**structural unemployment**) or by the introduction of new technology which replaces labour (**technological unemployment**).

A favourable balance of payments

A country's **balance of payments** is essentially the net balance of credits (earnings) and debits (payments) arising from its international trade over a given period of time (see Chapter 16). Where credits exceed debits, a balance of payments surplus exists, the opposite being described as a deficit. Understandably, governments tend to prefer either equilibrium in the balance of payments, or surpluses rather than deficits. For a government facing persistent balance of payments deficits, a sustained reduction in the size of the deficit may also be regarded as signifying a 'favourable' balance of payments situation.

Like other economic indicators, the balance of payments statistics come in a variety of forms and at different levels of disaggregation, allowing useful comparisons to be made not only on a country's comparative trading performance but also on the international competitiveness of particular industries and commodity groups or on the development or decline of specific external markets. Particular emphasis tends to be given to the balance of payments on current account, which measures imports and exports of goods and services and is thus seen as an indicator of the competitiveness of an economy's firms and industries. Sustained current account surpluses tend to suggest favourable trading conditions, which can help to boost growth, increase employment and investment and create a general feeling of confidence among the business community. They may also give rise to surpluses which domestic firms can use to finance overseas lending and investment, thus helping to generate higher levels of corporate foreign earnings in future years.

While it does not follow that a sustained current account deficit is inevitably bad for the country concerned, it often implies structural problems in particular sectors of its economy or possibly an exchange rate which favours importers rather than exporters. Many observers believe that the progressive decline of Britain's visible trading position after 1983 was an indication of the growing uncompetitiveness of its firms, particularly those producing finished manufactured goods for consumer markets at home and abroad. By the same token, Japan's current account trade surplus of around $120 billion in late 1995 was portrayed as a sign of the cut-throat competition of Japanese firms, particularly those involved in producing cars, electrical and electronic products, and photographic equipment.

Controlling public borrowing

Governments raise large amounts of revenue annually, mainly through taxation, and use this income to spend on a wide variety of public goods and services (see below). Where annual revenue exceeds government spending, a budget surplus occurs and the excess is often used to repay past debt (formerly known in the United Kingdom as the 'public sector debt repayment' or PSDR). The accumulated debt of past and present governments represents a country's **national debt**. In the UK this stood at around £1.16 trillion in 2013, which was more than 70 per cent of GDP.

Where governments face annual budget deficits rather than budget surpluses, they are said to have a 'public sector borrowing requirement' or PSBR (now known in the UK as **public sector net borrowing** or PSNB). While such deficits are not inevitably a problem, in the same way that a small personal overdraft is not necessarily critical for an individual, large-scale and persistent deficits are generally seen as a sign of an economy facing current and future difficulties which require urgent government action. The overriding concern over high levels of public borrowing tends to be focused on:

1. Its impact on interest rates, given that higher interest rates tend to be needed to attract funds from private sector uses to public sector uses.
2. The impact of high interest rates on consumption and investment and hence on the prospects of businesses.
3. The danger of the public sector 'crowding out' the private sector's search for funds for investment.
4. The opportunity cost of debt interest, especially in terms of other forms of public spending.
5. The general lack of confidence in the markets about the government's ability to control the economy and the likely effect this might have on inflation, growth and the balance of payments.
6. The need to meet the 'convergence criteria' laid down at Maastricht for entry to the single currency (e.g. central government debt no higher than 3 per cent of GDP).

The consensus seems to be that controlling public borrowing is best tackled by restraining the rate of growth of public spending rather than by increasing revenue through changes in taxation, since the latter could depress demand.

A stable exchange rate

A country's currency has two values: an internal value and an external value. Internally, its value is expressed in terms of the goods and services it can buy and hence it is affected by changes in domestic prices. Externally, its value is expressed as an **exchange rate**, which governs how much of another country's currency it can purchase (e.g. £1 = $2 or £1 = €1.20). Since foreign trade normally involves an exchange of currencies, fluctuations in the external value of a currency will influence the price of imports and exports and hence can affect the trading prospects for business, as well as a country's balance of payments and its rate of inflation (see Chapter 16).

On the whole, governments and businesses involved in international trade tend to prefer exchange rates to remain relatively stable, because of the greater degree of certainty this brings to the trading environment; it also tends to make overseas investors more confident that their funds are likely to hold their value. To this extent, schemes that seek to fix exchange rates within predetermined levels (e.g. the European Exchange Rate Mechanism (ERM)), or that encourage the use of a common currency (e.g. the euro), tend to have the support of the business community, which prefers predictability to uncertainty where trading conditions are concerned.

mini case: Digging in for the long term

For firms engaged in international trade, the strength of the currency (i.e. the exchange rate) is an important consideration (see, for example, Chapter 16). As the value of one currency changes against other currencies, this usually alters the price of imported/exported products and this can make them more/less attractive to potential customers. To mitigate the impact of exchange rate changes, some firms engage in a process known as hedging, which basically involves trying to reduce or eliminate exchange rate risks, for example by buying a proportion of a currency forward (i.e. before it is needed) at an agreed price. An alternative strategy is to consider producing the product in different locations (e.g. setting up manufacturing facilities in other countries), which can offset some of the impact of currency fluctuations, as well as providing other potential benefits to a business.

A good example of the latter approach is provided by JCB, the UK-owned private company famous for its yellow construction equipment (e.g. diggers). In the 1990s, the company's business was mainly based in the UK and parts of western Europe, but faced with a limited market and a strengthening pound, which made exporting difficult, the firm decided to seek a global presence by investing in manufacturing abroad. Focusing first on the USA, JCB built a plant in Georgia in the late 1990s to exploit the US market; this was followed by further plants in Sao Paulo in Brazil and new plants in India near Mumbai. It also acquired a German construction firm in 2005 and opened a further factory near Shanghai in 2006, thereby adding to its global reach.

Despite having to shed some jobs in the global recession, by 2013 the company's global workforce numbered around 10,000 based on four continents and it was selling its product in 150 countries via a network of dealerships. In September of that year the firm opened the world's biggest JCB dealer depot in Ekaterinberg, Russia, following a multi-million-pound investment.

In addition to the potential currency benefits of operating in different countries, JCB has gained a number of other advantages, including establishing a global brand name, access to low-cost suppliers and to developing markets, and reducing freight costs and tariff barriers. Globalisation, in short, can offer businesses many 'opportunities', but we must not forget that it can also give rise to substantial 'threats' at the corporate level, not least the danger of low-cost competitors invading one's own markets.

Government and the macroeconomy: policies

Governments throughout Europe and beyond play various key roles in their respective economies. These include the following functions:

- consumer of resources (e.g. employer, landowner);
- supplier of resources (e.g. infrastructure, information);
- consumer of goods and services (e.g. government spending);
- supplier of goods and services (e.g. nationalised industries);
- regulator of business activity (e.g. employment laws, consumer laws);
- regulator of the economy (e.g. fiscal and monetary policies); and
- redistributor of income and wealth (e.g. taxation system).

The extent of these roles, and their impact on the economy in general and on business in particular, varies from country to country as well as over time.

Despite the economic significance of these roles, in most market-based economies democratically elected governments prefer levels and patterns of production and consumption to be determined largely by market forces, with a minimum of government interference. At the same time, the recognition that market forces alone are unable to guarantee that an economy will automatically achieve the objectives established by governments has meant that state intervention – to curb inflation, encourage growth, reduce unemployment, correct a balance of payments or budgetary problem or restore currency stability – invariably occurs to some degree in all countries. In broad terms, this intervention usually takes three main forms, described as fiscal policy, monetary policy and direct controls. These policy instruments – or 'instrumental variables' – and their effects on the business community are discussed below.

Fiscal policy

As indicated above, each year governments raise and spend huge amounts of money. The UK government's estimates for 2013, for example, suggested that **government spending** would be about £720 billion and was to be allocated in the manner illustrated in Figure 5.8. This spending was to be funded mainly from **taxation (direct and indirect)** and national insurance contributions (see Figure 5.9). The PSNB was estimated at £108 billion.

Fiscal policy involves the use of changes in government spending and taxation to influence the level and composition of aggregate demand in the economy and, given the amounts involved, this clearly has important implications for business. Elementary circular flow analysis suggests, for instance, that reductions in taxation and/or increases in government spending will inject additional income into the economy and will, via the multiplier effect, increase the demand for goods and services, with favourable consequences for business. Reductions in government spending and/or increases in taxation will have the opposite effect, depressing business prospects and probably discouraging investment and causing a rise in unemployment.

Apart from their overall impact on aggregate demand, fiscal changes can be used to achieve specific objectives, some of which will be of direct or indirect benefit to the business community. Reductions in taxes on company profits and/or increases in tax allowances for investment in capital equipment can be used to encourage business to increase investment spending, hence boosting the income of firms producing industrial products and causing some additional spending on consumption. Similarly, increased government spending targeted at firms involved in exporting, or at the creation of new business, will encourage increased business activity and additionally may lead to more output and employment in the economy.

In considering the use of fiscal policy to achieve their objectives, governments tend to be faced with a large number of practical problems that generally limit their room for manoeuvre. Boosting the economy through increases in spending or reductions in taxation could cause inflationary pressures, as well as encouraging an inflow of imports and increasing the public sector deficit, none of which would be particularly welcomed by entrepreneurs or by the financial markets. By the same token, fiscal attempts to restrain demand in order to reduce inflation will generally depress the economy, causing a fall in output and employment and encouraging firms to abandon or defer investment projects until business prospects improve.

Figure 5.8　The allocation of UK government spending, 2013 budget

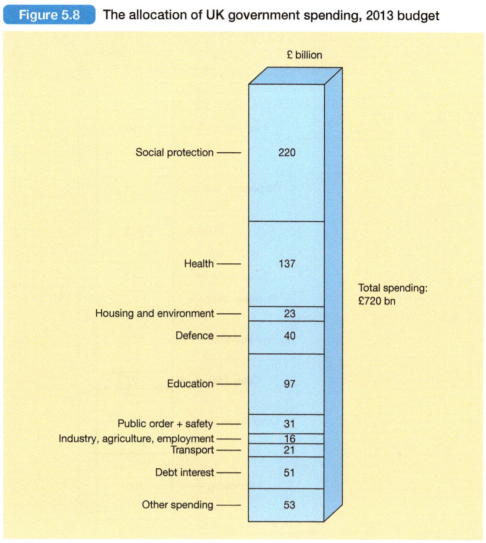

Source: Adapted from Budget Statement, 2013.

Added to this, it should not be forgotten that government decision-makers are politicians who need to consider the political as well as the economic implications of their chosen courses of action. Thus, while cuts in taxation may receive public approval, increases may not, and, if implemented, the latter may encourage higher wage demands. Similarly, the redistribution of government spending from one programme area to another is likely to give rise to widespread protests from those on the receiving end of any cuts, so much so that governments tend to be restricted for the most part to changes at the margin, rather than undertaking a radical reallocation of resources and they may be tempted to fix budgetary allocations for a number of years ahead (e.g. the introduction of the Comprehensive Spending Review in the UK).

Other factors too – including changes in economic thinking, self-imposed fiscal rules, external constraints on borrowing and international agreements – can play their part in restraining the use of fiscal policy as an instrument of demand management, whatever a government's preferred course of action may be. Simple prescriptions to boost the economy through large-scale cuts in taxation or increases in government spending

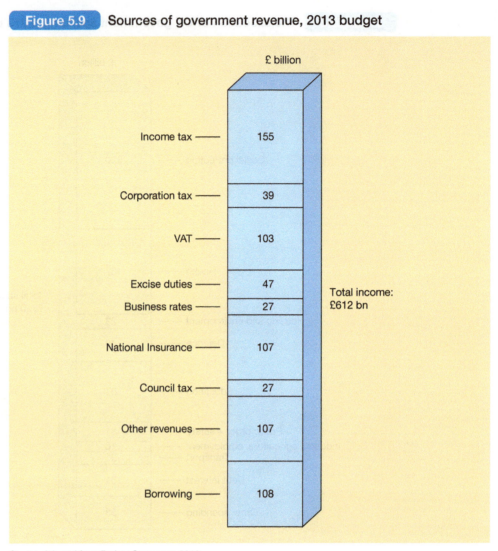

Figure 5.9 Sources of government revenue, 2013 budget

Source: Adapted from Budget Statement, 2013.

often fail to take into account the political and economic realities of the situation faced by most governments.

Monetary policy

Monetary policy seeks to influence monetary variables such as the money supply or rates of interest in order to regulate the economy. While the supply of money and interest rates (i.e. the cost of borrowing) are interrelated, it is convenient to consider them separately.

As far as changes in **interest rates** are concerned, these clearly have implications for business activity, as circular flow analysis demonstrates. Lower interest rates not only encourage firms to invest as the cost of borrowing falls, they also encourage consumption as disposable incomes rise (predominantly through the mortgage effect) and as the cost of loans and overdrafts decreases. Such increased consumption tends to be an added spur to investment, particularly if inflation rates (and therefore **'real' interest rates**) are low, and this can help to boost the economy in the short term, as well as improving the supply side in the longer term.[3]

Raising interest rates tends to have the opposite effect – causing a fall in consumption as mortgages and other prices rise, and deferring investment because of the additional cost of borrowing and the decline in business confidence as consumer spending falls. If interest rates remain persistently high, the encouragement given to savers and the discouragement given to borrowers and spenders may help to generate a recession, characterised by falling output, income, spending and employment and by increasing business failure.

Changes in the **money stock** (especially credit) affect the capacity of individuals and firms to borrow and, therefore, to spend. Increases in money supply are generally related to increases in spending and this tends to be good for business prospects, particularly if interest rates are falling as the money supply rises (see the case study at this end of this chapter). Restrictions on monetary growth normally work in the opposite direction, especially if such restrictions help to generate increases in interest rates which feed through to both consumption and investment, both of which will tend to decline.

As in the case of fiscal policy, government is usually able to manipulate monetary variables in a variety of ways, including taking action in the money markets to influence interest rates and controlling its own spending to influence monetary growth. Once again, however, circumstances tend to dictate how far and in what way government is free to operate. Attempting to boost the economy by allowing the money supply to grow substantially, for instance, threatens to cause inflationary pressures and to increase spending on imports, both of which run counter to government objectives and do little to assist domestic firms. Similarly, policies to boost consumption and investment through lower interest rates, while welcomed generally by industry, offer no guarantee that any additional spending will be on domestically produced goods and services, and also tend to make the financial markets nervous about government commitments to control inflation in the longer term (see below, 'The role of the central bank').

This nervousness among market dealers reflects the fact that in modern market economies a government's policies on interest rates and monetary growth cannot be taken in isolation from those of its major trading partners and this operates as an important constraint on government action. The fact is that a reduction in interest rates to boost output and growth in an economy also tends to be reflected in the exchange rate; this usually falls as foreign exchange dealers move funds into those currencies that yield a better return and that also appear a safer investment if the market believes a government is abandoning its counter-inflationary policy. As the UK government found in the early 1990s, persistently high rates of interest in Germany severely restricted its room for manoeuvre on interest rates for fear of the consequences for sterling if relative interest rates got too far out of line.

Direct controls

Fiscal and monetary policies currently represent the chief policy instruments used in modern market economies and hence they have been discussed in some detail. Governments, however, also use a number of other weapons from time to time in their attempts to achieve their macroeconomic objectives. Such weapons, which are designed essentially to achieve a specific objective – such as limiting imports or controlling wage increases – tend to be known as **direct controls**. Examples of such policies include:

- *incomes policies*, which seek to control inflationary pressures by influencing the rate at which wages and salaries rise;
- *import controls*, which attempt to improve a country's balance of payments situation, by reducing either the supply of, or the demand for, imported goods and services (see Chapter 16);
- *regional and urban policies*, which are aimed at alleviating urban and regional problems, particularly differences in income, output, employment, and local and regional decline (see Chapter 13).

A brief discussion of some of these policy instruments is found at various points in the text below. Students wishing to study these in more detail are recommended to consult the books referred to at the end of this chapter.

The role of financial institutions

Interactions in the macroeconomy between governments, businesses and consumers take place within an institutional environment that includes a large number of financial intermediaries. These range from banks and building societies to pension funds, insurance companies, investment trusts and issuing houses, all of which provide a number of services of both direct and indirect benefit to businesses. As part of the financial system within a market-based economy, these institutions fulfil a vital role in channelling funds from those able and willing to lend, to those individuals and organisations wishing to borrow in order to consume or invest. It is appropriate to consider briefly this role of financial intermediation and the supervision exercised over the financial system by the central bank, before concluding the chapter with a review of important international economic institutions.

Elements of the financial system

A financial system basically comprises three main elements:

1. *Lenders and borrowers* – these may be individuals, organisations or governments.
2. *Financial institutions*, of various kinds, which act as intermediaries between lenders and borrowers and which manage their own asset portfolios in the interest of their shareholders and/or depositors.
3. *Financial markets*, in which lending and borrowing take place through the transfer of money and/or other types of asset, including paper assets such as shares and stock.

Financial institutions, as indicated above, comprise a wide variety of organisations, many of which are public companies with shareholders. Markets include the markets for short-term funds of various types (usually termed **money markets**) and those for long-term finance for both the private and public sectors (usually called the capital market). Stock exchanges normally lie at the centre of the latter and constitute an important market for existing securities issued by both companies and government.

The vital role played by financial intermediaries in the operation of the financial system is illustrated in Figure 5.10 and reflects the various benefits that derive from using an intermediary rather than lending direct to a borrower (e.g. creating a large pool of savings, spreading risk, transferring short-term lending into longer-term borrowing, providing various types of funds transfer services). Lenders on the whole prefer low risk, high returns, flexibility and liquidity, while borrowers prefer to minimise the cost of borrowing and to use the funds in a way that is best suited to their needs. Companies, for example, may borrow to finance stock or work-in-progress or to meet short-term debts and such borrowing may need to be as flexible as possible. Alternatively, they may wish to borrow in order to replace plant and equipment or to buy new premises – borrowing which needs to be over a much longer term and which hopefully will yield a rate of return that makes the use of the funds and the cost of borrowing worthwhile.

The process of channelling funds from lenders to borrowers often gives rise to paper claims, which are generated either by the financial intermediary issuing a claim to the lender (e.g. when a bank borrows by issuing a certificate of deposit) or by the borrower issuing a claim to the financial intermediary (e.g. when government sells stock to a financial institution). These paper claims represent a liability to the issuer and an asset to the holder and can be traded on a secondary market (i.e. a market for existing securities), according to the needs of the individual or organisation holding the paper claim. At any point, financial intermediaries tend to hold a wide range of such assets (claims on borrowers), which they buy or sell ('manage') in order to yield a profit and/or improve their liquidity position. Decisions of this kind, taken on a daily basis, invariably affect

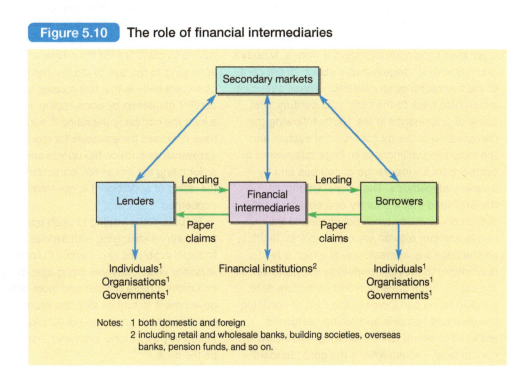

Figure 5.10 The role of financial intermediaries

Notes: 1 both domestic and foreign
2 including retail and wholesale banks, building societies, overseas banks, pension funds, and so on.

the position of investors (e.g. shareholders) and customers (e.g. depositors) and can, under certain circumstances, have serious consequences for the financial intermediary and its stakeholders (e.g. the bad debts faced by financial institutions in the wake of the sub-prime mortgage crisis in the USA from 2007–8 onwards).

Given the element of risk, it is perhaps not surprising that some financial institutions have historically been conservative in their attitude towards lending on funds deposited with them, especially in view of their responsibilities to their various stakeholders. In general, UK retail banks have a long-standing preference for financing industry's working capital rather than investment spending, and hence the latter has tended to be financed largely by internally generated funds (e.g. retained profits) or by share issues. In comparison, banks in Germany, France, the United States and Japan tend to be more ready to meet industry's medium- and longer-term needs and are often directly involved in regular discussions with their clients concerning corporate strategy, in contrast to the arm's length approach favoured by many of their UK counterparts.[4] As the global financial crisis has illustrated, however, the increasing complexity of financial instruments and the willingness of some traders to take risks in pursuit of higher corporate (and personal) rewards suggests that the past deregulation of the financial system may have come at a significant price.

mini case: A new kid on the block: the rise of the credit rating agency

Credit rating agencies have become powerful and influential organisations in world finance, rating the 'credit worthiness' of both companies and countries and thereby often helping to influence lending and investment decisions.

Of more than 150 agencies worldwide, the three best known are Standard & Poor's, Moody's and Fitch, which together rate about 95 per cent of the market for corporate debt. These agencies, which date back to the early 20th century, first came to prominence in the 1980s following the deregulation of the global financial system and the increasing willingness of large businesses to borrow from a wider range of sources and by a variety of methods. Their assessments of the likelihood that a country or a company will default on its debts are widely trailed in the media and can play an important role in deciding on the price (i.e. interest rate) at which a lender is prepared to provide funding to the borrower. In the case of both sovereign and corporate debt, a falling rating can increase the cost of servicing the debt and hence is something borrowers are keen to avoid. Once the rating falls below a certain level – where AAA is the gold standard – this is known as 'junk status', indicating that a default is more likely and invariably pushing up interest rates significantly.

It is interesting to note that credit rating agencies are funded by the companies they rate, with organisations wishing to acquire a rating having to pay a fee for the privilege, which varies according to the size of the business. Some observers believe that this creates a potential conflict of interest by encouraging an agency to award the company the rating it would like. Others have criticised the agencies for regularly inaccurate assessments both on the upside and the downside or for being too influential, particularly where the rating of sovereign (i.e. government) debt is concerned.

By potentially helping to push up interest rates for countries struggling with serious economic and financial problems (e.g. certain Eurozone countries in recent years), adverse rating agency judgements can make it more difficult and more costly for a government to turn its situation round. In the real economy, both firms and households may be forced to pay a higher price than might otherwise be the case.

The role of the central bank

A critical element in a country's financial system is its **central** or **state bank**; in the United Kingdom this is the Bank of England. Like most of its overseas counterparts, the Bank of England exercises overall supervision over the banking sector, with the aim of maintaining a stable and efficient financial framework as part of its contribution to a healthy economy. Its activities have a significant influence in the financial markets (especially the foreign exchange market, the gilts market and the sterling money market). These activities include the following roles:

- banker to the government;
- banker to the clearing banks;
- manager of the country's foreign reserves;
- manager of the national debt;
- manager of the issue of notes and coins;
- supervisor of the monetary sector; and
- implementer of the government's monetary policy.

Since 1997 the Bank has also been granted 'operational independence' to set interest rates and to conduct other aspects of monetary policy free from Treasury interference as part of its core purpose of ensuring monetary stability (e.g. controlling inflation and protecting the currency). Interest rates are set at the monthly meetings of the Bank's Monetary Policy Committee (MPC), which is chaired by the Bank governor. In order to facilitate forward planning by businesses and financial institutions and to promote market stability, the MPC also now provides forward guidance on aspects of monetary policy, particularly interest rates.

In response to the problems resulting from the global financial crisis, the Bank has recently acquired an enhanced role in promoting and developing greater financial stability. Under the Financial Services Act 2012, a Financial Policy Committee has been established with responsibility for taking action to remove or reduce systemic risks in the financial system and generally supporting government economic policy (i.e. a macro-level role). Alongside this new body is a Prudential Regulation Authority that has been set up to supervise the key financial institutions (e.g. banks, building societies, insurers) so as to protect policy-holders and investors and promote sound practices within the financial system (i.e. a micro-level role).

For further information on the Bank of England you should consult www.bankofengland.co.uk

While central banks are nationally-based institutions, the EU also has its own central bank, the **European Central Bank (ECB)**, which is based in Frankfurt. The main task of the ECB is to maintain the purchasing power of the euro and hence to promote price stability within the Eurozone. Among its key roles are defining and implementing monetary policy for the Eurozone, including foreign exchange operations and issuing euro banknotes. It has also been heavily involved in bond purchasing in struggling EU economies to support the value of the euro.

The ECB's website is *www.ecb.europa.eu*

International economic institutions and organisations

Given that external factors constrain the ability of governments to regulate their economy, it is appropriate to conclude this analysis of the macroeconomic context of business with a brief review of a number of important international economic institutions and organisations that affect the trading environment. Foremost among these is the European Union, which is examined at length in Chapters 4 and 16. In the discussions below we look at the International Monetary Fund (IMF), the Organisation for Economic Co-operation and Development (OECD), the European Bank for Reconstruction and Development (EBRD), the World Trade Organisation (WTO) and the World Bank (IBRD).

The International Monetary Fund (IMF)

The IMF is an international organisation currently of 184 member countries. It came into being in 1946 following discussions at Bretton Woods in the USA which sought to agree a world financial order for the post-Second World War period that would avoid the problems associated with the worldwide depression in the inter-war years. Its original role was to provide a pool of foreign currencies from its member states that would be used to smooth out trade imbalances between countries, thereby promoting a structured growth in world trade and encouraging exchange rate stability. In this way, the architects of the Fund believed that the danger of international protectionism would be reduced and that all countries would consequently benefit from the boost given to world trade and the greater stability of the international trading environment.

The IMF's website is www.imf.org

While this role as international 'lender of last resort' still exists, the IMF's focus in recent years has tended to switch towards international surveillance and to helping the developing economies with their mounting debt problems and assisting eastern Europe with reconstruction, following the break-up of the Soviet empire.[5] More recently it has played a major role in lending to countries caught up in the global financial crisis in order to boost the global economy. To some extent its position as an international decision-making body has been diminished by the tendency of the world's leading economic countries to deal with global economic problems outside the IMF's institutional framework. The United States, Japan, Germany, France, Italy, Canada, Britain and Russia now meet regularly as the Group of Eight (G8) leading industrial economies to discuss issues of mutual interest (e.g. the environment, eastern Europe). These world economic summits, as they are frequently called, have tended to supersede discussions in the IMF and as a result normally attract greater media attention. Key global and economic issues are also discussed at meetings of the G20, which includes the G8 countries and a number of other key players, including China, India and Brazil.

The Organisation for Economic Co-operation and Development (OECD)

The OECD came into being in 1961, but its roots go back to 1948 when the Organisation for European Economic Co-operation (OEEC) was established to coordinate the distribution of Marshall Aid to the war-torn economies of western Europe. Today it comprises 34 members, drawn from the rich industrial countries and including the G7 nations, Australia, New Zealand and most other European states. Collectively, these countries account for less than 20 per cent of the world's population but produce around two-thirds of its output – hence the tendency of commentators to refer to the OECD as the 'rich man's club'.

You can access the OECD's website at *www.oecd.org*

The OECD is the main forum in which the governments of the world's leading industrial economies meet to discuss economic matters, particularly questions concerned with promoting stable growth and freer trade and with supporting development in poorer non-member countries. Through its council and committees, and backed by an independent secretariat, the organisation is able to take decisions which set out an agreed view and/or course of action on important social and economic issues of common concern. While it does not have the authority to impose ideas, its influence lies in its capacity for intellectual persuasion, particularly its ability through discussion to promote convergent thinking on international economic problems. To assist in the task, the OECD provides a wide variety of economic data on member countries, using standardised measures for national accounting, unemployment and purchasing-power parities. It is for these data – and especially its economic forecasts and surveys – that the organisation is perhaps best known.

The European Bank for Reconstruction and Development (EBRD)

The aims of the EBRD, which was inaugurated in April 1991, are to facilitate the transformation of the states of central and eastern Europe and beyond from centrally planned to free-market economies and to promote political and economic democracy, respect for human rights and respect for the environment. It is particularly involved with the privatisation process, project financing, technical assistance, training and investment in upgrading of the infrastructure and in facilitating economic, legal and financial restructuring. It works in cooperation with its members, private companies and organisations such as the IMF, OECD, the World Bank and the United Nations.

Information on the EBRD can be obtained at *www.ebrd.com*

The World Trade Organisation (WTO)

The World Trade Organisation, which came into being on 1 January 1995, superseded the General Agreement on Tariffs and Trade (the GATT), which dated back to 1947. Like the IMF and the International Bank for Reconstruction and Development (see below), which were established at the same time, the GATT was part of an attempt to reconstruct the international politico-economic environment in the period after the end of the Second World War. Its replacement by the WTO can be said to mark an attempt to put the question of liberalising world trade higher up on the international political agenda.

The WTO can be accessed at www.wto.org

With a membership of more than 150 states (plus other observers), the WTO is a permanent international organisation charged with the task of liberalising world trade within an agreed legal and institutional framework. In addition it administers and implements a number of multilateral agreements in fields such as agriculture, textiles and services and is responsible for dealing with disputes arising from the Uruguay Round Final Act. It also provides a forum for the debate, negotiation and adjudication of trade problems and in the latter context is said to have a much stronger and quicker trade compliance and enforcement mechanism than existed under the GATT. See also Chapter 16.

The World Bank (IBRD)

Established in 1945, the World Bank (more formally known as the International Bank for Reconstruction and Development, or IBRD) is a specialised agency of the United Nations, set up to encourage economic growth in developing countries through the provision of loans and technical assistance. The IBRD currently has over 180 members.

The IBRD can be accessed at www.worldbank.org

The European Investment Bank (EIB)

The European Investment Bank was created in 1958 under the Treaty of Rome and is the financing institution of the European Union. Its main task is to contribute to the integration, balanced development and the economic and social cohesion of EU member states. Using funds raised on the markets, it finances capital projects which support EU objectives within the European Union and elsewhere. Its interests include environmental schemes, projects relating to transport and energy, and support for small and medium-sized enterprises.

For further information on the EIB see www.eib.org

Synopsis

Business and economics are inextricably linked. Economics is concerned with the problem of allocating scarce productive resources to alternative uses – a fundamental aspect of business activity. In market-based economies, this problem of resource allocation is largely solved through the operation of free markets, in which price is a vital ingredient. The existence of such markets tends to be associated primarily, though not exclusively, with democratic political regimes.

In all democratic states, government is a key component of the market economy and exercises considerable influence over the level and pattern of business activity – a point illustrated by the use of elementary circular flow analysis. A government's aims for the economy help to shape the policies it uses and these policies have both direct and indirect consequences for business organisations of all kinds.

In examining the economic context in which firms exist, due attention needs to be paid to the influence of a wide range of institutions and organisations, some of which operate at the international level. Equally, as markets become more open and business becomes more global, the fortunes of firms in trading economies become increasingly connected and hence subject to fluctuations that go beyond the boundaries of any individual state.

Summary of key points

- Business activity exists in and is affected by the broader macroeconomic environment; it also helps to shape that environment.

- Economics is concerned with how societies allocate scarce economic resources to alternative uses and the 'real costs' of the choices that are made.

- Broadly speaking, two main approaches to the problem of resource allocation exist: state planning and the market.

- Most economies in the world are market-based economies which operate through a price mechanism. Within such economies the state also plays a key role in some allocative decisions.

- In market economies, economic activity essentially involves 'real flows' and corresponding flows of income and expenditure between producers and consumers.

- Combining these flows into a simple model of the macroeconomy illustrates that income basically flows round the economy in a circular motion.

- Levels of income in the economy are related to levels of output, expenditure and employment.

- Changes in the level of economic activity can be explained by examining changes in one or more of the key economic variables such as consumer spending, saving, government decisions on state spending/taxation and external trade.

- Within the macroeconomy, governments often play a key role in influencing both the levels and patterns of demand in pursuit of their macroeconomic objectives.

- Key government objectives usually include controlling inflation, promoting economic growth, reducing unemployment, and creating a stable macroeconomic environment.
- To pursue these objectives governments use a range of policies, most notably fiscal and monetary policies.
- Government policy decisions take place within a broader economic and financial framework, which includes the influence of financial institutions and markets and the requirements that accrue from membership of different supranational and international organisations.

case study: Quantitative easing (QE)

As indicated by the analysis presented in this chapter, governments have a variety of options available when tackling a problem such as recession in the economy. Where monetary policy is concerned, a traditional approach has been to lower interest rates in the hope of boosting demand. This option has become increasingly difficult in recent years as interest rates in many countries have fallen to historically low levels in the wake of the global financial crisis that occurred after 2008.

An alternative approach that has become widely used in recent years (e.g. in Japan, the UK, the USA) is the policy known as quantitative (or credit) easing. In simple terms this involves a country's central bank 'creating' money electronically by crediting the accounts of financial institutions (e.g. banks, pension funds, insurance companies) in return for the purchase of assets, particularly government bonds held by these investors. By buying bonds, the central bank reduces their supply in the market, resulting in an increase in the price of these assets. Since bond prices move inversely to the yield they generate (i.e. the rate of interest on the asset), an increase in prices reduces long-term interest rates, thus making borrowing cheaper for businesses and mortgage holders. This, it is hoped, will help to stimulate demand, boost the housing and stock markets, and generally increase confidence among both firms and consumers.

The additional cash held by the financial institutions as a result of QE can also be used to purchase other assets, including equities and corporate bonds, and this could encourage firms to issue new stock to fund investment. In the case of the banks, this additional money can be lent on directly to consumers and businesses, thereby cascading through the economy and generally increasing economic activity. Coupled with low interest rates and a rising stock market, the conditions for a return to growth appear to be an inevitable consequence of this form of monetary stimulus to the economy.

Critics of QE tend to be less sanguine about its ability to achieve its objectives of boosting economic growth and reducing unemployment associated with a recession. One criticism is that there is no guarantee that the banks will pass on the additional cash to consumers and businesses. Instead, they may use it to speculate in, say, commodities (e.g. oil), thus pushing up commodity prices and making conditions even tougher for consumers, some of whom (e.g. pensioners about to invest in an annuity and savers generally) are already being adversely affected by low interest rates. Others have suggested that QE might be being used by a country surreptitiously to depress the value of its currency in the hope of making its exports more attractive on international markets. Given the tough global trading conditions that are affecting many countries at the moment, this development could prove highly controversial and could spark off an exchange rate and trading war.

A further concern has been that some of the global tidal wave of cheap money has found its way into emerging markets, such as India, and has helped to mask some underlying economic problems. With the Federal Reserve's announcement that it intends to taper off QE in the future – thereby reversing the huge investment flows – currencies such as the rupee have come under severe pressure in the currency markets as traders are beginning to question whether inflationary pressures can be contained and whether the country will be able to fund its trade deficit in the future. There are also fears that any phasing out of QE, if handled badly, could have adverse consequences for global bond markets and interest rates (see, for example, the IMF's Global Financial Stability Report, October 2013).

While it is probably too early to judge whether QE will work as intended, its adoption by central banks in different countries does at least underline the belief among policy-makers that it is sometimes necessary to intervene in the economy in order to tackle or fend off economic problems. As with most things in economics, what the best approach is tends to be a matter of opinion; matching ends and means is rarely free of controversy.

Case study questions

1 QE is seen as one way in which a government can stimulate the economy. What other approaches could it use?

2 Could QE lead to inflationary pressures in an economy, and if so, how?

Review and discussion questions

1 To what extent do you agree with the proposition that the market economy is the 'best' form of economic system? Do you have any reservations?

2 Explain how interest rates could be used to boost the economy. Why, then, do governments frequently hesitate to take such steps?

3 Using circular flow analysis, suggest why a large programme of capital expenditure by government (e.g. on new motorways, roads, railways) will benefit businesses. How could such a programme be financed?

4 Which businesses are likely to benefit from a recovery in a country's housing market?

Assignments

1 Imagine you work in the economic development unit of a local authority. Produce a draft report outlining the benefits to the local economy of encouraging direct inward investment. Indicate any disadvantages.

2 You are a trainee journalist on a regional or national newspaper. As part of your first big assignment, you have been asked to provide information on the 'privatisation' of eastern European economies. Using journals and newspapers, provide a scrapbook of information indicating the different ways in which western companies have sought to exploit business opportunities in eastern Europe.

Notes and references

1. Donaldson, P. and Farquhar, J., *Understanding the British Economy*, Penguin, 1988, p. 84.
2. See also the concept of gross value added (GVA), which is an important measure in the estimation of GDP. National Statistics Online has a good explanation of GVA.
3. Real interest rates allow for inflation.
4. See, for example, Neale, A. and Haslam, C., *Economics in a Business Context*, Chapman & Hall, 1991, p. 141.
5. The role of assisting reconstruction in eastern Europe is also undertaken by the European Bank for Reconstruction and Development (EBRD). See text below.

Further reading

Begg, D. and Ward, D., *Economics for Business*, 3rd edition, McGraw-Hill, 2009.

Donaldson, P. and Farquhar, J., *Understanding the British Economy*, Penguin, 1991.

Griffiths, A. and Wall, S. (eds), *Applied Economics*, 12th edition, Financial Times/Prentice Hall, 2011.

Griffiths, A. and Wall, S., *Economics for Business and Management*, 3rd edition, Financial Times/Prentice Hall, 2011.

Mulhearn, C., Vane, H. R. and Eden, J., *Economics for Business*, 2nd edition, Palgrave Macmillan, 2011.

Neale, A., Haslam, C. and Johal, S., *Economics in a Business Context*, Thomson Learning, 3rd edition, 2010.

Worthington, I., Britton, C. and Rees, A., *Economics for Business: Blending Theory and Practice*, 2nd edition, Financial Times/Prentice Hall, 2005.

Web links and further questions are available on the website at:
www.pearsoned.co.uk/worthington

6 The demographic, social and cultural context of business

Ian Worthington

As an integral part of society, businesses are subject to a variety of social influences. These influences, which include demography, social class and culture, can change over time and affect both the demand and supply sides of the economy. Marketing organisations recognise and make use of these factors when segmenting markets for consumer goods and services.

Learning outcomes

Having read this chapter you should be able to:

- explain the notions of demography, social class, lifestyles, reference groups, culture and sub-culture
- identify key demographic and social trends that can affect organisations in the private, public and voluntary sectors
- provide examples of how demographic, social and cultural factors can influence both the demand and supply sides of the economy
- outline the concept of market segmentation and demonstrate how marketing organisations can use demographic and socio-cultural variables to segment consumer markets

Key terms

ACORN
Ageing population
Birth rate
Cultural diversity
Culture
Death rate
Demographic time-bomb
Demography
Dependent population
Family life cycle
Geo-demographic segmentation
Lifestyle
Market segmentation
MOSAIC
Natural population change
Net migration
Primary reference group
Psychographic segmentation
Reference group
Secondary reference group
Social class
Social mobility
Sub-culture
VALS

Introduction

Previous chapters have demonstrated that human beings are a critical element of business activity, both in their role as producers (e.g. workers, managers, entrepreneurs) and as consumers of outputs provided by the private, public and voluntary sectors. Put simply, business activity ultimately takes place because of and for people, a point well illustrated by the concept of the circular flow of income (CFI) (Chapter 5) and by the systems model introduced in Chapter 1. In order to more fully understand the environment in which business organisations exist and operate, it is important to consider how broader 'social' influences affect business organisations by examining how they can impact upon both the demand and supply sides of the economy.

In this chapter we look at three such influences – demography, social aspects and the idea of culture – illustrating how these can affect both the amount and types of goods and services consumed within an economy and the different aspects of the production process. In the next chapter, on the resource context, we examine people as a key factor of production and look at a number of areas associated with the concept of the workforce.

As the CFI model clearly shows, the demand and supply sides of the economy are interrelated (e.g. consider the notion of 'derived demand'); the same is often true for demographic, social and cultural influences. In some countries, for example, changing attitudes to female participation in the workforce (a socio-cultural factor) have helped to influence family sizes (a demographic factor) and this in turn has had implications for the markets for goods and services and for human resources. To simplify the analysis, however, we have chosen to examine the different social influences and their impact on the economy separately, but would encourage you to think of the various ways in which the different factors can be interconnected, both in themselves and with other macroenvironmental variables (e.g. the political environment).

The examples provided below are by no means exhaustive and you might like to think of others based on your own interest and/or experience (e.g. public administration students should consider the impact of a changing demographic and socio-cultural environment on the supply of and demand for public sector services such as education, pensions and healthcare). Moreover, the analysis can also be applied across different countries and cultures and ideally should seek to demonstrate the impact of socio-cultural and demographic change on business activity in different national and cultural settings.

The demographic environment of business

Demography is the study of populations in terms of both their overall size and their structural characteristics. From a business point of view the key areas of interest include the age structure of a given population, its gender balance, its geographical distribution and the tendency for both the size and structure of the population to change over time. As noted above, demographic change can have important implications for both sides of the economy and hence for organisations of all types.

The size of the population

A country's population normally increases over time and will vary according to such factors as changes in the birth and death rates and in the rate of net migration. Take the UK population, which in 1971 was just under 56 million; by 2008 this had risen to 60 million. The most recent (2013) estimates suggest that over the next 25 years it will rise again, to 73.3 million, partly because of immigration and partly through natural change (see below). In comparison, Russia's current population of around 143 million is projected to fall by at least 25 million by 2050 as a result of a declining birth rate and a rising death rate in the wake of the country's economic collapse. If this occurs, the world's biggest country will have fewer people than countries such as Uganda and Egypt. It is worth remembering, however, that future population changes are only projections and that these can vary considerably over time as new data become available. For example, in late 2007 the UK's Office for National Statistics provided three projections for the UK population by 2081: 63 million (lowest estimate), 108.7 million (highest estimate), 85 million (most likely estimate). These estimates show considerable variation and indicate how future population changes are relatively unpredictable, which can make forward planning in areas such as education, housing and healthcare provision very difficult.

Table 6.1 indicates the wide variations that can occur in the size of national populations by examining a range of countries across the globe. Within the EU we can see that major member countries such as France, Germany, Italy and the UK all had populations over 50 million in 2012, while the majority of the new member states had populations below 10 million. These figures are dwarfed, however, by India and China, which had populations of around 1.24 billion and 1.35 billion respectively. Such differences in overall population size have important economic implications in areas such as potential market size, workforce availability, public expenditure, economic growth and international trade.

Table 6.1 Population size in selected countries, 2012

Country	Population (millions)
Germany	81.9
France	65.7
UK	63.2
Italy	60.9
The Netherlands	16.8
Greece	11.3
Poland	38.5
Hungary	9.9
Slovakia	5.4
Malta	0.4
USA	313.9
India	1236.7
China	1350.7

Source: Various (including World Bank).

The age and sex distribution of the population

In addition to examining the overall size of a country's population, demographers are interested in its structural characteristics, including the balance between males and females and the numbers of people in different age categories. Table 6.2 gives illustrative data for the UK population by age and gender for selected age groups and intervals over the period 1971–2021. As we can see from the figures in the right-hand column, women outnumber men in the UK population, despite the fact that the annual number of male births slightly exceeds that of female births. Moreover, the data clearly point to an **ageing population**, with an increasing percentage of the population in the over-65 group and a decreasing percentage in the under-16 category. Projections suggest that by 2061 the number of over-65s in the UK population will significantly exceed the number who are under 16, a trend which is sometimes described as the **demographic time-bomb**. This clearly has important implications for both the private and public sectors, not least in terms of the overall demand for goods and services, including 'public goods' such as education, healthcare, social services, state pensions and social security arrangements.

Table 6.2 Distribution of UK population by age and gender, 1971–2021, at selected intervals

	Under 16 (%)	35–44 (%)	55–64 (%)	Over 65 (%)	All ages (millions)
Males					
1971	27	12	11	10	27.2
2001	21	15	11	14	28.8
2021[1]	18	13	13	18	31.4
Females					
1971	24	11	12	16	28.8
2001	19	15	11	18	30.2
2021[1]	17	12	13	22	32.4

Note: [1] Projections.
Source: Adapted from *Social Trends*. Available via www.ons.gov.uk.

The UK's ageing population is a characteristic shared by many other countries, including those in the European Union. Data produced by Eurostat indicate similar trends in both the original EU-15 and in the new accession countries (Table 6.3). In comparison, both India and China have a much smaller percentage of the population

Table 6.3 Percentage of EU populations aged 65 and over for selected EU countries, 1970–2011

Country	1970	1991	2003	2011
Germany	13	15	17	21
Belgium	13	15	17	17
Spain	9	14	17	17
Finland	9	13	15	18
Denmark	12	16	15	17
Estonia	12	12	16	17
Lithuania	10	11	15	18
Czech Republic	12	13	14	16
Slovakia	9	10	12	13
EU-27 average	12	14	16	18

Source: Adapted from Eurostat available via epp.eurostat.ec.europa.eu/ © European Union, 1995–2014. Figures are rounded.

in the over-65 category, the figures being around 5 per cent and 9 per cent respectively for 2012.

Other structural characteristics

Populations can also be examined in a number of other ways, including their ethnicity and geographical distribution. For instance, in the 2001 population census in the UK, around 8 per cent of people surveyed described themselves as belonging to a minority ethnic group; a Leeds University study in 2010 predicts this will rise to 20 per cent by 2051. The census data show that, in general, minority ethnic groups in the UK have a younger age structure than those in the 'White Group' and tend to be highly concentrated in large urban centres, particularly London. For the UK population as a whole, the majority of people live in England, with significant concentrations in regions such as the south-east, the Midlands, the north-west and the north-east, a fact that has important economic, political and social ramifications. Moreover, inter-regional movements of population, together with other factors such as international migration and differential birth and death rates, can result in significant local and regional variations in population over time, with a knock-on effect for both the public and private sectors (for example, demand for housing and school places).

Population change

As the previous analysis indicates, populations can change in either size and/or structure, with important consequences for economic activity both within and between countries. The size and structure of a country's population depend on a number of variables, the most important of which are the birth rate, the death rate and the net migration rate.

The birth rate

Birth rates tend to be expressed as the number of live births per thousand of the population in a given year. In many countries this figure has been falling steadily over a long period of time for a number of reasons. These include:

- a trend towards smaller families as people become better off and health improves and death rates fall;
- the increased availability of contraception;
- the trend towards later marriages and later childbearing for social and/or economic reasons;
- declining fertility rates;
- changing attitudes towards women and work.

In some countries, governments have offered financial and other incentives to married couples to try to reduce the birth rate (e.g. China) as a means of controlling population growth. In others, incentives have been offered to try to reverse the actual or potential decline in the birth rate because of its economic consequences (e.g. France, Singapore). Changing birth rates are, of course, an important contributor to an ageing population, but they can also have other effects. For instance, a recent increase in the birth rate in the UK has led to a call by the Optimum Population Trust for British couples to restrict themselves to two children in order to reduce the impact of population growth on the natural environment.

The death rate

Like birth rates, **death rates** are usually measured per thousand of the population in a given year. For developed economies such as the UK this figure has tended to fall over time before reaching a plateau. Among the main contributors to this trend have been:

- rising living standards, including better housing, sanitation and nutrition;
- developments in medical technology and practice;
- better education;
- improved working conditions.

The difference between the birth rate and the death rate represents the **natural change** in the population (i.e. increase or decrease).

Net migration

Apart from the movement of population within a country (internal migration), people may move from one country to another for a variety of reasons. The balance between those leaving (emigrants) and those entering (immigrants) a country over a given period of time represents the rate of **net migration**. Along with changes in the birth and/or death rate, this can be a significant factor in population change and can have important consequences for the economy (e.g. the gain or loss of certain skills) and for the political system. In the UK, estimates by the Migration Observatory at Oxford University have suggested that around 50 per cent of the country's increase in population between 1991 and 2010 was due to the direct contribution of net migration, much of which was related to EU enlargement.

Influences on the rate of net migration include:

- legal barriers (e.g. immigration laws);
- economic migrancy;
- the numbers fleeing persecution;
- government policy;
- political developments.

Demographic change and business

Changes in the size and/or structure of a country's population can affect enterprises in all sectors, both in the short and the long term. Given increased globalisation and international trade, the impact of demographic change has an international as well as a national dimension for a growing number of trading organisations.

The following examples provide illustrations of how a changing demography can influence both the level and pattern of demand within an economy and in turn help to explain why changes can occur in a country's economic and industrial structure (see Chapter 12) and why some countries engage in international trade (see Chapter 16). Demographic change can also have important effects on the supply side of the economy. You should try to think of other examples.

- As populations grow in size, the demand for many types of goods and services also tends to grow (e.g. energy, consumer durables, food). A growing population also provides a larger workforce, other things being equal.
- An 'ageing population' increases the demand for a range of public, private and voluntary sector goods and services (e.g. healthcare, pensions, specialist holidays, sheltered housing). It also creates an increasingly **dependent population**. The Office for Budget Responsibility (OBR) in the UK has calculated that by 2018 the country's ageing population will be costing the Exchequer an additional £19 billion.
- A declining birth rate influences the demand for education, children's products, childcare, certain TV programmes, comics, toys, etc. It can also reduce the numbers of young people available to enter the workforce to replace those who retire.
- Changes in the ethnic make-up of the population can affect the demand for particular food products, clothing and media services and can place increased demands on public authorities (e.g. documents printed in different languages). Some researchers also argue that a more diverse workforce can improve an organisation's performance.
- The regional redistribution of the population will affect the consumption of a range of goods and services, including housing, education, healthcare, transport, energy and many day-to-day products. It can also affect prices (e.g. in the housing market) and the make-up of the local labour market.

On a more general level, it is also worth remembering that demographic change can impact on a country's social as well as its economic structure and that this can result in increased (or reduced) demands on a range of organisations, particularly those in the public sector. For example, the growing imbalance being experienced in many countries between an increasing and dependent elderly population and a diminishing population of working age touches on many areas of public policy, from healthcare and social provision on the one hand to pensions and fiscal policy on the other. Governmental responses to the consequences of demographic change can have both direct and indirect consequences for a wide variety of organisations across the economy.

The social context

Being part of society, organisations are subject to a variety of societal influences that operate at both a general and a specific level. In this section we consider some of the key factors within an organisation's social environment, starting with the concept of social class. The notion that organisations also have responsibilities to society is examined in Chapter 9.

Social class

Throughout history, all societies have normally exhibited a certain degree of social and economic inequality that has given rise to the tendency to classify individuals into different social categories. For example, in India the 'caste system' has been an important source of social differentiation and one that has exerted a key influence over the life and opportunities available to members of the different castes. In other countries, including the United Kingdom, the categorisation of individuals has often been based around notions of social class, the idea of grouping together people who share a similar social status which is related to certain common features such as educational background, income and occupation. Whereas in some types of social system, movement between groups is either very difficult or impossible (e.g. the caste system), in others social mobility is frequently observed, with some individuals able to move relatively quickly between the different social strata (e.g. upper class, middle class, working class) as their personal circumstances change.

The process of allocating individuals to a particular class category has generally been based on socio-economic criteria such as income, wealth and occupational status. Advertisers and market researchers – including the Institute of Practitioners in Advertising – have tended to favour a scheme known as 'ABC1' (see Table 6.4), which uses an individual's occupation as a basis for allocation, the assumption being that a person's job is closely linked to key aspects of her/his attitudes and behaviour, including their choice of car, clothes, home furnishings, holidays, reading material and so on. There is even evidence to suggest that class might be influential in an individual's choice of retail outlets (e.g. different UK supermarket chains appear to attract customers from different socio-economic groups).[1]

Table 6.4 The ABC1 system of social grading

Social grading	Social status	Occupation
A	Upper middle class	Higher managerial, administrative and professional
B	Middle class	Intermediate managerial, administrative and professional
C1	Lower middle class	Supervisory or clerical, junior managerial, administrative and professional
C2	Skilled working class	Skilled manual workers
D	Working class	Semi and unskilled manual workers
E	Lowest subsistence level	State pensioners or widows, casual workers, lowest grade workers

mini case A new class structure?

According to the Great British Class Survey (2013) – a collaboration between the BBC and academics from six universities – the traditional three-class model (working, middle and upper) may no longer be sufficient to describe the British class structure. Using economic, social and cultural indicators to define a person's social class, the researchers suggested that the following seven categories of class now seemed more appropriate to modern Britain. These are presented in descending (sic) order:

1 *Elite* – individuals educated at top universities, with average savings of more than £140,000 and possessing extensive social contacts. Members of this class constitute about 6 per cent of the population.

2 *Established middle class* – comprising around 25 per cent of the population, this group scores highly on economic, social and cultural capital, has a household income of £47,000 and some 'highbrow' tastes.

3 *Technical middle class* – a small new group of prosperous individuals, but who score lowly on social and cultural capital.

4 *New affluent worker* – people with middling levels of economic capital and who are young and socially and culturally aware.

5 *Traditional working class* – making up around 14 per cent of the population, this group tends to be property owners, largely middle-aged and with low scores on all forms of capital.
6 *Emergent social worker* – with a mean age of 34 and a high proportion of ethnic minority members, this group is relatively poor but has high social and cultural capital.
7 *Precariat* – or precarious proletariat, this group comprises about 15 per cent of the total population. Members have average savings of £800, an after tax income of £8,000 and are unlikely to be university graduates.

As with any new system of classification of this kind, there are inevitably going to be criticisms. In a letter to *The Guardian* (6 April 2013), two leading UK academics pointed out that the current NS-SEC scheme used by the ONS, public organisations and researchers alike currently identifies eight social classes based on a wide range of socio-economic indicators. They also suggested that the authors seemed to have started by choosing a set of outcomes and then allocating individuals to different groups on this basis. In short, outcomes seemed to have been used to determine social class, rather than class determining outcomes, the latter being the approach normally used by social researchers.

Similar systems of classification have also been/are used for official purposes (e.g. the UK ten-year census of population). In the 1990s in the UK, government statistics used what was called the Registrar General's Social Scale – subsequently renamed 'Social Class based on Occupation' – to group the UK population into seven different categories according to their occupation (e.g. Group I was professional; Group II was managerial and technical; Group V was unskilled occupations). This system has now been replaced by NS-SEC (the National Statistics Socio-Economic Classifications), which again focuses on occupation as the key criterion for class allocation. An example of NS-SEC is shown in Table 6.5. The figures in the right-hand column represent the socio-economic classification of the UK population of working age in autumn 2005.[2] Current figures are difficult to obtain as some revision to the approach has taken place in recent years.

While it would be unwise to assume that a factor such as a person's social class will invariably affect their choice of goods and services, empirical evidence reveals some interesting variations in the levels of expenditure on particular products among different groups in the UK population, a fact not lost on marketing organisations, which often use socio-economic criteria as one way to segment a market (see below). According to data produced by the Office for National Statistics (see Table 6.6), total expenditure was highest among the large employer and higher managerial group and was more than three times that of people in the never worked/long-term unemployed category. Within this overall pattern of expenditure some interesting data emerge, particularly with regards to priorities, as indicated by expenditure on different items by the different social groupings. For instance, expenditure on restaurants and hotels and on recreation and culture was significantly higher among the large employer/higher managerial group than other groups, while spending on housing, fuel and power was similar across most categories. Note that spending by people in the never worked/long-term unemployed group shows clear evidence of the impact of the prolonged recession in the UK economy after 2008.

Table 6.5 National Statistics Socio-Economic Classifications (NS-SEC)

Category	Occupation	Estimated % of working population in 2005
1	Higher managerial and professional occupations	11.1
1.1	Employers and managers in larger organisations (e.g. company directors, senior managers, senior civil servants, senior police and armed forces officers)	
1.2	Higher professionals such as doctors, lawyers, teachers, social workers, clergy	
2	Lower managerial/professional occupations, including nurses, midwives, journalists, actors, musicians, prison officers, etc.	22.4
3	Intermediate occupations, for example clerks, secretaries, driving instructors	10.0
4	Small employers and own-account workers such as publicans, farmers, taxi drivers, window cleaners, painters and decorators	7.6
5	Lower supervisory, craft and related occupations, including plumbers, printers, train drivers and butchers	9.1
6	Semi-routine occupations, for example shop assistants, hairdressers, bus drivers, cooks	12.8
7	Routine occupations such as labourers, couriers, waiters, refuse collectors	9.3
8	People who have never had paid work or are long-term unemployed	3.8

Source: Office for National Statistics.

Table 6.6 Household expenditure (£/week) by socio-economic classification of household reference person, by selected categories, 2011

	Large employers and higher managerial	Intermediate occupations	Routine occupations	Never worked and long-term unemployed[1]
Transport	137.30	67.90	48.10	15.10
Recreation and culture	115.30	62.30	46.80	25.90
Food and non-alcoholic drink	69.90	56.30	53.50	42.60
Housing, fuel and power	74.50	67.60	73.00	44.70
Restaurant and hotels	83.20	43.20	32.00	18.30
Clothing and footwear	40.80	23.80	20.80	9.80
Alcohol, tobacco and narcotics	17.80	10.60	16.60	8.00
Communication	15.90	14.50	13.00	7.40
Education	14.80	4.70	[0.70]	[3.00]
Health	12.50	8.00	5.00	0.60
All expenditure groups	703.90	426.20	365.90	196.80

Note: [1] This category excludes students. Figures in brackets are based on very small samples.
Source: Adapted from ONS, Family Spending, 2011.

Lifestyles

Another factor that can clearly affect people's attitudes and behaviour is the **lifestyle** that they choose to adopt. Lifestyles are basically concerned with the way in which people live and how they spend their money, decisions which are not necessarily always linked to their socio-economic position. Two individuals with the same occupation – and nominally in the same social class – may have entirely different lifestyles, a point well illustrated by examining two university lecturers. My own lifestyle is highly sophisticated, environmentally sensitive, artistic and cosmopolitan; that of a colleague – who happens to teach marketing – is narrow, parochial, philistine and consumption-driven. Then, what would one expect?!

Joking apart, lifestyle analysis provides another way of seeking to categorise and explain human behaviour, based on factors such as an individual's interests, activities and opinions as well as on their demographic characteristics. The proposition is that by examining distinctive patterns of consumer response, a marketing organisation can build up a clearer picture of an individual's habits, preferences and behaviour and by doing so can design more effective and appealing products, marketing programmes and/or communications that can be aimed at specific lifestyle groups. Data collected from an individual's use of social networking sites and from their expenditure choices (e.g. their supermarket bills) are particularly useful in this regard.

While we should be cautious of over-generalising, the evidence suggests that in many countries the way in which people spend their time and money has changed considerably in recent decades as a result of changes in demography, working patterns, technology, income and a range of other factors. Once again we can illustrate this by looking at longitudinal data collected through the annual survey of social trends in the UK. These data show, for example, that between 1971 and 2009:

- household spending on communication (including mobile phones) increased more than eleven-fold. Within this period, ownership of mobile phone equipment and services rose from 27 per cent in the late 1990s to 79 per cent in 2008, internet access by households rising from 10 per cent to 66 per cent during the same period;
- there was an eight times increase in spending on recreation and culture and a five-fold rise in spending on overseas holidays. Alcoholic drinks and tobacco was the only category of expenditure that fell during the period.

Other social trends data indicate that:

- by 2009–10 40 per cent of household waste per person was being recycled, composted or reused compared with less than 1 per cent in 1983–4;
- domestic energy consumption in the UK increased by 18 per cent between 1970 and 2009;
- there were 1.8 billion transactions by cheque in 1985 compared with only 0.6 billion in 2009 as a result of a rapid growth in the use of electronic payment methods;
- almost all (98 per cent) single music tracks were purchased digitally in 2009, with digital sales increasing more than 90 per cent between 2007 and 2009;

- in 2009–10 UK adults (16 and over) spent an average of 3.5 hours watching TV, 2.5 hours using a computer and 1 hour listening to the radio;
- sales of books by UK publishers fell by almost 6 per cent between 2007 and 2009. This trend is particularly worrying!

If we take changing expenditure patterns in the UK as an indication of changes in lifestyles, then there has been a discernible shift in emphasis from essential products such as food, housing, water and fuel to the less essential items such as communications, and recreation and culture. This can be seen in Table 6.7, which highlights the changing volumes of household spending in particular categories of goods and services over a 38-year period.

Table 6.7 Volume of household expenditure on selected items, 1971–2009, expressed as index numbers (base year 1971)

Category of spending	1971	1991	2001	2009
Food and non-alcoholic drink	100	117	137	151
Alcohol and tobacco	100	92	88	90
Housing, water, fuel	100	139	152	160
Health	100	182	188	229
Communication	100	306	790	1126
Recreation and culture	100	279	545	869
Transport	100	181	246	273

Source: Adapted from ONS.

In light of the discussion on inflation in Chapter 5, it is worth noting that such changes in spending patterns over time are reflected in changes in the official 'basket of goods and services' used to calculate the Retail Prices Index (and the CPI) in the UK. The 1980s saw CDs, CD players and condoms added to the basket, with computers, camcorders and mobile phone charges added in the next decade. By 2004–5 dishwater tablets had replaced dishwasher powder, wooden garden furniture sets had replaced plastic sets and leather sofas had replaced ordinary ones. More bizarrely, hamsters and popcorn bought in cinemas had been added to the index, while baguettes, corned beef and writing paper were dropped (see, for example, *The Guardian*, 22 March 2005, p. 20). By 2007–8, the RPI contained fruit smoothies, USB sticks, peppers, muffins and small oranges and had discarded microwaves, TV repairs, washable carpets and 35mm camera films. In 2013 it included e-books, continental meats, blueberries, vegetable stir fry and kitchen wall units. What does this tell us about the changing lifestyles and spending habits of UK citizens; are people in the UK getting healthier? Judging by the current statistics on obesity and alcohol consumption, we should be cautious about drawing this conclusion.

Many of the trends referred to above are, of course, mirrored in consumer aspirations and behaviour in other countries, particularly in respect of issues such as healthier lifestyles, increased foreign travel, greater access to communications technology and more environmentally friendly products (though not necessarily rodent purchases!). Thus, while some firms have benefited from the changing trends (e.g. Facebook, Twitter, Apple, Google), others have experienced a decline in business as a result of factors such as changes in habits, in the law or in competition (e.g. France has experienced a substantial fall in the number of bistros and cafés over the last decade). Where change occurs, there will always be winners and losers.

Other social influences

While it is important to consider the influence of broad social factors such as class and lifestyles, it is also worth remembering that consumers are individuals and that they are subject to influences that operate at a personal level. Such influences include the wide variety of individuals and groups with whom we come into contact during our lifetime and who may influence our attitudes, values, opinions and/or behaviour. Primary among these are our interactions within the family, with friends or work colleagues, and through our involvement with sports and social clubs, religious organisations, trade unions and so on. Such groups are sometimes referred to as reference groups.

Groups that have a regular or direct (i.e. face-to-face) influence on us are known as primary reference groups, while those whose influence tends to be more indirect and formal are known as secondary reference groups. The former, in particular, can be very influential in shaping our attitudes and behaviour, including our decisions on consumption.

The importance of reference groups – especially family and friends – is recognised by both economists and marketers, with the former using the notion of 'households' (see Chapter 5) to indicate that the consumption of goods and services often takes place within a collective family framework, as in the case of groceries, holidays, vehicles and many other everyday products. Marketers use concepts such as the family life cycle to show changing patterns of consumption as the individual moves from being a child in a family to being a parent with different needs and responsibilities.

While it is difficult to be precise about when and how far an individual's demand is shaped by the family and other reference groups, it is not difficult to think of particular examples when this is likely to be the case. For many services such as builders, restaurants, hotels, hairdressers and car repairs, consumers often rely on the advice of a trusted friend or colleague and firms can gain new business through such word-of-mouth recommendations. Equally, through membership and/or support of a particular group or club, individuals may be tempted to purchase particular goods and/or services (e.g. football kit, trainers, a CD, tickets), especially those with a desirable 'brand name' and endorsed by a well-known personality (e.g. sportsperson, musician, singer, film star). In such cases, the demand for the product is often less price sensitive (see Chapter 14) since it is a 'must-have' product.

The cultural environment

Culture

The term culture generally refers to a complex set of values, norms, beliefs, attitudes, customs, systems and artefacts, handed down from generation to generation through the process of socialisation, and which influences how individuals see the world and how they behave in it. Defined in this way, culture can be seen to have at least three important features:

- it comprises both material (e.g. human artefacts such as buildings, literature, art, music) and abstract elements (e.g. rituals, symbols, values);
- it is socially learned and transmitted over time; and
- it influences human behaviour.

As a concept, 'culture' is often applied in a variety of circumstances at both the macro and the micro level: terms such as 'western culture', 'Asian culture', 'European culture', 'New York City culture', 'youth culture', 'pop culture', 'entrepreneurial culture' and 'research culture' are just some of the examples of its usage in the modern world. What they have in common is that they imply certain shared aspects of human belief, understanding and behaviour that link individuals into some form of definable group and/or range of activities.

In a business context, it can be easy to underestimate the degree to which a person's perceptions, attitudes and behaviour can be shaped by cultural influences, some of which may be relatively enduring (e.g. certain 'core' values and beliefs) while others may be more open to change (i.e. secondary beliefs and values). In the United States, for example, American citizens believe in the right of individuals to bear arms and this is enshrined in the US Constitution. The buying and selling of handguns and rifles is thus acceptable within American society, despite the fact that they are frequently used in violent crimes, including robbery and murder. In other countries, trade in such weapons tends to be seen as highly questionable by most people and is usually heavily regulated by the government to certain types of weapons for use in acceptable pursuits such as hunting or rifle shooting. Cultural differences such as this can, of course, apply not only to the kinds of goods and services that are consumed (e.g. eating horsemeat in France is acceptable but not in the UK) but also to other aspects of both the production and consumption process and this can have important implications for an organisation's behaviour.

Examples include:

- who decides what is bought, how it is bought or where it is bought (e.g. in some cultures women have predominantly been the purchasers of household products);
- what colours are acceptable (e.g. the colour associated with bereavement varies across cultures);
- how far harmonisation of products and marketing activities is feasible (e.g. the EU's perennial debates over what constitutes an acceptable definition of certain products such as sausages, feta cheese, chocolate);
- what factors can enhance the prospect of a sale (e.g. bribes are acceptable in some cultures);
- how business is conducted (e.g. the length of negotiations, the meaning of a handshake);
- the method of communicating with the target audience (e.g. in the UK a single shared language allows organisations to use national media);
- how customer enquiries/complaints are dealt with (e.g. UK businesses using call centres in India often give their operators British names and train them to talk about everyday British preoccupations such as the weather and sport).

Culture not only influences an individual's response to products and the nature of the buying and selling process, it also exercises a significant influence on the structure of consumption within a given society. For companies that can gain acceptability on a global scale, despite cultural differences between countries, the potential benefits are huge (e.g. global brands such as Coca-Cola, McDonald's, Nike).

While the so-called 'Americanisation' of consumption is not to everyone's taste, other forms of cultural exportation are often more acceptable and can prove highly lucrative for the country concerned, exemplified by the UK's overseas earnings from culture and arts-related tourism (see Chapter 16). Many other countries benefit in similar ways.

mini case: National cultures

Recognising and responding to cultural differences between countries can have an important impact on how successful organisations are in international trade. But is it possible to generalise about a country's culture?

One academic who has made a significant contribution in this area is Professor Geert Hofstede, who has developed a theory of culture that allows comparisons to be made between the main cultural characteristics in different countries. Hofstede's research is based on data collected from IBM employees across the world while he was working at the company as a psychologist. On the basis of his research Hofstede identified four cultural dimensions; later he added a fifth. These dimensions can be used to compare value systems at different levels, from the family through to the state.

The five cultural dimensions are as follows:

1 *Power distance* – this is concerned with the degree to which the members of a society accept an unequal or hierarchical power structure. In societies where the power distance is large, there is a perception that inequality exists and subordinates tend to be more dependent on their superiors. This can result in an autocratic or paternalistic style of management or governance (e.g. in some African countries), which can evoke either positive or negative reactions. Where the power distance is small, individuals tend to see themselves more as equals and management/governance styles tend to be more consultative and less hierarchical (e.g. in northern European countries).

2 *Uncertainty avoidance* – this focuses on how members of society cope with uncertainty in their lives. Where levels of anxiety are generally high, this results in high uncertainty avoidance and people in these cultures are deemed to be more expressive and emotional (e.g. Latin American countries) than in low uncertainty avoidance countries (e.g. many Asian countries).

3 *Individualism* – this refers to the extent to which individuals in society see themselves as independent and autonomous human beings or as part of a collectivity. High individualist countries tend to be those such as the USA, the UK, Canada and Australia; low individualism is said to be prevalent in Asian and Latin American countries.

4 *Masculinity* – this is concerned with how far a society is predisposed to aggressive and materialistic behaviour and is linked to gender role. Hofstede associates masculinity with toughness, assertiveness and materialism and with a predisposition to conflict and competition. Femininity, in contrast, is characterised as caring, sensitive and concerned with the quality of life; the result is a more accommodating style based on negotiation and compromise. Hofstede's analysis suggests the more masculine countries include Austria and Japan, while Scandinavian countries tend to be the most feminine.

5 *Long-term orientation* – this relates to the degree to which a society embraces a long-term view and respect for tradition. In societies with a short-term orientation, people tend to stress the 'here and now', typified by western countries. Eastern cultures, by comparison, are generally held to have a longer-term orientation that emphasises concern for the future and for tradition as well as for the present.

One of the benefits of Hofstede's research is that it reminds us that cultural differences can and do occur between states and, as a result, there is no 'one-size-fits-all' style of management or governance that would be suitable across all countries. For companies that are multinational organisations, management styles and approaches in the country of origin may not necessarily be suitable in other parts of the organisation for cultural reasons. Vive la différence!

Sub-culture

A society is rarely, if ever, culturally homogeneous. Within every culture **sub-cultures** usually exist, comprising groups of individuals with shared value systems based on common experiences, origins and/or situations. These identifiable sub-groups may be distinguished by nationality, race, ethnicity, religion, age, class, geographical location or some other factor and their attitudes, behaviour, customs, language and artefacts often reflect sub-cultural differences. At times such differences can be relatively easily accommodated and ultimately may become institutionalised through the legal and/or political process (e.g. the Scottish and Welsh Assemblies – see Chapter 4). At other times sub-cultural differences can be the source of a considerable degree of conflict between various sub-groups, resulting in serious divisions within a society and even in civil war and genocide.

The UK provides a good example of the notion of **cultural diversity** and can be used to illustrate how this can influence the demand for goods and services. In addition to nationality groups such as the Irish, Scots and Welsh, the country has provided a home for successive generations of immigrants from around the globe and this has created a rich mix of ethnic and other sub-groups, often concentrated in particular parts of the country and having their own language, traditions and lifestyles. In Leicester, for instance, where a significant proportion of the population is of Asian origin, there is a substantial Asian business community, part of which has developed to cater specifically for the local ethnic population (e.g. halal butchers, saree shops), as well as attracting custom from the wider community (e.g. Indian restaurants). Many Asian businesses in Leicester are small, family-owned enterprises, employing members of the extended family in keeping with cultural traditions. Aspects such as the organisation and financing of the business, its network of relationships and the working conditions for staff are also frequently influenced by cultural values, traditions and norms, although changes in these areas are becoming more apparent, especially among second- and third-generation Asian-owned enterprises.

Application: market segmentation

Marketers have long recognised the importance of demographic, social and cultural factors in shaping people's demand for goods and services. This is exemplified by the concept of **market segmentation**.

Market segmentation refers to the practice of dividing a market into distinct groups of buyers who share the same or similar attitudes and patterns of behaviour and who might require separate products or marketing to meet their particular needs. By segmenting a market into its broad component parts, businesses should be able to focus their marketing efforts more effectively and efficiently by developing product offerings and marketing programmes which meet the requirements of the different market segments.

Markets can be segmented in a variety of ways and this tends to differ between consumer markets and those which involve business-to-business transactions. Table 6.8 outlines some of the major variables used in segmenting consumer markets. As the table indicates, demographic, social and cultural factors provide a basis for identifying distinct market segments within the markets for consumer goods and services. In practice, of course, marketers may use either one (e.g. demography) or a combination (e.g. age, location and social class) of different variables to segment a market they are seeking to target.

Table 6.8 Methods of segmenting consumer markets

Type of segmentation	Key segmentation variables	Examples
Demographic	Age, gender, religion, ethnic group, family size, family life cycle stage	Children's products, ethnic foods, 18–30 holidays, retirement homes, cars
Socio-economic	Social class, income, occupation	Luxury products, convenience services, discount goods
Geographic	Country, region, urban/suburban/rural, town/city, climate	Country clothing, air conditioning, regional specialities
Geo-demographic	House type and location	Conservatories, lawnmowers
Psychographic	Lifestyles, values, personality	Health/healthier products, cosmetics, cigarettes
Mediagraphic	Media habits (e.g. papers read)	Specialist magazines, eco-friendly holidays
Behavioural	Behavioural characteristics including time/occasion of purchase, loyalty, user status, benefits sought, attitude to product, etc.	Mother's Day products, disposable cameras, toothpaste

A good example of combining the different variables is provided by the notion of **geo-demographic segmentation**, which focuses on the relationship between an individual's geographical location and her/his demographic characteristics, given that close links frequently exist between a person's place and type of residence and factors such as income, family size and attitudes. One well-known scheme of this type is **ACORN** (A Classification of Residential Neighbourhoods), which uses 40 variables from population census data to differentiate residential areas. Another is **MOSAIC**, developed by Experian, which draws on a variety of data sources (e.g. census data, financial data, property characteristics, demographic information) and uses a range of sophisticated analytical techniques to produce household profiles at full postcode level. Under the MOSAIC scheme, UK households are divided into 11 groups with names such as 'Symbols of Success', 'Suburban Comfort' and 'Grey Perspectives' and these are then further sub-divided into 61 types, again with interesting and evocative names, including 'Golden Empty Nesters', 'Sprawling Subtopia' and 'Childfree Serenity'. For a fuller description of MOSAIC and Experian's other products (e.g. commercial MOSAIC) and methodology you should access the company's website at *www.experian.co.uk* and follow the links.

With regard to factors such as social class and lifestyles, these tend to be grouped under the notion of **psychographic segmentation**, an approach that has attracted considerable attention in recent years given the reciprocal link between lifestyles and consumption indicated above. Lifestyle segments can be developed either as 'off-the-shelf' products by marketing agencies/management consultancies or can be customised for/by individual companies, although the latter often tend to be both complex and expensive to design. One established and popular example of the former is **VALS** (Values and Lifestyles) developed by SRI International. Under this model, individuals are allocated to different categories on the basis of a combination of demographic and lifestyle factors such as age, education, income and levels of self-confidence, and then these categories are grouped into a number of broader segments, which reflect a category's predominant orientations. Thus, under VALS 2, the three broad groups identified were (1) people who were *principle-orientated* (i.e. guided by their views of how the world should be); (2) people who were *status-orientated* (i.e. guided by the opinions and actions of others); (3) people who were *action-orientated* (i.e. guided by the desire for social and physical activity, variety in life and risk taking). Again you can gain further information on this scheme by visiting the SRI website at *www.sri.com/*.

Synopsis

All organisations are an integral part of the society in which they exist and carry out their activities and as a result are affected by a range of influences emanating from the demographic, social and cultural environment. These influences can change over time and help to shape both the demand and supply sides of business activity. Businesses and other organisations need to be aware of and respond to the process of societal change and to the opportunities and threats that such change can engender.

Summary of key points

- Organisations exist and operate within society and are subject to a variety of demographic and socio-cultural influences.
- Demography is concerned with population variables, including population size, structure and distribution.
- Changes in demography are primarily related to changes in birth and/or death and/or net migration rates.
- Demographic change can affect both the demand and supply sides of the economy.
- The social context of business includes factors such as social class, lifestyles and reference group influences. The consumption of goods and services in an economy can be linked to such factors.
- The cultural environment of business comprises those institutions and other forces that help to shape society's basic attitudes, values, perceptions, preferences and behaviour.
- Societies usually also contain sub-cultures, which can influence a person's beliefs, attitudes and actions.
- Like demography and social factors, cultural influences can change over time and can affect organisations. Businesses need to be sensitive to such change.
- The importance of demographic, social and cultural factors in business can be illustrated by the concept of market segmentation.

case study: An invitation to 'tweet'

The last decade has seen a remarkable explosion in the use of social media/social networking sites by individuals, groups and organisations. Facebook, Twitter, YouTube and others now attract hundreds of millions of users across the globe on a daily basis, a growing number of whom use smartphones and tablets to access these media services. Interacting with others and creating and sharing content through internet-based communities has become relatively commonplace, as has shopping for products on the internet and accessing online music, videos and sports content.

Where businesses are concerned, social networking sites appear to provide substantial marketing opportunities for firms of all sizes. Media can be used to build stronger relationships with existing customers, attract new consumers, inform users about current and future goods and services, generally promote the business and the firm's brand name(s), and find out what customers think about the organisation and its performance, including the issue of customer satisfaction. Most major firms now have a Facebook site and/or use Twitter to communicate with existing and potential consumers who are encouraged to 'follow' the business via the different media and to receive regular updates on its products and activities.

As a tool for marketing communication, social media sites have a number of important advantages. They are often free to businesses; they have a broad (often global) reach; they are fast and easy to access; they can be used to target specific groups of individuals; they allow an organisation to communicate with particular customers or groups on a personal basis at any point in time and wherever they may be. Far from replacing other forms of marketing communication and promotion, social media usage has become an additional weapon in the armoury of participating businesses; many firms have been quick to recognise that for a rapidly growing number of individuals, accessing the different networking sites is an essential part of their daily lives and hence a potentially lucrative marketing opportunity that can be exploited by suppliers of goods and services.

For organisations that choose to use social media to market their businesses, there can be risks involved, a point illustrated by the following example. In October 2013, Britain's largest energy company, British Gas, announced its intention of increasing energy prices by 10 per cent, which was around three times the level of inflation. Faced with a consumer and political backlash over its decision, the company decided to use Twitter[1] to try to head off criticism of its price hike by inviting questions from concerned customers. In the event, the organisation's attempts to pacify angry consumers proved to be a PR disaster,[2] with almost 16,000 Twitter comments – most of which were vitriolic – raining down on the company within a few hours of the invitation. To compound the problem, British Gas evidently failed to answer customers' tweets, choosing instead to use the networking site to explain to customers the reason for the decision to raise energy prices substantially, despite an earlier promise by the parent group, Centrica, to use windfall profits from the previous winter to keep prices down.

As this example illustrates, communicating with customers through social media needs to be undertaken with care and forethought; bad news can spread as rapidly as good news, even if only 140 characters are available. It doesn't take much to get things wrong, however genuine the intention.

Notes

1 Twitter – which was established in 2006 – is a 'micro-blogging' service which allows individuals and organisations to send and receive short messages about all kinds of issues and topics, including world events (e.g. the 'Arab Spring'). Popular with ordinary individuals, celebrities and companies alike, it currently attracts hundreds of millions of users worldwide, who send around 1 billion tweets every two and a half days. Like Facebook, Twitter has recently become a public company and derives most of its revenue from advertising. By 2015 it is estimated that its advertising revenue is likely to be in the region of $1 billion, or almost double its earnings in 2013.

2 British Gas's experience is reminiscent of the wrath engendered by Starbucks' invitation to 'spread the cheer' via Twitter at Christmas time 2012. This prompted a plethora of angry tweets over the company's failure to pay UK corporation tax, which had received widespread media coverage.

Case study questions

1 What are the key advantages for firms of using social networking sites to market themselves and/or their products?

2 Is the use of social media by businesses size dependent, i.e. predominantly limited to larger firms?

Review and discussion questions

1 What is meant by an 'ageing' population? Examine some of the key ways in which an ageing population can affect the supply side of the economy.

2 In a country of your choice, identify some of the major social trends over the last decade. How are these trends reflected in changing patterns of consumption?

3 What is meant by the term 'culture'? To what extent do you agree with the proposition that globalisation could destroy local cultural diversity?

4 Why do marketers segment markets? Give examples of particular markets where demographic segmentation might be appropriate.

Assignments

1 Assume you work in the HR department of a large retail organisation that is seeking to replace staff who are about to retire. Because of demographic and other trends you anticipate problems in recruiting school leavers in sufficient numbers. Produce a report outlining the problem to senior executives and suggest possible solutions. Provide justifications for your recommendations.

2 Choose three countries from different continents. Produce data to show the age distribution of the population in each of the countries in a given year. Account for any differences in the age profile of the three countries and suggest ways in which these differences might affect their respective economies in both the short and the long term.

Notes and references

1 See, for example, Worthington, I., Britton, C. and Rees, A., *Economics for Business: Blending Theory and Practice*, 2nd edition, Financial Times/Prentice Hall, 2005, pp. 86–89.

2 The figure for long-term unemployment excludes students and others who are not officially in paid employment (e.g. housewives).

Further reading

Hofstede, G., *Culture's Consequences: Comparing Values, Behaviors, Institutions and Organizations Across Nations*, 2nd edition, Sage, 2003.

Hofstede, G., Hofstede, G. J. and Minkov, M., *Cultures and Organizations: Software of the Mind*, 3rd edition (Google eBook), McGraw-Hill Professional, 2010.

Kotler, P., Armstrong, G., Wong, V. and Saunders, J., *Principles of Marketing*, 5th European edition, Pearson Education, 2008.

Masterson, R. and Pickton, D., *Marketing: An Introduction*, 3rd edition, Sage, 2014.

Morrison, J., *The Global Business Environment: Meeting the Challenges*, 3rd edition, Palgrave Macmillan, 2011, Chapter 6.

Office for National Statistics, available free online (*www.statistics.gov.uk*).

Worthington, I., 'The social and economic context', in Rose, A. and Lawton, A., *Public Services Management*, Financial Times/Prentice Hall, 1999, pp. 26–43.

Web links and further questions are available on the website at:
www.pearsoned.co.uk/worthington

7 The resource context: people, technology and natural resources

Chris Britton

Businesses carry out a variety of activities, but their main activity is to produce goods and services to be sold on the market. In the production process, inputs are turned into outputs. Key inputs into the production process are people, technology and natural resources.

Learning outcomes

Having read this chapter you should be able to:

- illustrate the importance of people, technology and natural resources to business
- explain what determines the quality of labour in the economy
- demonstrate the effect of technological change on business
- outline the main issues affecting natural resources

Key terms

Capital	Land	Research and development
Computer-aided design (CAD)	Minimum wage	Resources
Derived demand	Natural resources	Social capital
Educated workforce	Negademand	Stock
Factor of production	Net investment	Technological change
Fixed capital	Non-renewable resources	Technological unemployment
Fracking	NVQs	Technology
Geographical immobility	Occupational immobility	Trade union
Gross investment	Occupational structure	Wage rate
Immobility of labour	Participation rate	Wages
Information technology	People	Workforce
Infrastructure	Process innovation	Working capital
Innovation	Product innovation	Working week
Investment	Renewable resources	
	Replacement investment	

Introduction

The main aim of business is to produce goods and services that people want. This production cannot take place without people, technology and natural resources. In economics, these three are called the factors of production and are categorised under the headings of labour, capital and land. This chapter will consider each of these in turn. **Resources** can be renewable or non-renewable. **Renewable resources** would include labour, water, fishing stocks, soil, air and solar power, even though many of these might not be renewable for a long period of time. **Non-renewable resources** would be most minerals, including oil, iron ore and coal, agricultural land, forests and electricity (in so far as most electricity is derived from minerals).

People

As indicated in Chapter 6, **people** are important in the economy as both producers and consumers of goods and services. For most products that are produced, people are the most important input into the production process. Therefore the quantity and quality of the people available in an economy will have a considerable impact upon the economy's ability to produce.

The quantity of people available for work depends upon a variety of factors:

- the size of the total population;
- the age structure of the population;
- the working population;
- the length of the working week;
- the wage level.

As well as the quantity of labour, productivity will be affected by its quality. This in turn depends upon:

- education and training;
- working conditions;
- welfare services (e.g. national insurance schemes, which cover sickness pay, the NHS, which maintains the health of workers; also many firms provide their own welfare services such as private pension plans, and so on);
- motivation;
- the quality of the other factors of production.

Some of the quantitative factors have already been discussed in the previous chapter. In this section we concentrate on the idea of the 'workforce' and associated issues, before considering the question of labour quality.

The workforce

The **workforce** is the number of people who are eligible and available to work and offer themselves up as such. The size of the workforce will be determined by the age at which people can enter employment, which in the United Kingdom is 18 years, and the age at which they leave employment. In the United Kingdom the retirement age for men is 65 years and for women will be 65 by 2020. Those included in the definition of the workforce are:

- those working in paid employment, even if they are over retirement age;
- part-time workers;
- the claimant unemployed;
- members of the armed forces;
- the self-employed.

The workforce in 2013 was 32.3 million, which is about 51 per cent of the total population. The importance of the workforce is two-fold: it produces the goods and services needed in the economy, and through the payment of taxes it supports the dependent population (i.e. the very old and the very young).

An important determinant of the size of the workforce is the **participation rate** (i.e. the proportion of the population who actually work). Table 7.1 shows that the participation rate for women in the UK was 75.3 per cent in the summer of 2013, somewhat lower than the male figure of 83.5 per cent. The figures have, however, been converging over the years. There has been a rise in participation rates for women at the same time as a fall in participation rates for men.

Table 7.1 Economic activity by gender (% men 16–64 and women 16–59), July 2013

	Men	Women
Economically active	83.5	75.3
In employment	76.4	69.7
Unemployed	8.5	7.4
Economically inactive	16.5	24.7

Source: Adapted from Table A03 Summary of National LFS Data, www.ons.gov.uk

The trend has been for increased participation rates for women over time as families have become smaller and because of the changing role of women in society as a whole, labour-saving devices in the home, government legislation to promote equal pay and treatment, and the increase in the pension age of women. Also important in this process are the changes in industrial structure which have led to more part-time service jobs (see Chapter 12).

There has been an increase in participation rates of married or cohabiting women with dependent children, from 67 per cent in 1996 to 70 per cent by 2013. There has been a similar increase in participation rates of lone mothers – from 43 per cent to 60 per cent over the same time period.

Table 7.2 gives some comparisons with other EU countries. The United Kingdom has the third-highest activity rates for men and women after Denmark and Germany. There are marked differences in the activity rates for women across the EU, but in every country they are lower than the male activity rate.

For more information on labour markets:
in the UK see *www.statistics.gov.uk/hub/labour-market/*
in Europe see *http://epp.eurostat.ec.europa.eu*
and in the world *www.oecd.org*

Table 7.2 Economic activity rates* by sex for selected EU countries (%), 2010

	Males	Females	All
UK	74.5	64.8	69.5
France	68.3	59.9	64.0
Germany	76.0	66.1	71.1
Belgium	67.4	56.5	62.0
Italy	67.7	46.2	56.9
Denmark	75.8	71.1	73.4
EU-27 average	70.1	58.6	64.2

Note: *As a percentage of the working-age population.
Source: Adapted from Table 2.2, http://epp.eurostat.ec.europa.eu/cache/ITY_OFFPUB/1, © European Union, 1995–2014.

The length of the working week

The average length of time for which people work is also a significant determinant of the quantity of labour that is available in an economy. Generally, the shorter the **working week**, the less labour there is available. There has been, over the last 100 years, a gradual reduction in the length of the working week; 40 hours is now roughly the norm, with a gradual increase in the number of holidays that people take. More recently, this trend has been reversed: the average working week in the UK was 42.8 hours in 2010. Table 7.3 shows the length of the average working week in selected EU countries.

Table 7.3 Average hours worked per week* for selected EU countries, 2010

	All
UK	42.8
France	41.1
Germany	41.8
Belgium	41.2
Italy	40.7
Denmark	41.8
Netherlands	41.0
EU 15 average	41.5
EU 25 average	41.6

Note: *Full-time employees.
Source: Table 2.8, http://epp.eurostat.ec.europa.eu/cache/ITY_OFFPUB/1, © European Union, 1995–2014.

Both men and women in the UK work a longer week than men and women in all other EU countries. A relatively new phenomenon in the UK is the use of zero-hours contracts – see mini case study.

mini case Zero-hours contracts

A growing trend in the UK is the use of the zero-hours contract (ZHC), where employees are not guaranteed any hours' work per week but are expected to be 'on call'. They can be called in as and when they are required. They often typically work much more than zero hours, but nothing is

Figure 7.1 Numbers employed on zero-hours contracts, Oct–Dec, UK, thousands

Source: Adapted from 'Working Zero Hours, 2005–2012', www.ons.gov.uk

guaranteed. They are only paid for the work they do and often have to ask their employer's permission to take other employment. These sorts of contracts are not new – there are some jobs which by their very nature require ZHCs, examination invigilation for example. Schools, colleges and universities have a big demand for invigilators at certain times of the year. It would be uneconomic for them to use permanent full- or even part-time employees for this job. In this case ZHCs benefit the employees as well, many invigilators being retired teachers who are happy with this working arrangement.

The Labour Force Survey (LFS) estimated that in quarter 4 of 2012, 0.8 per cent of the UK workforce (250,000) were on ZHCs. This number is disputed by the Chartered Institute of Personnel and Development (CIPD) and the Unite trade union as being a gross underestimate of the total (the Labour Force Survey data is based on a survey and there could be misunderstandings of the questions). The CIPD estimates that in 2013 3–4 per cent of the workforce was employed on ZHCs, approximately 1 million people. Even using the LFS data, there is a definite upward trend in the use of ZHCs, as Figure 7.1 shows.

ZHCs are more commonly used in large companies (23 per cent of companies with more than 100 employees compared with 11 per cent of those companies with 50–99 employees). There are differences between sectors: they are most common in hotels and restaurants (19 per cent in 2011), health (13 per cent in 2011) and education (10 per cent in 2011).[1] It is estimated that some retailers and hospitality companies have more than 80 per cent of their workers on ZHCs.

There are arguments for and against ZHCs:

1 ZHCs give flexibility to both employer and employee.
2 There is less security for employees.
3 Employees are open to possible exploitation by employers.
4 There are problems with arranging child care at short notice.

Although there is much bad press about ZHCs, it is not all negative. The CIPD found that the levels of job satisfaction of those on ZHCs were just as high as those of other employees. More than half of the employees surveyed by the CIPD said that they would not want to work longer hours (but they may be working more hours anyway). The debate continues in the press and has reached the level of government debate, with possible legislation on ZHCs in 2014.

Wages

It is clear that **wages** will affect how much people are willing to work and therefore the overall supply of labour in the economy. The analysis here will use the basic tools of demand and supply described in Chapter 14. It is advisable to review that chapter before proceeding.

The market for labour can be likened to the market for any other commodity, in that there will be a demand for and a supply of labour. The demand for labour will come from the firm that wishes to produce goods and services that can be sold in the market. The demand for labour is a '**derived demand**' as its demand is derived from the demand that exists for what it produces. The demand curve can be assumed to be a normal downward-sloping demand curve which indicates that – everything else being equal – as the wage rate goes up, the demand for labour goes down.[2] The supply of labour comes from people. It is equally likely that the total supply curve has the normal upward slope, indicating that as the wage rate increases the supply of labour increases. It is argued that as the wage rate increases past a certain level, people would prefer to substitute leisure for wages. The individual supply curve will therefore bend backwards at that wage rate. The total supply curve, however, will be upward sloping, indicating that those not working will be encouraged to offer their services and that those already working might be encouraged to work overtime.

Assuming for the time being that the labour market is a totally free market, the **wage rate** and the amount of labour being used will be determined by the forces of demand and supply, as in Figure 7.2. The equilibrium wage rate is £W and the equilibrium quantity of labour is L. If there is a change in the level of demand or supply, there will be a corresponding change in the wages and quantity of labour.

Trade unions and wages

In the UK there are four different types of **trade union**:

1 *Craft unions*. They represent one particular craft or skill, like the Boilermakers Union, which was formed in 1834 and was the longest-lived craft union in the TUC when it merged with the GMB in 1982. These were the earliest type of union.

Figure 7.2 The market for labour

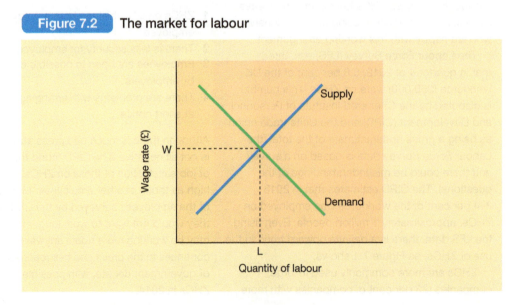

2 *Industrial unions.* They have members doing different jobs but in the same industry. Industrial unions are more common in other countries, but some UK unions come close to this type; for example, the National Union of Miners.
3 *General unions.* They contain members doing different jobs in different industries, such as the Transport and General Workers Union.
4 *White collar unions.* They represent the non-manual workers like teachers, social workers and so forth. An example is UNISON.

For information on trade unions in the UK see *www.tuc.org.uk*

One of the main aims for all types of union has been to counteract and protect their members from the power of the employer. As far as wages are concerned, this has been achieved through collective bargaining. Over the years a situation has been reached where hardly any wage contracts are negotiated individually. Rather, they are collectively negotiated by trade unions and employers. Although there does seem to be a trend away from collective bargaining, coinciding with the anti-trade union legislation of the 1980s and decline in the membership and power of the trade unions, the majority of wage increases are still negotiated by trade unions.

It is argued that the activities of trade unions through collective bargaining have served to increase the wage rate above its equilibrium level and thus cause unemployment. Figure 7.3 demonstrates this effect. Assume that the market clearing wage rate is £W and the quantity of labour being used is L. Assume now that a trade union enters the market that has the power to enforce a wage increase to £W_1. At this wage rate the market does not clear, the demand for labour is L_1 while the supply of labour is L_2. There is therefore excess supply of labour, or unemployment. In this way trade unions are blamed for keeping wages at too high a level so that the market cannot clear.

Figure 7.3 can be used to illustrate the argument of those who oppose the setting of a minimum wage. Although this argument seems plausible enough, it is not quite as simple

Figure 7.3 The effect of trade unions on the labour market

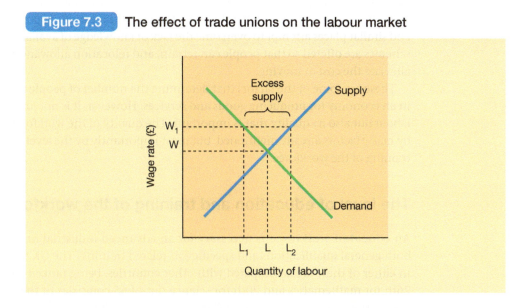

as it seems. There are other market imperfections which prevent the market from operating as smoothly as suggested and which contribute towards creating unemployment. There are some industries that have only one or two employers who can exercise a great deal of power over the market. The arguments over the **minimum wage** are also more complicated and centre on much wider economic and social issues. There are additional factors that may prevent people moving easily and smoothly between jobs. For example, people may not easily be able to change jobs if they are geographically or occupationally immobile.

Immobility of labour

People are **geographically immobile** (**immobility of labour**) for a variety of reasons:

- The cost of moving – it is an expensive business to move to another part of the country, particularly to areas where housing costs are high, such as London.
- There may be shortages of housing in certain areas, or it may be difficult or even impossible to sell a house in other areas.
- There will be many social ties in the form of family and friends that people may be reluctant to leave.
- For people with children, schooling will be important. For example, parents are reluctant to relocate when their children are working for important examinations.

People may also experience **occupational immobility** for the following reasons:

- Some jobs require some natural ability that an individual may not possess (e.g. entertainers, footballers and so on).
- Training is required by many occupations (e.g. doctors, engineers). Without this training an individual could not do the job and the length of training might be a deterrent.
- To enter some occupations (like starting up your own business), a certain amount of capital is required. In some cases the amount of capital needed will be very high (dry cleaning, for example, where the machines are expensive to purchase), and for many this might prove to be a barrier to mobility.

In order to help people to be more mobile so that the labour market works more smoothly, the government over the years has evolved a variety of policies. Job centres and similar places attempt to overcome the lack of knowledge of available jobs. Training schemes are offered so that people can retrain, and relocation allowances can be paid to alleviate the cost of moving.

These are some of the factors that determine the number of people who are available in an economy for producing goods and services. However, it is not just the quantity of labour but also its quality that is important. The quality of the workforce is determined by many factors already mentioned, but most importantly by the level of education and training of the workforce.

The level of education and training of the workforce

An **educated workforce** is necessary for an advanced industrial nation, in terms of both general qualifications and specific job-related training. The UK does not fare well in either of these areas compared with other countries, being ranked 23rd for reading, 26th for mathematics and 20th for science out of 65 countries in the Programme for International Student Assessment (PISA) produced by the OECD.[3]

In the UK, a stated aim of the government is to increase the proportion of young people staying on at school after the statutory minimum leaving age. In September 2013 the school leaving age was raised to 17 years and in 2015 it will rise again to 18 years old. The UK government also has put in place policies aimed towards vocational courses for the over-16s. Table 7.4 gives some examples of these over the last three decades.

Table 7.4 Examples of vocational courses for over-16s

Year	Scheme	Description
1983	Youth Training Scheme	Provided work-related training for 16- and 17-year-olds, both on and off the job. Largely introduced to fill the gap left by the demise of the traditional apprenticeships.
1985	Certificate of Pre-vocational Education	Full-time vocational courses for over-16s containing an element of work experience.
1992	National Vocational Qualifications (NVQs), General National Vocational Qualifications (GNVQs)	A comprehensive system of vocational qualifications at four levels of achievement.
1998	Work-based Training for Young People	This replaced the Youth Training Scheme with the aim of ensuring that young people have access to post-compulsory education or training.
2004	National Qualifications Framework	This brings together general and vocational qualifications into one framework.
2010	Qualifications and Credit Framework	National credit transfer system.

National Vocational Qualifications (**NVQs**) are qualifications that cover a specific skill, such as plumbing or carpentry, while General National Vocational Qualifications (GNVQs) are more general and indicate a broad knowledge of an area, such as the built environment. NVQ level 2 equates to GNVQ intermediate level and is equivalent to five GCSE grades A* to C. NVQ level 3 equates to GNVQ advanced level and is equivalent to two GCE A-levels, and level 4 equates to a degree or higher vocational qualification.

The Qualifications and Credit Framework (QCF) replaced the National Qualifications Framework in 2010. Under the QCF each qualification carries a credit value. There are three sizes of qualification: award, which equals 1–12 credits; certificate, which equals 13–36 credits; and diploma, which equals 37+ credits. The new system corresponds with the EU system so that the credits are internationally comparable. Part of the framework is shown in Table 7.5.

Table 7.5 National Qualifications Framework, up to level 3

Level	General	Vocational	Occupational
3 National Diploma, National Certificate	A level	BTEC national award	NVQ level 3
2 First Diploma	GCSE (grade A*–C)	BTEC first diploma	NVQ level 2
1 Foundation	GCSE (grade D–G)	BTEC introductory certificate	NVQ level 1

Source: Qualifications and Credit Framework, qca.org.uk, 2005.

The UK government has used a variety of policies in an attempt to increase educational attainment and training. These include:

- the National Literacy and Numeracy Strategy, launched in 1998, which provides for a dedicated literacy hour and one mathematics lesson every day for primary school children;
- the use of Education Action Zones in areas of educational disadvantage;
- the introduction of the Education Maintenance Allowance, which offers financial incentives to young people from low-income homes to remain in education;
- an increased number of Modern Advanced Apprenticeships;
- e2e (entry to employment), which is an entry to a level 1 programme that uses work-based learning;
- in 2001 43 Learning and Skills Councils were set up with responsibility for all post-16 education up to university level;
- in 2002 Sector Skills Councils were set up;
- in 2010 the Learning and Skills Council was replaced by the Skills Funding Agency.

As well as school and higher education, job-related training is important in improving the quality of the workforce. Training at work can be of two types: on-the-job training and off-the-job training. There has been the development of a competence-based approach to training, which partly stems from the introduction of NVQs. The system is designed to be easily understood and to provide workers with the skills that are needed by industry. It is designed to unify what is a very diverse system of qualifications existing in the United Kingdom at present. Recent developments include:

- the Commission for Employment and Skills was set up in 2008 to bring industry into the heart of decision-making;
- in 2011 the Work Programme was set up to help long-term unemployed people back into work through work experience and training;
- in 2013 the Help to Work scheme was introduced to offer training for those who had been unemployed for more than three years.

The government also sponsors training for young people. This includes Apprenticeships and Advanced Apprenticeships. These schemes are designed for the 16–25-year age group and aim to provide training leading to recognised vocational qualifications – Apprenticeships at NVQ level 2 and Advanced Apprenticeships at NVQ level 3.

The Investors in People initiative has had an impact on training as it is based on four principles:

- top-level commitment to develop all employees;
- regular reviews of training and development of all employees;
- action to train and develop employees throughout their employment; and
- evaluation of the outcome of training as a basis for continuous improvement.

By October 2013, more than 37,000 UK organisations had achieved recognition under the standard, representing 38 per cent of the UK workforce.

The number of women receiving job-related training has increased over the last 20 years relative to men, and there has been a gradual increase for both sexes over the time period. There are significant differences between industries, with, for example, the service sector having a much higher level of training than agriculture, forestry and fishing, and between occupations.

Training is an important issue not just for school leavers and the unemployed but for all employees. The *UK Employers' Skills Survey*, carried out in the UK in 2013, found that 31 per cent of vacancies were skill shortage vacancies. In 2013, only 38 per cent of establishments had a training plan, down from 48 per cent in 2007, although 60 per cent of establishments do provide training.

For information on training schemes see
www.gov.uk (Department for Business, Innovation & Skills)
www2.warwick.ac.uk/fac/soc/ier (Institute for Employment Research)
www.nfer.ac.uk (National Foundation for Educational Research)
www.ukes.org.uk
http://skillsfundingagency.bis.gov.uk/
www.ssda.org.uk

Occupational structure of the population

There will be changes in the **occupational structure** of the population over time. These will be caused by changes in industrial structure and technological change. There has been an increase in the number of non-manufacturing jobs at the same time as a fall in the number of manufacturing jobs. There are more women in the workforce now because there has been an increase in demand for the types of goods that have been produced by women. There has also been an increase in the availability and quality of labour-saving devices in the home, which has released women into the workforce. There has been a decrease in the average family size so that if women leave the workforce to look after their children, they now do so for a shorter period of time. There has also been a change in attitude towards women working.

Figure 7.4 shows the structure of occupations in the UK by gender. There is a higher percentage of men than women in the professional/managerial occupations and there are more men working in skilled trades than women. Women are clearly concentrated in clerical/selling-type occupations.

Figure 7.4 The structure of occupations in the UK by gender

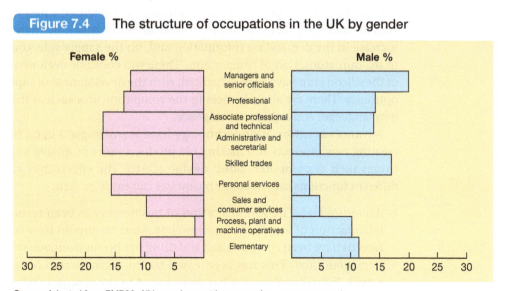

Source: Adapted from EMP08: All in employment by occupation, www.ons.gov.uk

There was a fundamental change in the nature of working life throughout the 1980s and on into the 1990s, and this has to do with the notion of 'flexibility'. There has been an increase in the incidence of part-time working, for both men and women, and an increased use of temporary contract and flexible working patterns. In 2013, 8 million people worked part time in the UK; this represents about a fifth of the workforce. Approximately 3 million people were self-employed (see mini case study on zero-hours contracts).

Technology

Technology is defined as 'the sum of knowledge of the means and methods of producing goods and services' (*Penguin Dictionary of Economics*). It is increasingly science based, encompassing subjects such as chemistry, physics and electronics, and refers to the organisation of production as well as the actual techniques of production itself. **Technological change** leads to the introduction of new products, changes in the methods and organisation of production, changes in the quality of resources and products, new ways of distributing the product and new ways of storing and disseminating information. Technology has a very big impact upon the world of business in all of these areas and has an important effect on the level and type of investment that takes place in an economy and therefore the rate of economic growth.

Technological change

There have been massive changes in technology in the past ten years. This section will consider a few of these and assess their impact upon business and the economy.

Information technology

Developments in **information technology** have had the effect of transforming existing business activities as well as creating entirely new ones, involving the collection, handling, analysis and transmission of information. There has been a huge increase in the demand for information and, on the supply side, continued advances in the miniaturisation of components. These will continue even when the capabilities of the silicon chip have been exhausted, with the development of superconductors and optronics. There are also advances in the computing area such as the development of new languages and artificial intelligence.

Advances in information technology have many impacts upon business. They are creating new products and making old products more profitable to produce through things such as **computer-aided design (CAD)**. The effects they are having on the different functions carried out by businesses can easily be seen:

- *Administration.* The administration of businesses has been revolutionised by the introduction of information technology. Most businesses have computer systems, records have been computerised and filing has become unnecessary.
- *Communication.* This has been eased by the introduction of fax machines and e-mail. Video conferencing has contributed to the change in working practices by making it possible for people to work anywhere. Telecommunications companies,

such as BT, are working on desktop video conferencing systems, where the video camera is attached to the desktop PC.
- *Production.* The use of CAD will shorten the design and planning phase of the product and shorten the life cycle of the product. Japan applied this very early on in the field of consumer electronics and many of the products are withdrawn from sale and redesigned within a very short period of time.
- *Storage and distribution.* The computerisation of stock control has had implications for the storage requirements of firms. It has made implementation of the just-in-time method of stock control possible. This is easily seen in the case of supermarkets where the use of bar-codes on products makes it possible to carry out a stock check of a whole supermarket in a matter of hours. The shelves can then be loaded up as the stock check continues. Similarly, the use of bar-codes with Electronic Point of Sale (EPOS) makes stock control simpler.
- *Electronic Funds Transfer at Point of Sale (EFTPOS).* This system has also had a revolutionary effect in the area of retailing. Most shops now accept credit cards or Switch cards where funds are immediately transferred from bank accounts to the supermarkets.
- *The internet.* The potential for the internet is enormous, although it is still, relatively speaking, in its infancy. In quarter 2 of 2012, there were an estimated 1.5 billion people wired to the internet. The highest percentage population penetration was in the US (78.6 per cent), the lowest in Africa (15.6 per cent). There are three projects operating that will provide a cable system under the Indian Ocean linking African countries.
- *Artificial intelligence.* As the mini case study shows, the developments in this area have been huge and the growth is exponential. The use of robotisation and artificial intelligence has implications for many areas of business and law.

One aspect of business where information technology has become particularly important is in providing opportunities for firms to interact immediately with their customers and suppliers, whoever and wherever they might be. Concepts such as e-commerce, e-business and e-markets are now part of the business lexicon and are an important area of study for undergraduate and postgraduate students alike.

mini case: The robots are coming

The pace of technological change over the past 50 years has been incredible and there is no sign of a slowdown. A few of these technological developments are discussed in this mini case study, together with their implications for the business world.

Robotisation

The increased use of robotisation can be seen in many areas of life: self-service checkouts at the supermarket; online education courses; hotels without reception staff; driverless cars. All of these replace people with machines so they have implications for the labour force: will the main occupation be designing and maintaining machines? What many argue will happen is the loss of jobs in the middle of the market (admin and logistics, for example) but an increase in jobs that are IT related at the top of the market and a continuing demand at the bottom end of the market for jobs that cannot be carried out by machines: care for the elderly and children, for example.

Some of these developments will have legal implications and often the law is slow to keep pace with technological change. A good example is the case of driverless cars – who will hold the insurance? The CEO of Amazon announced in November 2012 that within 5 years Amazon would be delivering parcels to customers using GPS-operated 'octocopters' – parcels could be delivered within 30 minutes of placing the order. This is another example that has huge implications for the labour force (loss of jobs) and the law – there are no rules in place for the use of commercial drones in the USA and there is much resistance from the general public. Several US states have banned the police from using drones.

Virtual wallets

In 2011 Google launched Google Wallet in the USA. It is a mobile payment system that allows consumers to pay for goods, use loyalty cards or gift cards, and receive special offers, all on their mobile phones. Its adoption has been very slow because of technical difficulties and consumer resistance, and it has not made it across to Europe. But now the three biggest mobile networks in the UK (EE, Vodafone and O2) have come together to form a company called Weve, which is developing the concept for the UK. The plan is that by using GPS, your mobile phone will know when you are outside a particular shop and will alert you of any special offers in that shop. This concept has clear implications for marketing and most commentators see this as the big development for 2014. The US market, which was estimated at £12.8 billion in 2012, is predicted to grow to $90 billion by 2017.

There are many other examples of technological developments, such as the 3D printer (see mini case in Chapter 12), and all of them will have a dramatic impact on business. It is clear that these developments will continue apace. Apple has been investing millions in developing supply chain robotisation and acquired Prime Sense, the company that developed 3D sensing technology. Amazon acquired Kiva Systems in 2012 – a company that developed warehouse automation. And in December 2013 Google bought Boston Dynamics, a military robot company, only the latest in a succession of similar purchases. Watch this space!

Other technological developments

- *New materials*. The new material being heralded as the 'miracle material' of the 21st century is graphene. It consists of a single layer of carbon atoms bonded together in hexagons and is the strongest material ever measured. It is a replacement for silicon and will revolutionise computers.
- *Biotechnology*. This is expected to have wide-ranging effects on many fields. The development of new products like computers that can imitate the activity of the brain can shorten the development process for certain products by speeding up existing processes.
- *Energy*. The kind of developments that can take place in this field are the use of superconductors to transport electricity and research that might make solar energy a viable source of energy.

Technology and investment

The second input into the production process after people is **capital**. In economics, capital has a special meaning: it refers to all man-made resources that are used in production. Capital is usually divided into **working capital** and **fixed capital**. Working capital consists of the stocks of raw materials and components used in producing things. Fixed capital consists of buildings, plant and machinery. The main difference between the two is that fixed capital gives a flow of services over a long period of time, while working capital needs to be replaced on a regular basis. Because of its nature, working capital is much more mobile than fixed capital (i.e. it can be used for other purposes much more easily). Capital is a '**stock**' of goods used in the production process, a stock which is continually being used and therefore needing to be replaced. This stock provides a flow of services for the production process.

Capital includes a wide diversity of items, including factory premises, machinery, raw materials in stock, transport vehicles and partly finished goods. As well as these, there is what is often called '**social capital**', which refers to capital that is owned by the community, such as schools and hospitals. There is also spending on the **infrastructure**, which is important to all businesses rather than being linked to one particular business. The main components of this are transport, energy, water and information. The transportation system is obviously very important to a developed economy. Road, rail, air and water are used to transport goods, services and raw materials. The capital stock in transport and communications in the UK was £345 billion in 2009. The same is true for energy and water; both are used by industry in great quantities, and a good infrastructure in these is essential. The information distribution system is also part of the infrastructure and would include telephone systems and the post.

Table 7.6 shows the capital stock of the United Kingdom in 2001 and 2009 by industry. The level of capital stock increased over the period by 21.7 per cent, but there are marked differences between industries, ranging from a growth of 75 per cent in other services to a fall of −11 per cent in mining and quarrying.

Table 7.6 Gross capital stock in 2001 and 2009 by industry at 2006 replacement costs in UK (£ billion)

Industry	2001	2009	% change
Agriculture, forestry and fishing	46.5	44.2	− 5.0
Mining and quarrying	133.6	118.9	− 11.0
Manufacturing	374.2	346.1	− 7.5
Electricity, gas and water supply	164.9	180.1	+ 9.2
Construction	27.4	44.2	+ 61.3
Distribution	17.3	284.8	+ 52.0
Hotels and restaurants	58.5	93.7	+ 60.0
Transport and communications	236.9	345.0	+ 45.1
Financial intermediation	101.6	130.8	+ 28.7
Dwellings	1786.1	2053.3	+ 15.0
Real estate, renting and business activities	210.5	311.8	+ 48.0
Public administration	339.7	407.5	+ 20.0
Education	138.7	186.9	+ 34.8
Health and social welfare	891.0	121.1	+ 35.9
Other services	137.3	240.2	+ 75.0
Total	**4032.3**	**4908.6**	**+ 21.7**

Source: Adapted from www.ons.gov.uk

The increase in the stock of capital over time is called **investment**. Investment will serve to increase the productive potential of the firm and the economy. Investment usually refers to the purchase of new assets, as the purchase of second-hand assets merely represents a change in ownership and therefore does not represent a change in productive potential. Investment is important for the firm as it is a mechanism for growth; it is an integral part of the **innovation** process and can have disastrous results for a firm if an

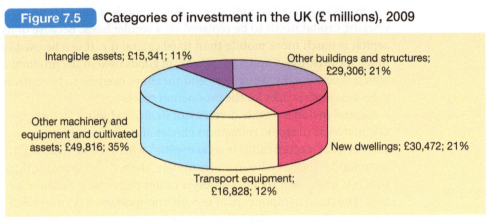

Figure 7.5 Categories of investment in the UK (£ millions), 2009

Source: Adapted from Table 4, Capital stocks, capital consumption and non-financial balance sheets, 2010, www.ons.gov.uk

investment goes wrong. Generally, the higher the level of investment in a country, the higher will be the level of economic growth.[4]

Total or **gross investment** can be broken down into **replacement investment**, which is investment to replace obsolete or worn-out machines, and new investment, which is any investment over and above this. This includes investment by firms, individuals (in dwellings mainly) and governments (see Figure 7.5). As might be expected, the level of investment is affected by the state of the economy. There was a fall in the level of investment in the early 1980s, again in the early 1990s, and a gradual fall in investment levels since 2005, all of these as a result of the recession in the economy (see Figure 7.6). The level of investment in 2009 represented 23 per cent of GDP.

Figure 7.6 Gross fixed investment in the UK manufacturing industry (2006 prices) 1979 to 2009

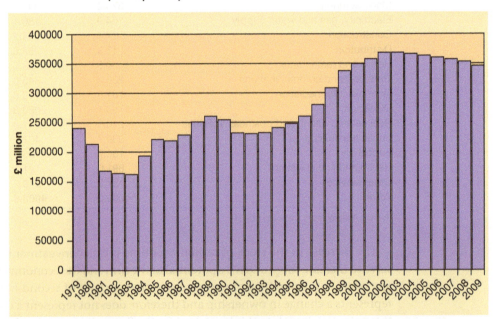

Source: Adapted from Table 2.2.2 Capital Stocks, capital consumption and non-financial balance sheets, 2010, www.ons.gov.uk

There is an important relationship between investment and technological change which runs in both directions. Investment can form the basis for improvements in technology, while improved technology, which brings about new ways of producing goods, will lead to greater investment. For private firms, the main determinants of the level of investment will be the rate of technological change and the scope for extra profit as a result of these changes.

Innovation and technology

There are two types of innovation that can occur as a result of technological change: **product innovation** and **process innovation**. Product innovation is the development of new products, such as the microprocessor, which will have far-reaching effects on business. New products impact upon the industrial structure of a country, as new industries grow and old industries disappear. This in turn will lead to changes in the occupational structure of the workforce, as we have seen. It has even had the effect of reducing the benefits large firms derive from economies of scale in cases where the technological change can be exploited by small firms as well as it can by large firms. Another example of product innovation which has affected the level of competition in the market is the development of quartz watches, which allowed Japan to enter the market and compete with Switzerland.

Process innovation, meanwhile, refers to changes that take place in the production process, such as the introduction of assembly-line production in the manufacture of cars. The two types of innovation are related, as the above examples show. The microprocessor (product innovation), which is a new product, has led to massive changes in the way that production and offices operate (process innovation).

Not all innovation is technological in nature; for example, changes in fashion in clothing are not technological. Innovative activity is important for all industry, whether manufacturing or non-manufacturing. In some industries (e.g. pharmaceuticals, computers), innovation is essential if firms wish to remain competitive.

For information on innovation see the Department for Business, Innovation & Skills website at *www.gov.uk*

Research and development

Most, but not all, technological changes have occurred through the process of **research and development (R&D)**. 'Research' can be theoretical or applied, and 'development' refers to the using of the research in the production process. Most research and development carried out by private companies is directed towards applied research and development. It is designed to develop new products and production processes that will render production more profitable. It is also aimed at improving existing products and processes. Most basic theoretical research carried out in the United Kingdom is financed from public sources and is undertaken in places like the universities.

Table 7.7 shows that the level of research and development expenditure in manufacturing industries in the UK in 2011 was £17,408 million, which represents around 1.2 per cent of GDP. Although total spending in real terms has risen over the past 20 years, the percentage share of R&D in GDP fell from 1.4 per cent in 1995 to 1.2 per cent in 2011. This is a long way short of the UK government target of 1.7 per cent by the end of 2014.

Table 7.7 Spending on R&D (£ million) in 2011 (2011 prices)

Product group	£ million	% of total
All product groups	17 408	100
All products of manufacturing industry	12 552	72
Chemical industries	5539	32
Mechanical engineering	1089	6
Electrical machinery	1199	7
Aerospace	1417	8
Transport	1833	10
Other manufactured products	1475	8
Non-manufactured products	4856	28

Source: Adapted from Table 15, Business Enterprise and Development, 2011, www.ons.gov.uk

It can be seen that there are wide differences in expenditure between industries, with manufacturing involved in a great deal more research and development spending than non-manufacturing. Even within the broad category of manufacturing there are wide differences, with chemicals accounting for more than a quarter of the expenditure. Table 7.8 shows the sources from which R&D is financed. As we can see, the majority of R&D is financed by companies themselves. If R&D is split into civil and defence spending, the government finances the majority of defence R&D, as would be expected.

Table 7.8 Sources of funds for R&D within industry in the UK for selected years

	1985	1990	1996	2000	2005	2006	2007	2008	2009	2010	2011
Total (£ million)	5 122	8 082	9 362	10 417	13 310	14 306	15 676	15 814	15 532	16 053	17 408
Government funds (%)	23	17	10	9	8	7.5	6.8	7.2	8.5	8.7	9.3
Overseas funds (%)	11	16	22	21	26	23	23	24	22	24	21
Mainly own funds (%)	66	68	69	70	66	66	70	70	70	68	69

Source: Adapted from Table 15, Business Enterprise and Development, 2012, www.ons.gov.uk

For information on R&D see www.oecd.org or http://epp.europa.eu.int/eurostat.eu

Figure 7.7 shows that the UK tends to fare badly in international comparisons of research and development spending.

Limits to technological change

Technological change has many effects on the economy and the environment and if uncontrolled can lead to problems, including high levels of unemployment or the exhaustion of natural resources. One area of concern is energy. The world's stock of energy is finite and we are still heavily dependent upon fuel that was formed millions of years ago. The development of nuclear power again represents a finite source of energy, and also carries with it other problems, such as the disposal of nuclear waste and the possibility of accidents. For these and other reasons the scale of technological change needs to be controlled.

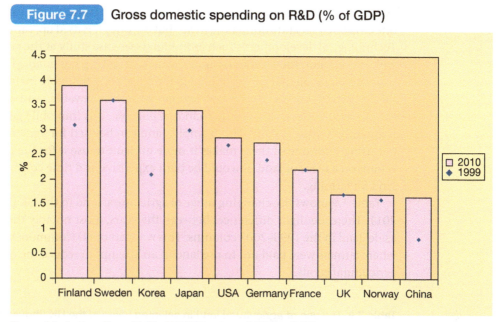

Figure 7.7 Gross domestic spending on R&D (% of GDP)

Source: Adapted from Figure 14, 'The UK R&D Landscape', CIHE and UK-irc

It is also the case that technological change can lead to high levels of unemployment in industries that are in decline. This type of unemployment often takes on a regional bias as the older traditional industries tend to be located in particular parts of the country. **Technological unemployment** is in some respects inevitable as in a changing world it would be expected that new industries would emerge and old industries die. The problem can be tackled by the government and industry through retraining, but what is also needed is a new and more flexible view of work where less time is spent working and more on leisure. Technological change can also give rise to the opposite problem of skill shortage in new industries, where particular skills are required. Technological change has not led to the massive increase in unemployment predicted by many in the 1970s and 1980s, but what might happen in the future is unknown.

Natural resources

In economics, **natural resources** are put under the heading of **land** as a **factor of production**. It would include all natural resources like the soil, minerals, oil, forests, fish, water, the sun and so on. The uneven distribution of natural resources throughout the world means that they can be used as economic and political weapons.

Although the area of land in a country is fixed, land as a factor of production is not completely fixed in supply as more land can be made available through land reclamation schemes and better irrigation. The productivity of agricultural land can be increased by the use of fertilisers. It is true, however, that our natural resources are in finite supply. And often their true extent is not known with certainty.

It is in the area of natural resources that the distinction between renewable and non-renewable resources is most important. Natural resources can be either. Land can often be used for more than one purpose – for example, agricultural land can be used to grow one crop one year and another the next – but oil, once it is used up, cannot be used again. Technological developments such as **fracking** (see case study at the end of the chapter) will impact upon the level of natural resources. Fracking has enabled the extraction of natural gas and oil that was bound up in the shale rock, therefore increasing the quantities of these resources. However, they remain non-renewable. And even though land can sometimes be used for more than one purpose, it is immobile geographically and frequently occupationally. For example, land can be used for agriculture or industry, but using it for one of these makes it more difficult to use it for the other. If a factory is built on a piece of land, it would be both expensive and time consuming to clear the land for farming.

Table 7.9 shows the changing usage of agricultural land in the UK between 1971 and 2011. There are slight differences between the years, most notably the inclusion of 'set aside' land in the 1993–2007 columns. This was part of EU Common Agricultural Policy where farmers were paid not to use land in an attempt to reduce the overproduction of agricultural goods.

Table 7.9 The use of agricultural land in selected years in the UK (thousand hectares)

	1971	1993	1997	2000	2003	2007	2011
Crops	4838	4519	4990	4709	4478	4350	4694
Bare fallow	74	47	29	33	29	165	–
Grasses	7240	6770	6687	6767	6884	7141	7343
Rough grazing*	6678	5840	5878	5803	5565	5552	5402
Set aside	–	677	306	572	689	440	–
Woodland and other land on agricultural holdings	285	678	763	789	792	954	1297
Total	19 115	18 531	18 653	18 579	18 438	18 602	18 736

Note: *Includes sole-right rough grazing and common rough grazing.
Source: Adapted from Table 21.3, *Annual Abstract of Statistics 2011*, www.ons.gov.uk

Protection of the environment

Increased knowledge of the effects of depletion of natural resources has led to increased environmental awareness among the population. There has been an increased interest in conservation and recycling and the search for alternative forms of energy. A survey by the Department of the Environment found that 90 per cent of the adult population in the UK was either 'fairly concerned' or 'very concerned' about the environment. The issues that have caused this concern include traffic congestion, global warming, air and water pollution and depletion of the ozone layer. This change in public opinion has already had a major impact on the way in which business operates and is likely to have even bigger effects.

Governments in the UK and elsewhere have a variety of targets for environmental protection relating to issues such as greenhouse gas emissions, biodiversity, renewable energy, recycling, packaging and so on. Some of these targets are set through negotiations with other countries at both international (e.g. Kyoto Protocol) and supranational (e.g. EU) levels and hence are influenced by political, economic, social and technological considerations and by a variety of state and non-state actors (see Chapter 4). Given the growing importance of environmental issues in business, a separate chapter on ethics and the natural environment has been added (see Chapter 9).

One important resource in business whose exploitation and use have a significant impact on the natural environment is energy. The UK is not well endowed with high-grade minerals; the main natural resource is energy. There is a good deposit of coal and the discovery of North Sea oil and gas made the UK self-sufficient in energy supplies, and now fracking might do the same again. The usage of energy has doubled since 1970, but as Table 7.10 shows, there has been a change in the relative importance of the different sources of energy.

Table 7.10 Final energy consumption by source in the UK (%)

	1950	1970	1980	1990	2000	2010	2012
Solid fuel	79	47	36	31	16	15	20
Gas	6	5	22	24	41	43	36
Oil	12	44	37	36	33	32	32
Electricity	3	4	5	8	9	7	9
Renewable energy	–	–	–	0.3	1	3.2	3.8

Source: Adapted from Table 1.02, Energy consumption in UK, 2013 updates, www.ons.gov.uk

Coal has lost its place to oil and gas as the most important sources of energy. The increase in the usage of both oil and gas is due to the discovery of North Sea oil and gas. The biggest single user of energy in the UK is the domestic sector (32 per cent of energy produced), followed by transport (28 per cent) and industry (22 per cent). A small but growing source of energy in the UK is renewables, with the government's target by 2020 being 15 per cent.

There is great variation in the fuels used for the generation of electricity across Europe, as Table 7.11 shows.

Table 7.11 Fuel used for electricity generation, selected EU countries (%), 2009

	Nuclear	Coal and ignite	Oil	Gas	Renewable energy	Other
France	74.9	4.7	1.1	4.4	14.0	1.0
Belgium	50.9	5.6	0.6	32.6	8.5	1.8
Sweden	38.1	0.9	0.5	1.4	58.9	0.2
Spain	17.4	11.9	5.5	35.8	26.2	3.0
Germany	22.3	41.5	1.6	14.0	17.4	3.1
UK	18.1	27.6	1.2	44.0	8.1	1.0
The Netherlands	3.7	21.4	1.3	62.6	10.9	0.2
EU-27	27.5	25.3	2.9	23.1	19.6	1.7

Source: Adapted from Figure 3, Electricity Production by Fuel, European Environment Agency, 2012.

There has been a fall in the amount of electricity generated by nuclear power since 2004, although some EU countries use it as their primary generator of electricity. While its use produces lower emissions of greenhouse gases, there is an increased risk of accidental leakage of radioactivity as well as the problem of the disposal of radioactive waste. Electricity generation from oil and gas has tended to fall and an EU Directive now requires 20 per cent of electricity (for the EU-27 countries) to come from renewable sources by 2020. The figure for 2009 is close to the target, but as Table 7.11 shows, there are huge differences between countries. There is clearly a growing demand for alternative sources of energy. The alternatives of hydro, wind and solar energy sources will also grow in importance. In the UK, the government has tried to promote the search for renewable energy sources through projects like the Renewables Obligation, which requires licensed electricity producers to obtain an increasing percentage of their electricity from clean sources (11 per cent in 2012). It also funds experimental work in the search for new sources of energy. One such source is 'biogas', which generates gas from household waste. The Committee on Climate Change claims that 1 in 20 of UK homes could be supplied with gas from this source. Biogas could also lead to fewer carbon emissions.

As well as recycling and searching for new sources of energy there is the concept of 'negademand', where the use of less produces negative demand for those commodities. This concept can be applied to energy and water saving, driving and shopping. It is possible that technological change (like the 3D printer) could reduce the demand for energy (see case study in Chapter 12).

For information on the natural environment in the UK see www.environment-agency.gov.uk or www.theccc.org.uk (the Committee on Climate Change)
In the EU see www.eea.europa.eu (the European Environment Agency)
In the world see www.oecd.org

Synopsis

This chapter looked at the three main inputs into the production process: people, technology and natural resources. It considered each in turn and examined their importance to business and the main factors that determine both the quality and the quantity of these factors of production.

People are important in two ways: they are the producers of goods and services, and also the consumers of goods and services. The quantity of human resources available in an economy depends upon things like total population size, participation rates, length of working week and wages. The quality depends upon such things as the level of health care, education and training. There have been significant changes in the labour market over recent years.

One of the main features of the last 50 years has been the immense changes in technology that have had an enormous impact upon business, resulting in new products and markets and new methods of production and distribution.

As far as natural resources are concerned, the traditional view was that they were fixed in supply and therefore did not receive much consideration. However, with increased environmental awareness there is growing concern that this is not the case and that many of our natural resources are non-renewable and therefore need to be conserved.

Each of the three inputs into the production process has been considered separately, but they are interlinked and difficult to separate in reality. It has already been said that the productivity of people will be affected by the technology at their disposal, and this is also true of natural resources. All of the three inputs are 'stocks', from which streams of resources flow to firms. These flows are crucial to business, as without them production could not take place. Both the quantities and qualities of our stocks of these resources are important, as too is the replacement of the stocks that are being used.

Summary of key points

- Three main resources are used in the production of goods and services – labour, capital and land.
- The quantity of labour available depends upon population size, regulations in the labour market, the length of the working week and wage levels.
- The level of education and training determines the quality of available labour.
- The quantity and quality of capital depends on the level and type of investment taking place, the extent of research and development and the level of innovation.
- The quantity and quality of land are important elements in the production process and will depend on many things, including environmental controls.

case study: Fracking

The world's stock of natural resources is finite and in the 1970s there was much talk of energy crises that might occur when the world's stock of fossil fuels ran out. Hubbert (1956) put forward the theory that there was a point (he called the 'peak') where maximum oil production is reached, after which it would decline and eventually run out. This is a supply-side factor, in addition to which there are demand factors in play – there have been massive increases in the demand for oil because of economic growth (in countries like China) and population growth. Both the demand and supply factors can lead to energy crises.

Hubbert predicted that peak oil would occur in the USA between 1965 and 1971. Modern-day peak oil theory suggests that peak oil production will be reached after 2020, and that reductions in the demand for oil and the search for alternative sources of energy continue to be essential.

The demand for and the supply of natural gas in the USA was in balance in 1986, after which demand exceeded supply, the excess being met by imported natural gas from Canada. This all changed in 2006 when new drilling techniques were used, which dramatically increased the output of natural gas. This technique is called hydraulic fracturing, or fracking. Natural gas extracted through fracking made up 10 per cent of all gas production in 2007 and this rose to 30 per cent by 2010.

Fracking involves the release of oil and gas which are bound up in shale rock through the use of high-powered water sprays mixed with sand being pumped into the rocks. The oil and gas are then pushed up into the wells. Fracking has been used extensively in the USA and has been credited with powering the economic recovery and driving down energy prices.

1 USA

Fracking is taking place across America from Ohio to Dakota and Texas. The production of oil in the country has increased by 30 per cent since 2008 and the production of natural gas has increased by 33 per cent. It is estimated that the USA will overtake Russia and Saudi Arabia in 2014 in becoming the world's largest oil producer. Since 2008 the price of gas has fallen by two-thirds; in 2013 it stood at $4 per million British Thermal Units. It is estimated that between now and 2020 shale gas and oil will add $380–690 billion to annual GDP (2–4 per cent) and will create 1.7 million permanent jobs. This will happen through growth in the energy industries – direct spending on fracking and pipelines and also indirect spending on infrastructure to support and distribute the fuels. Coal-fired electricity generation will be changed for the use of gas. Since gas is cleaner than coal in terms of CO_2 emissions, there was a 10 per cent fall in the emission of greenhouse gases in the USA between 2010 and 2012. It is estimated that by 2020 gas-generated electricity will constitute 33 per cent of total electricity production; it was 21 per cent in 2008.

Much of this is good news for the US economy. It is on its way to being energy independent and it can now be an exporter of coal. The falling cost of gas has a positive effect on manufacturing as its costs will be lower, and it is argued that this gives the USA a competitive advantage over other countries.

2 Europe

A recent report (Poyry Management Consulting and Cambridge Econometrics) estimated that the widespread use of fracking in the EU could produce 1 million new jobs and add £3 trillion to EU economies. It would also reduce the dependence of the EU on gas imports.

The attitude to fracking varies across the EU. The UK and Poland are very receptive to the idea, while France, Germany, Spain and Bulgaria are less keen. At present in the EU fracking is covered by the same environmental legislation that applies to full-scale oil drilling. This makes it an expensive process. The European Commission is considering the issue of fracking at the time of writing and aims to produce guidelines soon.

In the EU there is much more public opposition to fracking than in the USA. In the UK, exploratory drilling by Cuadrilla in Balcombe was halted in August 2013 because of local protests. Without exploratory investigation, it is impossible to determine how much oil and gas is contained in the shale rocks. In Poland, exploratory drilling was abandoned largely because of legislative uncertainties.

3 Pros and cons of fracking

The arguments against fracking include the following:

(a) Fracking requires huge amounts of water which needs to be transported to the site. This has environmental implications and for some countries (the UK, for example) many argue that water shortages would preclude fracking.
(b) It is argued that fracking could contaminate the water table through use of and generation of harmful chemicals and that it could lead to carcinogenic chemicals in the soil.
(c) Fracking can lead to earth tremors. In Blackpool in the UK, there were two small earthquakes in 2011 following fracking in the vicinity. Supporters of fracking argue that the possibility of earth tremors has more to do with the construction of the wells rather than the fracking itself.
(d) Opponents argue that the race towards fracking is stopping the energy companies looking at other renewable sources of energy. One such source that environmentalists argue is being ignored is biogas, where waste is used to generate gas.

The arguments in favour include:

(a) Fracking will increase the supply of oil and gas and provide for the world's growing energy needs.
(b) In the USA fracking has led to a fall in the price of gas and this is good for industry and consumers alike. Whether this would be true in the EU is unclear as not enough is known about the extent of the reserves or the cost of extraction. In the UK the cost of extraction under the North Sea will be very high.
(c) If prices did fall, the corresponding fall in costs to firms would increase international competitiveness.
(d) There will be energy security which could extend as far as the next 100 years. The facts are not known – the International Energy agency predicts that the USA will be the biggest oil producer from 2015 to 2030 and that its reserves will start to decline in the 2020s.
(e) The burning of gas produces half of the CO_2 emissions of burning coal, so the use of a natural gas is good for the environment. CO_2 emissions in the USA have fallen faster than in the EU.

The debate over fracking is a heated one, with strong proponents on both sides, and the debate is ongoing. Even the strong arguments used in favour in the USA can be qualified. For example, the one about the lower cost of gas – the price of gas in 2013 ($4 per million BTU) is lower than the cost of extraction ($6 per million BTU), which means that it is not sustainable unless natural gas is seen as a by-product of the extraction of oil. This makes the production of natural gas dependent upon the price of oil; if this were to fall, then what might happen to the production of natural gas? In Europe, the future of fracking depends upon public opinion; without exploratory studies it is impossible to know what reserves are present or what the cost of extraction might be. The guidelines being produced by the European Commission should prove interesting.

Case study questions

1 The debate on fracking was in its infancy at the time of writing. How has development continued? Has the general public accepted fracking? Have the predictions of quantities of oil and gas proved correct?

2 What impact will increased fracking have on OPEC and the price of oil?

Review and discussion questions

1 Why are industries such as electricity 'natural monopolies'? What other examples are there of natural monopolies?

2 Think of one technological advance that has been made recently. What have been the effects of that change on the economy, business and the consumer?

3 In what ways can the general and specific skills of the British workforce be improved?

4 What impact will increased use of the internet, both for customer information and purchasing, have on call centres?

Assignments

1 You work in the economic development unit of your local council. The unit is compiling a bid to central government in order to win some resources to improve the basic infrastructure in the locality. Your job is to identify the economic problems that exist in your local town and explain why an increase in resources would overcome the problems. Write a briefing paper to the management committee of the unit on your results.

2 You are a member of your local Chartered Institute of Personnel and Development branch and have been asked to give a talk on 'Flexibility in working practices' to a group of trainee managers from a variety of functional and industrial backgrounds. They are particularly interested in three questions:

- What is meant by flexibility?
- Why is flexibility needed?
- What are the implications of greater flexibility?

(Sources for this would include the second edition of this text and *People Management*, CIPD.)

Notes and references

1. See *Workplace Employment Relations Study*, BIS, July 2013, available at www.ons.gov.uk
2. For further reading on this area see Begg, D., Fischer, S. and Dornbusch, R., *Economics*, McGraw-Hill, 2011.
3. See PISA www.oecd.org/PISA
4. The relationship between investment and the rate of growth is difficult to prove, but there does seem to be high correlation between the level of investment in a country and its associated level of economic growth. It should be remembered, however, that high correlation does not prove that one thing causes another.

Further reading

Blowfield, M., *Business and Sustainability*, Oxford University Press, 2012.

Christensen, C. M., *The Innovator's Dilemma: When New Technologies Cause Great Firms to Fail*, Harvard Business Review Press, 2013.

Razin, A. and Sadka, E., *Population Economics*, MIT Press, 2013.

Worthington, I., Britton, C. and Rees, A., *Economics for Business: Blending Theory and Practice*, Financial Times/Prentice Hall, 2nd edition, 2005.

Web links and further questions are available on the website at:
www.pearsoned.co.uk/worthington

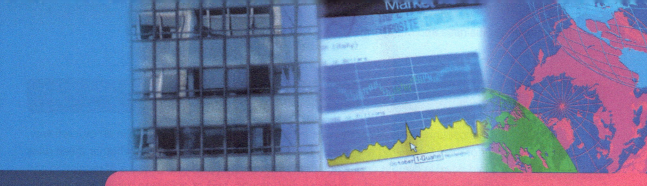

8 The legal environment

Martin Morgan-Taylor and Diane Belfitt

Businesses, like individuals, exist and carry on their activities within a framework of law which derives from custom and practice, from the judicial decisions of the courts and from statutes enacted by governments. This legal environment not only constrains and regulates a firm's operations, it also provides an enabling mechanism through which it is able to pursue its objectives, particularly the achievement of profits through entrepreneurial activity. Like the political and economic environment with which it is intertwined, the legal environment of business is a key influence on the business organisation and an important area of study for students of business. This can be demonstrated by an examination of a number of the fundamental areas in which the law impinges on the operations of an enterprise.

Learning outcomes

Having read this chapter you should be able to:

- understand the idea of 'law' and the sources from which laws are derived
- outline the court system, including the role of the European Court of Justice
- discuss the basic features of the laws of contract and agency
- analyse the reason for statutory intervention to protect the consumer and some of the principal pieces of legislation in this field

Key terms

Acceptance
Agent
Capacity
Case law
Codes of practice
Consideration
Criminal law
Customs
Delegated legislation
Intention to create legal relations
Judicial precedent
Legislation
Offer
Principal
Private law
Public law
Statute law
Tort
Trust

Introduction

It is almost universally accepted that for a society to exist and function in an ordered way, a set of rules is required to regulate human behaviour. Irrespective of whether these rules are laid down in custom or practice or in statute, they constitute a means of regulating and controlling the activities of individuals and groups, and of enforcing minimum standards of conduct – even though they may be ignored or flouted on occasions. This framework of rules and the institutions through which they are formulated and enforced represent what is normally understood as the 'law', which invariably evolves over time in response to changing social, economic and political circumstances (e.g. the influence of pressure groups). As one of the constraining (and enabling) influences on business organisations, this legal environment is an important area of study for students of business, hence the tendency for courses in business-related subjects to have specialist modules or units on different aspects of business law (e.g. contract, agency, property and so on).

The aim of this chapter is not to examine business law in detail or to provide a definitive insight into particular areas of the law as it relates to business organisations. Rather, it is to raise the reader's awareness of the legal context within which businesses function and to comment briefly on those aspects of law that regularly impinge on a firm's operations. Students wishing to examine business law in more detail should consult the many specialist texts in this field, some of which are listed at the end of this chapter.

Classification of law

Laws relating to both individuals and organisations can be classified in a number of ways: international and national, public and private, criminal and civil. In practice, there are no hard and fast rules to classification and some categories may overlap (e.g. where a person's behaviour is deemed to infringe different areas of law). Nevertheless, distinguishing laws in these terms serves as an aid to explanation and commentary, as well as helping to explain differences in liabilities and in legal remedies in England and Wales (e.g. a child under the age of ten cannot be held criminally liable).

Public and private law

Put simply, **public law** is the law that concerns the state, whether in international agreements or disputes or in the relationship between the state and the individual. Thus public law consists of international treaties and conventions, constitutional law, administrative law and criminal law. In contrast, **private law** is law governing the relationships between individuals and comprises laws in respect of contract, tort, property, trusts and the family.

Criminal law

Criminal law relates to a legal wrong (criminal offence) – a breach of a public duty, punishable by the state on behalf of society. Decisions on whether or not to bring a prosecution in a particular instance are taken by the Crown Prosecution Service (in England and Wales) and the matter may or may not involve trial by jury, according to the seriousness of the alleged offence and the plea of the defendant(s). In some cases, the consent of both magistrates and defendants is required for a case to remain in the magistrates' court, although this may change in the very near future. Moreover, while the criminal process may also arise from a private prosecution, such prosecutions are rare and, in these cases, the Attorney-General (the government's senior law officer) has the right to intervene if he or she sees fit.

Tort

A **tort** is a civil wrong other than a breach of contract or a breach of trust and is a duty fixed by law on all persons (e.g. road users have a duty in law not to act negligently). The law of tort, therefore, is concerned with those situations where the conduct of one party threatens or causes harm to the interests of another party and the aim of the law is to compensate for this harm. The most common torts are negligence, nuisance, defamation and trespass.

Trusts

A **trust** is generally defined as an 'equitable obligation imposing on one or more persons a duty of dealing with property, over which they have control, for the benefit of other persons who may enforce the obligation'. This property may be in the form of money or stocks and shares or in other types of asset, particularly land, where trusts have become a very common way of permitting persons who are forbidden to own legal estates in land to enjoy the equitable benefits of ownership. Partnerships, for example, cannot hold property as legal owners, so often several partners will act as trustees for all the partners (as a partnership has no separate corporate identity it cannot own property – see Chapter 10). Similarly, minors may not hold legal estates, so their interests must be protected by a trust, administered by an individual or an institution.

---

mini case — Banking on advice

Banks have duties as well as rights when dealing with the day-to-day affairs of their customers. Failure to discharge these duties, in some circumstances, may be deemed negligent behaviour.

In September 1995 the High Court ruled that Lloyds Bank had been negligent in lending money to two of its customers for use on a speculative property deal which had failed to come off because of a collapse in the property market in the late 1980s. In essence, the customers had claimed that the bank owed them a duty of care in advising them on the merits of a loan to invest in property speculation and that it had been in breach of its duty when agreeing to proceed with the loan. In effect, the claimants were arguing that they had been badly advised and that this had resulted in a loss which was not only suffered but also reasonably foreseeable.

In finding for the claimants – who were suing Lloyds under the tort of negligence – the judge ruled that the bank manager was in breach of his duty of care in advising them to proceed and that the couple had relied on his advice, including claims made in the bank's promotional literature. While a ruling of this kind sent shock waves through the financial community, it is, as yet, uncertain whether it set a legal precedent. Certainly, this is likely to prove a far more significant question to Lloyds (and other financial institutions) than the £77,000 compensation awarded to the claimants by the High Court.

Sources of law

Laws invariably derive from a number of sources, including custom, judicial precedent, legislation and international and supranational bodies (e.g. the EU). All of these so-called legal sources of the law can be illustrated by reference to English law, which applies in England and Wales. Where laws made by Parliament are to apply only to Scotland or Northern Ireland, the legislation will state this. Similarly, any Act which is to apply to all four home countries will contain a statement to this effect.

Custom

Early societies developed particular forms of behaviour (or **customs**), which came to be accepted as social norms to be followed by the members of the community to which they applied. In England many of these customary rules ultimately became incorporated into a body of legal principles known as the common law. Today customs would be regarded as usage recognised by law, whether by judicial precedent (**case law**) or through statutory intervention, and hence they are largely of historical interest. Occasionally, however, they are recognised by the courts as being of local significance and may be enforced accordingly as exceptions to the general law (e.g. concerning land usage).

Judicial precedent

Much of English law is derived from **judicial precedent** (previous decisions of the courts). The present system of binding precedent, however, is of fairly recent origin, dating from the latter part of the nineteenth century, when advances in recording legal judgments and a reorganisation of the court structure facilitated its general acceptance.

In essence, judicial precedent is based on the rule that the previous decisions of a higher court must be followed by the lower courts – hence the significance of the court structure. In any judgment will be found a number of reasons, arguments, explanations and cases cited and these must all be considered carefully by judges to determine whether there are material differences in the case before the court and the earlier decision. To reach a decision, the court must find what is termed the *ratio decidendi* of the previous case. Put very simply, the *ratio* of a case is the essential steps in the legal reasoning which led the court to make that particular decision. Anything which cannot be regarded as a *rationes* is termed *obiter dicta* or 'things said by the way'. The whole of a dissenting judgment in a case is regarded as *obiter*. *Obiter dicta* are not binding but may be regarded as persuasive arguments if the facts of the case permit.

Clearly there are times when, perhaps because of the position of a court in the hierarchy, decisions are not to be regarded as binding precedent. However, if the judgment has been delivered by a jurisdiction that has a common law system (e.g. Canada, Australia) or, most importantly, by the Judicial Committee of the Privy Council, then those decisions will be regarded as being of persuasive precedent and may be used to help the court reach its own decision.

Legislation

A substantial proportion of current law – including laws governing the operations of business organisations – derives from **legislation** or **statutes**, enacted by the Queen (or King) giving Royal Assent in Parliament. As Chapter 4 indicated, the initiative in this sphere lies effectively with the government of the day, which can virtually guarantee a bill will become law, if it has a working majority in the House of Commons.

Apart from a limited number of bills proposed by backbench MPs (private members' bills), the vast majority of legislation emanates from government and takes the form of Acts of Parliament or delegated legislation. Acts of Parliament are those bills that have formally been enacted by Parliament and have received the Royal Assent and, except where overridden by EU law, they represent the supreme law of the land. In addition to creating new laws (e.g. to protect the consumer), statutes may be used to change or repeal existing laws. In some instances they may be designed to draw together all existing law (a consolidating Act) or to codify it or to grant authority to individuals or institutions to make regulations for specific purposes (an enabling Act). Under the Consumer Credit Act 1974, for instance, the Secretary of State for Trade and Industry is permitted to make regulations governing the form and content of credit agreements under delegated authority from Parliament.

As its name suggests, **delegated legislation** is law made by a body or person to which Parliament has given limited powers of law-making – as illustrated by the example above. More often than not, authority will be delegated to a Minister of the Crown, but it may also be conferred on local authorities or other public undertakings, either through the use of a statutory instrument or by some other means of delegation. Since Parliament remains sovereign, such legislation is required to receive parliamentary approval and scrutiny, but time tends to prevent anything other than a cursory glance at a limited proportion of the legislation of this kind. It does, however, remain subject to judicial control, in so far as the body granted authority may be challenged in the courts for exceeding its powers (*ultra vires*).

In addition to these two principal forms of domestic legislation, developments in the law emanate from Britain's membership of the European Union. Under the Union's main treaties – or those parts to which the British government has agreed – Union legislation becomes part of the law and takes precedence over domestic legislation, although the latter may sometimes be required to implement it. Accordingly, law that is inconsistent with Union law is repealed by implication and British citizens, like their counterparts elsewhere in the EU, become subject to the relevant Union laws (unless an 'opt-out' has been negotiated).[1]

Whereas the provisions of the main treaties represent primary legislation, the regulations, directives and decisions emanating from the Union's institutions are secondary (or subordinate) legislation, made under the authority conferred by the Treaty of Rome (1957) as amended by subsequent Treaties (e.g. the Maastricht Treaty 1992, the Amsterdam Treaty 1997, the Nice Treaty 2001 and the Lisbon Treaty 2007). As Chapter 4 indicated, regulations are of general application throughout the member states and confer individual rights and duties that must be recognised by the national courts. Their purpose is to achieve uniformity throughout the EU, as in the requirement for heavy goods vehicles to fit tachographs to control drivers' hours.

Directives, by contrast, are not directly applicable; they are addressed to member states and not individuals, although a directive may create rights enforceable by an individual citizen, as they become directly applicable if a member state fails to implement its provisions within the prescribed time limits. The aim of EU directives is to seek harmonisation or approximation between national laws rather than to achieve uniformity; hence the method of implementation is left to the discretion of the individual state, usually within a given time limit (e.g. the Companies Act of 1981 implemented the Union's fourth directive on company accounts by allowing small and medium-sized companies to reduce the amount of information provided to the Registrar of Companies).

Decisions, too, are binding, but only on the member state, organisation or individual to whom they are addressed and not on the population generally. In practice, EU decisions become effective from the date stated in the decision, which is generally the date of notification, and they are enforceable in national courts if they impose financial obligations.

The legal system: the courts

A country's legal system can be said to have two main functions: to provide an enabling mechanism within which individuals and organisations can exist and operate (e.g. companies are constituted by law) and to provide a means of resolving conflicts and of dealing with those who infringe the accepted standards of behaviour. These functions are carried out by a variety of institutions, including the government and the courts, and a detailed analysis of the legal system within a state would require consideration of the interrelationship between politics and law. Since the political system has been examined in Chapter 4, the focus here is on the courts as a central element of a country's legal system, with responsibility for interpreting the law and administering justice in democratic societies. It is worth remembering, however, that political and governmental activity takes place within a framework of law and that framework is itself a product of the political process at a variety of spatial levels.

The English legal system

Under the English legal system, a useful distinction can be made between courts on the basis of their status. The superior courts are the Supreme Court (formerly named the House of Lords), the Court of Appeal and the High Court. Law reports generally emanate from the higher courts – these cases involve a major point of law of general public interest (e.g. *R v R,* 1991). Inferior courts, in contrast, have limited jurisdiction and are subject to the supervisory jurisdiction of the High Court. The current hierarchy of courts is illustrated in Figure 8.1. For domestic purposes (i.e. not concerning EU legislation), the highest court is the Supreme Court, which is the final court of appeal for both civil and criminal cases. Decisions reached by the Court are binding on all other courts, though not necessarily on the Court's judges themselves.

Like the Supreme Court, the Court of Appeal has only appellate jurisdiction. In the case of the Civil Division of the court, its decisions bind all inferior courts and it is bound by its own previous decisions and by those of the Supreme Court. The Criminal Division similarly is bound by the decisions of the Law Lords, but not by the Court of

Figure 8.1 The hierarchy of courts

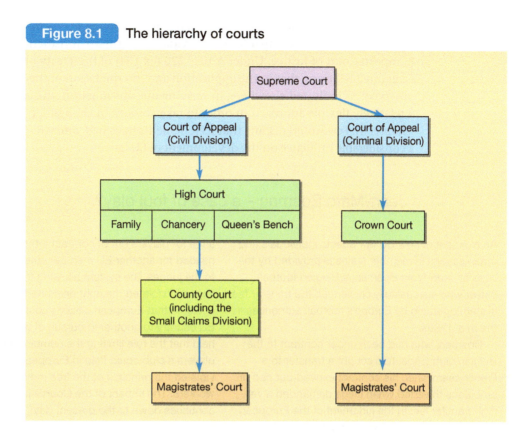

Appeal's Civil Division, nor is it bound by its own previous decisions where these were against a defendant, as exemplified in a number of celebrated cases in recent years.

The High Court is divided into three separate divisions – Chancery, Queen's Bench and Family – and has virtually unlimited original jurisdiction in civil matters, many of which are of direct relevance to business organisations. The Family court deals with such things as adoption, wardship and contested divorce cases, while the Chancery court deals with cases concerning trusts, property and taxation. Claims in contract and tort are the responsibility of the Queen's Bench division, which has two specialist courts to deal with commercial matters and with ships and aircraft. It also exercises the criminal jurisdiction of the High Court – the latter being entirely appellate in instances referred to it by the magistrates' courts or the Crown Court.

In criminal cases the Crown Court has exclusive original jurisdiction to try all indictable offences and can hear appeals against summary conviction or sentence from magistrates' courts. Broadly speaking, the latter largely deal with less serious offences (especially motoring offences), where trial by judge and jury is not permitted – an issue still under discussion following the publication of the Runciman Report (1993). Whereas magistrates' courts have both criminal and civil jurisdiction – with the emphasis towards the former – the jurisdiction of the county courts is entirely civil and derived solely from statute. Among the issues they deal with are conflicts between landlords and tenants and disputes involving small claims (e.g. concerning consumer matters) where a system of arbitration provides for a relatively inexpensive and quick method of resolving problems.

In disputes with a supranational dimension – involving EU member states, institutions, organisations, companies or individuals – ultimate jurisdiction rests with the European Court of Justice. Under Article 220 (ex 164) of the Treaty of Rome, the court is required to ensure that in the application and interpretation of the Treaty, the law is observed. As indicated elsewhere, in carrying out this function, the court has adopted a relatively flexible approach in order to take account of changing circumstances (see Chapter 4). Few would dispute that its judgments have had, and will continue to have, a considerable influence on the development of EU law.

mini case: Jean-Marc Bosman – a case of foul play?

An example of how EU law affects individuals and organisations in member states is provided by the case of Jean-Marc Bosman, a Belgian football player who successfully challenged the transfer fee system operated by Europe's football authorities in the mid-1990s.

Bosman, who had been under contract to the Belgian club Liège, had sought a transfer to a French team when his contract expired but had his ambitions thwarted when Liège demanded a very high transfer fee. In the judgment of the European Court of Justice, clubs could no longer demand a fee for players out of contract if the player was headed for another EU member state. According to the judges, the system allowing for a fee to be imposed violated the right enshrined in the Treaty of Rome that European citizens could go from one EU country to another in pursuit of work. They also held that the rule limiting the number of foreign players a club could field in European matches violated the principle of the free movement of workers. The impact of the Court's judgment continues down to the present day.

As a final comment, it is perhaps worth stating that while conflict remains an enduring feature of daily life, many disputes are settled without recourse to the courts, often through direct negotiation between the parties concerned. Moreover, even where negotiations fail or where one party declines to negotiate, a dispute will not necessarily result in court action but may be dealt with in other ways. Disputes over employment contracts, for example, tend to be dealt with by a specialist tribunal, set up by statute to exercise specific functions of a quasi-legal nature. Similarly, complaints concerning maladministration by public (and increasingly private) bodies are generally dealt with by a system of 'ombudsmen', covering areas as diverse as social security benefits and local authority services. Financial services such as banking and insurance are covered by the Financial Services Ombudsman.

Business organisations and the law

Business organisations have been described as transformers of inputs into output in the sense that they acquire and use resources to produce goods or services for consumption. As Table 8.1 illustrates, all aspects of this transformation process are influenced by the law.

It is important to emphasise from the outset that the law not only constrains business activity (e.g. by establishing minimum standards of health and safety at work which are enforceable by law), it also assists it (e.g. by providing a means by which a business unit can have an independent existence from its members), and in doing so helps an enterprise to achieve its commercial and other objectives. In short, the legal environment within which businesses operate is an enabling as well as a regulatory environment and one that provides a considerable degree of certainty and stability to the conduct of business both within and between democratic states.

Given the extensive influence of the law on business organisations, it is clearly impossible to examine all aspects of the legal context within which firms function. Accordingly, in the analysis below, attention is focused primarily on contract law, agency and some of the more important statutes enacted to protect the interests of the consumer, since these are areas fundamental to business operations. Laws relating to the establishment of an enterprise and to the operation of markets are discussed in Chapters 10 and 17 respectively.

Table 8.1 Law and the business organisation

Business activity	Examples of legal influences
Establishing the organisation	Company laws, partnerships, business names
Acquiring resources	Planning laws, property laws, contract, agency
Business operations	Employment laws, health and safety laws, contract, agency
Selling output for consumption	Consumer laws, contract, agency

Contract law: the essentials

All businesses enter into contracts, whether with suppliers or employees or financiers or customers, and these contracts will be important – and possibly crucial – to the firm's operations. Such contracts are essentially agreements (oral or written) between two or more persons that are legally enforceable, provided they comprise a number of essential elements. These elements are: **offer, acceptance, consideration, intention to create legal relations** and **capacity**.

Offer

An **offer** in law is a declaration by the offeror (offer maker) that they intend to be legally bound by the terms stated in the offer if it is accepted by the offeree (the person to whom the offer is made) – for example, to supply particular laptop computers, at a particular price within a specified time period. This declaration may be made orally or in writing or by conduct between the parties and must be clear and unambiguous. Simply writing 'offer for sale' is not in itself enough. Furthermore, it should not be confused with an 'invitation to treat', which is essentially an invitation to make an offer, and as such cannot be accepted. This is generally the case with advertisements, auctions and goods on display. Tenders are offers; a request for tenders is merely an invitation for offers to be made.

Termination of an offer can happen in several ways. Clearly an offer is ended when it is accepted, but that apart, an offer may be revoked at any time up to acceptance. It is of no consequence, legally, that an offer may be kept open for a certain time. It is only when some consideration is paid for 'buying the option' that the time factor is important and this 'buying the option' would generally be a separate contract in any case. If an offer is for a certain length of time, then later acceptance is ineffective, and even where there is no specified time limit, the courts will imply a reasonable time. Thus, in *Ramsgate Victoria Hotel* v *Montefiore* (1866), shares in the hotel were offered for sale. After several months the offer was 'accepted', but the court held that too much time had passed, bearing in mind that the purpose of the shares offer was to raise money.

Another way for an offer to come to an end is by the failure of a condition. Although a genuine offer is always held to be firm and certain, sometimes it may be conditional and not absolute. Thus, should A wish to buy a model car from B, B may agree but impose conditions on the deal, such as stating that A must collect at a specific time on a certain day at a particular place and must pay in cash. This is known as a 'condition precedent' and failure to complete the conditions will nullify the agreement. There is another type of condition, called a 'condition subsequent', where there is a perfectly good contract that runs until something happens. For instance, a garage may have a good contract with an oil company to buy petrol at £x per 1000 litres until the price of oil at Rotterdam reaches $x per barrel. It is only when oil reaches the stipulated price that the contract ends.

Acceptance

Just as an offer must be firm and certain, the **acceptance** of an offer by the person(s) to whom it was made must be unequivocal and must not contain any alterations or additions. Accordingly, any attempt to alter the terms of an offer is regarded as a counter-offer and thus a rejection of the original offer, leaving the original offeror free to accept or decline as he or she chooses.

While acceptance of an offer normally occurs either in writing or verbally, it may also be implied by conduct. In the case of *Brogden* v *Metropolitan Railways Co.* (1877), Mr Brogden had supplied the company for many years without formalities. It was then decided to regularise the position and a draft agreement was sent to him. He inserted a new term, marked the draft 'approved', and returned it to the company where it was placed in a drawer and forgotten about, although the parties traded with each other on the terms of the draft for more than two years. Following a dispute, Mr Brogden claimed there was no contract. The then House of Lords decided differently, saying that a contract had been created by conduct.

Inferring the acceptance of an offer by conduct is quite different from assuming that silence on the part of the offeree constitutes acceptance; silence cannot be construed as an acceptance. Equally, while the offeror may prescribe the method of acceptance (although this is regarded as permissive rather than directory), the offeree may not prescribe a method by which he or she will make acceptance. For instance, an offer may be made by fax, thus implying that a fast response is required; therefore a reply accepting the offer that is sent by second-class mail may well be treated as nugatory.

There are some rules about acceptance that are important. Postal acceptance, for example, is a good method of communication and one that is universally used by businesses, but to be valid for contractual purposes a communication must be properly addressed and stamped and then placed into the hands of the duly authorised person (i.e. the post box or over the counter). An acceptance sent to a home address may be nullified if there has been no indication that this is acceptable. Similarly, acceptance of the offer must be effectively received by the offeror where modern, instantaneous methods of communication are used. Thus, if a telephone call is muffled by extraneous sound, then the acceptance must be repeated so that the offeror hears it clearly.

Consideration

Together, offer and acceptance constitute the basis of an 'agreement' or meeting of minds, provided the parties are clear as to what they are agreeing about (i.e. a *consensus ad idem* exists). However, English courts will rarely enforce a 'naked promise'. As a result, a promise must have 'consideration'. **Consideration** has been defined as some right, interest, profit or benefit accruing to one party or some forbearance, detriment, loss or responsibility given, suffered or undertaken by the other. In commercial contracts, the consideration normally takes the form of a cash payment in return for the goods or services provided (i.e. the 'price' in a contract of sale). It does not need to be the full market value, but it must be something tangible. In contracts involving barter (exchange), however, which are sometimes used in international trade, goods are often exchanged for other goods or for some other form of non-pecuniary consideration (e.g. information or advice).

Intention to create legal relations

Not every agreement is intended to create a legally binding relationship. For example, most domestic agreements – such as the division of household chores – would not constitute a contract recognised in law. In commercial agreements, however, it is generally accepted that both parties intend to make a legally binding contract and therefore it is unnecessary to include terms to this effect. Should such a presumption be challenged, the burden of proof rests with the person who disputes the presumption.

Capacity

A contract may be valid, voidable or void and one of the factors that determines this is the contractual capacity of the respective parties to the agreement. Normally speaking, an adult may make a contract with another adult which, if entered into freely and without any defects, and which is not contrary to public policy, is binding upon them both (i.e. valid). However, the law provides protection for certain categories of persons deemed not to have full contractual capacity (e.g. minors, drunks and the mentally disordered); hence the practice by firms of excluding people under the age of 18 from offers of goods to be supplied on credit.

Concentrating on minors – those below voting age – the law prescribes that they can be bound by contracts only for 'necessaries' (e.g. food, clothing, lodging) and contracts of employment that are advantageous or beneficial, as in the case of a job which contains an element of training or education. In most other instances, contracts with minors are void or voidable and as such will be either unenforceable or capable of being repudiated by the minor.

In the case of business, legal capacity depends on the firm's legal status. Unincorporated bodies (e.g. sole traders, partnerships) do not have a distinct legal personality and hence the party to the agreement is liable for their part of the bargain. Limited companies, by contrast, have a separate legal identity from their members and hence contractual capacity rests with the company, within the limits laid down in the objects clause of its Memorandum of Association (see Chapter 10).

Other factors

To be enforceable at law a contract must be legal (i.e. not forbidden by law or contrary to public policy). Similarly, the agreement must have been reached voluntarily and result in a genuine meeting of minds. Consequently, contracts involving mistakes of fact, misrepresentation of the facts, or undue influence or duress may be void or voidable, depending on the circumstances. In insurance contracts, for instance, the insured is required to disclose all material facts to the insurer (e.g. health record, driving record), otherwise a policy may be invalidated. In this context a 'material fact' is one that would affect the mind of a prudent insurer, even though the materiality may not be appreciated by the insured.

Agency

As business activity has become more specialised and complex, firms have increasingly turned to other businesses to carry out specialist functions on their behalf, such as freight forwarding, the sale of goods, insurance broking and commercial letting. These parties (known as **agents**) are authorised by the individual or organisation hiring them (known as the **principal**) to act on their behalf, thus creating an agency relationship. As in other areas of commercial activity, special rules of law have evolved to regulate the behaviour of the parties involved in such a relationship.

In essence, the function of an agent is to act on behalf of a principal so as to effect a contract between the principal and a third party. The agent may be a 'servant' of the principal (i.e. under their control, as in the case of a sales representative) or an 'independent contractor' (i.e. their own master, as in the case of an estate agent) and will be operating with the consent of the principal, whether by contract or implication. Having established a contractual relationship between the principal and the third party, the agent generally leaves the picture and usually has no rights and duties under the contract thus made.

With regard to an agent's specific obligations under an agency agreement, these are normally expressly stated under the terms of the agreement, although some may also be implied. Traditionally, the common law of agency prescribes, however, that agents:

- *obey the lawful instruction of the principal,* otherwise they may be in breach of contract;
- *exercise due care and skill,* in order to produce a deal that is to the principal's best advantage;
- *act personally,* rather than delegate, unless expressly or implicitly authorised to do so;

- *act in good faith,* thus avoiding conflicts of interest or undisclosed profits and bribes;
- *keep proper accounts,* which separate the principal's funds from those that belong personally to the agent.

Moreover, in so far as an agent is acting under the principal's authority, the principal is bound to the third party only by acts that are within the agent's authority to make. Consequently, *ultra vires* acts affect the principal only if he or she adopts them by ratification and the agent may be liable for the breach of the implied warranty of authority to the third party.

In addition to these common law duties owed by the principal, the Commercial Agents (Council Directive) Regulations 1993 apply when an agent falls within the definition of a commercial agent (Reg. 2(1)). They apply to transactions involving the sale or purchase of goods and they bestow certain rights and obligations upon both the principal and the agent. It is clear that these duties overlap to some extent with the common law duties. Regulation 3 provides the agent's duties to their principal. A commercial agent must:

- look after the interests of her/his principal and act dutifully and in good faith;
- make proper efforts to negotiate and, where appropriate, conclude the transactions;
- communicate to their principal all the necessary information available to them;
- comply with reasonable instructions given by the principal.

Regulation 4 specifies the duties of the principal:

- to act dutifully and in good faith;
- to provide the commercial agent with the necessary documentation relating to the goods in question;
- to obtain necessary information for the agent. This is a higher standard, perhaps requiring searching for data, than under the common law, where all the principal needs to do is to disclose information in their possession;
- to notify the agent within a reasonable period of time if the usual volume of trade is likely to be significantly reduced;
- to inform the agent within a reasonable period of time of the principal's acceptance, refusal, or non-acceptance of a commercial transaction arranged by the agent.

Law and the consumer

Neo-classical economic theory tends to suggest that laws to protect the consumer are unnecessary. However, modern economists (in particular behavioural economists) have shown that the traditional assumption of working markets is not necessarily reliable, so regulation is sometimes required. If individuals were behaving rationally when consuming goods and services, they would arrange their consumption to maximise their satisfaction (or 'utility'), in the words of an economist. Products that because of poor quality or some other factor reduced a consumer's utility would be rejected in favour of those that proved a better alternative and this would act as an incentive to producers (and retailers) to provide the best products. In effect, market forces would ensure that the interest of the consumer was safeguarded as suppliers in a competitive market arranged their production to meet the needs and wants of rational consumers.

The 'ideal' view of how markets work is not always borne out in practice. Apart from the fact that consumers do not always act rationally, they often do not have access to information which might influence their choice of products; in some cases they may not even have a choice of products (e.g. where a monopoly exists), although this situation can change over time (e.g. through privatisation of state monopolies). Also, given the respective resources of producers and consumers, the balance of power in the trading relationship tends to favour producers who can influence consumer choices using a range of persuasive techniques, including advertising.

Taken together, these and other factors call into question the assumption that the consumer is 'sovereign' and hence the extent to which individuals have inherent protection in the marketplace from powerful (and, in some cases, unscrupulous) suppliers. It is in this context that the law is seen to be an important counterbalance in a contractual relationship where the consumer is, or may be, at a disadvantage, and this can be said to provide the basis of legal intervention in this area.

Existing laws to protect consumers come from both civil and criminal law. These rights, duties and liabilities have been created or imposed by common law (especially contract and tort) or by legislation. Significantly, as the examples below illustrate, a large element of current consumer law has resulted from statutory intervention, with much of it coming from the EU by way of directives. These laws – covering areas as diverse as commercial practices, the sale of goods and services, and consumer credit and product liability – indicate a growing willingness on the part of governments to respond to the complaints of consumers and their representative organisations and to use legislation to regulate the relationship between business organisations and their customers. Europe is keen to encourage consumers to take advantage of cross-border EU markets by harmonising consumer protection, as this boosts market access and consumer spending. To this end Europe has been adopting consumer protection directives, the most significant recent one being the Unfair Commercial Practices Directive, which has replaced a great deal of the pre-existing domestic law. However, major domestic law reform has been proposed with a Consumer Rights Bill, which was going through Parliament at the time of writing. This reform aims to consolidate the recent changes to consumer law.

The Consumer Affairs Directorate in the Department of Business, Innovation and Skills is a useful source of reference on consumer law – see *www.gov.uk/consumer-protection-rights*

The Consumer Protection from Unfair Trading Regulations 2008

The Trade Descriptions Act 1968 was a mainstay of consumer protection before it was largely superseded by the Consumer Protection from Unfair Trading Regulations (2008). These Regulations implemented the Unfair Commercial Practices Directive 2005–29/EC, and extend criminal liability beyond simply misleading practices. These changes ban five categories of unfair practices, namely, a general prohibition on unfair practices, promoting unfair practices in codes of conduct, misleading actions and misleading omissions, aggressive commercial practices, and practices always deemed unfair under a 'banned list' of 31 practices. The Office of Fair Trading (OFT) (see Chapter 17), local authorities and the enforcement bodies also have powers to seek 'stop now' orders against such practices.

The Consumer Credit Acts 1974–2006

The Consumer Credit Act 1974, which became fully operational in May 1985, controls transactions between the credit industry and private individuals (including sole traders and business partnerships) up to a limit of £15,000. This statute has been updated since, especially so as to include EU directives, and it has recently been augmented by the Consumer Credit Act 2006. The Financial Conduct Authority took over regulation of consumer credit from the OFT on 1 April 2014. Under the legislation a consumer credit agreement is defined as a personal credit providing the debtor with credit up to the accepted limit. This credit may be in the form of a cash loan or some other type of financial accommodation (e.g. through the use of a credit card). The Act also covers hire purchase agreements (i.e. a contract of hire which gives the hirer the option to purchase the goods), conditional sale agreements for the sale of goods or land, and credit sale agreements, where the property passes to the buyer when the sale is effected.

The main aim of this consumer protection measure is to safeguard the public from trading malpractices where some form of credit is involved. To this end the Act provides, among other things, for a system of licensing controlled by the OFT, which must be satisfied that the person seeking a licence is a fit person and the name under which he or she intends to be licensed is neither misleading nor undesirable. Providing credit or acting as a credit broker without a licence is a criminal offence, as is supplying a minor with any document inviting them to borrow money or obtain goods on credit. The Consumer Credit Act 2006 created a Financial Services Ombudsman to settle disputes between consumers and their lenders. It has also created an unfair credit test that makes it easier for debtors to challenge excessive interest rates with the Ombudsman.

A further protection for the consumer comes from the requirements that the debtor be made fully aware of the nature and cost of the agreement and his or her rights and liabilities under it. The Act stipulates that prior to the contract being made the debtor must be supplied with certain information, including the full price of the credit agreement (i.e. the cost of the credit plus the capital sum), the annual rate of the total charge for credit expressed as a percentage (i.e. the annual percentage rate), and the amounts of payments due and to whom they are payable. In addition, the debtor must be informed of all the other terms of the agreement and of their right to cancel if this is applicable. In the case of the latter, this applies to credit agreements drawn up off business premises, and is designed to protect individuals from high-pressure doorstep sellers who offer credit as an incentive to purchase.

Sale of Goods Act 1979

Under the Sale of Goods Act 1979 (as amended), the Unfair Contract Terms Act 1977 and the Unfair Terms in Consumer Contracts Regulations 1999, consumers are essentially seen as individuals who purchase goods or services for their personal use from other individuals or organisations selling them in the course of business. A computer sold to a student, for example, is a consumer sale, while the same machine sold to a secretarial agency is not, since it has been acquired for business purposes. This legal definition of a consumer is important as some laws are designed specifically to provide consumers with extra protection, as in the case of the Sale of Goods Act. This statute governs agreements where a seller agrees to transfer ownership in goods to a buyer in return for a monetary consideration, known as the 'price'. Where such an agreement or contract is deemed to exist, the legislation provides all buyers with rights in respect of items that are faulty or that do not correspond with the description given to them, by identifying a number of implied conditions to the sale. However, consumer buyers are given extra remedies. In the case of contracts for the supply of services (e.g. repair work) or which involve the supply of goods and services (e.g. supplying units and fitting them in a bathroom or kitchen), almost identical rights are provided under the Supply of Goods and Services Act 1982 (as amended).

The three main implied conditions of the 1979 Act are relatively well known, namely, sale by description, satisfactory quality and fitness for purpose. The quality and fitness obligations are owed only when goods are sold in the course of a business, while section 13 applies to all sales. Under section 13, goods sold by description must match the description given to them, even if the buyer has selected the goods, for example, from a shop shelf. This description may be on the article itself or on the packaging or provided in some other way, and will include the price and possibly other information (e.g. washing instructions) which the buyer believes to be true. The description must describe the commercial characteristics and not be mere sales hype. A shirt described as 100 per cent cotton, for instance, must be just that, otherwise it fails to match the description given to it and the consumer is entitled to choose either a refund or an exchange.

The second condition relates to the quality of the goods provided. While this applies to all buyers, it applies only where goods are sold in the course of a business. So it will not apply to private sales. Under section 14(2) of the Act, goods had to be of 'merchantable quality', but 'merchantable quality' was a matter of some controversy, and so the phrase was amended to 'satisfactory quality' by section 1 of the Sale of Goods and Services Act 1994. The general expectation is that a product should be fit 'for all the purposes for which goods of the kind in question are commonly supplied', bearing in mind questions of age, price and any other relevant factors (e.g. brand name). A new top-of-the-range car should have no significant defects on purchase, whereas it would be unreasonable to expect the same from a high-mileage used car sold for a few hundred pounds. The quality expected of sale goods will normally be the same as the full-priced item. Thus, while the implied condition of 'satisfactory' applies to sale goods and used goods as well as to full-price purchases of new goods, it needs to be judged in light of the contract description and all the circumstances of a particular case, including the consumer's expectations.

The third implied condition derives from section 14(3) of the legislation, namely that goods are fit for a particular purpose (i.e. capable of performing the tasks indicated by the seller). Section 14(3) comes into its own when a use or range of uses is made known to the seller. Accordingly, section 14(3) will be breached if the seller, on request from the purchaser, confirms that goods are suitable for a particular purpose made known by the buyer and this proves not to be the case. Equally, if the product is unsuitable for its normal purposes, then section 14(2) would also be breached.

It is worth noting that 'satisfactory' and 'fitness for a purpose' are closely related and that a breach of one may include a breach of the other. By the same token, failure in a claim for a breach of section 14(2) is likely to mean that a claim for a breach of section 14(3) will also fail. Moreover, if, on request, a seller disclaims any knowledge of a product's suitability for a particular purpose and the consumer is willing to take a chance, any subsequent unsuitability cannot be regarded as a breach of section 14(3). The same applies if the buyer's reliance on the skill or judgement of the seller is deemed 'unreasonable'.

There are two sets of remedies available for breach of these implied terms, namely, rejection under a short-term right to reject, and/or damages. The time permitted to reject depends on the circumstances of the case, but usually it should at the very least be several weeks. The only exception to this has traditionally been that of durability, that is, where the goods have failed before goods of that type could reasonably be expected to fail. Durability has always been treated as a damages-only breach, so as to avoid overcompensating the buyer. These are the only remedies applicable to business buyers.

However, the Sale and Supply of Goods to Consumers Regulations 2002 have granted the consumer/buyer a choice, where they can use the traditional remedies (above) or additional remedies. The Regulations come from the European Consumer Guarantees Directive (1999–44/EC) and seek to continue the move towards harmonising the cross-border sale of consumer goods. The DTI (now BIS), keen not to reduce the pre-existing levels of consumer protection, added the new remedies to those already existing. The result is that the consumer retains the short-term right to reject the goods for non-conformity. However, if this remedy is lost due to lapse of time, or the consumer chooses not to use this remedy, the consumer now has four new paired remedies: repair or replace, price reduction or rescission. These are often called 'the four Rs' and are dealt with in more detail below, in the case study section. Until these Regulations the consumer had no right to require a repair or a replacement, and could sue for damages only.

Moreover, the Regulations now remove the problem of goods damaged in transit. Risk previously passed to the consumer/buyer once the goods had been handed over to a third-party carrier, the result being that the purchaser would find the carrier and the seller blaming one another for the loss. Ultimately, the consumer would go uncompensated unless they decided to sue both parties. The Regulations now require that goods must actually be received by the consumer/buyer in conformity with the contract, so risk passes later. Lastly, manufacturers must honour any guarantee that they provide, and bear the return cost for any defective goods under a manufacturer's guarantee.

These new remedies apply only to consumers/buyers of goods sold in the course of a business. Section 15A of the Sale of Goods Act applies to business-to-business sales where there is only a slight breach of an implied condition of description or quality. The provision seeks to prevent a business buyer from rejecting goods due to a minor technical breach, and imposes an award of damages only. As damages are based on loss, damages for a technical breach will probably be very low. As a result, businesses that find that they can get the goods cheaper elsewhere will be less tempted to try to seek to reject goods for minor breaches. This also recognises that rejection of goods is not the norm in business; normally a recalculation of the price or payment conditions takes place. Having theoretical rights is one thing, but in business one may need to trade with the other party again and it is wise to consider the impact of any decision taken.

As a final comment, under the Sale and Supply of Goods and Services Act 1982, section 3, there is an implied condition that a supplier acting in the course of business must carry out the service with reasonable care and skill and within a reasonable time, where a specific deadline is not stated in the contract. Reasonable care and skill tends to be seen as that which might be expected of an ordinary competent person performing the particular task, though this will, of course, depend on the particular circumstances of the case and the nature of the trade or profession. As in the case of the Sale of Goods Act, any attempt to deprive the consumer of any of the implied conditions represents a breach of both the Unfair Contract Terms Act 1977 and the Unfair Terms in Consumer Contracts Regulations 1999.

Exclusion or limitation clauses in consumer contracts are subject to the Unfair Contract Terms Act 1977 and the Unfair Terms in Consumer Contracts Regulations 1999, which currently operate as a dual regime, giving the consumer the choice of actions. Under the former, any clause seeking to exclude or limit liability for personal injury/death or the statutory implied terms against a consumer is void, while all other clauses are subject to the test of reasonableness. Under the latter regulations a term that has not been individually negotiated will be unfair if it is contrary to good faith by causing a significant imbalance between the parties. The situation is a little different in business deals, although personal injury/death still cannot be excluded. Thus, where a reference is made on a product or its container or in a related document to a consumer's rights under sections 13 to 15 of the Sale of Goods Act, there must be a clear and accessible notice informing consumers that their statutory rights are not affected when returning an item deemed unsatisfactory. It is an offence under the Fair Trading Act 1974 to display notices stating 'no refunds' or 'no refunds on sale goods'. The aim is to ensure that buyers are made fully aware of their legal rights and are not taken advantage of by unscrupulous traders who seek to deny them the protection afforded by the law.

The Consumer Protection Act 1987

The Consumer Protection Act 1987 came into force in March 1988 as a result of the government's obligation to implement EC Directive 85–374, which concerned product liability. In essence, the Act provides for a remedy in damages for any consumer who suffers personal injury or damage to property as a result of a defective product by imposing a 'strict' liability on the producers of defective goods (including substances, growing crops, ships, aircraft and vehicles). Naturally, the onus is on the complainant to prove that any loss was caused by the claimed defect and a claim can be made where damage to property, personal injury or death has occurred. In the case of the latter, for example, a relative or friend could pursue an action and, if American experience is anything to go by, could be awarded substantial damages if liability can be proven. As far as property is concerned, damage must be to private rather than commercial goods and property and the loss must exceed £275.

While the Act is, *inter alia,* intended to place liability on the producers of defective goods, this liability also extends to anyone putting a name or distinguishing mark on a product which holds that person out as being the producer (e.g. supermarkets' own-brand labels). Similarly, importers of products from outside the EU are also liable for any defects in imported goods, as may be firms involved in supplying components or parts of the process of manufacture of a product. To prevent a firm escaping its liability as a supplier claiming it is unable to identify its own suppliers, the legislation provides a remedy: any supplier unable or unwilling to identify the importing firm or previous supplier becomes liable itself for damages under the Act.

Firms seeking to avoid liability for any claim have a number of defences under section 4 of the Act. Specifically these are:

- that the defendant did not supply the product in question;
- that the product was not manufactured or supplied in the course of business;
- that the defect did not exist at the time the product was distributed;
- that where a product has a number of components, the defect is a defect of the finished product or due to compliance with any instructions issued by the manufacturer of the finished product;
- that the defect is attributable to the requirement to comply with existing laws;
- that the state of scientific and technical knowledge at the time the product was supplied was not sufficiently advanced for the defect to be recognised.

Of these, the last – the so-called development risks or 'state of the art' defence – is the most contentious, given that it applies largely to products such as new drugs and new technology where the implications of their usage may not be apparent for some years. As recent cases have shown, manufacturers faced with damages from claimants who appear to have suffered from the use of certain products often decide to settle out of court without accepting liability for their actions.

The annual Report of the Office of Fair Trading contains useful commentary on consumer protection issues, including codes of practice and the powers of the OFT. See www.oft.gov.uk

Codes of practice

Alongside the protection provided by the law, consumers may be afforded a further measure of security when the organisation they are dealing with belongs to a trade association that is operating under a **code of practice** (e.g. the Association of British Travel Agents). In essence, codes of practice represent an attempt by trade associations to impose a measure of self-discipline on the behaviour of their members by establishing the standards of service customers should expect to receive and by encouraging acceptable business practices. In addition, such codes of conduct invariably identify how customer complaints should be handled and many offer low-cost or no-cost arbitration schemes to help settle disputes outside the more formal legal process.

While codes of practice do not in themselves have the force of law, they are normally seen as a useful mechanism for regulating the relationship between business organisations and their customers and accordingly they have the support of the Office of Fair Trading, which often advises trade associations on their content. Businesses, too, usually find them useful, particularly if through the establishment of a system of self-regulation they are able to avoid the introduction of restrictions imposed by the law.

Synopsis

All business activities, from the establishment of the organisation through to the sale of the product to the customer, are influenced by the law. This legal environment within which businesses exist and operate evolves over time and is a key influence on firms of all sizes and in all sectors, as illustrated by an examination of some of the main laws governing the relationship between a business and its customers. The majority of consumer laws are of relatively recent origin and derive from the attempts by successive governments to provide individuals with a measure of protection against a minority of firms that behave in ways deemed to be unacceptable. Concomitantly, they also provide reputable organisations with a framework within which to carry out their business and, as such, act as an incentive to entrepreneurial activity in market-based economies.

Summary of key points

- The legal rules within which businesses exist and operate are an important part of the external environment of business organisations.
- Laws affecting businesses derive from a variety of sources, including custom, the decisions of the courts and legislation.
- Laws are sometimes made at international and supranational level (including Europe).
- Contract, agency and consumer protection are three key areas governing the day-to-day work of businesses.
- Offer, acceptance, consideration, intention to create legal relations and capacity are central elements of contract law.
- Agency relationships are a common feature of business practice.
- The relationship between businesses and their customers is governed by a variety of laws, many of which derive from statute.
- In addition to the protection provided to consumers by the law, many organisations operate under agreed codes of conduct.

case study: The sale of goods on the internet

The sale of consumer goods on the internet (particularly those between European member states) raises a number of legal issues. First, there is the issue of trust, without which the consumer will not buy; they will need assurance that the seller is genuine, and that they will get the goods that they have ordered. Second, there is the issue of consumer rights with respect to the goods in question: what rights exist and do they vary across Europe? Last, the issue of enforcement: what happens should anything go wrong?

Information and trust

Europe recognises the problems of doing business across the internet or telephone and it has attempted to address the main stumbling blocks via directives which are incorporated into member states' own laws. The original Distance Selling Directive, implemented as the Consumer Protection (Distance Selling) Regulations 2000, was in the process of being replaced by the Consumer Rights Directive (2011–83/EU) at the time of going to press. The new directive is a 'maximum harmonisation' measure, meaning that the provisions are binding on, and cannot be modified by member states. Both directives attempt to address the issues of trust in distance sale. In short, the consumer who does not buy face to face may lack important information, which they may otherwise have easy access to if they were buying face to face.

Article 6 of the Consumer Rights Directive requires *inter alia* for the seller to identify themselves and an address must be provided if the goods are to be paid for in advance. Moreover, a full description of the goods and the final price (inclusive of any taxes) must also be provided. The new directive bans pre-ticked boxes (e.g. for insurance), and limits card transaction charges to those of the cost actually incurred by the trader. These provisions will help to cut hidden costs. The seller must also inform the buyer of the right of cancellation available under Article 9, where the buyer has a right to cancel the contract for 14 days starting on the day the consumer receives the goods or services (this was seven days under the Distance Selling Directive). This 'cooling off' period is intended to place the consumer in the position as if they had seen the goods in store. Failure to inform the consumer of this right automatically extends the period to a year and 14 days. While the seller can place the cost of returning goods on the buyer, the seller must refund the standard rate outgoing postage. The seller is not entitled to deduct any costs as a restocking fee. All of this places a considerable obligation on the seller; however, such data should stem many misunderstandings and so boost cross-border trade by increasing consumer faith and confidence in non-face-to-face sales.

Another concern for the consumer is fraud. The consumer who has paid by credit card will be protected by section 83 of the Consumer Credit Act 1974, under which a consumer/purchaser is not liable for the debt incurred if it has been run up by a third party not acting as the agent of the buyer. The Distance Selling Regulations extended this to debit cards, and removed the ability of the card issuer to charge the consumer for the first £50 of loss. Moreover, section 75 of the Consumer Credit Act 1974 also gives the consumer/buyer a like claim against the credit card company for any misrepresentation or breach of contract by the seller. This is extremely important in a distance-selling transaction, where the seller may disappear.

What quality and what rights?

The next issue relates to the quality that may be expected from goods bought over the internet. Clearly, if goods have been bought from abroad, the levels of quality required in other jurisdictions may vary. It is for this reason that Europe has attempted to standardise the issue of quality and consumer remedies, with the Consumer Guarantees Directive (1999–44/EC), thus continuing the push to encourage cross-border consumer purchases. The Sale and Supply of Goods to Consumer Regulations 2002 came into force in 2003, which not only lay down minimum quality standards but also provide the series of consumer remedies (the four Rs) across

Europe. The Regulations further amend the Sale of Goods Act 1979. The former DTI (now BIS), whose job it was to incorporate the directive into domestic law (by way of delegated legislation), ensured that the pre-existing consumer rights were maintained, so as not to reduce the overall level of protection available to consumers.

The directive requires goods to be of 'normal' quality, or fit for any purpose made known by the seller. This has been taken to be the same as our pre-existing 'satisfactory quality' and 'fitness for purpose' obligations owed under sections 14(2) and 14(3) of the Sale of Goods Act 1979. Moreover, the pre-existing remedy of the short-term right to reject is also retained. This right provides the buyer a short period of time to discover whether the goods are in conformity with the contract. In practice, it is usually a matter of weeks. After that time has elapsed, the consumer has four new remedies that did not exist before, which are provided in two pairs. These are repair or replacement and price reduction or rescission. The pre-existing law only gave a right to damages, which would rarely be exercised in practice. (However, the Small Claims Court would ensure a speedy and cheap means of redress for almost all contract claims brought under £10,000.) Now there is a right to a repair or a replacement, so that the consumer is not left with an impractical action for damages over defective goods. The seller must also bear the cost of return of the goods for repair. So such costs must now be factored into any business sales plan.

If these remedies are not suitable, deproportionate or actioned within a 'reasonable period of time' then the consumer may rely on the second pair of remedies. Price reduction permits the consumer to claim back a segment of the purchase price if the goods are still useable. It is effectively a discount for defective goods. Rescission allows the consumer to reject the goods, but they do not get the full refund that they would under the short-term right to reject; here money is knocked off for 'beneficial use'. This is akin to the pre-existing treatment for breaches of durability, where goods have not lasted as long as goods of that type ought reasonably be expected to last. The level of payment would take account of the use that the consumer has (if any) been able to put the goods to and a deduction made off the return of the purchase price. However, the issue that must be addressed is the length of time that goods may be expected to last. A supplier may state the length of the guarantee period, so a £500 television set guaranteed for one year would have a life expectancy of one year. However, a consumer may expect a television set to last ten years. Clearly, if the set went wrong after six months, the consumer would get back only £250 if the retailer's figure was used, but would receive £475 if their own figure was used. It remains to be seen how this provision will work in practice.

One problem with distance sales has been that of liability for goods that arrive damaged. The pre-existing domestic law stated that risk would pass to the buyer once the goods were handed over to a third-party carrier. This had the major problem in practice of who would actually be liable for the damage. Carriers would blame the supplier and vice versa. The consumer would be able to sue for the loss, if they were able to determine which party was responsible. In practice, consumers usually went uncompensated and such a worry has deterred many consumers from buying goods over the internet. The Sale and Supply of Goods to Consumer Regulations 2003 also modify the transfer of risk, so that now the risk remains with a commercial seller of goods to a consumer, until actual delivery. This will clearly lead to a slight increase in the supply of goods to consumers, with the goods usually now being sent by insured delivery. However, this will avoid the problem of who is actually liable and should help to boost consumer confidence.

Enforcement

Enforcement for domestic sales is relatively straightforward. Small-scale consumer claims can be dealt with expeditiously and cheaply under the Small Claims Court. Here, claims under £10,000 for contract-based claims are brought in a special court intended to keep costs down by keeping the lawyers out of the court room, as a victorious party cannot claim for their lawyers' expenses. The judge will conduct the case in a more 'informal' manner, and will seek to discover the legal issues by questioning both parties, so no formal knowledge of the law is required. The total cost of such a case, even if it is lost, is the cost of issuing the proceedings (approximately 10 per cent of the value claimed) and the other side's 'reasonable expenses'. Expenses must be kept down, and a judge will not award value which has been deliberately run up, such as first-class rail travel and stays in five-star hotels. Such claims may now be made online via the internet (www.courtservice.gov.uk outlines the procedure for MCOL, or Money Claims Online). Cases will normally be held in the defendant's court, unless the complainant is a consumer and the defendant a business.

There is now a European-wide Small Claims Court dealing with transnational European transactions valued at less than €2,000. The case will be handled by member states' existing small claims courts.

Case study questions

1 Consider the checklist of data which a distance seller must provide to a consumer purchaser. Is this putting too heavy a burden on sellers?

2 Is a consumer distance buyer any better off after the European legislation?

3 Are there any remaining issues that must be tackled to increase European cross-border consumer trade?

Review and discussion questions

1 Why are laws to protect the consumer felt to be necessary? What other means do consumers have of protecting their interests in the marketplace?

2 To what extent does the supranational structure of European Union law infringe the principle of the supremacy of Parliament?

3 Do you think that tobacco companies should be made retrospectively liable for the safety of their product? Justify your answer.

4 Examine the case for and against increased government control over business practices.

Assignments

1 You are a trading standards officer in a local authority trading standards department. You have been asked to talk to a group of school sixth-form students on the Sale of Goods Act 1979. Prepare suitable PowerPoint slides outlining the following:

(a) The main provisions of the 1979 Act.
(b) The customer's rights in the event of a breach of the implied conditions.
(c) The sources of help and advice available to an individual with a consumer problem.

2 Imagine you work for a Citizens' Advice Bureau. A large part of your work involves offering advice to individuals with consumer problems. Design a simple leaflet indicating some of the principal pieces of legislation in the field of consumer protection and their main provisions. Your leaflet should also give guidance on further specialist sources of help and advice.

Notes and references

1 'Opt-outs' may sometimes be negotiated, however. Britain initially opted out of the Social Chapter of the Maastricht Treaty, which includes a provision for a 48-hour maximum working week. Within the Union an attempt was made to treat this issue as a health and safety measure, which could then be applicable to British firms by majority (not unanimous) vote of the member states. After the 1997 election, the government decided to 'opt in' to the Social Chapter. The 48-hour working restrictions are now causing concern in a number of areas, notably transport, deep sea fishing and the health service.

Further reading

Atiyah, P., *The Sale of Goods,* 12th edition, Longman/Pearson, 2010.

Furmston, M. and Chuah, J. (eds), *Commercial and Consumer Law,* 2nd edition, Pearson, 2013.

Marson, J., *Business Law,* 3rd edition, Oxford University Press, 2011.

Web links and further questions are available on the website at:
www.pearsoned.co.uk/worthington

9 The ethical and ecological environment

Ian Worthington

There is a growing body of opinion that businesses have a duty to fulfil objectives that stretch beyond the simple well-being of the organisation and its owners to the promotion of greater corporate social responsibility, particularly with regard to the natural environment. This chapter looks at the emergence of this perspective and analyses why and how a firm may seek to improve on its environmental performance.

Learning outcomes

Having read this chapter you should be able to:

- define the concepts of business ethics and corporate social responsibility
- discuss the emergence of corporate environmentalism as a business issue
- differentiate between the drivers of, and motivations for, green behaviour by businesses
- analyse the reasons why a firm might seek to improve on its environmental performance and what forms this could take
- illustrate how firms both affect and are affected by the natural environment

Key terms

Business ethics
Circular economy
Competitive advantage
Corporate social responsibility
Cradle-to-cradle™ (C2C)
Eco-efficiency
Eco-label
Eco-Management and Audit Scheme (EMAS)
Environmental champions

Environmental management system (EMS)
Environmental subsidies
Environmental taxes
European Emissions Trading Scheme (ETS)
Gold plating
Inside-out view
Market niche
Negative externalities
Outside-in view
Polluter pays principle

Public voluntary programmes
Resource-based view
Stakeholders
Sustainable development
Tradeable (or marketable) pollution permits
Unilateral commitments
Unlevel playing field
Voluntary approach (VA)
Win-win philosophy

Introduction

In May 1999 the largest ever survey of global public opinion took place on the changing expectations of businesses in the twenty-first century. Twenty-five thousand people in 23 countries on 6 continents were interviewed about their perceptions of the roles and responsibilities of business organisations in the social and environmental as well as the economic spheres. This worldwide survey – known as the Millennium Poll on Corporate Social Responsibility (CSR) – confirmed what many business researchers and corporate leaders had come to recognise over the course of the previous decade or so. Namely, that a firm's social and environmental performance was no less important to the general public (and, therefore, customers) than its traditional roles of making profits, paying taxes and complying with the law. While there were differences in the strengths of opinions expressed in the countries surveyed, the overall message of the poll was clear: consumers believe that business organisations should behave in a socially and environmentally responsible way and should be held accountable for their actions across a range of areas, from protecting the health and safety of their employees, through avoiding unethical business practices, to protecting the natural environment. This remains a common perception.

In the analysis below, we discuss how ethical and ecological issues in business have become an increasingly important aspect of a firm's macroenvironmental context. This development can be illustrated in a number of ways. Many larger organisations now publish annual social and environmental reports, which are designed to highlight improvements in the firm's performance on a range of indicators (e.g. employee training, charitable donations, reduction in carbon emissions) to a variety of stakeholder groups (see below). To achieve these claimed improvements, a growing number of firms have appointed senior executives and managers with responsibility for directing, monitoring and auditing the social and environmental performance of the business and for communicating this both internally and externally to the various interested parties.

In the lexicon of business, concepts such as **corporate social responsibility**, social responsiveness, corporate social performance, corporate citizenship and corporate sustainability have become relatively commonplace, as have notions such as supply chain ethics, green marketing and triple bottom line accounting. Parallel developments have also taken place in the academic world as a growing number of business and management programmes now incorporate the study of **business ethics**, CSR and sustainable development into the curriculum, supported by a burgeoning literature in these fields and an expanding group of international journals focusing on the ethical and environmental aspects of business (e.g. *Journal of Business Ethics, Journal of Environmental Management, Business Strategy and the Environment*).

To provide an insight into how businesses can be affected by ethical and ecological pressures, the chapter begins with a general discussion of the notions of business ethics and corporate social responsibility before moving on to a more detailed examination of the very topical issue of environmental management in business. For students wishing to investigate these subjects in more detail, we have recommended some useful sources in the 'Further reading' section at the end of the chapter. You could also consult the websites of leading multinational corporations and bodies such as business representative organisations (e.g. Confederation of British Industry, Institute of Directors, Chambers of

Commerce), environmental NGOs (e.g. Greenpeace, Friends of the Earth, Forum for the Future), advocacy groups (e.g. Business in the Community) and the various international groups/agencies whose work includes consideration of ethical and environmental issues in business (e.g. the UN, World Bank).

Ethics and business

As we saw in the previous chapter, business organisations exist and function within a framework of law emanating from various sources, including government. In many areas of life, laws essentially direct what individuals and/or organisations can or cannot do and set minimum standards of behaviour based on underlying ethical principles. Not all ethical aspects of business, however, are covered by government legislation or the common law, as in the case of selling weapons to overseas governments or paying low wages to workers producing a product in other countries. By the same token, not all laws governing individual or organisational behaviour raise what would be regarded as important ethical issues.

As Crane and Matten (2004) suggest, business ethics is basically concerned with those issues in business that are not covered by law or where there is no definite consensus on what is 'right' or 'wrong' behaviour. Accordingly, they define business ethics as 'the study of business situations, activities and decisions where issues of right and wrong are addressed', stressing quite rightly that in terms of organisational behaviour right and wrong should be seen in a moral sense, not from a financial or strategic point of view. It might make financial sense, for instance, for an organisation to exploit cheap labour or flush its waste products into a river at no cost to the business, and it might not be illegal, but is it ethical? As the Millennium Poll (Available via www.ipsos-mori.com) and other surveys have illustrated, a firm's stance on ethical issues in business are an important aspect of its external environment and one that applies to enterprises of all kinds, in all sectors, and across different national jurisdictions.

While it is beyond the scope of this chapter to discuss all the potential ethical dilemmas faced by modern business organisations, it is worth noting that these have tended to intensify and broaden as business activity has become more globalised and as technological transformation has given rise to the globalisation of communications and the 24-hour instant news culture. Multinational corporations in particular are facing much closer scrutiny by different groups of stakeholders which are increasingly willing to pressurise larger businesses to behave in a more ethically and ecologically sustainable way. Allegations that some high-profile western companies are (sometimes unwittingly) exploiting child labour in the developing world or are involved in ethically questionable commercial practices (e.g. bribery, price fixing) or in environmentally damaging activities (e.g. illegal logging, oil exploration in unspoiled natural environments) inevitably attract media attention and can result in significant damage to a firm's reputation and, potentially, its bottom line. By the same token, firms recognised for having a good ethical stance may find favour with the different stakeholder interests and this could bring organisational benefits of various kinds, including increased sales, access to new customers/markets, improvements in labour recruitment and retention, lower insurance premiums and less scrutiny by governments and/or NGOs.

mini case: Illegal or unethical?

While definitions of business ethics focus on issues of right and wrong that are not covered by the law, the dividing line between behaviour that is evidently illegal and that which is unethical can sometimes be difficult to draw. Take the following recent cases of alleged and controversial business practices. Where would you draw the line?

1. Major banks – including UBS, Barclays, Standard Chartered, HSBC, RBS, J.P. Morgan and Lloyds – have been accused of, and sometimes fined for, a series of misdemeanours. These have included mis-selling of payment protection insurance; manipulating the key London inter-bank interest rate (LIBOR); breaches of money laundering rules and sanctions busting; selling of sub-prime mortgages; being involved in businesses that speculate on world food prices; manipulation of exchange rates. Not all of the above named banks have been accused of every one of these practices and some allegations are still being investigated.

2. Major international companies (e.g. Starbucks, Vodafone, Amazon, Apple, Facebook, Google) have been criticised for arranging their business affairs so as to minimise the tax paid to host governments.

3. GSK has been accused of paying bribes to win business in China. Rolls-Royce is facing similar allegations relating to past contracts in both Indonesia and China.

4. A number of major retailers – including Primark, Marks and Spencer, H&M, New Look – have come under pressure to investigate more fully the conditions in overseas factories supplying their garments following a fatal fire in a Bangladeshi supplier's premises. Most major retailers have now signed up to a UN-sponsored, legally binding agreement on worker safety and building regulations.

5. Some major food and drink firms have been exhorted to provide more accurate product labelling, particularly salt, sugar and calorie content, because of concerns over diabetes and obesity. Critics have accused some of the major companies in the food industry of providing unclear information and guidance to consumers.

As the above examples illustrate, there may be cases where a certain business practice may be judged to be both illegal and unethical in the moral sense of the word. Where businesses fail to provide an adequate system of corporate governance to address ethically questionable behaviour by their employees, governments are sometimes forced to intervene through the law. This is not necessarily easy, particularly if the issue is a cross-national problem (e.g. tax avoidance) requiring a coordinated approach by different national governments.

Whether 'good ethics' and 'good business' are always complementary has been the subject of considerable debate in both practitioner and academic circles and is one that is far from resolved.[1] That said, what is clear is that the question of ethics in business and the related concept of corporate social responsibility are no longer peripheral issues and have been rapidly moving up the corporate agenda in most large business organisations in recent years. If firms are to avoid the potential risks posed by a poor ethical performance (e.g. Enron) and/or exploit the anticipated opportunities offered by a positive ethical stance (e.g. The Body Shop), they need to put in place appropriate mechanisms for managing the ethical issues they face (e.g. values statements, codes of ethics, robust systems of corporate governance, accredited auditing and reporting systems). They also need to think more broadly about society's expectations of corporate behaviour and of their obligations and responsibilities beyond those to the immediate owners of the business. This notion of a firm's social responsibilities is the issue to which we now turn.

Corporate social responsibility (CSR)

The idea of CSR essentially means that business organisations have responsibilities that go beyond mere profit-making and encompass voluntary activities and actions that affect people, their communities and the natural environment. The question of whether, and how far, a firm should engage in such activities if they might adversely affect profitability remains a contested arena. A central theme in this debate has been the issue of the central purpose of the business organisation and the knowledge, abilities and responsibilities of those that run profit-seeking enterprises. Under the neo-classical view of the firm, private sector businesses exist to make profits for the owners (e.g. shareholders) and the responsibility of the firm's managers is to act in a way that enhances the position of the providers of capital, by maximising profits and/or shareholder value. Writing in *The New York Times* in 1970, the economist Milton Friedman basically echoed this perspective when he argued that the social responsibility of a business was to increase its profits so long as it obeyed the law and operated ethically.[2] In Friedman's opinion, a firm's directors were not only ill-equipped to make decisions on social and environmental matters but, as agents for the firm's owners (the principals), they also had a fiduciary responsibility to the shareholders, not to some broader conception of the social good. Under this interpretation, allocating some of the firm's resources to the pursuit of socially responsible objectives could effectively be construed as unethical since it involves spending money that belongs to other individuals.

This conventional view of the role of business in society has been challenged on a number of grounds and to many observers of the business scene now seems outdated, narrow and arguably naïve. As Chapter 1 has shown, businesses exist within and draw their resources from the broader society and therefore could be said to have a moral obligation to take account of their social and environmental performance. Added to this, shareholders are only one of the groups with which the firm interacts and consequently there are other stakeholder interests to which a business has responsibilities and obligations when carrying out its activities (see, for example, Chapter 10). Such **stakeholders** are both internal (e.g. employees) and external (e.g. customers) to the organisation and under the stakeholder view of the firm (see, for example, Freeman, 1984) businesses have a social responsibility to take into account the interests of all parties affected by their actions and decisions, not just the owners of the business. In contrast to the neo-classical view of the firm, the stakeholder approach stresses the necessity for managers to try to operate the business to the benefit of all stakeholder groups and to seek to gain an effective balance between the different interested parties. Using some of the firm's profits to achieve such an outcome is not necessarily detrimental to the firm's owners and indeed may ultimately help to enhance shareholder value, particularly over the longer term.

More recent discussions of why businesses should take account of their social and environmental responsibilities have tended to focus on the strategic benefits of CSR, how acting 'responsibly' can generate advantages for the business on both the demand and the supply sides (see, for example, McWilliams *et al.*, 2006). Writers such as Porter and Kramer (2002) have argued that a firm can gain a **competitive advantage** by investing in CSR, particularly if its actions in this area become an intrinsic part of its business and corporate differentiation strategies. One important element in this debate has been the application of a **resource-based view (RBV)** of the firm in which social and environmental responsibility are portrayed as an organisational resource/capability that can lead to sustained competitive advantage.[3] The claim is that engaging in CSR has the potential to enhance a firm's reputation with key stakeholder groups and this could give it an advantage over its rivals that is both valuable and potentially difficult to imitate. One arena where this might be particularly important is with regard to an organisation's environmental performance, given the growing international concerns over the impact of business activity on the natural environment. This is the subject we now investigate in more detail.

The 'environment' as a business issue: the emergence of corporate environmentalism

In Chapter 1 we portrayed goods and services as the outputs of business activity, the end result of transforming inputs into products to meet the needs and demands of individuals, organisations and governments. While such economic activity undoubtedly gives rise to significant individual and societal benefits, these desirable aspects of business come at a price; production generates 'bads' as well as 'goods', including damage to the natural environment and resource depletion. Hawken (1996) has suggested that the business community contributes to environmental degradation in three main ways – by what it takes, by what it makes and by what it wastes. This bad face of business is found at all stages of the transformation process (see, for example, Worthington, 2013) and involves environmental problems across all spatial levels from the local (e.g. litter) to the global (e.g. climate change).

Pressure on firms to accept responsibility for the negative impacts they have on the natural environment can be seen as part of the broader debate on corporate social responsibility. Worthington (2013) has argued that growing levels of corporate environmental awareness began to emerge in the closing decades of the twentieth century and can be linked to several key factors, including the publication of a number of influential books (e.g. Rachel Carson's *Silent Spring* in 1962), a series of high-profile ecological disasters (e.g. the chemical release at the Union Carbide plant in Bhopal in the 1980s), scientific discoveries (e.g. ozone depletion) and global media coverage of major environmental concerns (e.g. climate change). In helping to place the environment on both the public and political agendas, developments such as these helped to spawn a growing environmental movement and to encourage action at governmental and intergovernmental levels, both of which have had important implications for the business community and for the debate over how to reconcile the widespread demand for economic growth with the need for greater environmental protection.

As far as the latter question was concerned, what emerged from a lengthy and complex process of debate and discussion at an international level was the notion of **sustainable development**, the idea that when making choices designed to increase well-being today, countries should ensure that future generations are left no worse off than their current counterparts. In environmental terms, this implied, *inter alia,* the need to take steps to limit environmental damage and degradation, conserve the world's natural capital, preserve essential ecosystem functions and aim for qualitative rather than simply quantitative improvements over time. From a business point of view, this philosophical stance appeared to run counter to the traditional notion of 'business as usual', with its emphasis on year-on-year growth and unfettered access to the world's natural resources and environmental services.

The late twentieth century debate over sustainable development clearly poses an important question for the business community: how far should a firm be prepared to incorporate concern for the environment into its strategic decisions and day-to-day operations? Should environmental protection be seen as an inevitable additional cost to the business, or could it be leveraged for competitive advantage? As with CSR generally, opinions have tended to vary on this question, the latter view eventually gaining traction with business leaders of major international companies as the new millennium approached.

While it is impossible to pinpoint an exact time or event which helped to place the environment on corporate agendas, the available evidence indicates that its emergence as an important business issue has been gradual and largely incremental and has been shaped by a combination of pressures emanating from the regulatory, market and social domains of business. What these pressures have been and how and why firms have responded in different ways are the focus of the subsequent sections of this chapter.

Drivers of 'green' business

Academic researchers have long been interested in the factors that predispose businesses to engage in different forms of socially responsible behaviour (see, for example, Burke and Logsdon, 1996; McWilliams *et al.*, 2006). With regard to a firm's 'green' responses, these have been linked to four major influences: governmental action, other stakeholder pressures, economic opportunities and ethical considerations. We discuss each of these in turn.

Government action

As we saw in Chapters 4 and 5, government is a key actor and stakeholder in a firm's external environment. Its actions and decisions can play a formative role in promoting more sustainable forms of development and in encouraging businesses to improve on their environmental performance; to address, in effect, imperfections in the market system, including the existence of **negative externalities** such as pollution (for a discussion see Worthington, 2013).

Where environmental protection is concerned, three main approaches have been used: legislation and regulation, market-based instruments and voluntary agreements.

With regard to legal instruments, this basically involves the establishment of a system of direct control over organisations and their activities via the adoption of laws and other forms of regulatory measure, including the use of directives, permits, licences, and the creation of regulatory, inspection and enforcement regimes, backed by the application of sanctions in the event of non-compliance. Examples of environmental laws and regulations can be found in most, if not all, countries, and action may also be taken at an intergovernmental level, as in the case of the European Union.

While governments can and do use legislation/regulation to shape the environmental behaviour of firms, in practice instruments of this kind can vary substantially in style, content and degree of application; they are also aimed at a range of environmental problems from pollution control to resource management. Regulatory intervention can be used *inter alia* to outlaw or ban certain activities, apply particular standards, specify the characteristics required of certain products, determine the inputs to be used, mandate the techniques and/or technology a firm must apply, and identify its obligations regarding issues such as recycling and information disclosure. In short, they are generally imposed by a governing authority to produce outcomes that might otherwise not occur if decisions are left entirely to market forces. The evidence suggests that in this respect they have probably been the key driver of firm-level environmental behaviour (see, for example, Bansal and Roth, 2000; Etzion, 2007).

It is worth remembering that while governments are ultimately responsible for environmental laws and regulations, these are frequently shaped by different stakeholder interests, including the business community and its representative organisations. It is not uncommon for firms to lobby against proposed environmental legislation on the grounds that it will increase business costs and/or reduce international competitiveness, particularly if there are disparities in regulatory requirements between countries. Complaints that there is frequently an **unlevel playing field** or that **gold plating** of standards can occur are often used in this sphere; some businesses may even threaten to move their operations to locations (i.e. other countries) where environmental demands are less stringent, though it is unlikely that this consideration alone will be the determinant of such a strategic decision.

Turning to market-based or economic instruments, these involve the use of financial (or other) incentives or disincentives aimed at shaping business behaviour, **environmental taxes/subsidies** and **tradeable pollution permits** being two major examples. In simple terms, an environmental tax or charge seeks to take account of the negative environmental impact of business activity (e.g. pollution) by imposing a cost on firms that are responsible for the problem. Action taken by a business to reduce its environmental impact is rewarded by the reduction or removal of the financial penalty. Alternatively the organisation may be granted a financial gain in the form of an environmental subsidy or other type of fiscal reward (e.g. a reduction in corporate tax).

At the heart of this approach lies the use of the price mechanism to shape the behaviour of economic actors; to correct the market for negative externalities by endorsing the **polluter pays principle**. Whereas regulation basically involves government in deciding on the best course of action to address environmental problems, so-called green taxes and subsidies essentially leave businesses free to respond to certain stimuli in ways they themselves decide are most beneficial to the organisation, such as through investment in pollution reduction measures/technology or in changes in inputs or production or distribution methods. In this regard, taxes and subsidies can be said to work with the grain of the market and to act as a spur to innovation and investment. On the downside, they often tend to be viewed by firms as a revenue-raising exercise, can be difficult to design and implement and can, in some cases, have an adverse effect on firm, industry and national competitiveness.

Whereas environmental taxes and subsidies work by creating a price where none previously existed or by modifying an existing price, **tradeable** or **marketable pollution** permits are an example of market creation. Government establishes, in effect, a system of tradeable pollution rights, issues quotas, allowances or permits up to an agreed level and then allows the holders of those rights to trade them like any other commodity. The trading of rights (e.g. relating to greenhouse gas emissions) usually takes place under prescribed rules and may be external (e.g. between different enterprises or countries) or internal (e.g. between different plants within the same firm), within a free or controlled permit market. Gunningham and Grabosky (1998) have described this approach as a hybrid between direct regulations and free market environmentalism in that governments decide on the overall quantity of pollution permissible, while market forces determine the eventual distribution of rights between participating firms or countries.

As with green taxes/subsidies, a tradeable permit system – exemplified by the **European Emissions Trading Scheme (ETS)** – has both benefits and drawbacks. On the positive side, it offers firms a degree of flexibility in their responses and acts as an inducement to reducing their emissions, not least since any unused permits can be sold to businesses which have exceeded their quota. On the negative side, the system can be extremely bureaucratic and can be difficult to implement; there are also questions over its effectiveness and its impact on poorer nations.

Alongside regulation and market-based instruments, governments also use **voluntary approaches (VAs)** in an attempt to improve the environmental performance of firms beyond existing legal requirements. The three main types of instrument employed are:

- **public voluntary programmes** – which involve commitments devised by an environment agency and in which individual firms are invited to participate, the EU's **Eco-Management and Audit Scheme (EMAS)** being a prime example;
- **negotiated agreements** – which are initiatives that result from a process of bargaining between a public authority (e.g. national government) and an industry or industry sector, exemplified by the covenants that form part of the Netherlands National Environment Policy Plan;
- **unilateral commitments** – which are environmental programmes set up by firms independently of any public authority, but which may be aimed at forestalling government regulation, hence their inclusion here. An example of this form of self-regulation is the Chemical Manufacturers' Association Responsible Care Programme.

Since this approach to environmental protection provides firms with a substantial degree of flexibility regarding how far and in what ways they respond, it tends to be popular with the business community; it also has the potential to enhance stakeholder relationships (e.g. by improving the firm's image with customers) and possibly increase participants' competitiveness.

Other stakeholder pressures

In addition to the legislative, regulatory and fiscal demands imposed by governments, firms face pressures to reduce their environmental impact from other constituencies. Customers, competitors, suppliers, creditors, investors, shareholders, employees, civil society organisations and the media can all be instrumental in inducing a green response in businesses. Consumers, for instance, may actively seek out goods with a higher level of environmental performance or may boycott products deemed to have an adverse effect on the natural environment. Other examples include pressure exerted through the supply chain and/or by major investors, shareholder activism, adverse media publicity, lobbying by environmental NGOs and withdrawal by a public authority of a licence to operate. The extent to which stakeholder pressures are likely to prove effective in shaping firm-level behaviour is normally related to their impact on an organisation's bottom line, either directly or indirectly.

Economic opportunities

Organisations may also seek to improve on their environmental performance as a means of gaining an economic and commercial benefit, with opportunities potentially available on both sides of business. Gains could be generated by:

- reducing waste and generally increasing the efficiency of factor inputs, as highlighted by the concepts of **eco-efficiency** and acronyms such as Pollution Prevention Pays (PPP) and Waste Reduction Always Pays (WRAP);
- creating revenue-raising opportunities by developing green products and processes which may allow the firm to create a **market niche** by differentiating its offering to consumers who may be willing to pay a premium price;
- enhancing the organisation's resources and capabilities, including its corporate reputation with external stakeholders and its capacity to innovate;
- managing current and future environmental (e.g. accidents) and regulatory (e.g. stricter laws) risks with their associated costs.

As with CSR generally, the claim that environmental responsibility can pay remains hotly contested (see, for example, Worthington, 2013, Chapter 6).

Ethical considerations

A firm's green behaviour can also be driven by influences emanating from within the business itself, most notably the belief by organisational decision-makers that 'it is the right thing to do'. Initiatives may come from an organisation's owners and/or senior management team or from **environmental champions**, or the workforce generally. In some cases, the organisation's culture and values may be largely or wholly attuned to an ecologically responsible approach (e.g. environmental NGOs such as Greenpeace).

Why and how firms become more environmentally responsible

Whereas a discussion of the 'drivers' of corporate greening focuses on the factors that push a firm towards pro-environmental responses, examining its motivations for going in this direction raises a related, though slightly different, question: What is the underlying rationale for its behaviour?

In broad terms, the academic literature suggests three main reasons: it provides benefits or creates opportunities for the organisation; it reduces threats or risks to the enterprise; it accords with the firm's ethical stance. In practice, of course, an organisation's actions could reflect any or all of these motivations, each of which can be expressed in several ways.

Benefit-focused or opportunity-focused explanations link a firm's responses to the various strategic advantages thought to derive from a green response. These include meeting stakeholder or societal expectations, achieving market-related benefits through product differentiation, exploiting a green market niche, making cost savings or eco-efficiencies, and enhancing the organisation's image and/or corporate reputation. To what extent these claimed advantages represent *ex ante* explanations for a firm's actions or are *ex post* rationales aimed at persuading key stakeholders that there is a sound business case for investing in proactive green behaviour is not always clear.

Risk-focused or threat-focused arguments centre around the idea that corporate environmentalism is a way of protecting the organisation from adverse stakeholder reactions and/or the consequences of a negative or limited response to external pressures for change. Reduced current and future liabilities and risk – including fines, adverse publicity, loss of business, the danger of legislative sanctions and retrospective liabilities – may all be reasons why a firm might engage in pro-environmental behaviour. While this perspective suggests a predominantly defensive rationale, it is not always easy to separate risk-based explanations from the more proactive, opportunity-related motivations, given that investments in green responses may simultaneously reduce risks and create organisational benefits.

Whereas the two above explanations suggest that organisations are motivated primarily by economic and commercial considerations, some firms may believe that they have a moral obligation to protect the natural environment and this could explain their behaviour. As discussed previously, ethical explanations reflect the view that a business has obligations to the wider society not just to narrow, stakeholder interests such as shareholders or other investors. That said, as with other forms of corporate social responsibility, a firm's ethical stance could help it to gain a strategic advantage over its rivals, particularly if its actions are seen as an important aspect of doing business by powerful and influential stakeholder groups (see, for example, Porter and Kramer, 2002).

Turning to the question of what steps a firm may take to demonstrate its green credentials, these can range from relatively simple initiatives such as recycling or energy-saving measures to more complex practices and processes, including greening the supply chain, investing in new technology and developing an **environmental management system (EMS)**, the latter being a multi-stage process aimed at identifying, measuring and controlling a firm's environmental impact. Some businesses may also seek external recognition for their actions and decisions, whether by engaging in a strategic alliance with an environmental NGO (e.g. McDonald's and the Environmental Defense Fund), seeking certification for their products by a recognised and reputable body (e.g. the Forest Stewardship Council), or qualifying for the display of an **eco-label**, which certifies that a given product is environmentally safe or friendly (e.g. Germany's Blue Angel, Japan's Eco-Mark, the EU's European Eco-Label).

mini case: Going round in circles: Desso Carpets

Linear models of business activity – such as the systems approach presented in Chapter 1 – are essentially based on notions of 'take, make and dispose'. Inputs are acquired, a production process occurs, the product is consumed and then disposed of at the end of its life. Despite some opportunities for recycling, reclamation and re-use of materials and components, products produced in this way generate considerable levels of waste and pollution and consume large quantities of energy and raw materials, including non-renewables.

An alternative philosophy – currently exciting a degree of interest among forward-looking businesses (see below) – is the notion of the **circular economy**, a concept that focuses on waste eradication, rebuilding natural and social capital and adopting a renewable approach. Advocates of what is sometimes called the **cradle-to-cradle™ (C2C)** stance conceive of manufacturers continuing to own their own products, the use of which they sell to customers. These products are designed in a way that eliminates waste and involves manufacturing and distribution systems based around renewable sources of energy.

The Dutch company Desso is one of Europe's largest producers of commercial-grade carpet and carpet tiles used in a wide range of domestic and commercial situations. In 2007 the firm announced its intention of designing by 2020 a fully closed-loop system for all its products based on C2C principles. The company aims to produce products that are entirely biodegradable or are capable of being recycled to produce new goods. This will involve designing systems and processes that will allow the firm to purchase appropriate materials, use waste to provide a source of energy, reduce energy consumption, provide facilities for recycling, product take-back and composting, and completely modify the way it does business (e.g. renting rather than selling products). To achieve its ambitious aims, the firm is working in partnership with the Environmental Protection Encouragement Agency (EPEA), which has its headquarters in Hamburg.

web link See, for example, www.desso.com/c2c-corporate-responsibility

On the whole, it tends to be the case that smaller firms are more limited in their responses than their larger counterparts, given that they tend to lack the knowledge, resources and capabilities needed to invest in more advanced forms of environmental behaviour. Schemes such as General Electric's (GE) Ecomagination initiative and Marks and Spencer's Plan A (see the case study) are clearly beyond the reach of smaller businesses, many of which face substantial barriers to improved environmental performance and remain to be convinced that they have a negative impact on the natural environment or that they can benefit from investment in environmental protection measures.

Another perspective: the 'outside-in' view

In examining the interaction between firms and the natural environment, much of the focus has been on the pressures exerted on business to address the negative impacts that result from their activities, what might be called an **inside-out** view from the firm to the environment. It is important to recognise, however, that the natural environment also provides critical economic functions for the business community: it is a provider of inputs (e.g. raw materials), an assimilator of waste products (e.g. pollution) and a source of amenity value for individuals and organisations (e.g. landscape). When viewed in this way (i.e. the **outside-in** perspective), it is clear that economic activity and organisational competitiveness, both now and in the future, are intrinsically linked with the well-being of the natural environment (see, for example, Porter and Reinhardt, 2007). In 2006, for example, the Stern Report estimated that failure to tackle climate change could result in an up to 20 per cent decline in the size of the global economy and a plethora of recent authoritative reports by both national and international bodies paint a picture of how environmental problems – caused in part by business activity – can impact adversely on the business community.

To repeat the assertion made in Chapter 1, the business/environment relationship flows in both directions and is complex, interactive and dynamic, varying both between places and over time. In short, organisations not only affect the natural environment, they are affected by it and by what services it can provide. Protecting the environment may equally be a matter of self-interest, rather than simply a question of corporate social responsibility or inter-generational equity and social justice.

Synopsis Summary of key points

- Business ethics is concerned with issues of 'right' and 'wrong' behaviour in a business context.

- Corporate social responsibility (CSR) is the idea that organisations should be held accountable for the effects of their actions on people, their communities and the environment.

- CSR has become an important consideration for modern businesses, alongside traditional concerns with profitability and growth.

- Being socially responsible as a business does not preclude being profitable.

- Increasingly, business organisations have to take account of the views of their stakeholders on questions of social and environmental responsibility.

- One area where this has become particularly significant is with regard to the impact of business operations and decisions on the natural environment.

- The key 'drivers' of corporate environmental responsiveness are government intervention, other stakeholder pressures, economic opportunities and ethical considerations.

- Firms that implement environmental policies tend to be motivated by questions of organisational benefit or risk avoidance.

- Different businesses respond in different ways, ranging from reactive stances through to more proactive environmental approaches, which go beyond compliance with regulatory demands.

- Firms not only affect the natural environment, they are affected by it in a variety of ways.

case study: Doing well by doing good

As consumers have become increasingly aware of environmental issues, many organisations have felt compelled to demonstrate their commitment to a greener approach by announcing a range of high-profile environmental initiatives and programmes. This case study looks at two examples: GE's Ecomagination initiative and Marks and Spencer's Plan A.

GE's Ecomagination initiative

Launched in 2005, General Electric's Ecomagination initiative is an environmentally focused business strategy aimed at producing profitable growth by providing solutions to environmental problems such as the demand for cleaner sources of energy, reduced carbon emissions and access to cleaner water. Backed by a multi-million-dollar advertising campaign, the initiative emphasised that being 'good' and being commercially successful were complementary, what has been called a win-win situation, where both the environment and the firm benefit.

To qualify for inclusion in the firm's Ecomagination portfolio, a product or service must be able to demonstrate significant and measurable improvement in operational and environmental performance or in value proposition, additional value being provided for both investors and customers. Since the initiative began, products meeting these criteria have ranged from electric vehicles and aircraft engines to energy-efficient light bulbs and water-purification technologies.

During the first five years of the initiative it is estimated that Ecomagination products and services generated $85 billion for the business; there also appears to have been a number of less tangible benefits, such as creating customer trust in GE's brands and helping the business to attract and retain high-quality employees (see, for example, Esty and Winston, 2006; Laszlo and Zhexembayeva, 2011). The company has also been able to significantly reduce its environmental footprint during this period and it aims to achieve further reductions in environmental impact in the future and to increase its investment in clean technology research and development.

Marks and Spencer's 'Plan A'

M&S's Plan A was announced in early 2007 by the then chief executive Stuart Rose, who claimed that the initiative was so named because there was no Plan B. Under the new scheme the company committed itself to spending several hundred million pounds to reduce its environmental impact and to put social and environmental commitment at the heart of its commercial activities. Key aspects of the plan included reducing waste, saving energy, promoting animal welfare and trading fairly, goals which required it to consider a wide range of aspects of the business, including its logistics and retail operations, its relationship with suppliers and its sourcing policies. As the plan has been rolled out and incorporated into the fabric of the Marks and Spencer brand, additional aspects have been added or developed more fully, community engagement being one example.

According to a report in *The Guardian* on 8 July 2013, M&S had saved around £135 million through Plan A in the previous year alone and has evidently cut carbon emissions by 23 per cent since 2006, reduced waste by 28 per cent and made substantial savings in its use of glass. On the downside, the use of disposable plastic bags has been rising year-on-year and the company has had difficulties in reducing food packaging and in meeting its targets for converting to the use of Fairtrade cotton and for supplying more organic food and free-range products. There are also doubts as to whether it will reach its highly ambitious target of 20 million items of recycled clothing by 2015 through its Shwopping initiative.

For further information on these two companies and their social and environmental initiatives go to www.ge.com and www.marksandspencer.com and follow the links.

Case study questions

1 What do you think have been the key drivers of the two initiatives mentioned in this case study?

2 Will investors in these organisations benefit from or be disadvantaged by the two schemes?

Review and discussion questions

1 To what extent are governments responsible for establishing the parameters by which organisations conduct business? Should a business be free to decide its own level of corporate responsibility?

2 How can governments influence the environmental behaviour of firms?

3 Writers have argued that the only objective of business is to make profit, within the boundaries established by government. Do you agree?

Assignments

1 As a group, select an environmental issue (e.g. business or natural feature) and write a report to the leader of a local pressure group which details an environmental impact assessment of the issue. The report should make clear reference to:

   (a) a cost-benefit analysis, carried out by the group, of the salient factors;
   (b) any legislation/regulation that concerns the case; and
   (c) the provision of a stakeholder map that illustrates who the stakeholders are, their importance to the case and their ability to affect future decisions.

2 As a newly appointed trainee manager you have been asked to look afresh at the business, with particular reference to the implementation of an environmental management system. Your immediate superior has asked you to write a report. Accordingly, you are required to:

   (a) consult the available literature and identify what you consider to be the necessary processes and procedures that would comprise an environmental management system;
   (b) indicate the areas within the organisation that need to be addressed; and
   (c) explain how such a policy should be implemented within the organisation.

Notes and references

1 For a discussion see, for example, Vogel (2005).
2 Friedman, M., 'The social responsibility of business is to increase its profits', *New York Times Magazine,* 13 September 1970, pp. 7–13.
3 See, for example, Hart, S., 'A natural resource-based view of the firm', *Academy of Management Review,* 20, 1995, pp. 986–1014.

Further reading

Bansal, P. and Roth, K., 'Why companies go green: a model of ecological responsiveness', *Academy of Management Journal,* 43 (4), 2000, pp. 717–736.

Burke, L. and Logsdon, J. M., 'How corporate social responsibility pays off', *Long Range Planning,* 29 (4), 1996, pp. 495–502.

Cairncross, F., *Green Inc: A Guide to Business and the Environment,* Earthscan Publications, 1995.

Crane, A. and Matten, D., *Business Ethics,* Oxford University Press, 2004. A third edition was published in 2010.

Esty, D. C. and Winston, A. S., *Green to Gold: How Smart Companies Use Environmental Strategy to Innovate, Create Value and Build Competitive Advantage,* Yale University Press, 2006.

Etzion, D., 'Research on organizations and the natural environment, 1992–Present: a review', *Journal of Management,* 33 (4), 2007, pp. 637–664.

Frederick, W. C., Post, J. E. and Davis, K., *Business and Society: Corporate Strategy, Public Policy, Ethics,* 8th edition, McGraw-Hill, 1996.

Freeman, R. E., *Strategic Management: A Stakeholder Perspective,* Prentice Hall, 1984.

Gunningham, N. and Grabosky, P., *Smart Regulation: Designing Environmental Policy,* Clarendon Press, 1998.

Hawken, P., 'A teasing irony', in Welford, R. and Starkey, R. (eds), *Business and the Environment,* Earthscan, 1996, pp. 5–16.

Kolk, A., *Economics of Environmental Management,* Financial Times/Prentice Hall, 2000.

Laszlo, C. and Zhexembayeva, N. *Embedded Sustainability: The Next big Competitive Advantage*, 2011, Greenleaf Publishing.

McWilliams, A., Siegel, D. S. and Wright, P. M., 'Corporate social responsibility: strategic implications', *Journal of Management Studies,* 43 (1), 2006, pp. 1–18.

Pearce, D. and Barbier, E., *Blueprint for a Sustainable Economy,* Earthscan Publications, 2000.

Porter, M. E. and Kramer, M. R., 'The competitive advantage of corporate philanthropy', *Harvard Business Review,* 80 (12), 2002, pp. 56–69.

Porter, M. E. and Reinhardt, F. L., 'A strategic approach to climate change', *Harvard Business Review,* 85 (10), 2007, pp. 22–26.

Vogel, D., *The Market for Virtue: The Potential and Limits of Corporate Social Responsibility,* Brookings Institution, 2005.

Welford, R. and Gouldson, A., *Environmental Management and Business Strategy,* Pitman Publishing, 1993.

Worthington, I., *Greening Business: Research, Theory & Practice,* Oxford University Press, 2013.

Worthington, I., Britton, C. and Rees, A., *Economics for Business: Blending Theory and Practice,* 2nd edition, Financial Times/Prentice Hall, 2005, Chapter 14.

---

web link

Web links and further questions are available on the website at:
www.pearsoned.co.uk/worthington

International business in action

Migration

In an increasingly globalised world, companies often look to international migration of labour to fill jobs if they can no longer rely on their own domestic labour markets to do this. The international migration of labour is important – although it has no overall effect on the world population, it has significant effects for individual countries. There is a difference between stocks and flows of migration.

Flows vary from year to year for many economic and political reasons and some of these are considered later in the case study. Stocks represent the historical accumulation of migration built up over the long term. In 2013 the migrant population stock was 232 million, which represented 3.2 per cent of the world population (as opposed to 2.1 per cent in 1960).[1] In 2013 the USA accounted for 20 per cent of the total; the Russian Federation was second with 5 per cent. Between 1990 and 2013 the USA added 23 million international migrants (flows) to its population; the second highest gain (7 million) was the United Arab Emirates.

The World Bank identifies four pathways for international migration, as the figure shows. The figures in brackets indicate stocks of international migrants in 2013.

Pathways for international migration

- North to south – the stock has remained fairly constant since 1990 and the most common pathways are USA to Mexico, Germany to Turkey and Portugal to Brazil.

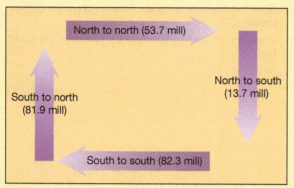

Source: Adapted from Total Population Facts, No 2013–3, September 2013, www.unpopulation.org

- North to north – has risen slightly since 1990 and the most common routes are Germany to the USA, UK to Australia and UK to Canada.
- South to north – the stock has risen consistently from 39 million in 1990 to 85 million in 2013,[2] with the most common routes being Mexico to the USA, Turkey to Germany and China to the USA.
- South to south – has remained fairly constant up to 2000, but has risen consistently since. The most common routes are Ukraine to the Russian Federation and vice versa, Bangladesh to Bhutan and Afghanistan to Pakistan.

There are push factors and pull factors, which give rise to labour migration: push factors include poverty in the home country, natural disasters and political fear; pull factors include the possibility of employment, better standards of living and better education. A recent push factor is political unrest in the Middle East – the migrant stock in the Arab countries increased by 1.8 million between 2005 and 2010, mainly due to displaced people from Iran, Iraq and later the Arab Spring. A pull factor is the increased opportunity and higher wages in western Europe compared with eastern Europe. The increase in migration from Portugal to Angola in 2013–14 can be seen as a push factor (high unemployment in Portugal) or a pull factor (high growth in Angola).

Migration can be permanent or temporary. In 2010 there were 4.1 million permanent migrants into the OECD countries and 1.9 million temporary migrants.[3] Permanent migration is dominated by family migration, where families join previous labour migrants. The rate of migration has slowed since 2007 because of the slowdown in the OECD countries.

The debate over labour migration is often heated and not based on fact, but the costs and benefits of migration need to be considered in both the sending countries and the receiving countries. It is often argued that immigrants take jobs away from people in the host country, but this is not sustained by research. In Western Europe, immigrants are often not in direct competition with the home population and take jobs at both ends of the spectrum: at the low-skill, high-risk and low-paid end, where it is difficult to fill vacancies from the home labour force, and at the high-skill, high-paid end, where home-grown skills may not be available. Research in the USA, for example, has shown that the average income of immigrants is around 20 per cent lower than that of the home workforce. Another argument often used, but again not borne out by research, is that immigration represents a drain on welfare, health and education spending in the host country. A recent report[4] found that immigrants who entered the UK since 2000 from the European Economic Area contributed 34 per cent more in taxes than they received in benefits; for immigrants from outside the EEA, the net contribution goes down to 2 per cent but it is still positive.

The migration of skilled labour is an obvious benefit to the host country, but for the sending country it represents a 'brain drain' – education, skills and knowledge are lost. This is not all negative, however, as migrants often return home, bringing with them newly acquired skills and knowledge – a 'brain gain'. The OECD estimates that between 20 per cent and 50 per cent of migrants return to their home countries within five years. There has been a big increase in the number of foreign students, which rose by 62 per cent from 2002 to 2009 globally, with the countries benefiting the most being the USA, the UK, Australia and Canada. This brings in short-term benefits in the form of extra income for fees, but this type of migration is often temporary as the students return home at the end of their studies.

One benefit of migration to the country of origin is what are called remittances – migrants sending money home to their families. These flows are expected to be $550 billion in 2013 globally and $700 billion by 2016.[5] The majority of this goes to the developing countries ($414 billion in 2013). These are important flows for developing countries as they are significantly bigger than official development aid, bigger than capital flows and bigger than FDI flows in some countries, and the weakening of the emerging nations will only serve to increase their importance. The biggest recipient in 2013 was India and the second biggest was Mexico. Diaspora associations (groups of émigrés from one country which link together in the host country) can also contribute to development and help relations between the host country and the country of origin. They are also instrumental in circular migration where émigrés return home.

International migration is important to business – it helps fill jobs that are hard to fill or require specialised skills. In 2013 it was estimated that over 200,000 more engineers were required in the UK to fill shortages over the next two years.[6] The UK Border Agency publishes a list of shortage occupations, and in 2014 half of the jobs were for engineers and more than one-fifth were other technical and scientific occupations.

At the other end of the job market, international migrants often fill the very low-skilled jobs that are difficult to fill from the UK population – fruit picking, for example. Farmers are worried that the opening up of the European jobs market to Romanians and Bulgarians at the beginning of 2014 will make it more difficult to fill these temporary jobs as they will be looking for more permanent employment. In 2007 and 2008, as there was a shortage of migrant labour to pick fruit, large amounts of crops remained unharvested. The price of fruit went up and supermarkets sourced more from outside the UK.

It is clear from the above discussion that the topic of migration is a complex one, and that there are interrelationships within countries and between countries. International migration is necessary for the smooth working of markets.

Notes

1. UN, Press release September 2012.
2. Population facts 2013–3, UN.
3. International Migration Outlook, 2012, OECD.
4. Recent Immigration to the UK, CReAM, University College London, 2013.
5. Migration and development brief 21, Oct 2013, the World Bank.
6. Sir James Dyson.

CHAPTER 4
MANAGING INTERNATIONALLY

Aim

To outline the factors shaping the work of managing internationally.

Objectives

By the end of your work on this chapter you should be able to outline the concepts below in your own terms and:

1. Contrast the ways in which organisations conduct international business
2. Explain, with examples, how PESTEL factors affect the decisions of those managing internationally
3. Summarise at least one aspect of EU policy (or of an international trade agreement) which is of interest to you for your career
4. Explain and illustrate the evidence on national cultures, and evaluate the significance of Hofstede's research for managers working internationally
5. Compare and contrast the features of national management systems
6. Summarise the forces stimulating the growth of international business
7. Show how ideas from the chapter add to your understanding of the integrating themes

Key terms

This chapter introduces the following ideas:

international management	pervasiveness (of corruption)
offshoring	arbitrariness (of corruption)
foreign direct investment	high-context culture
licensing	low-context culture
franchising	power distance
joint venture	uncertainty avoidance
multinational company	individualism
transnational company	collectivism
global company	masculinity
theory of absolute advantage	femininity
political risk	globalisation
ideology	

Each is a term defined within the text, as well as in the glossary at the end of the book.

Case study: Starbucks www.starbucks.com

Starbucks sells coffee, pastries, confectionery and coffee-related accessories through over 18,000 retail stores – about 13,000 in the United States and 5000 in more than 50 countries. In the financial year to the end of September 2012 its revenue was $13.3 billion (14 per cent more than in 2011), and profits were almost $2.0 billion. While sales in Europe had been weak, it had done especially well in Asia. Sales in its (main) US market had grown so strongly that it was planning to open 1500 new outlets there by 2017 – a strong recovery from the crisis in 2007 (see later instalments).

Three entrepreneurs created the company in 1971 to sell coffee in Seattle, and by 1981 they had five stores. The owners decided to sell the business in 1987 and Howard Schultz (a former employee) bought the company which he then expanded rapidly, so that by 1991 there were 114 Starbucks stores. The company introduced new products to attract customers – such as low-fat iced coffee for the diet conscious. It grew by about 20 per cent a year during the 1990s, but believed the US market had little more scope for growth.

To maintain rapid growth, the company began to expand overseas through Starbucks Coffee International, a wholly owned subsidiary. The company used joint ventures, licensing or wholly owned subsidiaries to enter new markets and by the end of 2009 it had 4000 stores (30 per cent of the total) outside the US. It entered the Asia Pacific rim first, as the eagerness of young people there to imitate western lifestyles made them attractive markets.

Initially it opened a few stores in trendy parts of the country, with the company's managers from Seattle handling the operation. Local *baristas* (brew masters) were trained in Seattle for 13 weeks, to ensure consistent standards across the world. Similar products were stocked, and all stores were 'No Smoking'.

The company's managers adapted the business to local tastes – such as offering curry puffs and meat buns in Asia, where people prefer to eat something while having coffee. In the Middle East the coffee shops had segregated sections for ladies. In 1998 the company opened in Europe, with stores in the UK, Switzerland, Germany and Greece. The company believed that it was successful not because it was selling coffee, but because it was selling an experience. In many markets it faces local competition and is subject to the same economic conditions as other businesses of its type.

Purestock/Alamy

It has attracted criticism in some overseas markets – in the UK for using a legal device to reduce the tax it pays. It has also faced criticism over the sources of its coffee. Advocates of fair trade argued that big coffee buyers like Starbucks should do more to ensure that they buy coffee at fair prices from growers who do not exploit workers – to which it has responded.

Sources: Schultz (2011); *Financial Times*, 6 December 2012; company website.

Case questions 4.1

- What encouraged managers at Starbucks to expand overseas, and what influenced their choice of countries in which to operate?
- What are the main risks that Starbucks faces in expanding rapidly in overseas markets?
- What does the case so far suggest about the management issues it will face in operating internationally?

> ### 4.1 Introduction

Managers at Starbucks decided to expand their business overseas, and in doing so are likely to face common problems in moving to a global operation. Having expanded rapidly in their home market, they believe that the best way to grow is to build the business overseas. 'Going international' will bring new challenges, including how to organise the overseas activities, how far, if at all, to adapt the Starbucks experience to local tastes, and how to ensure the company still delivers value to present customers as well as seeking new ones.

Other retailers like Tesco and Ikea face similar challenges of balancing the consistency of a global brand with what local customers expect. Manufacturers like Ford and Coca-Cola are investing heavily in China, Brazil and India where demand is growing rapidly. This will mean managing relationships with local companies as partners or competitors, and working in the local political and legal environment. They have to decide which countries to invest in, taking into account rules which may require them to work with a local partner – Ford has a joint venture with the Chong Qing Group in China to manufacture a compact family car. And as they do so, they know that many overseas ventures fail, reducing value rather than adding to it.

Other manufacturers and service providers have transferred some work to low-wage countries to remain competitive, but still face the challenges of managing such operations in unfamiliar countries. Managers investing overseas consider not only the economic aspects, but also whether the country's legal system will protect their investment and whether it is politically stable. They may also face local sensitivities: when Tata Motors bought Jaguar and Land Rover they pledged to retain their UK identities, and to invest in modern equipment.

There has been international trade since the earliest times. The merchants who created the East India Company in London in 1599 to trade with the spice islands in South-east Asia were formalising established practice, and by the nineteenth century there were many worldwide trading companies. International operations are inherent in transport and mineral businesses. Federal Express and Maersk move products around the world for their customers; BP and Rio Tinto Zinc necessarily secure resources in some parts of the world and sell them in others.

What is new is the high proportion of production that crosses national boundaries, much of it through businesses operating on a regional or global scale. One-third of all trade takes place within transnational companies, quite apart from external sales of foreign subsidiaries. Rapid economic development in China, India and other Asian countries is transforming them into major players in world trade, and providing opportunities for the shipping business – see Management in practice.

Management in practice — Maersk and global trade   www.maersk.com

Maersk is the world's largest container shipping line, and its growth has reflected that of world trade. Doug Bannister, Managing Director of Maersk Line (UK and Ireland) explained:

> We're involved in the transportation sector, about 90 per cent of world trade is done by sea-borne transportation, it is an incredible industry to be associated with: our primary mission is to create opportunities in global commerce.
>
> The scale of containerised shipping is enormous. Container shipping has been around for 40 years, and it's had incredible growth, 8 to 10 per cent a year. The types of stuff we bring in are anything from

lamps to furniture to bananas, about 90 per cent of anything that you'd see in any room was transported in by one of our ships.

Several external factors have really played into Maersk Line's growth, globalisation probably being the primary one, and the explosion of world trade has been incredible. This is down to efficient transport solutions, and to companies moving production to low cost countries.

Source: Interview with Doug Bannister.

From a career point of view, **international management** (managing business operations in more than one country) can mean:

- working as an *expatriate manager* in another country;
- joining or managing an *international team* with members from several countries;
- managing in a *global organisation* whose employees, systems and structures are truly international in that they no longer reflect its original, national base.

> **International management** is the practice of managing business operations in more than one country.

Companies expanding their overseas activities put time and money into managing the careers of staff working overseas, as well as developing adequate language and cultural skills.

This chapter begins by showing how companies conduct business internationally, and then introduces ideas on the context of international business, with sections on trade agreements and culture. It shows the differences between national management systems and examines the forces driving internationalisation. Figure 4.1 shows a plan of the chapter.

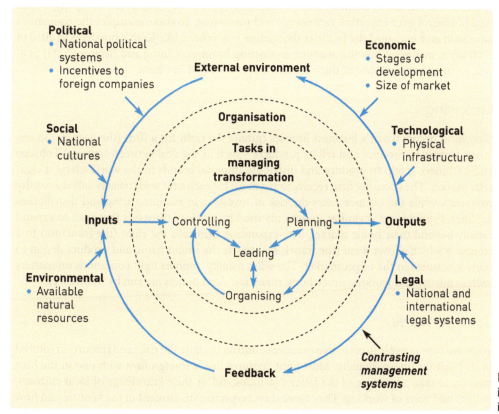

Figure 4.1 Themes in managing internationally

4.2 Ways to conduct business internationally

Companies which conduct international business do so by one or more of six methods.

Offshoring

Offshoring happens when managers decide to transfer activities to countries which will do them more cost-efficiently. This began when companies in developed Western economies transferred routine manufacturing activities to low-wage developing countries. Faster communication over the internet now enables companies to transfer some administrative activities (such as payroll or accounting) overseas, especially to India – though some firms there now also send work to economies where staff costs are even lower.

> **Offshoring** is the practice of contracting out activities to companies in other countries who can do the work more cost-effectively.

Exporting and importing

The longest established way of dealing with overseas customers and suppliers is by transporting physical products (raw materials or finished goods) or delivering services (a retail shop, consultancy or legal advice) across national boundaries. If the final distribution of exports is arranged through a dealer or agent in the receiving country, the implications for people in the exporting company are limited, apart from those directly involved in managing the transactions.

Foreign direct investment

Foreign direct investment (FDI) is when a firm builds or acquires facilities in a foreign country, and manages them directly. Motor companies often do this – Nissan manufactures at several sites in the UK, while General Motors built a plant in India to make the Chevrolet Spark. If the venture is a wholly-owned subsidiary profits stay within the company, which retains control over expertise, technology and marketing. In these examples the companies have built and managed the facilities themselves – in others, like Kraft's purchase in 2010 of Cadbury's, managers buy the assets of an existing business. Chung and Bruton (2008) provide an informative review of the scale and diversity of FDI in China.

> **Foreign direct investment (FDI)** is the practice of investing shareholder funds directly in another country, by building or buying physical facilities, or by buying a company.

Licensing

Licensing occurs when a business licenses (grants the right to) a firm (the licensee) in another country to produce and sell its products – such as the deal between Imperial Tobacco and a Chinese group to produce and distribute Imperial brands in the world's largest cigarette market. The licensing firm receives a payment for each unit sold (usually called a royalty payment), while the licensee takes the risk of investing in manufacturing and distribution facilities. **Franchising** is similar, commonly used by service businesses that wish to expand rapidly beyond their home market. The expanding firm sells the right (the franchise) to a company which allows them (the franchisee) to use the brand name and product design to build a business in the target market. The seller usually imposes tight conditions on matters such as quality and working procedures: many fast-food outlets are run by franchisees.

> **Licensing** is when one firm gives another firm the right to use assets such as patents or technology in exchange for a fee.
>
> **Franchising** is the practice of extending a business by giving other organisations, in return for a fee, the right to use your brand name, technology or product specifications.

Joint ventures

Joint ventures enable firms in two or more countries to share the risks and resources required to do business internationally. Most joint ventures link a foreign firm with one in the host country to take advantage of the latter's facilities and/or their knowledge of local customs, politics and ways of working. They agree their respective investment in the venture and how

> A **joint venture** is an alliance in which the partners agree to form a separate, independent organisation for a specific business purpose.

they will share the profits. Imax has a joint venture with Wanda Cinema Line, China's largest cinema operator, to open 75 cinemas in the country by 2014. Starbucks typically uses joint ventures in overseas markets: in Germany this is with KarstadtQuelle, a department store group. The hazards of joint ventures include cultural differences and misunderstanding between the partners.

Wholly-owned subsidiary

Managers who want to retain close control over their company's international activities they can create a subsidiary in another country. This is costly, but if the venture works all profits stay within the company. It retains control over its expertise, technology and marketing, and can secure local knowledge by employing local staff. The company may establish the subsidiary as a new entity, or, if time is scarce, it may acquire an existing company – which brings the problem of managing different cultures.

Which route to take (if any) is a significant decision. Johnson and Tellis (2008) found that the success depended on how much control the company retained over the venture. Exporting (cheap) gives very little control, as managers cannot control how their products are distributed and sold. A wholly-owned subsidiary (expensive) gives high control, as the company can deploy further resources such as finance or marketing knowledge if required. Firms with a high degree of control were consistently more successful than those without.

Companies also develop forms of organisation through which to conduct their international business – multinational, transnational and global.

Management in practice — Banco Santander www.santander.com

In less than twenty years Banco Santander has changed from being a Spanish regional bank into one of the world's largest banks. Parada *et al.* (2009) report that – unusually – international growth was profitable, due to the systematic way managers built their international presence, namely:

- **building capabilities** in the home market;
- **creating growth options** in foreign markets through small acquisitions (e.g. acquiring Alliance and Leicester in the UK) to become familiar with a country, and to identify possible larger acquisitions; and
- **large-scale foreign market entry** and rapid integration. If it decides to remain in the country it acquires local banks and quickly integrates them into its established ways of working.

The bank regards information systems as critical to its operations and invests heavily in them: for example in credit risk management. The system the bank developed in the home market enabled it to assess risk better than competitors and also to act swiftly and insistently when a client fell into arrears. As soon as Santander acquires a foreign bank all its systems are rapidly integrated, bringing further cost savings.

Source: Based on Parada *et al.* (2009).

Multinational companies are based in one country, but have significant production and marketing operations in many others – perhaps accounting for more than a third of sales. Managers in the home country make the major decisions.

Transnational companies also operate in many countries, but decentralise many decisions to local managers. They use local knowledge to build the business, while still projecting a consistent company image.

Global companies work in many countries, securing resources and finding markets in whichever are most suitable. Production or service processes are performed, and integrated, across many global locations – as are ownership, control and top management. Staff at Trend Micro, an anti-virus software company, must respond rapidly to new viruses that appear

> **Multinational companies** are managed from one country, but have significant production and marketing operations in many others.
>
> **Transnational companies** operate in many countries and delegate many decisions to local managers.

Global companies work in many countries, securing resources and finding markets in whichever country is most suitable.

anywhere and spread very quickly. Trend's financial headquarters is in Tokyo; product development is in Taiwan (a good source of staff with a PhD); and the sales department is in California – inside the huge US market. Nestlé is another example: although headquarters are in Switzerland, 98 per cent of sales and 96 per cent of employees are not. Such businesses are often organised by product, with those in charge of each unit securing resources from whichever country gives best value.

In 2012 General Electric (one of the first US multinationals to build significant operations in China and India) moved the headquarters for its global operations unit from the US to Hong Kong. This shift of senior management functions away from the home country to an international location is an example of a trend advocated by Prahalad and Lieberthal (2003):

> Success in the emerging markets will require innovation and resource shifts on such a scale that life within the multinationals will inevitably be transformed. (p. 110)

Activity 4.1 Choosing between approaches

Consider the different ways of expanding a business internationally.

- For each of the methods outlined above note the advantages and disadvantages.
- Identify a company with international operations, and gather evidence to help you decide which method it has used, and why.
- Compare your research with colleagues on your course, and prepare a short presentation summarising your conclusions.

Case questions 4.2

- Which of the modes of entry outlined above has Starbucks used?
- Using the definitions here, is Starbucks as a multinational, transnational or global firm?

4.3 The contexts of international business – PESTEL

People managing internationally pay close attention to the international aspects of the general business environment (Chapter 3), shown in Figure 4.2. Section 4.3 outlines four of these (beginning, for clarity, with the economic context), and Sections 4.4 and 4.5 present the socio-cultural and legal contexts.

Economic context

The **theory of absolute advantage** is a trade theory which proposes that by specialising in producing goods and services which they can produce more efficiently than others, and then trading them, nations will increase their economic wealth.

One area of economic theory aims to understand why nations trade with each other, rather than being self-sufficient. The **theory of absolute advantage** states that by specialising in the production of goods which they can produce more cheaply than other countries, and then trading them, nations will increase their economic well-being. If countries use the resources in which they have an advantage (such as fertile land, rich raw materials or efficient methods) to produce goods and services, and then exchange them with countries for things in which *they* are most efficient, they will collectively add more value than if everyone was self-sufficient. While being self-sufficient sounds attractive, it is more costly than buying things which someone else can produce more cheaply. The theory is of course a great deal more complex that (see Chapter 6 in Rugman and Hodgetts (2003) for a fuller treatment) – but

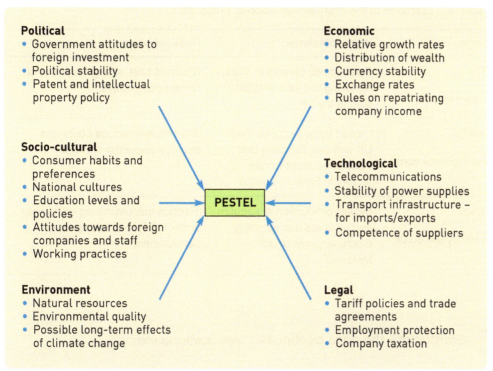

Figure 4.2 An international PESTEL analysis

even this simple account begins to explain why nations trade, even though each could make the goods themselves.

Evidence supporting this theory is the rapid internationalisation of production since the 1960s. At that time many firms in the developed world realised that labour intensive manufacturing was costly – especially in electrical goods, clothing, footwear and toys, which could not compete with imports. Managers looked for new sources of supply, and received a positive response from a small group of Asian countries – Taiwan, Hong Kong, South Korea and especially Singapore. In the years which followed they become major 'offshoring' centres, supplying goods and components to companies around the world. They also developed their education systems so that they now do work of higher value, widening their product range – including software development and administrative functions. Table 4.1 gives some examples.

Companies sometimes find that operations in remote locations require more management time than they expected, so reducing the cost advantage. Some also find that customers object to talking to a call centre operator in a distant country who may lack the local knowledge to conduct a transaction smoothly. They are then likely to 'repatriate' the outsourced activities: in 2012 General Electric announced that it was bringing some manufacturing work back to the United States, as Chinese manufacturing costs were becoming too high, and overseas manufacture was reducing GE's ability to respond quickly to changing demand.

The internationalisation of markets happens when companies from wealthier countries see market opportunities in less developed ones. Audi, BMW and Mercedes-Benz are increasing sales in India, where sales of luxury cars are expected to rise from 39,000 in 2012 to 133,000 by 2020 (*Financial Times*, 20 August 2012, p. 17). Brewers like Heineken, Diageo and SABMiller are investing heavily in Africa, where rising incomes and population stimulate demand. Tobacco maker Philip Morris sees good prospects in Malaysia and South Africa, whose high birth rates ensure more young smokers. Hong Kong Disneyland reflects the company's belief that Asia's media and entertainment market will grow rapidly: the Chinese government agreed, taking a 57 per cent stake. Disney hopes this will help it win good terms for other ventures – TV, films and consumer goods.

Table 4.1 Examples of the internationalisation of production

Company	Work transferred	Reasons given
BT www.bt.com	Opened call centres in India, replacing the jobs of 2000 staff in the UK	'To meet cost-saving targets and remain competitive'
Gillette www.gillette.com	Closed three factories (two UK and one German) and transferred work to new factory in Eastern Europe	'Significantly reduce costs and improve operating efficiency'
Dyson www.dyson.co.uk	Moved production of vacuum and cleaners and washing machines from UK to Malaysia	'Reduce manufacturing costs help protect UK jobs in design and development'

Case study: Starbucks – the case continues   www.starbucks.com

In 2007 Howard Schultz, founder and former chief executive saw signs of trouble:

Starbucks had begun to fail itself. Obsessed with growth, we took our eyes of operations and became distracted from the core of our business. No single decision or tactic was to blame. The damage was slow and quiet, incremental … Decision by decision, store by store, customer by customer, Starbucks was losing some of the signature traits it had been founded on. Worse, our self-induced problems were being compounded by external circumstances as the world went through unprecedented change on several fronts.

Most significantly, the economy was [moving into a financial crisis and global recession]. At the same time, a seismic shift in consumer behaviour was under way, and people became not just more cost conscious, but also more environmentally aware, health minded, and ethically driven. Consumers were holding the companies they did business with – including Starbucks – to higher standards.

And then there was the digital revolution and the sea change in how information flows – the proliferation of online media and social networks, as well as the rise of the blogosphere. Too often, in real time, worldwide exchange of opinion and news seemed to follow Starbucks every move.

Finally an onslaught of new coffee and espresso competitors … swept into the marketplace and targeted Starbucks, often with unprecedented vitriol. (Schultz, 2011, p. xi–xii)

In January 2008 Schultz returned to the position of chief executive (he had remained as chairman after giving up as CEO in 2000) and acted quickly to restore the business. He identified many small decisions that had combined to diminish 'the Starbucks experience', including:

- installing new espresso machines which were more efficient – but were so tall that the *baristas* could not engage properly with customers while they made their coffee;
- instead of staff scooping fresh coffee beans from bins and grinding it in front of the customers, the company had begun sending ground coffee to stores in bags – more efficient, but eliminating the aroma and atmosphere associated with freshly ground coffee;
- the stores' design, so critical to atmosphere, now seemed to lack the warm feeling of a neighbourhood gathering place.

Schultz then began a recovery programme, with less emphasis on growth, improving internal processes (taking care not to damage the customer experience), and improved customer service, coffee and food.

By March 2010 the company appeared to be recovering, which has continued. Speaking to a conference of store managers he congratulated them on 'one of the most historic turnrounds in corporate history' but warned against complacency:

> We can't allow mediocrity to creep back into the business. The worst thing we could do is not understand what happened three years ago.

Sources: Schultz (2011); Starbucks Corporation *Annual Report 2012*.

Case questions 4.3

- What are the likely implications for Starbucks management of the changing external factors that Schultz identifies in this extract?
- How might dealing with them in its core market (the United States) affect the strategy of international expansion?

The economic context of a country includes its stage of development as well as levels of inflation, exchange rates or levels of debt. The measure of economic development usually used is income per head of population – a measure of a country's total production, adjusted for size of population.

Key ideas — The complex forces behind China's transition to capitalism

Doug Guthrie (2006) presents a valuable insight into one of the major business developments in recent years – the transition of China from a state-run towards a market-based system. A distinctive feature of his analysis is the emphasis he places on the links between political, social, cultural and economic forces:

> Economic institutions and practices are deeply embedded in political, cultural and social systems, and it is impossible to analyse the economy without analysing the way it is shaped by politics, culture and the social world. The perspective is essential for understanding the complex processes of economic and social reform in any transforming society, but it is especially critical for understanding China's reform path and trajectory. This position may seem obvious to some, but ... for years, economists from the World Bank, the IMF, and various reaches of academia have operated from a different set of assumptions: they have assumed that a transition to markets is a simple and, basically, apolitical process ... In other words, 'don't worry about the complexities of culture or pre-existing social or political systems; if you put the right capitalist institutions in place (i.e. private property), transition to a market economy will be a simple process'. The perspective I present here is that the standard economic view of market transitions that defined a good deal of policy for the IMF and the World Bank in the late twentieth century could not be more simplistic or more wrong.

Source: Guthrie (2006), pp. 10–11.

Political context

Whatever economic theory may predict about the patterns of trade, political factors – such as the institutions and processes of the political system, the extent of government involvement in the economy, and a nation's record on corruption – also affect the pattern. They shape the **political risk** a company faces in a country – the risk of losing assets, earning power or managerial control due to political events or the actions of host governments. During the 1990s east European countries offered incentives to attract Western companies to build power plants in their territories: now they are members of the EU these incentives may be judged as illegal state aid, so the investing companies risk losing money.

Political risk is the risk of losing assets, earning power or managerial control due to political events or the actions of host governments.

> An **ideology** is a set of integrated beliefs, theories and doctrines that helps to direct the actions of a society.

The political system in a country influences business, and managers adapt to the prevailing **ideology**. Political ideologies are closely linked to economic philosophies and attitudes towards business. In the United States the political ideology is grounded in a constitution which guarantees the rights of people to own property and to have wide freedom of choice. This laid the foundations of a capitalist economy favourable to business. While countries such as Australia or the UK are equally capitalist in outlook, others such as Brazil or France have political ideologies which give more emphasis to social considerations.

There are close links between political and economic systems – especially in how they allocate resources and deal with property ownership. Governments set rules that establish what commercial activity takes place within their jurisdiction, and how it can be conducted – a capitalist way, a centrally-controlled way, or a mix. Political systems affect business life through:

- the balance between state-owned and privately-owned enterprises;
- the amount of state intervention through subsidies, taxes and regulation;
- policies towards foreign companies trading in the country, with or without local partners (the Indian government wants foreign retailers to invest in the country by opening modern stores, but faces opposition from Indian retailers to this competition: it has developed strict and complex rules governing foreign retailers);
- policies towards foreign companies acquiring local firms;
- policies on employment practices, working conditions and job protection (in 2010 the French government ordered Renault to make the new Clio in France, rather than move production to Turkey).

All states are affected to some degree by corruption – when politicians or officials abuse public power for private benefit. Coping with this is part of the job of managers operating internationally, but as Rodriguez et al. (2005) point out:

> while corruption is everywhere ... it is not the same everywhere. (p. 383)

> **Pervasiveness (of corruption)** represents the extent to which a firm is likely to encounter corruption in the course of normal transactions with state officials.
>
> **Arbitrariness (of corruption)** is the degree of ambiguity associated with corrupt transactions.

They introduce a framework to analyse the implications of corruption for business – based on its **pervasiveness** and **arbitrariness**. Pervasiveness is the extent to which a firm is likely to encounter corruption during transactions with officials. Arbitrariness is the degree of ambiguity associated with corrupt transactions. When corruption is arbitrary, officials apply rules haphazardly – perhaps enforcing them strictly in some areas but ignoring them elsewhere. Figure 4.3 illustrates this.

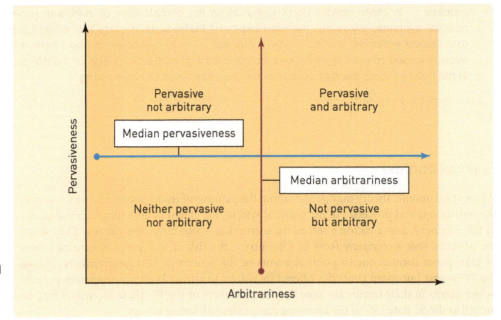

Figure 4.3 Two dimensions of corruption: pervasiveness and arbitrariness

Source: Based on Rodriguez et al. (2005).

> **Management in practice**   Towards a single market in Spain
>
> In early 2013 the Spanish government announced that it planned to reduce the burden on business of the many rules and regulations imposed by the country's 17 autonomous regions. At a time when the EU has been moving towards a single market, the opposite has been happening within Spain: road haulage companies, for example, are confronted with different regulations in each state as their trucks move across the country.
>
> Under the proposed change, any company that meets the rules in one region would automatically have the right to provide goods and services in any other – it would be a system of mutual recognition by the regions, not a centrally imposed uniformity. The new law would be part of a wider campaign to liberalise the economy and reduce the administrative burden on business.
>
> One aim of the government is to improve Spain's record as a country in which to do business. Spain ranks 44th in a list of countries compiled by the World Bank according to the ease of doing business, below Peru and just ahead of Colombia.
>
> Source: From an article by Tobias Buck, *Financial Times*, 25 January 2013, p. 6.

Technological context

Infrastructure includes all of the physical facilities that support economic activities – ports, airports, surface transport and telecommunications. Companies operating abroad, especially in less developed countries, are closely interested in the quality of this aspect of a country as it has a huge effect on the cost and convenience of conducting business.

> **Management in practice**   Power shortages benefit Aggreko   www.aggreko.com
>
> Many developing economies regularly experience severe shortages of power as demand for electricity exceeds their generating capacity. This provides opportunities for Aggreko, a UK company with about 2000 staff which rents power generation and temperature control equipment to businesses and governments. In 2012 it reported that its strongest-performing division that year had been International Power Projects, which provides long-term power generation capacity to countries without sufficient installed capacity. For example, the company provides almost half of Uganda's electricity, and also supplies Bangladesh and Kenya.
>
> Source: Company website.

A poor infrastructure is an opportunity for those supplying such facilities. European water companies have contracts to apply their expertise to providing water and sanitation services to many developing countries.

Developments in information technology stimulate international trade in two ways. The electronics industry requires billions of high-value, low weight components, produced in globally-dispersed factories and assembly plants – from which finished products are in turn transported around the world. These movements are a major source of growth in world trade. The internet makes it easier for managers to control international operations, which also encourages trade.

Environmental context

One aspect of the environment is an economy's natural resources – oil, coal and other minerals, agricultural land and the prevailing climate. Some resources are renewable but many are not. Water supplies are becoming scarce in many countries, and a major concern not only to local residents but to international food production companies.

These considerations affect the kind of businesses which people create in a country, and the pattern of world trade. Technological developments reveal previously unknown resources (new oil reserves in Central Asia) and the fuller use of some that were uneconomic (shale oil in North America). This benefits the country, and the companies who agree to extract the resources.

The process is also controversial, as when foreign mining or oil companies come into conflict with local populations whose land they occupy, or over the commercial terms of the concessions.

Some object to the environmental degradation associated with timber or mineral exploitation, whose effects spread widely (such as when rivers are polluted in one country before flowing to another). Economic development itself causes pollution – a problem for people in the area, and an opportunity for foreign businesses that specialise in environmental remediation.

Activity 4.2 Reflecting on contexts

Go to the website of a large company (such as BAE systems, www.bae.com) and see what examples you can find of managers responding to the factors in this section.

Alternatively, if you have worked in a company operating internationally, which of the contextual factors in this section have had most effect on the management of the venture?

- Within each heading, which items had most impact, and why?
- Which items that are NOT listed had a significant impact, and why?
- Evaluate the usefulness of the model as a guide to those managing internationally.

4.4 Legal context – trade agreements and trading blocs

Managers planning to enter an overseas market need to ensure they are familiar with local laws and regulations affecting business practice: they also seek to satisfy themselves that the local legal system will protect them in the event of disputes with customers or suppliers. Beyond conditions in an individual country, international managers engage in trade agreements and economic alliances.

GATT and the World Trade Organization

The General Agreement on Tariffs and Trade (GATT) reduces the tendency of national governments to put tariffs on physical goods to protect domestic companies. Its main tool is tariff concessions, whereby member countries agree to limit the level of tariffs they impose on imports. GATT has also sponsored a series of international trade negotiations aimed at reducing restrictions on trade – one of which established the World Trade Organization (www.wto.org). This monitors international trade and arbitrates in disputes between countries over the interpretation of tariffs and other barriers to trade. It is also seeking a world agreement on rules governing foreign investment.

European Union

Since the leaders of the original member states signed the Treaty of Rome in 1959 the aim of the European Union (EU) (**http://europa.eu**) has been to eliminate tariffs and other restrictions that governments use to protect domestic industries. The European Commission (responsible for proposing and implementing policy) is encouraging European trade by proposing changes in national laws to make it easier. Car companies such as BMW and DaimlerChrysler have plants in several countries, each specialising in some components or models. They import and export these between the countries as part of a European production system. The Single European Act of 1986 aimed to create a single internal market. Introducing the euro as a common currency for many of the members encouraged further changes in the European economy by unifying capital markets and making price comparisons more transparent. It is the world's biggest exporter and the second biggest importer.

The EU continues to deepen integration to enable the free movement of goods and services and so improve efficiency by:

- harmonising technical regulations between member states;
- creating a common industrial policy (e.g. eliminating subsidies for businesses);
- liberalising services (such as mail) across the EU;
- harmonising rules on employment and environmental protection;
- facilitating cross-border mergers; and
- recognising professional qualifications to enable freer movement of labour.

The EU is developing common policies on monetary and political matters, so that it can speak with a single voice on (for example) interest rates and financial regulation. The Lisbon Treaty (2009) aims to enable the EU to work more effectively by extending Qualified Majority Voting (QMV) to streamline decisions in technical areas (e.g. appointments to the European Central Bank's board). The UK insists on maintaining national control in areas of justice, home affairs, social security, tax, foreign policy and defence: the Lisbon Treaty clarified this.

Enlargement has long been a feature of the EU agenda, the greatest event being in 2004 when ten members (many from Eastern Europe) joined: discussions continue about Turkey.

Management in practice Competition for the Polish Post Office

Jerzy Jozkowiak, head of the Polish national postal operator, is unsparing in his criticism of the company he has led since March 2011:

> Our efficiency is four or five times lower than in western Europe. The Polish Post Office is one of the most inefficient post offices in the European Union.

> The Polish operator earns about €18,000 per worker, while the EU average is €72,600. Polish postal workers handle an average of 17,000 letters per year, while the European average is 63,600. That is a problem because, from this month, the Polish postal market has been deregulated and letter deliveries have been opened to competition. Finally buckling to pressure from Brussels, Poland is one of the last EU countries to undertake this step, but the long resistance to change has left the post office very vulnerable.

> This is the largest market in this part of Europe. If someone has already gone through the privatisation process then this is a natural market for them, says Mr Jozkowiak.

Source: *Financial Times*, 11 January 2013.

> **Activity 4.3** **Access the European Union website** http://europa.eu
>
> - Access the European Union website, and navigate to areas that interest you, such as those on European Policies, or on Jobs at the Commission.
> - Alternatively, gather information from the site that provides you with specific examples or evidence about one of the topics in this chapter, which you could use in an essay or assignment.
> - Make notes on what you have found, and compare it with a colleague on your course.

4.5 Socio-cultural context

Culture is distinct from human nature (features which human beings have in common) and from an individual's personality (their unique way of thinking, feeling and acting). It is a collective phenomenon, which people learnt and shared in a common social environment. Hofstede and Hofstede (2005) describe it as

> the collective programming of the mind which distinguishes one group or category of people from others (in which 'group' means a number of people in contact with each other, and a 'category' means people who have something in common, such as people born before 1940). (p. 4 and p. 377)

While humans share common biological features those in a particular society, nation or region develop a distinct culture. As a business becomes more international, its managers balance a similar approach to business across the world with the unique cultures of the places in which they operate.

Cultural diversity and evolution

Hofstede and Hofstede (2005) note the diversity of cultures between human societies, even though people have evolved from common ancestors. There are recognisable differences between people in geographically separate areas in how they communicate with each other, how they respond to authority, when they go to work – and in countless other aspects of social life. Societies develop these practices as they adapt to their environment, experience military or religious conquest, or exploit scientific discoveries. These are overlaid by the more recent creation of nations:

> strictly speaking, the concept of a common culture applies to societies, not to nations … yet rightly or wrongly, properties are ascribed to the citizens of certain countries: people refer to 'typically American', 'typically German', 'typically Japanese' behaviour. Using nationality is a matter of expediency. (pp. 18–19)

Nations develop distinct institutions – governments, laws, business systems and so on. Some argue that these in themselves account for differences in behaviour between countries, implying that institutions (such as a legal or banking system) that work in one country will do so elsewhere. A counter view is that institutions reflect the culture in which they developed: something that works in one country, may fail in another:

> Institutions cannot be understood without considering culture, and understanding culture presumes insight into institutions. (p. 20)

Culture and managing internationally

Managers working internationally are aware of the benefits of understanding and managing cultural differences. This is most evident when one company acquires, or enters into a joint venture with, a company in a country with a different culture. As one observer noted:

> A lot of companies are struggling to find the middle way. As a global company they would like to impose their view of the world. But being aware of cultural differences, you can't manage Chinese or Japanese employees the same way you manage Americans.

Another noted that Tesco (Part 6 Case) tries to understand the local culture in new markets:

> It's a very thoughtful company, the way it sees culture is continually evolving. It has had executives stay in people's homes is new markets, to stay with families to see their relationship with food.

The company has also tried to import foreign knowledge, bringing overseas managers to the UK to observe and document the company's culture in its home base – helping to build a more blended management team (*Financial Times*, 25 August 2011, p. 10).

Activity 4.4 Comparing cultures

Form a group amongst your student colleagues made up of people from different countries.

- Identify the main characteristics of the respective cultures in your group.
- Gather any evidence about how members think they affect the work of managing.
- Compare your evidence on cultural differences with that from Hofstede's research (below).

High-context and low-context cultures

Hall (1976) distinguished between high- and low-context cultures. In a **high-context culture** information is implicit, and can only be fully understood by those with the benefit of shared experience, assumptions and verbal codes. This happens when people live closely together, developing deep mutual understandings which provide a rich context for communication. In a **low-context culture** information is explicit and clear. These cultures occur where people are psychologically distant, and so depend more on explicit information to communicate:

> Japanese, Arabs and Mediterranean people, who have extensive information networks among family, friends, colleagues and clients and who are involved in close personal relationships, are examples of high context cultures. Low context peoples include Americans, Germans, Swiss, Scandinavians and other northern Europeans; they compartmentalise their personal relationships, their work and many aspects of day-to-day life. (Tayeb, 1996, pp. 55–6)

High-context cultures are those in which information is implicit and can only be fully understood by those with shared experiences in the culture.

Low-context cultures are those where people are more psychologically distant so that information needs to be explicit if members are to understand it.

Attitude to conflict and harmony

Disagreements and conflict arise in all societies. The management interest is in how societies vary in how people deal with it. Individualistic cultures such as the United States or the Netherlands see conflict as healthy, as everyone has a right to express their views. People are encouraged to bring disagreements into the open and to discuss them, rather than suppress them. Other cultures place greater value on social harmony and on not disturbing the peace:

> The notion of harmony is central in almost all East Asian cultures, such as Korea, Taiwan, Singapore and Hong Kong, through their common Confucian heritage. In ... Korea the traditional implicit rules of proper behaviour provide appropriate role behaviour for individuals in junior and subordinate roles. (Tayeb, 1996, p. 60)

Key ideas — **Overemphasising diversity?**

The chapter has illustrated the diversity of national cultures. There is another view that the underlying fundamentals of management outweigh cultural variations in detailed processes. One powerful constraint on diversity is the economic context of an essentially capitalist economic system. This places similar requirements on managers wherever they are. They have to provide acceptable returns, create a coherent organisational structure, maintain relations with stakeholders and try to keep control.

Further, if managers work in a multinational organisation that has developed a distinctive corporate culture (Chapter 3), will that influence their behaviour more than the local national culture?

Another constraint is the use of integrated information systems across companies (and their suppliers) operating internationally, which can place common reporting requirements on managers irrespective of their location. This ties units more closely together, and may bring more convergence in the work of management.

These are unresolved questions: look for evidence as you work on this chapter that supports or contradicts either point of view.

Several scholars have developed survey instruments to classify and compare national cultures, notably Trompenaars (1993), House *et al.* (2004) and Hofstede (2001). Hofstede's work has been widely used in management research (Kirkman *et al.*, 2006), and the next section outlines it.

4.6 Hofstede's comparison of national cultures

Geert Hofstede conducted widely quoted studies of national cultural differences. The second edition of his research (Hofstede, 2001) extends and refines the conclusions of his original work, which was based on a survey of the attitudes of 116,000 IBM employees, one of the earliest global companies. The research inspired many empirical studies with non-IBM employees in both the original countries in which IBM operated and in places where they did not. Kirkman *et al.* (2006) reviewed these and concluded that 'most of the country differences predicted by Hofstede were supported' (p. 308). Hofstede and Hofstede (2005, pp. 25–8) make a similar point and also provide an accessible account of the research method.

Hofstede (2001), as already noted, saw culture as a collective programming of people's minds, which influences how they react to events in the workplace. He identified five dimensions of culture and used a questionnaire to measure how people vary between countries in their attitudes to them.

Power distance

Power distance is the extent to which the less powerful members of organisations within a country expect and accept that power is distributed unevenly.

Power distance (PD) is 'the extent to which the less powerful members of ... organisations within a country expect and accept that power is distributed unevenly' (Hofstede and Hofstede, 2005, p. 46). Countries differ in how they distribute power and authority, and in how people view the resultant inequality. Some see inequality in boss/subordinate relationships as undesirable, while others people see it as part of the natural order. The questionnaire allowed the researchers to calculate scores for PD – high PD showing people accepted inequality. Those with high scores included Malaysia, Mexico, Venezuela, Arab countries, China, France and Brazil. Those with low PD scores included Australia, Germany, Great Britain, Sweden, and Norway.

Uncertainty avoidance

Uncertainty avoidance is 'the extent to which the members of a culture feel threatened by ambiguous or unknown situations' (Hofstede and Hofstede, 2005, p.167). People in some cultures are reluctant to move without clear rules or instructions – they avoid uncertainty. Others readily tolerate uncertainty and ambiguity – if things are not clear they improvise or use their initiative. Uncertainty avoidance scores were high in Latin American, Latin European and Mediterranean countries, and for Japan and Korea. Low UA (happy with ambiguity) scores were recorded in the Asian countries other than Japan and Korea, and in most of the Anglo and Nordic countries – United States, Great Britain, Sweden, and Denmark.

> **Uncertainty avoidance** is the extent to which members of a culture feel threatened by uncertain or unknown situations.

Individualism/collectivism

Hofstede and Hofstede (2005) distinguish between **individualism** and **collectivism:**

> Individualism pertains to societies in which the ties between individuals are loose: everyone is expected to look after himself or herself and his or her immediate family. Collectivism as its opposite pertains to societies in which people, from birth onwards, are integrated into strong, cohesive in-groups which throughout people's lifetime continue to protect them in exchange for unquestioning loyalty. (p. 76)

Some people live in societies which emphasise the individual, and his or her responsibility for their position in life. Others value the group, placing more emphasis on collective action, mutual responsibility, and on helping each other through difficulties. High individualism scores occurred in the United States, Australia, Great Britain and Canada. Low scores occurred in less developed South American and Asian countries.

> **Individualism** pertains to societies in which the ties between individuals are loose.
>
> **Collectivism** 'describes societies in which people, from birth onwards, are integrated into strong, cohesive in-groups which ... protect them in exchange for unquestioning loyalty' (Hofstede, 1991, p. 51).

Activity 4.5 Implications of cultural differences

- Consider the implications of differences on Hofstede's first two dimensions of culture for management in the countries concerned. For example, what would Hofstede's conclusions lead you to predict about the method that a French or Venezuelan manager would use if he or she wanted a subordinate to perform a task, and what method would the subordinate expect his or her manager to use? (Note: France is part of the Latin European cluster in Figure 4.4.)
- How would your answers differ if the manager and subordinates were Swedish?

Masculinity/femininity

A society is called **masculine** when emotional gender roles are clearly distinct: men are supposed to be assertive, tough and focussed on material success, whereas women are supposed to be more modest, tender and concerned with the quality of life. A society is called **feminine** when emotional gender roles overlap (i.e. both men and women are supposed to be modest, tender and concerned with the quality of life). (Hofstede and Hofstede, 2005, p. 120)

> **Masculinity** pertains to societies in which social gender roles are clearly distinct.
>
> **Femininity** pertains to societies in which social gender roles overlap.

The research showed that societies differ in the desirability of assertive behaviour (which he labels as masculinity) and of modest behaviour (femininity). Many expect men to seek achievements outside the home while women care for things within the home. Masculinity scores were not related to economic wealth: 'we find both rich and poor masculine countries, and rich and poor feminine countries' (p. 120). The most feminine countries were Sweden, Norway, the Netherlands and Denmark. Masculine countries included Japan, Austria, Germany, China and the United States.

Integrating the dimensions

These four dimensions describe the overall culture of a society, and each culture is unique. They also have similarities – for example the UK, Canada and the US all have high individualism, moderately high masculinity, low power distance, and low uncertainty avoidance. In these nations managers expect workers to take the initiative and assume responsibility (high individualism), rely on the use of individual (not group) rewards to motivate staff (moderate masculinity), treat their employees as valued people whom they do not treat officiously (low power distance) and keep bureaucracy to a minimum (low uncertainty avoidance). A systematic analysis of Hofstede's data for all the countries in his survey revealed that most of them (the exceptions being Brazil, Japan, India and Israel) fall into a particular cultural cluster. Figure 4.4 illustrates this.

Long-term and short-term orientation

In their 2005 work Hofstede and Hofstede added this fifth dimension:

> Long-term orientation (LTO) stands for the fostering of virtues orientated towards future rewards – in particular perseverance and thrift. Its opposite pole, short-term orientation, stands for the fostering of virtues related to the past and present – in particular respect for tradition, preservation of 'face', and fulfilling social obligations. (p. 210)

Countries with high LTO scores include China, Hong Kong, Taiwan and Japan. Great Britain, Australia, New Zealand, the United States and Canada have a short-term orientation, in which many people see spending, not thrift, as a virtue.

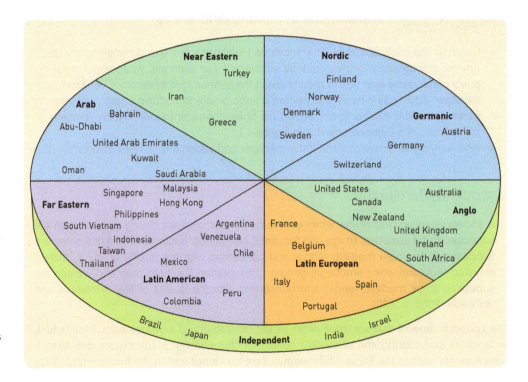

Figure 4.4 A synthesis of country clusters

Source: Ronen and Shenkar (1985).

Current status

Hofstede's work has limitations, including:

- the small (and so possibly unrepresentative) number of respondents in some countries;
- reducing a phenomenon as complex as a nation's culture (whose population includes many class, social, ethnic and religious divisions) to five dimensions;
- basing the original sample on the employees of one global company;
- the likelihood of differences of culture within IBM.

Others, like Thomas Friedman (2005) in his book *The World is Flat* believe that deep and persistent changes – globalisation, communications technologies such as social networking, spread of market economies – are diminishing differences in national values and beliefs. Managers are also aware that national culture is just one factor affecting the performance of overseas operations.

Hofstede's work, for all the limitations, provides a widely recognised starting point for those working internationally. They can use it to think about the culture in which they operate, to reflect on their cultural biases, and so begin to develop the skill of working across cultures.

Case questions 4.4

Here are some suggestions about how cultural differences may affect attitudes and behaviour at work.

- **Preferences for style of leadership**: people in individualist and low power distance cultures prefer participative leadership, while people in collectivist and high power distance cultures prefer more direct and charismatic leaders.
- **Team working**: people in collectivist cultures are more likely to prefer working in a team and to show commitment to other team members, while people with individualist values are less likely to conform to group pressures and have weaker affiliations to a team
- **Communication style**: people in masculine and individualist cultures are likely to use direct and open communication styles, while collectivist, feminist cultures are more associated with indirectness and modesty.

If these suggestions, based on Hofstede's analysis, are accurate, what may be the implications for a Starbucks manager who has to work with colleagues in several countries? Check the text for the cultural features which Hofstede identified for these countries, and then identify possible implications.

- United States
- Japan
- France
- United Kingdom

Source: Based on an idea in Taras et al. (2011).

Activity 4.6 Critical reflection on cultural differences

If you have worked in an organisation with international operations, reflect on whether your experience leads you to agree or disagree with the ideas in this section. For example:

- Can you recognise the differences in national cultures identified by Hofstede?
- If so, in what ways did they affect the way people worked?
- How did company culture and national culture interact?

4.7 Contrasting management systems

Despite the growth of international trade and the growing interdependence of business across the world, countries vary substantially in the way they organise economic activities. There are major differences in the way businesses are organised in different countries – even though all are capitalist economies. As Whitley (1999) explains:

> Different patterns of industrialisation developed in contrasting institutional contexts and led to contrasting institutional arrangements governing economic processes becoming established ... Partly as a result, the structure and practices of state agencies, financial organisations and labour-market actors ... continue to diverge and to reproduce distinctive forms of economic organisation. (p. 5)

Table 4.2 illustrates his ideas in relation to the United States and Europe. There are significant differences between countries within Europe, and in some respects the UK is closer to the United States model than to the rest of Europe.

He also examines the Japanese model with networks of interdependent relations, and a tradition of mutual ownership between different, but friendly, business units. Companies have close financial and obligational links with each other and the Ministry of Industry actively supports and guides the strategic direction of major areas of business. Firms create a network of mutually dependent organisations and decide strategy by negotiation with their stakeholders – other companies and financial institutions.

At the other extreme, firms in the United States and United Kingdom are more isolated, raising most of their funds from the capital markets. Some observers believe that investors in US and UK companies expect steadily increasing returns from the companies they invest in, which in turn leads those managing the companies to focus on short-term profits at the expense of the long-term health of the business. The collapse of some financial institutions in 2008 was in part blamed on executives taking excessive risks to meet capital market expectations.

Table 4.2 Contrasting business systems of the United States and Europe

	United States	Europe
Power of state	Relatively limited, with more scope for discretion by companies to provide employee and social benefits	Relatively strong, with more engagement in economic activity through state-owned companies.
Financial system	Stock market central source of finance for companies, with shareholdings dispersed. Corporations expected to be transparent and accountable to investors	Corporations in network of relations with small number of larger investors. Non-shareholders often play equal role to shareholders.
Education and labour system	Corporations have developed policies; relatively local and decentralised labour relations and collective bargaining.	Publicly led training and labour market policies, in which corporations participated; national collective bargaining.
Cultural systems	Traditions of participation, philanthropy, wary of government, moral value of capitalism; ethic of giving back to society.	Preference for representative organisations – political parties, trade unions, trade associations, state.

Source: Based on Whitley (1999 and 2009).

Managing Internationally

> **Management in practice** **The evolving Japanese management system**
>
> A special issue of *Long Range Planning* in 2009 outlined both continuity and change in what has become known as the Japanese management system. A brief summary provides a point of comparison with other systems – while acknowledging that the system is most prevalent amongst large firms, so that many Japanese workers do not benefit. Stiles (2009) noted the main features:
>
> - **Corporate governance and ownership** – large corporations have cooperative relationships with each other across industries and along the supply chain.
> - **Culture** – a collectivist society values attaining cooperation and trust with others in the workplace.
> - **Permanent employment** – core staff have high security of employment.
> - **Seniority wages** – pay and promotion are largely based on education level and years with the employer.
> - **Enterprise unions** – most firms have one union, and make changes in consultation with it.
> - **Production methods** – a relentless focus on quality and continuous improvement.
>
> Many of these practices are being challenged by intense competition from other Asian countries, and by dissenting views within Japan – from, for example women and non-core workers who are often denied the benefits of this system.
>
> Source: Stiles (2009).

4.8 Forces driving globalisation

The globalisation of markets?

If you travel to another country, you immediately see many familiar consumer products or services – examples of the idea that global brands are displacing local products. In several industries identical products (Canon cameras, Sony Walkman, Famous Grouse whisky) are sold across the globe. Theodore Levitt observed this trend towards **globalisation** – see Key ideas.

Globalisation refers to the increasing integration of internationally dispersed economic activities.

> **Key ideas** **The globalisation of markets**
>
> Theodore Levitt, a Professor at Harvard Business School, believed that advances in communications technology were inspiring consumers around the world to want the same things.
>
> **The world's needs and desires have been irrevocably homogenised. This makes the multinational corporation obsolete and the global corporation absolute. (p. 93)**
>
> He advised international companies to cease acting as 'multinationals' that customised their products to fit local markets and tastes. Instead they should become 'global' by standardising production, distribution and marketing across all countries. Sameness meant efficiency and would be more profitable than difference. Economies of scale would bring competitive advantage.
>
> Source: Based on Levitt (1983).

Practice in many global businesses soon appeared to support Levitt's theory. In the mid-1980s British Airways developed an advertisement ('The world's favourite airline') and (after dubbing it into 20 languages) showed it in identical form in all 35 countries with a developed

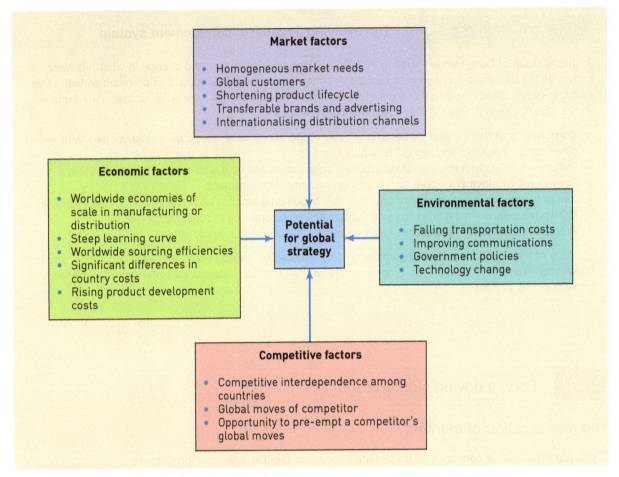

Figure 4.5 Factors driving globalisation in an industry
Source: Adapted from *Total Global Strategy II*, 2nd ed., Pearson Education, Upper Saddle River, NJ (Yip, G.S. 2003) p. 10, Copyright © 2003, reprinted by permission of Pearson Education, Inc., Upper Saddle River, NJ.

TV network. Consumer companies like Coca-Cola and McDonald's began promoting themselves as identical global brands, with standard practices and a centralised management structure.

What had led to this increasingly global business world? Yip (2003) developed a model (Figure 4.5) of the factors that drive globalisation in particular industries. Market factors were probably the most significant in Starbucks – such as the transferability of brands and advertising, and the ability to develop international distribution channels. In other industries cost factors are more prominent – car companies can benefit from economies of scale in manufacturing, and the ability to buy components around the world. In other cases government incentives for companies to relocate facilities away from their home base have encouraged globalisation. Developments in communication technologies also drive globalisation, by enabling the efficient flow of data on which international operations depend.

There is also evidence of resistance to the apparent inevitability of Yip's model. Local companies develop new products that may offer better value than global brands: so rather than 'going global' companies began to 'go local' – Coca-Cola now owns not one brand but 200, many of them in only one or two markets; Starbucks and McDonald's vary their offerings to suit local tastes; Nestlé has about 200 varieties of its instant coffee. The Management in practice feature shows contrasting approaches in the motor industry.

> **Management in practice** — Contrast Ford (www.Ford.com) with VW (www.VW.com)
>
> In 2008 Ford announced that it was trying to break down the 'regional fiefdoms' which managers of the company's businesses around the world had developed. Designers, engineers and marketing staff focussed primarily on their parts of the world producing, for example, a Ford Focus in Europe that was quite different from that sold in the United States. Alan Mulally, Ford's chief executive (who had joined the company from Boeing) saw this as inefficient:
>
> > We didn't make different 737s for France and China.
>
> Under his plan, by 2015 all cars of each model will share a common platform, irrespective of where they are sold, believing this will produce great economies of scale for it and its suppliers.
>
> In the same year Martin Winterkorn, chief executive of Volkswagen said that the days of building one car for the whole world were over:
>
> > We will make the VW group the world's most international car maker. The days of a 'world car' are dead and buried. Our customers in China or India expect us, as a global player, to offer entirely different solutions than we do in the US or western Europe.
>
> Source: *Financial Times*, 14 March 2008, and 25 July 2008.

Alan Rugman has noted that rather than becoming globalised, the world has divided into three regions – North America, the European Union and Japan/East Asia – see Key ideas. He notes that almost three-quarters of exports from EU members went to other EU countries, concluding that we are seeing is not globalisation but regionalisation:

> Only in a few sectors is globalisation a successful firm strategy ... For most manufacturers and all services, regionalisation is much more relevant than globalisation. (p. 18)

> **Key ideas** — Alan Rugman – the myth of globalisation
>
> It is widely accepted that multinationals drive globalisation. The top 500 multinationals dominate international business, accounting for over 90% of the world's FDI and nearly half its trade. But globalisation, as commonly understood, is a myth. Far from taking place in a single global market, business activity by most large multinationals takes place within any one of the world's three great trading blocs – North America, Europe, and Asia-Pacific.
>
> Of the world's 500 multinationals in 2001, 428 were in the USA, the EU, and Japan. Only [nine] were by my definition truly global. These took at least a fifth of their sales from each of the three regions, but less than half from any one region. Most – 320 out of 380 – were stay-at-home multinationals, deriving on average four-fifths of their sales from their home regions.
>
> Source: Rugman (2005), p. 6.

Concerns about globalisation

Supporters of more world trade cite the benefits which wider access to markets brings to both consumers and workers by encouraging innovation and investment. It gives many consumers a wide choice of goods from suppliers around the world, often more cheaply than those produced locally. Others are critical, believing that agreements reached in bodies such as the WTO serve the interests of multinational businesses and richer economies rather than indigenous local producers.

Case study: Starbucks – the case continues   www.starbucks.com

Activists in some countries criticise the company offering a global brand that tends to push out local companies and reduce the variety of shopping areas. Others question whether it treats coffee growers fairly. It has taken these criticisms seriously, and has for ten years been working with Conservation International to help farmers grow coffee in ways that are better for people and for the planet. The goal is that 100 per cent of coffee will be responsibly grown and ethically traded – at present about 75 per cent meets that standard. It also has a target that by 2015 all of the cups will be reusable or recyclable, and to contribute over one million community service hours each year. It expects all suppliers to comply with specified social responsibility standards covering worker health, safety, treatment, hours and pay, and environmental protection.

In 2012 it announced a plan to revitalise the European stores, led by Michelle Gass, president for the Europe, Middle East and Africa region. While its sales and profits continue to grow, the performance of the region was lagging behind the group. It planned to open 300 new outlets in the UK over the next five years (there were 760 in 2012) and to vary the offering to suit the different tastes in France, Greece and the UK. The company hoped this plan would help it improve performance in the area which Schultz acknowledged had been neglected:

From 2008 to 2010 my primary focus and that of the leadership was to strengthen and fix the US business. We unfortunately were not able at the same time to focus on this region. (Quoted in *Financial Times*, 2 April 2012, p. 22.)

In 2012 a UK Parliamentary Committee found that it paid very little tax in the UK, through arrangements described as 'legal but immoral'. Facing criticism from media and many customers, the company announced that it was reviewing its tax arrangements, and would now pay more UK tax.

It also announced that it was planning to open coffee shops in India, through a joint venture with the Indian company Tata Global Beverages. The company already had over 500 shops in China, believed to be the most profitable of the company's regions.

Sources: *Fortune*, 13 November 2006; *Financial Times*, 21 January 2012, 2 April 2012, 13 November 2012; 7 December 2012; company website.

Case questions 4.5

- List the management issues which this extract shows Starbucks faces.
- What hazards does it face in the new expansion plans?

Activity 4.7 Debating globalisation

Arrange a debate or discussion on these questions:

- Has globalisation increased people's power as consumers, or diminished their power as employees?
- Has it lifted millions out of poverty, or has it widened the gap between rich and poor?
- Has it widened consumer choice, or has it encouraged levels of industrialisation and consumption which make unsustainable demands on the earth's natural resources?
- Does globalisation heighten aesthetic awareness of different cultures, or does it expose people to a stream of superficial images?
- Does it enable more people to experience diversity, or does it lead to a bland homogenisation of local cultures into a global view?

All of these developments imply much greater patterns of contact between managers in different countries. Legislative changes and treaties remove some barriers to trade, but they do not solve the management problems of making those economic activities work efficiently. Above all, they bring many managers face to face with the need to manage cultural differences.

4.9 Integrating themes

Entrepreneurship

Entrepreneurial businesses, especially those in high-tech sectors such as software or bio-medicine, face an early decision on whether to focus on their home market or to expand overseas. Many (possibly most) international ventures fail, which makes them a risky move for a small company, since an overseas failure could wipe out their limited reserves.

Research by Coeurduroy *et al.* (2012) identified three factors in the success or failure of international ventures by small high tech firms. They studied 600 such firms in the UK and Germany over six years, to assess what they did to make a success of their international expansion. They found that survival rates were improved by:

- **High knowledge intensity**: firms whose products had a high research and development content, and who were able to learn fast as they met unexpected problems overseas did well. Small, young firms inevitably meet hazards in a new market – and need to be able to think and act quickly if they are to survive.
- **Close relations with specified customers**: high-tech products will be challenging to make and use, and overcoming early snags will be done most effectively if there are close relations between the supplier and their customer. Both benefit – the customer from close working with those who designed the product, and the designer from learning how the customer uses it.
- **Scale of international exposure**: the more a company has engaged in international ventures, the more likely it is that subsequent ones will succeed. While the first occasion will involve learning the first two factors, later ventures will be easier and less costly.

The authors suggest that underlying all these is an early decision by the entrepreneur to become an international business, and to devote resources to it. Without that commitment, they will lack the capacity to support these factors in success.

Sustainability

Effective action to combat climate change depends on political action – and given the global nature of the problem, that means that effective global policies must be in place. The core of the proposals put forward by Lord Stern (2009) is that global emissions of greenhouse gas must peak in the next 15 years, and then fall by at least 50 per cent, relative to 1990 levels, by 2050, when global emissions must on average be 2 tonnes per head.

Any set of policies to achieve this must be effective, efficient and equitable. The most difficult of these criteria to meet in this context is that of equity, principally between the developed (who emitted three-fifths of the stock of man-made greenhouse gases) and developing countries (who wish to develop their economies, which will mean more emissions). Persuading developing countries to accept binding limits even in 2020 is bound to be hard, given the gross inequity of the starting point.

While this is all very uncertain, the implication for business is that:

> both climate change, and ever tightening climate change policies by governments and international bodies, are realities. Managers should plan their long-term investments and their research and development priorities in this light. (Based on an article by Martin Wolf in a *Financial Times Supplement on Climate Change*, Part 3, 2 December 2008.)

Internationalisation

As business becomes increasingly international, do managers respond passively to aspects of the environment in the countries where they do business, or do they also try to shape it? The first view stresses how features of the political or other environments can constrain choice, especially in economies with a tradition of significant government involvement in business. It sees managers as having a passive role, reacting to pressures from their environment. An alternative view regards managers as proactive, influencing policies which are part of their context: the Management in practice feature reports a study which gives some empirical support for the proactive view.

> ### Management in practice — MNCs and environmental policy in China and Taiwan
>
> In a study of the interaction between companies and government institutions over environmental policy, Child and Tsai compared the experience of companies in China and Taiwan. They examined three multinational corporations (MNCs) in the chemicals sector, each with plants in China and Taiwan – which have different environmental policies. In examining how these policies affected companies, and how companies affected the policies, they found that:
>
> - MNCs took a broad view of the stakeholders to whom they paid attention, including suppliers, customers, local communities and especially non-governmental agencies (NGOs) who could affect public opinion.
> - Non-governmental organisations (NGOs) played a major role in mobilising public concerns.
> - MNCs engaged in proactive political action, often in conjunction with NGOs, to influence environmental policy.
>
> Source: based on Child and Tsai (2005).

Governance

Mallin (2013) notes that while Berle and Means' (1932) work on the implications of separating ownership from control in modern corporations influenced laws to protect shareholders, countries' legal systems mean they achieve this aim in different ways.

The US and the UK have legal systems which generally give good protection to shareholders, encouraging a diversified shareholder base. Other countries have different ownership systems – family firms, or a small number of large dominant shareholders, are more common in Continental Europe than in the UK. Banks often play a bigger role in financing companies, which they control by being members of the board. This implies that governance arrangements will fit the local institutional arrangements.

Mallin (2013) summarises the arrangements in many parts of the world, noting signs of convergence on some features, for example on the need for:

> more transparency and disclosure, accountability of the board, and the independence of at least a portion of the directors. (p. 253)

Summary

1 **Contrast the ways in which organisations conduct international business**
   - Offshoring, FDI, exporting, licensing, joint ventures, wholly owned subsidiaries.
   - Multinational (independent operations in many countries, run from centre); transnational (independent operations in many countries, decentralised); global (linked and interdependent operations in many countries, closely coordinated).

2 **Explain, with examples, how PESTEL factors affect the decisions of those managing internationally**

Managing Internationally   557

- This would involve gathering data and information about how one or more of the political, economic, socio-cultural, technological, environmental and legal factors had affected a company's policies and practices.

3 **Summarise at least one aspect of EU policy (or of an international trade agreement) which is of interest to you for your career**
   - The chapter outlined several EU policies and practices relevant to management, especially in the areas of freer trade and common industrial policies.

4 **Explain and illustrate the evidence on differences in national cultures, and evaluate the significance of Hofstede's research for managers working internationally**
   - Early work distinguished between low-context and high-context cultures. In the former, information is explicit and clear while in the latter it is more implicit, and can only be understood through shared experience, values and assumptions.
   - Hofstede distinguished between cultures in terms of power distance (acceptance of variations in power); uncertainty avoidance (willingness to tolerate ambiguity); individualism/collectivism (emphasis on individual or collective action); masculinity/femininity (preferences for assertive or modest behaviour); and long/short term orientation. Case question 4.4 encouraged you to identify how cultural differences could affect attitudes and behaviours towards some management practices.

5 **Compare and contrast the features of national management systems**
   - These shape the way people interpret generic activities of management:
   - US – individualistic, rational approach, contingent design of organisations;
   - Europe – collective, rational approach, pragmatic;
   - Japan – collective responsibility, secure employment, consensus building.

6 **Summarise the forces stimulating the growth of international business**
   - Yip proposes that these factors are market, economic, environmental and competitive.

7 **Show how ideas from the chapter add to your understanding of the integrating themes**
   - Research has identified management practices which support the survival of small high-tech firms wanting to expand internationally.
   - Reducing global emissions of greenhouse gases depends on regulations by governments and international bodies; while the shape of these is still uncertain, managers should plan their long-term investments in ways that anticipate these changes.
   - Managers are often active in influencing government policy and regulations in the countries in which they want to do business.
   - Governance arrangements vary between countries, reflecting the evolution of distinctive national systems.

Test your understanding

1 What factors are stimulating the growth in world trade?
2 Compare internationalisation and globalisation. Give a specific example of a company of each type about which you have obtained some information.
3 Identify three PESTEL factors which have affected Starbucks.
4 Outline the difference between a high- and a low-context culture and give an example of each from direct observation or discussion.
5 Explain accurately to another person Hofstede's five dimensions of national culture. Evaluate his conclusions on the basis of discussions with your colleagues in Activity 4.4.

6 Name two distinctive features of Japanese, European and US management systems respectively.
7 Compare the implications, if any, of globalisation for (a) national governments, (b) their citizens.
8 Summarise Yip's theory about the forces driving globalisation.
9 What is Rugman's contribution to perceptions about the spread of globalisation?
10 Summarise an idea from the chapter that adds to your understanding of the integrating themes.

Think critically

Think about the way managers in your company, or one with which you are familiar, deal with the international aspects of business. Review the material in the chapter, and make notes on these questions:

- What **assumptions** appear to guide the way people manage internationally? Do they assume that cultural factors are significant or insignificant?
- What aspects of the historical or current **context** of the company appear to influence your company's approach to international business? Do people see it as a threat or an opportunity, and why? Are there different views on how you should manage internationally?
- Can you compare your approach with that of other companies in which colleagues on your course work? Does this suggest any plausible **alternative** ways of managing internationally?
- What **limitations** can you see in the theories and evidence presented? For example, is Hofstede's analysis of different cultures threatened by the increasingly international outlook and interests of young people?

Read more

Chen, M. (2004), *Asian Management Systems*, Thomson, London.

Comparative review of the management systems in Japan, mainland China, overseas Chinese and Korean. These are compared with Western approaches to management.

Chung, M.L. and Bruton, G.D. (2008), 'FDI in China: What We Know and What We Need to Study Next', *Academy of Management Perspectives*, vol. 22, no. 4, pp. 30–44.

Excellent study of FDI in China, with many ideas that are also relevant to other countries.

Friedman, T. (2005), *The World is Flat: A Brief History of the Globalised World in the 21st Century*, Penguin/Allen Lane, London.

Best-selling account of the forces that are driving globalisation, and enabling greater collaboration between companies wherever they are. The same forces that assist company networks also assist terrorist networks.

Guthrie, D. (2006), *China and Globalisation: The Social, Economic and Political Transformation of Chinese Society*, Routledge, London.

An excellent review of China's transition towards a market economy, showing how the visible economic changes depend on supportive social, cultural and political changes.

Taras, V., Steel, P. and Kirkman, B.L. (2011), 'Three decades of research on national culture in the workplace: Do the differences still make a difference?', *Organisational Dynamics*, vol. 40, no. 3, pp. 189–98.

Clear overview of Hofstede's work, and of later studies developing the idea. It also traces carefully the implications for practice.

> ### Go online

These websites have appeared in the chapter:

www.starbucks.com
www.maersk.com
www.aggreko.com
www.wto.org
http://europa.eu
www.walmart.com
www.ford.com
www.VW.com

Visit two of the sites in the list, or others which interest you, and navigate to the pages dealing with recent news, press or investor relations.

- What signs are there of the international nature of the business, and what are the main issues in this area that the business appears to be facing?
- Compare and contrast the issues you identify on the two sites.
- What challenges may they imply for those working in, and managing, these organisations?

CHAPTER 3
ORGANISATION CULTURES AND CONTEXTS

Aim

To identify the cultures and contexts within which managers work, and to outline some analytical tools.

Objectives

By the end of your work on this chapter you should be able to outline the concepts below in your own terms and:

1. Compare the cultures of two organisational units, using Quinn's or Handy's typologies
2. Use Porter's Five Forces model to analyse an organisation's competitive environment
3. Collect evidence to make a comparative PESTEL analysis for two organisations
4. Compare environments in terms of their complexity and rate of change
5. Give examples of stakeholder expectations
6. Explain the meaning and purposes of corporate governance
7. Show how ideas from the chapter add to your understanding of the integrating themes

Key terms

This chapter introduces the following ideas:

internal environment (or context)   **task culture**
competitive environment (or context)   **person culture**
general environment (or context)   **Five Forces analysis**
external environment (or context)   **PESTEL analysis**
culture   **corporate governance**
power culture   **agency theory**
role culture

Each is a term defined within the text, as well as in the glossary at the end of the book.

Case study: Nokia www.nokia.com

In 2000 Nokia was the world's leading manufacturer of mobile phones and as late as 2008 it had 40 per cent of the world market. By 2012 that had fallen to 19 per cent: still a substantial share, but low enough for the company to be in such financial trouble that, without precedent, it paid no dividend to shareholders. Staff had been cut from 65,000 in 2011 to 45,000 by early 2013, and competitors were challenging its once dominant position. In lake 2013, Nokia sold its mobile phone business to Microsoft.

The Finnish company was founded in 1895 as a paper manufacturer, which grew into a conglomerate with wide interests in electronics, cable manufacture, rubber, chemicals, electricity and, by the 1960s, telephone equipment. In the early 1990s senior managers decided to focus on the new mobile phone industry.

Two factors favoured this move. First, the Finnish government had encouraged the growth of the telecommunication industry and Nokia was already supplying equipment to the national phone company. Second, the European Union (EU) adopted a single standard – the Global System for Mobile Telephony (GSM) – for Europe's second generation (digital) phones. Two-thirds of the world's mobile phone subscribers use this standard. Finland's links with its Nordic neighbours also helped, as people in these sparsely populated countries adopted mobile phones enthusiastically.

Nokia's management quickly realised that mobile phones had become a fashion accessory, as well as a communication device. By offering reliable devices with smart designs, different ring tones and coloured covers Nokia became the 'cool' mobile brand for fashion-conscious people.

While many competitors subcontract the manufacture of handsets, Nokia assembles them in its factories across the world, believing this gives a better understanding of the market and the manufacturing process. At its peak Nokia was buying about 80 billion components a year, and managing the complex global logistical task of moving these to assembly plants and the completed devices to customers.

Courtesy of Nokia

The company's leading position until 2008 owed much to Jorma Ollila, chief executive from 1992. He shaped the mobile phone industry by his vision of a mass market for voice communication while on the move. As he prepared to hand over to a new chief executive in 2006, he observed that the next challenge would be to enable users to access the internet, videos, music, games and emails through a new generation of 'smart' phones. This was prophetic, as Nokia was slow to respond to these new possibilities – even though its designers were already developing the software to do so.

Source: *The Economist*, 16 June 2001; *Financial Times*, 9 February 2012, 25 January 2013, 26 February 2013.

Case questions 3.1

- Visit Nokia's website, and read their most recent trading statement (under investor relations). What have been the main developments in the last year?
- How did the business environment favour the development of Nokia as a mobile phone maker?
- Which factors may have weakened the company in recent years?

3.1 Introduction

Nokia's performance depends on the ability of its managers to spot and interpret signals from consumers in the mobile phone market, and on ensuring the company responds more effectively than competitors. It also depends on identifying ideas emerging from its laboratories that have commercial potential – and ensuring these offer attractive features for consumers in the next generation of products. The early success of the company was helped by recognising that many users see a mobile as a fashion item, and by using its design skills to meet that need. Recent failures arose in part from a failure to spot consumer trends quickly enough, as well as by new competition from Apple – a new entrant to the industry.

All managers work within a context which both constrains and supports them. How well they understand, interpret and interact with that context affects their performance. Finkelstein (2003) (especially pp. 63–8) shows how Motorola, an early market leader in mobile communications, failed in the late 1990s, to see changes in consumer preferences (for digital rather than analogue devices). By the time they did, Nokia had a commanding lead. Years later, it was Nokia's turn to suffer when it failed to sense how quickly people would take to smartphones.

Figure 3.1 shows four environmental forces. The inner circle represents the organisation's **internal environment (or context)** – which is the manager's most immediate context. That includes its culture, which many regard as having a significant influence on managers.

The **internal environment (or context)** consists of those elements of the organisation or unit within which a manager works, such as it people, culture, structure and technology.

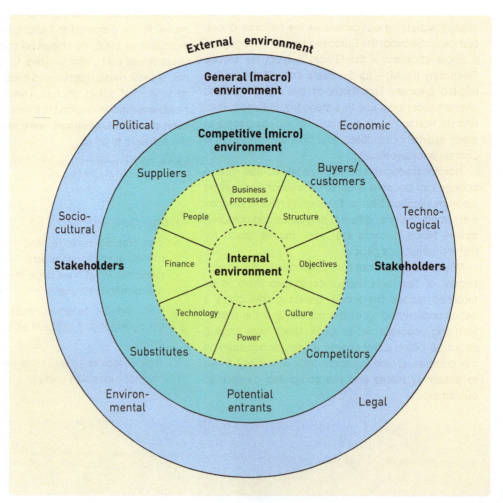

Figure 3.1 Environmental influences on the organisation

Beyond that is the **competitive environment (or context),** sometimes known as the microenvironment. This is the industry-specific environment of customers, suppliers, competitors and potential substitute products. The outer circle shows the **general environment (or context)**, sometimes known as the macro-environment – political, economic, social, technological, (natural) environmental and legal factors that affect all organisations.

Together these make up an organisation's **external environment (context)** – a constantly changing source of threats and opportunities: how well people cope with these affects performance (Roeder, 2011).

Forces in the external environment do not affect practice of their own accord. They become part of the agenda only when internal or external stakeholders act to place them on the management agenda. In terms of Figure 3.1, they are a fourth force. Managers (who are themselves stakeholders) balance conflicting interpretations of their context. They work within an internal context, and look outside for actual and potential changes that may affect the centre of Figure 3.1. The figure implies a constant interaction between an organisation's culture and its external environment.

Managers do not passively accept their external environment, but actively shape it by persuading governments and other agencies to act in their favour (known as 'lobbying'). Car makers and airlines almost routinely ask governments for subsidies, cheap loans or new regulations to help their businesses, while most industry bodies (such as the European Automobile Manufacturers Association – www.acea.be) lobby international bodies such as the European Commission – often employing professional lobbying business to support their case.

The next section presents ideas on organisational culture which is an immediate aspect of a manager's context. Beyond that managers need to interact intelligently with their competitive and general environments. The chapter contrasts stable and dynamic environments, outlines stakeholder expectations and introduces ideas on governance and control.

A **competitive environment (or context)** is the industry-specific environment comprising the organisation's customers, suppliers and competitors.

The **general environment (or context)** (sometimes known as the macro-environment) includes political, economic, social, technological, (natural) environmental and legal factors that affect all organisations.

The **external environment (or context)** consists of elements beyond the organisation – it combines the competitive and general environments.

Activity 3.1 Which elements of the business environment matter?

Write a few notes summarising aspects of the business environment of which you are aware. You may find it helpful to think of a manager you have worked with, or when you have been managing an activity.

- Identify two instances when they (or you) were discussing aspects of the wider context of the job – such as the culture of the organisation, or the world outside.
- How did this aspect of the context affect the job of managing?
- How did the way people dealt with the issue affect performance?

3.2 Cultures and their components

Developing cultures

Interest in organisation **culture** has grown as academics and managers have come to believe that it influences behaviour. Several claim that a strong and distinct culture helps to integrate individuals into the team or organisation, and so helps performance (Deal and Kennedy, 1982; Peters and Waterman, 1982). Deal and Kennedy (1982) refer to culture as 'the way we do things around here' and Hofstede (1991) sees it as the 'collective programming of the mind', distinguishing one group from another. Company mergers and acquisitions sometimes show that their different cultures affect aspects of performance, and that the process of integrating cultures may be disruptive (Teerikangas and Very, 2006).

Culture is a pattern of shared basic assumptions learnt by a group as it solved its problems of external adaptation and internal integration, which has worked well enough to be considered valid and, therefore, to be taught to new members as the correct way to perceive, think, and feel in relation to those problems (Schein, 2010, p. 18).

Someone entering a department or organisation for the first time can usually sense and observe the surface elements of the culture. Some buzz with life and activity, others seem asleep; some welcome and look after visitors, others seem inward looking; some work by the rules, while others are entrepreneurial and risk taking; some have regular social occasions while in others staff rarely meet except at work.

> **Management in practice**   **A culture of complaint in a bank**
>
> John Weeks (2004) spent six years working in a UK bank (believed to be NatWest, which the Royal Bank of Scotland acquired in 2000) as part of his doctoral research. He observed and recorded the bank's distinctive culture – which he described as one of 'complaint'.
>
> No one liked the culture – from the most senior managers to the most junior counter staff, people spent much of their time complaining about it. Weeks realised that this was a ritual, a form of solidarity amongst the staff: complaining about the culture *was* the culture. He noticed that most complaints were directed at other parts of the bank – not at the unit in which the complainer worked. He noted:
>
> **Local sub-cultures are sometimes described positively – usually to contrast them with the mainstream – but I never heard anyone [describe the bank's culture in positive terms]. It is described as too bureaucratic, too rules driven, not customer-focussed enough, not entrepreneurial enough, too inflexible, too prone to navel gazing, too centralised. (p. 53)**
>
> His detailed narrative shows, with many examples, how people in the bank made sense of their culture – using it to achieve their goals, while others did the same to them.
>
> Source: Weeks (2004).

Figure 3.2 illustrates how a distinctive culture develops: as people develop common values they use these to establish shared beliefs about how to behave towards each other and to outsiders. Positive outcomes reinforce their belief in the underlying values, which then become a stronger influence on how people should work and relate to each other: should people have job titles? How should they dress at work? Should meetings be confrontational or supportive?

A shared culture guides people on how they should contribute, and following these strengthens it.

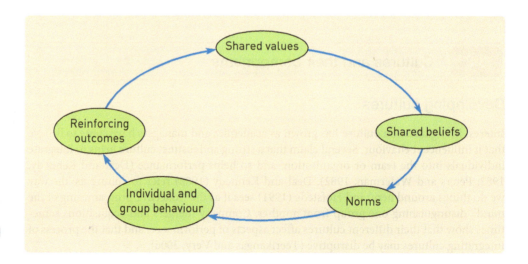

Figure 3.2 The stages of cultural formation

Components of cultures

Schein (2010) identifies three levels of a culture, 'level' referring to the degree to which the observer can see its components.

- **Artefacts** represent the visible level – elements such as the language or etiquette which someone coming into contact with a culture can observe:
  - architecture (open plan offices without doors or private space);
  - technology and equipment (Powerpoint presentations);
  - style (clothing, manner of address, emotional displays);
  - rituals and ceremonies (leaving events, awards ceremonies, away-days);
  - courses (to induct employees in the culture as well as the content).

  While it is easy to observe artefacts, outsiders will have trouble understanding what they mean to the group, or the beliefs and values they represent.

- **Beliefs and values** are the accumulated ideas that members hold about their work. As a group develops, members refine their ideas about 'what works here': how people make decisions, how teams work, how they solve problems. Practices that work become acceptable behaviours:
  - 'Quality pays.'
  - 'We should stick to our core business.'
  - 'Take personal responsibility.'
  - 'Work as a team.'
  - 'Challenge a proposal – whoever made it.'

  Some companies (Ikea is an example) codify and publish their beliefs and values, to help induct new members and to remind current staff. them. The extent to which employees internalise these beliefs probably depends on how closely they derive from shared underlying assumptions.

> **Key ideas**   **Values matter in management**
>
> The beliefs and values which shape an organisation's culture affect the practice and ultimately the reputation of their managers. The financial crisis which began in 2008 was in large part due to cultures in banks and other financial institutions which encouraged greed and self-interest above those of honesty and customer service. Companies who treat employees as self-interested opportunists who must be forced to do their job, tend to create employees who do just that. Conversely, managers who assume a reasonable degree of trust and cooperation create a system in which honest, cooperative people flourish. Prophecies are often self-fulfilling – so the prevailing values have a significant influence on how an organisation treats employees and customers, and for the reputation of those who work in it.

- **Basic underlying assumptions** are deeply held by members of the group as being the way to work together. As they act in accordance with their values and beliefs, those that work become embedded as basic underlying assumptions. When the group holds these strongly, members will act in accordance with them, and reject actions based on others:
  - 'We need to satisfy customers to survive as a business.'
  - 'Our business is to help people with X problem live better with X problem.'
  - 'People can make mistakes, as long as they learn from them.'
  - 'We employ highly motivated and competent adults.'
  - 'Financial markets worry about the short-term: we are here for the long-term.'

  Difficulties sometimes arise when people with assumptions developed in one group need to work with people from another. King *et al.* (2012) show how cultural differences between two healthcare professions prevented them from making good use of an information system which would save time and improve patient care. The groups viewed patient information in different ways, and would not accept information prepared by the other.

> **Management in practice**   Culture as an asset at Bosch   www.bosch.com
>
> Franz Fehrenbach was (in 2009) chief executive of Bosch, Germany's largest privately owned engineering group, and the world's largest supplier of car parts. He said:
>
> > The company culture, especially our high credibility, is one of our greatest assets. Our competitors cannot match us on that because it takes decades to build up.
>
> The cultural traditions include a rigid control on costs, an emphasis on team thinking, employees being responsibility for their errors, cautious financial policies, and long-term thinking. For example, to cope with the recession in 2009 Mr Fehrenbach explained that:
>
> > We have to cut costs in all areas. We will reduce spending in the ongoing business, but we will not cut back on research and development for important future projects.
>
> Source: Based on an article by Daniel Schaefer, *Financial Times*, 2 March 2009, p.16.

> **Activity 3.2**   Culture spotting
>
> - Identify as many components of culture (artefacts, beliefs and values, underlying assumptions) in an organisation or unit as you can.
> - What may the artefacts suggest about the deeper beliefs and values, or underlying assumptions?
> - Gather evidence (preferably by asking people) about how the culture affects behaviour, and whether they think it helps or hinders performance.
> - Analyse your results and decide which of the four types in the competing values framework most closely reflects that organisation's culture.

3.3 Types of culture

This section outlines three ways of describing and comparing cultures.

Competing values framework

The competing values model developed by Quinn *et al.* (2003) reflects inherent tensions between flexibility or control and between internal or external focus. Figure 3.3 (based on Figure 2.2) shows four cultural types.

Open systems

This represents a culture in which people recognise the significance of the external environment as a vital source of ideas, energy and resources. It also sees it as complex and turbulent, requiring entrepreneurial leadership and flexible, responsive behaviour. Key motivating factors are growth, stimulation, creativity and variety. Examples are start-up firms and new business units – organic, flexible operations.

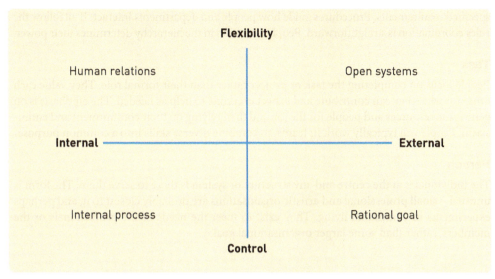

Figure 3.3 Types of organisational culture
Source: Based on Quinn et al. (2003).

Rational goal

Members see the organisation as a rational, efficiency-seeking unit. They define effectiveness in terms of economic goals that satisfy external requirements. Managers create structures to deal with the outside world and tend to be directive, goal-orientated and functional. Motivating factors include competition and achieving goals. Examples are large, established businesses – mechanistic.

Internal process

Members focus on internal matters with the goal of making the unit efficient, stable and controlled. Tasks are repetitive and methods stress specialisation, rules and procedures. Leaders tend to be cautious and spend time on technical issues. Motivating factors include security, stability and order. Examples include utilities and public authorities – suspicious of change.

Human relations

People emphasise the value of informal interpersonal relations rather than formal structures. They try to maintain the organisation and nurture its members, defining effectiveness in terms of their well-being and commitment. Leaders tend to be participative, considerate and supportive. Motivating factors include attachment, cohesiveness and membership. Examples include voluntary groups, professional service firms and some internal support functions.

Charles Handy's cultural types

Charles Handy (1993) distinguished four cultures – **power**, **role**, **task** and **person**.

Power

A dominant central figure holds power: others follow the centre's policy and interpret new situations in the way the leader would. Many entrepreneurial firms operate in this way, with few rules but with well-understood, implicit codes on how to behave and work. The firm relies on the individual rather than on seeking consensus through discussion.

Role

Typical characteristics of this culture are the job description or the procedure. Managers define what they expect in clear, detailed job descriptions. They select people for a job if they meet the

A **power culture** is one in which people's activities are strongly influenced by a dominant central figure.

A **role culture** is one in which people's activities are strongly influenced by clear and detailed job descriptions and other formal signals as to what is expected of them.

A **task culture** is one in which the focus of activity is towards completing a task or project using whatever means are appropriate.

A **person culture** is one in which activity is strongly influenced by the wishes of the individuals who are part of the organisation.

specified requirements. Procedures guide how people and departments interact. If all follow the rules coordination is straightforward. People's position in the hierarchy determines their power.

Task

People focus on completing the task or project rather than their formal role. They value each other for what they can contribute and expect everyone to help as needed. The emphasis is on getting the resources and people for the job and then relying on their commitment and enthusiasm. People will typically work in teams, to combine diverse skills into a common purpose.

Person

The individual is at the centre and any structure or system is there to serve them. The form is unusual – small professional and artistic organisations are probably closest to it, and perhaps experiments in communal living. They exist to meet the needs of the professionals or the members, rather than some larger organisational goal.

Activity 3.3 — Cultural examples

For each of Handy's four cultural types, identify an example from within this text that seems to correspond most closely to that form.

- What clues about the company have you used to decide that allocation?
- Why do you think that culture is suitable for that organisation?
- What evidence would you seek to decide if that culture was suitable?
- Compare the 'competing values' and Handy models: where are they similar, and where different?

Key ideas — Expressing and using cultures

A theme in studies of organisational culture is a move away from seeing it as an element which affects behaviour, to seeing it something that people use as part of other organisational processes. An example of this is a study by Kaplan (2011) of the way in which staff in a telecommunications equipment manufacturer used PowerPoint presentations as they engaged in a process to develop strategy. For Schein (2010), PowerPoint would be an example of a static cultural artefact representing a deeper cultural value – to use modern professional tools. From her empirical work in the company Kaplan found that using (or not) PowerPoint affected the strategy process. Staff who tried to express ideas without using PowerPoint received little attention, and Kaplan noted that some gave more attention to the quality of their PowerPoint show than to the quality of the ideas it contained. This affected the process of strategy formation, and reinforced the deeper cultural values represented by the PowerPoint artefact. The evidence in Table 3.1 is an example of a similar process in which members of a firm discuss their perception of the cultures within the business, and in so doing strengthen its fragmentary, rather than unitary, nature.

Source: Kaplan (2011).

Multiple cultures

Martin (2002) proposed that organisations have not one, but several cultures and that observers typically take one of three perspectives:

- **Integration** – a focus on identifying consistencies in the data, and using those common patterns to explain events.

- **Differentiation** – a focus on conflict, identifying different and possibly conflicting views of members towards events.
- **Fragmentation** – a focus on the fluid nature of organisations, and on the interplay and change of views about events.

Ogbonna and Harris (1998, 2002) provided empirical support for this view, based on interviews with staff in a retail company. They found that a person's position in the hierarchy determined their perspective on the culture (see Table 3.1). As consensus on the culture was unlikely, the authors advised managers to recognise the existence of sub-cultures, and only seek to reconcile those differences that were essential to policy. They also observed that culture remains a highly subjective idea, largely in the eye of the beholder

> and is radically different according to an individual's position in the hierarchy. (p. 45)

Culture and performance

Peters and Waterman (1982) believed that an organisation's culture affected performance, and implied that managers should try to change their culture towards a more productive one. Klein (2011) takes a similar approach by tracing the relation between culture and performance in three successful companies. Others are more sceptical, questioning whether, even if a suitable culture has a positive effect, managers can consciously change it. Kotter and Heskett (1992) studied 207 companies to assess the link between culture and economic performance. Although they were positively correlated, the relationship was weaker than advocates of culture as a factor in performance had predicted. Some observers believed Nokia's team culture helped it to grow, but is that case still strong?

Thompson and McHugh (2002), while critical of much writing on the topic, observe the potential benefits which a suitable culture can bring:

> Creating a culture resonant with the overall goals is relevant to any organisation, whether it be a trade union, voluntary group or producer co-operative. Indeed, it is more important in such consensual groupings. Co-operatives, for example, can degenerate organisationally because they fail to develop adequate mechanisms for transmitting the original ideals from founders to new members and sustaining them through shared experiences. (pp. 208–9)

Table 3.1 Hierarchical position and cultural perspectives

Position in hierarchy	Cultural perspective	Description	Example
Head office managers	Integration	Cultural values should be shared across the organisation. Unified culture both desirable and attainable	'If we can get every ... part of the company doing what they should be doing, we'll beat everybody.'
Store managers	Differentiation	Reconciling conflicting views of head office and shop floor. See cultural pluralism as inevitable	'People up at head office are all pushing us in different directions. Jill in Marketing wants customer focus, June in Finance wants lower costs.'
Store employees	Fragmented	Confused by contradictory nature of the espoused values. See organisation as complex and unpredictable	'One minute it's this, the next it's that. You can't keep up with the flavour of the month.'

Source: Based on Ogbonna and Harris (1998).

Case study

Nokia – the case continues www.nokia.com

One factor in Nokia's success over many years was believed to have been a culture which encouraged co-operation within teams, and across internal and external boundaries. Jorma Ollila, CEO until 2006, believed that Nokia's innovative capacity came from multi-functional teams working together to bring new insights to products and services. Staff work in teams which may remain constant for many years – but sometimes combine with others to work on a common task.

Informal mentoring begins when someone starts a new job: their manager lists at least 15 people in the organisation the employee should meet, and explains why they should establish a working relationship with them. The gift of time – in the form of hours spent on coaching and building networks – is at the centre of the collaborative culture. This helps them to build ties with many parts of the company – some of which continue during later work.

Another perspective on the culture was that it had become very bureaucratic, and many committees, boards and cross-functional meetings delayed decisions. Too many things were coming through headquarters: one local manager had emailed the CEO:

Look, I'm right here in the region. I can make this simple little decision, [but] I'm waiting for someone who is ten timezones away and has three bosses of their own. (From an article by Andrew Hill, *Financial Times*, 14 April 2011, p. 16.)

Nevertheless, one of the many successes of these teams was to see that mobile devices could carry data of all kinds. The company's engineers were leaders of early smartphone technology (and claim that Apple used some of their ideas in the iPhone) and Nokia has many valuable patents to prove it. Despite a leading position in 2007, and with the ingredients for further success at its fingertips, Nokia failed to create a device as sleek and user friendly as the iPhone, which Apple launched in 2007. Consumers liked the iPhone, and by 2011 Nokia was losing sales not only to Apple but also to Samsung devices using the Android operating system.

Sources: Grattan and Erickson (2007); Doz and Kosonen (2008); *Financial Times*, 14 April 2011, 15 June 2011, 3 May 2012, 15 June 2012; company website.

Case questions 3.2

- Which of the cultural types identified by Quinn *et al.* (2003) appear to exist within Nokia's handset business?

As managers work within an organisational culture, they also work within an external context – whose members will have expectations of the organisation. They need some tools with which to analyse that external world.

3.4 The competitive environment – Porter's Five Forces

Managers are most directly affected by forces in their immediate competitive environment. According to Porter (1980a, 1985) the ability of a firm to earn an acceptable return depends on Five Forces – the ability of new competitors to enter the industry, the threat of substitute products, the bargaining power of buyers, the bargaining power of suppliers and the rivalry amongst existing competitors. Figure 3.4 shows Porter's **Five Forces analysis**.

Five Forces analysis is a technique for identifying and listing those aspects of the Five Forces most relevant to the profitability of an organisation at that time.

Porter believes that the *collective* strength of the Five Forces determines industry profitability, through their effects on prices, costs and investment requirements. Buyer power influences the prices a firm can charge, as does the threat of substitutes. The bargaining power of suppliers determines the cost of raw materials and other inputs. The greater the collective strength of the forces, the less profitable the industry: the weaker they are, the more profitable.

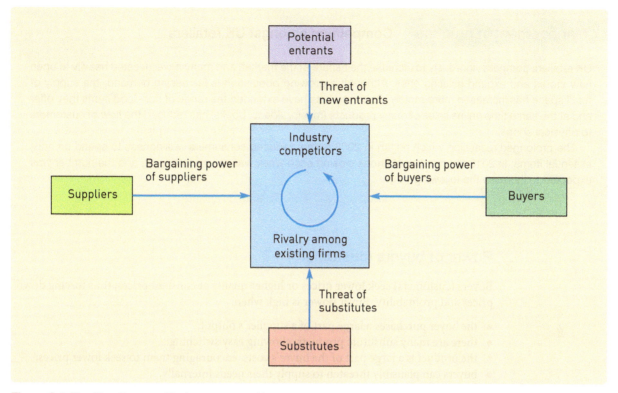

Figure 3.4 The Five Forces of industry competition

Source: Competitive Strategy: Techniques for Analyzing Industries and Competitors, Free Press, New York (Porter, M.E. 1980) p. 5, Copyright © 1980, 1998 by The Free Press, all rights reserved, reprinted with the permission of Simon and Schuster Publishing Group from the Free Press edition.

Threat of new entrants

Factors which affect how easily new entrants can enter an industry include:

- the need for economies of scale (to compete on cost), which are difficult to achieve quickly;
- the amount of capital investment required;
- available distribution channels;
- subsidies and regulations which benefit existing firms;
- need for tangible and intangible resources which existing firms control; and
- how loyal customers feel about existing firms.

Developments in technology have made it easier for companies successful in one industry to enter others: Apple and Samsung have both moved from their original industries (computer manufacturing and electronic components respectively) to enter the mobile phone industry.

Intensity of rivalry amongst competitors

Strong competitive rivalry lowers profitability, and occurs when:

- there are many firms in an industry;
- there is slow market growth, so companies fight for market share;
- fixed costs are high, so firms use capacity and overproduce;
- exit costs are high; specialised assets (hard to sell) or management loyalty (in old family firms) deter firms from leaving the industry, which prolongs excess capacity and low profitability;
- products are similar, so customers can easily switch to other suppliers.

The airline, print media and food retailing are examples of industries with intense competitive rivalry – and low profitability.

> **Management in practice** — Competition amongst UK retailers
>
> UK retailers compete vigorously to increase their share of the market, and many have invested heavily to open new stores and expand existing ones. Although a growing population is increasing demand, the supply of retail space has increased more rapidly. Supermarkets have extended the range of non-food items they offer and at the same time online sales of many products (music, videos, books) has reduced the flow of customers to physical shops.
>
> The prolonged recession which began in 2008 further reduced consumers' willingness to spend on non-essential items. In 2013 the number of shops closing each week was at a record level, and the number was expected to increase the following year.

Power of buyers (customers)

Buyers (customers) seek lower prices or higher quality at constant prices, thus forcing down prices and profitability. Buyer power is high when:

- the buyer purchases a large part of a supplier's output;
- there are many substitute products, allowing easy switching;
- the product is a large part of the buyer's costs, encouraging them to seek lower prices;
- buyers can plausibly threaten to supply their needs internally.

> **Management in practice** — Walmart's power as a buyer   www.walmart.com
>
> Walmart (which owns Asda in the UK) is the world's largest company, being three times the size of the second largest retailer, the French company Carrefour. Growth has enabled it to become the largest purchaser in America, controlling much of the business done by almost every major consumer-products company. It accounts for 30 per cent of hair care products sold, 26 per cent of toothpaste, 20 per cent of pet food and 20 per cent of all sales of CDs, videos and DVDs. This gives it great power over companies in these industries, since their dependence on Walmart reduces their bargaining power.
>
> Source: *Business Week*, 6 October 2003, pp. 48–53, and other sources.

Bargaining power of suppliers

Conditions that increase the bargaining power of suppliers are the opposite of those applying to buyers. The power of suppliers relative to customers is high when:

- there are few suppliers;
- the product is distinctive, so that customers are reluctant to switch;
- the cost of switching is high (e.g. if a company has invested in a supplier's software);
- the supplier can plausibly threaten to extend their business to compete with the customer;
- the customer is a small or irregular purchaser.

Aircraft manufacture (dominated by Boeing and Airbus), pharmaceutical companies with medicines protected (temporarily) by patents, or computer operating systems (Microsoft) are examples of suppliers with high bargaining power.

Threat of substitutes

Substitutes are products in other industries that can perform the same function – for example, using cans instead of bottles – and close substitutes constrain the ability of firms to raise prices. This threat is high when:

- technological developments reduce the advantages of existing providers or open the way to new ones;
- buyers are willing to change their habits; and
- existing firms have no legal protection for their position.

Physical retailers and travel agents have lost market share to substitutes – online suppliers – as have print media.

Analysing the forces in the competitive environment is a useful way for companies to assess their strengths and weaknesses, and as part of their planning when considering which new markets to enter – the Virgin case illustrates this (Part 3 Case). They can consider how to improve their position by, for example, building barriers to entry: the speed and quality of Google's search responses is a high barrier for a potential competitor to overcome.

Activity 3.4 Critical reflection on the Five Forces

Conduct a Five Forces analysis for an organisation with which you are familiar. Discuss with a manager of the organisation how useful he or she finds the technique.

- Evaluate whether it captures the main competitive variables in his or her industry.
- Review the analysis you did for Nokia, and revise it to take account of the Five Forces model.

3.5 The general environment – PESTEL

Forces in the wider world also shape management policies, and a **PESTEL analysis** (short for political, economic, socio-cultural, technological, environmental and legal) helps to identify these – which Figure 3.5 summarises. When these forces combine their effect is more pronounced – pharmaceutical companies face problems arising from slower progress in transferring scientific knowledge into commercial products, regulators who require more costly trials, companies offering cheap alternatives to patented drugs, and governments trying to reduce the costs of healthcare.

PESTEL analysis is a technique for identifying and listing the political, economic, social, technological, environmental and legal factors in the general environment most relevant to an organisation.

Political factors

Political systems shape what managers can and cannot do. Most governments regulate industries such as power supply, telecommunications, postal services and transport by specifying, amongst other things, who can offer services, the conditions they must meet, and what they can charge. These influence managers' investment decisions.

When the UK and most European governments altered the law on financial services, non-financial companies like Virgin and Sainsbury's began to offer banking services. Deregulating air transport stimulated the growth of low-cost airlines, especially in the US (e.g. Southwest Airlines), Europe (easyJet), Australia (Virgin Blue) and parts of Asia (Air Asia). The European Commission is developing regulations to manage the environmentally friendly disposal of the millions of personal computers and mobile phones that consumers scrap each year.

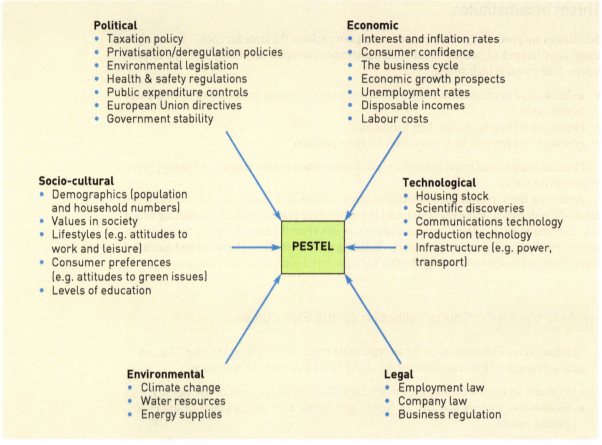

Figure 3.5 Identifying environmental influences – PESTEL analysis

Managers aim to influence these political decisions by employing professional lobbyists, especially at international institutions. The European Commission relies on ideas from interested parties to inform its decisions, and lobbying firms provide this. They focus on those people who have decision-making power, often members of the European Parliament. Hillman et al. (2004) trace the forms of political influence which companies exercise to support their position.

Economic factors

Economic factors such as wage levels, inflation and interest rates affect an organisation's income and costs. Ikea reported increased sales in 2012 since, as people were short of money during the recession, more of them were choosing to shop at the Swedish company's large out-of-town stores because of their low prices. Other companies doing well in the recession were those employing relatively unskilled staff in service occupations, where wage costs were increasing little if at all.

The state of the economy is also major influence on capital investment decisions. Managers planning capital investments follow economic forecasts: if these suggest slower growth, they may postpone the project. Many people in India are becoming more prosperous, encouraging Tata (www.Tata.com), the Indian conglomerate, to invest in launching a low-cost car, the Nano.

Socio-cultural factors

Demographic change affects most organisations, apart from those most clearly affected by the ageing population – healthcare and pharmaceuticals businesses. A growing number of single people affects the design of housing, holidays and life assurance. Demographic change affects an organisation's publicity to ensure, for example, that advertising acknowledges racial diversity. Leading banks develop investment and saving schemes that comply with *sharia* law, to attract devout Muslims as customers.

> **Management in practice** — Changing tastes challenge pubs
>
> Across Europe people are drinking more alcohol at home and less in pubs. The trend is particularly marked in Britain, where about 40 pubs close each week. They are gradually being usurped as the biggest sellers of beer in the UK, with supermarkets supplying most ale and lager. Many pub managers have adapted to this change by selling more food, some of whom have become gastro-pubs – offering high quality food in the simple 'public house' environment. A manager at a company with several gastro-pubs said:
>
> > Our pubs are doing really well and we want to raise our exposure to this market. The new pubs are in good areas such as west London where people are going to eat out two or three times a week, and want a relaxed place where they can meet their friends without [having to spend too much].
>
> Source: *Financial Times*, 26 August 2008, and other sources.

Changes in consumer habits open new business opportunities. As people buy more goods online, parcel delivery services experience growing demand: in 2012 ParcelForce (part of Royal Mail Group) announced it was recruiting more staff to take advantage of this growth.

> **Key ideas** — Grown Up Digital
>
> In his latest book (subtitled *How the Net Generation is Shaping your World*) Don Tapscott proposes that senior managers need to understand what he calls the 'net generation' – people born between 1977 and 1997 – sometimes called 'generation Y'. His research team interviewed thousands of 16-to-19 year olds in 12 countries, as well as doing comparative interviews with older people. He notes that the net generation grew up using a wider range of media than its parents: they typically spend hours on their computer - while also talking on the phone, listening to music, doing homework and reading. Technology is shaping their minds to access information in a different way. Rather than absorb information sequentially from a limited number of sources, they are more likely to 'play' with information by clicking, cutting, pasting and linking to interesting material.
>
> Tapscott suggests that this challenges established educational methods, and also media companies whose established products may not match the way young people expect to interact with information.
>
> Source: Tapscott (2009).

Technological factors

Companies pay close attention to the physical infrastructure - such as the adequacy of power supplies and transport systems. Even more, they monitor advances in information technology, which are dramatically changing the business environment of many companies. Computers traditionally handled data, while other systems handled voice (telephones) and pictures (film and video). Digitisation – the packaging of data, images and sounds into a single format – has profound implications for many industries – see Table 3.2.

Bernoff and Li (2008) show how social networking (Facebook) and user-generated content sites (YouTube) change the technological context – to which companies respond.

Table 3.2 Examples of digital technologies affecting established businesses

Technology	Application	Businesses affected
Digital Versatile Discs (DVDs)	Store sound and visual images	Sales of stereophonic sound systems decline sharply
iPOD, MP3 and smartphones	Digital downloads of music and films	Threat to retailers like HMV - almost went out of business in 2013
Broadband services delivering online content	Enables readers and advertisers to use online media rather than print or television	Circulation and advertising revenue of newspapers decline - some move online
Voice over Internet Protocol (VoIP)	Enables telephone calls over the internet at very low cost	Growth of new providers like Skype
Digital photography	Enables people to store pictures electronically and order prints online	Photographic retailers such as Jessops go out of business

Case study: Nokia – the case continues   www.nokia.com

The iPhone rapidly attracted millions of users to a device which had all the features of design and quality which people associated with Apple. It quickly brought out improved models, severely threatening Nokia's position: although at first smartphones were a small proportion of handset sales, they sold for higher prices than basic models and were very profitable. Demand grew much more rapidly then expected, so Nokia was now weak in a growing market segment – its share of the total world smartphone market fell from 18 per cent in 2011 to 9 per cent in 2012.

The convergence of mobile and computing technologies which enabled smartphone developments attracted other new entrants. Some, like Samsung, adopted Google's Android software to develop devices.

Nokia also faced competition in the market for basic handsets. It had had a high share of the market for these in emerging economies, but local companies were launching competitive models at lower prices.

By 2010 it was clear that Nokia was in trouble, and shareholders demanded that Nokia's board of directors should confront the crisis. They dismissed the then Chief Executive (who had taken over from Jorme Ollila in 2006), and replaced him with Steve Elop, who had worked for Microsoft. He quickly acknowledged the difficulties, writing to staff in March 2011:

> We fell behind, we missed big trends, and we lost time. We now find ourselves years behind ... Nokia, our platform is burning.

He also announced an alliance with Microsoft to develop a new range of smartphones using the Windows Phone 8 operating system. Microsoft's mobile devices had not been successful, and the company saw the alliance as a solution. Nokia had neglected to develop its own Symbian operating system sufficiently, even though designing both software and hardware improved user experience (as Apple had shown). The crisis led the company to abandon this asset in favour of an alliance with Microsoft.

This led to the launch in 2012 of the Lumia range, to compete with Apple and Samsung. Observers noted that the company had delivered this within eight months of the deal with Microsoft – a big improvement on the eighteen months Nokia usually took to launch a product. Under Mr Elop, it was learning to move quickly.

Later in 2012 Samsung overtook Nokia as the world's leading mobile phone maker.

Sources: *Financial Times*, 27 October 2011, 3 May 2012, 15 June 2012, 26 February 2011; company website.

Case questions 3.3

- Use Porter's Five Forces model to outline Nokia's competitive (micro) environment.
- Which PESTEL factors are most affecting the macro environment of the industry? Are they likely to be positive or negative for Nokia?

Environmental factors

The natural resources available in an economy – including minerals, agricultural land and the prevailing climate – affect the kind of businesses that managers create. Many senior managers know that climate change has major implications for their organisations, and are working out how best to respond. Some businesses will face serious risks from droughts, floods, storms and heat waves – less rainfall in some places, more in others. For some this represents a threat – insurance companies, house builders and water companies are only the most visible examples. For others sustainability brings opportunities – alternative energy suppliers, emission control businesses and waste management companies are all experiencing rising demand for their products and services.

Management in practice   An advocate for sustainability at Unilever
www.unilever.com

Paul Polman became chief executive of Unilever in 2009 and is a strong advocate of the principle of sustainability in business.

> Our ambitions are to double our business, but to do that while reducing our environmental impact and footprint. We say this publicly and it causes some discomfort ... But you see, you cannot go on in this world the way we're doing.
>
> But the road to well-being doesn't go via reduced consumption. It has to be done via more responsible consumption ... So that's why we're taking such a stand on moving the world to sustainable palm oil. That's why we go to natural refrigerants in our ice-cream cabinets. That's why we work with small farmers, to be sure that people who don't have sufficient nutrition right now have a chance to have a better life. Because at the end of the day, I think companies that take that approach have a right to exist.

Source: *Financial Times*, 5 April 2010.

Legal factors

Competent governments assert their authority over the territory, creating a stable legal framework embodying the rule of law, commercial contracts and property rights (including intellectual property covering patents and inventions). Without these tools, organisations find it difficult and expensive to operate, which led the UK parliament to pass the Joint Stock Companies Act in 1862. Previously investors were personally liable for the whole of a company's debts if it failed. The Act limited their liability to the value of the shares they held in the company – they could lose their investment, but not the rest of their wealth. This stimulated company formation and other countries soon passed similar legislation, paving the way for the countless 'limited liability' companies that exist today (Micklethwait and Wooldridge, 2003).

The PESTEL analysis is just as relevant to public and voluntary sector organisations. Many public service organisations do things that the market does not, so a PESTEL analysis can identify emerging issues that need attention. An example is the age structure: a country with an ageing population has to finance changes in community care services, social services and hospitals. Public organisations are often unable to expand their operations to meet identified needs, but can use the information to lobby for funds or to make the case for cutting other services.

The PESTEL framework is a useful starting point for analysis if managers use it to identify factors that are relevant to their business, and how they are changing.

> **Activity 3.5**   **Critical reflection on a PESTEL analysis**
>
> Conduct a PESTEL analysis for your organisation, or one with which you are familiar.
>
> - Which of the external forces you have identified has most implications for the business?
> - Evaluate the extent to which the organisation's policy has taken account of these forces.
> - Compare your analysis with that which you did for Nokia, and present a summary of similarities and differences in the forces affecting the companies.

3.6 Environmental complexity and dynamism

Perceptions of environments

The axes in Figure 3.6 show two variables (Duncan, 1972) which affect how people see their environment – the degree of complexity and the degree of dynamism. Complexity refers to the number and similarity of factors which people take into consideration when making a decision – the more of these, and the more different they are, the more complex the situation. Dynamism refers to the degree to which these factors remain the same or change.

To consider just the most contrasting cells in Figure 3.6, those who perceive themselves to be in a *simple-stable* environment will experience stability. Competitors offer similar products, newcomers rarely enter the market and there are few technological breakthroughs. Examples could include routine legal work such as house sales and wills, or the work of local tradesmen like joiners and builders. The information they need for a decision is likely to be available, so they can assess likely outcomes quickly and accurately, using the past to predict the future with reasonable confidence. Some aspects of health and education, where demand is driven largely by demographic change, may also fit this pattern: the capacity needed in primary and secondary schools is easy to predict several years ahead.

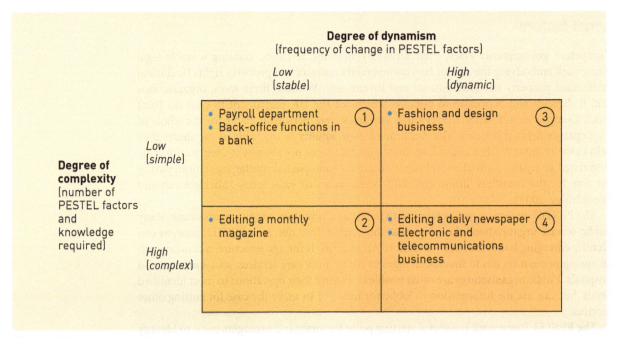

Figure 3.6 Types of environment

Organisation Cultures and Contexts 579

> **Key ideas** — Don Sull – active waiting in unpredictable markets
>
> Donald Sull (2005) has studied more than 20 pairs of comparable companies in unpredictable industries such as airlines, telecommunications and software development. By comparing similar companies he was able to show how they responded differently to unforeseen threats and opportunities. Successful companies regularly responded more effectively to unexpected shifts in regulation, technology, competitive or macro-environments. They did this by what he termed 'actively waiting', using techniques which included:
>
> - keeping priorities clear to avoid dissipating energy and resources;
> - conducting reconnaissance to identify gaps in the market;
> - keeping a reserve of cash to fund major opportunities when they emerge;
> - using lulls to push through operational improvements;
> - declaring that an opportunity is the company's main effort to seize it faster than rivals.
>
> Source: Based on Sull (2005).

At the other extreme, those working in complex-dynamic environments face great uncertainty. They have to monitor many diverse and changing factors. Companies in the mobile phone or entertainment industries are like this. Multinationals like Shell and BP experience great complexity, operating across diverse political, legal and cultural systems. Eric Schmidt (until 2012 CEO of Google) has said that in many high tech industries:

> the environment is changing so fast that it requires improvisation in terms of strategy, products and even day-to-day operations. Just when you think you understand the technology landscape, you see a major disruption.

> **Activity 3.6** — Critical reflection on type of environment
>
> Use Figure 3.6 to analyse the environment in which your unit of the organisation works. Then try to do the same analysis for one or two other units of the organisation.
>
> - Compare the nature of these environments.
> - What are the implications of that for managing these departments, and the organisation?
>
> Managers who work in dynamic and complex situations face great uncertainty historical analysis is unlikely to be a useful guide to the future – see Don Sull in Key ideas above.

> **Case question 3.4**
>
> - How would you classify the environment in which Nokia operates? Which factors contributed to your answer?

3.7 Stakeholders and corporate governance

Stakeholders

Stakeholders are groups of constituents (individuals, groups or other organisations) with a legitimate claim on an organisation (Freeman, 1984). This legitimacy arises because they

Table 3.3 Contributions and expectations of stakeholders

Stakeholders	Contributions	Expectations
Shareholders	Capital	Adequate dividend payments and/or rising share value
Creditors	Loans	Timely repayment
Managers	Time and skill	Fair income and adequate working conditions
Employees	Time and skill	Fair income and adequate working conditions
Customers	Revenues from sale of goods	Value for money
Suppliers	Inputs of materials and other resources	Fair prices and dependable buyers
Local communities	Sites, local infrastructure, perhaps tax incentives	No damage to quality of life
General public	National infrastructure	No damage to quality of life and obey law

Source: Based on Hill and Jones (1992, p.133).

have contributed resources and expect something in return. Hill and Jones (1992) set out these mutual obligations for an illustrative set of stakeholders, as shown in Table 3.3.

Each stakeholder is part of a nexus of implicit and explicit contracts (of contributions and rewards) which make up the organisation. However, as a group, managers are unique in this respect because of their position at the centre of the nexus of contracts. Managers are the only group of stakeholders who enter into a contractual relationship with all other stakeholders. Managers are also the only group of stakeholders with *direct* control over the decision-making apparatus of the firm (Hill and Jones, 1992, p. 134).

Since stakeholders provide the (diverse) resources, managers allocate the resources available in the hope of meeting expectations – which inevitably means some compromise when they conflict. Nutt (2002) shows the dangers: he studied 400 strategic decisions, and found that half of them 'failed' – in the sense that they were not implemented or produced poor results – largely because managers failed to attend to stakeholders.

Allocating resources to meet the interests of one stakeholder will often mean a loss to another. A topical example is the conflict between managers and shareholders over executive rewards, especially when business performance has been poor. One way to resolve such conflicts is through corporate governance.

Case study Nokia – the case continues   www.nokia.com

Nokia has moved much of the work to manufacture mobile phones from Finland to low-cost locations, mainly in Asia. This also reflects the fact that much of the company's revenue comes from cost-conscious emerging markets, which are developing their own sources of supply.

This is leading the Finns to reassess their high dependence on the industry. An economist at the Bank of Finland:

Nokia's profits, and the tax revenues they have generated for Finland, have exceeded our wildest dreams in the past 10 years. But it is disappointing that the production has not provided the highly paid, large-scale source of employment we hoped for.

By 2012 it had also slipped to become only the third most valuable company in Finland, as the share price continued to decline. The company had been worth 110 billion Euros at the end of 2007, but was now valued at only 11.4 billion Euros. As it became clear in 2011 that the company was losing ground, a Finnish newspaper wrote:

> For the first time, the modern Finnish economy now lacks a credible locomotive. Finland needs an economic saviour.

At its peak Nokia accounted for 4 per cent of Finnish GDP and 21 per cent of corporation tax revenues. Cuttings staff at its factories had a devastating effect on local communities.

All handset makers depend on software providers to develop attractive applications which the phones will run, and on network operators to sell the devices. Apple has been more successful at attracting developers to design apps than Nokia, partly because it has a smaller range of devices. As Nokia cut prices to increase demand, this cut the income of the network operators, who asked for better terms.

Source: *Financial Times*, 13 April 2012.

Case questions 3.5
- Who are the stakeholders in Nokia?
- What are their interests in the success of the company?
- How can management ensure it maintains the support of the most important stakeholders?

Corporate governance

Scandals and failures in prominent organisations lead people to question the adequacy of their systems of **corporate governance**. Berle and Means (1932) first raised the issue when they described the dilemma facing owners who become separated from the managers they appoint to run the business. The shareholders (principals) have financed, and own, the business, but delegate the work of running it to managers (agents). The principals then face the risk that managers may not act in their (the principals) best interests: they may take excessive investment risks, or withhold information so that the state of the business appears to be better than it is. The principal is then at a disadvantage to the agent (the manager), who may use this to personal advantage. Their observations led to what is now termed **agency theory**, which seeks to explain what happens when one party (the principal) delegates work to another party (the agent). Failures at major financial institutions, caused in part by lending money to risky borrowers in the hope of high returns, show that the separation of ownership from management, of principal from agent, is as relevant as ever.

Corporate governance refers to the rules and processes intended to control those responsible for managing an organisation.

Agency theory seeks to explain what happens when one party (the principal) delegates work to another party (the agent).

Management in practice — The interests of managers and shareholders

While senior managers often claim to be trying to align their interests with those of shareholders, the two often conflict. Mergers often appear to benefit senior managers and their professional advisers rather than shareholders. Acquiring companies often pay too much for the target, but executives inside the enlarged company receive higher pay. Professional advisers (investment bankers) make money on both the merger and the break-up.

Using company money to buy the company's shares in the market uses money that can't be spent on dividends. From the vantage point of many CEOs, paying dividends is about the last thing they would want to do with corporate earnings. In theory, a CEO is carrying out shareholder wishes. In practice, as the spate of recent scandals has shown, the interests of chief executives and their shareholders can widely diverge.

Source: Based on extracts from an article by Robert Kuttner, *Business Week*, 9 September 2002.

Widening recognition that managers have responsibilities not only to shareholders but to a wider group of stakeholders means that corporate governance now usually refers to arrangements designed to make senior managers formally accountable for their actions.

Similar issues arise in the public sector, where elected members are nominally in charge of local authorities, health boards and other agencies – but who appoint professional managers to run the organisation on behalf of the citizens. Elected members face the risk that the people they appoint act in their personal interests, rather than the electors'. Hartley *et al.* (2008) write:

> A new awareness of the social, economic and cultural contribution of government, public organisations and public services has resulted in a significant period of reform and experimentation. At the heart of these initiatives is the idea that improvements to the way public services can be governed, managed and delivered will produce improved outcomes for citizens. (p. 3)

Stakeholder theory is the term used for ideas trying to explain the evolving relationship between an organisation and its stakeholders. Governance systems are based on the principle that those managing an organisation are accountable for their actions, and create mechanisms to do that.

Mechanisms of corporate governance

Mallin (2013, p. 8) suggests that to provide adequate oversight of managers, governance systems should have:

- an adequate system of internal controls which safeguards assets;
- mechanisms to prevent any one person having too much influence;
- processes to manage relationships between managers, directors, shareholders and other stakeholders;
- aim to balance the interests of shareholders and other stakeholders; and
- aim to encourage transparency and accountability, which investors and many external stakeholders expect.

The book examines governance as one of the integrating themes at the end of each chapter.

3.8 Integrating themes

Entrepreneurship

Barringer and Ireland (2010) stress the significance of opportunity recognition – the process of perceiving the possibility of a new business or a new product. They identify some of the characteristics shared by those who excel at recognising opportunities which others miss.

- **Prior experience.** The authors cite studies showing the significance of prior experience in an industry to opportunity recognition. One study of 500 entrepreneurs found that almost half got their new business idea while working for companies in the same industry – this enables them to spot unsolved problems that represent opportunities, and to build a network of advice and information.
- **Cognitive factors.** Some believe that entrepreneurs have a sixth sense which allows them notice things without engaging in deliberate search. Entrepreneurial alertness is a learnt skill, and people who know an industry are more alert to opportunities and more able to assess a market.
- **Social networks.** People who build a substantial network of social and professional contacts are exposed to more opportunities and ideas than those with sparse ones. A survey of 65 startups showed that half of the entrepreneurs obtained their initial business idea from social contacts.
- **Creativity.** The fourth factor is the person's ability to generate a novel or useful idea from the information gleaned from the other factors.

Sustainability

Nicholas Stern (Stern, 2009) advises the UK government on climate change, and calls for urgent action to mitigate the effects. The paragraphs below summarise some of his points.

Climate change is not a theory struggling to maintain itself in the face of problematic evidence. The opposite is true: as new information comes in, it reinforces our understanding across a whole spectrum of indicators. The subject is full of uncertainty, but there is no serious doubt that emissions are growing as a result of human activity and that more greenhouse gases will lead to further warming.

The last 20 years have seen special and focussed attention from the Intergovernmental Panel on Climate Change (IPCC – www.ipcc.ch) which has published four assessments, the most recent in 2007. With each new report, the evidence on the strength and source of the effects, and the magnitude of the implications and risks, has become stronger. The basic scientific conclusions on climate change are very robust and for good reason. The greenhouse effect is simple science: greenhouse gases trap heat, and humans are emitting ever more greenhouse gases. There will be oscillations, there will be uncertainties. But the logic of the greenhouse effect is rock-solid and the long-term trends associated with the effects of human emissions are clear in the data.

In 2010 a report by the UK Meteorological Office (Stott, 2010) confirmed these conclusions, saying that the evidence was stronger now than when the Intergovernmental Panel on Climate Change carried out its last assessment in 2007. The analysis assessed 110 research papers on the subject, concluding that the earth is changing rapidly, probably because of greenhouse gases. The study found that changes in Arctic sea ice, atmospheric moisture, saltiness of parts of the Atlantic Ocean and temperature changes in the Antarctic are consistent with human influence on our climate.

Internationalisation

Models of national culture (see Chapter 4) are highly generalised summaries of diverse populations. Their value is to give some clues about broad differences between the places in which those managing internationally will be working. They encourage people to be ready to adapt the way they work to local circumstances.

The Management in practice feature shows how Iris, a rapidly growing advertising agency with a very strong and distinctive company culture AND many global clients seeks to gain the benefits of the diversity of its international staff and combine this to add more value for the client.

Management in practice   Gaining from cultural differences   www.irisnation.com

Iris was founded in 1999 and has established a distinctive position as an independent media and advertising agency, with a growing international business. An innovative technique which is very popular with global clients is 'Project 72'. Steve Bell, chief executive of Iris London, and one of the founding partners, explains:

> Project 72 is a very simple concept, and probably the purest way of bringing different agencies in the group together as one with a common goal and a common vision. [Suppose] Iris Miami is working on a brief for a client: they say 'right, let's engage a Project 72 on this one'. So the brief will go to the other agencies around the world, it will be handed to London for example, we will work on it for twelve hours, we will then [hand the baton] to Sydney, they will work on it for twelve hours, baton change to Singapore, so you can see how within 72 hours we've got the best freshest brains working on a brief to the common goal of developing the best creative work that we possibly can do. It's been fantastic …

> Project 72 benefits hugely from the cultural differences, and when I say cultural differences I don't mean within the agency but the societal cultural differences that happen within different areas around the world. So tapping into the fact that Singapore has a certain view around mobile telecomms enables us to look at things in a slightly different way, so it just allows fresh thinking, fresh outlooks, fresh cultures to inject some pace and some innovation around a particular brief at a given time.
>
> Source: Interview with Steve Bell.

Governance

This chapter has examined the culture of organisations and their external contexts: governance links the two. There are many high profile examples of organisations whose culture has encouraged managers and staff to act in their interests, rather than in the interests of those they were expected to serve – usually shareholders but also customers or members of the public.

Barings Bank is one example (see also Mallin, 2013) – one of Britain's oldest banks when it collapsed in 1995. Nick Leeson, a trader based in Singapore, had built a reputation for gambling successfully on the stock market, and his senior managers in London were happy to provide him with funds to do this, as they were earning large profits. When his luck ran out he asked for more funds which the bank continued to provide: he continued to invest in shares that then fell in value, making the situation worse. He was able to hide the losses from senior management for several months as he controlled the administrative processes – the trading and financial records – to conceal what was happening. The bank eventually collapsed, essentially because senior management had not imposed and enforced sufficiently robust controls, either through direct supervision or through transparent reporting procedures.

This illustrated the folly of trusting an apparently successful employee and being unwilling to scrutinise what they are doing. These lessons were ignored a decade later, when some senior traders in the investment division at The Royal Bank of Scotland engaged in very risky trading in securities derived from US home loans. Again the board (including the independent directors) was unable or unwilling to control the people who were making these trades, in part because they did not understand what they were doing – and were impressed by the profits they were earning.

Such cases (which happen in all sectors, though less spectacularly than in finance) draw attention to governance, which is part of the manager's context.

Summary

1 **Compare the cultures of two organisational units, using Quinn's or Handy's typologies**
   - Quinn *et al.* (2003) – open systems, rational goal, internal process and human relations.
   - Handy (1993) – power, role, task and person.

2 **Use Porter's Five Forces model to analyse the competitive environment of an organisation**
   - This identifies the degree of competitive rivalry, customers, competitors, suppliers and potential substitute goods and services.

3 **Collect evidence to make a comparative PESTEL analysis for two organisations**
   - The PESTEL model of the wider external environment identifies political, economic, social, technological, environmental and legal forces.

4 **Compare environments in terms of their complexity and rate of change**
   - Environments can be evaluated in terms of their rate of change (stable/dynamic) and complexity (low/high).

5 **Give examples of stakeholder expectations**
   - These are shown in Table 3.3.

6 **Explain the meaning and purpose of corporate governance**
   - Corporate governance is intended to monitor and control the performance of managers, to ensure they act in the interests of stakeholders, not just of themselves.

7 **Show how ideas from the chapter add to your understanding of the integrating themes**
   - Entrepreneurs depend on being quick to see opportunities, and research shows that this is increased by prior experience, cognitive factors (like intuition) and wide social networks.
   - A major feature of the natural environment relevant to managers is the accumulating evidence that climate change is due to human activities, leading to pressure for organisations and people to work and live more sustainably.
   - While culture has a powerful effect on what people do in an organisation, when they operate in internationally it provides an opportunity to benefit from diverse perspectives.
   - Some cultures encourage staff to take excessive risks, damaging companies and economies: this is leading stakeholders to press for tighter governance and control mechanisms.

Test your understanding

1. Describe an educational or commercial organisation that you know in terms of the competing values model of cultures.
2. What is the significance of the idea of 'fragmented cultures' for those who wish to change a culture to support performance?
3. Identify the relative influence of Porter's Five Forces on an organisation of your choice and compare your results with a colleague's. What can you learn from that comparison?
4. How should managers decide which of the many factors easily identified in a PESTEL analysis they should attend to? If they have to be selective, what is the value of the PESTEL method?
5. Since people interpret the nature of environmental forces from unique perspectives, what meaning can people attach to statements about external pressures?
6. Illustrate the stakeholder idea with an example of your own showing their expectations of an organisation.
7. Explain at least two of the mechanisms which Mallin (2010) recommends should be part of a corporate governance system.
8. Summarise an idea from the chapter that adds to your understanding of the integrating themes.

Think critically

Think about the culture which seems to be dominant in your company, and how managers deal with the business environment and their stakeholders. Alternatively gather information from another company which interests you. Review the chapter material, and make notes on these questions:

- What **assumptions** appear to guide the culture, and the factors in the external environment which managers believe matter to the business? How do these views affect the managers' task?
- What factors in the **context** appear to shape the prevailing view about which parts of the environment matter most to the business? Do people have different views?
- Can you compare your business environment with that of colleagues on your course. Does this show up **alternative** ways to see the context and to deal with stakeholders?
- What are the **limitations** of the ideas on culture and stakeholders which the chapter has presented. For example, are the cultural types transferable across nations, or how may they need to be adapted to represent different ways of managing?

Read more

Frooman, J. (1999), 'Stakeholder Influence Strategies', *Academy of Management Review*, vol. 24, no. 2, pp. 191–205.

Pajunen, K. (2006), 'Stakeholder Influences on Organisational Survival', *Journal of Management Studies*, vol. 43, no. 6, pp. 1261–88.

> These two articles provided a comprehensive theoretical background to case studies of stakeholder management.

Roeder, M. (2011), *The Big Mo: Why Momentum Now Rules Our World,* Virgin Books, London.

> An account of how forces such as those discussed in the chapter sometimes gain progressively greater momentum, often with devastating results for businesses affected by them, and how difficult it is to react against them.

Tapscott, E. and Williams, A.D. (2006), *Wikinomics: How Mass Collaboration Changes Everything*, Viking Penguin, New York.

> Best-selling account of the radical changes which convergent technologies bring to society, especially the relationship between producers and consumers.

Go online

These websites have appeared in the chapter:

> www.nokia.com
> www.bosch.com
> www.walmart.com
> www.unilever.com
> www.irisnation.com
> www.ipcc.com
> www.tata.com

Visit some of these, or any other companies which interest you, and navigate to the pages dealing with recent news, press or investor relations.

- What can you find about their culture?
- What are the main forces in the environment which the organisation appears to be facing?

- What assessment would you make of the nature of that environment?
- Compare and contrast the issues you identify on the two sites.
- What challenges may they imply for those working in, and managing, these organisations?

CHAPTER 6
PLANNING

Aim

To describe the purposes of planning in organisations, and illustrate the iterative tasks in planning.

Objectives

By the end of your work on this chapter you should be able to outline the concepts below in your own terms and:

1. Explain the purposes of planning and the content of several types of plan
2. Compare alternative planning processes, and evaluate when each may be most suitable
3. Outline five iterative tasks in planning, and describe techniques used in each
4. Use theory to evaluate the motivational effect of the goals stated in a plan
5. Use a framework to evaluate whether a plan is sufficiently comprehensive
6. Evaluate the context which will affect the ability of managers to implement a plan
7. Show how ideas from the chapter can add to your understanding of the integrating themes

Key terms

This chapter introduces the following ideas:

planning
goal (or objective)
business plan
strategic plan
strategic business unit
operational plans
enterprise resource planning
planning system
SWOT analysis

critical success factor
optimism bias
strategic misrepresentation bias
sensitivity analysis
scenario planning
stated goal
real goal
organisational readiness

Each is a term defined within the text, as well as in the glossary at the end of the book.

Case study
Crossrail   www.crossrail.co.uk

Crossrail is a new railway for London and the south-east of England which will connect the City, Canary Wharf, the West End and Heathrow Airport to commuter areas east and west of the capital. It aims to be a world-class, affordable railway, with high frequency, convenient and accessible services across the capital. The railway is intended to:

- relieve congestion on many Underground and rail lines;
- provide new connections and services on modern trains;
- provide eight new stations in central London.

It will add 10 per cent to London's transport capacity and provide 40 per cent of the extra rail capacity London needs. Main construction of the railway began in 2010, with services planned to begin in 2017. Crossrail will use main line size trains, each carrying more than 1500 passengers, to make travelling in the area easier and quicker as well as reducing crowding on London's transport network.

It is the largest civil engineering project in the UK and the largest single addition to the London transport network for over 50 years. It will run 118 km from Maidenhead and Heathrow in the west to Shenfield and Abbey Wood in the east, joining the Great Western and Great Eastern railway networks; 21 km of the route will be in new twin tunnels under Central London.

The project has a long history – it was first proposed in 1990, but amidst considerable opposition it was cancelled in 1996. Supporters, especially national and London business groups, continued to advocate the line as a contribution to London's transport, and eventually gained sufficient political support. Parliament passed the Crossrail Act in July 2008 giving authority to build the railway, and in December of that year the Government and the Mayor of London signed funding agreements.

The Crossrail website points out that it is a multiple worksite programme with construction works running concurrently across the route. It depends on co-operation amongst many organisations including Crossrail Central, London Underground, Network Rail, Docklands Light Railway, Canary Wharf Group and Berkeley Homes. Major construction features include:

Getty Images/Bloomberg

- using five tunnelling drives to bore the tunnels under central London;
- shipping the excavated material to Wallasea Island in Essex to build a new nature reserve;
- building eight new Underground stations to connect with the Underground and rail network; and
- building four overground lines from the central section, including one to Heathrow Airport.

The tunnel section needs to cross above the Jubilee Line but below the Central and Circle Lines, weaving around buried utilities and deep building foundations.

The Learning & Skills Council agreed to provide £5 million towards the cost of a Tunnelling and Underground Construction Academy which opened in October 2011, increasing the supply of the skilled workers the project requires. In 2013 the project entered the peak construction period, with two tunnel boring machines approaching the new Canary Wharf station.

Source: Company website and other published sources.

Case questions 6.1
Visit the Crossrail website (see above).
- What are the main items of recent news about the progress of the project?
- What kind of environment do you think the company is operating in? (Chapter 3, Section 3.6)
- What are the main planning challenges which Crossrail managers face?

6.1 Introduction

Crossrail is an example of a major project which managers can only achieve by a great deal of planning. From the early political processes to secure support from many interested parties (Glaister and Travers, 2001) – some in favour of the project, some against – then raising capital and securing public consent, managers have continually been developing plans to guide the project towards completion in several years time. That continues during construction, with work guided by the very detailed plans required to drive a new railway beneath the centre of a capital city. The complex organisation of clients, main contractors and sub-contractors also needs to be planned, so that Crossrail can be sure that the hundreds of firms working on the project have the right staff in place to do the work (Scott, 2011). The case will illustrate how Crossrail's managers dealt with these challenges and opportunities, some of which are still unforeseen.

Brews and Purahit (2007) show empirically that as business conditions become unstable, companies do more planning. Change creates uncertainty, and planning helps people adapt to this by clarifying objectives, specifying how to achieve them, and monitoring progress. Plans include both ends (what to do) and means (how to do it).

Informal plans (not written down, nor widely shared) work perfectly well in many situations – but as the number of people involved in an activity increases they need something more to guide them. That is the focus here – on more formal plans, which put into writing the goals of a business or unit, and who will do what to achieve them. When senior managers at Hiscox, a small insurance company, decided to add an online service to its traditional way of selling services through insurance brokers, it needed not only a plan to construct the website, but also a plan to reassure the brokers that they would still have a role. When two entrepreneurs decided to create the City Inn hotel chain they planned in detail the kind of hotels they would be – contemporary, city centre, newly built, 'active and open' atmosphere, and a consistent room design across the group. They then communicate their plan to those working on the project to ensure they act consistently.

Figure 6.1 provides an overview of the themes. At the centre are five generic tasks in planning – which people do not perform in sequence. They typically move rapidly between them, using the results of work at a later stage to go back and revise decisions they made earlier – the process is iterative, not linear. People also vary in how much time and attention they give to each.

The chapter outlines why people plan and the range of issues for which they plan – the content of plans. It examines the process of planning and five generic tasks – stressing throughout that this is iterative and depends on context.

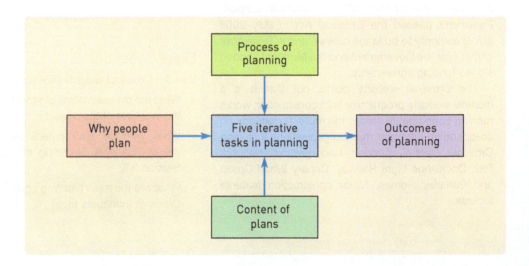

Figure 6.1 An overview of the chapter

6.2 Why people plan

A planner is an individual contemplating future actions: the activity of **planning** involves gathering relevant information about the task and its context, establishing **goals** (or **objectives**), specifying how to achieve them, implementing the plan and evaluating the results. Goals are the desired future state of an activity or unit, and achieving that end depends on deciding the means – what needs to be done, by when, and by whom?

Planning, if done well:

- clarifies direction;
- motivates people;
- uses resources efficiently; and
- increases control, by enabling people to measure progress against targets.

> **Planning** is the iterative task of setting goals, specifying how to achieve them, implementing the plan and evaluating the results.
>
> A **goal** (or **objective**) is a desired future state for an activity or organisational unit.

The act of planning may itself add value by ensuring that people base decisions on more evidence than they otherwise would. Gireaudeau (2008) shows how planning in one of Renault's divisions enhanced debate, and stimulated managers' strategic imagination. Closely observing a project to build a plant in Brazil (which produced its first cars in 2012), the author shows how providing detailed draft plans to other managers (unfamiliar with the country) led them to visualise opportunities the planners had not considered. If done badly, planning has the opposite effect, leading to confusion and delay.

Good plans give direction to those doing the work. If all know the purpose of a larger activity and how they fit in, they work more effectively. They adjust their work to the plan (sometimes suggesting changes), and co-operate and co-ordinate with others. If they know the end result (the big picture) they can respond to unexpected changes without waiting to be told, and are likely to have more interest in the activity and take more responsibility.

Management in practice   Maersk – planning key to strategy   www.maersk.com

Maersk is the world's largest container operator, and depends on planning. Mark Cornwall, Operations Manager, explains:

> Maersk operates 470 container ships with 1.9 million individual containers that are all travelling around the world, and our job is to build efficiencies into the system – moving the cargo to the customer on time.
>
> Part of our strategy is to deliver unmatched reliability, and operations is key to that. From the top of the company right down to the clerks on the desk, everybody's focussed on meeting deadlines and the requirements of the customer every step of the way. So whether it's a ship arriving in a port on time, or a container loading on a ship on time, or a truck delivery to a warehouse, everybody's focussed all the way through the chain on making sure that everything happens against the deadline as planned.
>
> Efficiency's all about making the best use of your assets, so whether it's putting as many containers as possible on a ship, or maximising your utilisation of a particular train, or getting as many miles out of a truck as you can during a shift, it's all about planning your assets to get the biggest use out of them during that period.

Source: Interview with Mark Cornwall.

Planning reduces overlap and at the same time ensures that someone is responsible for each activity. A plan helps people coordinate their separate tasks, so saving time and resources; without a plan they may work at cross-purposes. If people are clear on the goal they can spot inefficiencies or unnecessary delays and act to fix them.

> **Key ideas** — **Does planning help entrepreneurial behaviour and new ventures?**
>
> Delmar and Shane (2003) studied whether planning helps new ventures, by gathering data from over 200 new firms in Sweden. They hypothesised that planning would support new ventures by:
>
> - enabling quicker decisions;
> - providing a tool for managing resources to minimise bottlenecks;
> - identifying actions to achieve broader goals in a timely manner.
>
> They gathered data from the firms at their start-up in 1998, and then at regular intervals for three years. The results supported each of their hypotheses, leading them to conclude that planning did indeed support the creation of successful new ventures.
>
> Source: Delmar and Shane (2003).

Setting final and interim goals lets people know how well they are progressing, and when they have finished. Comparing actual progress against the intended progress enables people to adjust the goal or change the way they are using resources.

Sometimes plans have a ceremonial function. Kirsch *et al.* (2009) in a study of entrepreneurs seeking funding from venture capitalists found that

> neither the presence of business planning documents nor their content serve a communicative role for venture capitalists [in the sense of conveying information that influences the funding decision]. With some qualifications, we find that business planning documents may serve a limited ceremonial role [in the sense of showing that the entrepreneur understands how the venture capitalist expects them to behave].

The content of a plan is the subject – *what* aspect of business it deals with: strategic, business unit, operational, tactical or special purpose. The next section deals with those topics, and that which follows focuses on *how* the planning process is carried out.

> **Activity 6.1** — **Reflection on the purpose of plans**
>
> Find an example of a plan that someone has prepared in an organisation – preferably one of the types listed in the next section.
>
> - Ask someone what its purpose is, and whether it achieves that.
> - Ask whether the plan is too detailed, or not detailed enough.
> - What do they regard as the strengths and weaknesses of the planning process?
> - Refer to your notes as you work on this chapter.

6.3 The content of plans

A **business plan** is a document describing the markets a business intends to serve, how it will do so and what finance they require.

People starting a new business or expanding an existing one prepare a **business plan** – a document which sets out the markets the business intends to serve, how it will do so and what finance they require (Sahlman, 1997; Blackwell, 2008). It does so in considerable detail as it needs to convince potential investors to lend money. Managers seeking capital investment or other corporate resources need to convince senior managers to allocate them – which they do by presenting a convincing plan. People in the public sector do the same – a director of roads (for example) needs to present a plan to convince the chief executive or elected members that planned expenditure on roads will be a better use of resources than competing proposals from (say) the director of social work. Service managers inevitably compete with each other for limited resources, and develop business plans to support their case.

Strategic plans apply to the whole organisation. They set out the overall direction and cover major activities – markets and revenues, together with plans for marketing, human resources and production. Strategy is concerned with deciding what business an organisation should be in, where it wants to be and how it is going to get there. These decisions involve major resource commitments and usually require a series of consequential operational decisions – which a plan summarises: see the Volvo in the Management in practice feature.

In a large business there will be divisional plans for each major unit. If subsidiaries operate as autonomous **strategic business units** (SBUs) they develop their plans with limited inputs from the rest of the company, as they manage distinct markets.

> A **strategic plan** sets out the overall direction for the business, is broad in scope and covers all the major activities.
>
> A **strategic business unit** consists of a number of closely related products for which it is meaningful to formulate a separate strategy.

Management in practice **Volvo plans recovery** www.volvo.com

In 2012 Volvo's new chief executive Hakan Samuelsson outlined his plan to recover from a period of falling sales – about 380,000 units in 2012 compared to over 440,000 two years earlier. His plan for 2013 was to defend market share in Europe, and to cut costs quickly to compensate for the lost sales. Consultants, IT, commercial ads, PR – all will be cut as the focus is placed on developing new models for the end of 2014.

His plan for Volvo in the longer term has three elements:

- First, to strengthen Volvo's brand. Mr Samuelsson wants it to stand not just for safety but Scandinavian design and functionality as well.
- The second strand is new products. A new XC90, Volvo's large SUV, will be introduced at the end of 2014 (and a new saloon is expected soon afterwards).
- The final part is cultural and based on its small size, selling just 450,000 cars a year compared with 1.7 million for BMW:

We have to be nimble, dynamic and faster as an organisation. We can't afford to be as bureaucratic or [have such long] decision-making processes as a 4m car company.

Source: *Financial Times*, 18 December 2012, p. 23.

Strategic plans usually set out a direction for several years, though in businesses with long lead times (energy production or aircraft manufacture) they look perhaps 15 years ahead. Ryanair plans to increase its share of the European short-haul passenger market from 12 per cent in 2012–13 to 18 per cent in ten years' time. That implies the company will increase the fleet from 300 aircraft to 450 by 2022: replacing some older aircraft means it will probably buy about 300 aircraft – so will have a plan showing the financial and other implications of enlarging the fleet, recruiting staff and opening new routes. Such plans are not fixed: managers regularly update them to take account of new conditions, so they are sometimes called 'rolling plans'.

Operational plans detail how managers expect to achieve their strategy by showing what they expect each department or function to do. They create a hierarchy of related plans – a strategic plan for the organisation and main divisions, and several operational plans for departments or teams. In 2011 Royal Dutch Shell announced ambitious production targets to meet rising demand from emerging markets. It planned to invest £62 billion in new projects over the next four years – with liquid natural gas production expected to contribute most: within that there were development plans for each oil and gas field. These will contain linked objectives and become more specific as they move down the organisation – eventually specifying small pieces of work that someone needs to do in each site – but consistent with the wider expansion strategy. Table 6.1 shows this hierarchical arrangement, and how the character of plans changes at each level.

> **Operational plans** detail how the overall objectives are to be achieved, by specifying what senior management expects from specific departments or functions.

Table 6.1 A planning hierarchy

Type of plan	Strategic	Operational	Activity
Level	Organisation or business unit	Division, department, function or market	Work unit or team
Focus	Direction and strategy for whole organisation	Functional changes or market activities to support strategic plans	Actions needed to deliver current products or services
Nature	Broad, general direction	Detail on required changes	Specific detail on immediate goals and tasks
Timescale	Long term (2-3 years?)	Medium (up to 18 months?)	Very short term (hours to weeks?)

Case study

Crossrail – the case continues   www.crossrail.co.uk

The company has published its outline plans for building the stations and tunnels – the schedule below lists a small selection of these works. At some locations enabling works (such as the diversion of utilities like gas mains, and demolition of existing buildings) need to be scheduled before main works.

Plans also need to cover all the details of fitting out the structures ready for use.

Stations

The table gives examples of the planned start of station enabling works, and of the start and completion dates of the station themselves (correct at 2011).

Location	Enabling works started	Construction starts/ started	Works complete
Canary Wharf	December 2008	May 2009	Third quarter 2017
Tottenham Court Road	January 2009	Early 2010	Fourth quarter 2016
Farringdon	July 2009	Third quarter 2011	First quarter 2018
Custom House	First quarter 2012	Third quarter 2012	Third quarter 2014

Tunnelling works

The completion dates shown in the following table refer to the completion of the tunnel. Fit out will take place beyond these dates. Note that only the first three tunnels to be bored are shown here.

Location of tunnel drive	Boring begins	Tunnel drive complete
Royal Oak to Farringdon (Drive X)	Second quarter 2012	Third quarter 2013
Limmo to Farringdon (Drive Y)	Third quarter 2012	Third quarter 2014
Plumstead to North Woolwich (Drive H)	Fourth quarter 2012	Second quarter 2014

'On network' works

Network Rail is doing the work required on existing stations and tracks which Crossrail will use.

Other works

Press releases in 2012 about recently awarded contracts give further insight into the scale and diversity of the tasks which have to be planned. They included contracts for:

- design and construction of 13 stations on the Western section of the line;
- signalling enabling works;
- ensuring the central tunnel meets EU legislation on the interoperability of railway operations (several train companies will use the line);
- shipping material excavated from the tunnels to Wallasea Island in Essex, to create a bird reserve;
- design and manufacture of the last two tunnel boring machines.

Source: company website.

> ### Case questions 6.2
> - Visit the company website and look for information about progress on these (or other) plans.
> - Can you identify any plans mentioned that are clearly at strategic, operational or activity levels?
> - While on the website, identify and list three other pieces of work for which plans will have been made – especially any involving other organisations.

Most organisations prepare annual plans which focus on finance and set budgets for the coming year – these necessarily include sales, marketing, production or technology plans as well. Activity plans are short term plans which deal with immediate production or service delivery – a sheet scheduling which orders to deliver next week, or who is on duty tomorrow. Standing plans specify how to deal with routine, recurring issues like recruitment or customer complaints. Some use a method called **enterprise resource planning (ERP)** to integrate the day-to-day work of complex production systems – this technique is described later (Chapter 12, Section 12.5).

Figure 6.2 contrasts specific and directional plans. Specific plans have clear, quantified objectives with little discretion in how to achieve them. When Tesco opens a new store, staff

Enterprise resource planning (ERP) is a computer-based planning system which links separate databases to plan the use of all resources within the enterprise.

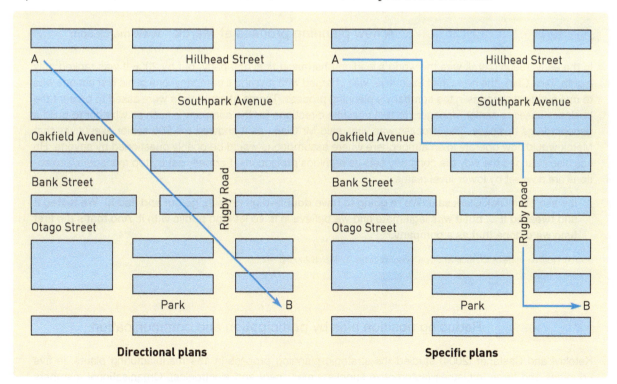

Figure 6.2 Specific and directional plans

follow defined procedures detailing all the tasks required to ensure that it opens on time and within budget. Where there is uncertainty about what needs to be done to meet the objective managers will use a directional plan, setting the objective, but leaving staff to decide how to get there. Hamm (2007) describes how in the early days of Wipro (a successful Indian information technology company) the founder, Azim Premji, held weekly telephone conversations with his regional managers, in which he set their targets for the following week – but they decided how to meet them. They were accountable for meeting the target, not for how they did so, provided they met his high ethical standards.

Wise managers also prepare plans for dealing with unexpected disasters such as product failures, accidents and explosions. Online communication implies that organisations need to plan how to deal with possibly hostile media at the same time as implementing a plan to minimise the effects of the disaster itself. This requires not only having worked out a recovery plan but also training people every few months in how to use it, and ensuring that it is instantly available online.

6.4 The process of planning

A **planning system** refers to the processes by which the members of an organisation produce plans, including their frequency and who takes part in the process.

The process of planning refers to how an organisation produces its plans – from the top of the organisation, or the bottom? who creates them? how frequently are they revised? A **planning system** organises and coordinates the activity, so shaping the quality and value of plans. Designing and maintaining a planning system is part of planning.

Participation is one issue – who is involved? One approach is to appoint one or more people to produce a plan, with or without consultation with the line managers or staff concerned. Others believe the quality of the plan, and especially the ease of implementing it, will be increased if those familiar with local conditions produce the plan – and even more so if they seek the views of others affected by it.

Management in practice — A new planning process at Merck www.merck.com

In the early 1990s Merck was the world's leading pharmaceutical company, but by 2006 it was ranked only eighth. Dick Clark, the new Chief Executive, was charged with reviving a company: one of his first actions was to make radical changes in the company's planning process. Teams of employees were asked to present the business cases to senior managers to test possible directions for the company – such as whether to build a generic drugs business. This process was vital, said Mr Clark, as it showed the 200 senior executives that Merck would now operate in an atmosphere where assumptions would be openly questioned by anyone. He has also changed the way the company sets its earnings projections. Formerly set by top managers, projections are now set by lower-level teams.

It wasn't like Dick Clark said 'We're going to have double-digit growth, go out and find it!' We tested it and tweaked it ... but it was legitimate and we believe in it, so let's go public with it. And that's the first time we'd done that as a company.

Source: From an article by Christopher Bowe, *Financial Times*, 27 March 2006, p. 10.

Key ideas — Reducing position bias by participation and communication

Ketokivi and Castaner (2004) studied the strategic planning process in 164 manufacturing plants, in five countries and three industries (automotive supplies, machinery and electronics). Organisational members

> tend to focus on the goals of their unit or function, rather than to those of the enterprise – known as 'position bias'. The study sought to establish empirically whether position bias existed, and, more importantly, whether strategic planning reduced this. The evidence confirmed the tendency to position bias. It also showed that having employees participate in strategic planning, and communicating the outcome to them, significantly diminishes it. If top management wants to reduce position bias, they can do so by designing the planning process so that it allows for such participation and communication.
>
> Source: Ketokivi and Castaner (2004)

A related debate (see Chapter 8, Section 8.3) is between those who advocate a rational approach to planning, and those who favour a learning perspective. The latter believe that in dynamic contexts plans must be provisional, so that managers can adapt them to suit changing circumstances, drawing on new information from a range of participants (Papke-Shields 2006). Andersen (2000) reconciled these views by studying strategic planning in three industries with different external conditions. He concluded that strategic planning was associated with superior performance in all settings: companies that planned performed better than those that did not. He also found that in complex dynamic industries a formal planning process was accompanied by autonomous actions by managers, which further enhanced performance.

Planning and doing may seem like separate activities, and in stable conditions they may be. In volatile conditions people conduct them almost simultaneously. In their study of strategic planning, Whittington *et al.*(2006) show that strategising and organising:

> become very similar, or even common: in the heat of the moment practitioners may be unable to distinguish the two. (p. 618)

Jennings (2000) shows how companies change their approach to planning as conditions change. A study of the UK electricity generating company PowerGen (now owned by the German company E.on) traced the evolution since privatisation of the company's corporate planning process. It retains a formal process with a five-year planning horizon, but it is more devolved. A small central team focuses on overall strategy while business units develop local plans within the larger plan. These changes created a more adaptive style of planning which suited the (new) uncertainty of the business. Grant (2003) shows how planning systems of large oil companies changed to deal with uncertainty.

Figure 6.3 shows the five generic tasks which people perform as they plan. They use them iteratively, often returning to an earlier task when they find new information that implies, say, that they should change the original goal. And they may spend too little or too much time on a task.

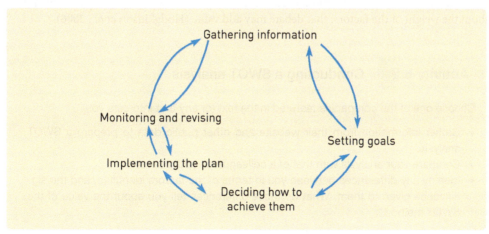

Figure 6.3 Five iterative tasks in planning

6.5 Gathering information

Any plan depends on information – including informal, soft information gained from casual encounters with colleagues, as well as formal analyses of economic and market trends.

Competitive and general environments feature prominently in business plans. External sources information about these include government economic and demographic statistics, industry surveys and general business intelligence services. Managers also commission market research on, for example, individuals' shopping patterns, attitudes towards particular firms or brand names, and satisfaction with services. Many firms use focus groups to test consumer reaction to new products.

Management in practice Inamo – planning the start-up www.inamo-restaurant.com

Danny Potter, Managing Director, explained the information they needed before they started:

> Well, in terms of market research, we looked at other interactive ordering restaurants and concepts there might be, a lot of research on the world wide web and just going round London to various restaurants. We also looked at good guides which give you a quick summary. Meeting people in the industry, going to shows and exhibitions are quick ways of learning a great deal. Also a few brainstorming sessions to get feedback on what people thought of the concept – one piece of feedback was that this would not fit a formal French dining environment. We came to the conclusion that Oriental fusion was the appropriate cuisine type.
>
> We spent a great deal of time finding the right location. We went through the government statistics database and built a database of our own, analysing demographics of the whole of London. What we found was that a very small area around central London is really where all the buzz happens, where all of the restaurants want to be. And then we focussed on finding the right location in this area.

Source: Interview with Danny Potter.

SWOT analysis

A **SWOT analysis** is a way of summarising the organisation's strengths and weaknesses relative to external opportunities and threats.

At a strategic level, planning usually combines internal analysis of strengths and weaknesses with external analysis to identify opportunities and threats – a **SWOT analysis.** Internally, managers look at the resources within, or available to, the organisation – unusually skilled staff, a distinctive research capability, or skill in integrating acquired companies. They probably base their external analysis on PESTEL and Porter's (1980) Five Forces model to identify relevant trends.

While the method appears rational, it is a human representation, so participants will differ about the weight of the factors: that debate may add value (Hodgkinson et al., 2006).

Activity 6.2 Conducting a SWOT analysis

Choose one of the companies featured in the text (or any that interests you).

- Gather information from their website and other public data to prepare a SWOT analysis.
- Compare your analysis with that of a colleague on your course.
- Identify any differences between you in terms of the factors identified, and the significance given to them. What do those differences tell you about the value of the SWOT method?

Given the diversity and complexity of organisational environments it is easy to have too much information. Managers need to focus on the few trends and events that are likely to be most significant. De Wit and Meyer (2004) report that planners at Royal Dutch Shell focus on critical factors such as oil demand (economic), refining capacity (political and economic), the likelihood of government intervention (political) and alternative sources of fuel (technological).

Critical success factors analysis

In considering whether to enter a new market, a widely used planning technique is to assess the **critical success factors** (Leidecker and Bruno, 1984) in that market. These are the things which customers in that market most value about a product or service – useful information for someone planning to enter it. Some value price, others quality, others some of the product's features – but in all cases they are things that a company must do well to succeed.

Critical success factors are those aspects of a strategy that *must* be achieved to secure competitive advantage.

Forecasting

Forecasts or predictions usually analyse trends in relevant factors, and assumptions about things that may change, to try to foresee the future. In stable environments people can reasonably assume that past trends will continue, but in uncertain ones they have to consider radical alternatives. Newspaper publishers face difficult decisions as they plan how much (if any) print capacity to retain as more readers obtain news online.

Forecasting is big business, with companies selling analyses to business and government, using techniques such as time-series analysis, econometric modelling and simulation. Some believe that uncertain conditions reduce the value of detailed forecasts: Grant (2003) reports that oil companies have significantly reduced the resources they spend on preparing formal forecasts of oil demand and prices, preferring to rely on broader assumptions about possible trends. Forecasts in public projects are also unreliable – see Key ideas.

Optimism bias refers to a human tendency to judge future events in a more positive light than is warranted by experience.

Strategic misrepresentation is where competition for resources leads planners to underestimate costs and overestimate benefits, to increase the likelihood that their project gains approval.

> **Key ideas**   **The planning fallacy in large projects**
>
> Large infrastructure projects regularly cost more and deliver less than their promoters promised: Flyvbjerg (2008) shows that the average cost inaccuracy for rail projects is 44 per cent, for bridges and tunnels 34 per cent, and roads 20 per cent. He then draws on work by Lovallo and Kahneman (2003) which identified a systematic fallacy in planning, whereby people underestimate the costs, completion times and risks of planned actions, whereas they overestimate their benefits. This 'planning fallacy' has two sources:
>
> - **optimism bias** – a human tendency to judge future events more positively than experience warrants; and
> - **strategic misrepresentation** – where competition for resources leads planners to underestimate costs and overestimate benefits, making it more likely that their project gains approval and funding.
>
> These biases lead planners to take an 'inside view', focussing on the constituents of their plan, rather than an 'outside view' – guided by information about the outcomes of similar plans that have been completed.
>
> Source: Flyvbjerg (2008).

Sensitivity analysis

One way to test assumptions is to make a **sensitivity analysis** of key variables in a plan. If this assumes a new product will gain (say) a 10 per cent market share within a year, a sensitivity analysis calculates what the effect on returns would be if they secure 5 per cent, or 15 per cent? What if interest rates rise, increasing the cost of financing the project? Planners can then compare the options and assess the risks. Johnson *et al.* (2011) give a worked example (pp. 372–3).

A **sensitivity analysis** tests the effect on a plan of several alternative values of the key variables.

Scenario planning

An alternative to forecasting is to consider possible scenarios. Cornelius *et al.* (2005) note:

> scenarios are not projections, predictions or preferences; rather they are coherent and credible stories about the future.

Scenario planning is an attempt to create coherent and credible alternative stories about the future.

Scenario planning typically begins by considering how external forces such as the Internet, an ageing population, or climate change might affect a company's business over the next five–ten years. Doing so can bring managers new ideas about their environment, enabling them to consider previously unthinkable possibilities. Advocates (Van der Heijden, 1996) claim that it discourages managers from relying on a single view of the future, and encourages them to develop plans – to cope with a variety of possible outcomes. Few companies use the technique regularly, as it is time consuming and costly, but Shell is an exception (report in *Financial Times*, 30 November 2010):

> Scenario thinking ... underpins the established way of thinking at Shell. It has become a part of the culture, such that people throughout the company, dealing with significant decisions, normally will think in terms of multiple, but equally plausible futures to provide a context for decision making. (Van der Heijden, 1996, p. 21)

A combination of PESTEL and Five Forces analysis should ensure that managers recognise major external factors. Forecasting and scenario planning can help them to consider possible implications for the business – provided their boards take account of the signals.

Management in practice DSM – Business Strategy Dialogue www.dsm.com

DSM is a Dutch chemical company which has developed a planning process which requires each Business Group to conduct a Business Strategy Dialogue (BSD) every three years. This ensures a consistent method and terminology for the planning process across the company. The reviews have five phases:

- **Characterising the business situation:** Collecting information on what business you are in, the competitors, how attractive is the industry (growth, profitability), how do you compare with competitors?
- **Analysing the business system (macro):** Analysing the industry in which the group competes, using Porter's Five Forces model.
- **Analysing the business system (micro):** The internal processes of the business, including its value chain, and strengths and weaknesses.
- **Options and strategic choice:** This uses the earlier phases to allow the business managers to choose which strategic option to pursue and what it requires.
- **Action planning and performance measurement:** The chosen strategy is then turned into a plan and linked to performance measurement. The team sets performance indicators such as market share, new product development, customer satisfaction and cost per unit of output. These enable managers to monitor implementation.

Source: Based on Bloemhof, M., Haspeslagh, P. and Slagmulder, R. (2004), *Strategy and Performance at DSM*, INSEAD, Fontainebleau (Case 304-067-1, distributed by The European Case Clearing House); company website.

6.6 Setting goals (or objectives) – the ends

A clear plan depends on being clear about the intended goal – whether for an organisation or a unit. This seems obvious, but managers favour action above planning (Stewart, 1967) – especially the ambiguities of agreeing on goals. Yet until people clarify these they make little progress.

Goals (or objectives)

Goals give a task focus – what will we achieve, by when? Setting goals is difficult as people need to look beyond a relatively known present to an unknown future. Bond *et al.* (2008) asked people to set objectives for a personally relevant task (finding a good job) – and they consistently omitted nearly half of the objectives they later identified as important when these were drawn to their attention. The researchers secured the same results in a software company.

Goals, with a set timetable in which to meet them, provide the reference point for other decisions, and the criteria against which to measure performance. At the business level they include quantified financial objectives – earnings per share, return on shareholders' funds and cash flow. At the project level the targets will be expressed in other ways – see Management in practice.

Management in practice — Environmental targets at Heathrow Terminal 5

Building Terminal 5 was an opportunity to embed environmentally sustainable practices into every aspect of the terminal's operation. An environmental assessment group identified several sustainability focus areas, which evolved into the project requirements and then into environmental targets such as:

Aspect	Key performance indicator	Target
Water	Potable water use	70% cut in potable water use (more from other sources)
	Water consumption	25 litres/passenger
Pollution control	Total harmful emissions to water	Capture 25% of surface water runoff for re-use
Waste	Waste recycled/composted	40% by 2010, 80% by 2020
Resource use	Compliance with T5 materials	40% of coarse aggregate in concrete to be re-cycled

Source: Lister (2008).

Activity 6.3 — Developing goals

- Go to the websites of companies which interest you and collect examples of planning goals.
- Does the organisation or unit for which you work have stated planning goals. If so, how were they developed?
- Gather examples of goals at either organisational, operational or activity levels. If you can, ask about the process of setting them, and whether this has affected attitudes towards the goals.

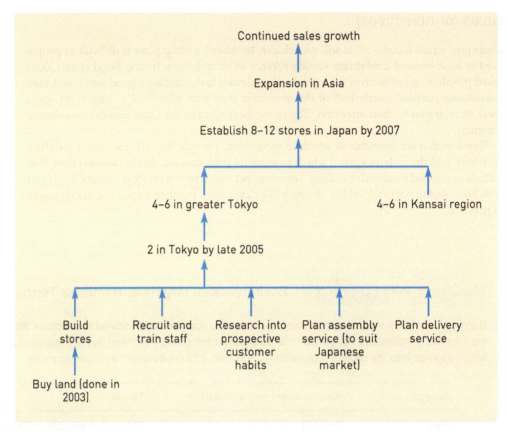

Figure 6.4
Developing a plan for Ikea (Japan)

A hierarchy of goals

A way of relating goals to each other is to build them into a hierarchy, in which organisational goals are transformed into specific goals for functions like marketing or human resources. Managers in those areas develop plans defining what they must do to meet the overall goal. Figure 6.4 illustrates this using Ikea's plan to expand in Japan – itself part of a wider plan to sell more in Asia. That evolved into a plan for their probable location, and then into a precise plan for two near Tokyo. Managers then developed progressively more detailed plans for the thousands of tasks that need to be complete to support the high level goal.

Plans like this need to be flexible to cope with changes in conditions between design and completion. Managers may be committed to achieving high level goals – but leave staff to decide on intermediate goals that will meet them.

Effective goal setting (producing goals which guide action) involves balancing multiple goals, ensuring they are SMART, and evaluating how they affect motivation.

Single or multiple goals?

Statements of goals – whether long-term or short – are usually expressed in the plural, since a single measure cannot indicate success or failure. Emphasis on one goal, such as growth, ignores another, such as dividends. Managers balance multiple, possibly conflicting goals: Gerry Murphy, who became chief executive of Kingfisher (a UK DIY retailer), recalled:

> Alan Sheppard, my boss at Grand Metropolitan and one of my mentors, used to say that senior management shouldn't have the luxury of single point objectives. Delivering growth without returns or returns without growth is not something I find attractive or acceptable. Over time we are going to do both. (*Financial Times*, 28 April 2004, p. 23)

As senior managers try to take account of a range of stakeholders they balance diverse interests. This can lead to conflict between **stated goals**, as reflected in public announcements, and the **real goals** – those to which people give most attention. The latter reflect senior managers' priorities, expressed through what they say and how they reward and discipline managers.

Stated goals are those which are prominent in company publications and websites.

Real goals are those to which people give most attention.

Criteria for assessing goals

The SMART acronym summarises some criteria for assessing a set of goals. What form of each is effective depends on circumstances (specific goals are not necessarily better than directional ones). The list simply offers some criteria against which to evaluate a statement of goals.

- **Specific** Does the goal set specific targets? People who are planning a meeting can set specific goals for what they hope to achieve, such as:

  By the end of the meeting we will have convinced them to withdraw their current proposal, and to have set a date (within the next two weeks) at which we will start to develop an alternative plan.

  A clear statement of what a meeting (or any other activity) should achieve helps to focus effort.

- **Measurable** Some goals may be quantified ('increase sales of product X by 5 per cent a year over the next three years') but others, equally important, are more qualitative ('to offer a congenial working environment'). Quantitative goals are not inherently more useful than qualitative ones – what can be measured is not necessarily important. The aim is to define goals precisely enough to measure progress towards them.
- **Attainable** Goals should be challenging, but not unreasonably difficult or people will not be committed. Equally goals should not be too easy, as that too weakens motivation. Goal-setting theory (see Key ideas) predicts the motivational effects of goal setting.
- **Rewarded** If people know that if they attain a goal they will receive a reward they will be more committed.
- **Timed** Does the goal specify the time over which it will be achieved, and is that also a reasonable and acceptable standard?

Key ideas — Practical uses of goal-setting theory

Goal theory has practical implications for those making plans:

- **Goal difficulty**: set goals for work performance at levels that will stretch employees but are just within their ability.
- **Goal specificity**: express goals in clear, precise and if possible quantifiable terms, and avoid setting ambiguous or confusing goals.
- **Participation**: where practicable, encourage staff to take part in setting goals to increase their commitment to achieving them.
- **Feedback**: provide information on the results of performance to allow people to adjust their behaviour and perhaps improve their achievement of future plans.

Source: Locke and Latham (2002).

> **Activity 6.4 Evaluate a statement of goals**
>
> - Choose a significant plan that someone has produced in your organisation within the last year. Are they SMART? Then try to set out how you would amend the goals to meet these criteria more fully. Alternatively, comment on how the criteria set out in the text could be modified, in the light of your experience with these goals.

6.7 Deciding how to achieve the goals – the means

This part of planning is about deciding what needs to be done, who will do it, and communicating that. In a small activity such as planning a project in a club this would mean listing the tasks and dividing them clearly amongst able and willing members. At the other extreme, Ford's plan to build a new car plant in China probably runs to several volumes.

Identifying what has to be done, by whom

Figure 6.5 (based on Figure 1.3) provides a model to help envisage the implications of a goal, by enabling managers to ask what, if any, changes do they need to make to each element.

If the goal is to launch a new product, the plan could identify which parts of the organisation will be affected (structure), what investment is needed (finance), how will production fit with existing lines (business processes), and so on. New technology projects often fail because planners pay too much attention to the technological aspects, and too little to contextual elements such as structure, culture and people (Boddy et al., 2009b). Each main heading will include further actions that people can identify and assign.

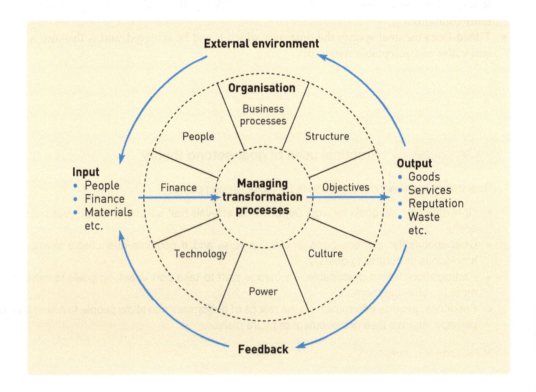

Figure 6.5
Possible action areas in a plan

Lynch (2003) found that managers handle this aspect of planning comprehensively, incrementally or selectively.

- **Comprehensive (specific) plan** This happens if managers decide to make a clear-cut change in direction, in response to a financial crisis or a technological development. They assume that success depends on driving the changes rapidly and in a co-ordinated way across the organisation – and make a comprehensive plan.
- **Incremental (directional) plan** People use this approach in uncertain conditions – such as when direction depends on the outcomes of research and development. Tasks, times and even the objective are likely to change as the outcomes of current and planned activities become known – 'Important strategic areas may be left deliberately unclear until the outcomes of current events have been established' (Lynch, 2003, p. 633).
- **Selective plan** This approach may work when neither of the other methods is the best way forward – such as when managers wish to make a comprehensive change, but are unable to do so because of opposition in some areas. They may then try to implement the change in those areas which, while not ideal, may enable them to make some progress towards the objectives.

Communicating the plan

In a small organisation or where the plan deals with only one area, communication in any formal way is probably unnecessary. Equally, those who have been involved in developing the objectives and plans will be well aware of it. However, in larger enterprises managers will probably invest time and effort in communicating both the objectives and the actions required throughout the areas affected. They do this to:

- ensure that everyone understands the plan;
- allow them to resolve any confusion and ambiguity;
- communicate the judgements and assumptions that underlie the plan;
- ensure that activities around the organisation are coordinated in practice as well as on paper.

6.8 Implementing, monitoring and revising

Implementing

However good the plan, nothing worthwhile happens until people implement it, making visible, physical changes to the organisation and the way people work. This is often challenging when the plan comes into contact with the processes and people which are expected to change. Those implementing the plan sometimes encounter objections – and perhaps find that some of the assumptions in the plan are incorrect.

Organisations are slower to change than plans are to prepare – so events may overtake the plan. Miller *et al.* (2004) tracked the long-term outcomes of 150 strategic plans to establish how managers put them into action and how that affected performance. They defined implementation as:

> all the processes and outcomes which accrue to a strategic decision once authorisation has been given to ... put the decision into practice. (Miller *et al.*, 2004, p. 203)

They concluded that success was heavily influenced by:

- managers' experience of the issue, and
- **organisational readiness** for a change.

Organisational readiness refers to the extent to which staff are able to specify objectives, tasks and resource requirements of a plan appropriately, leading to acceptance.

Having relevant experience of what has to be done ... enables managers to assess the objectives [and to] specify the tasks and resource implications appropriately, leading [those affected to accept the process]. (p. 206)

Readiness means a receptive organisational climate that enables managers to implement the change within a positive environment.

They illustrated the statistical results with cases showing, for example, how managers in a successful company were able to implement a plan to upgrade their computer systems because they had *experience* of many similar changes. They were 'able to set targets, detail what needed doing and allocate the resources ... That is, they could plan and control the implementation effectively'. In another illustration, a regional brewer extending into the London area had no directly relevant experience, and so was not able to set a specific plan. But people in the organisation were very *receptive* to new challenges, and could implement the move with little formal planning.

The authors concluded that the activities of planning do not in themselves lead to success, but are a means for gaining acceptance of what has to be done when it is implemented. Planning gives people confidence in the process, leading to high levels of acceptability:

Planning is a necessary part of this approach to success, but it is not sufficient in itself. (Miller *et al.*, 2004, p. 210)

Monitoring and revising

The final stage in planning is to set up a system that allows people to monitor progress towards the goals. This happens at all levels – from a Crossrail project manager monitoring whether a supplier delivered material today, to the board at the Co-op Bank monitoring progress on the LloydsTSB acquisition. In complex projects such as that (sometimes called a programme) monitoring focuses mainly on the interdependencies between the many smaller plans that make up the whole.

Project plans define and display every task and activity, but someone managing a programme of linked projects would soon become swamped with such detail. The programme manager needs to maintain a quick-to-understand snapshot of the programme. This should show progress to date, the main events being planned, interdependencies, issues, and expected completion dates. This also helps the programme manager to communicate with senior executives and project managers. One way to do this is to create a single chart (sometimes called a Gantt chart) with a simplified view of each project on a timeline. Figure 6.6 illustrates this. Details vary but the main features are usually:

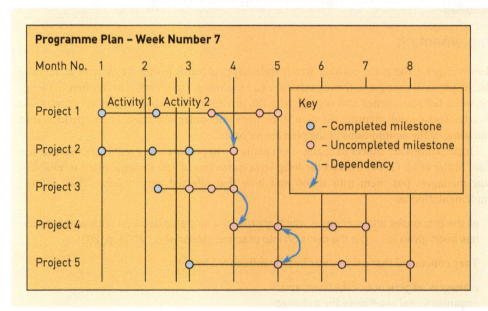

Figure 6.6 A programme overview chart

Source: *Managing Information Systems: Strategy and Organisation*, 3rd ed., FT/Prentice Hall, Harlow (Boddy, D., Boonstra, A., and Kennedy, G. 2009) p. 258, Figure 9.5, Copyright © Pearson Education Ltd. 2002, 2005, 2009.

- a timeline, showing its passage;
- a list of the tasks or sub-projects, with a symbols showing planned and actual completions or major milestones in each project;
- indications of interdependencies between projects.

Case study: Crossrail – the case continues   www.crossrail.co.uk

An article in *Civil Engineering* explained how a construction company and their client used some unusual planning practices to increase the speed and reduce the cost of building Canary Wharf Crossrail Station.

Crossrail had developed outline designs for every station, but in this case the station was to be built on land owned by Canary Wharf Group – a major property company which had developed other nearby sites (and an advocate of Crossrail). They offered to contribute £150 million towards the cost if they were given full responsibility for designing and building it. Crossrail agreed and those managing the project claimed that:

- involving the designers (Arup) of the station and the client (Canary Wharf Group) in early discussions enabled significant improvements to the original plan – such as reducing the size of the station without any loss of functionality, and adding a retail outlet;
- drawing on the long local experience of Canary Wharf Group, who had constructed more than 30 buildings in the area, enabled radical innovations in the design, such as changing the original Crossrail plan to fill a dock on the site before building the station – the developer believed this solution was too costly and raised severe environmental issues. They proposed a plan to avoid filling the dock, which would be less costly. They also assessed groundwater conditions using information prepared for the original development of Canary Wharf;
- commissioning a trial of a new type of piling machine which provided valuable data to help the team plan the time required for that piece of work. The trial cost £250,000 but saved many times that in time and construction cost;
- good communications between client and designers enabled them to adapt the design as work progressed, using the experience gained during implementation;
- in all, they claimed that the arrangements helped to reduce the cost of the station to 58 per cent of the expected cost, and to have reduced the time required for the work by one year.

Source: Yeow *et al.* (2012).

Case questions 6.3

- This part of the case gives examples of which approach to planning? (Section 6.4)
- What examples do you see here of managers acting to reduce 'optimism bias'? (Section 6.5)
- Consider the risks and benefits of radical innovation in one part of an unprecedented project such as this.

6.9 Integrating themes

Entrepreneurship

The discipline of producing a written business plan seems likely to help inexperienced entrepreneurs to clarify their ideas before making expensive mistakes, but Burke *et al.* (2010) noted that empirical evidence for this was uncertain, especially for other types of entrepreneur. 'Portfolio entrepreneurs' (those who already manage several businesses) may benefit if preparing a business plan helps them to clarify systematically how a new opportunity fits their other ventures, for example by identifying operating synergies. 'Serial entrepreneurs' (who have created one or more new ventures before the present one) may find spending time to produce a detailed business plan is a costly diversion if they can draw quickly on their experience.

Using documentary and interview data from over 400 new ventures in three English counties – led by inexperienced, portfolio or serial entrepreneurs – they found that:

> ventures with written business plans grew faster than those without business plans [probably because they] help raise entrepreneurial capabilities and, thereby, enhance performance. (Burke *et al.*, 2010, p. 406)

Results differed slightly depending on the type of entrepreneur, but consistently showed:

> that a written business plan improves employment growth in new ventures ... By articulating goals and identifying strategies for exploiting entrepreneurial opportunities, written business plans appear to enhance entrepreneurial decision making. (p. 407)

Sustainability

Many companies are responding to the challenges posed by climate change, and are developing policies to reduce carbon emissions and other environmentally damaging practices. Such policy statements depend on the quality of the plans which managers develop – unless they make detailed plans, they will be no more than good intentions. In 2007 Marks & Spencer announced 'Plan A' – and in 2010 extended this into a programme to become the world's most sustainable retailer by 2015. To achieve this it will extend Plan A to cover all of its 36,000 product lines, so that each carries at least one sustainable or ethical quality, and to fully embed sustainability into the way the company and its suppliers do business. The Plan A commitments are in seven areas:

1. **Customers and Plan A:** to help customers to live more sustainable lives.
2. **Make Plan A part of how we do business:** to accelerate our moves to make Plan A 'how we do business'.
3. **Tackling climate change:** to make operations in UK and Republic of Ireland carbon neutral.
4. **Packaging and waste:** to stop sending waste to landfill from stores, offices and warehouses, reduce the use of packaging and carrier bags, and find new ways to recycle and reuse the materials.
5. **Being a fair partner:** to improve the lives of hundreds of thousands of people in the supply chain and local communities.
6. **Natural resources:** to ensure that key raw materials come from the most sustainable source possible, in order to protect the environment and the world's natural resources.
7. **Health and wellbeing:** to help thousands of customers and employees choose a healthier lifestyle.

In November 2012 it published an update on progress report, claiming it was already achieving the majority of its objectives, including being the first retailer to be carbon neutral, and sending zero waste to landfill (**www.marksandspencer.com**).

Activity 6.5   **Progress towards the goals of Plan A**

- Visit the Marks & Spencer's website and navigate to the Plan A pages. That explains the plan fully, and includes current information on progress.
- Identify a theme that interests you and find out what progress they have made on the plan.

Internationalisation

As managers engage in international business they inevitably begin to work with colleagues from other national cultures in planning new products, joint ventures or merging information systems. The contrasts in national cultures which Hofstede observed (see Chapter 4) implies that some combinations of cultural types in cross-national teams may work better than others.

A manager working on a project at EADS (the European consortium which included BAE Systems until 2006) studied the relations between British, French and German staff working on the A380 project. In particular he considered how the dimensions 'power distance' and 'uncertainty avoidance' differed amongst team members, and how this affected the way they worked together in the planning process.

He found that French managers tended to be distant from their subordinates, while British and German employees felt they had greater freedom to talk back. Indeed, the British and German 'power distance' scores were identical. By contrast, the British had higher tolerance for uncertainty than the Germans or the French. While the French and German scores differed, they both showed less comfort with ambiguity and a greater desire for procedures. The British were good at contributing ideas to the planning process, but weaker at implementation (private communication).

Governance

Glaister and Travers (2001) describe the range of interests who invested significant capital or other resources in Crossrail, and who were closely interested in its progress. Decisions which those driving the project have to make could have serious consequences for one or more parties. They have therefore put in governance arrangements to ensure that as far as possible the project team acts in the interests of all the Crossrail sponsors.

The most obvious of these mechanisms is the company structure. Crossrail Limited is the company charged with delivering Crossrail. It was created in 2001 to promote and develop new lines and is a wholly-owned subsidiary of Transport for London (TfL). The ten members of the Crossrail Board include representatives of the project sponsors and partners, as well as those appointed for their relevant expertise in, say, finance or law. Sponsors are the Mayor of London (through Transport for London) and the Department of Transport. Other partners are Network Rail, British Airports Authority (BAA), The City of London, Canary Wharf Group (property developers) and Berkeley Homes (residential property developers). The executive team managing the project report regularly to the Main Board.

Among the issues which they will seek regular reassurance is on the financial control of the project. Earlier (Section 6.5) we showed the common tendency of public infrastructure projects to cost more than expected. A function of the Main Board will be to monitor how executives manage the project to ensure it stays within budgeted costs, especially as public funds to cover any excess costs will be very hard to secure in the current financial climate.

Summary

1 **Explain the purposes of planning and the content of several types of plan**
   - Effective plans can clarify direction, motivate people, use resources efficiently and allow people to measure progress towards objectives.
   - Plans can be at strategic, tactical and operational levels, and in new businesses people prepare business plans to secure capital. Strategic business units also prepare plans relatively independently of the parent. There are also special-purpose or project plans, and standing plans. All can be either specific or directional in nature.

2 **Compare alternative planning processes and evaluate when each may be most suitable**
   - Plans can be formal/rational/top down in nature, or they can be adaptable and emergent; a combination of approaches is most likely to suit firms in volatile conditions.

3 **Outline the five iterative tasks in planning and describe techniques used in each**
   - Recycling through the tasks of gathering information, deciding goals, deciding and what needs to be done, doing it, and revising.
   - Planners draw information from the general and competitive environments using tools such as Porter's Five Forces Analysis. They can do this within the framework of a SWOT analysis, and also use forecasting, sensitivity analysis, critical success factors and scenario planning techniques.

4 **Use theory to evaluate the motivational effect of the goals stated in a plan**
   - Goal-setting theory predicts that goals can be motivational if people perceive the targets to be difficult but achievable.
   - Goals can also be evaluated in terms of whether they are specific, measurable, attainable, rewarded and timed.

5 **Use a framework to evaluate whether a plan is sufficiently comprehensive**
   - Figure 6.5 provides a model for recalling the likely areas in an organisation which a plan should cover, indicating the likely ripple effects of change in one area on others.

6 **Evaluate the context which will affect the ability of managers to implement a plan**
   - The value of a plan depends on people implementing it, but Miller's research shows this depends on their experience, and the receptivity of the organisation to change.

7 **Show how ideas from the chapter can add to your understanding of the integrating themes**
   - All entrepreneurs can benefit from taking the time to write a business plan.
   - Long-term sustainability depends on organisations making equally long-term plans, which many organisations now do.
   - Companies operating internationally usually try to customise their products for local markets to reflect customer preferences. This affects not only the product but also product advice, packaging and distribution methods – and is a significant planning activity in such firms.
   - Complex, one-off, projects such as those in construction require governance and control systems to help ensure that conflicting interests work together.

Test your understanding

1 What types of planning do you do in your personal life? Describe them in terms of whether they are (a) strategic or operational, (b) short or long term, (c) specific or directional.
2 What are four benefits that people in organisations may gain from planning?
3 What are the main sources of information that managers can use in planning? What models can they use to structure this information?
4 What are SMART goals?
5 In what ways can a goal be motivational? What practical things can people do in forming plans that take account of goal-setting theory?
6 What is meant by the term 'hierarchy of goals', and how can the idea help people to build a consistent plan?

7 Explain the term 'organisational readiness', and how people can use the idea in developing a plan that is more likely to work.
8 What are the main ways of monitoring progress on a plan, and why is this so vital a task in planning?
9 Summarise an idea from the chapter that adds to your understanding of the integrating themes.

Think critically

Think about the way your company, or one with which you are familiar, makes plans. Review the material in the chapter, and perhaps visit some of the websites identified. Then make notes on these questions.

- What examples of the themes discussed in this chapter are currently relevant to the company? What types of plans are you most involved with? Which of the techniques suggested do you and your colleagues typically use, and why? What techniques do you use that are not mentioned here?
- In responding to these issues, what **assumptions** about the nature of planning in business appear to guide your approach? Are the prevailing assumptions closer to the rational or learning perspectives? Why do you think that is?
- What factors in the **context** of the company appear to shape your approach to planning – what kind of environment are you working in, for example?
- Have you compared your planning processes with those in other companies to check if they use **alternative** methods to yours? How do they plan?
- Have you considered the **limitations** of your approach – such as whether you plan too much or too little? What limitations can you see in some of the ideas presented here – for example the usefulness of scenario planning or SWOT analysis

Read more

Grant, R. M. (2003), 'Strategic planning in a turbulent environment: evidence from the oil majors', *Strategic Management Journal*, vol. 24, no. 6, pp. 491–517.

Empirical study of the strategic planning systems in major international oil companies, and how these aim to cope with uncertainty in that industry.

Latham, G. P. and Locke, E. A. (2006), 'Enhancing the Benefits and Overcoming the Pitfalls of Goal Setting', *Organisational Dynamics*, vol. 35, no. 4, pp. 332–40.

Leidecker, J. K. and Bruno, A. V. (1984), 'Identifying and Using Critical Success Factors' *Long Range Planning*, vol. 17, no.1, pp. 23–32.

This useful article identifies eight possible sources for identifying critical success factors, gives examples, and suggests ways of assessing their relative importance.

Sahlman, W. A. (1997), 'How to Write a Great Business Plan', *Harvard Business Review*, vol. 75, no. 4, pp. 98–108.

Valuable guidance by an experienced investor, relevant to start-ups and established businesses.

Whittington, R., Molloy, E., Mayer, M. and Smith, A. (2006), 'Practices of Strategising/Organising: Broadening Strategy Work and Skills', *Long Range Planning*, vol. 39, no. 6, pp. 615–29.

> ### Go online

These websites have appeared in the chapter:

www.crossrail.co.uk
www.dsm.com
www.volvo.com
www.merck.com
www.marksandspencer.com
www.inamo-restaurant.com
www.maersk.com

Visit two of the sites in the list, and navigate to the pages dealing with corporate news, or investor relations.

- What planning issues can you identify that managers in the company are likely to be dealing with?
- What kind of environment are they likely to be working in, and how will that affect their planning methods and processes?

CHAPTER 8
MANAGING STRATEGY

Aim

To describe and illustrate the processes and content of managing strategy.

Objectives

By the end of your work on this chapter you should be able to outline the concepts below in your own terms and:

1. Explain why the process, content and context of strategy matters, and how the issues vary between sectors
2. Compare planning, learning and political views on strategy
3. Summarise evidence on how managers develop strategies
4. Explain how tools for external and internal analysis help managers develop strategy
5. Use the product/market matrix to compare corporate level strategies
6. Use the generic strategies matrix to compare business level strategies
7. Illustrate the alternative ways in which managers deliver a strategy
8. Show how ideas from the chapter add to your understanding of the integrating themes

Key terms

This chapter introduces these ideas:

strategy
competitive strategy
emergent strategy
relational resources
unique resources
strategic capabilities
dynamic capabilities

value chain
mission statement
cost leadership strategy
economies of scale
differentiation strategy
focus strategy

Each is a term defined within the text, as well as in the glossary at the end of the book.

Case study: GKN   www.gkn.com

GKN is an internationally successful engineering company based in the UK's West Midlands. It supplies components to automobile and aircraft manufacturers around the world, employing about 40,000 people at over 35 locations. In 2012 the company reported sales of £6,904 million, and profit before tax of £497 million – both significant increases on the year before. A strategically important decision in 2011 had been to spend £633 million on purchasing Volvo's aircraft engineering division, strengthening the company's position in that market.

In 1759 nine entrepreneurs built a blast furnace at Dowlais, high in a Welsh valley, powered by water from a stream. Eight years later they appointed John Guest to manage their business, which he did successfully, and was later followed by his son, Thomas, and grandson, Josiah John Guest – whose wife Charlotte led the business for several years after his death in 1852. They and their successors continued to invest in modern technology and to enter new markets – such as a steam engine in place of water in 1798, a transport link to Cardiff docks, and a mill that allowed it to supply large quantities of iron rails for the rapidly growing railway network – including those in Russia and the US (Lorenz, 2009, p. 9).

In 1900 the iron company which Guest had founded merged with a major customer – Arthur Keen's nut and bolt company – to form Guest, Keen and Co. In 1902 this company acquired Nettlefold's to create the company which traded for many years as Guest, Keen and Nettlefolds.

By 1963 the company was mainly a steel producer, though also making semi-finished castings and forgings and huge quantities of screws, nuts and bolts. In 1967 the Labour government nationalised the UK steel industry, including the part owned by GKN. Senior management assumed that when the Conservatives returned to power they would denationalise the industry and the company would buy back the steel plants.

Trevor Holdsworth, who had recently joined the company in a senior finance role, believed that returning to steel would be a serious strategic error. He saw the potential value of a resource the company had acquired a few years earlier – Birfield, an engineering company supplying components to the motor industry. This in turn owned a minority stake in Uni-Cardan – a German supplier to Volkswagen and other European car manufacturers. Holdsworth concluded the company should not return to the UK commodity steel business but instead should focus on supplying high-technology components to the international motor industry.

Lorenz (2009) shows it was only with great difficulty that Holdsworth, a courteous man who led by reason rather than charisma, persuaded the then Chairman to change his mind. Holdsworth prevailed: the board of directors decided not to return to steel, and to buy full control of Uni-Cardan. Over the next 20 years GKN was able to establish a powerful position in Europe's strongest motor industry: Holdsworth had a clear idea of what sectors GKN should be in, and what it should leave.

Source: Lorenz (2009).

Getty Images/Bloomberg

Case questions 8.1

Visit the company website and note recent events and developments in the company.

- Note the sales and profit performance in the most recent period compared to an earlier one.
- What do the chairman and chief executive write about the company's current strategy?
- What challenges do they say the company is facing?

> **Activity 8.1 Describing strategy**
>
> Before reading this chapter, write some notes on what you understand 'strategy' to be.
>
> - Think of one organisation with which you have had contact, or about which you have read, in the last week.
> - Make brief notes summarising what they do and how they do it.
> - What clues does that give you about the strategic decisions they have made?
> - Record your ideas as you may be able to use them later.

8.1 Introduction

GKN illustrates the value of managing strategy. At successive periods in its long history it has faced major decisions about where to allocate financial resources – replacing water power with steam, investing in a mill to meet rising demand for rails, deciding to merge with other businesses to create GKN, and then the decision to stay out of steel and to focus on supplying the booming European car industry. These, and later, strategic investment decisions shaped the company.

All organisations face these issues of where to allocate effort and resources, and depend on senior management providing strategic leadership – see Management in practice.

> **Management in practice A new strategist at easyJet www.easyJet.com**
>
> Carolyn McCall became chief executive of easyJet in 2010 when the company was in disarray. She quickly stabilised the immediate problems, and embarked on a strategy to improve core operations and rebuild a demoralised management team by stemming departures and making some good new appointments. The company has since reduced capacity in line with economic conditions, and has worked hard to attract a wider range of customers, including business travellers – attracting them away from airlines like BA. By early 2013 the share price was around 990p, and the company was on the verge of entering the FTSE 100 index. One observer said:
>
> > Before Carolyn arrived, the easyJet team were very nervous and reactive to what Ryanair did. Now you see them doing their own thing – and you see Ryanair even following easyJet. The world really has changed.
>
> Source: *Financial Times*, 19 February 2012, p. 21.

Should Virgin continue to extend the brand into more areas of activity, or would it gain more by building profits in the existing areas, and achieving more synergies across the group? Some charities face declining income – should their managers continue as they are now, or will they serve their cause better by providing fewer services or delivering them in a different way?

Strategic management enables companies to be clear about how they will add value to resources, even as their situation changes. Strategy links the organisation to the outside world, where changes in the competitive (micro) and general (macro) environment bring opportunities and threats. Table 8.1 gives some examples of organisations managing their strategies.

Managing Strategy 617

Table 8.1 Examples of organisations making strategic changes

Organisation and strategic issue	Strategic decisions or moves
Tesco (Part 6 case) – wanting to widen overseas business to achieve faster growth (www.tesco.com)	In 2005 opens Fresh and Easy chain in US. Invests over £1 billion but makes no profit. In 2012 begins strategic review – may lead to closure.
Procter and Gamble (world's largest supplier of consumer goods (like soap and toothpaste) – how to ensure long term growth (www.p&g.com)	Changed from focus on people in rich economies to those in poor countries – affects R&D, market research and manufacturing to identify and make suitable products.
Nestlé (global food and drinks) – how to stimulate sales and profits in a mature business (www.nestle.com)	Increased emphasis on healthy foods, by adapting current products and buying companies with established reputations for healthy products.

The first sections of this chapter outline the strategy process, how managers develop strategy, and the tools they use to analyse external and internal environments. Two sections then focus on corporate and business unit strategies respectively, followed by a presentation of the ways in which managers choose to deliver their strategy.

8.2 Strategy – process, content and context

What is strategy?

Strategy is about how people decide to organise major resources to enhance the performance of an enterprise. It is about resource decisions that are large, relatively long-term, expensive and visible – with correspondingly large implications for performance: decisions that are not strategic are operational or tactical. Elaborating on the definition:

- **People**: Strategy is typically the responsibility of senior management, but some believe that in times of rapid change engaging more people in decisions will improve the result.
- **Decide**: In formal planning processes and/or informal conversations amongst managers.
- **Organise**: How to divide and coordinate activities to add most value.
- **Major**: Significant, expensive, visible – decisions with long-term implications.
- **Resources**: Inputs the enterprise needs – including those in other organisations.
- **To enhance performance**: The intended outcome of strategic decisions.
- **Enterprise**: All kinds of organisation can benefit from managing their strategy.

Strategy is about how people decide to organise major resources to enhance performance of an enterprise.

The definition is consistent with the view of Johnson *et al.* (2007) who suggest that strategy is something people do (their strategy process) *and* that organisations have (their strategy content).

Process

People, usually senior managers, talk and email and argue about their present and future strategy – this is their strategy process. In this sense, strategy is something that people *do* (Johnson *et al.*, 2007). Understanding this perspective implies finding out who creates strategy, what information they gather and how they use the tools available. Do they work in formal settings leading to rationally-based plans – or is the process more fluid and iterative?

Are strategies set for years, or do they emerge, alter and disappear, sometimes very quickly. Sections 8.3 and 8.4 introduce ideas on strategy processes.

Content

The current strategy is the starting point of, and the new one emerges from, the strategy process – so in this sense strategy is something that organisations *have* (Johnson *et al.*, 2007). Something stimulates managers to question current strategy, such as a hostile takeover bid, or an idea for a new service, but which requires investment. If the investment will be significant, then the decision will be 'strategic'. Managers develop strategy to perform well against competitors. They try to identify what gives their enterprise an edge, to define their **competitive strategy** and support it with suitable resources. Competitive strategy includes deciding what to offer, to which markets, using what resources. Sections 8.5 and 8.6 will deal with these topics.

Competitive strategy explains how an organisation (or unit within it) intends to achieve competitive advantage in its market.

Context

The organisation's context affects the issues those managing strategy will face. Not-for-profit (NFP) or public sector organisations share some characteristics with commercial businesses (they need to attract and retain enthusiastic and capable staff) and differ in others (their performance criteria and sources of funding). Table 8.2 illustrates these differences.

Whatever their context, strategists hope to enhance performance by clarifying and unifying purpose, linking short term actions to long term goals, and measuring performance.

Table 8.2 Examples of strategic issues in different settings

Type of organisation	Distinctive strategic issues	Examples in this text
Large multinational corporations (MNCs)	Structure and control of global activities Allocating resources between units	Prector and Gamble (this chapter); BP (Part 2 case)
Small and medium enterprises (SMEs)	Strongly influenced by founders or owners; lack of capital limits choices	innocent drinks (Chapter 2)
Manufacturing	Relative contribution to competitive advantage of the manufacturing (physical product) or service aspect (delivery, customer support) of the offer	BMW (Chapter 11)
Firms in innovative sectors	Adding value depends on rapid innovation, so strategy aims to create a culture of questioning and challenge	Nokia (Chapter 3)
Public sector	Competing for resources, and so aim to demonstrate best value in outputs; most problems require co-operation between agencies, complicating strategy	Crossrail (Chapter 6)
Voluntary and NFP sector	Balancing ideology and values with interests of funding sources; balancing central control (consistency) with local commitment (volunteers and local staff).	The Eden Project (Chapter 15)

> **Activity 8.2** **Think about the definition**
>
> Reflect on an organisation you have worked in, or ask a friend or relative who works in an organisation to help.
>
> - Can you/they identify examples of people in that organisation working on some or all of the items in the definition of strategy?
> - Did you/they do other things that were seen as 'managing strategy' but which are not mentioned?
> - Decide if the definition accurately describes 'strategy'.
> - If not, how would you change it?

8.3 Planning, learning and political perspectives

Table 8.3 shows three perspectives on the strategy process, comparing their approach, content, nature and outcomes – and the context in which they may be suitable.

Planning

The 'planning view' is prescriptive, based on the idea that the complexity of strategic decisions requires a formal approach to guide managers through the process of making them. Ansoff (1965) presented strategy development as a systematic process, following a prescribed

Table 8.3 Alternative perspectives on the strategy process

	Planning	Learning	Political
Approach	Prescriptive; assumes rationality	Descriptive; based on bounded rationality	Descriptive; based on bounded rationality
Content	Analytical tools and techniques; forecasting; search for alternatives, each evaluated in detail	Limited use of tools and techniques, limited search for options: time and resources don't permit	As learning view, but some objectives and options disregarded as politically unacceptable
Nature of process	Formalised, systematic, analytical; top down – centralised planning teams	Adaptive, learning by doing; top down and bottom up	Bargaining; use of power to shape strategies; top down and bottom up
Outcomes	Extensive plans made before work begins; plans assumed to be achieved with small changes	Plans are made but not all are 'realised'; some strategies are not planned but emerge in course of 'doing'	Plans may be left ambiguous to secure agreement; need interpretation during implementation; compromises
Context/environment	Stable environment; assumption that future can be predicted; if complex, use of more sophisticated tools	Complex, dynamic, future unpredictable	Stable or dynamic, but complex; stakeholders have diverging values, objectives and solutions

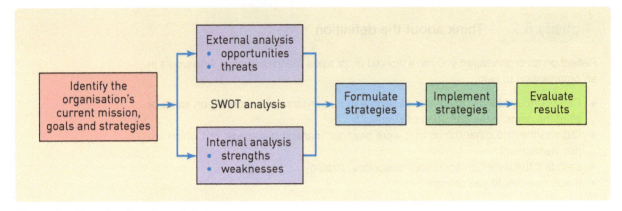

Figure 8.1 The planning view of strategy

sequence of steps and making extensive use of analytical tools and techniques – shown in Figure 8.1. Those favouring this method assume that events and facts can be expressed objectively, and that people respond rationally to such information.

Those who challenge these assumptions of objectivity and rationality advocate two alternative views – the learning and the political.

Learning

Mintzberg (1994a, b) regards formal strategic planning as a system developed during a period of stability to suit the centralised bureaucracies typical of western manufacturing industry in the mid-twentieth century. This works well in those conditions, but not when businesses need to respond quickly to external changes.

He therefore distinguished between intended and **emergent strategy** (Figure 8.2). This shows an intended strategy, some parts of which are realised (deliberate strategy) – but also that some of the plans are not implemented (unrealised strategy). It is also likely that

Emergent strategies are those that result from actions taken one by one that converge in time in some sort of consistent pattern.

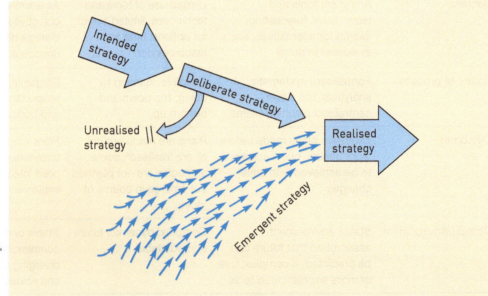

Figure 8.2 Five forms of strategy

Source: The Rise and Fall of Strategic Planning, Pearson Education Ltd. (Mintzberg, H. 2000) p. 24, Figure 1-1, Copyright © Pearson Education Ltd. 2000, with permission of Pearson Education Ltd.

other moves or investments take place that were not expressly intended when the plan was made – he describes these as 'emergent strategies' which result from:

> actions taken one by one, which converged in time in some sort of consistency or pattern. (Mintzberg, 1994a, p. 25)

The realised strategy is a combination of surviving parts of the intended strategy, and of the emergent strategy.

Management in practice **Emergent strategy at Ikea** www.ikea.com

Barthélemy (2006) offers an insight into the strategy process at Ikea. Their strategy has clearly been highly successful, but how did it come about? A close examination of the company's history shows that many of the specifics of the strategy were not brought about through a process of deliberate formulation followed by implementation:

> **Instead, the founder, Ingvar Kamprad started with a very general vision. Ikea's specific strategy then emerged as he both proactively developed a viable course of action and reacted to unfolding circumstances. (p. 81)**

Examples include:

- The decision to sell furniture was an adaptation to the market, not a deliberate strategy – furniture was initially a small part of the retail business, but was so successful that he soon dropped all other products.
- The flat pack method which symbolises the group was introduced to reduce insurance claims on the mail order business – its true potential only became clear when the company started opening stores, and realised that customers valued this type of product.
- The company only began to design its own furniture because other retailers put pressure on established furniture companies not to sell to Ikea.

Source: Barthélemy (2006).

This view of strategy recognises that:

> the real world inevitably involves some thinking ahead of time as well as some adaptation *en route*. (Mintzberg, 1994a, p. 26)

The essence of the learning view is adaptation, reacting to unexpected events, experimenting with new ideas 'on the ground'. Mintzberg gives the example of a salesperson coming up

> with the idea of selling an existing product to some new customers. Soon all the other salespeople begin to do the same, and one day, months later, management discovers that the company has entered a new market. (Mintzberg, 1994a, p. 26)

This was not planned but learned, collectively, during implementation. While advocating a learning view, Mintzberg notes the value of planning:

> Too much planning may lead us to chaos, but so too would too little, more directly. (Mintzberg, 1994a).

Political view

Strategy as an emergent process has much in common with political perspectives, since both draw on the concepts of bounded rationality and satisficing behaviour. While the learning view reflects the logic that planning can never give complete foresight, the political view adds dimensions of power, conflict and ambiguity.

Drawing on his experience in the public sector, Lindblom (1959) drew attention to political influences on strategy, especially as value judgements influence policy and how stakeholders' conflicting interests frustrate attempts to agree strategy. He concluded that strategic management is not a scientific, comprehensive or rational process, but an iterative, incremental process, featuring restricted analysis and bargaining between the players. Lindblom called this the method of 'successive limited comparisons' whereby 'new' strategy is made by marginal adjustments to existing strategy that are politically acceptable and possible to implement:

> Policy is not made once and for all; it is made and remade endlessly . . . [through] . . . a process of successive approximation to some desired objectives.

Activity 8.3 Gather evidence about the three perspectives

Read one of these case studies – Crossrail (Chapter 6), Apple (Part 1), BP (Part 2) – or any other organisation of interest to you.

- Identify two or three strategic moves made by the company, and write a brief note of each.
- Can you find evidence to show which of the three perspectives on strategy they used – planning, learning or political?
- On reflection, does that seem to have been the best method for the situation?
- Compare your answers with other students on your course, and try to identify any common or contrasting themes.

Case study GKN – the case continues www.gkn.com

Commenting later on his disagreement over strategy with the then Chairman, Trevor Holdsworth said:

> Thank goodness he gave in, or the constant velocity technology – which became central to our strategy – would have been lost. (Lorenz, 2009, p. 140)

This decision to invest in Uni-Cardan was the basis of GKN's future in driveline systems (equipment to control vehicle steering) and also changed the company's geographical balance. It was previously confined mainly to the British Commonwealth, but the new business brought a new range of customers and locations. By the mid-1980s the automotive business made 68 per cent of group profits.

For several years the company invested time and energy in building close links with the Japanese motor industry. To reduce their reliance on the only significant local driveline supplier, they invited GKN to supply these. Rather than build a plant in Japan, the company offered Toyota, Nissan and then Honda the right to make the components they required under licence, on condition that if they started to produce outside of Japan, they would buy these components from GKN.

As demand for Japanese cars grew in the US, each company built factories there – which GKN then supplied. This process was repeated in the UK when Nissan set up a plant in Sunderland, followed by Honda in Swindon. Both honoured their commitment to buy drivelines from GKN. By 1984, 75 per cent of GKN's auto component sales were to non-UK customers: it was becoming an international company making innovative engineering products (Lorenz, 2009, pp. 225–39).

The group was also implementing an earlier strategic decision to diversify into services, such as auto parts distribution, and wooden pallet supply.

Source: Lorenz (2009).

Case questions 8.2

- What external developments have affected the company's strategy?
- What examples are there in the case of the three perspectives on strategy?

8.4 How do managers develop strategies?

Grant (2003) offers insights into the way managers develop strategy from his study in eight major oil companies, especially how a more uncertain environment has affected them. In the relatively stable conditions of the 1970s staff at corporate HQ developed formal planning systems which included much analysis of economic trends, detailed forecasts of energy demand and price, and documents setting out long term plans for the businesses to follow.

At the time of Grant's study, all used a clear planning process – the details varied but Figure 8.3 shows the common components. Corporate HQ set the overall direction, which provided a framework within which business unit staff developed their strategy proposals. They discussed these with corporate staff, and the revised plans then informed both the annual financial budget, and the corporate plan. After board approval the corporate plan formed the context for annual performance targets, and for appraising their achievement.

As expected, all the companies said that the more turbulent environment (volatile oil prices, economic uncertainty, competition) had changed the strategy process. There was now:

- less detailed forecasting, more broad scenario planning (see below), more making assumptions about significant variables;
- less formality and documentation, more face-to-face discussion between corporate and business unit staff;
- shorter planning meetings; and
- a shift in responsibility from corporate to business unit management, and from planning staff to line management.

The content of strategic plans had also changed in that they now covered shorter periods, dealt with direction not detail, and emphasised performance by setting:

- financial targets;
- operating targets;

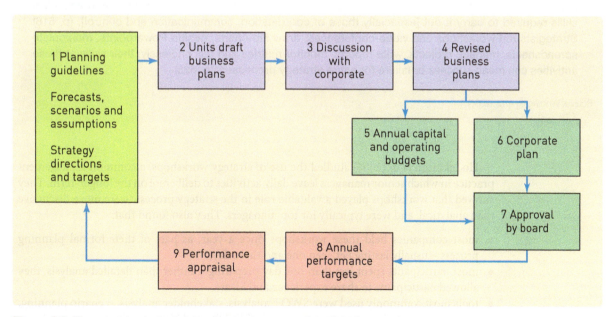

Figure 8.3 The generic strategic planning cycle among the oil majors
Source: Grant (2003), p. 499.

- safety and environmental targets;
- strategic mileposts; and
- capital expenditure limits.

Grant's final conclusion was that strategic planning processes were mainly concerned with coordinating the strategies emerging from the business units, and with monitoring implementation:

> Strategic planning has become less about strategic decision making and more a mechanism for coordination and performance managing . . . permitting increased decentralisation of decision making and greater adaptability and responsiveness to external change. (p. 515)

The eight oil companies are not typical organisations – but studies in other sectors present a similar picture of contemporary strategic planning as a process combining elements of formality and informality, of demanding targets and intelligent flexibility. Whittington *et al.* (2006) and Johnson *et al.* (2007) add to this with their view of 'strategy as practice', showing how people craft strategy, and how their context influences this – see Key ideas.

Key ideas — **Strategy as practice**

Whittington *et al.*(2006) conducted qualitative research in ten organisations to examine how they developed their strategies. They conclude that in a world of accelerating change the linked activities of formulating strategy and designing organisation are best conducted as tightly linked practical activities. They focussed on three specific tools – strategy workshops (or away-days), strategic change projects, and symbolic artefacts (things that people develop to represent and communicate strategy). Their observations showed the transitory nature of strategies and organisational forms, leading them to suggest that verbs ('strategising' and 'organising' respectively) capture the nature of the work people do as they develop strategy.

They also found that practical crafts of strategising and organising were as important as analytical tools:

Formal strategy can be renewed by a greater appreciation of the everyday, practical, non-analytical skills required to carry it out [especially those of coordination, communication and control]. (p. 616) Strategists run workshops and video-conferences, draw flip-charts, design Powerpoints, manipulate spreadsheets, manage projects, write reports, monitor metrics and talk endlessly: their skills at these activities can mean success or failure for entire strategy processes. (p. 625)

Source: Whittington *et al.* (2006).

Hodgkinson *et al.*(2006) studied the use of strategy workshops, a common management practice in which senior managers leave daily activities to deliberate on the longer-term. They showed that workshops played a valuable role in the strategy process, were more discursive than analytical, and were typically for top managers. They also found that:

- most companies held these workshops once a year, as part of their formal planning process – usually lasting between one and three days;
- most participants spent less than one day preparing – rather than detailed analysis, they allowed participants to share experience and ideas;
- tools most commonly used were SWOT analysis, stakeholder analysis, scenario planning, market segmentation, competence analysis, PESTEL, and Value Chain Analysis; and
- top managers were more likely to attend than middle managers.

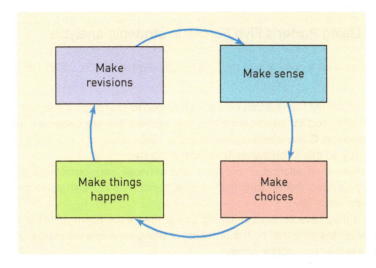

Figure 8.4 The strategy loop
Source: Sull (2007), p. 33.

They observed that since the main benefit of such workshops was to communicate and coordinate strategy, the absence of middle managers made this difficult. Hendry *et al.*(2010) studied the respective roles in forming strategy of boards of directors and chief executives in 21 Australian businesses. They distinguished between *procedural strategising* in which the board approved the strategy which the chief executive presented, and *interactive strategising* in which board members and CEO collaborated to create strategy. Some companies used both approaches, with choice of method probably reflecting the relative power of the chief executive and the board.

Sull (2007) believes that since volatile markets throw out a steady stream of opportunities and threats, managers cannot predict the form, magnitude or timing of events. This makes the planning view of strategy inadequate, as it may deter people from incorporating new information into action. He therefore sees the strategy process as inherently iterative – a loop instead of a line:

> According to this view, every strategy is a work in progress that is subject to revision in light of ongoing interactions between the organisation and its shifting environment. To accommodate those interactions, the strategy loop consists of four major steps: making sense of a situation, making choices on what to do (and what not to do), making those things happen and making revisions based on new information. (p. 31)

Figure 8.4 shows the strategy loop, the most important feature of which is that it implies that managers incorporate and use new information as it becomes available, closely linking strategy formation and implementation.

Sull stresses the importance of conversations – formal and informal, short and long, one-on-one and in groups – as the key mechanism for coordination. To put the strategy loop into practice managers at every level must be able to lead discussions about the four steps. The following sections provide ideas and examples about each:

- making sense – using information about external and internal environments;
- making choices – deciding strategy at corporate and business unit levels;
- making things happen – ways to deliver strategy; and
- making revisions – reflecting on results, and taking in new information.

8.5 Making sense – external analysis

Chapter 3 outlined Porter's Five Forces model, showing the forces which affect the profitability of an industry – see Key ideas.

> **Key ideas** — Using Porter's Five Forces in strategic analysis
>
> Analysing the likely effects on a company of the Five Forces (Porter, 1980a; 2008) can show potential action points.
>
> - **Threat of entry:** what are the barriers that new entrants need to overcome if they are to compete successfully? High barriers are good for incumbents: they fear barriers that are becoming lower, as this exposes them to more competition. Government legislation in the 1980s reduced the barriers protecting banks from competition, and allowed other companies to enter the industry.
> - **Threat of substitutes:** what alternative products and services may customers choose? Many people choose to receive their news online rather than in print, seriously threatening print newspapers, who need to build strategies for survival.
> - **Power of buyers:** if they have strong bargaining power they force down prices and reduce profitability. Small food companies are attracted by the prospect of doing business with large retailers – but are wary of the power of the retailers to dictate prices.
> - **Power of suppliers:** if suppliers have few competitors they can raise prices at the expense of customers. Companies that have few alternative sources of energy or raw materials are exposed when stocks are low.
> - **Competitive rivalry:** the four forces combine to affect the intensity of rivalry between an organisation and its rivals. Factors such as industry growth or the ease with which companies can leave it also affect this.
>
> The model remains popular, and Porter published a revised version in 2008 – mainly by adding current examples: the Five Forces remain the same. They help strategists to understand the fundamental conditions of their industry, and to work out how to make their company less vulnerable and more profitable.
>
> Source: Porter (1980, 2008).

The PESTEL framework helps companies to identify factors in the general environment that may affect strategy. As an example, cuts to local authority budgets have encouraged many to outsource services to companies in the private sector – in the belief they will deliver them at lower cost: Care UK, a privately-owned business, runs many care homes for the elderly for local authorities.

Companies vary widely in how they respond to external change. Engau and Volker (2011) illustrate this in a study of their reaction to the 1997 Kyoto Protocol. This is an international agreement setting national targets for lowering greenhouse gas emissions, but

> policy makers left many regulatory issues open, explicitly referring their resolution to subsequent negotiations. [This] created high regulatory uncertainty for firms. (p. 43)

The authors distinguished three types of response to this uncertainty – offensive, defensive and passive. Using survey data from 133 global companies in carbon-intensive industries, and interview data from 27 European airlines, they found that responses ranged from 'daredevils', who put all their resources into one type of response (such as influencing national policy makers to accept their point of view) to 'hedgers' who combined practices from all three (such as using an influencing strategy, but also making contingency plans to alter their business if influence failed).

External signals are often unclear, but the ability to process vast amounts of information about customers may bring opportunities to companies who are able to use it: see Key ideas.

> **Key ideas** — Opportunities in 'big data'?
>
> 'Big data' is the term used to describe the large volumes of data generated by traditional business activities and from new sources such as social media. Typical big data includes information from point-of-sale terminals,

cash machines, Facebook posts and YouTube videos. Companies use sophisticated software to analyse this data, looking for hidden patterns, trends or other insights they can use to better tailor their products and services to customers, anticipate demand and improve performance.

Companies and governments have been doing this for years with 'structured data' that is already well-organised – such as sales records – but recently there has been an explosion of 'unstructured data', such as Facebook posts. Their lack of an identifiable structure makes them harder to analyse – but could provide the most useful insights about, for example, what people and their friends think of a brand, or about their intentions towards trying a new product.

Many companies are developing models to capture and process this data, which they believe will be valuable to companies in areas such as consumer goods, insurance, consumer loans, small business lending and home loans who need to understand better the many linked factors in the business environment affecting consumers' decisions. The biggest gainers may be those who make the computer systems and software that do the analytical work – established players like IBM, Oracle and SAP.

Source: From an article by Richard Waters in the *Financial Times*, 10 December 2012, p. 19.

Strategy links an organisation's external relationships with its internal capabilities, so managers need an internal analysis to show how they may cope with external changes.

Activity 8.4 Using Porter's Five Forces to analyse a competitive environment

- Identify an industry which features in one of the case in this book, such as airlines or retailing.
- Gather specific evidence and examples of each of the Five Forces, and of how it affects competition.
- Try to identify how one company in the industry has changed their strategy to take account of this change in one or more of the Five Forces.

8.6 Making sense – internal analysis

Resources, competences and dynamic capabilities

Managers analyse the internal environment to identify strengths and weaknesses – what the organisation does well, where it might do better and where it stands in relation to competitors.

Chapter 1 introduced the idea of strategic capability as the ability to perform at the level required to survive and prosper, and showed how this depends on the resources available to the organisation, and its competence in using them. Tangible resources are the physical assets such as buildings, equipment, people or finance, while intangible resources include, following De Wit and Meyer (2010, pp. 115–16), relational resources and reputation – see Figure 8.5.

Relational resources are all the means available to a firm from its interaction with the environment – cultivating relationships with influential customers, government agencies, media organisations, research centres and so on provides management with valuable

Relational resources are intangible resources available to a firm from its interaction with the environment.

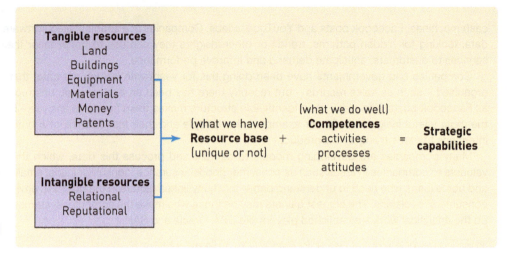

Figure 8.5
Resources, competences and capabilities

Unique resources are resources which are vital to competitive advantage and which others cannot obtain.

information. Reputation amongst other players in the environment is also a resource – a reputation for quality, trust or innovation will be more useful than one for sharp practice and poor delivery. A firm also benefits if it has **unique resources** – those which others cannot obtain such as a powerful brand, access to raw material or a distinctive culture. Joe Morris, operations director at TJ Morris, a Liverpool-based chain of discount stores (in 2010 the second largest independent grocer in the UK) claims that their IT system (which his brother Ed designed) gives them a competitive advantage:

> It is our own bespoke product. It is extremely reliable and simple. We can do what we want to do very quickly.

While the amount and quality of resources matter, how people use them matters more. Successful firms add value to resources by developing competences – activities and processes which enable them to deploy their resources effectively. If managers encourage staff to develop higher skills, cooperate with each other, be innovative and creative, the company is likely to perform better than one where managers treat staff indifferently. Johnson *et al.* (2011) show that resources and competences combine to provide a firm with what they call capabilities – the things that an organisation is able to do in a reliable, efficient way. They define **strategic capabilities** as the capabilities of an organisation that contribute to its long-term survival or competitive advantage – stressing that a capability (such as regularly introducing attractive new products, or consistently delivering services at low cost) typically combines both resources ('what we have') and competences ('what we do well').

Strategic capabilities are the capabilities of an organisation that contribute to its long-term survival or competitive advantage.

Ryanair has prospered not because it has resources (a fleet of modern, standard aircraft) – other airlines have similar resources, but are unprofitable. The difference is that Ryanair has developed competences – such as quick turn-arounds which enable it to use aircraft more efficiently. GlaxoSmithKline has a strategy to acquire half of its new drugs from other organisations: for this to work, it will develop a competence of identifying and working with suitable partners.

Management's task in internal analysis is to identify those capabilities (resources and competencies) that distinguish it to customers. At the *corporate level*, this could be the overall balance of activities that it undertakes – the product or service portfolio. Does it have sufficient capabilities in growing rather than declining markets? Does it have too many new products (which drain resources) relative to established ones? Are there useful synergies between the different lines of business? At the *divisional or strategic business unit level*, performance again depends on having adequate resources (physical, human, financial and so on) and competences (such as design, production or marketing).

In uncertain conditions factors which once brought success may no longer be enough. A company may need to create new capabilities better suited to the new conditions – such as the ability to bring new products to the market more rapidly than competitors, or to develop skills of developing alliances with other businesses. These are called **dynamic capabilities** – which enable it to renew and recreate its strategic capabilities to meet the needs of a changing environment. As described by Teece (2009) they include:

> the capacity (1) to sense and shape opportunities and threats, (2) to seize opportunities, and (3) to maintain competitiveness through enhancing, combining, protecting, and when necessary, reconfiguring the business enterprise's intangible and tangible assets. (p. 4)

These capabilities may be relatively formal, such as systems for sensing and responding to market opportunities or for identifying and acquiring firms with valuable skills or products. They may also be informal, such as the ability to reach decisions quickly when required, or the ability of staff to work well in constantly changing multi-professional teams.

Dynamic capabilities are an organisation's abilities to renew and recreate its strategic capabilities to meet the needs of a changing environment.

Case study: GKN – the case continues   www.gkn.com

One unexpected benefit of close, long-term links with the Japanese motor industry was that the driveline operation developed a cultural affinity with Japanese ways of working. This includes the concept of *kaizen* – continuous, incremental improvement in production processes.

> By the early 1980s GKN's drivelines operations had ingrained into their *modus operandi* a culture of continuous improvement [and] invested consistently in incremental improvements to both the joints themselves and their methods of manufacture. (Lorenz, 2009, p. 231)

In 1995 the company decided to leave one significant part of its industrial services business (and by 2001 had left industrial services altogether). The 1995 decision was to dispose of the automotive parts distribution business which, after 16 years of trying, had not fulfilled the company's expectations. The CEO at the time:

> Autoparts was like steel stock holding – it's a branch operation. And GKN was never any good at running branch operations. You have to do it by numbers through branch managers. You've got to have good branch managers . . . and reward them if they do well. You have to be monitoring them constantly, on a daily, weekly basis. We never had the drive or the people capable of running branches. We didn't have the experience, frankly . . .

Reflecting on the original decision to diversify, and to overestimate the company's ability to manage a different kind of business:

> Possibly we also had a slight delusion of grandeur. With the benefit of hindsight, that was a pretty bad mistake. (Lorenz, 2009, pp. 281–2)

The company's website reports (in 2013) that it seeks to recruit talented individuals with the skills and energy to become leaders of the future. Each employee's role is related to the group strategy and the job purpose and its business context is explained. In 2012 it recruited over 100 graduates, and employed over 800 apprentices. GKN Academy, an online training resource, enables all employees to access over 360 courses in eight languages.

Sources: Lorenz (2009); GKN website.

Case questions 8.3
- Visit the GKN website and look for information about how it develops the resources it needs to deliver the current strategy.
- What examples have you seen in the case about the company's resources and competences
- How have these interacted with strategy?

Value chain analysis

A **value chain** 'divides a firm into the discrete activities it performs in designing, producing, marketing and distributing its product. It is the basic tool for diagnosing competitive advantage and finding ways to enhance it' (Porter, 1985).

The concept of the **value chain**, introduced by Porter (1985), is derived from an accounting practice that calculates the value added at each stage of a manufacturing or service process. Porter applied this idea to the activities of the whole organisation, as an analysis of each activity could identify sources of competitive advantage.

Figure 8.6 shows primary and support activities. *Primary* activities transform inputs into outputs and deliver them to the customer:

- **inbound logistics**: receiving, storing and distributing the inputs to the product or service; also material handling and stock control etc;
- **operations**: transforming inputs into the final product or service, by machining, mixing and packing;
- **outbound logistics**: moving the product to the buyer collecting, storing and distributing; in some services (as sports event) these activities will include bringing the customers to the venue;
- **marketing and sales**: activities to make customers aware of the product;
- **service**: enhancing or maintaining the product – installation, training, repairs.

These depend on four *support* activities:

- firm infrastructure; organisational structure, together with planning, financial and quality systems;
- human resource management; recruitment, training, rewards etc.;
- technology development: relate to inputs, operational processes, outputs;
- procurement – acquiring materials and other resources.

Value chain analysis enables managers to consider which activities benefit customers, and which are more troublesome – perhaps destroying value rather than creating it. It might, say, be good at marketing, outbound logistics and technology development – but poor at operations and human resource management. That awareness may lead managers to consider

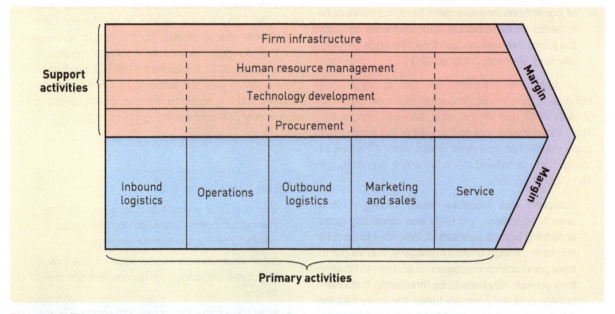

Figure 8.6 The value chain

Source: Competitive Advantage: Creating and Sustaining Superior Performance, The Free Press, New York (Porter, M.E. 1985) Copyright © 1985, 1988 by Michael E. Porter, all rights reserved, reprinted with the permission of Simon and Schuster Publishing Group from the Free Press edition.

which activities the business should do itself, and which it should outsource to other firms. Each activity in the chain can contribute to a firm's relative cost position and create a basis for differentiation (Porter, 1985) – the two main sources of competitive advantage. Analysing the value chain helps management to consider:

- Which activities have most effect on reducing cost or adding value? If customers value quality more than costs that implies a focus on quality of suppliers.
- What linkages do most to reduce costs, enhance value or discourage imitation?
- How do these linkages relate to cost and value drivers?

SWOT analysis

Strategy follows a 'fit' between internal capabilities and external changes – managers try to identify key issues from each and draw out the strategic implications. A SWOT analysis (**see Chapter 6**) summarises the internal and external issues and helps identify potentially useful developments – shown schematically in Figure 8.7.

Hodgkinson *et al.* (2006) found that managers often use the technique in strategy workshops, though like any technique the value depends on how thoroughly they do so – by, for example, taking time to gather evidence about the relative significance of factors, rather than simply listing them.

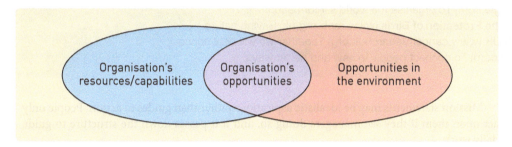

Figure 8.7
Identifying the organisation's opportunities

If the SWOT analysis is done thoroughly, it is useful to managers as they develop and evaluate strategic alternatives, aiming to select those that make the most of internal strengths and external opportunities. Managers in large enterprises develop strategies at corporate, business and functional levels, though in smaller organisations there will be less complexity. Figure 8.8 shows this.

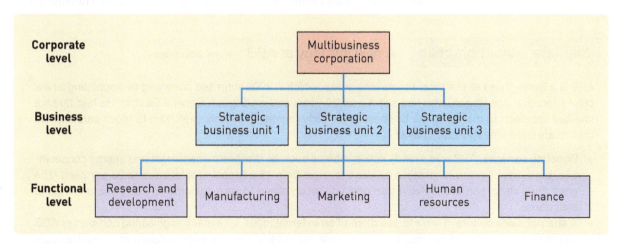

Figure 8.8 Levels of strategy

> **8.7** Making choices – deciding strategy at corporate level

At corporate level the strategy reflects the overall direction of the organisation, and the part which the respective business units will play. What is the overall mission and purpose? Should it focus on a small range of activities or diversify? Should it remain a local or national business, or seek to operate internationally? These decisions establish the direction of the organisation.

The corporate mission

A **mission statement** is a broad statement of an organisation's scope and purpose, aiming to distinguish it from similar organisations.

Defining the mission is intended to provides a focus for work. A broad **mission statement** can guide those setting more specific goals and the strategies to achieve them, by expressing the underlying beliefs and values held within the organisation – see the examples in the Management in practice feature.

Management in practice — Examples of missions and visions

IKEA (www.ikea.com) A better everyday life.
Google (www.google.com) To organise the world's information.
Royal Society for the Protection of Birds (www.rspb.org.uk) Saving nature.
Cancer Research UK (www.cancerresearchuk.org) Together we will beat cancer.
Nokia (www.nokia.com) To connect people in new and better ways.

Mission statements may be idealistic aspirations rather than guides to action. People only act upon them if they see managers doing so, and if it passes down the structure to guide daily work.

Setting a strategic direction

Strategies can aim for growth, stability or renewal. Growth strategies try to expand the number of products offered or markets served. Stability is when the organisation offers the same products and services to much the same group of customers. Renewal often follows a period of trouble and involves significant changes to the business to secure the required turnaround.

Management in practice — A new strategy at ABB www.abb.com

ABB is a Swiss-Swedish electrical engineering group, which in 2009 surprised observers by appointing a new chief executive, Joe Hogan, who had spent over 20 years at the US giant, General Electric. He had taken a low-key approach to managing the business in his early months in the job, preferring to move carefully. He then made three strategic adjustments:

- **Boosting services.** ABB was already active in areas such as facilities management and energy conservation, but Hogan wanted to increase services revenue from 16 per cent of total sales to 25 per cent: 'The great thing about services is that it also gets you much closer to your customer, helping you understand their needs.'
- **A sharper sales culture.** 'I want to see more of an external focus. Like many engineering companies ABB has tended to be inward looking.' It must become more sensitive to market signals and immediate customer needs.

- **Plugging geographic weaknesses.** ABB is admired for having moved early into China and India. Mr Hogan believes the group can deepen its activities in existing markets and grow where it is weak. 'We need to improve our global footprint. ABB has always been heavily focussed on Europe.'

Source: *Financial Times*, 8 June 2009.

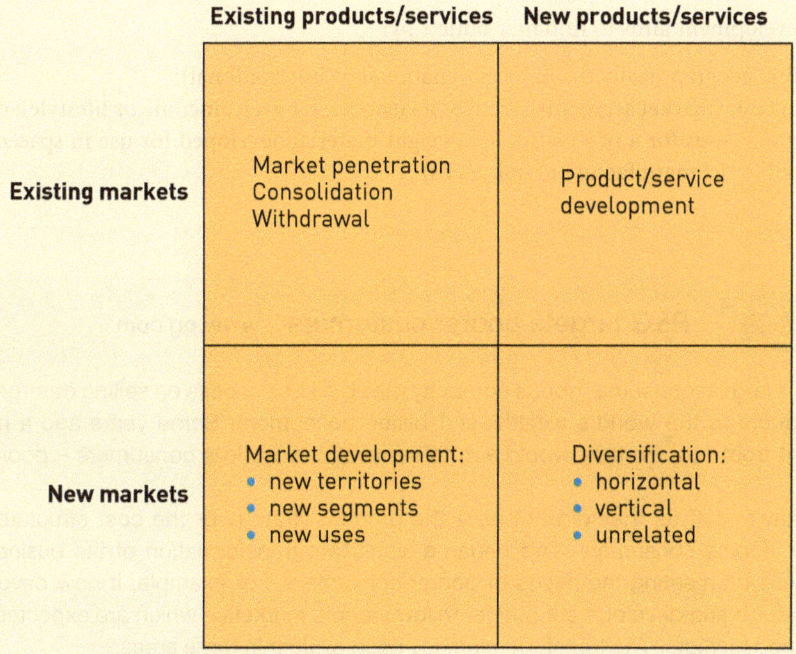

Figure 8.9
Strategy development directions – the product/market matrix

Source: As adapted in Johnson *et al.* (2011) from Chapter 6 of H. Ansoff, *Corporate Strategy*, published by Penguin 1988.

	Existing products/services	New products/services
Existing markets	Market penetration Consolidation Withdrawal	Product/service development
New markets	Market development: • new territories • new segments • new uses	Diversification: • horizontal • vertical • unrelated

Managers can decide how to achieve their chosen option by using the product/market matrix, shown in Figure 8.9. They can achieve growth by focussing on one or more of the quadrants; stability by remaining with existing products and services; and renewal by leaving some markets followed by entry into others.

Existing markets, existing product/service

Choice within this segment depends on whether the market is growing, mature, or in decline. Each box shows several possibilities:

- A market penetration strategy aims to increase market share, which will be easier in a growing market. It could be achieved by reducing price, increasing advertising or improving distribution.
- Consolidation aims to protecting the company's share in existing markets. In growing or mature markets this could mean improving efficiency and/or service to retain custom. In declining markets management might consolidate by acquiring of other companies.
- Withdrawal is a wise option when, for instance, competition is intense and the organisation is unable to match its rivals: staying in that line of business would destroy value, not create it. In the public sector, changing priorities lead to the redeployment of resources. Health boards have withdrawn accident and emergency services from some hospitals to make better use of limited resources.

Existing markets, new products/services

A strategy of product or service development allows a company to retain the relative security of its present markets while altering products or developing new ones. In retail sectors such as fashion, consumer electronics and financial services, companies continually change products to meet perceived changes in consumer preferences. Car manufacturers compete by adding features and extending their model range. Some new products, such as 'stakeholder pensions' in the United Kingdom, arise out of changes in government policy. Many new ideas fail commercially, so product development is risky and costly.

New markets, existing products/services

Market development aims to find new outlets by:

- extending geographically (from local to national or international);
- targeting new market segments (groups of customers, by age, income or lifestyle); or
- finding new uses for a product (a lightweight material developed for use in spacecraft is also used in the manufacture of golf clubs).

Management in practice   P&G targets poorer customers   www.pg.com

Procter & Gamble, the world's largest consumer goods company, has built its success on selling detergent, toothpaste and beauty products to the world's wealthiest 1 billion consumers. Some years ago a new chief executive declared that from now on they would aim to serve all the world's consumers – poor as well as rich.

This surprised the company's staff as they did not have the product strategy or the cost structure to be effective in serving lower income consumers. This began a significant transformation of the business, in which all the functions focus on meeting the needs of poorer consumers. For example, it now devotes 30 per cent of the annual research and development budget to low income markets – which are expected to grow twice as fast as developed markets. The transformation has been evident in three areas:

- how the company finds out what customers want;
- how this affects R&D; and
- manufacturing facilities.

Source: Company website.

New markets, new products/services

Often described as diversification, this can take three forms:

- **Horizontal integration** Developing related or complementary activities, such as when mortgage lenders extend into the insurance business, using their knowledge of, and contact with, existing customers to offer them an additional service. The advantages include the ability to expand by using existing resources and skills – such as Kwik-Fit's use of its database of depot customers to create a motor insurance business.
- **Vertical integration** Moving either backwards or forwards into activities related to the organisation's products and services. A manufacturer might decide to make its own components rather than buy them from elsewhere. Equally, it could develop forward into distribution.
- **Unrelated diversification** Developing into new markets outside the present industry. Virgin has used its strong brand to create complementary activities in sectors as diverse as airlines, media and banking. The extension by some retailers into financial services is another

example. It is a way to spread risk where demand patterns fluctuate at different stages of the economic cycle, and to maintain growth when existing markets become saturated.

Alternative development directions are not mutually exclusive: companies can follow several at the same time. Apple has a clear strategy to move away from being a computer manufacturer and into areas which would give their products a very wide appeal. One observer predicted, at the time of the iPad launch in 2010:

> Get on any train in five years' time, and people will be reading the newspaper (downloaded at home or automatically when they walk through Waterloo Station on the way home), books, watching TV, playing games (quite possibly with fellow passengers!) on their iPads.

8.8 Making choices – deciding strategy at business unit level

At the business unit level, firms face a choice about how to compete. Porter (1980b, 1985) identified two types of competitive advantage: low cost or differentiation. From this he developed the idea that firms can use three generic strategies: cost leadership, differentiation and focus, which Figure 8.10 shows. The horizontal axis shows the two bases of competitive advantage. Competitive scope, on the vertical axis, shows whether company's target market is broad or narrow in scope.

Cost leadership

Cost leadership is when a firm aims to compete on price rather than, say, advanced features or excellent customer service. They will typically sell a standard product and try to minimise costs. This requires **economies of scale** in production and close attention to reducing operating costs – including the benefits of what is known as the experience curve – the tendency for the unit cost of making a product to fall as experience of making it increases. Low costs alone will not bring competitive advantage – consumers must see that the product represents

A **cost leadership** strategy is one in which a firm uses low price as the main competitive weapon.

Economies of scale are achieved when producing something in large quantities reduces the cost of each unit.

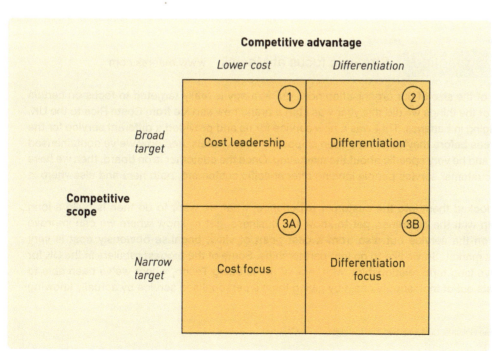

Figure 8.10
Generic competitive strategies

Source: Competitive Advantage: Creating and Sustaining Superior Performance, The Free Press, New York (Porter, M.E. 1985) Copyright © 1985, 1998 by Michael E Porter, all rights reserved, reprinted with the permission of Simon and Schuster Publishing Group from the Free Press edition.

value for money. Retailers which have used this strategy include Walmart (Asda in the UK), Argos and Superdrug; Dell Computers is another example, as is Ryanair (Chapter 1 Case).

Differentiation

> **Differentiation strategy** consists of offering a product or service that is perceived as unique or distinctive on a basis other than price.

A **differentiation strategy** is seen when a company offers a service that is distinct from its competitors, and which customers value. It is 'something unique beyond simply offering a low price' (Porter, 1985) that allows firms to charge a high price or retain customer loyalty. Chatterjee (2005) shows the strategic benefits of identifying very clearly the outcomes that customers value, and Sharp and Dawes (2001) contrast companies' methods of differentiation:

- Nokia achieves differentiation through the individual design of its product.
- Sony achieves it by offering superior reliability, service and technology.
- BMW differentiates by stressing a distinctive product/service image.
- Coca-Cola differentiates by building a widely recognised brand.

The form of differentiation varies. In construction equipment durability, spare parts availability and service will feature in a differentiation strategy, while in cosmetics differentiation is based on images of sophistication, exclusivity and eternal youth. Cities compete by stressing differentiation in areas such as cultural facilities, available land or good transport links.

Focus

> A **focus strategy** is when a company competes by targeting very specific segments of the market.

A **focus strategy** (sometimes called a 'niche' strategy) targets a narrow market segment, either by consumer group (teenagers, over-60s, doctors,) or geography. The two variants – cost focus and differentiation focus – are simply narrow applications of the broad strategies. Examples include:

- Saga (www.saga.co.uk) offers travel and insurance for those over 50.
- Croda (www.croda.com) produces speciality chemicals used in other products, including cosmetics.
- NFU Mutual offers insurance for farmers.

Management in practice   Strategic focus at Maersk   www.maersk.com

I think because of the size of our organisation now, our strategy is really targeted to focus on certain segments. One of the things we did this year was start a brand new service from Costa Rica to the UK, specifically bringing in bananas. That was a new service for us and provided a different service for the customer, whereas before they've always been shipped in bulk vessels, and now we've containerised them. So we try and be very specific about the marketing. Once the customer is on board, then we have small teams of customer service people looking after specific customers, both here and elsewhere in the world.

Once we've locked them into the customer experience, what we want to do then is build a long term relationship with the customer, get to know the business, get to know where we can improve them. Not just on the service but also from a cost point of view, because obviously cost is very important in this market. So we like to go into partnerships. Some of the biggest retailers in the UK for instance we have long term relationships with, one of those being Tesco, where we've been able to take a lot of costs out of their supply chain by giving them a personalised service by actually knowing their business.

Source: Interview with Brian Godsafe, Customer Services Manager.

> **Activity 8.5 Critical reflection on strategy**
>
> - Select two companies you are familiar with, and in each case gather evidence to help you decide which generic strategy they are following.
> - Then consider what features you would expect to see if the company decided to follow the opposite strategy.

Porter initially suggested that firms had to choose between cost leadership and differentiation. Many disagreed, observing how companies often appeared to follow both strategies simultaneously. By controlling costs better than competitors, companies can reinvest the savings in features that differentiate them. Porter (1994) later clarified his view:

> Every strategy must consider both relative cost and relative differentiation . . . a company cannot completely ignore quality and differentiation in the pursuit of cost advantage, and vice versa . . . Progress can be made against both types of advantage simultaneously. (p. 271)

However, he notes there are trade-offs between the two and that companies should 'maintain a clear commitment to superiority in one of them'.

Functional level strategy

Business level strategies need the support of suitable functional level strategies (Chapters 9, 11 and 12 give examples).

8.9 Making things happen – delivering strategy

Organisations deliver their strategies by internal development, acquisition, or alliance – or a combination: the choice affects the success of the strategy.

Internal development

The organisation delivers the strategy by expanding or redeploying relevant resources that it has or can employ. This enables managers to retain control of all aspects of the development of new products or services – especially where the product has technologically advanced features. Microsoft develops its Windows operating system in-house.

Public sector organisations typically favour internal development, traditionally providing services through staff whom they employ directly. Changes in the wider political agenda have meant that these are often required to compete with external providers, while some – such as France Telecom, Deutsche Post or the UK Stationery Office – have been partially or wholly sold to private investors.

Merger and acquisition

One firm merging with, or acquiring, another allows rapid entry into new product or market areas and is a quick way to build market share. It is also used where the acquiring company can use the other company's products to offer new services or enter new markets. Companies like Microsoft and Cisco Systems frequently buy small, entrepreneurial companies and incorporate their products within the acquiring company's range. Outside of their main domain, the researchers found that companies acquired firms to help them move quickly in a new direction. Vodafone made several large acquisitions in its quest to become the world's largest mobile phone company. Others take over companies for their knowledge of a local market.

Mergers and acquisitions frequently fail, destroying rather than adding value. When Sir Roy Gardner took over as chairman of Compass (a UK catering company) at which profits and the share price had fallen rapidly, he was critical of the previous management:

> (They) concentrated far too much on growing the business through acquisition. They should have stopped and made sure (that) what they had acquired delivered the expected results. Compass was being run by its divisional managers, which resulted in a total lack of consistency. (*Financial Times*, 19 January 2007, p. 19)

Case study: GKN – the case continues   www.gkn.com

Since the early 1990s the company had been building a presence in Aerospace, from an earlier investment in Westland helicopters. Kevin Smith had joined the company in 1999 as head of the Aerospace division and began to integrate a disparate group of companies and facilities. He had worked in the aircraft industry and knew Boeing managers well, soon learning they were about to outsource a large fabrication plant. Smith saw this as a major opportunity – but the board had banned further aerospace purchases. Smith persuaded them to lift the ban, bought the plant, and persuaded Boeing to appoint GKN as a preferred supplier of aerostructures – such as wings and fuselages (Lorenz, 2009, p. 315).

At a stroke, Smith had significantly increased GKN's presence in US military aerospace and by 2012 aerostructures accounted for 24 per cent of group sales. In that year it agreed to take over Volvo's aero-engine unit. Mr Stein, then GKN's CEO, said the deal meant that GKN components would be fitted in engines made by all three main aero-engine companies (General Electric, Pratt and Whitney and Rolls-Royce).

In 2011 GKN completed the purchase of Stromag which makes components such as electromagnetic brakes and hydraulic clutches, and of Getrag Driveline which supplies all-wheel drive transmission systems. Chief executive Nigel Stein said that both high margin businesses had been successfully integrated into the Driveline division and had already made a positive contribution.

Sources: Lorenz (2009); group website, *Financial Times*, 19 April 2012, 6 July 2012.

Case questions 8.4

- Review the other instalments of the case and list the ways it has chosen to deliver strategy against each of the headings in this section.
- Combine your results with the work you have done on Activity 8.6.

Joint ventures and alliances

Joint ventures to develop products or enter new countries range from highly formal contractual relationships to looser forms of cooperation. One attraction is that they limit risk. UK construction firm John Laing has a joint venture the Commonwealth Bank of Australia to invest in UK hospital and European road projects: rather than borrow funds for a project, Laing shares the risk (and the reward) with the bank.

A second reason for joint ventures (JVs) is to learn about new technologies or markets. Alliances also arise where governments want to keep sensitive sectors, such as aerospace, defence and aviation, under national control. Airbus, which competes with Boeing in aircraft manufacture, was originally a JV between French, German, British and Spanish manufacturers. Alliances – such as the Star Alliance led by United Airlines of the United States and Lufthansa of Germany – are common in the airline industry, where companies share revenues and costs over certain routes. As governments often prevent foreign ownership of airlines, such alliances avoid that barrier.

Other forms of joint development include franchising (common in retailing – like Ikea), licensing and long-term collaboration with suppliers.

Alliances and partnership working have also become commonplace in the public sector. In many cities alliances or partnerships have been created between major public bodies, business and community interests. Their main purpose is to foster a coherent approach to planning and delivering services. Public bodies often act as service commissioners rather than as direct providers, developing partnerships with organisations to deliver services on their behalf.

Activity 8.6 Critical reflection on delivering strategy

- Select two companies you are familiar with, and in each case gather evidence to help you decide which of the available options (or a combination) they have chosen to deliver their strategy.
- What are the advantages of the route they have chosen compared to the alternatives?
- Compare your evidence with other students on your course, and identify any common themes.

8.10 Making revisions – implementing and evaluating

Implementation turns strategy into action, moving from corporate to operational levels. Many strategies fail to be implemented, or fail to achieve as much as management expected. A common mistake is to assume that formulating a strategy will lead to painless implementation. Sometimes there is an 'implementation deficit', when strategies are not implemented at all, or are only partially successful. A common reason for this is that while formulating strategy may appear to be a rational process, it is often a political one. Those who were content with the earlier strategy may oppose the new one if it affects their status, power or career prospects.

Evaluate results

Managers, shareholders (current and potential) and financial analysts routinely compare a company's performance with its published plans. Only by tracking results can these and other interested parties decide if performance is in line with expectations or if the company needs to take some corrective action. Many targets focus on financial and other quantitative aspects of performance, such as sales, operating costs and profit.

Although monitoring is shown as the last stage in the strategy model, it is not the end of the process. This is continuous as organisations adjust to changes in their business environment. Regular monitoring alerts management to the possibility that they will miss a target unless they make some operational changes. Equally, and in conjunction with continuous scanning of the external environment, performance monitoring can prompt wider changes to the organisation's corporate and competitive strategies.

Donald Sull (2007) advises that in any discussions to revise strategy, people should treat actions as experiments:

> they should analyse what's happened and use the results to revise their assumptions, priorities and promises. As such, the appropriate time to have such conversations is after the team has reached a significant milestone in making things happen... Managers must acknowledge that their mental models are merely simplified maps of complex terrain based on provisional knowledge that is subject to revision in the light of new information (p. 36–7)

8.11 Integrating themes

Entrepreneurship

Strategic change in public organisations provides opportunities for private entrepreneurs. The National Health Service continues to have difficulty in achieving the standards of care expected within available budgets, and sometimes decides to outsource services. In 2012 it gave the task of running Hinchingbrooke hospital in Cambridgeshire, which was failing to attract sufficient patients to cover its costs, to Circle (www.circlepartnership.co.uk). This is a private company founded in 2004, and (in 2013) employing 4000 staff. Just under half of the shares are owned by the clinicians and staff who work there, with the remainder owned by private investors.

Circle's management believes its ability to take on the challenge of improving the performance of hospitals like Hinchingbrooke is due in part to its mutual structure, which incentivises staff though a share-ownership scheme. One senior manager said:

> Without this model of ownership we couldn't do what we are doing. We brought in employee engagement and entrepreneurial drive. We empowered people to feel they could conquer the world and run the hospital. Companies do need capital, but you also need employee engagement. (*Financial Times*, 3 July 2012)

The company runs several day surgery units within NHS hospitals, and has built a privately funded hospital in Bath. Further expansion is planned, following a successful effort to raise additional funds from investors.

Sustainability

If managers are to enhance the sustainability of their activities, they need to ensure it becomes part of their strategic discussions. A perspective that can help to clarify the issue was suggested by Vogel (2005), namely that while advocates of corporate responsibility (in this context, sustainability) are genuinely motivated by a commitment to social goals, it is only sustainable if 'virtue pays off'. Responsible action is both made possible and constrained by market forces.

Virtuous behaviour can make business sense for some firms in some areas in some circumstances, but does not in itself ensure commercial success. Companies who base their strategy on acting responsibly may be commercially successful, but equally they may fail – responsible behaviour carries the same risks as any other kind of business behaviour. While some consumers or investors will give their business to companies that appear to be acting responsibly, others will not. Some customers place a higher priority on price, appearance or any other feature than they do on whether goods are produced and delivered in a sustainable way. As Vogel (2005) observes:

There *is* a place in the market economy for responsible firms. But there is also a large place for their less responsible competitors. (p. 3)

While some companies can benefit from a strategy based on acting responsibly, market forces alone cannot prevent others from having a less responsible strategy, and profiting from doing so. Hawken *et al.* (1999) and Senge *et al.* (2008) provide abundant evidence that sustainable performance can be both good for the planet and good for profits.

Internationalisation

As the business world becomes ever more international, companies inevitably face difficult strategic choices about the extent to which they develop an international presence, and the way in which they develop their international strategy. The nature of the challenge is shown by the fact that while many companies have done very well from international expansions, many overseas ventures fail, destroying value rather than creating it.

Chapter 4 outlined the nature of the challenges faced as companies respond to what they perceive to be international opportunities. They need, for example, to deal with complex structural and logistical issues when products are made and sold in several countries, ensure that there are adequate links between research, marketing and production to speed the introduction of new products, and facilitate the rapid transfer of knowledge and ideas between the national components of the business. These are complex enough issues in themselves, but the extra dimension is that solutions which work in one national context may not work as well in another. Differences in national culture mean that people will respond in perhaps unexpected was to strategies and plans, especially if these are perceived in some way to be inconsistent with the local culture (as the examples cited in Chapter 4 testify).

The content of an international strategy will be shaped by the process of its production – and the extent to which different players in the global enterprise take part in it.

Governance

Pye (2002) sees a close link between what she terms the process of governing and strategising. Having conducted long-term research with the boards of several large companies she notes:

i. in 1987–9, no one talked of corporate governance, whereas now most contributors raise this subject of their own volition, implying greater awareness of and sensitivity to such issues; and
ii. relationships with major shareholders have changed considerably across the decade and directors now see accounting for their *strategic direction* as crucial in this context. (p. 154, emphasis added).

She distinguished between governance and governing:

Corporate governance is often identified through indicators such as board composition, committee structure, executive compensation schemes, and risk assessment procedures etc, which offer a snapshot view of governance practice, rather than the dynamic process of governing. To explore governing, i.e. how governance is enacted, means unravelling the complex network of relationships amongst [the board] *as well as* relationships with 'outsiders' who observe [the board's governance]. (p. 156)

She refers to strategising as the process by which directors go about deciding the strategic direction of the organisation, though this is primarily shaped by the executive directors. She found that almost all directors agreed that what is crucial is not so much the words on paper as the process of dialogue and debate by which those words are created – the strategising process is more important than the final document.

Summary

1. **Explain the significance of managing strategy and show how the issues vary between sectors**
   - Strategy is about the survival of the enterprise; the strategy process sets an overall direction with information about the external environment and internal capabilities. Defining the purposes of the organisation helps to guide the choice and implementation of strategy.

2. **Compare planning, learning and political perspectives on the strategy process**
   - The planning approach is appropriate in stable and predictable environments; while the emergent approach more accurately describes the process in volatile environments, since strategy rarely unfolds as intended in complex, changing and ambiguous situations. A political perspective may be a more accurate way of representing the process when it involves the interests of powerful stakeholders. It is rarely an objectively rational activity, implying that strategy models are not prescriptive but rather frameworks for guidance.

3. **Summarise evidence on how managers develop strategies**
   - The evidence is accumulating that companies in turbulent environments follow a strategy process that is relatively informal, with shorter planning meetings, and greater responsibility placed on line managers to develop strategy rather than on specialist planners.
   - Formulating strategy and designing the organisation appear to be done as closely linked practical activities.
   - Sull uses the 'strategy loop' to describe how managers continually develop and renew their strategy.

4. **Explain the tools for external and internal analysis during work on strategy**
   - External analysis can use Porter's Five Forces model and the PESTEL framework to identify relevant factors.
   - Internally managers can use the value chain to analyse their current organisation.
   - The two sets of information can be combined in a SWOT diagram.

5. **Use the product/market matrix to compare corporate level strategies**
   - Strategy can focus on existing or new products, and existing or new markets. This gives four broad directions, with options in each – such as market penetration, product development, market development or diversification.

6. **Use the concept of generic strategies to compare business level strategies**
   - Strategic choices are cost leader, differentiation or a focus on a narrow market segment.

7. **Give examples of alternative methods of delivering a strategy**
   - Strategy can be delivered by internal (sometimes called organic) development by rearranging the way resources are deployed. Alternatives include acquiring or merging with another company, or by forming alliances and joint ventures.

8. **Show how ideas from the chapter add to your understanding of the integrating themes**
   - Changes in a public organisation can represent opportunities for entrepreurial professionals.
   - Sustainable performance in the environmental sense only works in the economic sense if it is part of the organisation's strategy, i.e., that it makes business sense as well as environmental sense. There are many examples of companies which have done this.

- International expansion and diversification strategies often fail, probably when managers underestimate the complexity of overseas operations.
- Pye (2002) found that directors were more likely to be taking responsibility for strategic direction of the business as well as for their narrower governance responsibilities – emphasising the benefits of the process as much as of the final outcomes.

Test your understanding

1. Why do managers develop strategies for their organisation?
2. How does the planning view of strategy differ from the learning and political views respectively?
3. Describe what recent research shows about how managers develop strategy.
4. Draw Sull's strategy loop, and explain each of the elements.
5. Discuss with a manager from an organisation how his or her organisation developed its present strategy. Compare this practice with the ideas in the chapter. What conclusions do you draw?
6. What are the main steps to take in analysing the organisation's environment? Why is it necessary to do this?
7. Describe each stage in value chain analysis and illustrate them with an example. Why is the model useful to management?
8. The chapter described three generic strategies that organisations can follow. Give examples of three companies each following one of these strategies.
9. Give examples of company strategies corresponding to each box in the product/market matrix.
10. What are the main ways of delivering strategy?
11. Summarise an idea from the chapter that adds to your understanding of the integrating themes.

Think critically

Think about the way your company, or one with which you are familiar, approaches issues of strategy. Review the material in the chapter, and perhaps visit some of the websites identified. Then make notes on these questions:

- What examples of the issues discussed in this chapter are currently relevant to your company – such as whether to follow a differentiation or focus strategy?
- In responding to these issues, what **assumptions** about the strategy process appear to have guided people? To what extent do these seem to fit the environmental forces as you see them? Do they appear to stress the planning or the learning perspectives on strategy?
- What factors such as the history or current **context** of the company appear to have influenced the prevailing view? Is the history of the company constraining attempts to move in new directions?
- Have people put forward **alternative** strategies, or alternative ways of developing strategy, based on evidence about other companies?
- What **limitations** can you see in any of the ideas presented here? For example does Porter's value chain adequately capture the variable most relevant in your business, or are there other features you would include?

> ### Read more

Ackermann, F. and Eden, C. (2011), 'Strategic Management of Stakeholders: Theory and Practice', *Long Range Planning*, vol. 44, no. 3, pp. 179–96.

> Shows how to use some empirically-grounded analytical tools to take stakeholder interests into account during the strategising process.

Lorenz, A. (2009), *GKN: The Making of a Business*, Wiley, Chichester.

> An account of how the company has evolved over more than 250 years, with many examples of strategic decisions along the way.

Mintzberg, H., Ahlstrand, B. and Lampel J. (1998), *Strategy Safari*, Prentice Hall Europe.

> Excellent discussion of the process of strategy making from various academic and practical perspectives.

Moore, J. I. (2001), *Writers on Strategy and Strategic Management* (2nd edn), Penguin, London.

> Summarises the work of the major contributors to the fields of strategy and strategic management – Part One contains a useful overview of the work of the 'movers and shakers', including Ansoff, Porter and Mintzberg.

> ### Go online

These websites have appeared in the chapter:

> www.gkn.com
> www.ikea.com
> www.tesco.com
> www.nestle.com
> www.motorola.com
> www.abb.com
> www.pg.com
> www.maersk.com
> www.circle.com
> www.easyJet.com
> www.circlepartnership.co.uk

Visit two of the business sites in the list, or any other company that interests you, and navigate to the pages dealing with news or investor relations.

- What are the main strategic issues they seem to be facing?
- What information can you find about their policies?

CHAPTER 10

ORGANISATION STRUCTURE

Aim

To introduce terms and practices that show the choices managers face in shaping organisations.

Objectives

By the end of your work on this chapter you should be able to outline the concepts below in your terms and:

1 Outline the links between strategy, organisation and performance
2 Give examples of how managers divide and co-ordinate work, with their likely advantages and disadvantages
3 Compare the features of mechanistic and organic forms
4 Summarise the work of Woodward, Burns and Stalker, Lawrence and Lorsch and John Child, showing how they contributed to this area of management
5 Use the 'contingencies' outlined to evaluate the form of a unit
6 Explain and illustrate the features of a learning organisation
7 Show how ideas from the chapter add to your understanding of the integrating themes

Key terms

This chapter introduces the following ideas:

organisation structure
organisation chart
formal structure
informal structure
vertical specialisation
horizontal specialisation
formal authority
responsibility
delegation
span of control
centralisation and decentralisation
formalisation

functional, divisional and matrix structures
outsourcing
collaborative network
mechanistic structure
organic structure
technology
differentiation
integration
contingency theories
determinist
structural choice
learning organisation

Each is a term defined within the text, as well as in the glossary at the end of the book.

Case study: GlaxoSmithKline (GSK) www.gsk.com

GSK is one the world's largest pharmaceutical companies, formed in 2000 by the merger of GlaxoWellcome and SmithKlineBeecham. In 2011 it had sales of £27.4 billion, with over 97,000 staff in 100 countries – including 16,000 in Research & Development. The company has 74 manufacturing sites in 32 countries, with research sites in the UK, US, Spain, Belgium and China.

Over £18 billion (68 per cent) of sales comes from Pharmaceuticals Division (medicines to treat serious and chronic diseases), 13 per cent from Vaccines and 19 per cent from Consumer Healthcare (over-the-counter products including Panadol and Lucozade).

Like other major pharmaceutical companies, the company's survival depends on developing new drugs which it can sell profitably. New products are discovered, developed and launched – and are protected by patents for about ten years. Patents prevent other companies from taking the idea and manufacturing and selling an equivalent product. While the drug has patent protection the company has a monopoly over its supply – enabling it to make high profits if doctors prescribe the drug for their patients. When the patent expires, other companies can copy the drug and produce what are known as 'generic' versions which sell at very low prices.

Companies like GSK are finding it increasingly difficult to maintain the flow of new drugs. Diseases that are relatively easy to treat have adequate drugs to do the job. The rising costs of every aspect of scientific research and tighter regulations have increased the cost of getting approval from regulators to sell a drug. Discovering and developing a new medicine takes about 12 years before it begins to produce revenue – and during that time it is draining resources from the company. In 2013 GSK announced it would make the results of its drugs trials available to the 'Cochrane' group of independent scientists to enable them to check the validity of its claims about the effectiveness of drugs.

In the 1960s GSK employed fewer than a 1000 scientists, who worked in a functional structure – chemists, pharmacologists, clinical development, and so on. There were few management layers, few projects, and most scientists worked on a single campus. Communication, co-ordination and the exchange of ideas with colleagues was quite easy.

Getty Images/AFP

In the following decades the number of employees grew many times, and it gradually became clear that the traditional way of organising the business was unsatisfactory.

The company has faced criticism for the prices it charges for medicines in emerging countries. It now relates prices to a country's wealth and ability to pay. This has led to

> significant reductions in price and increases in demand for our products in emerging economies, representing a good outcome for patients, governments and our shareholders. (GSK Annual Report 2011, p. 5)

Senior managers had also been concerned about the high cost and low productivity of its research expenditure. Scientists were spread over several sites and countries, so communication was difficult and slow – the opposite of that required in a research community.

Sources: Company Annual Report 2011, *British Medical Journal*, 9 March 2013.

Case questions 10.1

- Visit the company website and note any recent announcements about the development of new medicines or vaccines.
- What type of working environment is likely to encourage scientific creativity?
- What type of working environment is likely to ensure that safety testing and clinical trials required by national regulatory bodies are carried out accurately, consistently and reliably?

10.1 Introduction

Managers at GlaxoSmithKline (GSK) aim to create a context which encourages different and perhaps contradictory types of behaviour. If the company is to survive they need to have a steady flow of new pharmaceuticals that deal with a disease or condition effectively. This depends on encouraging, and paying for, sustained scientific imagination and creativity over many years, in the hope that research teams develop useful products. New products with commercial potential must go through rigorous processes of clinical trials to satisfy national and international regulators about safety and effectiveness. Products which survive then enter a disciplined manufacturing process to deliver them to a precise specification, while sales staff aim to persuade enough doctors prescribe them to earn a return on the investment. The company aims to create a working environment which encourages both creativity (in research) and order (in production and sales), seeking a balance between having enough structure to get things done, but not so much structure that it stifles creativity.

One reason for the success of Virgin Group may be the relationship between the central management group and the operating companies with which we are familiar. Those in charge of companies whose performance is below expectations often change the structure. Nokia was losing sales rapidly, and in 2011 announced a joint venture with Microsoft to develop a new mobile operating system. Others follow a policy of frequent small changes. The (then) Chairman of L'Oréal, the world's biggest beauty company referred to its

> culture of permanent mini-restructuring. I don't think there has ever been a major restructuring in the whole of L'Oreal's corporate history … but there have been hundreds of little ones. What we do is try to live a life of permanent small change to avoid the major disasters. (*Financial Times*, 3 March 2008)

When an owner-manager is running a small business he or she decides what tasks to do and co-ordinates them. If the enterprise grows the entrepreneur passes work to newly recruited staff, though the division will probably be flexible and informal. Owner and staff can easily communicate directly with each other, so co-ordination is easy. If the business continues to grow, informality will cause problems, so people begin to introduce more structure. This often means clarifying tasks to ensure people know where to focus, and finding ways to ensure they communicate well. As scientific developments enable people to create new services, they need to devise suitable forms of organisation through which to deliver them.

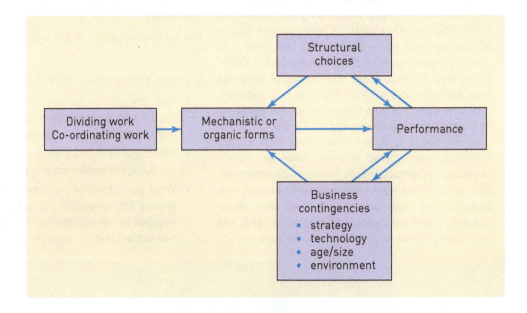

Figure 10.1
Alternative structures and performance

Many organisations are not only productive enterprises but also fulfilling places to work and contributing to the wider community. This happens when those involved combine identifiable elements of structure in appropriate ways – rather than in ways that produce inefficiency and discontent. The chapter illustrates the main choices for dividing and co-ordinating work. It contrasts 'mechanistic' and 'organic' forms, and presents a theory about when each is likely to be suitable. The chapter concludes with ideas on learning organisations. Figure 10.1 shows these themes.

10.2 Strategy, organisation and performance

Alfred Chandler (1962) traced the evolution of America's largest industrial firms, showing how their strategies of growth and diversification placed too many demands on their centralised structures. As the diversity of products and geographies grew, issues arose which those at the (increasingly remote) centre could not handle, as they lacked the knowledge of local circumstances. Chandler's historical analysis of du Pont, General Motors, Standard Oil and Sears, Roebuck shows how they responded by creating decentralised, divisional structures – a significant organisational innovation which many companies use today. It allowed managers at corporate headquarters to provide overall guidance and control, leaving the detailed running of each division to local managers (strategy shaped structure).

Chandler also shows that structure could influence strategy. A new legal requirement to break Standard Oil into small regional companies encouraged one of these – Standard Oil (New Jersey) to expand into foreign markets as a way of increasing profits (structure shaped strategy). Chandler's aim was to study the interaction of strategy and structure in a changing business environment. In successive cases he traces how strategies to launch new products or enter new regions strained current structures, and how managers responded by gradually, through trial and error, developing new variants of the decentralised divisional form.

That research tradition continues in, for example, research by Whittington *et al.* (2006) who trace how managers re-think strategies and structures. Table 10.1 gives examples of visible, corporate changes. While senior managers discuss these prominent changes,

Table 10.1 Examples of Strategic and Organisational decisions

Example	Strategic issue	Organisational issue
Royal Dutch Shell, 2009 (www.shell.com)	New CEO decided the present structure was too complex and costly. Aimed to cut costs and speed up large projects.	Combined two largest divisions into one; common functions (such as IT) moved from divisions to a central service.
McGraw-Hill, 2011 (www.mcgrawhill.com)	Pressure from investors for the company to increase earnings for shareholders	Chairman announced division of company – one part to focus on services for financial markets, the other on textbooks. In 2012 announces sale of textbook division to private investors.
Top Right Group (previously Emap) 2012 Media (www.topright-group.com)	Originally a printed magazine company, it had moved into other areas of business, and new CEO wanted these to have more visibility and responsibility.	Changed name, split into three companies – events, information services, and the original print media. Central functions (IT, HRM, finance) decentralised into the new businesses.

those at other levels work on fundamentally similar issues within their respective units, such as:

- Should we divide a job into three parts and give each to a separate employee, or have them work as a team with joint responsibility for the whole task?
- Should Team A do this task, or Team B?
- Should that employee report to supervisor A or supervisor B?

Whether the issue is at a multinational business or a small company, the organisational task is the same – where to focus resources and how best to divide and coordinate the roles of people using them.

The next section introduces the main tools which people use as they create and re-create their organisation.

10.3 Designing a structure

Organisation structure
'The structure of an organisation [is] the sum total of the ways in which it divides its labour into distinct tasks and then achieves co-ordination among them' (Mintzberg, 1979).

Organisation structure describes how managers divide, supervise and co-ordinate work. It gives someone taking a job a reasonably clear idea of what they should do – the marketing assistant should deal with marketing, not finance. The topic relates closely to culture and to human resource management, since the more coherence there is between these three elements the more they will support the strategy.

The organisation chart

An **organisation chart** shows the main departments and senior positions in an organisation and the reporting relations between them.

The **organisation chart** shows departments and job titles, with lines linking senior executives to the departments or people for whose work they are responsible. It shows who people report to, and clarifies four features of the **formal structure**:

- tasks – the major activities of the organisation;
- subdivisions – how they are divided;
- levels – the position of each post within the hierarchy;
- lines of authority – these link the boxes to show who people report to.

Formal structure consists of guidelines, documents or procedures setting out how the organisation's activities are divided and co-ordinated.

Informal structure is the undocumented relationships between members of the organisation that emerge as people adapt systems to new conditions and satisfy personal and group needs.

Organisation charts give a convenient (though transient) summary of tasks and who is responsible for them. Figure 10.2 shows that for an aircraft factory which was then part of BAE Systems, a UK defence contractor, there are six departments – design, production engineering, purchasing, inventory, production and human resources. It also shows the chain of command within the plant and the tasks of the respective departments (only some of which are shown). In this case the chart includes direct staff such as operators and engineers, and shows the lines of authority throughout the factory. It does *not* show the **informal structure** – the many patterns of work and communication that are part of organisational life.

Work specialisation

Within the formal structure managers divide work into smaller tasks, in which people or departments specialise. They become more expert in one task than they could be in several and are more likely to come up with improved ideas or methods. Taken too far it leads to the negative effects on motivation (described in Chapter 15).

Management in practice   Multi-show Events

Multi-show Events employs 11 people providing a variety of entertainment and promotional services to large businesses. When Brian Simpson created the business there were two staff – so there was no formal structure. He reflected on the process of growth and structure:

While the company was small, thinking about a structure never occurred to me. It became a consideration as sales grew and the complexity of what we offered increased. There were also more people around and I believed that I should introduce a structure so that clear divisions of responsibility would be visible. It seemed natural to split sales and marketing from the actual delivery and production of events as these were two distinct areas. I felt that by creating 'specialised' departments we could give a better service to clients as each area of the company could focus more on their own roles. [Figure 10.3 shows the structure.]

We had to redesign the office layout and introduce a more formal communication process to ensure all relevant information is being passed on – and on the whole I think this structure will see us through the next stage of business growth and development.

Source: Private communication.

Figure 10.2 shows specialisation in the BAE factory – at the top it is between design, production, purchasing and so on. It shows a **vertical specialisation** in that people at each level deal have distinct responsibilities, and a **horizontal specialisation**. Within production engineering some specialise in electrical problems and others in mechanical: within the latter,

Vertical specialisation refers to the extent to which responsibilities at different levels are defined.

Horizontal specialisation is the degree to which tasks are divided among separate people or departments.

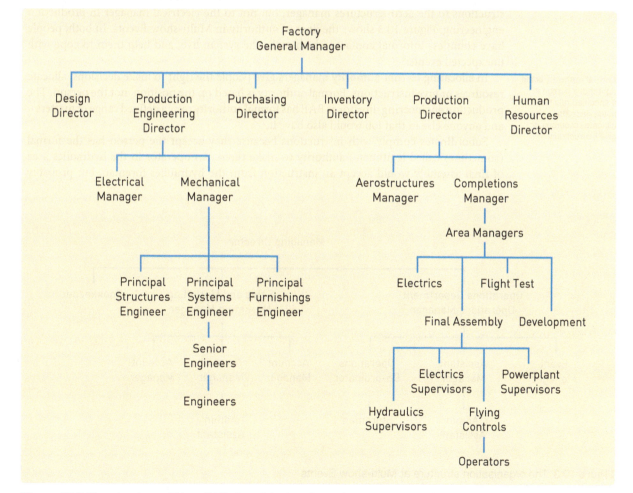

Figure 10.2 The structure within a BAE aircraft factory (www.baesystems.com)

people focus on structures, systems or furnishings. Though Multi-show Events is still a small company, they too have begun to create a structure showing who is responsible for which tasks.

> **Activity 10.1 Draw a structure**
>
> Select a job you have held (such as in a pub, call centre or shop), and draw a chart showing the structure of your area such as:
>
> - your position;
> - the person(s) to whom you reported;
> - who reported to them;
> - the person(s) to whom they reported.

Chain of command

The lines of authority show the links between people – who they report to and who reports to them. It shows who they can ask to do work, who they can ask for help – and who will be expecting results from them. Figure 10.2 shows that the production director can give instructions to the aero-structures manager, but not to the electrical manager in production engineering. Figure 10.3 shows the lines of authority in Multi-show Events. In both, people have countless informal contacts which make the system live, and help them to cope with unexpected events.

Formal authority is the right that a person in a specified role has to make decisions, allocate resources or give instructions.

In allocating **formal authority** managers give people the right to make decisions, allocate resources or give instructions. Formal authority is based on the position, not the person. The production engineering director at BAE has formal authority over a defined range of matters – and anyone else in that job would also have it.

Subordinates comply with instructions because they accept the person has the formal (sometimes called legitimate) authority to make them. An operator in the hydraulics area of final assembly would accept an instruction from the hydraulics foreman, but probably

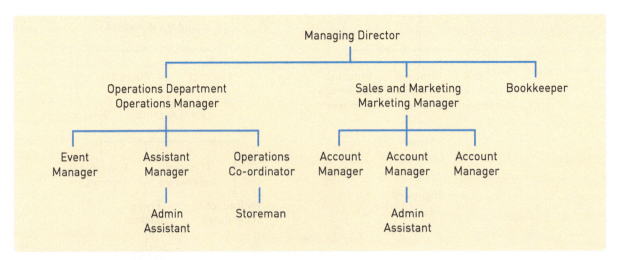

Figure 10.3 The organisation structure at Multi-show Events

not from the powerplant foreman (they may help as a personal favour, but that is different from accepting formal authority). If managers give instructions beyond their area of formal authority, they meet resistance.

Responsibility is a person's duty to meet the expectations associated with a task. The production director and the hydraulics foreman are responsible for the tasks that go with those positions. To fulfil those responsibilities they require formal authority to manage relevant resources.

Responsibility refers to a person's duty to meet the expectations others have of them in their role.

Accountability means that people with formal authority over an area are required to report on their work to those above them in the chain of command. The principal systems engineer is accountable to the mechanical manager for the way he or she has used resources: have they achieved what was expected as measured by the cost, quantity, quality or timeliness of the work?

Delegation occurs when people transfer responsibility and authority for part of their work to people below them in the hierarchy. The production director is responsible for all work in that area, and can only do this by delegating. They must account for the results, but pass responsibility and necessary authority to subordinates – and this continues down the hierarchy. Delegating to subordinates enables quicker decisions, though some managers are reluctant to do this as they fear it will reduce their power.

Delegation occurs when one person gives another the authority to undertake specific activities or decisions.

The span of control

The **span of control** is the number of subordinates reporting to a supervisor. If managers supervise staff closely there is a narrow span of control – as shown in the top half of Figure 10.4. If they allow staff wider responsibilities that means less supervision, so more can report to the same manager: the span of control becomes wider, and the structure flatter – the lower half of Figure 10.4.

A **span of control** is the number of subordinates reporting directly to the person above them in the hierarchy.

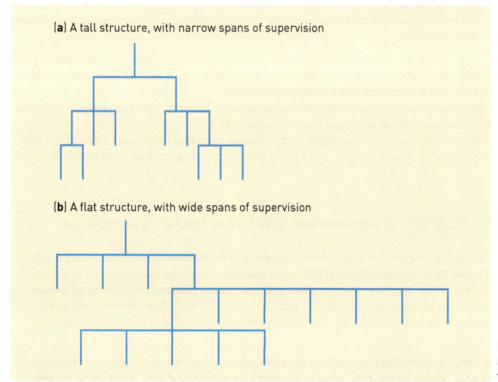

Figure 10.4 Tall and flat organisation structures

> **Key ideas** Joan Woodward's research
>
> Joan Woodward's study of 100 firms in Essex found great variety between them in the number of subordinates managers supervised (Woodward, 1965). The number of people reporting directly to the chief executive ranged from 2 to 18, with the median span of control being 6. The average span of control of the first line supervisors varied from 10 to 90, with a median of 37. Woodward explained the variation by the technological system used (more in Section 10.7, page 234).

Centralisation and decentralisation

As an organisation grows managers divide work vertically, as they delegate decisions to those below them – and so begin to create a hierarchy as in Figure 10.4. Growth brings complexity, but it is usually possible to see three levels – corporate, divisional and operating – such as at The Royal Bank of Scotland (RBS) (www.rbs.com):

- **Corporate** The most senior group, such as the board of directors, has overall responsibility for leading and controlling the company. It approves strategy across the group, monitors performance at major units, and maintains links with significant external institutions such as regulators and political bodies.
- **Divisional** Responsible for implementing policy and for allocating budgets and other resources. RBS is organised partly by customer (UK Personal and UK Corporate); partly by product (RBS Insurance); and partly geographically (US Retail and Commercial Banking). Division managers are responsible for meeting the targets which the board sets. They represent the division's interests to the board and monitor performance in the operating units.
- **Operating** Responsible for the technical work of the organisation – making products, catching thieves, caring for patients or delivering services. Within UK Personal at RBS there are teams responsible for ensuring that, for example, branches and cash machines work smoothly.

> **Centralisation** is when a relatively large number of decisions are taken by management at the top of the organisation.
>
> **Decentralisation** is when a relatively large number of decisions are taken lower down the organisation in the operating units.

The vertical hierarchy establishes what decisions people at each level can make. This theme is especially relevant in multinational companies, which experience constant tension between global consistency and local responsiveness.

Centralisation is when those at the top make most decisions, with managers at divisional level ensuring those at operating level follow the policy.

Decentralisation is when people in divisions or operating units make many of the business decisions. Branch managers in a chain of retail travel agents had considerable freedom

> **Management in practice** A decentralised structure at Roche   www.roche.com
>
> Roche, based in Switzerland, is one of the world's most successful and profitable pharmaceutical companies. The board appointed a new chief executive, Severin Schwan (a graduate in business and law) who, at the age of 40, has spent his career in the company. The group has a decentralised structure which analysts believe has been a major factor in its success, by encouraging each subsidiary to focus their research on specific diseases, while collaborating on marketing. Mr Schwan says teamwork is essential in this knowledge-based business:
>
>> When I toured our labs, I grasped the potential and the enthusiasm of our people. We have to capitalise on that. If you tell your people all the time what to do, don't be surprised if they don't come up with

> new ideas. Innovative people need air to breathe. Our culture of working together at Roche is based on mutual trust and teamwork. An informal friendly manner supports this: at the same time this must not lead to negligence or shoddy compromises – goals must be achieved and, at times, tough decisions have to be implemented.'
>
> Source: *Financial Times*, 4 August 2008.

over pricing and promotional activities, but were required to follow very tight financial reporting routines. KPMG, the auditing and consulting firm announced in 2012 that the European division would decentralise more decisions to national offices.

Many organisations display a mix of both. Network Rail (responsible for the railway track and signals) has highly standardised processes and highly centralised control systems, but local managers have high autonomy in deciding how to organise their resources. They can co-ordinate track improvements and engineering schedules to meet the needs of local train operating companies (*Financial Times*, 23 July 2007).

This tension between centralising and decentralising is common, with the balance at any time reflecting managers' relative power and their views on the advantages of one direction or the other – see Table 10.2.

Formalisation

Formalisation is when managers use written or electronic documents to direct and control employees. These include rules, procedures, instruction manuals, job descriptions – anything that shows what people must do. Operators in call centres use scripts to guide their conversation with a customer, ensuring they deal with each one consistently and in accordance with regulatory requirements.

> **Formalisation** is the practice of using written or electronic documents to direct and control employees.

There is always tension between flexibility and control. People who want to respond to individual needs or local conditions favour informal arrangements with few rules. Industry regulators or consumer protection laws often specify detailed procedures to protect customers against unsuitable selling methods, or to protect staff against unfounded complaints. This leads to more formal systems and recording procedures.

Table 10.2 Advantages and disadvantages of centralisation

Factor	Advantages	Disadvantages
Response to change	Thorough debate of issues	Slower response to local conditions
Use of expertise	Concentration of expertise at the centre makes it easier to develop new services and promote best practice methods	Less likely to take account of local knowledge or innovative people
Cost	Economies of scale in purchasing – efficient administration if use common systems	Local suppliers may be better value than corporate suppliers
Policy implications	Less risk of local managers breaching legal requirements	More risk of local managers breaching legal requirements
Staff commitment	Backing of centre ensures wide support	Staff motivated by more responsibility
Consistency	Provides consistent image to the public – less variation in service standards	Local staff discouraged from taking responsibility – can blame centre

> **Activity 10.2 Critical reflection on structures**
>
> Select an organisation with which you are familiar, or which you can find out about. Gather information about aspects of the structure, such as:
>
> - Does the organisation chart look tall, or flat?
> - What evidence is there of high or low levels of formality?
> - Which decisions are centralised, and which are decentralised?
> - Share your information with colleagues on your course, to increase your awareness of the range of ways in which people have designed structures.

10.4 Dividing work internally – functions, divisions and matrices

Work specialisation divides the larger tasks of an organisation (develop new pharmaceuticals) into smaller tasks for designated units (in functional, divisional or matrix forms), within which further specialisation divides those tasks into jobs for individuals. Another approach shares the work amongst networks of collaborating, but independent, organisations. Figure 10.5 shows these alternatives.

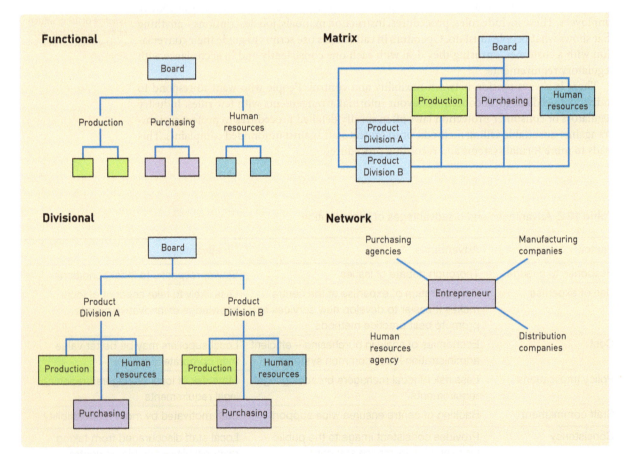

Figure 10.5 Four types of structure

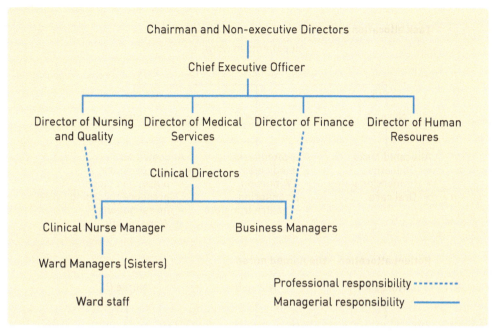

Figure 10.6
Partial organisation structure in a hospital

Specialisation by function

When managers divide staff according to profession or function (finance, marketing) they create a **functional structure.** The BAE chart shows design, production engineering, purchasing, inventory, production, and human resources functions. Figure 10.6 shows a hospital chart, with a functional structure at senior level.

The functional approach can be efficient as people with common expertise work together, and follow a professional career path. It can lead to conflict if functions have different perceptions of organisational goals. Le Meunier-FitzHugh and Piercy (2008) show how staff in sales and marketing experienced this – the former stressing immediate sales, the latter long term customer relations. Functional staff face conflicts when product managers compete for access to functional resources such as information technology.

A **functional structure** is when tasks are grouped into departments based on similar skills and expertise.

Specialisation by divisions

Managers create a **divisional structure** when they arrange the organisation around products, services or customers, giving those in charge of each unit the authority to design, make and deliver the product. Functions within the division are likely to co-operate as they depend on satisfying the same set of customers.

A **divisional structure** is when tasks are grouped in relation to their outputs, such as products or the needs of different types of customer.

Product or customer

Divisional structures enable staff to focus on a distinct group of customers – Shell UK has a division (Shell Gas Direct) which supplies industrial companies, and another (UK Retail) which manages the petrol stations. Hospitals can use the 'named-nurse' system, in which one nurse is responsible for several identified patients. That nurse is the patient's contact with the system, managing the delivery of services to the patient from (functional) departments. Figure 10.7 contrasts 'task' and 'named-nurse' approaches.

Geographic divisions

Here managers in companies with many service outlets – like Waitrose or Weatherspoon's – group them by geography. This allows front-line staff to identify local needs, and makes it easier for divisional managers to monitor performance – see Table 10.3.

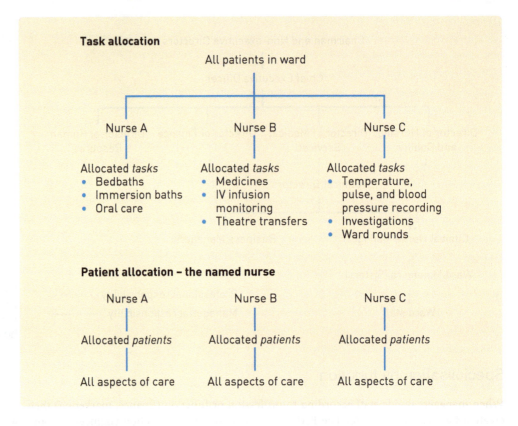

Figure 10.7 Task and named-nurse structures

Matrix structure

A **matrix structure** is when those doing a task report both to a functional and a project or divisional boss.

A **matrix structure** combines functional and divisional structures: function on one axis and products, projects or customers on the other. Functional staff work on one or more projects as required. They report to two bosses – a functional head and the head of the current project(s). They usually work in teams – the matrix form in Figure 10.5 implies that a team made up of people from the production, purchasing and human resources functions respectively could work on Product A, another on Product B and so on.

Table 10.3 Advantages and disadvantages of functional and divisional structures

Structure	Advantages	Disadvantages
Functional	Clear career paths and professional development	Isolation from wider interests damages promotion prospects
	Specialisation leads to high standards and efficiency	Conflict over priorities
	Common professional interests support good internal relations	Lack of wider awareness damages external relations
Divisional	Functional staff focus on product and customer needs	Isolation from wider professional and technical developments
	Dedicated facilities meet customer needs quickly	Costs of duplicate resources
	Common customer focus enables good internal relations	Potential conflict with other divisions over priorities
		Focus on local, not corporate, needs

This method works well in organisations which depend on a flow of new products: managers delegate significant responsibility and authority to an identifiable team, which is then accountable for results. Cisco (Chapter 17 Case Study), is an example, as is Apple (Part 1 Case).

Activity 10.3 Choosing between approaches

Go to the website of a company which interests you, and gather information about the structure of the company.

- Decide whether it has a functional or a divisional structure – and if the latter, is that based on products or geography?
- If it has international operations, how are they shown in the structure?
- Compare your research with colleagues on your course, and prepare a short presentation summarising your conclusions

---

Case study GlaxoSmithKline – the case continues www.gsk.com

Senior management at GSK believed that part of the problem with research was the way they organised it. R&D had become large and bureaucratic, which damaged the creative atmosphere in which scientists work best. The company had lost the clear accountability, transparency and personal enthusiasm essential for drug discovery.

The then chief executive (Jean-Paul Garnier) concluded that the functional structure was obsolete, while a matrix structure would become too complex with continued growth. He therefore replaced it with 'Centres of Excellence for Drug Discovery' (CEDDs). Each is focussed on a family of related diseases (such as Alzheimer's or obesity), has a CEO with the authority to initiate and end projects, and employs several hundred scientists. There are only two or three management layers between the CEO and the 'bench' scientists.

The intention was to increase the speed of decision making and restore freedom of action to the scientist conducting the research. It also changed the incentive system, to ensure that those who made the discoveries could expect a share in the financial rewards. By 2008 it had 12 CEDDs, and the results appeared promising. When it began changing to this divisional type of structure in 2005 GSK had only two products in the 'late stage development' phase: by 2011 it had about 30.

Sources: Garnier (2008); *GSK Annual Report*, 2011, p. 6.

Case question 10.2

- Review this and the previous instalment of the case, and list which of the structural types mentioned in this and the previous section the company has used.

10.5 Dividing work externally – outsourcing and networks

Creating a structure includes deciding which tasks in the value chain the organisation will do itself, and which it will secure from other organisations – sometimes expressed as the 'make or buy' decision. Many companies outsource work to others, and in some sectors companies engage in collaborative networks.

Outsourcing

Outsourcing refers to the practice of delegating selected value chain activities to an external provider.

Outsourcing happens when managers delegate certain activities in the value chain to external providers – to cut costs or to access expertise.

The remaining organisation concentrates on activities such as marketing and integrating the supply chain. Companies routinely outsource transport, distribution work and information processing. New businesses outsource functions as this allows them to grow more quickly: innocent drinks (Chapter 2 Case Study) outsource all their manufacturing to established producers. A growing volume of UK public services is outsourced: analysis of the Official Journal of the European Union database shows that the value of outsourcing contracts rose from £9.6 billion in 2008 to £20.4 billion in 2012 (quoted in *Financial Times*, 1 February 2013, p. 4).

One disadvantage of outsourcing is that the company depends on others working to their required standard. When the oil rig on BP's well in the Gulf of Mexico exploded in 2010, the fact that BP neither owned the rig nor employed the contractors did not absolve it of responsibility. A company withdrawing from an area of work will also lose the skills in that area, which may become more critical.

Collaborative networks

A **collaborative network** is when tasks required by one company are performed by other companies with expertise in those areas.

A **collaborative network** (sometimes called a 'virtual organisation') refers to a situation in which organisations remain independent but agree to work together in defined areas of work. There is not necessarily a 'hierarchical' relationship between the players – they work together because they share common goals in some aspects of their business, and hope to gain by contributing their respective skills. The approach is most common in high-technology sectors with a large research component – an example, such as that of ARM Holdings will help to clarify how they can work – see Management in practice.

Management in practice   ARM Holdings www.arm.com

ARM Holdings is a leading designer and supplier of digital electronic products founded at Cambridge in1990. It has grown from twelve people then to more than 2,000, with a market value of about £8 billion.

The founders realised that in a sector which experiences very rapid technological development, a new entrant like Arm could not compete with established companies to manufacture complete IT systems. They decided to concentrate on their strength – designing microprocessors – and to position Arm as an enabler working in partnership with other companies. Rather than make things itself, it would be central to an 'ecosystem' of IT design and manufacture. To make this happen, Arm had to develop both a business approach and a workplace culture based on collaboration, whether internally between colleagues or externally with other organisations.

The founders developed a 'Connected Community of Partners' that includes its customers and their customers as well as suppliers and even rivals. The vision was to cement Arm's position in the value chain by enabling all stakeholders to collaborate in developing and using microprocessors. There are now about 1000 companies in the Connected Community.

Source: *Financial Times*, 24 January 2012; company website.

Miles *et al.* (2010) review the structural forms outlined in these two sections and draw on their research into what they call 'collaborative communities' to identify common properties:

Shared interests	Shared resources or common goals
Collaborative values	Willingness to share knowledge and contribute to the success of fellow community members, and seek fairness in community contributions and the distribution of rewards

Community-oriented leadership	A focus on facilitating community growth and sustainability, member collaboration and promotion of collaborative values and practices
Infrastructure to support member collaboration	Systems, processes, and norms that support both direct and pooled collaborative relationships among members
Expandable resources	Knowledge and other resource pools that all members contribute to and draw from.

Mixed forms

Large organisations typically combine functional, product and geographical structures within the same company – see for example BP (Part 2 Case) or RBS (Part 4 Case).

The counterpart of dividing work is to coordinate it, or there will be confusion and poor performance.

Case study   GlaxoSmithKline – the case continues   www.gsk.com

A more recent structural innovation is to work more closely with external partners. To speed up the development process GSK will no longer depend on its own research: by 2020 half of the new drug discovery projects at the company may be undertaken by external partners as part of a radical overhaul designed to improve the pipeline of new drugs at the group. The company's research director estimated that between one-quarter and one-third of GSK's research on new drugs already involved working with external partners and the CEDD would play a growing role by managing a 'virtual' portfolio of research run by such companies:

> In the future we are going to have many more external projects.

In 2010 it announced a further change: a group of 14 scientists would move into a separate company specialising in pain relief. They will take with them the rights to several patents, in exchange for GSK holding an 18 per cent stake in the company. This will enable GSK to reduce overhead costs, while benefiting from the new company's profits. They expect that the scientists will be more highly motivated in their own company than as a small group within a large one.

Sources: *Financial Times*, 31 May 2006; 5 October 2010; Garnier (2008).

Case questions 10.3

- What may be the implications for control of these latest stages in the way the company organises research?
- What may be the effects for individual scientists of outsourcing much of its R&D?

Activity 10.4   Comparing structures

Think of an organisation in which you have worked, or about which you can gather information.

- To which of the five structural forms did it correspond most closely?
- What were the benefits and disadvantages of that approach?
- Compare your conclusions with colleagues on your course, and use your experience to prepare a list of the advantages and disadvantages of each type of structure.

10.6 Co-ordinating work

Co-ordination is necessary in routine, ongoing activities and Lechner and Kreutzer (2010) show how companies also need to coordinate their diverse units as they grow.

Direct supervision

A manager can ensure co-ordination by directly supervising his or her staff to check they are working as expected. The number of people whom anyone can supervise effectively reflects the idea of the span of control – that beyond some (variable) point direct supervision is no longer sufficient.

Hierarchy

If disputes or problems arise between staff or departments, they can put the arguments to their common boss in the hierarchy, making it the boss's responsibility to reach a solution. At BAE (Figure 10.2), if the engineer responsible for structures has a disagreement with the systems engineer, they can ask the mechanical manager to adjudicate. If that fails they can escalate the problem to the production engineering director – but this takes time. In rapidly changing circumstances the hierarchy cannot cope, and this delays decisions.

Standardising inputs and outputs

If the buyer of a component specifies exactly what is required, and the supplier meets that specification, coordination between users is easy. If staff receive the same training they will need less direct supervision, as their manager can be confident they will work consistently. All new staff at Pret A Manger must complete a very precise training course before they begin work, which is then constantly reinforced once they are in a post.

Rules and procedures

Another method is to prepare rules or procedures, like that in the Management in practice feature. Organisations have procedures for approving capital expenditure, with instructions on the questions a bid should answer, how people should prepare a case, and to whom they should submit it. Software developers face the challenge of co-ordinating the work of the designers working on different parts of a project, so they use strict change control procedures to ensure that the sub-projects fit together.

Management in practice — Safety procedures in a power station

The following instructions govern the steps that staff must follow when they inspect control equipment in a nuclear power station:

1. Before commencing work you must read and understand the relevant Permit-to-Work and/or other safety documents as appropriate.
2. Obtain keys for relevant cubicles.
3. Visually inspect the interior of each bay for dirt, water and evidence of condensation.
4. Visually inspect the cabling, glands, terminal blocks and components for damage.
5. Visually check for loose connections at all terminals.
6. Lock all cubicles and return the keys.
7. Clear the safety document and return it to the Supervisor/Senior Authorised person.

Information systems

Information systems help to ensure that people who need to work in a consistent way have common information, so that they can coordinate their activities. Computer systems and internet applications enable different parts of an organisation, as well as suppliers and customers, to work from common information, helping co-ordination.

Key ideas — **Co-ordinating sales and marketing**

Large organisations typically create separate sales and marketing departments, which must then co-ordinate their work to ensure co-operation, customer satisfaction and profitability. Homberg *et al.* (2008) concluded (from a survey of German firms in financial services, consumer goods and chemicals) that the best performance was in firms where managers had:

- developed strong structural links between the two functions, especially by using teams, and requiring staff to plan projects jointly; and
- ensured that staff in both functions had high market knowledge – by rotating them between other functions in the firm to develop knowledge about customers and competitors, which then helped the two functions to work effectively together.

Source: Homberg *et al.* (2008).

Most companies purchase goods and services electronically, ensuring that orders and payments to suppliers flow automatically to match current demand. This co-ordinates a laborious task where mistakes were common.

Direct personal contact

The most human form of co-ordination is when people talk to each other. Mintzberg (1979) found that people use this method in both the simplest and the most complex situations. There is so much uncertainty in the latter that information systems cannot cope – only direct contact can do this, by enabling people to making personal commitments to across business units (Sull and Spinosa, 2005) – see Key ideas and Management in practice.

Management in practice — **Co-ordination in a social service**

The organisation cares for the elderly in a large city. Someone who had worked there for several years reflected on co-ordination:

> Within the centre there was a manager, two deputies, an assistant manager, five senior care officers (SCOs) and 30 officers. Each SCO is responsible for six care officers, allowing daily contact between the supervisor and the subordinates. While this defines job roles quite tightly, it allows a good communication structure to exist. Feedback is common as there are frequent meetings of the separate groups, and individual appraisals of the care officers by the SCOs. Staff value this opportunity for praise and comments on how they are doing.
>
> Contact at all levels is common between supervisor and care officers during meetings to assess the needs of clients – for whom the care officers have direct responsibility. Frequent social gatherings and

> functions within the department also enhance relations and satisfy social needs. Controls placed on the behaviour of the care officers come from senior management, often derived from legislation such as the Social Work Acts or the Health and Safety Executive.
>
> Source: Private communication.

> **Activity 10.5 Comparing co-ordination**
>
> Think of an organisation you have worked in, or about which you can gather information.
>
> - Which forms of co-ordination did it use?
> - What were the benefits and disadvantages of that approach?
> - Compare your conclusions with colleagues on your course, and use your experience to prepare a list of the advantages and disadvantages of each method of co-ordination.

Managers make a succession of decisions on any or all of these ways to divide and coordinate work: as they do so they build a structure which in varying degrees corresponds to a mechanistic or organic form.

10.7 Mechanistic and organic forms

*A **mechanistic structure** means there is a high degree of task specialisation, people's responsibility and authority are closely defined and decision-making is centralised.*

*An **organic structure** is one where people are expected to work together and to use their initiative to solve problems; job descriptions and rules are few and imprecise.*

Some organisations emphasise the vertical hierarchy by defining responsibilities clearly, taking decisions at the centre, delegating defined tasks and requiring frequent reports. This enables those at the centre to know what is happening and whether staff are working correctly. The organisation presents a uniform image and ensures that customers receive consistent treatment. Communication is mainly vertical, as the centre passes instructions down and staff pass queries up. Burns and Stalker (1961) called this a **mechanistic structure**.

Others develop a structure with broadly defined, flexible tasks, many cross-functional teams, and base authority on expertise rather than position. Management accepts that the centre depend on those nearest the action to find the best solution. Communication is mainly horizontal amongst those familiar with the task. There may not be an organisation chart, as the division of work is so fluid. Burns and Stalker (1961) called this an **organic structure**. Table 10.4 compares mechanistic and organic forms.

Table 10.4 Characteristics of mechanistic and organic systems

Mechanistic	Organic
Specialised tasks	Contribute experience to common tasks
Hierarchical structure of control	Network structure of contacts
Knowledge located at top of hierarchy	Knowledge widely spread
Vertical communication	Horizontal communication
Loyalty and obedience stressed	Commitment to goals more important

Source: Based on Burns and Stalker (1961).

> **Management in practice** An organic structure at Pixar www.pixar.com
>
> The company's string of successful movies depends not only on the creative people which it employs, but on how it manages that talent. Ed Catmull (co-founder of Pixar, and president of Pixar and Disney Animation Studios) has written about what he calls the 'collective creativity' of the process, and how the senior team fosters this. Something that he believes sets Pixar apart from other studies is the way that people at all levels support each other. An example of how they do this is the process of daily reviews. He writes:
>
> > The practice of working together as peers is core to our culture, and it's not limited to our directors and producers. One example is our daily reviews, or 'dailies', a process for giving and getting constant feedback in a positive way ... People show work in an incomplete state to the whole animation crew, and although the director makes decisions, everyone is encouraged to comment. There are several benefits. First, once people get over the embarrassment of showing work still in progress, they become more creative. Second, director or creative leads ... can communicate important points to the entire crew at the same time. Third, people learn from and inspire each other: a highly creative piece of animation will spark others to raise their game. Finally, there are no surprises at the end: when you're done, you're done. People's overwhelming desire to make sure their work is 'good' before they show it to others increases the possibility that their finished version won't be what the director wants. The dailies process avoids such wasted efforts.
>
> Source: Catmull (2008), p. 70.

Within a large organisation some units will correspond to a mechanistic form and others to an organic. A company may have a centralised information system and tightly controlled policies on capital expenditure – while also allowing business units autonomy on research or advertising budgets. Why do managers favour one form of structure rather than another? One (though disputed) view is that it depends on how they interpret contingencies – the environment in which it works:

> the essence of the contingency paradigm is that organisational effectiveness results from fitting characteristics of the organisation, such as its structure, to contingencies that reflect the situation of the organisation. (Donaldson, 2001, p. 1)

Successful organisations appear to be those in which managers maintain a good fit between contingent factors and the structure within which people work. (Figure 10.1 showed four such factors – strategy, technology, age/size and environment.)

Strategy

We looked earlier (Chapter 8) at Porter's view that firms adopt one of three generic strategies – cost leadership, differentiation or focus. With a cost leadership strategy managers try to increase efficiency to keep costs low. A mechanistic structure is likely to support this strategy, with closely defined tasks in an efficient functional structure. A hierarchical chain of command ensures people work to plan and vertical communication keeps the centre informed.

A differentiation strategy focuses on innovation – developing new products rapidly and imaginatively. An organic structure is most likely to support this, by enabling ideas to flow easily between people able to contribute, regardless of their function – Pixar is an example.

Figure 10.8 expresses the idea that different strategies require different structures. The more the strategy corresponds to cost leadership, the more likely it is that managers will support it with a functional structure. If the balance is towards differentiation, the more likely there will be a divisional, team or network structure.

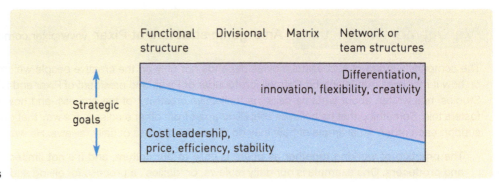

Figure 10.8
Relationship between strategies and structural types

Technology

Technology is the knowledge, equipment and activities used to transform inputs into outputs.

Technology refers to the knowledge, tools and techniques used to transform inputs into outputs. It includes buildings, machines, computer systems and the knowledge and procedures associated with them.

Joan Woodward (1965) gathered information from 100 UK firms to establish whether structural features such as the span of control or the number of levels in the hierarchy affected performance. The researchers saw no pattern until they analysed companies by their manufacturing process, which showed a relationship between technical complexity and company structure.

- **Unit and small batch production** Firms make unique goods to a customer's order. It is similar to craft work, as people and their skills directly shape the process – custom-built cycles, designer furniture, luxury yachts.
- **Large batch and mass production** Many standard products move along an assembly line, with people complementing the machinery – mobile phones, Ford cars or Electrolux washing machines.
- **Continuous process** Material flows through complex technology which makes the product as operators monitor and generally oversee the process and fix faults – a Guinness Brewery, a BP refinery or a Mittal steel plant.

Woodward concluded that the different technologies impose different demands on people. Unit production requires close supervision to ensure that staff meet the customer's unique requirements. Supervisors communicate directly with staff on direct operations and so manage the uncertainties involved in producing one-off items – which takes time. Assembly line work is routine and predictable so a supervisor can monitor more staff: there is a wide span of control. Commercially successful firms were those where managers had created an organisational form providing the right amount of support for the technology in use.

Technology also delivers services, and managers create structures to shape the way staff interact. When Steve Jobs was at Pixar, he designed the building

> to maximise inadvertent encounters. At the centre is a large atrium which contains the cafeteria, meeting rooms, bathrooms, and mailboxes. As a result, everyone has strong reasons to go there repeatedly during the course of the workday. It's hard to describe just how valuable the resulting chance encounters are. (Catmull, 2008, p. 71)

Environment

We looked earlier (Chapter 3) at how environments vary in terms of their complexity and dynamism: does this mean that firms need a structure which suits the nature of their environment? Burns and Stalker (1961) compared the structure of a long-established rayon plant in Manchester with the structures of several new electronics companies then being created in the east of Scotland. Both types of organisation were successful – but had different structures.

The rayon plant had clearly set out rules, tight job descriptions, clear procedures, and co-ordination was primarily through the hierarchy. There was a high degree of specialisation, with tasks divided into small parts. Managers had defined responsibilities clearly and discouraged people from acting outside of their remit. They had centralised decisions, with information flowing up the hierarchy, and instructions down.

The small companies in the newly created electronics industry had few job descriptions, while procedures were ambiguous and imprecise. Staff were expected to use their initiative to decide priorities and to work together to solve problems. Communication was horizontal, rather than vertical (see Table 10.3).

Burns and Stalker (1961) concluded that both forms were appropriate for their circumstances. The rayon plant had a stable environment, as its purpose was to supply a steady flow of rayon to the company's spinning factories. Delivery schedules rarely changed and the technology of rayon manufacture was well known. The electronics companies were in direct contact with their customers, mainly the Ministry of Defence. The demand for commercial and military products was volatile, with frequent changes in requirements. The technology was new, often applying the results of recent research. Contracts were often taken in which neither the customer nor the company knew what the end product would be: it was likely to change during the course of the work.

Case study: GlaxoSmithKline – the case continues   www.gsk.com

The company's Annual Report for 2011 states that:

We have broken up the traditional hierarchical pharmaceutical R&D business model, creating instead smaller units to encourage greater entrepreneurialism and accountability for our scientists.

We are striving to develop new partnerships and approaches, adopting a different mindset, that is more innovative, open-minded, flexible and consultative. We value the new and different perspectives that other groups can bring to our thinking. We are open to working with research charities, academia, companies and non-governmental organisations. We are also increasing consultation with patients and payers to ensure the medicines we are developing provide improvements that healthcare systems will value and reward. (GSK Annual Report, 2011, p. 5)

The same report also explained the international structure of this global business. Pharmaceuticals and Vaccines are organised geographically by large regions – for example European Pharmaceuticals and Vaccines, Japanese P&V and so on. Consumer Healthcare is managed as a single global unit. Global Support Functions such as property, IT and procurement had been merged into one centralised group.

Source: GSK Annual Report, 2011.

Case questions 10.4

- GSK has had both mechanistic and organic structures: what prompted the change?
- Why may the new structure improve business performance?
- What co-ordination issues or other risks may arise in the new structure?

Burns and Stalker (1961) concluded that stable, predictable environments were likely to encourage a mechanistic structure. Volatile, unpredictable environments were likely to encourage an organic structure. This recognition that environmental conditions place different demands upon organisations was a major step in understanding why companies adopt contrasting structures – an idea which Figure 10.9 illustrates.

	Structure	
	Mechanistic	*Organic*
Environment — *Uncertain (unstable)*	**Incorrect fit:** Mechanistic structure in uncertain environment. Structure too tight	**Correct fit:** Organic structure in uncertain environment
Certain (stable)	**Correct fit:** Mechanistic structure in certain environment	**Incorrect fit:** Organic structure in certain environment. Structure too loose

Figure 10.9 Relationship between environment and structure

Activity 10.6 — Comparing mechanistic and organic forms

Think of a department you have worked in, or about which you can gather information.

- Was it broadly mechanistic or organic?
- Why has that form evolved, and is it suitable?
- How does it compare to other departments in the organisation?

Management in practice — Organic problem solving in a mechanistic structure

The organisation I work for has just come through a short-term cash-flow crisis. The problem arose because, while expenditures on contracts are relatively predictable and even, the income flow was disrupted by a series of contractual disputes.

The role culture permeates the head office, and at first the problem was pushed ever upwards. But faced with this crisis all departments were asked for ideas on how to improve performance. Some have been turned into new methods of working, and others are still being considered by the 'ideas team', drawn from all grades of personnel and departments. This was a totally new perspective, of a task culture operating within a role culture – that is, we developed an organic approach. What could be more simple than asking people who do the job how they could be more efficient?

To maintain the change in the long run is difficult, and some parts have now started to drift back to the role culture.

Source: Private communication.

Organisations do not face a single environment. People in each department try to meet the expectations of players in the wider environment, and gradually develop structures which help them to do that. A payroll section has to meet legal requirements on, amongst other things, salary entitlements, taxation and pensions records. Staff must follow strict rules, with little scope to use their initiative: they work in a mechanistic structure. Staff in product development face different requirements – and will expect to work in a structure which encourages creativity and innovation: they expect to work in an organic structure.

An implication is that co-ordination between them will be difficult as they work in different ways. Paul Lawrence and Jay Lorsch explored this – see Key ideas.

> **Key ideas**   **Lawrence and Lorsch: differentiation and integration**
>
> Two American scholars, Paul Lawrence and Jay Lorsch, developed Burns and Stalker's work. They observed that departments doing different tasks face a separate segment of the environment – some relatively stable, others unstable. Lawrence and Lorsch predicted that to cope with these varying conditions departments will develop different structures and ways of working. Those in stable environments would move towards mechanistic forms, those in unstable environments would move towards organic.
>
> Empirical research in six organisations enabled Lawrence and Lorsch to show that departments did indeed differ from each other, and in ways they had predicted. Those facing unstable environments (research and development) had less formal structures than those facing stable ones (production). The greater the **differentiation** between departments the more effort was needed to integrate their work. Successful firms achieved more **integration** between units by using a variety of integrating devices such as task forces and project managers with the required interpersonal skills. The less effective companies in the uncertain environment used rules and procedures.
>
> Source: Lawrence and Lorsch (1967).

Size and life cycle

Small organisations tend to be informal – people work on several tasks and coordinate with each other by face-to-face contact or direct supervision. Weber (1947) noted that larger organisations had formal, bureaucratic structures: research by Blau (1970) and Pugh and Hickson (1976) confirmed that as organisations grow they develop formal structures, hierarchies and specialised units. Like the head of Multi-show Events, as managers divide a growing business into separate units they need more controls such as job descriptions and reporting relationships.

Differentiation The state of segmentation of the organisation into subsystems, each of which tends to develop particular attributes in response to the particular demands posed by its relevant external environment.

Integration is the process of achieving unity of effort amongst the various subsystems in the accomplishment of the organisation's task.

> **Management in practice**   **Growth and structure in a housing association**
>
> A manager in a housing association, which was created to provide affordable housing for those on low incomes, describes how its structure changed as it grew:
>
> > Housing associations have to give tenants and their representatives the opportunity to influence policy. In the early days it had few staff, no clear division of labour and few rules and procedures. It was successful in providing housing, which attracted more government funds, and the association grew. Managing more houses required a more formal structure to support the work. The association no longer served a single community, but several geographical areas. Staff numbers grew significantly and worked in specialised departments. The changes led to concerns amongst both staff and committee that the organisation was no longer responsive to community needs and that it had become distant and bureaucratic.
>
> Source: Private communication from the manager.

This implies that organisations go through stages in their life cycle, with structures adapting to suit. The entrepreneur creates the business alone, or with a few partners or employees. They operate informally with little division of labour – tasks overlap (for a discussion of the unique structural issues facing entrepreneurs in high technology industries, see Alvarez and Barney (2005)). There are few rules or systems for planning and co-ordination. The owner makes the decisions, so they have a centralised structure. If the business succeeds it will need to raise more capital to finance growth. The owner no longer has sole control, but shares decisions with members of the growing management team. Tasks become divided by function or product, creating separate departments and more formal controls to ensure co-ordination. Many small companies fail when they expand rapidly, but fail to impose controls and systems for managing risks – as an executive of a publishing company which got into difficulties recalled:

> We were editors and designers running a large show, and we were completely overstretched. Our systems were simply not up to speed with our creative ambitions.

If a business continues to grow, it almost inevitably becomes more bureaucratic with more division of responsibilities and more rules and systems to ensure co-ordination. Mature, established firms tend to become mechanistic, with a strong vertical system and well-developed controls. More decisions are made at the centre – bringing the danger of slower responses to change and, in some industries, a less competitive position than newer rivals. The managing director of Iris, an advertising agency:

> Iris London is our oldest and our most mature office – about 300 people. When an agency grows to that sort of size there are things about it that start to become dysfunctional. You start to have to invent admin systems, processes, bureaucracy, and that's countercultural and it stops you being any good, it stops you getting closer to clients and being creative. So in London we've reorganised around clients [with five groups] of between 30 and 60 people: the creative, the planning, the commercial guys are all sat together, all around dedicated clusters of client type. And that we think will make us more efficient, more effective, more instinctive as an agency.

Contingencies or managerial choice?

Contingency theories propose that the most effective structure will depend (be contingent) upon the situation in which the organisation is operating:

> The organisation is seen as existing in an environment that shapes its strategy, technology, size and innovation rate. These contingent factors in turn determine the required structure; that is, the structure that the organisation needs to adopt if it is to operate effectively. (Donaldson, 1996, p. 2)

Contingency theories propose that the performance of an organisation depends on having a structure that is appropriate to its environment.

Effective management involves formulating an appropriate strategy and developing a structure which supports that strategy by encouraging appropriate behaviour. The emphasis is **determinist** (the form is determined by the environment) and functionalist (the form is intended to serve organisational effectiveness). Management's role is to make suitable adjustments to the structure to improve performance as conditions change – such as by increasing formality as the company grows.

Determinism is the view that the business environment determines an organisation's structure.

John Child (2005) disagrees, suggesting that contingency theorists ignore the degree of **structural choice** which managers have. The process of organisational design is not a solely rational matter but one also shaped by political processes. The values and interests of powerful groups are able to influence the structure that emerges even if this reduces performance to some degree. The standards used to assess performance are in any case not always rigorous, and people may tolerate some under-performance caused by an inappropriate structure. There is other evidence that managers have choice over the structure they design without necessarily damaging performance – see Management in practice.

Structural choice emphasises the scope which management has to decide the form of structure, irrespective of environmental conditions.

Organisation Structure   671

> **Management in practice**   Retailers' response to the internet
>
> The internet enables online grocery shopping, initially allowing customers to order online and receive home delivery. Sainsbury's responded by creating a new division to handle this business, with a separate management structure, warehouses and distribution system. Tesco chose to integrate the online business with existing stores – staff pick the customer's order from the shelves of a conventional store. Other chains offer the choice of doing the whole transaction in-store, ordering online and collecting from the store, or ordering online for home delivery. The underlying internet technology is the same for all, but managers have chosen to use it in different ways.

> **Activity 10.7**   Critical reflection – contingency or choice?
>
> - Recall some significant changes in the structure of your organisation. Try to establish the reasons for them, and whether they had the intended effects. Do those reasons tend to support the contingency or management choice perspectives?

> **Case questions 10.4**
> - Does the GSK example support contingency or management choice approaches?
> - Does the role of management in the company support either of these approaches?

Another consideration is that the direction of causality is not necessarily from strategy to structure. It is also possible that an organisation with a given structure finds that that makes it easier to embark on a particular strategy.

10.8   Learning organisations

Innovation is the main reason why many advocate the development of 'learning organisations', since organisations which operate in complex and dynamic environments can only be successful innovators if they develop the capacity learn and respond quickly to changing circumstances. The term **learning organisation** is used to describe an organisation that has developed the capacity to continuously learn, adapt and change. In a learning organisation the focus is on acquiring, sharing and using knowledge to encourage innovation.

A learning organisation is one that has developed the capacity to continuously learn, adapt and change.

According to Nonaka and Tageuchi (1995) the ability to create knowledge and solve problems has become a core competence in many businesses. In their view, everyone is a knowledge worker – someone dealing with customers, for example, quickly finds out about their likes and dislikes, and their view of the service. Because they are typically in low-paid jobs far from corporate headquarters, this valuable intelligence is overlooked.

Table 10.5 (based on Pedler *et al.* (1997) presents a view of the features of an ideal learning organisation – features to which managers can aspire. These features cluster under five headings, shown in Figure 10.10.

In a learning organisation members share information and collaborate on work activities wherever required – including across functional and hierarchical boundaries. Boundaries between units are either eliminated or are made as porous as possible to ensure that they do

Table 10.5 Features of a learning organisation

Feature	Explanation
A learning approach to strategy	The use of trials and experiments to improve understanding and generate improvements, and to modify strategic direction
Participative policy-making	All members are involved in strategy formation, influencing decisions and values and addressing conflict
Informative	Information technology is used to make information available to everyone and to enable front-line staff to use their initiative
Formative accounting and control	Accounting, budgeting and reporting systems are designed to help people understand the operations of organisational finance
Internal exchange	Sections and departments think of themselves as customers and suppliers in an internal 'supply chain', learning from each other
Reward flexibility	A flexible and creative reward policy, with financial and non-financial rewards to meet individual needs and performance
Enabling structures	Organisation charts, structures and procedures are seen as temporary, and can be changed to meet task requirements
Boundary workers as environmental scanners	Everyone who has contact with customers, suppliers, clients and business partners is treated as a valuable information source
Inter-company learning	The organisation learns from other organisations through joint ventures, alliances and other information exchanges
A learning climate	The manager's primary task is to facilitate experimentation and learning in others, through questioning, feedback and support
Self-development opportunities for all	People are expected to take responsibility for their own learning, and facilities are made available, especially to 'front-line' staff

Source: Based on Pedler *et al.* (1997).

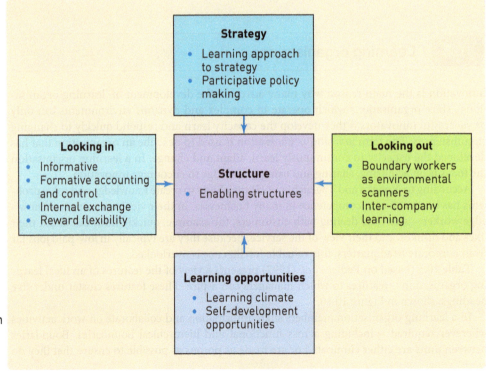

Figure 10.10 Clusters of learning organisation features

Source: Pedler *et al.* (1997).

not block the flow of ideas and information. Learning organisations tend to emphasise team working, and employees operate with a high degree of autonomy to work as they think will best enhance performance. Rather than directing and controlling, managers act as facilitators, supporters and advocates – enabling their staff to work and learn to the greatest degree possible.

Learning depends on information, so there is an emphasis on sharing information amongst employees in a timely and open manner. This too depends on managers creating a structure which encourages people to pass information in this way. Leadership is also important in the sense that one of their primary roles is to facilitate the creation of a shared vision for the business, and ensuring employees are enabled to work continually towards that. Finally the culture is one in which all agree on a shared vision and understands how all aspects of the organisation – its processes, activities, environment are related to each other. There is a strong sense of community and mutual trust. People feel free to share ideas and communicate, share and experiment – able to learn without fear of criticism or punishment.

Argyris (1999) distinguished between single-loop and double-loop learning. The classic example of single-loop learning is the domestic thermostat which, by detecting temperature variations, takes action to correct deviations from a predetermined level. In single-loop learning, the system maintains performance at the set level, but is unable to learn that the temperature is set too high or too low. Learning how to learn involves double-loop learning – challenging assumptions, beliefs and norms, rather than accepting them and working within their limitations. In single-loop learning, the question is 'how can we better achieve that standard of performance?' In double-loop learning the question becomes: 'is that an appropriate target in the first place?' In the context of developing the skills to cope more effectively with change, the aim is to enhance the ability of members to engage in double-loop learning.

Li and Kozhikode (2012) provide an excellent example towards the end of their article showing how TCL, the Chinese consumer electronics group, used ideas of organisational learning to enter the mobile phone market, despite being a relatively late entrant to the industry.

10.9 Integrating themes

Entrepreneurship

Ambos and Birkenshaw (2010) observed that the nature and evolution of new ventures cannot be analysed by using the traditional core elements of organisation such as dividing and co-ordinating tasks, or decision processes. To develop an accurate and contextually relevant way of describing their evolution they studied nine new ventures (all with a science base and often connected to a university) over several years. They identified three 'archetypes' – patterns of mutually supporting organisational elements – which all firms exhibited at some time during the observations:

- **Aspiration driven**: the desire to build a company: when this archetype was dominant, leaders focussed their energy on forming the venture and legitimising it to key stakeholders.
- **Market driven**: here the leader(s) focussed on market challenges and on meeting the specific needs of customers for the venture's products.
- **Capability driven**: here they focussed on technology and capability development – turning ideas into prototypes and then into saleable products, or developing required marketing knowledge.

The organisational elements which came together to 'define' these archetypes were specific to new ventures, namely:

- primary driver of action – the issue of most direct concern at the time;
- key stakeholders – the one or two whose support was vital to the next phase;
- key knowledge development – something they needed to develop at the time.

The authors claim their study offers a novel perspective on the evolution of new ventures, which does not try to understand them by reference to structural elements associated with large organisations, but arises from a common understanding of the venture's situation.

Sustainability

As earlier chapters have shown, many senior managers accept that the long-term viability of their organisation business depends on being effective in environmental as well as financial terms. Lawler and Worley (2010) contend that achieving this is not a matter of good intentions, but of locating sustainability within the organisation's strategy and supporting it with suitable structures. They studied companies with good reputations for sustainability to identify some of the ways in which they had ensured that their structures encouraged sustainable behaviour by managers and staff.

For a start, they found that sustainable effectiveness requires an external focus – structures that put as many people as possible in touch with the external environment so that they can experience what is happening and be able to make sound contributions to strategy and operations. General Electric required that each business strengthened their marketing teams, so that managers were more aware of how the environment was changing and how GE had to change to achieve sustainable effectiveness. They also refer to Cisco's 'eco-board' which is accountable for achieving the company's green objectives across the organisation. BP (Part 2 Case) is another example of an organisation which has made significant structural changes to ensure that safety and environmental issues are reported directly to senior management, rather than to heads of production units who may have other priorities.

Internationalisation

The growth of multinationals – based in one country but with significant production and sales in many others – continues, as managers see new opportunities beyond their home territory. At the same time they have to defend their position against new entrants from other countries. A perennial topic in multi-nationals is the balance between global integration and local responsiveness. Bartlett and Ghoshal (2002) show how managers at some firms – such as the Japanese Kao and Matsushita – sought to integrate worldwide operations to achieve global efficiency through economies of scale. Others, including Philips and Unilever, were more sensitive to local differences, permitting national subsidiaries high levels of autonomy to respond to local conditions.

They go on to suggest that as global pressures increase, companies needed to develop a more complex range of capabilities:

> To compete effectively, a company had to develop global competitiveness, multinational flexibility, and worldwide learning capability simultaneously. Building these [capabilities] was primarily an organisational challenge, which required organisations to break away from their traditional management modes and adopt a new organisational model. This model we call the transnational. (Bartlett and Ghoshal, 2002, p. 18)

They also present evidence and research on the organisational challenges which companies face if they wish to perform effectively in the international economy.

Governance

The financial crises which began in 2008 showed that many bankers had been taking great risks with the bank funds by investing in loans that were not only very risky, but packaged in such a complex way that others had difficulty understanding them. The bankers' behaviour had been encouraged in part by an incentive structure which rewarding them handsomely for profits, even if these were short-lived. This was not intentional fraud, but a sign of the negligence which failed to pay enough attention to banks' governance and control structures.

The Combined Code (2006) gives clear guidance to companies on how to structure their boards to ensure adequate governance and control. This is a voluntary Code of Best Practice, with which the boards of all companies listed on the London Stock Exchange are expected to comply. It includes guidance on matters such as:

- **The Board**: Every company should be headed by an effective board, which is collectively responsible for the success of the company.
- **Chairman and chief executive**: There should be a clear division of responsibilities between the running of the board and the executive responsible [for running the business]. No one individual should have unfettered powers of decision.
- **Board balance**: The board should include a balance of executive and [independent] non-executive directors so that no individual or small group can dominate the board's decision taking.
- **Board appointments**: There should be a formal, rigorous and transparent procedure for appointing new directors to the board.

Paradoxically, while this Code is widely seen as a valuable aid to corporate governance, it did not prevent the financial crisis: all the banks which had to be rescued by the government had complied with the Code.

Summary

1 **Outline the links between strategy, structure and performance**
   - The structure signals what people are expected to do within the organisation, and is intended to support actions that are in line with strategy, and so enhance performance. Equally, a structure may enable a new strategy to emerge which a different structure would have hindered.

2 **Give examples of management choices about dividing and co-ordinating work, with their likely advantages and disadvantages**
   - Managers divide work to enable individuals and groups to specialise on a limited aspect of the whole, and then combine the work into related areas of activity. Task division needs to be accompanied by suitable methods of co-ordination.
   - Centralisation brings consistency and efficiency, but also the danger of being slow and out of touch with local conditions. People in decentralised units can respond quickly to local conditions but risk acting inconsistently.
   - Functional forms allow people to specialise and develop expertise and are efficient; but they may be inward looking and prone to conflicting demands.
   - Divisional forms allow focus on particular markets of customer groups, but can duplicate facilities thus adding to cost.
   - Matrix forms try to balance the benefits of functional and divisional forms, but can again lead to conflicting priorities over resources.
   - Networks of organisations enable companies to draw upon a wide range of expertise, but may involve additional management and co-ordination costs.

3 **Compare the features of mechanistic and organic structures**
   - Mechanistic – people perform specialised tasks, hierarchical structure of control, knowledge located at top of hierarchy, vertical communication, loyalty and obedience is valued.
   - Organic – people contribute experience to common tasks, network structure of contacts, knowledge widely spread, horizontal communication, commitment to task goals more important than to superiors.

4 **Summarise the work of Woodward, Burns and Stalker, Lawrence and Lorsch, and John Child, showing how they contributed to this area of management**
- Woodward: appropriate structure depends on the type of production system ('technology') – unit, small batch, process.
- Burns and Stalker: appropriate structure depends on uncertainty of the organisation's environment – mechanistic in stable, organic in unstable.
- Lawrence and Lorsch: units within an organisation face different environmental demands, which implies that there will be both mechanistic and organic forms within the same organisation, raising new problems of co-ordination.
- John Child: contingency theory implies too great a degree of determinism – managers have greater degree of choice over structure than contingency theories implied.

5 **Use the 'contingencies' believed to influence choice of structure to evaluate the suitability of a form for a given unit**
- Strategy, environment, technology, age/size and political contingencies (Child) are believed to indicate the most suitable form, and the manager's role is to interpret these in relation to their circumstances.

6 **Explain and illustrate the features of a learning organisation**
- Learning organisations are those which have developed the capacity to continuously learn, adapt and change. This depends, according to Pedler *et al.* (1997), on evolving learning-friendly processes for looking in, looking out, learning opportunities, strategy, and structure.

7 **Show how ideas from the chapter add to your understanding of the integrating themes**
- Ambos and Birkenshaw (2010) traced the development of nine new businesses and identified three 'archetypes' – patterns of mutually supporting organisational elements which all firms exhibited – namely that they were driven by aspiration, markets and capabilities.
- The drive for sustainable performance is another example of the dilemma between central and local control. Decentralisation may harm the company if local managers ignore corporate policy, or may lead to more sustainable performance if local managers use their knowledge to find better solutions
- Bartlett and Ghoshal (2002) trace the many dilemmas companies face in creating a structure for their international operations.
- The financial crisis led many to call for tighter systems of governance and control – but many troubled banks already appeared to have such systems in place, which were not used.

Test your understanding

1 What did Chandler conclude about the relationship between strategy, structure and performance?
2 Draw the organisation chart of an organisation or department that you know. Compare it with the structures shown in Figure 10.2, writing down points of similarity and difference.
3 List the advantages and disadvantages of centralising organisational functions.
4 Several forms of co-ordination are described. Select two that you have seen in operation and describe how they work – and how well they work.
5 Explain the difference between a mechanistic and an organic form of organisation.
6 Explain the term 'contingency approach' and give an example of each of the factors that influence the choice between mechanistic and organic structures.

7 If contingency approaches stress the influence of external factors on organisational structures, what is the role of a manager in designing an organisation?
8 What is the main criticism of the contingency approaches to organisation structure?
9 What examples can you find of organisational activities that correspond to some of the features of a learning organisation identified by Pedler *et al.* (1997)?
10 Summarise an idea from the chapter that adds to your understanding of the integrating themes.

Think critically

Think about the structure and culture of your company, or one with which you are familiar, then make notes on these questions:

- What type of structure do you have – centralised or decentralised; functional or divisional, etc? What, if any, structural issues arise that are not mentioned here?
- In responding to issues of structure, what **assumptions** about the nature of organisations appear to guide your approach? If the business seems too centralised or too formal, why do managers take that approach?
- What factors in the **context** of the company appear to shape their approach to organising – what kind on environment are you working in, for example? To what extent does your structure involve networking with people from other organisations – and why is that?
- Have managers seriously considered whether the present structure is right for the business? Do they regularly compare your structure with that in other companies to look for **alternatives**?
- What **limitations** can you identify in any of the ideas and theories presented here? For example how helpful is contingency theory to someone deciding whether to make the organisation more or less mechanistic?

Read more

Woodward, J. (1965), *Industrial Organisation: Theory and practice*, Oxford University Press, Oxford. 2nd edition 1980.

Burns, T. and Stalker, G.M. (1961), *The Management of Innovation*, Tavistock, London.

Lawrence, P. and Lorsch, J.W. (1967), *Organisation and Environment*, Harvard Business School Press, Boston, MA.

These influential books give accessible accounts of the research process, and it would add to your understanding to read at least one of them in the original. The second edition of Woodward's book (1980) is even more useful, as it includes a commentary on her work by two later scholars.

Bartlett, C. A. and Ghoshal, S. (2002), *Managing Across Borders: The Transnational Solution*, (second edition) Harvard Business School Press, Boston, Ma.

Applies ideas on organisations and their structure to international management.

Catmull, E. (2008), 'How Pixar Fosters Collective Creativity', *Harvard Business Review*, vol. 86, no. 9, pp. 64–72.

The co-founder explains how it works.

Homburg, C., Jensen, O. and Krohmer, H. (2008), 'Configurations of Marketing and Sales: A Taxonomy', *Journal of Marketing,* vol. 72, no. 2, pp. 133–54.

An account of research into one of the continuing questions in organisation structure, of particular interest to students with an interest in marketing.

Go online

These websites have appeared in the chapter:

www.philips.com
www.lilly.com
www.reid-elsevier.com
www.sony-ericsson.com
www.roche.com
www.emi.com
www.rbs.com
www.communityhealthpartnerships.co.uk
www.gore.com
www.monsanto.com

Visit two of the business sites in the list, and navigate to the pages dealing with corporate news, investor relations or 'our company'.

- What organisational structure issues can you identify that managers in the company are likely to be dealing with? Can you find any information about their likely culture from the website?

- What kind of environment are they likely to be working in, and how may that affect their structure and culture?

CHAPTER 7
DECISION MAKING

Aims

To identify major aspects of decision making in organisations and to outline alternative ways of making decisions.

Objectives

By the end of your work on this chapter you should be able to outline the concepts below in your own terms and:

1. Outline the (iterative) stages in a systematic, decision making process and the tasks required in each
2. Explain, and give examples of, programmed and non-programmed decisions
3. Distinguish decision-making conditions of certainty, risk, uncertainty and ambiguity
4. Contrast rational, administrative, political and garbage-can decision models
5. Give examples of common sources of bias in decisions
6. Explain the contribution of Vroom and Yetton, and of Irving Janis, to our understanding of decision making
7. Show how ideas from the chapter add to your understanding of the integrating themes

Key terms

This chapter introduces the following ideas:

decision
decision making
problem
opportunity
decision criteria
decision tree
programmed (or structured) decision
procedure
rule
policy
non-programmed (or unstructured) decision
certainty
risk
uncertainty

ambiguity
rational model of decision making
administrative model of decision making
bounded rationality
satisficing
incremental model
political model
heuristics
prior hypothesis bias
representativeness bias
optimism bias
illusion of control
escalating commitment
groupthink

Each is a term defined within the text, as well as in the glossary at the end of the book.

Case study: Ikea www.ikea.com

In early 2013 Ikea employed 139,000 co-workers and had over 300 home furnishing stores in 44 countries: in the 2012 financial year it had generated sales of over €27 billion. It offers a limited online service in ten of the countries in which it operates – in the UK online sales rose by 25 per cent in 2012. Mikael Ohlsson became CEO in 2009, but had always said that he would only stay for four years. In September 2013 he would be replaced by Peter Agnefjall, the current head of Ikea in Sweden.

The Ikea vision 'to create a better everyday life for the majority of people' developed from a decision by Ingvar Kamprad, a Swedish entrepreneur, to sell home furnishing products at prices so low that many people could afford them. He aimed to achieve this not by cutting quality, but by applying simple cost-cutting solutions – products are designed, manufactured, transported, sold and assembled to support the vision. This has evolved into the 'Ikea Concept', elements of which include:

- focus on younger people and young families, and on modern innovative design;
- operate large stores on the outskirts of cities;
- customers serve themselves and assemble the furniture at home;
- purchasing 90 per cent of stock from global suppliers;
- buy the land and build the store; and
- emphasise responsible and sustainable operations.

The first showroom opened in 1953 and until 1963 all stores were in Sweden. International expansion began with a store in Norway – it has entered one new country in almost every year since, and is now planning to open three stores in China every year.

The Ikea Group manages the worldwide stores and associated businesses. It is owned by Stichting INGKA Foundation, based in the Netherlands: Ingvar Kamprad and a family member have two of the five board seats. They also control the Interogo Foundation in Liechtenstein, which has links with the company.

The company calls its employees 'co-workers', and aims to enable them to grow individually and professionally, taking care to recruit people who share the company's values. The website explains

© Inter Ikea Systems BV 2006.

that it seeks people with personal qualities such as a strong desire to learn, the motivation to continually do things better, common sense, able to lead by example, efficiency and cost-consciousness:

These values are important to us because our way of working is less structured than at many other organisations.

Ikea gives a substantial amount of money to charitable causes mostly focussed on women and children in south Asia – it is one of the biggest donors to child welfare in India, where it expects that within four years about 100 million people will have received support worth €125 million. It is also a major donor to Unicef and Save the Children, and in 2010 gave €47 million to charity.

Sources: *Financial Times*, 1 January 2011 (p. 23); company website.

Case questions 7.1
- Make a note of the decisions that have been taken in the story so far.
- Reflect on the elements of the Ikea Concept: do they have a common characteristic?
- How are they, and other decisions in the case study, likely to have affected the development of the business?
- Visit the company's website, and note examples of recent decisions shaping the company.

7.1 Introduction

The case study introduces one of Europe's biggest and most successful companies, now a global player in the home furnishing market. To move a small Swedish general retailer to its present position, senior managers at Ikea needed to decide where to allocate time, effort and other resources. Over the years their decisions paid off and they now face new issues, such as how to attract customers and well-qualified staff against competition from other retailers. They also face questions from environmental campaigners about their sources of timber (they are the world's third largest user of timber), and need to decide how to respond: this will shape Ikea's future.

Choice creates tension in individuals if they worry about 'what if' they had selected the other option (Schwartz, 2004). Good decisions add value, poor ones do the opposite: Tesco's decision to enter the US market had destroyed about £1 billion of the company's value by 2012. Hewlett-Packard, the computer company, appears to destroy value regularly by deciding to buy other companies – including EDS, Palm and Autonomy – and then finding that they are less valuable than the purchase price. These three acquisitions alone are believed to have lost HP shareholders some $20 billion (*Financial Times*, 22 November 2012, p. 13).

The complexity of decision making in organisations arises from structural divisions (see Buchanan and O'Connell (2006) for a review of the study of decision making). People at all levels and in all units make (often independent) choices about problems they believe need attention, or ideas they can use. These decisions establish which resources to use for which tasks, which resources they should build, which they no longer need. They arise throughout the management task: inputs (how to raise capital, who to employ), outputs (what to make, how to distribute them) and transformations (how to deliver a new service, how to manage the finances). Decisions affect what resources the organisation obtains and develops, how it uses them, and whether it adds value to them.

The 'content' (*what*) of these decisions is the result of a process – *how* the decisions are made. People make many discrete decisions every day, reflecting personal and local priorities, and what they believe to be the wider strategy. If these separate decisions do not reinforce each other in a reasonably consistent way the organisation will not perform well. Whether they appear coherent and mutually reinforcing reflects, in large part, the decision-making process – the systems managers create to guide staff as they make decisions – who to involve, what information to seek, and to aim for decisions that support the wider strategy.

> Like management itself, decision making is a generic process that is applicable to all forms of organised activity. (Harrison, 1999, p. 8)

An aspect of the process is speed: this is sometimes more important than certainty, and people need to understand the difference. The chief executive of Eli Lilly (pharmaceuticals) recalled that when he took over he realised the company needed to make decisions more quickly:

> We've had the luxury of moving at our own pace. Sometimes you can think for so long that your competitors pass you by. We need to act with 80 per cent, not 99.5 per cent, of the information. (From an article by John Lechleiter, *Financial Times*, 6 April 2009.)

Figure 7.1 illustrates the themes of the chapter, showing that making a decision involves:

- identifying the type of decision;
- identifying the conditions surrounding it;
- using one or more models to guide the process;
- selecting a decision-making style; and
- working through the decision process.

Decision Making   683

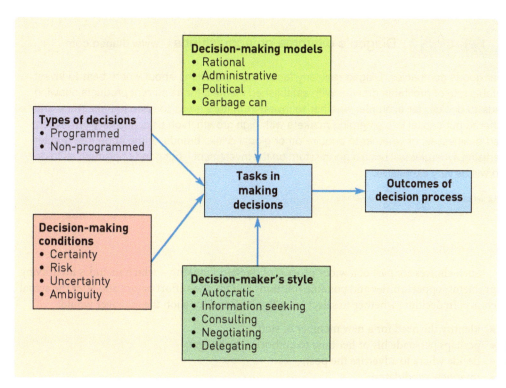

Figure 7.1 An overview of the chapter

The chapter contrasts 'programmed' and 'non-programmed' decisions, identifies four conditions surrounding a decision, compares four models, shows how bias affects decisions, and how managers can shape the context of decision making. It begins by outlining a simple, systematic model of the process which later sections elaborate.

Activity 7.1 Questions about a decision

Identify a management decision of which you are aware. You may find it helpful to discuss this with a manager you know, or use an activity have managed.

- Note what the decision involved, and what was decided.
- Was it an easy decision to make, or complex and messy? What made it so?
- How did those involved make the decision? Note just two or three main points.
- Did you (and they) consider the outcome of the decision satisfactory or not? Why was that?

7.2 Tasks in making decisions

A **decision** is a specific commitment to action (usually a commitment of resources). People make such choices at all levels – some affecting the business significantly (Ikea deciding to expand overseas, Nokia to enter a partnership with Mirosoft). Others affect local operations – whether to recruit staff, how much to spend on advertising next week.

A **decision** is a specific commitment to action (usually a commitment of resources).

> **Management in practice** — Diageo's dilemma on acquisitions www.diageo.com
>
> Like many consumer goods companies, Diageo regularly faces major decisions about where best to invest to ensure an acceptable rate of profitable growth. With established markets for its current products showing slow growth, it needs to decide, for example, whether to invest in mature areas to raise market share and reduce costs; whether to put capital into emerging markets with high growth, high risks and very few synergies with established businesses: or whether to acquire other global drinks brands, in the hope that greater marketing and advertising synergies will bring a good return on the investment – but good opportunities to do this are rare, and so will be very expensive.
>
> Source: *Financial Times*, 12 January 2011, p.17; company website.

Decision making is the process of identifying problems and opportunities and then resolving them.

Such choices are part of a wider process of **decision making** – which includes identifying problems, opportunities and possible solutions and involves effort before and after the actual choice. In deciding whether to select Jean, Bob or Rasul for a job the manager would:

- identify the need for a new member of staff;
- perhaps persuade his or her boss to authorise the budget;
- decide where to advertise the post;
- interview candidates;
- select the preferred candidate;
- decide whether or not to agree to their request for a better deal; and
- arrange their induction into the job so that they work effectively.

During each of these tasks the manager may go back in the process to think again, or to deal with another set of decisions – such as who to include on the selection committee. Samsung's decision about which new models to offer follows many earlier decisions about the target market, the design concept, how much to invest in design, production volumes and price. A manager makes small but potentially significant decisions all the time – which of several urgent jobs to do, whose advice to seek, which report to read, which customer to call. These shape the way people use their time, and the issues to which they attend.

Figure 7.2 shows a systematic sequence of tasks that people can work through to make a decision, with the direction of the arrows showing that it is an iterative process. As we do

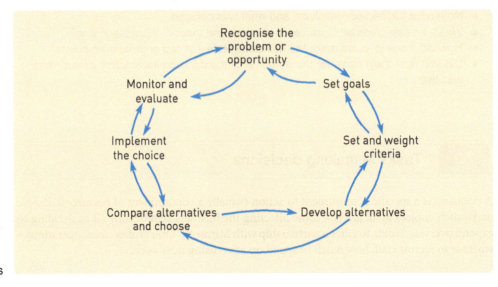

Figure 7.2 Tasks in making decisions

one task we find new information, reconsider, revisit an earlier task and perhaps decide on a new route. People may miss a task, give too much attention to one and too little to others.

Some adopt a completely different approach, moving quickly, and perhaps intuitively (see Section 7.5), from problem awareness to decision without formal analysis. For familiar or routine decisions this makes sense, as the alternatives and relevant information are well known. Some people depend mainly on their intuition to decide major issues, without formal analysis. Figure 7.2 shows a systematic way to reach a decision, but Section 7.5 will introduce other methods.

> **Key ideas** — Paul Nutt on 'idea discovery' and 'idea imposition'
>
> Paul Nutt studied over 400 decisions involving major commitments of resources. He distinguished between an 'idea discovery process' which usually led to success, and an 'idea imposition process' which usually led to failure. Decision processes correspond to one or other of these alternatives.
>
> Those following a discovery process spend time at the start looking beyond the initial claim that 'a problem has arisen that requires a decision': they spend time *understanding the claims* – by talking to stakeholders to judge the strength of their views. This leads to a clearer view of the 'arena of action' on which to take a decision. They also identify at the outset the forces that may block them from *implementing the preferred idea*, as this helps to understand the interests of stakeholders whose support they need.
>
> These early actions enable decision makers *to set a direction* – an agreed outcome of the decision. Dealing thoroughly with these three stages makes the remaining stages – *uncovering and evaluating ideas* – comparatively easy, as they help build agreement on what the decision is expected to achieve.
>
> Those following an idea imposition process
>
> **skip some stages ... jump to conclusions and then try to implement the solution they have stumbled upon. This bias for action causes them to limit their search, consider very few ideas, and pay too little attention to people who are affected, despite the fact that decisions fail for just these reasons.** (Nutt, 2002, p. 49)
>
> Analysis of more decisions (Nutt, 2008) confirmed that decision makers were as likely to use the failure-prone 'idea imposition process' as they were to use the (usually more successful) 'discovery process'.
>
> Source: Nutt (2002, 2008).

Recognising a problem or opportunity

People make decisions which commit time and other resources towards an objective. They do so when they become aware of a **problem** – a gap between an existing and a desired state of affairs, or an **opportunity** – the chance to do something not previously expected. Suppose a manager needs to decide whether to buy new mobile devices for the sales team, who say the models they have lack useful features and waste time – so they are presenting the manager with a clear problem. Most situations are more ambiguous, and people will have different views about the significance of an event or a piece of information: labelling a problem as significant is a subjective, possibly contentious matter. Before a problem gets onto the agenda, enough people have to be aware of it and feel sufficient pressure to act. The Nokia case (in Chapter 3) includes an acknowledgement by their new CEO that they were too slow to build on their early lead in smartphones.

A **problem** is a gap between an existing and a desired state of affairs.

An **opportunity** is the chance to do something not previously expected.

> **Management in practice**   **The opportunity for Iris**   www.irisnation.com
>
> Ian Millner explains the decision to start Iris:
>
> We started about ten years ago, and we were essentially a group of friends all working within a really large advertising agency group, and we just decided that we could do it better. And then I guess one thing led to another and before we knew it we were having conversations with one of the clients that we had at the time which was Eriksson. Once we had that conversation Iris was quite quickly born, and then over a period of months myself and those friends, we sort of left the building and set Iris up.
>
> I think without doubt the biggest success that we've had is around momentum and being able to keep the momentum high and continue to change as we've gone from being a small company, which is just defined by a group of friends, to a large company that is global, expanding really quickly and driving the strategic agenda of a lot of clients all over the world. We've always had a strong kind of entrepreneurial streak, we've always been willing to try things and learn quickly.
>
> Source: Interview with Ian Millner.

Managers become aware of a problem as they compare existing conditions with the state they desire. If things are not as they should be – the sales reps are complaining that their current mobiles prevent them doing their jobs properly – then there is a problem. People are only likely to act if they feel pressure – such as a rep threatening to leave or a customer complaining. Pressure comes from many sources – and people differ in whether they pay attention: some react quickly, others ignore uncomfortable information and postpone difficult (to them) decisions.

Set goals and weight criteria

The goals (or objectives) of the decision may seem obvious in view of the problem, but it is worth spending time to ensure they are clear and that all involved have a common understanding of which specific aspects of the problem a decision is intended to settle. The main issue is probably to clarify the scope of the decision. Continuing the selection decision mentioned above, at an earlier phase – when the previous job holder said they were leaving – the manager and perhaps some colleagues would decide what to do:

- Do we need to replace the person who has left?
- Shall we alter the terms of the job before we recruit?
- Shall we try find an internal replacement first?
- Which recruitment method shall we use?
- Who will interview the candidates?

All are valid questions but it is worth being clear which bit of the problem a particular process is intended to solve: this is clarified by setting a goal, such as:

- *Do we need to appoint a replacement and if so, at what grade?*

That is separate from other decisions, such as:

- *Which recruitment agency should we appoint?*

Spending time clarifying this will help to prevent people talking at cross purposes, or discussing issues which logically only arise once other decisions are known.

To decide between options people need **decision criteria** – the factors that are relevant to the decision. Without these they cannot choose: in the 'new mobile' case, criteria could include usefulness of features, price, delivery, warranty, and ease of use. Some criteria are more important than others, and the decision process can represent this by (say) assigning 100 points between the factors depending on their relative importance. We can measure some criteria (price or delivery) objectively, while others (features, ease of use) are subjective.

Like problem recognition, setting criteria is subjective: people differ over the factors to include, and their relative weight. They may also have private and unexpressed criteria – such as 'will cause least trouble', 'will do what the boss wants', 'will help my career'. Changing the criteria or their weights will change the decision – so the manager in the mobile case has to decide whether to set and weight the criteria herself, or to ask the reps.

Decision criteria define the factors that are relevant in making a decision.

Develop alternatives

Another task is to identify solutions: in the mobile case this is a list of available brands. In more complex problems alternatives need to be developed – at a cost. Too few will limit choice, too many will be costly. Schwartz (2004) found that giving people more choices beyond a certain point is counter-productive as it leads to stress, frustration and anxiety about making the wrong decision – there is an example in Key ideas.

> **Key ideas** Too many jams to choose
>
> Iyengar and Lepper (2000) demonstrated that consumers protect themselves from the stress of too much choice by refusing to purchase. In an experiment conducted in a food store, they set up a tasting booth offering different types of jam. When 24 types were on display, about 60 per cent of passers-by stopped at the booth, compared with just 40 per cent when only six jams were shown. But when it came to choosing a pot of jam to buy, the proportions changed. Only 3 per cent of visitors to the 24-jam booth made a purchase, while 30 per cent of those visiting the smaller display did so. The limited selection was the most effective in converting interest into sales.
>
> Source: Iyengar and Lepper (2000).

Compare alternatives and choose between them

Management decisions need a system for comparing and choosing. Figure 7.3 illustrates the decision stages through a simple example – though setting and weighting criteria is tricky, especially if several people take part.

Another way to structure a situation in which there are several alternative actions is to draw a **decision tree**. This helps to assess the relative suitability of the options by assessing them against identified criteria – successively eliminating the options as each relevant factor is introduced. Figure 7.8 is an example: it shows how a manager can decide the most suitable method of solving a problem by asking a succession of questions about the situation, leading to the most likely solution for those circumstances. The main challenge in using the technique is to identify the logical sequence of intermediate decisions and how they relate to each other.

A decision tree helps someone to make a choice by progressively eliminating options as additional criteria or events are added to the tree.

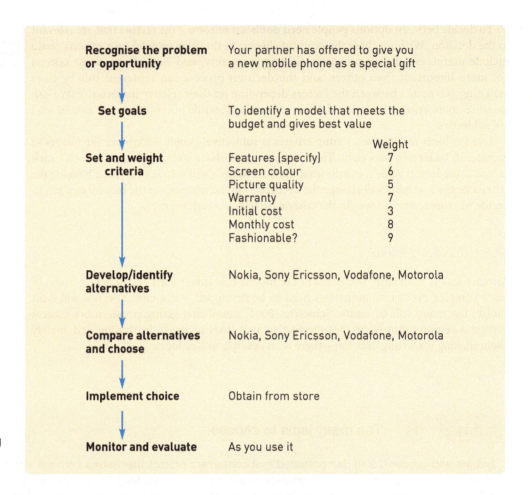

Figure 7.3 Illustrating the decision-making tasks – a new mobile phone

---

Key ideas — Mintzberg's study of major decisions

Henry Mintzberg and his colleagues studied 25 major, unstructured decisions in 25 organisations, finding that rational techniques could not cope with the complexity of strategic decisions. They concluded that:

- whether people recognised the need for a decision depended on the strength of the stimuli, the reputation of the source, and the availability of a potential solution;
- most decisions depended on designing a custom-made solution (a new organisation structure, a new product or a new technology); and
- the choice phase (see Figure 7.2), was less significant than the design phase: it was essentially ratifying a solution that was determined implicitly during design.

Source: Mintzberg *et al*. (1976).

Implement the choice

In the mobile case this is a simple matter if the manager has conducted the process well. In bigger decisions this will be a much more problematic stage as it is here that the decision commits scarce resources – and perhaps meets new objections. So implementation often takes longer than expected, and depends on people making other decisions. It also shows the effects of the decision process: if the promoter involved others they may be more willing to cooperate with the consequential changes – for example, in the way they work.

> **Management in practice**   **Entrepreneurial decisions – data or intuition?**
>
> Luke Johnson is a successful entrepreneur who runs Risk Capital Partners (www.riskcapitalpartners.co.uk), a private equity firm. Reflecting on how entrepreneurs reach decisions he writes:
>
> > Do highly rational individuals make better entrepreneurs? I'm not so sure. I think a strong emotional quotient can matter more. Successful business builders know that for most companies, the core of any achievement will depend on personal relationships – with employees, customers, bankers, shareholders, suppliers and others. Managing these interactions is more dependent upon charisma than calculation.
> >
> > Statistical analysis cannot handle the multiple issues involved in a start-up. One can get lost in the hundreds of pages of verbiage and spreadsheets and forget about critical issues such as culture and the big picture. When I bough Patisserie Valerie it was barely profitable, but the brand and business model felt valuable. On strict criteria it was hard to justify the purchase price. Yet it has turned into one of the best investments I've ever made.
>
> Source: *Financial Times*, 3 October 2012, p. 18.

Monitor and evaluate

The final stage is evaluation – looking back to see if the decision has resolved the problem, and what can be learnt. It is a form of control, which people are often reluctant to do formally, preferring to turn their attention to future tasks, rather than reflect on the past. That choice inhibits their ability to learn from experience.

> **Activity 7.2**   **Critical reflection on making a decision**
>
> Work through the steps in Figure 7.3 for a decision you currently face – such as where to go on holiday, which courses to choose next year, or which job to apply for. Then do the same for a decision that involves several other people, such as which assignment to do in your study group or where to go for a night out together.
> If you work in an organisation, select two business decisions as the focus of your work.
>
> - How did working through the steps affect the way you reached a decision?
> - Did it help you think more widely about the alternatives?
> - How did the second decision, involving more people, affect the usefulness of the method?
> - Then reflect on the technique itself – did it give insight into the decision process? What other tasks should it include?

7.3 Programmed and non-programmed decisions

Many decisions which managers face are straightforward and need not involve intense discussion.

Programmed decisions

Programmed (or structured) decisions (Simon, 1960) deal with problems that are familiar, and where the information required is easy to define and obtain – the situation is well

> A **programmed (or structured) decision** is a repetitive decision that can be handled by a routine approach.

structured. If a store manager notices a product is selling well they use a simple, routine procedure to decide how much new stock to order. Decisions are 'structured' if they arise frequently and people deal with them by following a **procedure** – a series of steps, often online, to deal with that problem. They may use a **rule** setting out what to do, or not do, in a given situation or refer to a **policy** – which sets out general principles to follow.

Programmed decisions deal with routine matters – ordering supplies, appointing a junior member of staff, lending money to a retail bank customer. Once managers formulate procedures, rules or policies, others can usually make the decisions. Computers handle many decisions of this type – the checkout systems in supermarkets link to systems recording sales and ordering stock.

> A **procedure** is a series of related steps to deal with a structured problem.
>
> A **rule** sets out what someone can or cannot do in a given situation.
>
> A **policy** is a guideline that establishes some general principles for making a decision.

Non-programmed decisions

Simon (1960) also observed that people make **non-programmed (unstructured) decisions** to deal with situations that are novel or unusual, and so require a unique solution. The issue has not arisen in quite that form, and the information required is unclear, vague or open to several interpretations. Major management decisions are of this type – such as the choice which managers at Marks & Spencer faced in 2010 in deciding whether to launch their programme to become the world's most sustainable retailer by 2015. Whatever benefits this may bring, it will be challenging and time-consuming to introduce as it involves changing the way suppliers work. While the company will have done a lot of research before making the decision, they could not know how customers and competitors would respond, or how long any benefit would last. Most issues of strategy are of this type, as they involve great uncertainty and many interests.

> A **non-programmed (unstructured) decision** is a unique decision that requires a custom-made solution when information is lacking or unclear.

Management in practice — Inamo – choosing a designer — www.inamo-restaurant.com

Inamo is a London restaurant where customers place their order directly to the kitchen from an interactive ordering system on their table. Selecting the designer for such a novel idea was a big step. Noel Hunwick, Chief Operating Officer:

> An early and crucial decision we had to make was to select our interior design company. The way we've always worked is to make sure that we always [have] options from which to choose so, based on recommendations and on web research, and going to various shows and events, I put together a large portfolio of work … to get a rough price per square foot that these companies generally charged.
>
> We then selected eight companies to give us a full design brief, and then cut that down to three – who came out with three entirely different concepts so I think that then allowed us to narrow it down to two and have a final showdown. [Given out our ordering system was so novel] I think that was a crucial decision – we had to make sure it wasn't an overload on the customer, so I think that was a very delicate and difficult business decision. We always want options. Every single decision, whether it's the cleaning company that we use, everything, we want three options at least. I think that's very important.

Source: Interview with Noel Hunwick.

While analytical techniques are good for programmed decisions, non-programmed decisions depend on judgement and intuition. Many decisions have elements of each type – complex non-programmed decisions probably contain elements that can be handled in a programmed way.

Decision Making 691

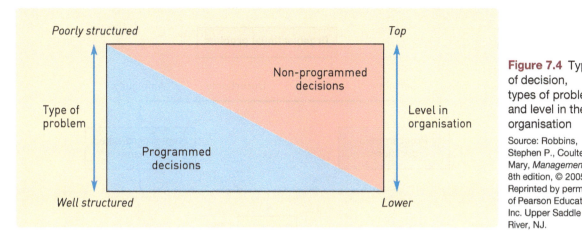

Figure 7.4 Types of decision, types of problem and level in the organisation

Source: Robbins, Stephen P., Coulter, Mary, *Management*, 8th edition, © 2005. Reprinted by permission of Pearson Education, Inc. Upper Saddle River, NJ.

Figure 7.4 relates the type of decision to the levels of the organisation. People at lower levels typically deal with routine, structured problems by applying procedures. As they move up the hierarchy they face more unstructured decisions – junior staff hand decisions that do not fit the rules to someone above them, while the latter pass routine matters to junior staff.

Activity 7.3 Programmed and non-programmed decisions

Identify examples of the types of decision set out above. Try to identify one example of your own to add to those below or that illustrates the point specifically within your institution:

- **Programmed decision** – whether to reorder stock.
- **Non-programmed decision** – whether to launch a new service.

Compare your examples with those of other students and consider how those responsible made each decision. How easy is it to distinguish decisions as fitting one or other of these categories?

7.4 Decision making conditions

Decisions arise within a context whose nature, measured by the degree of **certainty**, **risk**, **uncertainty** and **ambiguity**, materially affects the decision process. Figure 7.5 relates the nature of the problem to the type of decision. Whereas people can deal with conditions of certainty by making programmed decisions, many situations are both uncertain and ambiguous. Here people need to be able to use a non-programmed approach.

Certainty

Certainty is when the decision maker has all the information they need – they are fully informed about the costs and benefits of each alternative. A company treasurer wanting to

Certainty describes the situation when all the information the decision maker needs is available.

Risk refers to situations in which the decision maker is able to estimate the likelihood of the alternative outcomes.

Uncertainty is when people are clear about their goals, but have little information about which course of action is most likely to succeed.

Ambiguity is when people are uncertain about their goals and how best to achieve them.

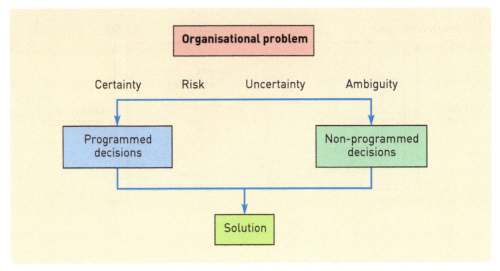

Figure 7.5 Degree of uncertainty and decision-making type

place reserve funds can readily compare rates of interest from several banks, and calculate exactly the return from each. Few decisions are that certain, and most contain risk and/or uncertainty.

Risk

Risk refers to situations in which the decision maker can estimate the likelihood of the alternative outcomes, possibly using statistical methods. Banks have developed tools to assess credit risk, and so reduce the risk that the borrower will not repay the loan. The questions on an application form for a loan (home ownership, time at this address, employer's name, etc.) enable the bank to assess the risk of lending money to that person.

Uncertainty

Uncertainty means that people know what they wish to achieve, but do not have enough information about alternatives and future events to estimate the risk confidently. Factors that may affect the outcomes of deciding to launch a new product (future growth in the market, changes in customer interests, competitors' actions) are difficult to predict.

Managers at GlaxoSmithKline, the pharmaceutical group, experience great uncertainty in allocating research funds. Scientists who wish to develop a range of vaccines have to persuade the board to allocate resources to the project. Uncertainties include rapid change in the relevant science, what competitors are doing, and how many years will pass before the vaccines begins to earn revenue (if any).

Ambiguity

Ambiguity describes a situation in which the intended goals are unclear, and so the alternative ways of reaching them are equally fluid – leading to stress. Students would experience ambiguity if their teacher created student groups, told each group to complete a project, but gave them no topic, direction, or guidelines. Ambiguous problems are often associated with rapidly changing circumstances, and unclear links between decision elements – see Management in practice.

Decision Making 693

> **Management in practice** — Nokia's decision on the joint venture with Microsoft
>
> As Nokia struggled to regain its once dominant position in the mobile phone industry, one issue was what to do about its proprietary operating system, Symbian. This had in part helped it gain a strong position, since designing the software and the device in the same company enhanced the user experience – as in Apple devices. Symbian was no longer competitive with the operating system in the iPhone, or with Google's Android software, used by Samsung. Rebuilding Symbian would take time, so a joint venture with Microsoft seemed attractive. But it is highly uncertain: the goal is clear, but when teams develop new software under extreme time pressure they cannot be sure of the quality of the product. Nor can they be sure how it will work in devices designed in another company (Nokia). And Nokia will never know if an alternative decision, such as an alliance with Google, would have produced a better result.
>
> Source: Chapter 3 case.

Dependency

Another way to categorise decisions is by their dependency (or not) on other decisions. People make decisions in a historical and social context and so are influenced by past and possible future decisions, and by events in other parts of the organisation. Legacy computer systems (the result of earlier decisions) frequently constrain how quickly a company can adopt new systems.

Some decisions have few implications beyond their immediate area, but others have significant ripples around and beyond the organisation. Changes in technology usually require consistent, supportive changes in structures and processes if they are to be effective – but decisions on these areas are harder to make than those on technology. Figure 7.6 illustrates this.

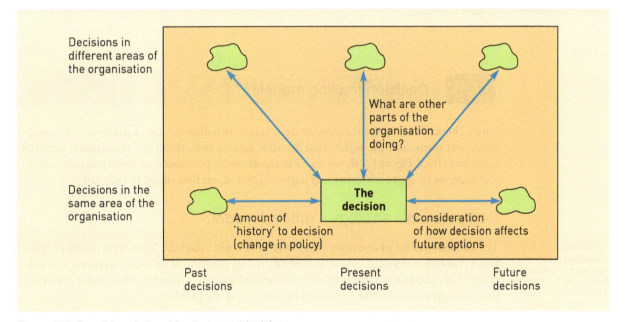

Figure 7.6 Possible relationships between decisions

Source: Making Management Decisions, 2nd ed., Prentice Hall, Hemel Hempstead (Cooke, S. and Slack, N. 1991) p. 24, Copyright © Pearson Education Ltd. 1991.

> **Case study**   Ikea – the case continues   www.ikea.com

Mikael Ohlsson, who joined Ikea in 1979, became CEO in 2009. One of his early decisions was to renew the company's efforts to open stores in India, which it had been trying to do for several years. In 2011 he spent ten days in the country, from which it obtains many of its products, especially soft furnishings. He is aware that the stores are still concentrated in Europe, and wants to drive expansion into large developing countries like India, China and Russia. Governments in these countries want to attract the revenues and modernising influences of international companies, but also face pressure from domestic retailers trying to protect their interests. Ikea's Asia-Pacific retail manager:

> We still face a very high level of uncertainty. It is a very sensitive political issue in India and it may take a new government more time to negotiate with the different parties and agree the changes that are required to open up and develop the retail sector.

In 2012 the project moved another step forward as the Indian government relaxed some requirements on sourcing from small local companies (Ikea already sources goods from many Indian companies, but inevitably they tend to become large). The company plans to open one store a year in India over the next decade. Mr Ohlsson has also decided to triple the rate of expansion in China to three stores a year, and also to expand more rapidly in Russia.

The stores have a common design, intended to reflect the company values – and also to encourage people to stay there for a long time. Any outlet that wishes to organise the store in a particular way has to obtain permission from head office. The company spent five years planning its entry into the Japanese market, before opening the first store in 2006. It wanted to reduce the risks of the decision by understanding Japanese culture as it relates to the home – how people use their home, which of them has most influence on purchases, and how parents and their children spend time.

Ikea made quite significant changes to the concept to suit the needs of Japanese customers; indeed [these] have been greater than in any other country that Ikea has entered in recent years. (Edvardsson and Enquist, 2009, p. 73)

Sources: Edvardsson and Enquist (2009); *Financial Times*, 23 January 2012, p.21.

Case question 7.2

- Reflect on IKEA's decision to invest in Russia and China, and its attempts to enter India. What risks, uncertainties, ambiguities or dependencies were probably associated with these situations? Use Figure 7.5 to structure your answer on dependencies.

7.5 Decision making models

James Thompson (1967) distinguished decisions on two dimensions – agreement or disagreement over goals, and the beliefs that decision makers hold about the relationship between cause and effect. Figure 7.7 shows that a decision can be positioned on these two dimensions, and suggests an approach to making decisions that seems best suited to each cell.

Computational strategy – rational model

The **rational model of decision making** is sometimes called the 'economic model of rationality' because economists use it to analyse pricing, investment or other decisions in conditions where the goal is clear, but there are several ways to achieve it. The model prescribes that managers should make a decision by structuring the problem:

- specify the goal and the intended economic outcome;
- gather information about the likely costs and benefits of each route to achieving the goal; and
- select the route that will probably bring the greatest economic return.

*The **rational model of decision making** assumes that people make consistent choices to maximise economic value within specified constraints.*

	Agreement on goals?	
	High	Low
Certainty	**I** Computational strategy Rational model	**III** Compromise strategy Political model
Beliefs about cause-and-effect relationships		
Uncertainty	**II** Judgemental strategy Administrative, incremental and intuitional models	**IV** Inspirational strategy Garbage-can model

Figure 7.7 Conditions favouring different decision processes

Source: Based on Thompson (1967), p.134.

The model depends on the assumption that the decision maker is rational and logical in setting preferences, assigning values to costs and benefits, and evaluating alternatives.

The rational model is normative, in that it defines how a decision maker *should* act – it does not necessarily describe how managers *do* act. It aims to help people to act more rationally, rather than relying on intuition and personal preferences. If they are able and willing to gather the required information and to agree criteria for choice, the approach is likely to add value – see Management in practice.

Management in practice — How Google decides between features www.google.com

Google depends on the brilliance of its engineers to create search features which will enhance users' experience. They work in small teams and typically have a technical lead (the smartest engineer) and an Assistant Product Manager (APMs – and intended, in the broadest sense, to connect the team with the market). The company had great difficulty clarifying the APM role as the founders believed that engineers did not want to be managed. Others insisted they did – even if only to have someone to go to if they reached an impasse over a decision – most often over whether to develop, and then include, a new search feature.

> A product manager ... did not give orders. His (or her) job was to charm the engineers into a certain way of thinking ... The way to do that, of course, was by hard numbers. Information was a great leveller at Google. [APMs can only gain authority over senior, experienced engineers if they] gather the data, lobby the team, and win them over by data.

That process became an asset for Google, by making sure that data was at the centre of decision making. An APM:

> could order up a 1 per cent A/B experiment (in which one out of a hundred users gets a version of the product with the suggested change), then go to the team and say, 'users with this new experience are doing 11 per cent more page views and clicking on ads 8 per cent more'. With ammunition like that, a decision to include the new feature in the product wouldn't be based on a power struggle but on a mathematical calculation. Nothing personal. It was data.

Source: Based on Levy, 2011, pp. 161–2.

Table 7.1 Examples of automated decision systems by types of decision

Type of decision	Example of automated decision systems
Solution configuration	Mobile phone operators who offer a range of features and service options: an automated programme can weigh all the options, including information about the customer, and present the most suitable option to the customer.
Yield optimisation	Widely used in the airline industry to increase revenue by enabling companies to vary prices depending on demand. Spreading to other transport companies, hotels, retailing and entertainment.
Fraud detection	Credit card companies, online gaming companies and tax authorities use automated screening techniques to detect and deter possible fraud.
Operational control	Power companies use automated systems to sense changes in the physical environment (power supply, temperature or rainfall), and respond rapidly to changes in demand, by redirecting supplies across the network.

Source: Based on Davenport and Harris (2005).

Davenport and Harris (2005) describe how computer-based decision support systems analyse large quantities of data, with complex relationships – such as in power supply, transport management and banking. Automated decision systems:

> sense online data or conditions, apply codified knowledge or logic and make decisions – all with minimal amounts of human intervention. (Davenport and Harris, 2005, p. 84)

Table 7.1 gives examples.

Such applications give managers objective, quantitative methods to deal with some types of decision. Other decisions require other methods, sometimes in combination with rational ones.

Judgemental strategies – administrative, incremental and intuitional

Administrative models

The **administrative model of decision making** describes how people make decisions in uncertain, ambiguous situations.

Bounded rationality is behaviour that is rational within a decision process which is limited (bounded) by an individual's ability to process information.

Satisficing is the acceptance by decision makers of the first solution that is 'good enough'.

Simon's (1960) **administrative model of decision making** describes how managers make decisions in situations which are uncertain and ambiguous. Many management problems are unstructured (goals, and routes to achieve them, are unclear) and so not suitable for the precise quantitative analysis of the rational model. People rely on judgement to resolve such issues.

Simon based the model on two concepts – bounded rationality and satisficing. **Bounded rationality** expresses the fact that people have mental limits, or boundaries, on how rational they can be. We cannot comprehend all the options, so select from what is available – so our selection represents a limited part of the whole. We cannot then make a rational decision, so instead we decide by **satisficing** – choosing the first solution that is 'good enough'. Searching for other options may produce a better return but identifying and evaluating them would cost more than the benefits. Suppose you are in a strange city and need coffee before a meeting. You look for the first acceptable coffee shop that will do the job – you satisfice. In a similar fashion, managers seek solutions only until they find one they believe will work.

> **Key ideas** **A behavioural theory of decision making**
>
> Richard Cyert, James March and Herbert Simon (Simon, 1960; Cyert and March, 1963; March, 1988) developed an influential model of decision making. It is sometimes referred to as the behavioural theory of decision making since it treats decision making as an aspect of human behaviour. Also referred to as the administrative model, it recognises that in the real world people are restricted in their decision processes, and therefore have to accept what is probably a less than perfect solution. It introduced the concepts of 'bounded rationality' and 'satisficing' to the study of decision making.

The administrative model focuses on the human and organisational factors that influence decisions. It is more realistic than the rational model for non-programmed, ambiguous decisions. According to the administrative model, managers:

- have goals that are typically vague and conflicting, and are unable to reach a consensus;
- have different levels of interest in the decision, and interpret information subjectively;
- rarely use rational procedures fully;
- limit their search for alternatives;
- accept satisficing rather than maximising solutions.

The administrative model is descriptive, showing how managers decide complex issues.

> **Management in practice** **Satisficing in e-health projects**
>
> Boddy *et al.* (2009) studied the implementation of several 'e-health' projects, in which modern information and communication technologies assist clinicians in delivering care. These include applications like remote diagnostic systems, in which a consultant, assisted by video-conferencing equipment, examines the condition of a patient in a clinic hundreds of miles away. Such methods offer significant savings in patient travel time, and make better use of consultants' time, especially in remote parts of the country. Despite this, the health service has been slow to use e-health systems on a national scale.
>
> To secure the fullest benefits managers and staff also need to make significant changes throughout the organisation. The processes for interacting with patients change, as does the work of consultants, nurses and other medical staff. These changes are harder to implement than a decision to buy the technology. Pilot projects are producing modest benefits, but nothing like those which could flow from a national programme. A reasonable conclusion is that managers have unconsciously decided to satisfice – they can show they are trying the new methods and producing benefits: to secure the full potential would require more effort than they are willing to give.
>
> Source: Boddy *et al.* (2009b).

Incremental models

Charles Lindblom (1959) developed an **incremental model**, which people use when they are uncertain about the consequences of their choice. He built on Simon's idea of bounded rationality to show that people typically make only a limited search until they find an option that is reassuringly close to what already exists. Current choices are heavily influenced by past choices.

On this view, policy unfolds not from a single event, but from the accumulation of small decisions. These help people to minimise the risk of mistakes, and they can reverse the decision if necessary. He called this incrementalism, or the 'science of muddling through'. Lindblom contrasted what he called the 'root' method of decision-making with the 'branch' method. The root method required a comprehensive evaluation of options in the light of defined objectives. The branch method involved building out, step-by-step and by small degrees, from the current

*People use an **incremental model** of decision making when they are uncertain about the consequences. They search for a limited range of options, and policy unfolds from a series of cumulative small decisions.*

situation. He claimed that the root method is not suitable for complex policy questions, so the practical person follows the branch approach – the science of muddling through. The incremental model (like the administrative one) recognises human limitations.

Intuitional models

Klein (1997) studied how effective decision makers work, including those working under extreme time pressure like surgeons, fire fighters and nurses. He found they rarely used classical decision theory to weigh the options: instead they used pattern recognition to relate the situation to their experience. They acted on intuition – a non-conscious mental process of basing decisions on experience and accumulated judgement – sometimes called 'tacit knowledge'. Klein concluded that effective decision makers use their intuition as much as formal processes – perhaps using both as the situation demands. Experienced managers act quickly on what seems like very little information – rather than formal analysis, they rely on judgement to make decisions. Hodgkinson *et al.* (2009) quote the co-founder of Sony, Akio Mariata, the driving force behind one of the great innovations of the 20th century:

> Creativity requires something more than the processing of information. It requires human thought, spontaneous intuition and a lot of courage. (p. 278)

They stress that intuition is not the same as instinct (autonomous reflex actions or inherited behaviour patterns), nor is it a random process of guessing.

Compromise strategy – political model

> The **political model** is a model of decision making that reflects the view that an organisation consists of groups with different interests, goals and values.

The **political model** examines how people make decisions when managers disagree over goals and how to pursue them (Pfeffer, 1992b; Buchanan and Badham, 1999). It recognises that an organisation is a working system, and a political system, which establishes the relative power of people and functions. A decision will enhance the power of some and limit that of others. People pursue goals supporting personal and sub-unit interests, as well as those of the organisation, evaluating a decision in terms of its likely effects on these interests.

They will often support their position by building a coalition with those who share their interest. This gives others the opportunity to contribute their ideas and enhances their commitment if the decision is adopted.

The political model assumes that:

- organisations contain groups with diverse interests, goals and values. Managers disagree about problem priorities and may not understand or share the goals and interests of other managers;
- information is ambiguous and incomplete. Rationality is limited by the complexity of many problems as well as personal interests; and
- managers engage in the push and pull of debate to decide goals and discuss alternatives – decisions arise from bargaining and discussion.

Inspirational strategy – garbage-can model

Cohen *et al.* (1972) suggested that decisions are made when four independent streams of activities meet – usually by chance. The four streams are:

Choice opportunities	Occasions at which people make decisions – such as budget or other regular management meetings, and chance encounters
Participants	A stream of people who are able to decide
Problems	A stream of problems which people recognise as significant – a lost sale, a new opportunity, a vacancy
Solutions	A stream of potential solutions seeking problems – ideas, proposals, information – that people continually generate

Table 7.2 Four models of decision making

Features	Rational	Administrative/incremental	Political	Garbage can
Clarity of problem and goal	Clear problem and goals	Vague problems and goals	Conflict over goals	Goals and solutions independent
Degree of certainty	High degree of certainty	High degree of uncertainty	Uncertainty and/or conflict	Ambiguity
Available information on costs and benefits	Much information about costs and benefits	Little information about costs and benefits of alternatives	Conflicting views about costs and benefits of alternatives	Costs and benefits unconnected at start
Method of choice	Rational choice to maximise benefit	Satisficing choice – good enough	Choice by bargaining amongst players	Choice by accidental merging of streams

In this view, the choice opportunities (scheduled meetings and chance encounters) act as the container (garbage can) for the mixture of participants, problems and solutions. One combination of the three may be such that enough participants are interested in a solution which they can match to a problem – and take a decision accordingly. Another group of participants may not have made those connections, so would not have reached that decision.

This may at first sight seem an unlikely way to run a business, yet creative businesses depend on a rapid interchange of ideas, not only about specific, known problems but also about new discoveries, research at other companies, what someone heard at a conference. They depend on people bringing these solutions and problems together – but will lose opportunities if chance meetings don't happen. So it makes sense to create a context which increases the likelihood of creative exchange – which companies do when they construct buildings that give many opportunities for face-to-face contact, and build a culture that can make decisions quickly if necessary.

Table 7.2 summarises these four models – which are complementary in that a skilful manager or a well-managed organisation will use all of them, depending on the decision and the context. A new product idea may emerge from a process resembling the garbage can – but someone then needs to be able to build a rational case to persuade the board to invest resources in it.

Activity 7.4 Decide which approach to making decisions is most suitable

Here are some decisions which Virgin (see Part 3 Case) has faced:

- What fare structure to set for the unregulated services it operates (where it is free to set fares without involving the rail regulator).
- Whether to bid to retain its railway franchise to run the UK West Coast Main Line.
- Whether to bid for about 300 branches which the EU requires RBS to sell.
- Whether to order further airliners for Virgin Atlantic.

In each case, decide which of the four decision models best describe the situation, and explain why.

Compare your answers with colleagues on your course, and prepare a short report summarising your conclusions from this activity.

7.6 Biases in making decisions

Heuristics Simple rules or mental short cuts that simplify making decisions.

Since people have a limited capacity to process information they use **heuristics** – simple rules, or short cuts, that help us to overcome this constraint (Khaneman and Tversky, 1974). While they help us to make decisions, they bring the danger of one or more biases - prior hypothesis, representativeness, optimism, illusion of control, escalating commitment and emotional attachment.

Prior hypothesis bias

People who have strong prior beliefs about the relationship between two alternatives base their decisions on those beliefs, even when they receive evidence that their beliefs are wrong. This is the **prior hypothesis bias**, which is strengthened by paying more attention to information which supports their beliefs, and ignoring what is inconsistent.

Prior hypothesis bias results from a tendency to base decisions on strong prior beliefs, even if the evidence shows that they are wrong.

Representativeness bias

This is the tendency to generalise from a small sample or a single episode, and to ignore other relevant information. Examples of this **representativeness bias** are:

- predicting the success of a new product on the basis of an earlier success;
- appointing someone with a certain type of experience because a previous successful appointment had a similar background.

Representativeness bias results from a tendency to generalise inappropriately from a small sample or a single vivid event

Optimism bias

Lovallo and Kahneman (2003) believe that a major reason for poor decisions is because people systematically underestimate the costs and overestimate the benefits of a proposal. This is **optimism bias** – a human tendency to exaggerate their talents and their role in success. Hodgson and Drummond (2009) give an example of a brewery whose senior managers were over-confident about their ability to acquire and re-build a brewery that had closed down. What seemed like a good way to increase capacity turned out to be a poor decision, as the property required more expenditure than expected, which led to the failure of the purchasers' business.

Optimism bias is a human tendency to see the future in a more positive light than is warranted by experience.

Case study: Ikea – the case continues   www.ikea.com

Managers in Ikea have placed great emphasis on developing a strong culture, transmitting this to new employees and reinforcing it for existing ones. They believe that if co-workers develop a strong sense of shared meaning of the Ikea Concept, they deliver good service wherever they work. Edvardsson and Enquist (2002) explain:

> The strong culture in IKEA can give IKEA an image as a religion. In this aspect the Testament of a Furniture Dealer [written by Kamprad and given to all co-workers] is the holy script. The preface reads: *Once and for all we have decided to side with the many. What is good for our customers is also good for us in the long run.*

After the preface the testament is divided into nine points:

(1) The Product Range – our identity, (2) The IKEA Spirit. A Strong and Living Reality, (3) Profit Gives us Resources, (4) To Reach Good Results with Small Means, (5) Simplicity is a Virtue, (6) The Different Way, (7) Concentration of Energy – Important to Our Success, (8) To Assume Responsibility – A Privilege, (9) Most Things Still Remain to be Done. A Glorious Future! (Edvardsson and Enquist, 2002, p. 166)

Mikael Ohlsson decided to break with the tradition of secrecy that surrounds Ikea. Although as a private company it does not need to publish financial results, he made them available for the first time soon after he became CEO. The octogenarian founder still gives advice, but senior executives manage the business – some in functional roles, others leading one of the overseas operations.

Cultural reasons may be holding back the company's promotion of online sales. It promotes the idea of a visit to one of the stores as a shopping experience, involving not just looking at furniture but eating at the restaurant, putting the children in a special playroom and walking round the maze-like floors. It is difficult to replicate that model online, and customers buy many smaller items on impulse.

Sources: Edvardsson and Enquist (2002); *Financial Times*, 23 January 2012, p.21 and 14 November 2012, p.14.

> **Case questions 7.3**
> - How may the culture described here affect decision-making processes in Ikea?
> - The company has been slow to promote online shopping across the group. This is a major decision – which of the decision making models appear to best reflect the nature of this choice?

Illusion of control

The **illusion of control** is the human tendency to overestimate our ability to control activities and events. Those in senior positions with a record of success overestimate their chances of future success. The Part 4 Case on the Royal Bank of Scotland shows how a several profitable acquisitions encouraged Fred Goodwin to bid for ABN-Amro Bank. Some questioned the value of the deal anyway, but a wider financial crisis (beyond Goodwin's control) ensured that it became a major cause of the RBS collapse.

> The **illusion of control** is a source of bias resulting from the tendency to overestimate one's ability to control activities and events.

Escalating commitment

Managers may also fall into the trap of **escalating commitment**, which happens when they decide to increased their commitment to a previous decision despite evidence that it may have been wrong (Drummond, 1996 – see Management in practice). People are reluctant to admit mistakes, and rather than search for a new solution, they increase their commitment to the original decision.

> **Escalating commitment** is a bias which leads to increased commitment to a previous decision despite evidence that it may have been wrong.

Management in practice — A study of escalation – Taurus at the Stock Exchange

Helga Drummond studied the attempt by management at the London Stock Exchange to implement a computerised system to deal with the settlement of shares traded on the Exchange. The project was announced in May 1986 and was due to be completed by 1989 at a cost of £6 million. After many crises and difficulties, the Stock Exchange finally abandoned the project in March 1993. By that time the Exchange had spent £80 million on developing a non-existent system. Drummond interviewed many key participants to explore the reasons for this disaster – which occurred despite the skill and willing efforts of the system designers.

She concluded that the project suffered from fundamental structural problems, in that it challenged several powerful vested interests in the financial community, each of whom had their own idea about what should be done. Each new demand, reflecting this continuing power struggle, made the system more complicated. However, while many interests needed to work together, structural barriers throughout the organisation prevented this. There was little upwards communication, so that senior managers were largely unaware of staff concerns about the timetable commitments being made.

Senior managers continued to claim the project was on track, and to invest in it, until a few days before it was finally, and very publicly, terminated. The lack of proper mechanisms to identify pressing issues lulled those making decisions into a false sense of security about the state of the project.

Source: Drummond (1996).

Guler (2007) found evidence of the same phenomenon in the venture capital industry – firms which lend money to entrepreneurs to start and build a business. They typically provide money in instalments over several years, which limit their risk: yet the study showed that investors became less likely to terminate an investment as they paid further instalments, despite evidence that returns were declining. Three factors caused this – social (losing face amongst colleagues), political (pressure from other investors) and institutional (damage to the firm's reputation if it pulled out).

Emotional attachment

Finkelstein *et al.* (2009a, 2009b) note that people are frequently influenced by emotional attachments to:

- family and friends;
- communities and colleagues;
- objects – things and places which have meaning for us.

These attachments (negative or positive) bring us meaning and happiness and are bound to influence our decisions. Most of the effects are insignificant, but sometimes a manager's emotional attachments can lead them to make bad business decisions. They give examples such as Samsung's disastrous investment in car manufacturing (widely opposed as a poor use of resources, but initiated and supported by a chairman who liked cars); and the chairman who justified the retention of a small and unprofitable design consultancy because:

> I like it! It's exciting. I enjoy it … So I'm keeping it! (Finkelstein *et al.*, 2009a, p. 87)

Key ideas — **Daniel Kahneman and the danger of biases**

Nobel Prize-winning psychologist Daniel Kahneman has demonstrated the effects of cognitive biases on decisions, such as an aversion to loss that makes us cautious, and a tendency to anchor decisions on certain assumptions that may no longer be relevant. We fear being contradicted, so seek out information that confirms our established opinions. In his book *Thinking, Fast and Slow* Prof. Kahneman recommends that managers create a form of quality control round important decisions to avoid the negative effect of these biases, as well as the self-interest and political considerations of everyone involved. The goal is to liberate decision makers from wrong-headed bias, mistaken analogies and emotional attachment. Since human judgement is so badly flawed, the aim is to find ways to limit its worst consequences.

Source: Kahneman (2011).

Activity 7.5 — **Examples of bias**

- List the six sources of bias.
- Try to identify one example of each which you have personally experienced in your everyday discussions with friends, family or colleagues.
- What (be specific) did they (or you) say which led you to label it as being of that type?
- Compare your results, so that, if possible, you have a clear example of each type of decision bias.

7.7 Group decision making

While people often make decisions as individuals, they also do so within the context of a group. This section looks at two ideas – Vroom and Yetton's decision model and Irving Janis' identification of groupthink.

Vroom and Yetton's decision model

The idea behind Vroom and Yetton's (1973) contingency model of decision making is to influence the quality and acceptability of decisions. This depends on the manager choosing how best to involve subordinates in making a decision – and being willing to change their style to match the situation. The model defines five leadership styles and seven characteristics of problems. Managers can use these characteristics to diagnose the situation. They can find the recommended way of reaching a decision on that problem by using the decision tree shown in Figure 7.8. The five leadership styles defined are:

- **AI (Autocratic)** You solve the problem or make the decision yourself using information available to you at that time.
- **AII (Information-seeking)** You obtain the necessary information from your subordinate(s), then decide on the solution to the problem yourself. You may or may not tell your subordinates what the problem is in getting the information from them. The role played by your subordinates in making the decision is clearly one of providing the necessary information to you rather than generating or evaluating alternative solutions.
- **CI (Consulting)** You share the problem with relevant subordinates individually, getting their ideas and suggestions without bringing them together as a group. Then *you* make the decision that may or may not reflect your subordinates' influence.
- **CII (Negotiating)** You share the problem with your subordinates as a group, obtaining their collective ideas and suggestions. Then *you* make the decision that may or may not reflect your subordinates' influence.
- **G (Group)** You share the problem with your subordinates as a group. Together you generate and evaluate alternatives and attempt to reach agreement (consensus) on a solution. Your role is much like that of a chairperson. You do not try to influence the group to adopt 'your' solution, and you are willing to accept and implement any solution that has the support of the entire group.

The idea behind the model is that no style is in itself better than another. Some believe that consultative or delegating styles are inherently preferable to autocratic approaches, as being more in keeping with democratic principles. Vroom and Yetton argue otherwise. In some situations (such as when time is short or the manager has all the information needed for a minor decision) going through the process of consultation will waste time and add little value. In other situations, such as where the subordinates have the relevant information, it is essential to consult them. The point of the model is to make managers more aware of the range of factors to take into account in using a particular decision-making style.

The problem criteria are expressed in seven diagnostic questions:

- Is one solution likely to be better than another?
- Does the manager have enough information to make a high-quality decision?
- Is the problem structured?
- Is acceptance of the decision by subordinates critical to effective implementation?
- If the manager makes the decision alone, is it likely to be accepted by subordinates?
- Do subordinates share organisational goals?
- Is conflict likely amongst subordinates over preferred solutions?

704 Introduction to Business and Marketing

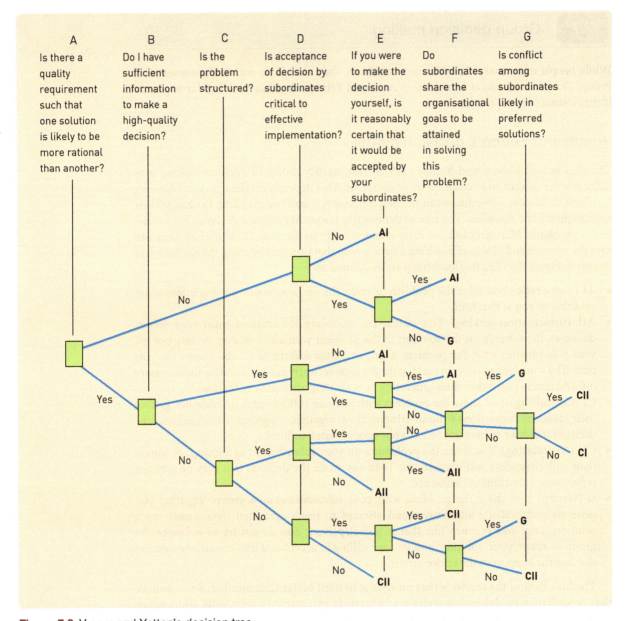

Figure 7.8 Vroom and Yetton's decision tree

Source: Reprinted from Vroom and Yetton (1973), p. 188 by permission of the University of Pittsburgh Press, copyright © 1973 by University of Pittsburgh Press.

The Vroom–Yetton decision model implies that managers need to be flexible in the style they adopt. The style should be appropriate to the situation rather than consistent amongst all situations. The problem with this is that managers may find it difficult to switch between styles, perhaps several times a day. Although the approach appears objective, it still depends on the manager answering the questions. Requiring a simple yes or no answer to complex questions is too simple, and managers often want to say 'it all depends' – on other historical or contextual factors.

Nevertheless the model is used in management training to alert managers to the style they prefer to use and to the range of options available. It also prompts managers to consider systematically whether that preferred style is always appropriate. They may then handle situations more deliberately than if they relied only on their preferred style or intuition.

> **Management in practice** Decision making in a software company

This Swedish company was founded in 1998, and now concentrates on developing software for mobile phones, such as an application which sends text messages from a computer to a mobile. It sells the products mainly to the operating companies who use them to add value to their services. The business depends on teams of highly skilled software developers, able to produce innovative, competitive products very rapidly. The Chief Technology Officer commented:

> As well as technical decisions we regularly face business decisions about where to focus development effort, or which customers to target. In this highly industrialised technocratic environment I am highly influenced by the experts in the team, and routinely consult them about the preferred course of action.

Source: Private communication from the Chief Technology Officer.

Irving Janis and groupthink

Groupthink is a pattern of biased decision making that occurs in groups that become too cohesive – members strive for agreement among themselves at the expense of accurately and dispassionately assessing relevant, and especially disturbing information. An influential analysis of how it occurs was put forward by the social psychologist Irving Janis. His research (Janis, 1972) began by studying major and highly publicised failures of decision making, looking for some common theme that might explain why apparently able and intelligent people were able to make such bad decisions – such as President Kennedy's decision to have US forces invade Cuba in 1961. One common thread he observed was the inability of the groups involved to consider a range of alternatives rationally, or to see the likely consequences of the choice they made. Members were also keen to be seen as team players, and not to say things that might end their membership of the group. Janis termed this phenomenon 'groupthink', and defined it as:

> a mode of thinking that people engage in when they are deeply involved in a cohesive in-group, when the members' striving for unanimity overrides their motivation to realistically appraise alternative courses of action. (Janis, 1972, p. 9)

He identified eight symptoms of groupthink, shown in Key ideas.

Margin note: **Groupthink** is 'a mode of thinking that people engage in when they are deeply involved in a cohesive in-group, when the members' striving for unanimity overrides their motivation to realistically appraise alternative courses of action' (Janis, 1972).

> **Key ideas** Irving Janis on the symptoms of groupthink

Janis (1977) identified eight symptoms that give early warning of groupthink developing – and the more of them that are present, the more likely it is that the 'disease' will strike. The symptoms are:

- **Illusion of invulnerability** The belief that any decision they make will be successful.
- **Belief in the inherent morality of the group** Justifying a decision by reference to some higher value.
- **Rationalisation** Playing down the negative consequences or risks of a decision.
- **Stereotyping out-groups** Characterising opponents or doubters in unfavourable terms, making it easier to dismiss even valid criticism from that source.
- **Self-censorship** Suppressing legitimate doubts in the interest of group loyalty.
- **Direct pressure** Strong expressions from other members (or the leader) that dissent to their favoured approach will be unwelcome.
- **Mindguards** Keeping uncomfortable facts or opinions out of the discussion.
- **Illusion of unanimity** Playing down any remaining doubts or questions, even if they become stronger or more persistent.

Source: Based on Janis (1977).

> **Management in practice** — **Groupthink in medicine**
>
> An experienced nurse observed three of the symptoms of groupthink in the work of senior doctors:
>
> - **Illusion of invulnerability** A feeling of power and authority leads a group to see themselves as invulnerable. Traditionally the medical profession has been very powerful and this makes it very difficult for non-clinicians to question their actions or plans.
> - **Belief in the inherent morality of the group** This happens when clinical staff use the term 'individual clinical judgement' as a justification for their actions. An example is when a business manager is trying to reduce drug costs and one consultant's practice is very different from those of his colleagues. Consultants often reply that they are entitled to use their clinical judgement. This is never challenged by their colleagues, and it is often impossible to achieve change.
> - **Self-censorship** Being a doctor is similar to being in a very exclusive club, and none of the members want to be excluded. Therefore doctors will usually support each other, particularly against management. They are also extremely unlikely to report each other for mistakes or poor performance. A government scheme to encourage 'whistle-blowing' was met with much derision in the ranks.
>
> Source: Private communication.

When groupthink occurs, pressures for agreement and harmony within the group have the unintended effects of discouraging individuals from raising issues that run counter to the majority opinion (Turner and Pratkanis, 1998). An often-quoted example is Challenger disaster in 1986, when the space shuttle exploded shortly after take-off. Investigations showed that NASA and the main contractors, Morton Thiokol, were so anxious to keep the Shuttle programme on schedule that they ignored or discounted evidence that would slow the programme down. On a lighter note, Professor Jerry Harvey tells the story of how members of his extended family drove 40 miles into town on a hot day, to no obvious purpose – and everyone was miserable. Discussing the episode with the family later, each person admitted that they had not wanted to go, but went along to please the others. Harvey (1988) coined the term 'Abilene paradox' to describe this tendency to go along with others for the sake of avoiding conflict.

7.8 Integrating themes

Entrepreneurship

Small entrepreneurial firms lack the resources of larger firms to support their decision making process, so the question arises of how they make strategic decisions. Liberman-Yacone *et al.* (2010) studied this in the software industry, wanting to know what patterns small firms followed in making decisions, what factors shaped their decision processes, and what methods they used to gather and process data. Their research in 14 very small firms in web design or IT support enabled them to develop a model which synthesised their findings with earlier research.

The challenge facing the small firm is that any strategic decision such as to develop a new product, will use significant resources. The entrepreneur cannot know the outcome: failure could destroy the firm. Yet by definition they do not have the resources to gather relevant information. The authors concluded that strategic decision making in these firms had these characteristics:

- more centralised and less formalised than is typical in larger firms;
- examples of iterative and garbage-can models;

- indicated bounded rationality and an intuitive process rather than a rational one; and
- gathered information from sources external to the firm, especially through informal business and social relationships.

Sustainability

In 2012 Ikea revealed its sustainability strategy up to 2015, in which it tries to give concrete targets for several green undertakings, such as producing as much renewable energy as it consumes by the end of the decade. Steve Howard, chief sustainability officer, said it was keen to 'close the loop' in the supply chain where possible and encourage customers to return products at the end of their useful life to be reused.

> Some things are best recycled by local authorities. But others, we can help, like kitchens, wardrobes, mattresses. Maybe we should have low-cost leasing of kitchens and see a product offering become a service one. We want a smarter consumption, and maybe people are less attached to ownership. People have needs to be met – they need wardrobes, sofas, kitchens. The most important thing is to meet those needs in the most sustainable way possible.

In some countries the company already collects certain products from customers to get the raw materials back into its production system – there is a factory in France where 50 per cent of the wood comes from former products that are ground down to make new bookshelves or tables.

It has also decided to encourage consumers to use light-emitting diodes, and will stop selling other kinds of light bulbs by 2016. The company claims LEDs give a better quality of light, cost less to use over their 20 year life, and do not contain the harmful chemical mercury.

There is however debate in green circles about whether a company such as Ikea, one of the world's largest users of wood, as well as other raw materials including leather and cotton can be classed as sustainable. Critics point to its low-priced furniture as encouraging a throwaway mentality when it breaks. (Based on articles in the *Financial Times*, 2 October 2012, p. 18; 23 October 2012, p. 23)

Internationalisation

The structure of decision-making processes change as companies become international. Decisions will cross the boundaries between managers at global headquarters and those in local business units. Neither of the extreme possibilities is likely to work. If decision making tilts too far in favour of global managers at the centre, local preferences are likely to be overlooked, and local managers are likely to lack commitment to decisions in which they have had no say. Leaving too many decisions to local managers can waste opportunities for economies of scale or opportunities to serve global clients consistently.

A solution may be to identify the major ways in which the company adds value to resources, and align the decision-making processes to make the most of them. For example, if procurement is a critical factor *and* can best be done on a global scale, that implies that those at the centre should make these decisions. Once supply contracts are agreed, however, responsibility for operating them could pass back to local level. Conversely, they might leave decisions on pricing or advertising expenditure to local managers. The central issue is to spend time on the difficult choices about the location of each set of decisions, to achieve an acceptable balance between global and local expectations.

Governance

Several themes in this chapter highlight the traps which await decision makers, and at the time show how good governance arrangements can help to protect them and the organisation.

The top level strategic decisions which shape an organisation's future are inherently unprogrammed, unstructured decisions which no-one has dealt with in quite that form. Senior managers make these decisions in conditions of risk, uncertainty and ambiguity – further placing at risk the assets and resources of the business. They are prone to any and all of the biases the chapter set out: a good example is the failure of the Taurus project at the London Stock Exchange, where those in charge continued to commit additional resources to the project, despite evidence that the project would not be able to deliver a solution acceptable to the main players. This was as much as anything a failure of governance.

More generally, the evidence on groupthink shows the delusions to which powerful senior managers are susceptible, as they come to believe in the soundness of their decisions, and are dismissive of those who question their views. This was evident in the 2008 banking crisis, where not enough, if any, of the non-executive directors were able and willing to provide the necessary challenges to the over-enthusiasm of executives taking too many risky decisions. Put another way, these companies had, on the face of it, put in place the governance procedures recommended in the Combined Code (see Chapter 3, Section 3.9) – but those with the power to do so did not exercise those responsibilities.

Summary

1 Outline the (iterative) tasks in a systematic decision making process and the tasks required in each

Decisions are choices about how to act in relation to organisational inputs, outputs and transformation processes. The chapter identifies seven *iterative* tasks:
- Recognise the problem – which depends on seeing and attending to ambiguous signals.
- Set goals – the kind of result the decision process should produce.
- Set and weight criteria – the features of the result most likely to meet problem requirements, and that can guide the choice between alternatives.
- Develop alternatives – identify existing, or develop custom-built, solutions to the problem.
- Compare alternatives and choose – use the criteria to select the preferred alternative.
- Implement – the task that turns a decision into an action.
- Monitor and evaluate – check whether the decision resolved the problem.

Most decisions affect other interests, whose response will be affected by how the decision process is conducted, in matters such as participation and communication.

2 Explain, and give examples of, programmed and non-programmed decisions
- Programmed decisions deal with familiar issues within existing policy – recruitment, minor capital expenditure, small price changes.
- Non-programmed decisions move the business in a new direction – new markets, mergers, a major investment decision.

3 Distinguish decision making conditions of certainty, risk, uncertainty, ambiguity, and dependence
- Certainty – decision makers have all the information they need, especially the costs and benefits of each alternative action.
- Risk – where the decision maker can estimate the likelihood of the alternative outcomes. These are still subject to chance, but decision makers have enough information to estimate probabilities.
- Uncertainty – when people know what they wish to achieve, but information about alternatives and future events is incomplete. They cannot be clear about alternatives or estimate their risk.

- Ambiguity – when people are unsure about their objectives and about the relation between cause and effect.
- Dependence – when a decision affects, and is affected by, decisions by others around the organisation.

4 **Contrast rational, administrative, political and garbage-can decision models**
- Rational models are based on economic assumptions which suggest that the role of a manager is to maximise the economic return to the firm, and that they do this by making decisions on economically rational criteria.
- The administrative model aims to describe how managers actually make decisions in situations of uncertainty and ambiguity. Many management problems are unstructured and not suitable for the precise quantitative analysis implied by the rational model.
- The political model examines how people make decisions when conditions are uncertain, information is limited, and there is disagreement among managers over goals and how to pursue them. It recognises that an organisation is not only a working system, but also a political system.
- The garbage-can model identifies four independent streams of activities which enable a decision when they meet. When participants, problems and solutions come together in a relevant forum (a 'garbage can'), then a decision will be made.

5 **Give examples of common sources of bias in decisions**
- Sources of bias stem from the use of heuristics – mental short cuts which allow us to cope with excessive information. Six biases are:
- Representativeness bias – basing decisions on unrepresentative samples.
- Optimism bias – over-confidence in own abilities.
- Prior hypothesis bias – basing decisions on prior beliefs, despite evidence they are wrong.
- Illusion of control – excessive belief in one's ability to control people and events.
- Escalating commitment – committing more resources to a project despite evidence of failure.
- Emotional attachment – to people or things.

6 **Explain the contribution of Vroom and Yetton, and of Irving Janis, to our understanding of decision making in groups**
- Vroom and Yetton introduced the idea that decision-making styles in groups should reflect the situation – which of the five ways of involving subordinates in a decision (Autocratic, Information-seeking, Consulting, Negotiating and Delegating) to use depended on identifiable circumstances – such as whether the manager has the information required.
- Irving Janis observed the phenomenon of groupthink, and set out the symptoms which indicate that it is affecting a group's decision-making processes.

7 **Show how ideas from the chapter add to your understanding of the integrating themes**
- Liberman-Yacone et al. (2010) showed that strategic decision making in small firms relies is rational and intuitive in nature, relying heavily on informal business and social contacts for information.
- Ikea is an example of the ways in which many companies are changing the may they operate to make them more sustainable.
- Those managing internationally constantly search for the best balance between central and local decision making.
- The chapter shows the many traps and biases that afflict decision makers – good governance can protect them and their organisations from these, by subjecting them to close external scrutiny. Groupthink is likely to have been a factor when management teams made bad decisions which damaged their firms and the economy.

Test your understanding

1. List three decisions you have recently observed or taken part in. Which of them were programmed, and which non-programmed?
2. What did Mintzberg's research on decision making contribute to our understanding of the process?
3. Explain the difference between risk and ambiguity. How may people make decisions in different ways for each situation?
4. What are the major differences between the rational and administrative models of decision making?
5. What is meant by satisficing? Can you illustrate the concept with an example from your experience? Why did those involved not try to achieve an economically superior decision?
6. List and explain three common biases in making decisions.
7. The Vroom–Yetton model describes five styles. How should the manager decide which style to use?
8. Recall four of the symptoms of groupthink, and give an example to illustrate each of them.
9. Summarise an idea from the chapter that adds to your understanding of the integrating themes.

Think critically

Think about the ways in which your company, or one with which you are familiar, makes decisions, and make notes on these questions:

- Are people you work with typically dealing mainly with programmed or non-programmed decisions? What **assumptions** about the nature of decision making appear to guide their approach – rational, administrative, political or garbage can? On balance, do their assumptions accurately reflect the reality you see?
- What factors such as the history or current **context** of the company appear to influence how people are expected to reach decisions? Does the current approach appear to be right for the company in its context – or would a different view of the context lead to a different approach?
- Have people put forward **alternative** approaches to decision making, based on evidence? If you could find such evidence, how may it affect company practice?
- Can you identify **limitations** in the ideas and theories presented here – for example are you convinced of the garbage-can model of decision making? Can you find evidence that supports or challenges that view?

Read more

Bazerman, M.H. (2005), *Judgment in Managerial Decision Making* (6th edn), John Wiley, New York.

> Comprehensive and interactive account, aimed at developing the skill of judgement, and so enabling people to improve how they make decisions.

Buchanan, L. and O'Connell, A. (2006), 'A Brief History of Decision Making', *Harvard Business Review*, vol. 84, no. 1, pp. 32–41.

> Informative overview, placing many of the ideas mentioned in the chapter within a historical context. Part of a special issue of the *Harvard Business Review* on decision making.

Finkelstein, S., Whitehead, J. and Campbell, A. (2009), 'How Inappropriate Attachments can Drive Good Leaders to Make Bad Decisions', *Organisational Dynamics*, vol. 38, no. 2, pp. 83–92.

Revealing insights into this source of bias in decision making.

Harvey, J. B. (1988), 'The Abilene Paradox: The Management of Agreement', *Organisational Dynamics*, vol. 17, no. 1, pp.17–43.

First published in the same journal in 1974, this reprint also includes an epilogue by Harvey, and further commentaries on this classic paper by other management writers.

Hodgson, J. and Drummond, H. (2009), 'Learning from fiasco: what causes decision error and how to avoid it', *Journal of General Management,* vol. 35, no. 2, pp. 81–92.

An accessible account of the topic which draws on the authors' extensive knowledge of, and research into, the hazards of making decisions in organisations.

Schwartz, B. (2004), *The Paradox of Choice*, Ecco, New York.

An excellent study of decision making at the individual level. It shows how people in modern society face an ever-widening and increasingly bewildering range of choices, which is a source of increasing tension and stress. Many of the issues the author raises apply equally well to decision making in organisations.

Go online

These websites have appeared in the chapter:

www.ikea.com
www.diageo.com
www.nokia.com
www.irisnation.com
www.riskcapitalpartners.co.uk
www.google.com
www.inamo-restaurant.com

Visit two of the business sites in the list, or any other company that interests you, and navigate to the pages dealing with recent news or investor relations.

- What examples of decisions which the company has recently had to take can you find?
- How would you classify those decisions in terms of the models in this chapter?
- Gather information from the media websites (such as **www.FT.com**) which relate to the companies you have chosen. What stories can you find that indicate something about the decisions the companies have faced, and what the outcomes have been?

CHAPTER 13
CREATIVITY, INNOVATION AND CHANGE

Aim

To outline theories of creativity and innovation, and of how context affects whether they add value.

Objectives

By the end of your work on this chapter you should be able to outline the concepts below in your own terms and:

1 Explain the meanings of creativity and innovation, with examples
2 Explain the management significance of creativity and innovation
3 Illustrate the organisational factors believed to support creativity and innovation
4 Explain how the interaction of change and context affects how people implement an innovation
5 Compare life cycle, emergent, participative and political theories of change
6 Show how ideas from the chapter add to your understanding of the integrating themes.

Key terms

This chapter introduces the following ideas:

creativity
innovation
open innovation
perceived performance gap
performance imperatives
organisational change
receptive contexts
non-receptive contexts
life cycle model
emergent model
participative model
political model

Each is a term defined within the text, as well as in the glossary at the end of the book.

Case study
Pixar Animation   www.pixar.com

Pixar Animation is unusual among movie studios in that it has generated a succession of box office hits. Although many companies have tried to break into the animation market, only two had (by 2011) produced animated movies taking more than $100 million – Disney and Pixar. Disney purchased Pixar in 2006 but the two companies still work independently.

Pixar originated at the University of Utah in the 1970s, where Edwin Catmull studied computer science before being recruited by the New York Institute of Technology. He then joined Lucasfilm and soon met John Lasseter, a young animator at Disney – whom he persuaded to move to Lucasfilm.

In 1986 Steve Jobs bought that part of Lucasfilm, known as Pixar. This unit then focussed on developing proprietary computer-generated imaging technology to represent images, backgrounds and movement. The ability of this animation technology to generate life-like 3D images and backgrounds gives Pixar a significant advantage over potential competitors who could not buy equivalent technology. The company licensed the digital tools it developed (RenderMan, Ringmaster and Marionette) to companies such as Disney and DreamWorks.

In May 1991 Disney and Pixar signed an agreement for three full-length 3D animated films. The films would be made by Pixar and distributed by Disney. On its release in 1995 *Toy Story* was considered revolutionary both from a technological and artistic perspective. Animated films were usually aimed at children, but teenagers and adults also enjoyed *Toy Story* – and most of Pixar's productions since.

Pixar's first tool, Renderman, was used to create high-quality, photo-realistic images, and its first major application was in James Cameron's movie *The Abyss* (1989). Cameron wanted a sea creature to explore its surroundings realistically, and to interact with the live characters of the film. Cameron also used it in his movie *Terminator 3*, another innovative work in computer-generated special effects. Experts believe that almost every film since 1993 using special effects has used Renderman – ensuring a steady income for Pixar. Jobs, Catmull and Lasseter shared the ambition to make the first computer-animated feature film and in 1991 they persuaded Disney to back the venture.

Rex Features/Buena Vista

Ed Catmull (co-founder with Steve Jobs of Pixar, and now president of Pixar and Disney Animation Studios) has written about the 'collective creativity' at the company: many of its methods are relevant to other organisations. He emphasises the uncertainty of the creative process – the idea which starts the process may not work – by definition it is new, and the innovator cannot know at the start if it will lead to a worthwhile result:

> at the start of making [*Ratatouille*] we simply didn't know if [it] would work. However, since we're supposed to offer something that isn't obvious, we bought into somebody's initial vision and took a chance. (Catmull, 2008, p. 66)

'Taking chances' that consistently succeed is not due to luck, but to the principles and practices that Pixar uses to support the people who turn the creative idea into a useful product.

Sources: Catmull (2008); company website.

Case questions 13.1
- What examples of creativity and innovation has the case mentioned?
- What professions or disciplines have contributed to them?
- How do you think creativity differs from innovation?

13.1 Introduction

Pixar is an example of a company which lives by creativity – audiences watch the films because they expect something new, so each one must meet the heightened expectations created by the previous success. It depends on individuals using their creativity to develop new technologies, stories or presentations and on them being able to work productively in teams drawn from several professions with different creative talents. The company has been highly successful in turning that energy into products that have brought a sustainable flow of income – they have used creativity in ways that add value. The initial idea for a movie is merely one step in a long, arduous process that takes four to five years – generating thousands of further creative moves along the way as they produce a stream of innovative experiences for audiences.

Other technology companies like Facebook and Google depend equally strongly on innovations to meet their customers' ever-rising expectations. The same is true of established businesses in completely different industries – GlaxoSmithKline and GKN both depend on creative work by their scientists and engineers to develop new pharmaceuticals and solve customers' engineering problems. Managers in the public sector face the same challenge: the British Museum has been creative in finding innovative ways to transform its financial position (see Chapter 14 case study).

Companies that fail often do so because they have become unable to innovate. Kodak understood digital imaging technologies that were eventually to destroy the business, but managers were unable to use them in new products to replace the obsolete film and camera businesses. Sony has become vulnerable to new products like the iPod and the iTunes store. Disruptive shifts in technology, shortening product life cycles and the arrival of new competitors means that in many areas of the economy the primary task of senior managers is to nurture creativity and innovation – even if others do not yet see the need for change.

Implementing radical innovation usually depends on changing established practices and ways of working. Successful businesses learn to manage this as they repeatedly reinvent the business: GKN does this. They succeed in creating a culture in which people see change as the norm – one intervention in a continuing flow – rather than as a disruption after which the stability they prefer will return. Managers cannot leave these activities to chance: they

Management in practice
Dyson Appliances www.dyson.co.uk

Dyson Appliances is one of the UK's most innovative engineering businesses, owned and managed by its founder, Sir James Dyson. Following his first major success with a bagless vacuum cleaner, he has led the company to create a constant stream of innovations in the consumer appliance market. The vacuum cleaner is estimated to have about 30 per cent of the US market, and almost 50 per cent of the UK market.

Design and creativity are the foundations of the company's success, and about half of the annual profits are invested in the Research, Design and Development Centre in Wiltshire. It ensures good use of this money by using a coherent set of management practices to encourage the design of high quality products. Care is taken to recruit only the most talented designers and engineers from university, typically the Royal College of Art, Brunel or Loughborough, and to pay them well.

About 650 engineers, scientists and designers work together, as Sir James believes all can learn from each other. They are located at the centre of the well-designed facility, emphasising the significance of their roles. Teamwork is central to the system, with all engineers and designers being members of frequently changed teams. The culture emphasises dialogue, seen as the foundation of progress. Sir James speaks to employees daily not just about design but also about marketing and financial issues, and the overall progress of the business.

Source: company website.

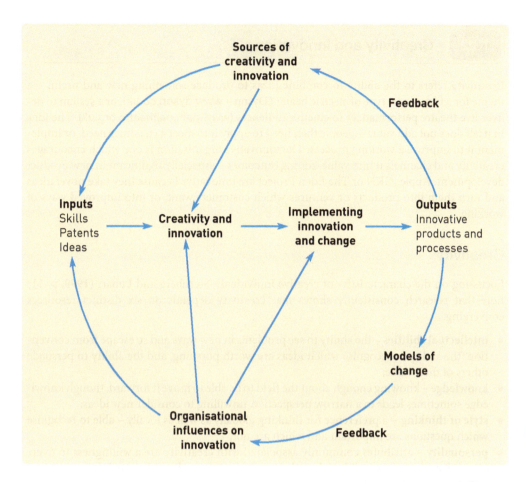

Figure 13.1 An overview of the chapter

depend on building a setting in which creativity and innovation add value to their changing organisation.

The chapter presents theories about the nature of creativity, innovation and change – which affect both products and processes. It begins by explaining the distinction between creativity and innovation, presents evidence about their sources, and on the organisational factors that influence innovation. Innovative ideas only add value when people implement them, which happens as they interact with external and internal contexts, drawing on complementary models of change. Figure 13.1 shows the themes.

Activity 13.1 Recording an innovation

From discussion with colleagues or managers, identify a major attempt at innovation in an organisation. Make notes on the following questions and use them as a point of reference throughout the chapter.

- What was the innovation?
- Why did management introduce it?
- What were the objectives?
- How did management plan and implement it?
- How well did it meet the objectives?
- What lessons about change have those involved taken from the experience?

13.2 Creativity and innovation

Creativity is the ability to combine ideas to produce something new and useful.

Creativity refers to the ability to combine ideas to produce something new and useful – a theme for a film, a new type of electric heater (Dyson – **www.dyson.co.uk**), or a system to deliver live theatre performances to cinema audiences (**www.nationaltheatre.org.uk**). The idea in itself does not add value – people then need to apply it to meet a customer need, or implement it to improve a working process. The innovative organisation is one which encourages creativity and channels it into value-adding outcomes – especially significant in new product development. Apple, GKN or The Eden Project are innovative because they take novel ideas and turn them into products or ventures which customers want, or into improved ways of working.

Creativity

Focussing on the characteristics of creative individuals, Sternberg and Lubart (1999, p. 11) note that research consistently shows that creativity depends on six distinct resources converging:

- **intellectual abilities** – the ability to see problems in new ways and so escape from convention, the ability to recognise which ideas are worth pursuing, and the ability to persuade others of their value;
- **knowledge** – knowing enough about the field to be able to move it forward, though knowledge sometimes leads to a narrow perspective, unwilling to consider new ideas;
- **style of thinking** – a preference for thinking globally as well as locally – able to recognise which questions are important and which are not;
- **personality** – attributes commonly associated with creativity are a willingness to overcome obstacles, take sensible risks, tolerate ambiguity, and be willing to defy convention;
- **motivation** – intrinsic, task-focussed motivation is essential to creativity – a focus on and commitment to the work being done, rather than potential rewards; and
- **environment** – a context which supports the creative person, if only by providing a forum in which to express ideas, and to encourage their discussion amongst colleagues.

The reference to 'environment' shows that creativity in organisations depends not only on individual characteristics but on the context. Amabile *et al.* (1996) developed and validated an instrument to assess the stimulants and obstacles to creativity in business, on the assumption that the social environment affects this. Table 13.1 shows the factors and describes each briefly.

Amabile and her team (Amabile *et al.*, 1996) conclude that:

> Creative ideas from individuals and teams within organisations sow the seeds of successful innovation [and that their instrument] highlights the psychological context of innovation ... that can influence the level of creative behaviour displayed in the generation and early development of new products and processes. (p. 1178)

Unsworth and Clegg (2010) focussed not on the outcomes of creativity, but on the factors which motivate employees to begin acting in a creative way – rather than staying safely within their role. They interviewed 65 design and development engineers in four aerospace factories, whose work was to design solutions to problems identified by test engineers. They too found that the working context influenced staff views about whether the effort of producing a creative solution was worth it: perceptions of context moderate personal influences. The authors suggested that management policy could influence these perceptions by making creativity a more explicit part of the engineers' role; providing time, resources and a degree of autonomy; and creating a supportive culture.

Table 13.1 Factors in KEYS: assessing the climate for creativity

Scale name	Description (partial)	Sample survey item
Stimulant scales		
Organisational encouragement	A culture that encourages creativity through fair, constructive judgement of ideas, reward and recognition of creative work	People are encouraged to solve problems creatively in this organisation
Supervisory encouragement	A supervisor who serves as a good work model, sets goals appropriately, supports the work group	My supervisor serves as a good work model
Work group support	A diversely skilled group in which people communicate well, are open to new ideas, constructively challenge each other's work	There is free and open communication within my work group
Sufficient resources	Access to appropriate resources including funds, materials, facilities and information	Generally, I can get the resources I need for my work
Challenging work	A sense of having to work hard on challenging tasks and important projects	I feel challenged by the work I am currently doing
Freedom	Freedom in deciding what work to do or how to do it: a sense of control over one's work	I have the freedom to decide how I carry out my projects
Obstacle scales		
Organisational impediments	A culture that impedes creativity through internal political problems, harsh criticism of new ideas, avoidance of risk	There are many political problems in this organisation
Workload pressures	Extreme time pressures, unrealistic expectations for productivity, distractions	I have too much work to do in too little time

Source: Amabile *et al.* (1996, p.1166).

Innovation

In the management context it is useful to think of **innovation** as the process of implementing something new and useful: that is, adding value by incorporating creative solutions in products and/or implementing changes in organisational processes.

Innovation is the process of applying or implementing something new and useful.

The systems model introduced earlier (Chapter 1) helps us to understand how organisations can become more innovative. Figure 13.2 shows that getting the desired outputs (innovative products or work methods) depends on both inputs and on transforming those inputs.

Inputs include having creative people and groups who are able to generate novel ideas and methods, but they only flourish in a favourable context. Managers create a context which they hope encourages creative people and the application of their ideas into goods and services that people want to buy.

Some radical innovations – such as the aerofoil that allows heavier than air flight and the transistor that is the basis of all modern electronics – have fundamentally changed society. Others such as Velcro or the ball-point pen are useful, but have modest effects on the lives of most people.

While discussion of innovation often centres on dramatic breakthroughs like the Walkman or the iPad, incremental innovations are more useful to most customers. They are generally more interested in quality products, good service or timely delivery than in dramatic new features. Most people buy a brand they expect will meet their needs a bit better, or more conveniently, than the competition. Much innovation is incremental.

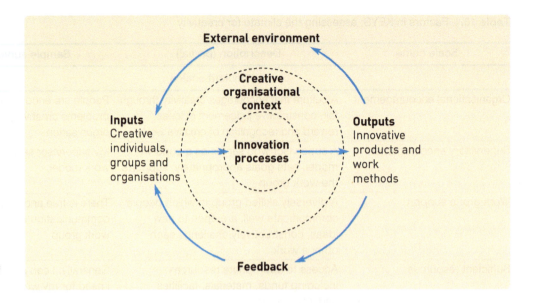

Figure 13.2 Systems view of innovation

Innovations become manifest in one or more of four areas: product, process, positioning in the market and the paradigm of the business.

Product innovations

An innovation here could be a change in the function or feature of a product such as the incorporation of a music player within a mobile phone or, in relation to a service, the incorporation of the facility to carry out personal banking on the internet. These innovations are intended to enhance the utility of the offering to make sales more likely.

Process innovations

An innovation here could be the addition of a self-service checkout at a supermarket where customers can scan their purchases using a barcode reader or an online banking system to allow customers to manage their finances. Examples in manufacturing would be using robots for assembly to give higher quality and more efficiently produced products.

Case study — Pixar – the case continues   www.pixar.com

Pixar initially developed three proprietary technologies: RenderMan, Marionette, and Ringmaster. In 1989 the company released RenderMan, a software system that applied texture and colour to 3D objects and was used for visual effects. Pixar used RenderMan itself and sold it to Disney, Lucasfilm, Sony and DreamWorks, which used it to create effects like the dinosaurs in *Jurassic Park*. The programme served as Pixar's main source of revenue during the company's early years. In 2001 Ed Catmull, along with two other Pixar scientists, won an Oscar for RenderMan and its contribution to motion picture rendering: it is the industry standard animation software.

Marionette, the primary software tool for Pixar animators, was designed specifically for character animation and articulation, compared with other animation software that was designed to address product design and special effects. Ringmaster was a production management system used to track internal projects and served as the overarching system to coordinate and sequence the animation, tracking the vast amount of data employed in a three-dimensional animated film.

The company values the three creative disciplines (computer technologists, artists and producers) equally, and deliberately breaks down walls between them:

> One way [we do this] is a collection of in-house courses we offer, which we call Pixar University. It is responsible for training and cross-training people as they develop in their careers. It also offers . . . optional classes that give people from different disciplines the opportunity to mix and appreciate what everyone else does . . . PU helps to reinforce the mindset that we're all learning and that it's fun to learn together.
>
> Our building is another way we try to get people from different departments to interact. It is structured to maximise inadvertent encounters. At the centre is a large atrium which contains cafeteria, meeting rooms, bathrooms, mailboxes. As a result, everyone has strong reasons to go there repeatedly during the course of the workday. It's hard to describe just how valuable the resulting chance encounters are. (Catmull, 2008, p. 71)

Source: The Walt Disney Company and Pixar Inc., p. 5; Catmull (2008).

Case questions 13.2

- Visit the Pixar website and read the timeline summarising the company's development.
- Which of the types of innovation mentioned on these pages can you see in the case?

Position innovations

These are changes in the target market or customer base for a product or service. Nokia repositioned mobile devices from being a communication tool to one that was also a fashion item. Another example is the four-wheel drive: originally used for off-road work, but now sold as fashionable family cars to carry large loads.

Paradigm innovations

These are changes in how companies frame what they do; for example the reframing of a supermarket such as Tesco from a seller of food products to a provider of many more of a family's needs such as petrol, clothing and financial products. Here the reframing has provided synergies where shoppers can buy food, clothes and petrol, paying for it all on their Tesco credit card.

13.3 Sources of innovation

Figure 13.3 illustrates the main sources of innovation.

Accidents and the unexpected

Many innovations have been accidental – from Fleming's discovery of Penicillin to the Post-It Note which arose when Art Fry used a recently invented 'sticky but not too sticky' adhesive to keep his book mark in place. This gave him the idea for the Post-It Note which, after a process of design and development, became the familiar product range. The Management in Practice feature describes a recent example. The innovative gyro which makes the Segway possible was developed in BAE Systems defence laboratories. Terrorist attacks have led to innovations in safety and security products – like the biometric scanning device. One of the largest service industries in the world – personal insurance – developed from the need to guard against unplanned events.

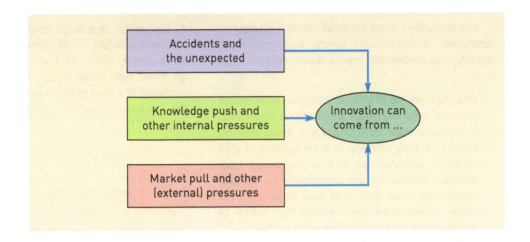

Figure 13.3 Sources of innovation

Management in practice

Plugging a 'mole' in the market www.magnamole.co.uk

Sharon Wright had her eureka moment while having a phone-line installed in her home. Under pressure for time she offered to help the engineer thread the cable through the wall of her house. To Sharon's surprise the engineer produced a makeshift tool made out of a wire coat-hanger. As well as being difficult to use Sharon's experience in Health and Safety management told her this device was unsuitable and hazardous. Market research showed there were no alternative tools available for cable threading.

Within hours she had sketched the design of the Magnamole tool, a plastic rod with a magnet at one end and an accompanying metallic cap for attaching to the wire to be threaded through the wall. She soon had a prototype, and orders followed from large customers around the world.

What is remarkable about Sharon is that she had little knowledge or experience of this area of business, but that did not stop her from taking advantage of an obvious gap in the market.

Source: Company website.

Market pull and other external pressures

No matter how innovative a new product might be it will not make money unless there is a market. Before investing significant resources in developing a new product, managers need a sense of the likely need. This may not be as straightforward as it seems: before lightweight digital music players and headphones became available, sportsmen and women trained without equipment to combat boredom. However this technology is now an essential part of a runner's or cyclist's training kit, and versions are now available for swimmers.

Companies spend heavily to understand changing customer needs – Unilever has several Innovation Centres devoted to just that. Many parts of the UK pub industry are highly innovative: the smoking ban and rapid increases in beer duty has prompted them to look out for new ways to attract customers. Many now offer coffee and breakfast while others take bookings on Twitter, have mystery visitors or offer takeaway food: one industry observer said:

> they keep surviving and they reinvent themselves.

Management in practice

The Segway www.segway.com

The Segway Personal Transporter is a two-wheeled, self-balancing electric vehicle produced by Segway Inc. Users lean forward to go forward, lean back to go backward, and turn by leaning it left or right. Computers and motors in the base of the device keep the Segway upright – in fact it has been jokingly said that the

> Segway is built simply to stay balanced in one place. The Segway is packed full of technological innovation including cutting-edge batteries, proprietary software and gyroscopic sensors initially developed for the defence industry.
>
> Despite the initial hype concerning the innovative nature of this product the Segway was not an immediate hit as limited capabilities and safety legislation reduced its appeal to the intended market. However by being innovative in finding new applications Segway has been able to sell them as transportation for police departments; military bases; warehouses; and large corporate campuses. It has also designed a range of models around the basic product platform for use with rough terrain and heavy loads.
>
> Source: company website.

Regulation changes

The makers of the Segway encountered regulatory problems in relation to safety and traffic laws, and regulations often hinder innovation. Other regulations trigger innovation by requiring change – those on environmental pollution are a current example, in that they have encouraged the search for renewable sources of energy. On a smaller scale regulations intended to improve road safety have led to the development of speed cameras and air bags.

> **Management in practice** Philip Morris www.philipmorristobacco.com
>
> Legislative change can also have indirect effects on innovation. Restrictions on advertising and other actions to curb smoking have encouraged tobacco companies to invest heavily in alternatives to tobacco aiming for a new 'safe' cigarette such as the Philip Morris Accord.

Users as innovators

Users are a source of ideas for innovation, especially in hi-tech industries, where three categories are particularly important:

- **Lead users** – people who not only use the product but help in its development.
- **User communities** – are groups of users who congregate around a product or product platform, such as early personal computer users, and find new and innovative ways to use the systems.
- **Extreme users** – push products to their limit creating a need for improved performance. The bicycle is an example, with the relentless drive for more durable and higher performing machines.

Knowledge push – and other internal pressures

Organisations which depend on innovation implement deliberate systems to ensure an adequate flow. Figure 13.4 shows a model of the traditional innovation process showing it as a filter through which ideas are gathered, channelled and focussed before selecting those believed to have most potential. Generating the initial idea is necessarily random – but thereafter firms try to create order from this randomness as quickly as possible. They apply resources and effort to these promising ideas to develop them into something that can be implemented. The steps in this system are sequential but their duration and complexity will vary – some may require a significant research and development, others merely a change in the focus of the sales effort. Ramirez *et al.* describe how Shell uses a process resembling this – see Management in practice.

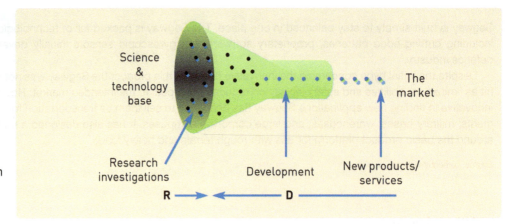

Figure 13.4 A closed innovation model
Source: Chesbrough et al. (2006), p. 3.

Management in practice — Shell's 'Gamechanger2' process   www.shell.com

Since 1998 Shell has used what it calls the Gamechanger process to develop, and select between, innovation projects. In the nine years to 2007 over 2050 innovation projects were submitted to Gamechanger, and of these 1950 had been stopped at some point in the gated funnel. 100 had survived as successes. All projects are submitted to be part of one of six 'domains' – which can be seen as 'stepping stones' that link potential company futures to where Shell is today. They reveal the areas which Shell needs to explore to realise those futures. Each domain consists of a small set of strategic propositions, and houses a small number of innovation projects that have been chosen to test those propositions. Proposed projects must go through a rigorous process before they are accepted as live projects for a domain.

For example, the 'bio-fuel' domain could include an ethanol project and an algae project and these projects, together with several similar initiatives in the domain would give Shell the option to move to a future where fuels are 'grown', not 'mined'.

A particular strength of the system is believed to be the tight connections it develops between innovation projects and company strategy, as domains ensure staff attend to three concerns – strategic options, opportunities offered by R&D, and the company's external environment. Since introducing the discipline of the domains in 2003, the proportion of projects surviving the first gate fell from 60 per cent to 30 per cent (more projects were killed off earlier than before), with no fall in the number of successful outcomes. The system has led to more focussed development and the earlier selection of winners.

Source: Ramirez et al. (2011).

Staff as innovators

The Japanese system of *kaizen* or 'Continuous Improvement' (Imai, 1986) encourages employees to question work processes and look for incremental improvements in all that they did is one example of how valuable staff can be as source of innovation, especially in processes. While suggestion schemes are not new, the more systematic and proactive approach of the Japanese was a key factor in the success of CI. *Kaizen* has been joined by other systems such as Total Quality Management (George and Weimerskirch, 1998) and Lean Manufacturing (Womack and Jones, 1996). While differing slightly in emphasis the common theme is to involve employees in innovation to help generate profitable ideas.

Open innovation

Large companies spend significant sums on their R&D laboratories in the hope of finding new products or profitable developments of old ones – Apple regularly spends 2 per cent of turnover

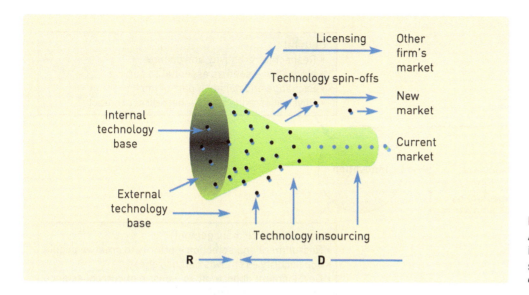

Figure 13.5
An open innovation model
Source: Chesbrough et al. (2006), p. 3.

on R&D, and Nokia three times that proportion. External changes are reducing dependence on these internal sources. Their cost, the preference of many good scientists to create their own research companies, and above all the need to present new products to customers very quickly is encouraging companies to use 'open innovation' (Chesbrough *et al.*, 2006). This happens as managers recognise that however good their research and development staff, useful knowledge is widely distributed and that they can benefit if they find ways to draw on that wider resource. This approach is shown in Figure 13.5 where the internal technology base is supplemented by an external technology base – throughout the innovation process. It also shows that there are more external interactions throughout the process, by bringing in technology from other sources, and earning revenues by licensing technology to other companies.

GlaxoSmithKline (GSK) plans to source half of their new products from external laboratories by 2015. Unilever relies on external input for 60 per cent of its innovations – up 25 per cent from when it established an **open innovation** team in 2009. Roger Leech, Unilever's director of external research:

> We are extremely interested in being able to tap into external sources of new ideas and capabilities. To find solutions in the external world has been extremely important to us, and we are looking at different ways of tapping into that. (*Financial Times*, 11 October 2012)

Procter and Gamble (P&G) – an acknowledged leader in consumer products innovation aims to increase the number of customers who buy its products from 2.5 billion to 3.5 billion, and will do so is by more innovation – often based on other people's good ideas. It is becoming common for consumer goods companies to innovate with outside partners – but P&G has probably made the largest deliberate effort since launching its Connect & Develop programme in 2001. A.G. Laffley, then chief executive, said he wanted at least 50 per cent of new products to involve an outside partner and it met that goal by 2006. Major successes include Tide's Total Care detergent which it developed in conjunction with the University of Lund in Sweden and two smaller partners.

Open innovation is based on the view that useful knowledge is widely distributed and that even the most capable R&D organisation must identify, connect to, and draw upon external knowledge as a core process in innovation.

13.4 Organisational influences on innovation

Organisations who depend on innovation aim to create an environment that encourages all staff (not just those with specific R&D responsibilities) to help create and implement a strong flow of successful new things. Figure 13.6 summarises how the organisational context affects innovation.

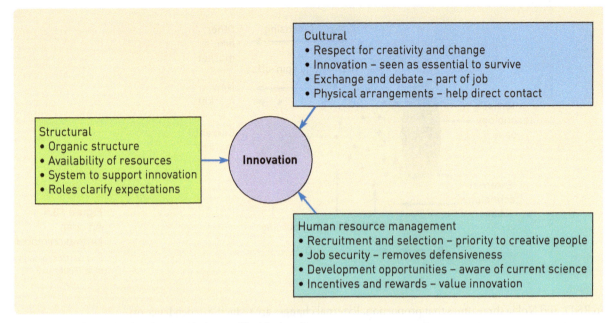

Figure 13.6 Organisation factors that can affect innovation

Structure

- An organic structure (Chapter 10) with extensive horizontal communication, team-based working and broadly defined roles that encourage people to use initiative is more likely to help innovation than a mechanistic form.
- Plentiful resources enable the company to recruit the best staff, and to give them the budget to invest in equipment, conduct trials and experiments, commission research – and be able to absorb the inevitable failures. A successful innovation will take time to introduce and earn revenue – and until then it is draining resources, which the company must sustain.
- Systems to support the innovation process – like Shell's 'Gamechanger' – increase the chances that innovations occur, and that they support the company strategy. Systems need to strike the balance between encouraging innovation and monitoring it ensure it supports the strategy.
- Role clarity – this can help by ensuring that innovation is clearly specified as an aspect of the role, that roles are not cluttered with non-essential tasks, and that there are suitable reward systems to incentivise those responsible for significant innovations.

Key ideas — Innovation and speed in R&D teams

One aspect of innovation is the speed at which a research team produces results, especially in developing new products. Pirola-Merlo (2011) found that the context within R&D research teams significantly affected performance as judged by managers and customers. West's Team Climate for Innovation (team climate being the norms and expectations that individuals perceive to operate in a social context) measures four aspect of a team's context that are expected to support innovation:

- **vision:** team members share clear and valued objectives;
- **participative safety:** a non-threatening environment where members can influence discussions and decisions;
- **task orientation:** concern with achieving excellence through high-quality work and critical appraisal; and

- **support for innovation:** valuing innovation, and supporting work practices aimed at achieving innovation. (p.1077)

The author suggests that an R&D project (lasting months or often years) is not a single innovation event, but a set of (overlapping or sequential) innovation-requiring episodes. It is plausible that prior conditions within the team – team climate – influence how they deal with these, and hence the speed and quality of the outcome. Data from 33 R&D teams in four organisations collected over nine months showed that, as predicted, teams with positive ratings on the TCI progressed significantly faster towards project completion, and produced more innovative outcomes, than those with lower ratings.

Source: Pirola-Merlo (2011).

Culture

Innovative organisations tend to have these characteristics.

- Respect and positive encouragement for all types of creativity – Pixar shows that technologists, creative and production staff are equally valued. A culture which discourages ideas and suggestion or which always raises obstacles will soon discourage people from trying to innovate
- Value open debate and criticism of ideas. They encourage people to challenge – but all know they are challenging the idea, not the person.
- Open systems approach (Chapter 2), making it clear that innovation is central to the business, with an emphasis on the external world and flexible responses to it.

Case study: Pixar – the case continues   www.pixar.com

This practice of working together as peers is core to our culture and it's not limited to our directors and producers. One example is our daily reviews, or 'dailies', a process of giving and getting constant feedback in a positive way. People show work in an incomplete state to the whole animation crew, and although the director makes decisions, everyone is encouraged to comment. One benefit is that the director or creative leads can communicate important points to the entire crew at the same time. People learn from and inspire each other – they spark each other to raise their game. [And] there are no surprises at the end: people's overwhelming desire to make sure their work is good before they show it to others increases the possibility that their finished version won't be what the director wants. The dailies process avoids such wasted efforts.

We believe the creative vision compelling each movie comes from one or two people and not from either corporate executives or a development Department. Instead of coming up with new ideas for movies (its role at most studios) the Department's job is to assemble small incubation teams to help directors refine their ideas to a point where they can convince senior filmmakers that those ideas have some potential to be great films. Each team consists of a director, a writer, some artists and some storyboard people.

Source: Catmull (2008, p. 68).

Case questions 13.3
- What examples are there in the case of how Pixar encourages creativity and innovation?

Human resource management

- Training and development – investment here to build skills and confidence to ensure knowledge is current, including the increasing use of online resources available to staff.

- Job security – ensuring people feel secure in their job is likely to encourage innovation – anxiety and stress tends to encourage people to stick with what they know, rather than risk doing something new which will threaten their career if it fails.
- Ensuring that recruitment is focussed on identifying people who are likely to be innovative and proactive.

Case study: Pixar – the case continues   www.pixar.com

Ed Catmull believes that Pixar's success is due to the work environment they have created, and the close collaboration and interaction between work groups – the technology group delivers computer graphics tools, the creative department which creates stories and the production group which coordinates the film making process. Practices include:

- **Getting talented people to work effectively with each other** … [by constructing] an environment that nurtures trusting relationships and unleashes everyone's creativity. If we get that right, the result is a vibrant community where talented people are loyal to one another and their collective work. (p. 66)
- **Everyone must be free to communicate with anyone** … the most efficient way to deal with numerous problems is to trust people to work out the difficulties directly with each other without having to check for permission. (p. 71)
- **We must stay close to innovations happening in the academic community**. We strongly encourage our technical artists to publish their research and participate in industry conferences. Publication may give away ideas . . . but the connection is worth far more than any ideas we may have revealed: it helps us attract exceptional talent and reinforces the belief throughout the company that people are more important than ideas. (p. 71)
- **[Measure progress]**. Because we're a creative organisation, people [think that what we do can't be measured]. That's wrong. Most of our processes involve activities and deliverables that can be quantified. We keep track of the rates at which things happen, how often something had to be reworked, whether a piece of work was completely finished or not when it was sent to another department . . . Data can show things in a neutral way, which can stimulate discussion. (p. 72)

Source: Catmull (2008).

Case questions 13.4
- To what extent are the practices used at Pixar likely to be unique to that industry?
- Which of them could managers in any organisation which values creativity use?

13.5 Implementing innovation and change

Creativity and innovation only add value when they are implemented – either through offering new goods and services or through changes in the way the organisation works.

Perceived performance gap

A **perceived performance gap** arises when people believe that the actual performance of a unit or business is out of line with the level they desire. If those responsible for transforming resources into outputs do so in a way that does not meet customer expectations, there is a performance gap. Cumulatively this will lead to other performance gaps emerging – such as revenue from sales being below the level needed to secure further resources. If uncorrected this will eventually cause the business to fail.

In the current business climate, two aspects of performance dominate discussion – what Prastacos *et al.* (2002) call '**performance imperatives**': the need for flexibility and the need

*A **perceived performance gap** arises when people believe that the actual performance of a unit or business is out of line with the level they desire.*

Performance imperatives are aspects of performance that are especially important for an organisation to do well, such as flexibility and innovation.

for innovation. In a very uncertain business world the scope for long-term planning is seriously limited. Successful businesses develop a high degree of strategic and organisational flexibility, while also being efficient and stable. This apparent paradox reflects the fact that while companies need to respond rapidly they also need to respond efficiently. This usually depends on having developed a degree of stability and predictability in the way they transform resources into goods and services.

The other imperative identified by Prastacos *et al.* (2002) is innovation:

> to generate a variety of successful new products or services (embedding technological innovation), and to continuously innovate in all aspects of the business. (p. 58)

The internal context

Earlier (Chapter 1) we introduced the internal context (Figure 1.4, repeated here as Figure 13.7) as the set of elements within an organisation that influence behaviour. Change begins to happen when sufficient people believe, say, that outdated technology or a confusing structure is causing a performance gap, by inhibiting flexibility or innovation. They notice external or internal events and interpret them as threatening the performance that influential stakeholders expect. This interpretation encourages them to propose changing one or more aspects of the organisation, shown in Figure 13.7.

They then have to persuade enough other people that the matter is serious enough to earn a place on the management agenda. People in some organisations are open to proposals for change, others tend to ignore them.

People initiate organisational change for reasons other than a conscious awareness of a performance gap – fashion, empire building or a powerful player's personal whim can all play a part. Employees or trade unions can propose changes in the way things are done to improve working conditions. The need for change is subjective – what some see as urgent others will leave until later. People can affect that process by managing external information – magnifying customer complaints to make the case for change, or minimising them if they wish to avoid change.

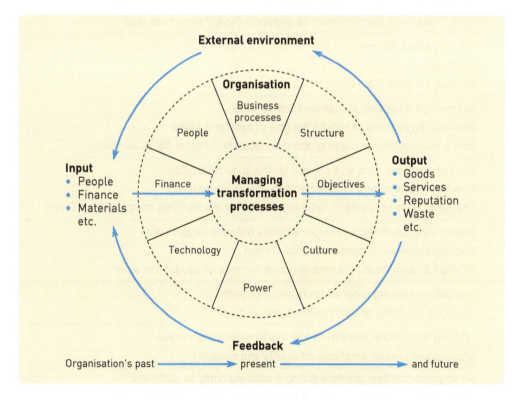

Figure 13.7
Elements of the internal context of management

Organisational change is a deliberate attempt to improve organisational performance by changing one or more aspects of the organisation, such as its technology, structure or business processes.

Whatever the underlying motivations, **organisational change** is an attempt to change one or more of the elements shown in Figure 13.7. Table 13.2 illustrates specific types of change that people initiate under each element, including some which appear elsewhere in this book.

Change in any of these areas will have implications for others – and these interconnections make life difficult. When Tesco introduced its online shopping service alongside its established retail business the company needed to create a website (technology). Managers also needed to decide issues of structure and people (would it be part of the existing stores or a separate unit with its own premises and staff?) and about business processes (how would an order on the website be converted to a box of groceries delivered to the customer's door?). They had to manage these ripples initiated by the main decision. Managers who ignore these consequential changes achieve less than they expect. Context affects the ability to change

While people managing a project aim to change the context, the context within which they work will itself help or hinder them. All of the elements of Figure 13.7 will be present as the project begins, and some of these will influence how people react. Managers who occupy influential positions will review a proposal from their personal career perspective, as well as that of the organisation. At Tesco the existing technology (stores, distribution systems, information systems) and business processes would influence managers' decisions about how to implement the online shopping strategy.

The prevailing culture – shared values, ideals and beliefs – influences how people view change. Members are likely to welcome a project that they believe fits their culture or subculture, and to resist one that threatens it.

Table 13.2 Examples of change in each element of the organisation

Element	Example of change to this element
Objectives	Developing a new product or service
	Changing the overall mission or direction
	GKN increasing its commitment to aviation – buys Volvo's business
Technology	Building a new factory
	Creating an online community
	Building Terminal 5 at Heathrow
Business processes	Improving the delivery of maintenance services
	Redesigning systems to handle the flow of cash and funds
	Zara's new system for passing goods to retailers (Chapter 18, Case study)
Financial resources	A set of changes, such as closing a facility, to reduce costs
	New financial reporting requirements to ensure consistency
	The Royal Bank of Scotland reducing costs after the NatWest merger (Part 4 Case)
Structure	Reallocating functions and responsibilities between departments
	Redesigning work to increase empowerment
	BP (Part 2 case) creating a new structure to make oil production safer
People	Designing a training programme to enhance skills
	Changing the tasks of staff to offer a new service
Culture	Unifying the culture between two or more merged businesses
	Encouraging greater emphasis on quality and reliability
Power	An empowerment programme giving greater authority to junior staff
	Centralising decisions to increase the control of HQ over subsidiaries

Creativity, Innovation and Change

> ### Management in practice
> **Culture and change at a European bank**
>
> While teaching a course to managers at a European bank, the author invited members to identify which of the four cultural types identified in Chapter 2 best described their unit within the bank. They were then asked to describe the reaction of these units to an Internet banking venture that the company was introducing.
>
> Course members observed that colleagues in a unit that had an internal process culture (routine back-office data processing) were hostile to the Internet venture. They appeared to be 'stuck with their own systems', which were so large and interlinked that any change was threatening. Staff in new business areas of the company (open systems) were much more positive, seeing the Internet as a way towards new business opportunities.
>
> Source: Data collected by the author.

> ### Case study
> **Pixar – the case continues** www.pixar.com
>
> One thing that's unique about our culture is that we recognise that the artistic side and the technical side are equal. We've set it up so that each has the potential to earn the same compensation . . . I look at other places and see that one group is considered first-class citizens, another second-class. . . . I think there's a lot of unhealthiness in cultures that let one side predominate.
>
> He also believes that hiring the right people is essential to nurture the culture of innovation at Pixar. It now hires people on the basis of where they are going rather than what they have achieved already. Sometimes Pixar hires people who could be a disruptive influence. While hiring Brad Bird, who went on to direct *The Incredibles*, Jobs, Lasseter and Catmull told him in clear terms, 'The only thing we're afraid of is getting complacent. We need to bring in outside people so we keep throwing ourselves off-balance'. Quips Bird, 'So I was brought here to cause a certain amount of disruption. I've been fired for being disruptive several times, but this is the first time I've been hired for it.'
>
> Source: Text extracts on pages 393-409 from How Pixar fosters collective creativity, *Harvard Business Review*, Vol. 86 (9), pp. 64-72 (Catmull, E. 2008), Copyright © 2008 by Harvard School Publishing Corporation, all rights reserved, reprinted by permission of Harvard Business Review..

Culture is a powerful influence on the success or failure of innovation – see Jones *et al.* (2005) for evidence of how it affected the acceptance of a new computer system. Some cultures support change: a manager in Sun Microsystems commented on that fast-moving business:

> A very dynamic organisation, it's incredibly fast and the change thing is just a constant that you live with. They really promote flexibility and adaptability in their employees. Change is just a constant, there's change happening all of the time and people have become very acclimatised to that, it's part of the job. The attitude to change, certainly within the organisation, is very positive at the moment.

At companies such as Google or Facebook the culture encourages change, while elsewhere it encourages caution. Cultural beliefs are hard to change, yet shape how people respond. Managers learn to be guided by these beliefs because they have worked successfully.

> ### Key ideas
> **Receptive and non-receptive contexts**
>
> Pettigrew *et al.* (1992) sought to explain why managers in some organisations were able to introduce change successfully, while others in the same sector (the UK National Health Service) found it very hard to move away from established practices. Their comparative research programme identified the influence of context on ability to change:

> **receptive contexts** are those where features of the context 'seem to be favourably associated with forward movement. On the other hand, in **non-receptive contexts** there is a configuration of features that may be associated with blocks on change. (p. 268)
>
> Their research identified seven such contextual factors, which provide a linked set of conditions that are likely to provide the energy around change. These are:
>
> 1. quality and coherence of policy;
> 2. availability of key people leading change;
> 3. long-term environmental pressure – intensity and scale;
> 4. a supportive organisational culture;
> 5. effective managerial–clinical relations;
> 6. cooperative interorganisational networks;
> 7. the fit between the district's change agenda and its locale.
>
> While some of these factors are specific to the health sector, they can easily be adapted to other settings. Together these factors give a widely applicable model of how the context affects ability to change.
>
> Source: Pettigrew et al. (1992).

Receptive contexts are those where features of the organisation (such as culture or technology) appear likely to help change.

Non-receptive contexts are those where the combined effects of features of the organisation (such as culture or technology) appear likely to hinder change.

The distribution of power also affects receptiveness to change. Change threatens the status quo, and is likely to be resisted by stakeholders who benefit from the prevailing arrangements. Innovation depends on those behind the change developing political will and expertise that they can only attempt within the prevailing pattern of power.

The context has a history, and several levels

The present context is the result of past decisions and events: Balogun *et al.* (2005) show how internal change agents adapted practice to suit aspects of their context, such as the degree of local autonomy, senior management preferences, rewards systems and financial reporting systems. Management implements change against a background of previous events that shaped the context. The promoter of a major project in a multinational experienced this in his colleagues' attitudes:

> They were a little sceptical and wary of whether it was actually going to enhance our processes. Major pan-European redesign work had been attempted in the past and had failed miserably. The solutions had not been appropriate and had not been accepted by the divisions. Europe-wide programmes therefore had a bad name. (Boddy, 2002, p.38)

Beliefs about the future also affect how people react. Optimists are more open to change than those who feel threatened and vulnerable.

The context represented by Figure 13.7 occurs at (say) operating, divisional and corporate levels. People at any of these will be acting to change their context – which may help or hinder those managing change elsewhere. A project at one level may depend on decisions at another about resources, as this manager leading an oil refinery project discovered:

> One of the main drawbacks was that commissioning staff could have been supplemented by skilled professionals from within the company, but this was denied to me as project manager. This threw a heavy strain and responsibility on myself and my assistant. It put me in a position of high stress, as I knew that the future of the company rested upon the successful outcome of this project. One disappointment (and, I believe, a significant factor in the project) was that just before commissioning, the manager of the pilot plant development team was transferred to another job. He had been promised to me at the project inception, and I had designed him into the working operation. (Boddy, 2002, pp. 38–9)

Acting to change an element at one level will have effects at this and other levels, and elements may change independently. The manager's job is to create a coherent context that encourages desired behaviour, by using their preferred model of change.

13.6 Models of change

There are four complementary models of change, each with different implications for managers – life cycle, emergent, participative and political.

Life cycle

Much advice given to those responsible for managing projects uses the idea of the project **life cycle**. Projects go through successive stages, and results depend on managing each one in an orderly and controlled way. The labels vary, but common themes are:

1 Define objectives.
2 Allocate responsibilities.
3 Fix deadlines and milestones.
4 Set budgets.
5 Monitor and control.

This approach (sometimes called a 'rational–linear' approach) reflects the idea that people can identify smaller tasks within a change and plan the (overlapping) order in which to do them. It predicts that people can make reasonably accurate estimates of the time required to complete each task and when it will be feasible to start work on later ones. People can use tools such as bar charts (sometimes called Gantt charts after the American industrial engineer Henry Gantt, who worked with Frederick Taylor), to show all the tasks required for a project, and their likely duration (see the example in Figure 6.6 on page 192). These help to visualise the work required and to plan the likely sequence of events.

In the life cycle model, successfully managing change depends on specifying these elements at the start and then monitoring them to ensure the project stays on target. Ineffective implementation is due to managers failing to do this. Figure 13.8 shows the stages in the life

Life cycle models of change are those that view change as an activity which follows a logical, orderly sequence of activities that can be planned in advance.

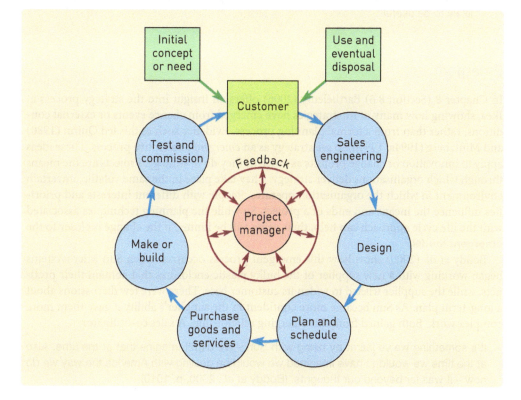

Figure 13.8 A project life cycle
Source: Lock (2007) p. 8.

cycle of a small project (Lock, 2007) – cyclical because they begin and end with the customer. He emphasises this is an oversimplification of a complex, iterative reality, but that it helps identify where decisions arise:

> Travelling clockwise round the cycle reveals a number of steps or *phases*, each of which is represented by a circle in the diagram. The boundaries between these phases are usually blurred in practice, because the phases tend to overlap. (pp. 8–9)

Many books on project management, such as Lock (2007), present advice on tools for each stage of the life cycle. Those advising on IS changes usually take a similar approach, recommending a variety of 'system development life cycle' approaches (Chaffey, 2003). For some changes the life cycle gives valuable guidance. It is not necessarily sufficient in itself, since people may not be able at the start to specify the end point of the change – or the tasks which will lead to that. In uncertain conditions it may make little sense to plan the outcomes in too much detail. It may be wiser to set the general direction, and adapt the target to suit new conditions that develop during the change. Those managing such change need an additional theory to cope with emergent change.

Activity 13.2 Critical reflection on the project life cycle

You may be able to gain some insight into the project life cycle by using it on a practical task. For example:

- If you have a piece of work to do that is connected with your studies, such as an assignment or project, sketch out the steps to be followed by adapting Figure 13.7; alternatively do the same for some domestic, social or management project.
- If you work in an organisation, try to find examples of projects that use this approach, and ask those involved when the method is most useful, and when least useful.
- Make notes summarising how the life cycle approach helps, and when it is most likely to be useful.

Emergent

In Chapter 8 (Section 8.6) Barthélemy (2006) offers an insight into the strategy process at Ikea, showing how many of its strategies have emerged from chance events or external conditions, rather than from a formal planning process. Evidence such as this led Quinn (1980) and Mintzberg (1994a, 1994b) to see strategy as an *emergent* or adaptive process. These ideas apply to innovation or change projects as much as they do to strategy. Projects are the means through which organisations deliver strategy. They take place in the same volatile, uncertain environment in which the organisation operates. People with different interests and priorities influence the means and ends of a project. So while the planning techniques associated with the life cycle approach can help, their value will be limited if the change is closer to the emergent model.

Emergent models of change emphasise that in uncertain conditions a project will be affected by unknown factors, and that planning has little effect on the outcome.

Boddy *et al.* (2000) show how this emergent process occurred when Sun Microsystems began working with a new supplier of the bulky plastic enclosures that contain their products, while the supplier wished to widen its customer base. There were few discussions about a long-term plan. As Sun became more confident in the supplier's ability it gave them more complex work. Both gained from this emerging relationship. A sales co-ordinator:

> It's something we've learnt by being with Sun – we didn't imagine that at the time. Also at the time we wouldn't have imagined we would be dealing with America the way we do now – it was far beyond our thoughts. (Boddy *et al.*, 2000, p. 1010)

Participative

Those advocating **participative models** stress the benefits of personal involvement in, and contribution to, events and outcomes. The underlying belief is that if people can say 'I helped to build this', they will be more willing to live and work with it, whatever it is. It is also *possible* that since participation allows more people to express their views the outcome will be better. Ketokivi and Castañer (2004) found that when employees participated in planning strategic change, they were more likely to view the issues from the perspective of the organisation, rather than their own position or function. Participation can be good for the organisation, as well as the individual.

> The **participative model** is the belief that if people are able to take part in planning a change they will be more willing to accept and implement the change.

While participation is consistent with democratic values, it takes time and effort, and may raise unrealistic expectations. It may be inappropriate when:

- the scope for change is limited, because of decisions made elsewhere;
- participants know little about the topic;
- decisions must be made quickly;
- management has decided what to do and will do so whatever views people express;
- there are fundamental disagreements and/or inflexible opposition to the proposed change.

Participative approaches assume that a sensitive approach by reasonable people will result in the willing acceptance and implementation of change. Some situations contain conflicts that participation alone cannot solve.

Activity 13.3 Critical reflection on participation

Have you been involved in, or affected by, a change in your work or studies?
If so:

- What evidence was there that those managing the change agreed with the participative approach?
- In what way, if any, were you able to participate?
- How did that affect your reaction to the change?

If not:

- Identify three advantages and three disadvantages for the project manager in adopting a participative approach.
- Suggest how managers should decide when to use the approach.

Political

Change often involves people from several levels and functions pulling in different directions:

> Strategic processes of change are ... widely accepted as multi-level activities and not just as the province of a ... single general manager. Outcomes of decisions are no longer assumed to be a product of rational ... debates but are also shaped by the interests and commitments of individuals and groups, forces of bureaucratic momentum, and the manipulation of the structural context around decisions and changes. (Whipp *et al.*, 1988, p. 51)

Several analyses of organisational change emphasise a **political model** (Pettigrew, 1985, 1987; Pfeffer, 1992a; Pinto, 1998; Buchanan and Badham, 1999). Pettigrew (1985) was an early advocate of the view that change requires political as well as rational (life cycle)

> **Political models** reflect the view that organisations are made up of groups with separate interests, goals and values, and that these affect how they respond to change.

skills. Successful change managers create a climate in which people accept the change as legitimate – often by manipulating apparently rational information to build support for their ideas.

> **Key ideas** — **Tom Burns on politics and language**
>
> Tom Burns (1961) observed that political behaviour in the organisation is invariably concealed or made acceptable by subtle shifts in the language that people use:
>
> > Normally, either side in any conflict called political by observers claims to speak in the interests of the corporation as a whole. In fact, the only recognised, indeed feasible, way of advancing political interests is to present them in terms of improved welfare or efficiency, as contributing to the organisation's capacity to meet its task and to prosper. In managerial and academic, as in other legislatures, both sides to any debate claim to speak in the interests of the community as a whole; this is the only permissible mode of expression. (p. 260)
>
> Source: Burns (1961)

Pfeffer (2010) shows that power and political skill is essential to get things done, since decisions in themselves change nothing – people only see a difference when someone implements them. Projects frequently threaten the status quo: people who have done well are likely to resist the change. Innovators need to ensure the project is put onto the senior management agenda, and that influential people support and resource it. Innovators need to develop a political will, and to build and use their power. Buchanan and Badham (1999) conclude that the roots of political behaviour:

> lie in personal ambition, in organisation structures that create roles and departments which compete with each other, and in major decisions that cannot be resolved by reason and logic alone but which rely on the values and preferences of the key actors. Power politics and change are inextricably linked. Change creates uncertainty and ambiguity. People wonder how their jobs will change, how their work will be affected, how their relationships with colleagues will be damaged or enhanced. (p. 11)

Reasonable people may disagree about means and ends, and fight for the action they prefer. This implies that successful project managers understand that their job requires more than technical competence, and are able and willing to engage in political actions.

The political perspective recognises the messy realities of organisational life. Major changes will be technically complex and challenge established interests. These will pull in

> **Key ideas** — **Henry Kissinger on politics in politics**
>
> In another work Pfeffer (1992b) quotes Henry Kissinger:
>
> > Before I served as a consultant to Kennedy, I had believed, like most academics, that the process of decision-making was largely intellectual and all one had to do was to walk into the President's office and convince him of the correctness of one's view. This perspective I soon realised is as dangerously immature as it is widely held. (p. 31)
>
> Source: Pfeffer (1992b).

Table 13.3 Perspectives on change and examples of management practice

Perspective	Themes	Example of management practice
Life cycle	Rational, linear, single agreed aim, technical focus	Measurable objectives; planning and control devices such as Gantt charts and critical path analysis
Emergent	Objectives change as learning occurs during the project, and new possibilities appear	Open to new ideas about scope and direction, and willing to add new resources if needed
Participative	Ownership, commitment, shared goals, people focus	Inviting ideas and comments on proposals, ensuring agreement before action, seeking consensus
Political	Oppositional, influence, conflicting goals, power focus	Building allies and coalitions, securing support from powerful players, managing information

different directions and pursue personal as well as organisational goals. To manage these tensions managers need political skills as well as those implied by life cycle, emergent and participative perspectives.

Management in practice — Political action in hospital re-engineering

Managers in a hospital responded to a persistent performance gap (especially unacceptably long waiting times) by 're-engineering' the way patients moved through and between the different clinical areas. This included creating multi-functional teams responsible for all aspects of the flow of the patient through a clinic, rather than dealing with narrow functional tasks. The programme was successful, but was also controversial. One of those leading the change recalled:

> I don't like to use the word manipulate, but . . . you do need to manipulate people. It's about playing the game. I remember being accosted by a very cross consultant who had heard something about one of the changes and he really wasn't very happy with it. And it was about how am I going to deal with this now? And it is about being able to think quickly. So I put it over to him in a way that he then accepted, and he was quite happy with. And it wasn't a lie and it wasn't totally the truth. But he was happy with it and it has gone on.

Source: Buchanan (2008), p. 13.

These perspectives (life cycle, emergent, participative, political) are complementary in that successful large-scale change is likely to require elements of each. Table 13.3 illustrates how each perspective links to management practice.

13.7 Integrating themes

Entrepreneurship

Drucker (1985) comments that 'Entrepreneurs see change as normal and healthy ... the entrepreneur always searches for change, responds to it, and exploits it as an opportunity' (p. 25). He stresses that entrepreneurship is at least as common, and as necessary, in existing business and public services as it is in new ventures, and this is equally true of innovation. Existing businesses depend on innovation just as much as new ventures.

Drucker sets out policies and practices which entrepreneurial management use in established organisations to foster a healthy flow of innovation, one of which is the Business X-Ray – which furnishes the information need to define how much innovation a business needs, in what areas, and within what time frame.

> In this approach a company lists each of its products or services, [and the market each serves] to estimate their position on the product life cycle. How much longer will this product still grow? How much longer will it still maintain itself in the marketplace? . . . When will it become obsolescent? This enables the company to estimate where it would be if it confined itself to managing to the best of its ability what already exists. And this then shows the gap between what can be expected realistically, and what a company still needs to do to achieve its objectives, whether in sales, market standing, or profitability.
>
> That gap is the minimum that must be filled if the company is not to go downhill . . . But innovative efforts . . . have a high probability of failure and an even higher one of delay. A company should have underway at least three times the innovative efforts, which, if successful, would fill the gap. [Hitches and delays are certain in innovation] so to demand innovative efforts which . . . yield three times the minimum results needed is only elementary precaution. (p. 141)

Sustainability

Across the world governments and international agencies are setting targets with the aim of reducing greenhouse gas emissions: an example is that by the European Union to aim for a 20 per cent reduction by 2020. This is a significant opportunity for innovative businesses in developing new technologies that reduce CO_2 emissions. As well as the existing hydro-electric power infrastructure, wind farms are steadily becoming a larger source of electric power in the UK. In addition significant investment is now being made in marine forms of generation such as wave, tidal and current.

Innovation opportunities are not limited to the generation of power but also arise in infrastructure and especially transport. Hydrogen fuel cells for use in personal vehicles are maturing as a technology and solar powered vehicles for public transport are being developed. Unilever is seeking help from companies and universities around the world to help in producing an environmentally friendly detergent – which will work without requiring large quantities of heated water – and more sustainable forms of packaging.

Internationalisation

The growing internationalisation of business has implications for the way international or global firms manage change and innovation. The issue here reflects one of the central themes within Chapter 4, namely the balance between a unified, global approach seeking to establish a common identity across all operations, or an approach that adapts the way the company operates to local conditions. Managers of local business units will have local priorities, and are likely to be unreceptive to change that the centre, or even another unit, appears to be imposing. This balancing act faces all companies operating internationally.

The same dilemma arises in relation to innovation: companies often want to allow research teams autonomy, yet to do could lead to expensive duplication of scientific resources and potentially harmful competition between national units. As an example an associate at innovative textile company W.L. Gore (**www.gore.com**) commented:

> One challenge is to retain the team-working ethos while working globally. There is a danger of duplication if the interests of separate teams in different parts of the world evolve in such a way that they are working on similar products. Yet at the same time we don't want to create structures or processes that stifle creativity. We don't want to say

that people should focus on specific areas of research. We need to find ways of sharing expertise globally. (Private communication)

Governance

The financial crisis in 2008 is an example of innovation out of control. Its origins lay in some banks selling mortgages to (sub-prime) customers who could not afford the repayments. The innovation was the way in which the companies making the loans 'packaged' these loans and sold them to other players in the financial supply chain. Innovative bankers converted the original (very dubious) loans into financial products called mortgage-backed securities. These were sold on to hedge funds and investment banks which saw them as high return investments. When borrowers started to default on their loans, the value of the investments fell, leading to huge losses. Investors then became nervous about buying any investment linked to mortgages, no matter how high their quality, so that lenders found it increasingly difficult to borrow money in the capital markets – with the familiar results.

Much of the blame was placed on the lack of governance within the banking industry that allowed innovative ideas to be implemented without regard to the risks they posed, or their longer term consequences. The Management in practice feature gives an example of a bank with very tight governance and control systems.

Management in practice   Governance and control at Santander   www.santander.com

In a speech to the first Santander Conference on International Banking, Emilio Botin, the chairman said:

Banks must focus on customers, focus on recurring business based on long-term relationships and be cautious in managing risk. You do not need to be innovative to do this well. You do not need to invent anything. You need to dedicate time and attention at the highest level.

Many are surprised to learn that the Banco Santander board's risk committee meets for half a day twice a week and that the board's ten-person executive committee meets every Monday for at least four hours, devoting a large portion of that time to reviewing risks and approving transactions. Not many banks do this. It consumes a lot of our directors' time. But we find it essential and it is never too much.

Source: *Financial Times*, 16 October 2008.

Summary

1 **Explain the meaning of creativity and innovation, with examples**
   - Creativity is the ability to combine ideas and information in unusual ways to create something new and useful. Innovation refers to the processes of implementing such new and useful things into an organisation where they add value.

2 **Explain the management significance of creativity and innovation**
   - As markets and customers preferences change with increasing speed, most companies need to be able to encourage creativity and innovation among their staff to meet these market expectations.
     - Product innovation – the changes in the things that the organisation offers for sale.
     - Process innovation – the changes in the process that creates the product.
     - Position innovation – the changes in the way the product is offered or targeted.
     - Paradigm innovation – the changes in how a company frames what it does.

3 **Illustrate the organisational factors believed to support creativity and innovation**
   - Cultural, structural and HR factors influence the context within which creative people work, and which managers can shape.
   - Strategy – innovation is explicitly called for in the corporate strategy.
   - Structure – roles and jobs are defined to aid in innovative behaviour.
   - Style – management empowers the workforce to behave innovatively.
   - Support – IT systems are available to support innovative behaviour.

4 **Explain what the links between change and context imply for those managing a change**
   - A change programme is an attempt to change one or more aspects of the internal context, which then provides the context of future actions. The inherited context can itself help or hinder change efforts.

5 **Compare life cycle, emergent, participative and political theories of change**
   - Life cycle: change projects can be planned, monitored and controlled towards achieving their objectives.
   - Emergent: reflecting the uncertainties of the environment, change is hard to plan in detail, but emerges incrementally from events and actions.
   - Participative: successful change depends on human commitment, which is best obtained by involving participants in planning and implementation.
   - Political: change threatens some of those affected, who will use their power to block progress, or to direct the change in ways that suit local objectives.

6 **Evaluate systematically the possible sources of resistance to change**
   - Reasons can be assessed using the internal context model, as each element (objectives, people, power, etc.) is a potential source of resistance. Analysing these indicates potential ways of overcoming resistance.
   - The force field analysis model allows players to identify the forces driving and restraining a change, and implies that reducing the restraining forces will help change more than increasing the driving forces.

7 **Show how ideas from the chapter add to your understanding of the integrating themes**
   - Drucker shows how entrepreneurship is as important in large companies as in new ventures, and that all depend on innovation. The example from his books illustrates one practice uses to manage innovation in a disciplined way, to ensure an adequate flow of new and useful things.
   - The search for sustainable performance offers significant opportunities to innovators who can find ways of reducing the use of energy throughout the value-adding chain.
   - International companies often wish to encourage local units to be innovative but, as the W.L. Gore example shows, they also need to avoid wasteful duplication if several sites work on similar projects.
   - The 2008 financial crisis showed the negative side of innovation, when it is not balanced by effective governance and control systems – such as those at banks like Santander whose managers take risk seriously.

Test your understanding

1 Think of products and services that are currently successful; determine the innovations that created that success and categorise them using the 4Ps model.
2 Can managers alter the receptiveness of an organisation to change? Would doing so be an example of an interaction approach?

3 What does the term 'performance gap' mean, and what is its significance for change?
4 What are the implications for management of the systemic nature of major change?
5 Outline the life cycle perspective on change and explain when it is most likely to be useful.
6 How does it differ from the 'emergent' perspective?
7 What are the distinctive characteristics of a participative approach, and when is it likely to be least successful?
8 What skills are used by those employing a political model?
9 Summarise an idea from the chapter that adds to your understanding of the integrating themes.

Think critically

Think about the way people handle major change in your company, or one with which you are familiar. Review the material in the chapter, and perhaps visit some of the websites identified. Then make notes on these questions:

- In implementing change, what **assumptions** about the nature of change in organisations appear to guide the approach? Is one perspective dominant, or do people typically use several methods in combination?
- What factors in the **context** of the company appear to shape your approach to managing change – is your organisation seen as being receptive or non-receptive to change, for example, and what lies behind that?
- Has there been any serious attempt to find **alternative** ways to manage major change in your organisation – for example by comparing your methods systematically with those of other companies, or with the theories set out here?
- Does the approach typically used generally work? If not, do managers recognise the **limitations** of their approach, and question their assumptions?

Read more

Balogun, J., Gleadle, P., Hailey, V.H. and Willmott, H. (2005), 'Managing change across boundaries: boundary-shaking practices', *British Journal of Management*, vol. 16, no. 4, pp. 261–78.

An empirical study of the practices that change agents used to introduce major cross-boundary changes in large companies, and how the context shaped their use.

Catmull, E. (2008), 'How Pixar Fosters Collective Creativity', *Harvard Business Review*, vol. 86, no. 9, pp. 64–72.

The co-founder explains how it works.

Christensen, C. M. and Raynor, M. E. (2003), *The Innovator's Solution: Creating and Sustaining Successful Growth*, Harvard Business School Press, Boston, Mass.

Sets innovation in the context of strategy, combining scholarship and practice to show the benefits of using good theory to guide action.

Pettigrew, A., Ferlie, E. and McKee, L. (1992), *Shaping Strategic Change*, Sage, London.

A detailed, long-term analysis of major changes in several units within the UK National Health Service. Although old, it still provide useful empirical insights into the task of managing change.

Tidd, J. & Bessant, J. (2009), *Managing Innovation: Integrating Technological, Market and Organisational Change*, Chichester, Wiley.

Combines a comprehensive account of innovation theories with many contemporary examples.

Go online

These websites have appeared in this and other chapters:

www.pixar.com
www.gknplc.com
www.magnamole.co.uk
www.segway.com
www.philipmorristobacco.com
www.santander.com
www.dyson.co.uk
nationaltheatre.org.uk
www.shell.com
www.gore.com

Visit two of the business sites in the list, and navigate to the pages dealing with corporate news, investor relations or 'our company'.

- What signs of major changes taking place in the organisation can you find?
- Does the site give you a sense of an organisation that is receptive or non-receptive to change?
- What kind of environment are they likely to be working in, and how may that affect their approach to change?

PART 4 CASE
THE ROYAL BANK OF SCOTLAND
www.rbs.co.uk

The company

For many years RBS offered traditional banking services to retail and business customers, mostly in the UK. It took deposits, made loans and provided payment services. During the 1990s the company's senior management took advantage of changes in UK and international banking regulations to widen the scope, and increase the size, of the business. It began to provide more services to UK customers, expand overseas, and increase its trading activities – using bank funds to trade in assets on behalf of the bank itself, rather than on behalf of customers.

In 2007 RBS was innovative and profitable, providing good returns to shareholders. Fred Goodwin became chief executive in 1997, and managed a rapid growth in size and profitability. This was publicly recognised in 2004 when he was awarded a knighthood for services to banking. By 2008 RBS was on the point of collapse, and only survived because the UK government invested £45.5 billion in the bank (at about 50 pence a share), in return for an 84 per cent stake in the business. Sir Fred had presided over the biggest bank failure in history.

In 2013 managers and staff were trying to rebuild the business so that the government could sell its shares profitably, returning RBS to private ownership. The shares were worth much less than the price the government had paid for them, implying it would be several years before taxpayers would recover their investment (in a public relations move in 2012, every ten of the original shares then trading at 25p were converted into one new share valued at 250p). Sir Fred had become so unpopular with the public that there was little opposition when the government arranged to remove his knighthood in 2012.

What happened to bring about this change? Before 2007 management, under Goodwin, made many internal changes, including:

Alamy Images/Tim Ayers

- segmenting customers into three groups – retail, commercial and corporate;
- creating new management roles, structures and an aggressive, results-based culture;
- HRM policies to hire more entrepreneurial managers who could deliver the vision of expanding in the UK and overseas, and to base appointment and rewards on achievement and ability.

This transformed the bank, and provided the base for a period of successful growth and acquisitions – and for the later crisis. The table shows the main financial indicators of performance in the two most recent financial years.

Measures of financial performance in year ending 31 December

	2012	2011
Total income (£m)	25,787	27,709
Operating expenses (£m)	(14,619)	(15,478)
Profit before insurance claims and impairment losses (£m)	11,168	12,231

741

	2012	2011
Insurance claims and impairment losses (£m)	(7,706)	(10,407)
Operating loss before tax (£m)	(5,165)	(1,190)
Tax (£m)	(469)	(1,127)
Loss from continuing operations (£m)	(5,634)	(2,317)

Source: *RBS Annual Reports*.

Managing to add value
Diversifying the business

Since the early 1990s the bank had diversified from traditional UK banking operations into a range of businesses and countries – so that by early 2008 it had eight 'customer-facing' divisions:

- UK Retail (RBS and NatWest – two divisions);
- Wealth Management (including Coutts Bank);
- Retail Direct (mainly online banking);
- RBS Insurance;
- US Retail and Commercial;
- Ulster Bank Group;
- Corporate Banking and Financial Markets.

These were supported by six Group divisions – Finance, Risk and Internal Audit; Manufacturing; Legal; Strategy; Communications, and Human Resources.

Growth by acquisition

RBS gained a reputation for acquiring other financial institutions and integrating them profitably. The most notable of these was the acquisition of NatWest Bank in 2000 – three times the size of RBS at the time. When RBS completed the acquisition, senior management quickly established the 'Integration Programme' to merge the two companies' operations, which it achieved early in 2003. This successful acquisition (Kennedy *et al.*, 2006) enhanced the reputation of Fred Goodwin and his team though, having made 23 acquisitions since 2000, they claimed they would now focus on building existing businesses.

However, senior management, supported by the board, completed another deal (in partnership with a consortium of banks) in late 2008 – which was disastrous. In the biggest deal in banking history the consortium acquired ABN Amro, a Dutch bank. Many doubted the wisdom of the deal since RBS would need to raise £12 billion to make the purchase, especially as senior management did not conduct a rigorous analysis of ABN Amro before buying it. In 2012 a group of investors claimed the bank's directors had misled them about the financial state of the group. The defendants denied this, arguing that it was made with the benefit of hindsight, and that in early 2008 the directors could not have foreseen the economic crisis that was to occur later in the year.

HRM policies

Goodwin expected the Head of Group HRM to develop policies and cultures that supported his goals. Goodwin's style was highly directive, holding executives personally, and publicly, accountable for performance in their area. Personal direction was reinforced by a performance management and reward system that reflected the CEO's emphasis on data to guide decisions – reward was closely tied to objective financial measures of the performance of a manager's team. HRM also ran a leadership development programme attended by the top 300 executives in the bank to reinforce Goodwin's approach to leadership, and to spread it throughout the bank. Martin and Gollan (2012) believe this helped to spread the aggressively confident style of the chief executive widely in the bank, which perhaps led them to ignore cautionary voices advising against the ABN Amro bid.

Investing to improve efficiency

The bank has for many years developed information technology systems to centralise administration. The clearest example is Manufacturing Division which deals with routine functions such as clearing cheques and opening accounts – and which has a mechanistic structure. The bank created the division in 1999 by transferring most administrative tasks from the branches to a central location. To select staff for the new division they used personality tests to identify those more comfortable with processes and systems. Those who were more interested in people remained in the branches. The branches themselves had been mechanistic, with staff working on strictly defined tasks. Now they are more organic, with staff trying to meet customers' diverse needs and interest them in other products, within an open layout.

RBS was quick to exploit the opportunities that information technology offered to change the way it dealt with customers. It was an early innovator when it launched Direct Line as one of the first examples of delivering financial services by telephone and online, and (in 2012) the UK's largest provider of motor insurance. An online bank complements the services offered by the branches.

In 2012 many customers were unable to access their accounts for several days due to it a technical fault during a routine software upgrade. The Financial Services Authority demanded a 'complete account' of the debacle, and RBS had to pay millions of pounds in compensation to customers.

Trading innovative products

Under Goodwin's leadership the bank built a substantial trading operation in which traders dealt with complex products, often based on 'sub-prime US mortgages'. These were loans which banks had made to low-income families in the US to buy a home – as with any mortgage, they borrow the money and gradually repay the capital, with interest, over perhaps 25 years. Financial companies devised complex schemes which turned a familiar product into a financial instrument which could be traded on financial markets.

RBS chose to enter this market, not by using the funds of its depositors, but by using short term loans from other banks. HRM policies, especially those relating to pay and bonuses, encouraged its traders. The FSA report into the collapse of RBS stated that while building up this risky business Goodwin vigorously resisted FSA procedures, which he saw as unnecessary interference. It also found that while the bank claimed to have in place suitable control mechanisms, there was 'a spectacular lack of understanding [about the nature of this business] at the very highest ranks of the bank' (*Financial Times*, 13 December 2011, p. 4). Deteriorating financial conditions (including the collapse of a major US bank) in 2008 reduced confidence amongst lenders – so that RBS was no longer able to borrow money for this business – many of whose assets were now of little value.

This led to a crisis in October 2008 when the UK government transferred taxpayers' money to RBS so that it could continue trading – and in return received an 83 per cent stake in the company. They demanded management changes, including the dismissal of Sir Fred Goodwin and most of the board. New managers were appointed to rebuild the bank so that it could be returned to private ownership.

Aspects of the RBS context
Competition

RBS is an example of a diversified bank providing a wide range of financial services. It therefore competes not only with other national (such as Barclays) and international (such as HSBC) banks offering a similar range, but also with businesses which focus on just one area (such as Royal Insurance Group or Fidelity Investments). It also faces competition from new entrants like Virgin Money, Metrobank and other smaller specialist lenders (such as Close Brothers) which avoided risky investments during the boom.

Governments in most countries see many benefits in a thriving banking sector providing employment, income and tax revenues. They often encourage innovation by those in the industry, and encourage overseas banks to enter their market. Since the mid-1980s the UK government had encouraged the growth of the financial services sector by removing restrictions on who could offer banking services – encouraging many new banks, including those based overseas, to set up in the UK.

The authorities also see the risks, especially when banks sell inappropriate products, make excessive charges and, above all, invest in risky ventures which, if they fail, threaten the financial stability of the economy. The media regularly draws attention to bankers' high rewards and irresponsible behaviour, which increases demands for government action to prevent these perceived abuses.

Regulation

All governments try to regulate banks (and the rest of the financial services sector), hoping that this will ensure they benefit customers and their national economies. Regulators aim to balance the economic benefits of a strong banking sector against the risks to consumers, business and the wider economy if banks' innovative practices and policies fail. They develop guidelines on acceptable practice by banks and apply sanctions against those which breach them.

In 2001 the UK government created the Financial Services Authority (FSA) (www.fsa.gov.uk) with the aim of regulating financial services. All firms providing a financial service must be authorised by the FSA – which sets the standards they must meet, and can act against them if they fail to do so.

The FSA report into the collapse of RBS acknowledges that there were at least four occasions between 2005 and 2007 when it failed to take a hard enough line:

> They show that the FSA allowed the bank to run high risks with low stocks of capital and liquid assets and left it vulnerable to a loss of investor confidence. These factors reveal how the regulator's 'light touch' approach, emphasising cooperation rather than confrontation, helped RBS down the road to failure. (*Financial Times*, 13 December 2011, p. 4)

In 2012 the UK government announced that it was accepting most of the recommendations of a report from the Independent Commission on Banking (chaired by Sir John Vickers), which sought to protect relatively safe retail banking from riskier investment activities. The government also said that RBS would reduce the size of its investment bank. These reforms mean the deposits of retail consumers and small businesses cannot be used to fund risky trading activities. Implementing them will take many years.

International

Financial services are such an important aspect of modern economies that most countries, seek a share of the employment, income and tax revenues which they provide. They compete with each other to attract international firms to their country. This (along with developments in IT that enable the rapid transmission of data across the world) has encouraged many (though not all) financial services companies to become international businesses.

While national governments want to regulate the industry, those in the industry try to shape these decisions in their favour. They imply that if regulations become unfavourable in one country they will move some or all of their operations to those with more favourable conditions. There is constant interaction between financial service firms and national governments over the form and stringency of regulations.

Governments counter this by pressing for common international agreements across the world, or for common regional policies, such as within the European Union. Such international regulations are additional to those which national governments create. The EU in 2012 announced that it would impose a limit on bank bonus levels, possibly limiting them to the same level as salaries. The rules were expected to apply to a relatively small number of staff – senior managers and traders who have significant influence on profits. Banks outside the EU were expected to benefit, as they would find it easier to recruit good senior staff.

Current management dilemmas

The management of RBS is grappling with the challenge of returning the bank to profit, in the face of an EU requirement to reduce the size of the bank (it has to sell 316 retail branches by the end of 2013), increase its reserves, reform the pay and bonus system, and introduce new systems to balance innovation with control.

Range of services

Stephen Hester replaced Goodwin as chief executive, and has been trying to rebuild the bank. He aims to focus on its traditional strengths such as UK retail banking, wealth management, and global payments and insurance. The investment banking business will be halved in size, and RBS will dispose of other parts of the business such as the Direct Line insurance business and 316 retail branches. In 2013, Ross McEwan took over as chief executive.

Pay and bonuses

Despite having had to seek a government bail-out, and to the fury of public and politicians alike, Fred Goodwin insisted that he was entitled to his full pension of over £700,000 a year, due at once although he is only 50. The bank's remuneration committee agreed to Sir Fred's massive payoff as part of the negotiations to remove him – he had a contract.

Others pointed out that bankers' pay during the bubble was too high, but that it would be a mistake for the state to impose pay limits. Finance relies on individuals, and employers compete for their skills. If taxpayers were to get their money back, RBS would need to become profitable, and it was unlikely to do so if it could not pay competitive salaries. This view appeared to prevail, as in 2009 Mr Hester reached a new pay deal, which was agreed by UK Financial Investments (which manages the state's shareholding). While the headline figure of £9.6 million attracted wide criticism, defenders pointed out that most of it depended on the share price rising from 35p to 70p – which would benefit taxpayers. In 2012 the bank awarded him a bonus (in shares) worth £963,000, in addition to a salary of £1.2 million. Mr Hester decided not to accept the bonus.

Mr Hester believes that the bank's ability to keep and motivate executives who can make it profitable is the biggest single problem he faces. Many of the HRM policies built before 2008 have been dismantled.

Internal governance

Banks, perhaps more than most organisations, need balance innovation and control. For years they have attracted very bright graduates from universities and business schools, and encouraged them to develop innovative and profitable products.

RBS itself had all of the formal mechanisms of corporate governance in place – independent non-executive directors, audit and risk committees, a remuneration committee. In the years before 2008 none of the people on these boards and committees appears to have been able and willing to stand up to Fred Goodwin. Whatever misgivings they may have had in private, they continued to support the management team in public – 90 per cent of shareholders approved the ABN AMRO deal.

Sources: Kennedy et al. (2006); *Economist*, 14 February 2009; *Financial Times*, 13 October 2008, 6 May 2009, 23 June 2009, 14 September 2011, 13 December 2011, 23 January 2012, 1 February 2012, 20 June 2012, 27 June 2012; RBS website; Martin and Gollan (2012).

Part case questions

(a) Relating to Chapters 10 to 13

1. Refer to Chapter 7 (Section 7.6 and Section 7.7). Do they offer insights into possible explanations for the troubles at RBS?
2. Which aspects of the banks operations were mechanistic, and which organic? (Section 10.7)
3. Outline how the HRM practices introduced in the years following Goodwin's arrival contributed to the bank's rise and fall. (Section 11.6 and Section 11.7)
4. Describe two examples of the bank using IT to change the way it operates. What organisational changes did it make to support this? (Section 12.4 and Section 12.5)
5. What did it do during the boom years to encourage innovation, especially by traders? What external factors encouraged this risk-taking culture? (Section 13.3 and Section 13.4)
6. Why do you think the board were unable to influence Fred Goodwin and the senior team – what sources of power did Goodwin possess? (Section 14.6)

(b) Relating to the company

1. Visit the RBS Group website (www.rbs.com), including the pages for 'investor relations' and read one or more of the management reports you will find there. Note recent events that add to material in this case.
2. Access the websites of *Economist*, *Financial Times* or *BBC News* (Business pages) and make notes about how, if at all, the dilemmas identified in the case are still current, and how the company has dealt with them.
3. What new issues appear to be facing RBS which the case did not mention?
4. The issue of bank bonuses was still highly topical and contentious in early 2013. Summarise how it has responded since to calls for it to limit the rewards to senior staff.
5. What information can you find on the website, or in the annual report, about the company's governance systems, and the issues faced in reaching a balance between innovation and control?
6. What progress has the bank made towards enabling the government to sell its shareholding?
7. For any one of those issues it faces, how do you think it should deal with it? Build your answer by referring to one or more features of the company's history outlined in the case.

PART 4
EMPLOYABILITY SKILLS – PREPARING FOR THE WORLD OF WORK

To help you develop useful skills, this section includes tasks which relate the themes covered in the Part to six employability skills (sometimes called capabilities and attributes) which many employers value. The layout will help you to articulate these skills to employers and prepare for the recruitment processes you will encounter in applications forms, interviews, and assessment centres.

Task 4.1 | Business awareness

If a potential employer asks you to attend an assessment centre or a competency-based interview, they may ask you to present or discuss a current business topic to demonstrate your business or commercial awareness. To help you prepare for this, write an individual or group report on ONE of these topics and present it to an audience. Aim to present your ideas in a 750-word report and/or ten PowerPoint slides at most.

1. Using data from one or more websites or printed sources, outline significant recent developments in RBS, especially regarding their:
   - range of activities (including their international presence);
   - human resource management policies, including reward systems;
   - regulation and internal governance; and
   - progress towards the intended sale of the government's stake in the business.

   Include a summary of commentators' views on the bank's progress.

2. Gather evidence on the interaction between RBS and their political and regulatory context, including specific examples of interventions by the regulator to influence the bank, and vice versa. Critically evaluate the actions of both parties. What generally relevant lessons can you draw from this example of business-government interaction?

3. Choose another financial services company that interests you – and which you may consider as a career option.
   - Gather information from the website and other sources about its strategy and structure.
   - What can you find about the role of HRM policies in supporting the strategy?
   - How have technological developments affected the business?
   - How innovative has the company been in products and/or processes?
   - What career options does it offer, and how attractive are they?

When you have completed the task, write a short paragraph giving examples of the skills (such as in information gathering, analysis and presentation) you have developed from this task. You can transfer a brief note of this to the table at Task 4.7.

Task 4.2 Solving problems

Reflect on the way that you handled Task 4.1, and identify problems which you encountered in preparing your report, and how you dealt with them. For example:

1. How did you identify the relevant facts which you needed for your report?
2. Were there alternative sources which you could have used, and if so, how did you decide between them? Were there significant gaps in the data, and how did you overcome this?
3. What alternative courses of action did you consider at various stages of your work?
4. How did you select and implement one of these alternatives?
5. How did you evaluate the outcomes, and what lessons did you draw from the way you dealt with the problem?

Write a short paragraph, giving examples of the problem solving skills (such as finding and accessing information sources, deciding which to use, and evaluation) you have developed from this task. You can transfer a brief note of this to the Table at Task 4.7.

Task 4.3 Thinking critically

Reflect on the way that you handled Task 4.1, and identify how you exercised the skills of critical thinking (Chapter 1, Section 1.8). For example:

1. Did you spend time identifying and challenging the assumptions implied in the reports or commentaries you read? Summarise what you found then, or do it now.
2. Did you consider the extent to which they took account of the effects of the context in which managers are operating? Summarise what you found then, or do it now.
3. How far did they, or you, go in imagining and exploring alternative ways of dealing with the issue?
4. Did you spend time outlining the limitations of ideas or proposals which you thought of putting forward?

When you have completed the task, write a short paragraph giving examples of the thinking skills you have developed (such as identifying assumptions, seeing the effects of context, identifying alternative routes and their limitations) from this task. You can transfer a brief note of this to the template at Task 4.7.

Task 4.4 Team working

Chapter 17 includes ideas on team working. This activity helps you develop those skills by reflecting on how the team worked during Task 4.1.

Use the scales below to rate the way your team worked on this task – circle the number that best reflects your opinion of the discussion.

1. How effectively did the group obtain and use necessary information?

1	2	3	4	5	6	7
Badly						Well

2 To what extent was the group's organisation suitable for the task?

1	2	3	4	5	6	7
Unsuitable						Suitable

3 To what extent did members really listen to each other?

1	2	3	4	5	6	7
Not at all						All the time

4 How fully were members involved in decision taking?

1	2	3	4	5	6	7
Low involvement						High involvement

5 To what extent did you enjoy working with this group?

1	2	3	4	5	6	7
Not at all						Very much

6 How did team members use their time?

1	2	3	4	5	6	7
Badly						Well

You could compare your results with other members of the team, and agree on specific practices which would help the team work better together.

When you have completed the task, write a short paragraph, giving examples of the team working skills (such as observing a group to identify good and bad practices, evaluating how a team made decisions, and making practical suggestions to improve performance) you have developed from this task. You can transfer a brief note of this to the template at Task 4.7.

Task 4.5 Communicating

Chapter 16 outlines ideas on communicating. This activity helps you to learn more about the skill by reflecting on how the team communicated during Task 4.1. For example:

1 What did people do or say that helped or hindered communication within the group?
2 What communication practices did you use to present your report to your chosen audience?
3 How did you choose them, and were they satisfactory for the circumstances?
4 What were the main barriers to communication which the group experienced?
5 What would you do differently to improve communication in a similar task?

Present a verbal summary of your report to a fellow student, and help each other to improve your work.

When you have completed the task, write a short paragraph giving examples of the communicating skills (such as observing communication to identify good and bad practices, evaluating how a team communicated, and making practical suggestions to improve performance) you have developed from this task. You can transfer a brief note of this to the template at Task 4.7.

Task 4.6 Self-management

This activity helps you to learn more about managing yourself, so that you can present convincing evidence to employers showing, amongst other things, your willingness to learn, your ability to manage and plan learning, workloads and commitments, and that you have a well-developed level of self-awareness and self-reliance. You need to show that you are able to accept responsibility, manage time, and use feedback to learn.

Reflect on the way that you handled Task 4.1, and identify how you exercised skills of self management. For example:

1. Did you spend time planning the time you would spend on each part of the task?
2. Did this include balancing the commitments of team members across the work, so that all were fully occupied, and that no one was under-used?
3. Can you identify examples of time being well used, and of when you wasted time? Who did what to improve the way you used time?
4. Were there examples of team members taking responsibility for an area of the work, and so helping to move the task forward?
5. Did you spend time reviewing how the group performed? If so, what lessons were you able to draw on each of the questions above, which you could use in future tasks?

When you have completed the task, write a short paragraph, giving examples of the communicating skills (such as observing communication to identify good and bad practices, evaluating how a team communicated, and making practical suggestions to improve performance) you have developed from this task. You can transfer a brief note of this to the template at Task 4.7.

Task 4.7 Recording your employability skills

To conclude your work on this Part, use the summary paragraphs above to make a summary record of the employability skills you have developed during your work on the tasks set out here, and in other activities. Use the format of the table below to create an electronic record that you can use to combine the list of skills you have developed in this Part, with those in other Parts.

Most of your learning about each skill will probably come from the task associated with it – but you may also gain insights in other ways – so add those in as well.

Template for laying out record of employability skills developed in this Part.

Skills/Task	Task 4.1	Task 4.2	Task 4.3	Task 4.4	Task 4.5	Task 4.6	Other sources of skills
Business awareness							
Solving problems							
Thinking critically							
Team working							
Communicating							
Self-management							

To make the most of your opportunities to develop employability skills as you do your academic work, you need to reflect regularly on your learning, and to record the results. This helps you to fill any gaps, and provides specific evidence of your employability skills.